How Audiences Decide

How Audiences Decide: A Cognitive Approach to Business Communication draws on a vast research literature and summarizes relevant theories and findings from the fields of social cognition, consumer behavior, decision science, behavioral finance, affective science, cognitive science, and neuroscience.

It delves into the hearts and minds of a breath-taking array of audiences: from Wall Street analysts to viewers of the evening news, from army officers to hospital patients, from venture capitalists to grocery shoppers, from CEOs to college admissions officers, from corporate recruiters to mock jurors.

This book surveys a broad range of communication techniques—including those concerning persuasion, leadership speaking, writing, content, style, typography, non-verbal behaviors, charts, images, rational arguments, and emotional appeals—and examines the empirical evidence supporting each of them.

Dr. Richard Young is Associate Teaching Professor of Management Communication at the Tepper School of Business at Carnegie Mellon University where he has taught for over twenty years. He received a Ph.D. in Rhetoric from Carnegie Mellon in 1989 with a dissertation on the cognitive processes of consultants and their clients.

How Audiences Decide

A Cognitive Approach to Business Communication

Richard O. Young

Routledge
Taylor & Francis Group

NEW YORK AND LONDON

First published 2011
by Routledge
270 Madison Ave, New York, NY 10016

Simultaneously published in the UK
by Routledge
2 Park Square, Milton Park, Abingdon, Oxon OX14 4RN

Routledge is an imprint of the Taylor & Francis Group, an informa business

© 2011 Richard O. Young

Typeset in Aldine and Helvetica Neue by
Florence Production Ltd, Stoodleigh, Devon
Printed and bound in the United States of America
on acid-free paper by Edwards Brothers, Inc.

Library of Congress Cataloging in Publication Data
Young, Richard O.
   How audiences decide: a cognitive approach to business communication/
   Richard O. Young.—1st ed.
       p. cm.
   1. Business communication—Psychological aspects.   I. Title.
   HF5718.Y686 2010
   658.4′5—dc22   2010010835

ISBN13: 978–0–415–87899–9 (hbk)
ISBN13: 978–0–415–87900–2 (pbk)
ISBN13: 978–0–203–84330–7 (ebk)

Contents

Detailed Contents

Acknowledgments

How Audiences Decide could not have been written without Professor Herbert Simon's work in human cognition, or without the aid and support of my family, friends, colleagues, students, and publisher. Among the friends and colleagues who generously came to my aid, I am particularly grateful to professors Evelyn Pierce, Patricia Carpenter, Priscilla Rogers, and Sandra Collins who read and commented on early drafts of the book and who encouraged me to keep working on it. I also owe a tremendous debt of gratitude to professors John R. Hayes, David Kaufer, Frank Demmler, James Stratman, Jeffrey Williams, Thomas Hajduk, Millie Myers, John R. Anderson, and Duane Seppi, as well as to Dr. Karen Schriver, Thomas G. Young, Colleen B. Frank, Deborah S. Magness, and Dr. Ilker Baybars for the many ways they supported my quest to better understand audience decision making. I am especially indebted to Dr. Cliff Parsons for his friendship and the substantive contributions he made to this book.

Perhaps my best teachers over the last twenty years have been the MBA students at the Tepper School of Business at Carnegie Mellon. I greatly appreciate all those students who collected think-aloud comments of audience members, who tested, wrote, and revised business presentations and documents, and who shared their work-related stories with me. The think-aloud comments Kirk Botula collected so many years ago opened my eyes to the significance of audience decision-making expertise. This volume also owes a special debt to Aaron Oh and his teammates, Andrew Bennett and his teammates, Kurt Ernst, Alan Michaels, and Matt Lysaught and their teammates, to Vero Anderson, Raphael Matarazzo, and Louis Zaretsky and their teammates, to Eric Schwalm, Stephen Kraus, Kalpesh Dadbhawala, Dominic Joseph, Laurie Barkman, Pradeep U. N., William Pomper, Sung-Ju Pak, Kirk Pond, Jack Deem, and Noriko Sasaki, and to several other wonderful former students whose names now escape me.

Rosemarie Lang, Bobbie Goettler, and my copy editor Gail Welsh all put in many long hours preparing the manuscript for publication. And thanks to my publisher John R. Szilagyi, his assistant Sara Werden, and my production editor Alfred Symons, the manuscript made its way from acquisition to publication without a hitch.

Barbara J. O'Brien Young helped me every step of the way, listening patiently to me explain each new problem I encountered and rejoicing with me in each new insight. To her I am forever grateful.

Introduction

It's a commonly held belief that knowing your audience—your readers, listeners, viewers, and conversational partners—is the key to persuasive communication. But what does "knowing your audience" really mean? Does it mean knowing your audience's name, age, gender, and socioeconomic status?

This book presents business communication as a type of persuasive communication. It shows that if you want to be persuasive in business organizations, or indeed in almost any organization, the most important thing you need to know about your audience is how your audience makes decisions. And it demonstrates with numerous examples and research findings that when experienced and otherwise highly skilled professionals—CEOs, medical doctors, magazine publishers—fail to grasp how their audiences make decisions they also fail to persuade them.

Part I encompasses the first four chapters of the book and describes how audiences make rational decisions. Chapter 1 explains what audiences already know about making rational decisions. Whether you ask your audience to try out a new product, vote for a political candidate, approve a loan, take a prescribed medicine, convict a felon, acquire a new firm, or reply to an ad in the personal columns, many members of your audience will already know what type of information they need in order to make a good decision. What's more, they will expect you to provide that information to them.

Chapter 2 describes 13 major types of decisions that professionals from a wide range of fields routinely ask their audiences to make and outlines the audience's information requirements for each decision type. Chapter 3 presents a simple model of audience decision making and explains why you need to attend to each of the six cognitive processes in it. Chapter 4 reviews communication techniques that help make rational decision making easy for audiences and demonstrates that different techniques enable different cognitive processes to operate more efficiently.

If audiences were entirely logical, an understanding of how they make rational decisions would suffice. But audiences base their decisions on intuitions and emotions as well as sound reasoning. Part II consists of Chapters 5 and 6 and describes how audiences make intuitive decisions, decisions based on their subjective feelings. Chapter 5 shows that the same communication techniques that make audience decision making easy also make your messages to them more intuitively appealing. Chapter 6 explains how your audience's subjective feelings about you as a person, as opposed to the information you communicate to them, influence and bias their decisions.

Part III consists of the final chapter of the book and describes the role of emotions in audience decision making. It demonstrates that when you are able to evoke the values of your audience, their decision-making process becomes truncated and their emotions come to dominate the decisions they make. Moreover, it shows that different emotions affect audience decisions in different ways. Taken together, the three parts of the book give a complete picture of audiences as decision makers. The three parts explain how audiences make decisions with their head, gut, and heart, based on appeals to what the ancient Greeks termed *logos*, *ethos*, and *pathos*.

Most of the chapters of the book include *think-aloud protocols* of real audience members using real documents to make decisions. Think-aloud protocols are verbatim transcripts of people thinking aloud as they make decisions or solve problems. Think-aloud protocols have been used to investigate decision making in an ever-increasing number of areas including chess (e.g., de Groot 1965), writing (e.g., Flower & Hayes 1978), policy-making (e.g., Voss, Greene, Post, & Penner 1983), business (e.g., Hall & Hofer 1993), and law (e.g., Wright & Hall 2007).

In this book think-aloud protocols provide a unique window on audience decision making. They reveal the information an audience considers to be important when making a particular decision, as well as the information it considers to be irrelevant, the information it has difficulty comprehending, and much more. Exposure to think-aloud protocols of audiences has been shown to improve communication skills. Schriver (1992) found that college students who were given think-aloud protocols of audiences reading one set of documents made dramatic gains in their ability to predict problems that audiences would have with another set of documents of the same genre.

The book as a whole draws on a vast research literature and summarizes relevant theories and findings from the fields of social cognition, leadership, consumer behavior, decision science, behavioral economics, psycholinguistics, sociolinguistics, affective science, cognitive science, and neuroscience. It delves into the hearts and minds of a wide array of audiences: from Wall Street analysts to viewers of the evening news, from army officers to hospital patients, from venture capitalists to grocery shoppers, from CEOs to college admissions officers, from corporate recruiters to mock jurors. It surveys a broad range of communication techniques—including those concerning speaking and writing, interviews and group meetings, leading and critical thinking, content and style, verbal and nonverbal behaviors, the use of charts and images, the construction of rational arguments and emotional appeals—and examines the empirical evidence supporting each of them.

If you believe business communication is a form of persuasive communication and that the key to persuasive communication is knowing your audience, if you are looking for techniques to influence the decisions your audiences make, and if you want a scientific understanding of why those techniques work, then *How Audiences Decide* is the introduction to business communication for you.

PART I

Understanding Rational Decision Making

CHAPTER 1

Audience Decision-Making Expertise

In June 2008 a sourcing manager for a large networking company was asked to find a subcontractor capable of designing a hardware component for one of the firm's multi-million dollar networking projects. Although the firm had never contracted out the design of this particular component before, the sourcing manager soon found three interested design firms who appeared to be good candidates for the job.

In his initial discussions with the salespeople from each design firm via e-mail or telephone, the sourcing manager explained the goals of the project and gave them the information they would need to evaluate the opportunity they were being offered such as the forecasted demand, the timeline expectations, and the technical performance requirements. In order to expedite his selection process, the sourcing manager also sent each sales team the following questions to be answered in a crisp one-hour meeting:

- How would you describe your company?
- How complex were your past projects and when were they completed?
- How long did it take you to complete the projects?
- Were they completed on schedule?
- What kind of issues came up, and how did you overcome them?
- What do you see as the biggest risks and how would you mitigate them?

The VP of Sales for the first design firm and his team of technical experts spent most of their hour-long meeting presenting an overview of their company. The sourcing manager reiterated his need to get answers to the rest of his questions. So the VP requested another meeting to answer them. The manager told the VP that he did not have time for another meeting. Later, when the VP sent e-mails and left voicemails asking for another meeting, the sourcing manager politely declined once again.

The salespeople who represented the second design firm were equally disappointing. They spent about half their allotted time giving an overview of their company and then asked the sourcing manager to supply more details about his firm's project. The sourcing manager declined to tell them more and spent the remainder of the hour re-asking his initial questions. After the meeting he wondered whether he wanted to work with a company that needed him to repeat his criteria for choosing a subcontractor.

The sales team for third design firm was different. They addressed every one of the sourcing manager's questions during their one-hour meeting with him. They willingly disclosed the issues that had come up on similar projects just as the manager had requested, giving them added credibility in the manager's eyes. In addition, the third sales team asked relevant questions about the firm's objective for pursuing this particular networking project, the firm's required pricing, desired features, and availability.

It should come as no surprise that the sourcing manager recommended the third design firm to his upper management. The favorable impression made by that firm's sales team led to two significant contracts for the design firm totaling $15 million per year or $80 million over the lifetime of the project.

Although most audiences do not spell out their information requirements as clearly as the sourcing manager did for the three sales teams who presented to him, we can still learn several lessons from this true story. One of the most important lessons we can learn is that experienced audiences, like the sourcing manager, already know what information they need from other professionals in order to make the types of decisions they make routinely. What's more, experienced audiences may judge the quality of a recommendation or firm on the basis of how thoroughly, efficiently, and honestly business people and other professionals address their information needs. Chapter 1 amplifies these lessons. It describes the nature of audience expertise in decision making and what professionals in all industries need to know about it in order to be persuasive.

The audiences of professionals include all the people who read the documents professionals write, attend the presentations professionals give, and listen to what professionals have to say either in person or on the phone. Some important audiences of business executives are board members, stockholders, customers, employees, bankers, suppliers, distributors, and Wall Street analysts. Some important audiences of physicians are patients, staff, and colleagues. A few of the important audiences of attorneys are clients, judges, and jurors.

Audiences use the documents, presentations, and other information that professionals convey to make informed decisions. Board members use executives' strategic plans to decide whether to allow management to pursue a new strategic direction. Consumers use manufacturers' advertisements, packaging, product brochures, and warranties to decide whether to purchase a product. Bankers use entrepreneurs' proposals for credit lines to decide whether to extend credit. Undecided voters use politicians' campaign speeches to decide whether to vote for a particular candidate. Even US Army personnel do not blindly obey the orders of superior officers but use their directives to make decisions, decisions that might surprise the officers who issued the orders (cf., Shattuck 1995).

Researchers have found that 78 to 85% of all the reading employees do at work is for the purpose of making decisions and taking immediate action. In contrast, only 15% of the reading students do is for that purpose—students read primarily to learn and to recall later (Mikulecky 1981; Sticht 1977). Table 1.1 lists a few of the audiences with whom professionals communicate. In addition, it lists one type of document or presentation professionals produce for each audience, or one type of interaction they have, as well as the decision the document, presentation, or interaction should elicit from that audience. Of course, the list of audience decisions in Table 1.1 represents only a small fraction of the total number professionals must be ready to recognize and address.

Sometimes audience members make decisions as individuals and at other times they make decisions as a group, usually after much discussion and debate. For example, jurors decide as a group whether defendants are guilty or innocent, school board members decide as a group which curricula can be taught in local schools, legislators decide as a group which bills to pass into law, and faculty selection committee members decide as a group which candidates to hire. Most strategic business decisions are made by groups, as opposed to individuals (Levine, Resnick, & Higgins 1993; Orasanu & Salas 1993). In all of these cases, group members interact with each other, playing the roles of both communicators and audience members. As communicators, group members make arguments to the other group members for or against alternative proposals. As audience members, group members help decide which of the proposals made to the group is best.

Understanding audiences as decision makers differs dramatically from viewing them as passive receivers or decoders of information, the conventional view unintentionally inspired by the field of information theory (cf., Schriver 1997, pp. 6–8). Understanding that many audience members are expert at making the decisions professionals want them to make differs even more profoundly from the conventional view of audiences as empty cups waiting to be filled with the communicator's knowledge about a topic.

Audiences gain decision-making expertise as they make a particular type of decision repeatedly. For example, consumers, a primary audience of computer manufacturers, develop expertise that helps them choose the best computer after buying and using several different computers. Board members, a primary audience of business executives, develop expertise that helps them decide which new management proposal merits their approval by attending numerous board meetings. Voters, a primary audience of politicians, develop expertise that helps them decide which political candidate most deserves their vote by reading the news and voting regularly. With time and experience many audience members learn how to make good decisions. More specifically, they learn what information to look for in a document or presentation and what questions to pose

Table 1.1 Audiences Use Professionals' Documents and Presentations to Make Decisions

Professional	Audience	Document, presentation, or interaction	Audience decision
Politicians	Voters	Campaign speeches	Vote for candidate or not
Job applicants	Recruiters	Job interview responses	Hire applicant or not
Attorneys	Jurors	Defense arguments	Acquit defendant or not
Consultants	Clients	Project proposals	Hire consultants or not
Executives	Board members	Strategic plans	Approve strategy or not
Army officers	Subordinates	Intent statements	Follow orders or not

in meetings and conversations. Of course, audiences will sometimes lack the expertise they need to make some decisions. In these cases, audience members are dependent upon others to tell them what information they will need to consider in order to ensure that their decisions are well informed.

This chapter shows that professionals who understand audience decision-making expertise are in a good position to give novice or inexperienced audiences the information they need to make informed decisions. The before and after examples of documents in this chapter and others show that professionals who understand audience decision-making expertise are also in a good position to select and deliver the information expert audiences will find most relevant and persuasive.

DECISION CRITERIA OF EXPERT AUDIENCES

Decision Criteria: The Audience's Mental Checklist of Questions

As audience members become expert at making a particular type of decision, they develop a set of *decision criteria*. For example, expert consumers typically decide whether to purchase products based on decision criteria regarding the product's price, quality, reliability, warrantee, and so forth. Similarly, experienced board members decide whether to approve management's plans based on decision criteria regarding the plan's projected profitability, strategy, action items, and proposed source of financing. As the examples above illustrate, different types of decisions require audiences to use different decision criteria. A job applicant does not use the same decision criteria to decide whether to accept a new job that a banker uses to decide whether to call an overdue loan.

Decision criteria for any particular type of decision can be thought of as a mental checklist of questions expert audience members want answered before they make that decision (Goldstein & Weber 1995; Hitt & Tyler 1991; Wells 1974). For example, experienced used car buyers want answers to questions such as "What is the car's make, model, and year?" "What is its mileage?" "What condition is the car in?" "What is the car's maintenance history?" "What accessories are included?" and "What is the asking price?" before they are willing to purchase a used car. Decision criteria such as these guide the information search of expert audiences for the relatively small amounts of specific information upon which their decisions will be based (cf., Bouwman 1980; Brucks 1985; Johnson & Russo 1984).

Because expert audiences possess decision criteria, they notice when important information about any option or alternative they are considering is missing (Kardes & Sanbonmatsu 1993; Sanbonsatsu, Kardes, & Herr 1992). If important information about an alternative is not available, they tend to discount the value of that alternative or reject it outright (e.g., Beaulieu 1994; Markman & Medin 1995). For example, if an experienced used car buyer is unable to determine the mileage on a particular used car, it is unlikely that she will consider purchasing it.

Because expert audiences know exactly what type of information they are looking for, they may not read a document from start to finish but may jump around in it in order to more rapidly acquire the information each decision criterion demands (Bouwman,

Frishkoff, & Frishkoff 1987; Johnson 1988a; Libby & Frederick 1989). For example, expert business appraisers jump around in the documents they are given to more quickly locate the information they need to evaluate the worth of a company (Paek 1997). During a presentation, expert audiences may ask questions or interrupt a presenter to more quickly gain the information they require (Collins, Brown, & Larkin 1980; Serfaty, MacMillan, Entin, & Entin 1997).

As soon as they find the answers to their decision criteria or mental checklist of questions, expert audience members stop searching and make their decisions (Nickles 1995; Saad & Russo 1996). For instance, Lipp and colleagues (1992) asked experts in corporate real estate disposition to decide how to dispose of different marketable properties. The real estate experts asked many short-answer questions about each property and made their decisions as soon as they acquired all of the answers to their questions.

The Number of Decision Criteria in Audience Decisions

Audiences' mental checklists of decision criteria do not appear to be long or complex. For most decisions, audiences seem to seek answers to only six or seven basic questions (cf., Bouwman 1980; Elstein, Shulman, & Sprafka 1978; Libby & Frederick 1989). For example, expert investors selecting stock use six "general evaluative factor categories," or decision criteria, that include both accounting and non-accounting information (Kercsmar 1985). CFOs and VPs of Development use six basic criteria, or "lines of reasoning," to make acquisition decisions as they read company descriptions: The strategic fit of the candidate with the acquirer, the competitive environment of the candidate, the management expertise of the candidate, the financial condition of the candidate and terms of the deal, the operational capabilities of the candidate, and the synergies between the candidate and the acquirer (Melone 1987, 1994). Pfeffer (1987) finds that the overwhelming majority (94%) of comments expert venture capitalists make when screening business plans focus on only seven factors other than the way the plan is presented: the market, the product, the management, the company, the financials, the board of directors, and the terms of the deal.

Other expert audiences also rely on a finite list of criteria to make decisions. In a study of the selection criteria of more than 400 top executives, Sessa and colleagues (1998; Sessa 2001) find that top executives have 6.7 requirements on average that they look for in candidates for top leadership positions in business. Listed in order the top seven requirements are: specific functional background, managerial skills, interpersonal skills, communication skills, technical knowledge, leadership skills, and team skills. US Army officers use a core set of six criteria to evaluate noncommissioned officers: initiative, responsibility, organizational skills, technical proficiency, assertive leadership skills, and supportive leadership skills (Borman 1987). In a study of 10 experienced real estate banking lenders and 10 experienced private banking lenders making two commercial lending decisions, Hardin (1996) finds that on average the real estate lenders spend more than 30 seconds on just seven pieces of information—the guarantor's income statement, the guarantor's balance sheet, the project's rent roll, the project's profit/loss statement, the market demographics, the project's pro forma profit/loss statement, and the market rents. Private banking lenders, on the other hand, spend more than 30 seconds on only two pieces of information—the guarantor's income statement and balance sheet. Both groups of lenders use other available pieces of information much less if it all.

Consumers also use a limited number of decision criteria when deciding to purchase goods and services. Although the typical American consumer is exposed to 300 advertisements per day (Britt, Adams, & Miller 1972), consumers consider only a small proportion of the available information relevant to the products and services they buy (Russo 1977; Russo, Staelin, Nolan, Russell, & Metcalf 1986). Even when they are presented with a great deal of product information, consumers usually rely upon a common, small set of criteria to make their decisions (Alpert 1971; Green & Srinivasan 1978).

Under time constraints audiences may use even fewer criteria when making a decision. For example, in a study of consumers selecting refrigerators, Verplanken and Weenig (1993) find that most consumers do not use information about refrigerators' energy efficiency when under time pressure to make a choice. Consumers neglect to use energy efficiency information even though it indicates the refrigerator's relative cost of operation and is usually prominently displayed on each refrigerator's door.

Although audiences seem to seek answers to only six or seven basic questions, each question may subsume several related or follow-up questions that operationalize it. Audiences operationalize and elaborate on their decision criteria via *metrics* and *tests*. Metrics and tests indicate more specifically what audiences are looking for when they ask a decision-making question. Metrics are quantitative in nature and provide results that can be measured and compared with other quantitative data. For example, many car buyers make their purchasing decision in part on the basis of the car's reliability. Metrics of the reliability of the various models under consideration might include the average number of days in the shop per year, the average number of repairs per year, and the average cost of repairs per year. Metrics of a firm's profitability might include its net income for the year, its return on equity, its return on assets, and its economic value added, to name a few. Metrics used by buy-side analysts to determine a firm's future value include the firm's earnings per share, return on investment (ROI), working capital, and liquidity (Frishkoff, Frishkoff, & Bouwman 1984).

Unlike metrics, tests are qualitative in nature. For example, to test if management has recommended a reasonable competitive strategy, board members may try to determine if the strategy builds on the firm's core competency, offers a distinct competitive advantage, and matches the management's corporate objectives.

The Similarity of Decision Criteria Among Audience Members

What makes knowing an audience's decision criteria so useful to professionals is the fact that different expert audience members tend to use the same decision criteria to make similar types of decisions. Knowing how expert audiences make decisions would not be very useful if every individual audience member used different criteria when making the same type of decision. But studies of experienced audience members making decisions show they are highly constrained by the type of decision they make. For example, experienced investors of any age, nationality, political party, gender, education level, or income bracket all use the same basic criteria to evaluate a business plan before writing the entrepreneur a check (cf., Hall & Hoffer 1993; Sandberg, Schweiger, & Hofer 1988). If they forget to evaluate the nature of the new business, the management team's experience, the projected sales, ROI, and so on, then they know from experience that they are very likely to lose their money. And this is one thing few investors care to do! Similarly, studies of jurors making decisions find that most demographic variables—including the juror's gender, age, intelligence, marital status, race, and occupation—rarely have any significant impact on the verdicts jurors hand down (Becker 1998; Goodman, Loftus, & Greene 1990; McCoy 1997).

The commonality of decision criteria among experts in a field is a robust research finding. Public school administrators use similar decision criteria to make budget decisions (Smotas 1996). Computer experts use similar decision criteria and give each criterion similar weight when selecting hardware and software products (Galletta, King, & Rateb 1993). In a study of finance directors from both US and UK multinationals making overseas financing decisions, Hooper (1994) finds that neither their decision criteria nor the relative importance of their decision criteria differ significantly. Consumers use similar decision criteria for deciding among brands of exercise equipment in different product categories and use them consistently (Graonic 1995). Consumers also use similar decision criteria, in this case similar product attributes, when choosing among brands within other product classes (Haines 1974; Palmer & Faivre 1973).

Experts in other fields also use similar criteria to make similar decisions. For example, pharmacists use the same four to six criteria when deciding whether to counsel a patient on a prescription: indication, the patient's age, drug interactions, adverse reactions, new prescription versus refill, and the number of medications currently being taken (Kier 2000). In a study of financial analysts using financial statements to assess companies' earning power, Biggs (1984, p. 313) finds that financial analysts employed by different financial institutions reveal "considerable similarity on the amount and type of information searched." Kuperman (2000) also finds a high level of similarity among analysts: "They seemed to be discussing many of the same issues and offering similar insights to one another" (p. 12). And in their review of the research on venture capitalists' decision making, Sandberg and colleagues (1988, p. 12) report that among the three most complete studies they review (MacMillan, Siegal, & Narasimha 1985; Robinson 1985; Tyebjee & Bruno 1984) "the most important area of consensus is the identity of the venture capitalists' criteria."

Audience Expectations Based on Decision Criteria

Expert audiences expect professionals to address their decision criteria. Both corporate recruiters and line managers rate job applicants' résumés more highly when the résumés address the criteria for success at the specific job (Brown & Campion 1994). Buyers are more likely to purchase from salespeople who accurately ascertain and explain the product attributes that are important to them (Weitz 1978). Like the sourcing manager in the story at the beginning of this chapter, purchasing agents rate salespeople's effectiveness more highly the more accurate the salespeople are in determining their purchasing criteria (Frame 1990). Surprisingly, the salesperson's level of motivation has a negative relationship to the purchasing agent's evaluation of that salesperson's effectiveness. Other attributes of salespeople such as their personality traits, job tenure, and selling experience have little if any effect on their performance (Baehr & Williams 1968; Ghiselli 1969, 1973; Tanofsky, Shepps, & O'Neill 1969).

Wall Street analysts expect firms to disclose specific financial and nonfinancial information pertaining to their decision criteria and may penalize firms that fail to do so (Kuperman 2000). As one analyst notes, "Analysts are always skeptical that if you're not giving out the information perhaps it's because you overpaid for something or there's some other reason." Another analyst observes that when firms "didn't provide us with a lot of information, it was normally a sign that they didn't have a lot of good information themselves" (Kuperman 2000, p. 39).

One important function of management consultants is to inform clients of the decision criteria of the clients' audiences. In a study comparing an expert management consultant to a freshly minted MBA who had just been hired by a top consulting firm, Young (1989) asked both the expert and novice consultants to analyze two actual business plans and to give advice to the entrepreneurs who wrote them. The expert consultant based his advice on the decision criteria of venture capitalists—entrepreneurs often send their business plans to venture capitalists in hopes of raising money for their new businesses. The expert consultant first explained to the entrepreneur the problems a venture capitalist would have with her current plan. He then helped her discover how she could change her business plan to satisfy the venture capitalist's decision criteria. For example, she could find a partner who possessed the business experience she lacked. In contrast, the new MBA relied on his function area or textbook knowledge to advise his client and never mentioned venture capitalists or their decision criteria to his client. For the expert consultant the client's business problem was identical to her rhetorical problem—how to satisfy a venture capitalist's decision criteria. For the new MBA, the client's business problems were independent of the audience. From the new MBA's perspective, his client simply needed to plan his new business "correctly."

Some business audiences put an extremely high premium on getting information that addresses their decision criteria. In a study of the responses of business executives to two business communication students' memos, Nicholas (1983) actually found an inverse relationship between the students' level of knowledge of and skill in business communication and the executives' ratings of the two students' memos. To her surprise, the executives rated the memo composed by the high-knowledge, highly skilled business communication student as ineffective. And despite the less skilled student's poor spelling, incorrect grammar, tortured syntax, lack of knowledge about business communication, and inability to defend a point of view, the executives rated his memo as highly effective. Why? As one of the executives explained, the strength of the less skilled student's memo was that it included "sufficient information for decision making" (p. 89).

Expert audiences also expect professionals to avoid presenting information that does not address their decision criteria. Frame (1990) finds that purchasing agents react negatively to sales presentations that include information irrelevant to their decision criteria. For instance, two purchasing agents in his study had especially negative reactions to salespeople who began their initial sales calls with in-depth descriptions of the selling firm's organization chart. Similarly, Carenini (2001) finds apartment seekers are more persuaded by recommendations that exclude features or benefits that are irrelevant to their decision criteria than by recommendations that include such features. In their think-aloud study of venture capitalists reading business plans, Hall and Hofer (1993) found "the thrust of the [venture capitalists'] protocol comments was that venture proposals should be short documents that provide the major pieces of information the venture capitalist needs to make a decision" (p. 40).

Techniques for Discovering and Using Audience Decision Criteria

Two of the more commonly used techniques for teasing out experts' decision criteria and their weights, or degree of importance, are Multi-Attribute Utility Analysis (Keeney & Raiffa 1976, 1993) and the Analytical Hierarchy Process (Saaty 1980). Both techniques first elicit a set of decision criteria from the experts and then elicit information that determines the weights experts assign them. Decisions computed by the resulting models tend to agree with experts' actual decisions with an average convergent validity ranging from 0.70 to 0.95 (Beach, Campbell, & Townes 1979; Borcherding & Rohrmann 1990; Von Winterfeldt & Edwards 1973). Not surprisingly, the models that both techniques elicit tend to yield similar decisions (Stillwell, Barron, & Edwards 1983).

Persuasive documents based on the models elicited by these techniques have been empirically tested by real audience members. For example, Carenini (2001) used multi-attribute utility models of renters' decision criteria to automatically generate arguments for choosing specific apartments. The arguments generated successfully persuaded real renters to choose the apartment the model recommended. Similarly, Carter and coauthors (1986) used a multi-attribute utility model of several hundred hospital patients' decision criteria to write a brochure that persuaded many to get flu shots. Of those patients who received the model-based brochure, 64% obtained flu shots compared to only 34% of the control group who received a brochure written, as is typically done, without the benefit of the model. A second model-based brochure improved patient compliance rates to Pap smear procedures by approximately 15% over rates achieved with conventionally produced brochures.

Another technique for teasing out experts' decision criteria is to ask experts to think out loud as they make decisions (cf., Ericsson 2001, 2006; Ericsson & Simon 1993). On the following five pages, an experienced investor's think-aloud comments about two versions of the same business plan's executive summary (note: The product and its attributes, the dates and numbers, and the entrepreneur's name and background have been changed) illustrate the dramatic difference that addressing the audience's decision criteria can make. The comments the investor made while reading the plan and "thinking aloud" were recorded, transcribed, numbered, and inserted into the text of the executive summary in bold and brackets.

As can be seen, the investor's comments about the original version are quite negative. They indicate the investor is not interested in investing his money in the new business. Missing from the original plan's summary are the answers to the investor's mental checklist of questions or decision criteria.

Notice that the investor spontaneously listed his decision criteria in comments 26 through 36 after he finished reading the original version. The decision criteria he lists concern the tax ramifications of the investment, the nature of the project, the amount of the investment required, the projected revenue and profit, the qualifications of the entrepreneur, and the plan for cashing out of the investment. When the investor read the revised version about a week later, he came away with a much more positive impression. Notice that the writer of the revision explicitly addressed each of the investor's decision criteria and used section headings to highlight them.

Original Executive Summary of a Business Plan with an Investor's Comments

Smartphone MBA

January 15, 2005
Limited Partnership Interests for $350,000
Copy 12

Executive Summary

The following is a business plan for a new company to be titled *Smartphone MBA* that will develop, sell, and deliver via smartphones a line of educational modules in the form of three-minute videos each of which briefly addresses an important topic covered in the curricula of top twenty business schools. This business plan provides a description of the new service, a look at the market for subscribers and advertisers, as well as action plans for starting operations.

The target market for Smartphone MBA consists of three main groups of subscribers: current MBA students who are presently enrolled in an MBA program, graduated MBAs who want a quick and easy refresher, and prospective MBA students who are planning to get an MBA in the near future **[current MBA students, graduated MBAs, and prospective MBA students.[1]]** Taken together, these three groups are expected to total over 2 million potential subscribers by 2010. Currently, there are no smartphone services targeted specifically to people who are enrolled in, plan to enroll in, or have graduated from an MBA program. This creates a significant opportunity for subscription sales as well as for advertisement of a wide range of elite business and consumer goods and services.

Sales projections for *Smartphone MBA* estimate a subscriber base of 40,000 for the premier installment. **[What's this 40,000 for the premier installment?[2]]** Subscription sales are expected to quadruple to 160,000 within five years. **[They say there are two million potential subscribers out of this group, these three categories. And they have a goal of reaching an initial subscription of 40,000 and 160,000 within five years. Okay. That's understandable.[3]]** The management's five-year projections concerning *Smartphone MBA*'s profits from subscriptions and advertisements can be found in the attachments provided at the end of this document. **[Management's projections? What the management of Smartphone MBA projects? That's what they're talking about. Okay.[4]]** However, as is explained in the section titled "Scenario Analysis," no guarantees about these projections can be made. **[Now where in the heck's the "Scenario Analysis"? See the way they've got this organized, they say they'll start off with the Scenario Analysis. But then they begin with editorial concepts. Then they refer to the Scenario Analysis. Now you've got to go dig out the Scenario Analysis.[5]]**

Seven interests in a limited partnership to be organized under the laws of the State of California and to be known as Smartphone MBA Company (the "Partnership") are being offered by Pallav Srisuwanporn (the "General Partner"). Purchasers of such interests shall be referred to herein as Limited Partners. The General Partner will contribute the concept and vision of the subscription service. The entire capital of the Partnership will be contributed by the Limited Partners. **[He doesn't have any risk in it. He has no risk at all.[6]]** The total profit-sharing interests in the Partnership for the Limited Partners will be 15.05000%. The General Partner will reserve a 84.95000% profit-sharing interest in the Partnership. **[That sounds extraordinarily high for the General Partner. He doesn't have anything at risk. All he has is an idea and he's asking the limited partners to take 85% of the risk. That's outrageous! I mean this would have to be a sure thing.[7]]**

The General Partner may raise additional capital by selling additional Limited Partnership Interests in the Partnership up to a maximum amount, including the amount hereunder, of $900,000 without the consent of any of the Limited Partners. **[Oh, he's only trying to raise $900,000. It's not that big a partnership, is it? It doesn't require much capital.[8]]** The sale of these Partnership Interests shall not dilute the Partnership Interests of the Limited Partners. **[In essence, what's he doing? He has 85%. Okay, so he sells off interest in his 85% interest.[9] It doesn't say anything about his background, does it?[10] Oh, here's the Scenario Analysis on another page. Just let me jump around here a minute to see what we've got ... Educational Concepts ... This thing isn't put in the order it's listed.[11] When I read these things I like to start off with the people involved. Is there anything in here about the background of the guy who is going to be the General Partner? (The investor then finds the General Partner's résumé in an appendix.) Oh, here he is.[12]]** With the consent of Limited Partners holding as a group a 50% Partnership Interest in the Partnership, the General Partner may raise capital in excess of such amount by selling additional Limited Partnership Interests. **[What the heck does that mean? It says your Limited Partnerships start out with 15% of the partnership. This is really poorly written.[13]]**

The purpose of the Partnership formation is to perform a test market advertisement campaign to determine if starting *Smartphone MBA* makes economic sense. For a subscription service, a greater than 3% positive response to a test market campaign is generally necessary before going to the next phase. If the response to the test marketing falls below this percentage, the plans for the service will be terminated and no remuneration to the Limited Partners will be provided. If the response is greater than 3%, the next step will be full-scale production of the educational modules. To start full-scale production will require the rental of office space, the recruitment of qualified educators, technical staff, and advertisement salespeople, the acquisition of office equipment, the selling advertising space, the creation of relations with vendors, **[Etcetera, etcetera.[14]]** and the raising of additional capital (see the section entitled "Phase One"). Purchase of servers and other equipment necessary to establish an online presence will be delayed until Phase Two is complete. Monies from the sale of interests in the Partnership will be expended on design of the MBA modules ($11,500), legal services ($10,000), advertising expenses ($240,000), production equipment ($60,000), and other ($28,500), for a grand total of $350,000. **[So ... you've got 350 thou' but he's raising 900.[15]]**

No person is authorized to give any information or representation not contained in this memorandum. Any information or representation not contained herein **[Etcetera, etcetera.[16]]** must not be relied upon as having been authorized by the Partnership or the General Partner. **[Blah, blah, blah.[17]]**

[This guy wants to raise 900 thousand dollars. He's going to spend 350 thousand on this. He says if Phase One isn't successful based on the test market, that the Partnership will be disbanded. There's no mention of what happens with the difference between 900 and the 350 thousand.[18]]

He doesn't have anything to risk. I mean how much incentive is there for this guy? How heavily tied is he to the success of the project? What's his incentive to watch expenses?[19]

This is a lousy deal.[20]

Wait a minute. It says 350,000 Partnership interest, I misread this. They're going to raise 350,000 initially, and then they can sell additional Partnership Interests to bring it up to the 900,000. I see.[21]

But still he has nothing at risk. One of the things I look at is what the General Partners have at risk. If they don't have anything at risk, move on. It reflects how enthusiastic he is about his idea. I mean a guy like this ought to mortgage his home.[22]

I want to see "John Doe", his background in the business, what he's done. Now his background is back here, you could dig it out.[23]

Telling you who their market is, is a good idea.[24]

But I want to see right out front what kind of money this Srisuwanporn guy is putting up of his own.[25]

I'd like to see what the tax ramifications are right up front. If you buy a 50,000 dollar unit, how much of a tax write off, if any, do you get the first year or the second year?[26]

I want to know what the project is,[27] the amount of the required investment,[28] what the tax ramifications are,[29] projected revenue and profit.[30]

The expenses he lists aren't necessary to include.[31] I want something on him.[32]

I want to be able to look at this and say, in five years, my $50,000 will be worth $250,000 or whatever.[33] I want to look at ventures that will potentially give me five times my investment within five years, that's an extreme example. What I would say is that I want to look at projects that will give me a 20% return on my money in four years at the very least. Today I can get 12% and 13% in a mutual fund, why should I go into a venture that doesn't double my money in four years?[34]

So I want to know right off the top what the profit potential is.[35]

Once you know what the profit potential is, how do you get out of this thing?[36]

These are the things that would tell me how much I want to dig into it.[37]]

Revised Executive Summary of a Business Plan with an Investor's Comments

Smartphone MBA

January 15, 2005
Seven Limited Partnership Interests for $50,000 each
Copy 12

Executive Summary

Objective: This is a brief overview of some of the critical characteristics of a unique investment opportunity. It covers the nature of the investment, who is behind the project, as well as the expected returns on the project. All of the topics covered in the summary, as well as other subjects not addressed here, are discussed in greater detail in the body of the business plan. [Okay.[1]]

What is the venture?

We are presently offering limited partnerships in a new educational subscription service to be delivered via smartphones called *Smartphone MBA*. **[Right.²]** An educational subscription service developed specifically for smartphone owners does not yet exist. *Smartphone MBA* will target an audience of over 2 million potential subscribers:

Current MBA students—students currently enrolled in an MBA program.
Graduates of MBA programs—executives who have already earned an MBA.
Prospective MBA students—people interested in enrolling in an MBA program.

Who is doing this?

Pallav Srisuwanporn is the General Partner of this project as well as being the president of this subscription service. He is a thirty-year-old graduate of the Stanford Business School. His experience includes positions with the McGraw-Hill Companies, publishers of *Business Week, Aviation Week,* **[That's impressive.³]** and other consumer and business communications. Mr. Srisuwanporn was also Vice President of Planning and Finance of Condé Nast Publications. Among the Condé Nast magazines were *Vogue, W, GQ, Brides* and others. He is currently the Senior Vice President of the Wiley Computer Publishing Division. **[Well, this guy ought to know what he's doing.⁴]**

How much can I invest?

Seven limited Partnership Interests are being sold for $50,000 each. You can buy as many of the Interests as you like. Once the project is underway you will have opportunities to contribute additional capital.

What is the projected return?

Each of your limited Partnerships represents a 2.15% profit-sharing interest. All together the seven interests will receive 15.05% of the profit-share. The General Partner accounts for an 84.95% share. The projected return over the next five years is:

YEAR	NET CASHFLOW	A 2.15% SHARE
Initial Phase	–$4,985,000	–$107,260
2006	–$3,187,000	–$68,570
2007	$4,193,000	$90,220
2008	$12,247,000	$263,530
2009	$25,988,000	$559,200
2010	$38,132,000	$820,520

[They've got to be kidding. For a $50,000 investment? I'll have to look at that more closely in the plan.⁵]

How will this affect my taxes?

A Partnership is not a taxable entity. Instead, each item of partnership income, gain, loss, deduction, or credit flows through to you and Mr. Srisuwanporn.

For example: You own a 2.15% profit-share of *Smartphone MBA*. During the initial phase you will experience a $107,260 loss from the Partnership. Since you are in the 35% tax bracket **[Yup, yup, yup.[6]]** you save $37,541 in taxes because of the write off. If the projected returns continue to prove accurate you will save $24,000 the first year of business because of losses. The second year you will be entitled to a $90,220 profit which, after taxes, will leave you with $58,643. So it will continue into the coming years.

What if I want out?

This partnership is only for the serious investor who does not plan to immediately resell his share. The Interests are not freely transferable. **[Hmmmm.[7]]**

Is this investment right for me?

This project is only for those who share the true spirit of the entrepreneur. Because of the lack of liquidity and the high degree of risk involved in starting Smartphone MBA you should only consider this project if you can afford to lose it all! To be sure if this investment could be for you, read the entire plan. **[Okay, I'll read this thing. It could be good.[8]]**

BENCHMARKS OF EXPERT AUDIENCES

Benchmarks: The Comparative Information Audiences Require

Audiences not only use decision criteria to ask relevant questions about the person, product, proposal, or performance under consideration, they also use decision criteria to ask relevant questions about their alternatives, or options, as well as about averages and norms. Audiences then use this comparative information to evaluate the relative benefits of the recommended alternative. For example, used-car buyers would be foolish to purchase a used car immediately after the seller addressed their decision criteria. To make a good decision, that is, a fully informed decision, the car buyers must first acquire comparative information about similar used cars and the fair market value of that make and model as quoted in the *Blue Book*.

A common term for the comparative information audiences seek in order to evaluate the responses to their decision criteria is *benchmark*. For example, a common benchmark investors use to decide how well their stock portfolio is doing is the current value of the S&P 500. Investors know something is wrong if the value of their portfolio has declined while the value of the S&P 500 has skyrocketed.

Some benchmarks are organization specific, such as predefined quotas and hurdle rates. Others are audience member specific, such as comparisons to one's own previous experience. The benchmark most commonly used when audiences consider only one alternative and simply decide whether to accept or reject it is the status quo (cf. Kahneman, Knetsch, & Thaler 1990; Schweitzer 1994; Svenson 2003). Ultimately, audiences need comparative data in order to make rational decisions. For most decisions, a value, such as the price of a car, is good or bad only relative to another value, not in the absolute.

Table 1.2 Audiences Use Benchmarks when Making Decisions

Audience	Decision	Benchmarks
Investors	To hold a mutual fund or not	Performance of other mutual funds; performance of S&P 500; current interest rates for CDs
Consumers	To buy a laptop or not	Competitors' laptops; firm's other models; computer currently owned
Board members	To approve a strategy or not	Competitors' strategies; alternative competitive strategies; current strategy
Job applicants	To accept a job offer or not	Other job offers; current salary; past salary; job offers of peers

All types of audiences use benchmarks to make decisions (see Table 1.2). Expert auditors from large international accounting firms compare their client firm's performance and practices to industry norms before making their audit decisions (Lauer & Peacock 1992). When asked to evaluate their MBA program, MBA students compare their program to other MBA programs (Burgoyne 1975). Patients' reactions to information about risks to their health depend on the comparative information that is available to them (e.g., Rothman, Haddock, & Schwarz 2001; Windschitl & Weber 1999; see Klein & Weinstein 1997 for a review). Not surprisingly, patients tend to search selectively for comparative information that casts their health situation in a favorable light (Wood, Taylor, & Lichtman 1985a). In a study of security analysts making investment decisions based on company descriptions, Gunderson (1991) shows that expert security analysts use a number of benchmarks to evaluate a company's current results, including the firm's historical results, the current value of the S&P 500, competitor results, overall industry results, and the state of the general economy.

The finding that audiences depend on benchmarks to make decisions has been especially robust in the area of consumer decision making. In a study of expert consumers reading both comparative and non-comparative ads, Lee (1989a) shows that expert consumers actively seek comparative product information when choosing among brands with which they are not already familiar. Consumers choosing among non-comparable items base their choices on abstract decision criteria such as necessity and enjoyment (Bettman & Sujan 1987; Johnson 1986, 1988b). These more abstract criteria allow consumers to make comparisons among otherwise non-comparable alternative products, just as they would if they were choosing among comparable products. When evaluating a new product, consumers tend to rely on prototypical products from the product category as comparative standards (Jung 1996).

Audience Expectations about Benchmark Information

Audiences expect professionals to provide them with benchmark information. On the next page, two excerpts from a board meeting of a simulated detergent manufacturing firm illustrate the importance of benchmarks to an experienced audience (adapted from Stratman & Young 1986). MBA students comprised the top management team of the simulated firm. In the board meeting the MBA students presented their report of last year's performance and their plans for the next year to a board of directors composed of experienced top managers. The board members' questions in bold and italics are requests for benchmark information.

The fact that the board members had to request benchmark information from the student team indicates the students were unaware of the crucial role benchmarks play in the audience's decision-making process (note: The names of the students have been changed). In the first excerpt, a board member requests benchmark information in order to evaluate the interest rate and type of loan the team secured. Given that interest rates rose the previous year, locking in the lower rate seemed to be a good decision for the team. In the second excerpt, the chairman of the board requests benchmark information about competitors' financial results. Initially the team's financial results sound outstanding. But when compared to their competitors' results, the team's results turn out to be about average.

Two Excerpts from a Presentation Given by MBA Students to an Experienced Board of Directors

Excerpt 1: A request for interest rate benchmarks

Student VP of Finance: Just give you a quick overview of the way we went about funding our expansion. Cost of our expansion was approximately $36,600,000. We had 15 million of long-term debt that we renewed at 14% fixed-rate amortized for the next five years. We wanted to finance construction [of a plant expansion] with as much internal generated funds as possible. And we had 19.2 million in cash from market securities at the end of last year. We negotiated a 20 million dollar line of credit with the bank to help us finance the expansion and also to help with the operating expenses. As a result, using our cash and our line of credit we were able to fund the expansion, and since then the line of credit has now been reduced to 12.5 million. And if we can, we hope to continue to reduce this as fast as possible.

Board Member: *How does the 14% fixed-rate compare to what benchmark rates or government rates were at the time for the same term?*

Student VP of Finance: The prime rate at the time was 12% with a prime plus two. And talking to people in our bank this was an average and much more favorable rate in relation to our competitors.

Board Member: You have prime plus two fixed though for five years, not floating with the prime?

Student VP of Finance: Right, yes. Prime was at 12% at the time that we negotiated.

Student VP of Marketing: It is now at 19.

Board Member: It's now 19. So the outlook for rates was that they were going to be rising.

Student VP of Finance: Right. Inflation was running at a fairly good clip and we thought the best thing to do was to try to lock in a rate. If you don't have any questions I would like to go over the results of the labor negotiations.

Excerpt 2: A request for competitive benchmarks

Student CEO: Okay. Fine. Okay. Very quickly I want to just give you the highlights from 1986. That is on July first we opened the new 38 million dollar factory and warehouse. Also during the year we submitted in our new advertising campaign, and we participated in the labor negotiations which Aditya just went through. Currently, we are producing two products for the commercial market inside the nation. A high sudser detergent, a medium sudser, and we're producing one product in the industrial market.

Right now, we have overall a 31% market share. And on a financial note net income rose 6.9 million last year to 23.7 million this year. This was on an increase to retained earnings of 22.5 million versus last year at 5.7 million. Much of this increase is due as Robert mentioned to the additional capacity that we have with the factory, with the new factory. It allowed us to do two things. One was to produce more goods for sale within the commercial end of the business and the other allows us to also get into the industrial market.

Stock price rose from last year roughly at this time from the low 50s to almost $90.00 per share right now. And earnings per share climbed from $6.96 last year to $23.68. Return on investment for the year was 23%, and return on equity was 42%. So with that in mind what we would like to do is present to you our main concerns for 1987.

Chairman of the Board: No. We would like to discuss that a little more. ***Do you have any comparative numbers for the competitors in our nation? What did the competitors' stock prices do?***

Student CEO: In our nation, Team 3, Yun Wang's team is at $90.00 stock price and Brenda Kelley, the third competitor, is at $110.00, I think it is. She's number one in the nation and in the world right now which is at $110.00. We are in at $90.00. We are sort of in the thick of things.

Audience-Provided Benchmarks

Audiences sometimes compare recommended alternatives to personal or subjective standards or benchmarks. In a study of renters' decision making, Svenson (1974) gave renters descriptions of seven houses with each house described in a separate booklet. Of all the comparisons the renters made, 71% were comparisons to a subjective standard, the remaining 29% were comparisons among alternative houses. A study of recruiters screening résumés for a supervisory position finds that recruiters use themselves as benchmarks: The more similar the applicant's background is to the background of the recruiter evaluating that applicant, the higher the probability the applicant will be hired (Ruck 1980). Consumers often generate a subjective reference price for a product based on its quality, and then evaluate different brands by comparing the subjective reference price to the actual price (Ordonez 1994).

Expert audiences may supply comparative information about alternatives when it is missing from a document or presentation. When consumers retrieve comparative information from their memories, the information they retrieve has a stronger effect on their decisions than does comparative information provided by an external source

(Dhar & Simonson 1992). When the missing information is not retrievable, audiences may infer it. Sanbonmatsu and coauthors (1992) gave expert and novice consumers of bicycles written descriptions of bicycles in which important information such as the weight of the bicycle was missing for some of the bicycles. Although novices were unconcerned that information was missing, experts who understood the importance of the missing information tried to guess what it would be for each bicycle model before making their decisions. However, even experts may not take the time necessary to infer missing attribute values of alternatives if the number of missing values is large or if they are not confident in their ability to make the inferences accurately (Burke 1992).

DECISION SCHEMATA OF EXPERT AUDIENCES

Decision Schemata: The Audience's Decision-Making Framework

When experts' decision criteria and benchmarks are plotted out, they form a grid or *decision matrix*. Figure 1.1 shows an example of a decision matrix for deciding on a new car in 2007. The first column of the matrix lists possible decision criteria. The first row indicates the recommended car and benchmark, or alternative, cars. The cells of the matrix give the values for the recommended and benchmark vehicles. But do such matrix representations have any psychological reality? Do they reflect something about the underlying structure of decision-making expertise? Research suggests the answer is *yes*. Expert decision makers appear to have decision-specific knowledge structures (cf., Walsh 1995), or mental representations, stored in their long-term memories that correspond to decision matrices. It is these knowledge structures that lead experts to mentally represent each alternative they consider as values along a number of attributes or decision criteria (e.g., Svenson 1979; Wallsten 1980).

Decision criteria	Recommendation (Car under consideration)	Benchmark 1 (Comparable car)	Benchmark 2 (Current car to be traded in)
Year, make, and model	2007 Lexus RX350	2007 Mercedes-Benz M-Class	1999 Ford Taurus
Type of car	Sport utility vehicle	Sport utility vehicle	Sedan
Overall miles per gallon	19	19	21
Reliability	Very good	Poor	Good
Safety record	Good	Good	Good
Depreciation rate			Very good
Suggested retail price	$34,500	$52,000	$21,500 (new)

Figure 1.1 Decision Matrices Incorporate Both Decision Criteria and Benchmarks

Cognitive scientists call such knowledge structures *schemata* (Carlston & Smith 1996; Chi & Ohlsson 2005; Markman 1999). Schemata are mental frameworks that reside in an expert's long-term memory into which new information can be fitted and made sense of (Fiedler 1982). Other terms for schemata include *scripts* (Schank & Abelson 1977), *frames* (Minsky 1975), *mental models* (Johnson-Laird 1980), and *knowledge representations* (Markman 1999). Grafman (1995) proposes that schema-level representations are stored in the frontal cortex of the brain. More recently, Mason and Just (2006) find evidence for schema-level representations being distributed over different areas of the cortex. Schemata, like the decision matrix illustrated in Figure 1.1, consist of slots that indicate the expert's knowledge relevant to a particular decision as well as empty slots that can be filled with situation-specific information called *slot values* (Brewer & Nakamura 1984; Marshall 1995; Minsky 1975). In Figure 1.1 the slot values for the car under consideration are 2007 Lexus RX350, Sport utility vehicle, 19, Very Good, Good, and $34,500. Sometimes the slots in an expert's schema may already be filled with default values. But when experts start to instantiate their schemata, they usually replace those default values with the actual values of the alternatives under consideration (Brewer & Tenpenny 1996).

Long-term memory is composed largely of schemata (Neisser 1976) and much of what we call expertise is schema-driven. Expertise has been shown to be schema-driven in accounting (Bhaskar 1978), physics (Larkin, McDermott, Simon, & Simon 1980), algebra word problems (Hinsley, Hayes, & Simon 1977), and medicine (Heller, Saltzstein, & Caspe 1992). Expertise in making parole decisions has been shown to be schema-driven (Carroll 1978), as has expertise in chess, law, and business. Wall Street analysts' ability to value firms and their acquisitions has been shown to depend on the analysts' schemata (Kuperman 2000). In addition, the ability of business leaders and military officers to effectively lead their subordinates has been shown to depend on their possessing complex and highly organized schemata (Connelly et al. 2000; Mumford, Marks, Connelly, Zaccaro, & Reiter-Palmon 2000; Wofford, Goodwin, & Whittington 1998).

The knowledge experienced consumers have about evaluating brands in a product class may also be thought of as schemata (Gardner 1981). A consumer's schemata for particular brands "largely determine how the consumer reacts to advertising" (Sentis & Markus 1986, p. 133).

Researchers agree that schemata are critical to decision making and high-level thought. In concluding their study of 713 product decisions made by second-year MBA students in the context of a marketing simulation, Walsh and colleagues (1988, p. 207) contend that "Decisions reflect the schemata employed in the decision-making process." Ritchhart and Perkins (2005) argue that "a rich collection of schemata constitutes an essential engine for high-level thinking in a domain" (p. 790). Anderson (2000), a leader in the field of cognitive science, identifies both reasoning and decision making as "schema-based inference processes" that can approach the level of normative principles if people "lock into the right schema" (p. 351); moreover, he has since confirmed this view (J. R. Anderson, personal communication, July 19, 2010).

Perhaps in part because of the similarities between internal schemata and decision matrices, consumers spontaneously create alternative-by-attribute decision matrices when deciding among different products and sources of credit (Ranyard & Williamson 2005). Figure 1.2 shows the decision matrix one consumer created while trying to decide among five different brands of do-it-yourself storage buildings (Coupey 1994). Not only

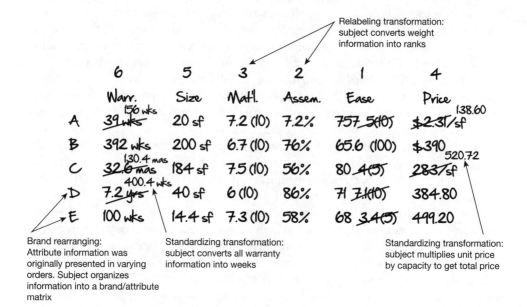

Figure 1.2 Decision Makers Spontaneously Create Decision Matrices (source: Coupey 1994, p. 90).

did the consumer rearrange randomly presented information, she also made calculations to fill empty schema slots, re-scaled slot values that were hard to compare, and ranked each of the six attributes or decision criteria.

Decision Schemata as Guides to the Decision-Making Process

Schemata not only store important information in an organized way, they also guide the process of decision making. "Once cued, schemas affect how quickly we perceive, what we notice, how we interpret what we notice, and what we perceive as similar and different" (Fiske & Taylor 1991, p. 122). Schemata direct attention during information search, specify which information is relevant and which is irrelevant, code information, organize it in memory, direct the retrieval of information from memory, and specify which important information is missing (Carlston & Smith 1996; Lipshitz & Shaul 1997). Voters' schemata can affect their attention to, interpretation, and recall of political information (Haste & Torney-Purta 1992; Price & Zaller 1993; Sniderman, Brody, & Tetlock 1991). The schemata of experienced voters lead them to give attention to and to seek information about political events that inexperienced voters tend to overlook (Fredin, Kosicki, & Becker 1996).

Well-developed schemata provide many advantages for the expert audience. For example, voters with more highly developed political schemata are able to produce higher quality arguments about the issues than are less sophisticated voters (Rhee & Cappella 1997). The ability of experienced physicians to recognize the significance of secondary physiological measurements (Alberdi et al. 2001) can be credited to their more complete schemata (Chi 2006). Schemata help experienced consumers recall product information, make accurate inferences about the product information with which they are presented, and put new information into context quickly (Brewer & Nakamura 1984). Internal knowledge structures, or schemata, allow expert business appraisers to quickly search for and assess the information they need to evaluate the worth of a company (Paek 1997).

Limitations of Decision Schemata

The schemata of expert audiences can sometimes have negative effects on their decisions. Expert audiences may lack the relevant schemata for novel situations within their domains and distort the information they acquire in order to fit it into their existing schemata (Endsley 2006; Tolcott, Marvin, & Lehner 1989). Schemata can blind audiences to new or unexpected information and may incline them to acquire only the type of information with which they are familiar, regardless of the problem setting (Frensch & Sternberg 1989; Staw 1981; Tversky & Kahneman 1988). For example, business executives have been found to define problems largely in terms of their functional expertise, such as marketing, finance, or operations, and not recognize business problems outside their function area (Dearborn & Simon 1958). Furthermore, because schemata are context specific, there is little transfer of expertise from one domain to another even when the domains appear to be similar (Ericsson & Lehmann 1996; Feltovich, Prietula, & Ericsson 2006; Glaser & Chi 1988).

Such limitations may lead to biased decisions, particularly when an expert's schema is not a good fit with the problem, as is often the case when experts try to make non-routine decisions or to solve ill-structured problems (Schwenk 1984). Schema-driven expert audiences do not necessarily make better decisions than novices if they face unfamiliar tasks within their domain of expertise (Camerer & Johnson 1991; Chan 1982; Lichtenstein, Fischhoff, & Phillips 1982). Schemata can also incline expert audiences to overlook information that is not formatted in the typical way. For example, expert, but nonprofessional, investors have been found to use comprehensive income information only when it is presented in the format they have come to expect (Maines & McDaniel 2000).

The Shared Decision Schemata of Groups

Shared schemata guide the decision-making processes of effective groups and teams (Rentsch & Hall 1994). In a study of 25 four- to six-person groups of business executives making hiring decisions, Vaughan (1999) found that the executives in each group shared the same schema concerning the characteristics of suitable applicants, tended to search for the same information about each applicant, mentioned that same information in group discussions, and used that same information to make group decisions. In addition, she found that if group members repeated information during their discussions, they were more likely to repeat information that was schema-relevant than schema-irrelevant. Vaughan also found that any information that was unshared, or known by only one group member, was more likely to be mentioned in group discussions if it were schema-relevant information than if it were schema-irrelevant. Finally, Vaughan observed that the most influential person in each group was the group member with the most complete knowledge of information relevant to the group's shared schema.

Factions within a group who are initially in a minority can successfully advocate their preferred alternative by appealing to shared knowledge structures or schemata upon which all members agree (Laughlin & Ellis 1986). These shared schemata help group members understand the logic behind the minority's preference for a given alternative. Any alternative consistent with a schema or task representation that the group shares is easier for a minority to defend and more likely to be chosen by the group as a whole, even when that alternative is not demonstrably correct as is often the case with jury decisions (Tindale, Smith, Thomas, Filkins, & Sheffey 1996). If group members do not share a schema, or if they possess multiple and conflicting schemata, the group will tend to choose an alternative on the basis of majority/plurality rule (Tindale, Kameda, & Hinsz 2003).

Shared mental models, a type of shared schema, may explain coordinated perform-ance in teams, especially when teams experience high workloads (Cannon-Bowers, Salas, & Converse 1993; Rouse, Cannon-Bowers, & Salas 1992). A shared mental model of the task their team must complete helps team members anticipate one another's information needs, communicate efficiently, work in sync, and also improves the team's performance overall (e.g., Lim & Klein 2006; Mathieu, Heffner, Goodwin, Cannon-Bowers, & Salas 2005; Minionis 1995). In many cases, shared mental models about the task are necessary if teams are to complete their tasks successfully (Lee 2008). Further-more, as the variance among the team members' task-related shared mental model decreases, team performance increases. High-performing teams tend to have not only more widely shared mental models than low-performing teams but also more elaborate ones (Carley 1997). Teams that do not share mental models tend to be uncoordinated and to perform poorly (HelmReich 1997; Langan-Fox, Anglim, & Wilson 2004).

DECISION SCHEMATA OF NOVICE AUDIENCES

Novices' Less Well-Developed Decision Schemata

What, if any, are the differences between expert and novice audiences? That there are significant differences there can be little doubt. Important differences have been dis-covered between expert and novice consumers and the decisions they make (Bettman & Sujan 1987; Maheswaran & Sternthal 1990; Simonson, Huber, & Payne 1988). Important differences have been discovered between other expert and novice audiences and their decisions as well (Carroll 1997; Peskin 1998; Rouet, Favart, Britt, & Perfetti 1997).

Perhaps the most fundamental difference between expert and novice audiences is that, in contrast to experts, novice audiences come to documents, presentations, and group meetings without well-developed or appropriate schemata in mind. As Holyoak (1984, p. 205) points out, expert/novice differences in problem solving can be attributed to "quantitative and qualitative differences in their respective stores of relevant problem schemas" (cf., Chi, Feltovich & Glaser, 1981; Chi, Glaser, & Rees 1982; Larkin, McDermott, Simon, & Simon 1980).

Thus, novice audience members may lack the well-formed and matrix-like decision schemata they need to make a good decision. Instead of a matrix-like schema, a novice's schema may consist of a simple list of reasons for the alternative they prefer and against the non-preferred alternative as the one-sided schema in Figure 1.3 illustrates. If the novice has more experience, her schema may consist of a random list of pros and cons for several alternatives as the two-sided schema in Figure 1.4 illustrates (Cassie & Robinson 1982). Thus, instead of attempting to estimate each alternative's overall value along a specific set of dimensions or decision criteria, novices try to find unique reasons for and against each alternative they consider (Shafir, Simonson, & Tversky 1993). In addition, novice consumers may not process information pertinent to an expert's decision criteria (e.g., the fact that a computer has 100 GB RAM) even when that information is provided to them in ads (Maheswaran & Sternthal 1990). Unless given incentives, novices will process only the benefit information ads contain (e.g., the computer is "Great for gamers").

Not surprisingly, novice audiences employ fewer decision criteria when making a decision than experts do (Mulvey, Olson, Celsi, & Walker 1994; Walker, Celsi, & Olson 1986). For example, novice consumers of insurance evoke fewer decision criteria than do experts when trying to choose the best insurance policy (Kuusela, Spence, & Kanto 1998). Novice consumers of newspapers search for information about fewer attributes, or decision criteria, than do more knowledgeable consumers when choosing among newspapers (Polansky 1987).

Even when novice audiences have access to the decision criteria that experts possess, they may not weight those criteria appropriately. For example, novice investors weight the decision criteria provided by analysts' forecasts less appropriately than do expert

Preferred alternative	Non-preferred alternative
Positive reasons + +	Negative reasons – –

Figure 1.3 One-Sided Novice Schemata Fail to Take an Impartial View

Alternative A	Alternative B	Alternative C
Positive reasons + +	Positive reasons + +	Positive reasons + +
Negative reasons - -	Negative reasons - -	Negative reasons - -

Figure 1.4 Two-Sided Novice Schemata Fail to Compare Alternatives Along the Same Dimensions (source: Cassie & Robinson 1982)

investors (Bonner, Walther, & Young 2003). Similarly, novice consumers are more likely to give weight to nonfunctional dimensions such as a product's brand name and packaging than are expert consumers (Park & Lessig 1981). Because novices lack the pre-stored decision criteria that experts possess, they sometimes try, without much success, to create them (Bettman & Sujan 1987).

Novice audiences also use fewer benchmarks and make fewer comparisons than experts do when making decisions. Novice consumers of insurance are less likely to make pair-wise comparisons of one policy to another than are experts (Kuusela et al. 1998). Novice consumers in general make fewer comparisons because they have less knowledge about alternative products, an important category of benchmarks, than expert consumers have (Bettman & Park 1980; Johnson & Russo 1984). Novice security analysts using company descriptions to value firms are less likely to compare a firm's financials to internal norms or benchmarks than are expert analysts (Gunderson 1991). Even when novice audiences have access to the benchmarks that experts rely on, they may not use them. In his study of consumers reading comparative and non-comparative ads in order to choose among brands, Lee (1989a) finds that, unlike the expert consumers, novice consumers fail to use the comparative product information the comparative ads provide.

Not only do novices possess less well-developed schemata than do experts, novices are also less likely than experts to agree among each other about the appropriate decision criteria that comprise their schemata (Graonic 1995; O'Shaughnessy 1987). In addition, novices are less likely than experts to use decision criteria consistently when making a decision (Marks & Olson 1981; McKeithen, Reitman, Rueter, & Hirtle 1981). For example, when screening résumés for a supervisory position, recruiters with less hiring experience are less consistent in applying their decision criteria than are more experienced recruiters (Ruck 1980). When selecting hardware and software products, technical novices not only agree less on decision criteria than do technical experts, they also apply them less consistently (Galletta et al. 1993).

Consequences of Less Well-Developed Decision Schemata

What happens when an audience lacks the appropriate schemata to make a good decision? In a survey of 43 officers and enlisted personnel who trained new platoon leaders, Strater and colleagues (2001) find that the root cause of many problems experienced by novice platoon leaders is their lack of well-developed schemata. Novice platoon leaders are quickly overwhelmed by incoming information and are slow to comprehend which information is important. They often fail to request and to communicate schema-relevant information. Without the appropriate schemata to support their decision making, the novices have difficulty integrating information into a coherent picture and specifying alternate courses of action (COAs).

Without the experts' well-developed schemata, novice audiences are unable to make as many inferences about the messages they read (Lee 1989b; Lee & Olshavsky 1995), to ask as many pertinent questions (Serfaty et al. 1997), or to recall as much of the information they do obtain (Alba & Hutchinson 1987; Lee 1989b; Srull 1983). Ultimately, novices make decisions that are inferior to those of experts (Shanteau 1988).

When audiences lack or fail to activate the appropriate decision schema, they may rely more on intuitive forms of decision making. For example, Gardner and coauthors (1985) exposed two groups of consumers to the same product advertisements. They asked the first group to evaluate the products advertised. They asked the second group to evaluate the entertainment value of each ad. Later, the researchers asked both groups to describe the content of the ads. The second group took longer to verify product information, generated fewer product-related thoughts, did not generate arguments either for or against purchasing the products, and yet formed more positive attitudes toward the products than did the first group. The researchers conclude that the second group had not activated the appropriate schemata and thus never fully comprehended the ads in terms of their messages' implications about the products. Instead, the second group relied on its subjective feelings toward the ads to guide its evaluation of the products.

Without the appropriate schema, novice audiences may also rely more on emotional forms of decision making. Srull (1983) demonstrates that when audiences lack the appropriate knowledge structures or schemata, emotional cues may be used in response to a message. A mood manipulation affected the responses of audience members with little knowledge about automobiles to car ads. In contrast, expert audience members were unaffected by the mood manipulation and made their decisions based on the quality of the ads' contents.

The differences between the schemata of expert and novice audiences can lead to big differences in the way the two groups search for information. A study of expert and novice home buyers choosing a mortgage reveals that home buyers' level of expertise strongly affects their search effort, search patterns, and alternative elimination (Gomez Borja 2000). Whereas experts actively search for specific information in a top-down fashion using their domain knowledge, or schemata, to structure the search, novices examine information in the way it is presented (Johnson 1981). Thus, product novices are more influenced by the way the contents of ads are displayed than are product experts (Lee 1989b). Lacking the expert's schemata, novices may only search for information that confirms their underdeveloped schemata. With somewhat more developed schemata, audiences are more likely to notice information that disconfirms components of their schemata and to revise their schemata accordingly (Roese & Sherman 2007). As expertise grows, audiences find fewer instances of disconfirming information and the need to revise their schemata lessens (Karniol 2003).

Without a well-developed schema to guide search, decision making by novice audiences is less efficient than that of expert audiences (Brucks 1985; Kardash, Royer, & Greene 1988). Novice audiences process more information than experts when making similar decisions (Brucks 1985; Johnson 1988a; Johnson & Russo 1984). Novice audiences have trouble identifying information that is irrelevant and safe to ignore (Shanteau 1988). For this reason, novice newspaper consumers take longer to choose between newspapers than more knowledgeable newspaper consumers (Polansky 1987). Expert consumers, on the other hand, are able to use search strategies that reduce their effort without compromising the quality of their decisions (Boyle 1994).

The Development of Expert-like Decision Schemata

How do novice audience members become experts? In order to acquire expertise in a domain, novices must develop expert schemata (Alba & Hutchinson 1987; Fredrickson

1985; Isenberg 1986). Novices begin to develop a schema of a task or decision as they repeat it (Chase & Simon 1973). It is possible for novices to construct a schema after performing a task or making a decision only twice by identifying what the two experiences have in common (Martin 1982; Nelson 1980). Abstract diagrams that highlight the necessary decision criteria can aid the formation of schemata (Beveridge & Parkins 1987; Gick & Holyoak 1983) as can access to decision matrices (Swaney, Janik, Bond, & Hayes 1991).

Exposure to analogies can also help novices formulate schemata (Kotovsky & Gentner 1996; Loewenstein, Thompson, & Gentner 1999; Ross & Kennedy 1990). Novices can acquire a schema by comparing just two analogs to one another (Gick & Holyoak 1983). They may also develop a schema as a side effect of applying what they learned from solving one problem to an unsolved target problem (Novick & Holyoak 1991; Ross & Kennedy 1990). Not surprisingly, novices' schemata become more developed and complex with additional experience (Chi & Koeske 1983; Kardash et al. 1988; Rouse & Morris 1986). Novices may also develop more complex schemata by unconsciously combining several simpler existing schemata into one (Chi & Ohlsson 2005; Ohlsson & Hemmerich 1999; Ohlsson & Lehtinen 1997). Moreover, schemata can be developed through instruction. Helping novice leaders create expert-like schemata is the focus of many leadership training programs (cf., Brown, Scott, & Lewis 2004; London 2002; Smither & Reilly 2001).

Although truly novice audience members do not possess predefined schemata to guide their decision making, they sometimes have the ability to appreciate experts' decision criteria and benchmarks when they are available to them. Note consumers' widespread reliance on *Consumer Reports* to make purchasing decisions. *Consumer Reports* provides novice consumers with experts' decision criteria on a range of products and rates each product according to how well it meets the experts' criteria for that product category. Each product attribute that is rated—quality, capacity, efficiency, reliability, and so on—corresponds to one of the experts' decision criteria. *Consumer Reports* also provides consumers with benchmark information, comparing the ratings and prices of many different products within the same product category. In addition, *Consumer Reports* computes an overall score for each product using the weighted sums method. Rosen and Olshavsky (1987) find that when novice consumers are given information such as is found in *Consumer Reports*, they become "instant experts." As Yates and colleagues (2003) observe, the online version of *Consumer Reports* amounts to a personal decision support system.

Figure 1.5 presents an example of a decision matrix from *Consumer Reports.org*, December 16, 2009, that at the time allowed novices to determine which AT&T smartphone provided the best quality for the money. The matrix compares 10 different smartphones on the basis of eight different decision criteria in addition to price: display, navigation, voice quality, phoning, messaging, web browsing, multimedia, and battery life with the Apple iPhone 3GS (16 GB) scoring the highest overall.

Consumer Reports is not the only source of instant expertise. Providing novice buyers of liability insurance policies with a decision matrix that describes and contrasts different types of insurance can help them make more informed decisions (Swaney et al. 1991). Adding such a matrix to the beginning of a policy can help new insurance buyers develop the schema they need in order to understand the policy and pose the right questions

Brand and Model	Price	Ratings and Test Results											
AT&T smartphones	Approximate retail price	Overall score (0 P F G VG 100 P)	Overall score	Navigation	Voice quality	Phoning	Messaging	Web browsing	Multimedia	Battery life	Size	Operating system
Apple iPhone 3G S (16 GB) ✓	$200	74	●	●	◗	◖	◖	●	◖	●	Mid-size	iPhone OS
Apple iPhone 3G S (8 GB) ✓	$100	71	●	●	◗	○	◖	●	◗	◗	Mid-size	iPhone OS
Nokia iN97	$570	70	●	○	○	●	◖	●	●	●	Mid-size	Symbian
BlackBerry Bold ✓	$200	69	◗	◗	○	◗	●	●	●	○	Mid-size	BlackBerry
ATC Pure ✓	$150	69	◗	○	◗	◖	●	●	●	○	Small	Windows Mobile
Samsung Jack	$80	68	○	○	◐	◖	●	●	●	●	Mid-size	Windows Mobile
LG Incite	$80	66	○	○	◗	◖	●	●	●	◗	Small	Windows Mobile
Nokia E71x	$50	63	○	○	◗	◖	◐	●	●	●	Mid-size	Symbian
Garmin Nuvifone G60	$200	62	◗	○	○	○	○	●	◗	◗	Mid-size	Linux
Nokia Surge	$30	57	○	◐	◗	◖	◖	◗	◗	◗	Small	Symbian

Figure 1.5 Decision Matrices from *Consumer Reports* can Provide Instant Expertise.

about it. Providing patients with basic healthcare information can help them develop schemata they can use to find and integrate new information about health-related issues (Cameron & Leventhal 2003). Providing novice consumers with decision criteria for choosing among both comparable and non-comparable products can significantly improve the quality of their purchasing decisions (Bettman & Sujan 1987).

Novices are usually happy to base their decisions on whatever decision criteria are presented to them (Sanbonmatsu, Kardes, Houghton, Ho, & Posavac 2003). Basing one's decision on another's criteria may not always be a good idea, however. Whittler (1994) finds that during the course of a sales interaction, sales representatives may use expressions that encourage consumers to consider decision criteria not necessarily relevant to the purchase decision (e.g., what others will think, the possibility of a missed opportunity). Thus, consumers' thoughts are diverted from more important criteria such as the price and quality of the product.

The Development of Shared Decision Schemata in Groups

Groups and teams become more expert and more cohesive when members coordinate their individual schemata with those of other team members and develop shared schemata, or shared mental models, to structure their decisions and other tasks

(Cannon-Bowers & Salas 2001; Gutwin & Greenberg 2004). The number and complexity of teams' shared mental models relevant to the task increase significantly over time and are vital to the coordination of team efforts (Espinosa & Carley 2001). In order to develop such shared schemata, team members must have the ability to coordinate the potentially different mental models of all the members of the team (Levine et al. 1993).

Team members may consciously coordinate divergent schemata by negotiating which decision criteria are relevant to the team's decisions (Walsh et al. 1988). The schemata of groups formed to make strategy decisions converge more quickly and completely when groups are asked to justify their decisions (Crespin 1997). Strategy groups asked to justify their decisions also report more common ground than other groups. As team members interact and acquire greater expertise in making specific types of decisions over time, their shared mental models, or shared schemata, change and become more refined (Eccles & Tenenbaum 2004; Kraiger & Wenzel 1997; McIntyre & Salas 1995). However, the ability to use the shared mental models that teams develop varies among team members. More highly skilled team members tend to use shared mental models more successfully than low-skill team members (Mohammed & Dumville 2001; Smith-Jentsch, Campbell, Milanovich, & Reynolds 2001).

EXPERT AUDIENCES VERSUS LINEAR MODELS AND NORMATIVE RULES

Linear Models: The Gold Standard of Rational Decision Making

As we have seen, expert audiences typically consider multiple decision criteria when making decisions and their decisions typically produce superior outcomes to those of novices. But do experts consistently make the best decisions possible given their decision criteria? And do experts consistently follow the rules of normative, or proper, decision making? If experts followed normative rules, such as those prescribed by multi-attribute utility theory (MAUT), they would consistently choose those alternatives that maximized their values (Einhorn & Hogarth 1981).

To answer the first question—"Do expert audiences consistently make the best decisions possible given their decision criteria?"—researchers use a statistical technique called *multiple regression analysis* to identify how much weight (if any) the experts should ideally give to each of their decision criteria in order to choose the best alternative. The result is called a *linear model*. Linear models are usually represented as equations, but they can also be expressed in the form of value trees, or, like decision schemata, in the form of decision matrices. Figure 1.6 shows the same linear model for selecting the best job applicant for an imaginary management position depicted in those three different ways.

The decisions experts make are usually inferior to those computed by linear models. Linear models are more accurate than clinical psychologists in diagnosing psychiatric patients (Goldberg 1968). Linear models are more accurate than medical doctors in diagnosing medical patients (Einhorn 1972). Linear models are better than faculty

As an equation

Applicant value = 0.2(GMAT) + 0.3(GPA) + 0.4(Communications skills) + 0.1(Work experience)

As a value tree

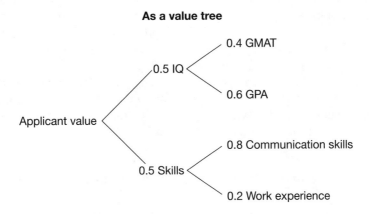

As a decision matrix

Decision criteria	Weight	Applicant 1	Applicant 2	Applicant 3
GMAT	0.2			
GPA	0.3			
Communications skills	0.4			
Work experience	0.1			
Applicant value				

Figure 1.6 The Same Linear Model for Choosing the Best Applicant can be Represented in Different Ways.

members on admissions committees at choosing the best students for graduate school (Dawes 1971). Linear models are more accurate than commercial bankers in deciding which firms are most likely to go bankrupt (Libby 1976). Linear models are more accurate than expert investors in predicting stock prices (Johnson & Sathi 1984; Wright 1979). In fact, Dawes and coauthors (1989) find in their review of the research that the decisions produced by linear models consistently outperform those of experts in all of the domains studied.

Even *bootstrapped models*, improper linear models that use the same weights experts give their decision criteria, produce better decisions than the experts they model (Camerer 1981; Dawes & Corrigan 1974; Johnson & Sathi 1984). A bootstrapped model can be expressed in the same three ways as is the linear model in Figure 1.6. Figure 1.6 could just as easily illustrate a bootstrapped model as a linear model. Bootstrapped models are called improper because, unlike linear models, they cannot produce an optimal decision. Surprisingly, another type of improper linear model, the equal-weight additive model, which weights all of the decision criteria equally, also produces better decisions than experts do (Dawes & Corrigan 1974).

The Causes of Individual Experts' Normally Inferior Performance

One reason linear and bootstrapped models outperform experts is that experts rarely abide by the normative rules of decision making when choosing among alternatives (cf., Edwards & Newman 1986; Keeney & Raiffa 1976, 1993; Massaro & Friedman 1990). To apply the rules of normative decision making, one must first create a model, i.e., identify the appropriate decision criteria and weights for a decision matrix, value tree, or equation. Once the model has been generated, one must enter the correct values for each alternative, calculate the total value for each alternative, and select the alternative with the highest value.

Unlike linear models, experts do not consistently follow the rules. Experts weight criteria inconsistently and routinely make errors when adding them (Camerer 1981). A study of the career decisions of graduating MBAs finds that weighting does not appear to enter into the graduates' job selection process (Soelberg 1967). Other anomalies crop up in the decision-making processes of expert audiences as well. In their study of expert security analysts predicting stock prices, Johnson and Sathi (1984) find that analysts neglect base-rate benchmark information and focus exclusively on case-specific information. Experts may make different decisions based on the way their choice was elicited (Lichtenstein & Slovic 1971). For example, experts may make different decisions when asked to select instead of reject one of two alternatives (Shafir 1993). They may also make different decisions when asked to evaluate one alternative at a time as opposed to all alternatives concurrently (Hsee, Loewenstein, Blount, & Bazerman 1999).

In addition, experts may not exclusively use a compensatory strategy—a method of deciding that involves trading off a low value on one criterion (e.g., poor gas mileage) for a high value on another (e.g., excellent safety features)—when making decisions as the normative rules of decision making dictate. Instead, experts often use a non-compensatory strategy and simply eliminate from consideration any alternative that has

Decision criteria	Car A	Car B
Comfort	Above average	Below average
Reliability	Above average	Below average
Style	Above average	Below average
Horsepower	Above average	Below average
Clean emissions	Below average	Above average
Overall score:	Above average	Below average

Figure 1.7 A Non-Compensatory Strategy can Result in a Non-Normative Decision.

a low value on an important decision criterion prior to computing the remaining alternatives' overall values (Russo & Dosher 1983; Tversky 1972).

Figure 1.7 describes two cars rated on five criteria—comfort, reliability, style, horsepower, and clean emissions—and can be used to illustrate the difference between compensatory and non-compensatory strategies. If a car buyer followed a compensatory strategy in deciding between the two cars, she would choose Car A since it has a higher score overall. On the other hand, if the car buyer felt that driving a car with clean emissions were imperative, then she would use a non-compensatory strategy to decide on Car B. In the study of MBAs selecting jobs cited above, Soelberg (1967) observes that although the MBAs had been taught to use compensatory strategies, the MBAs did *not* use the strategy to make their real job decisions. However, he finds that the MBAs did use the strategy to justify their already-made decisions. Similarly, Kahn and Baron (1995) find that teaching undergraduates how to use compensatory strategies does not increase their use of them. However, it does increase their desire for their agents, e.g., their doctors and advisors, to use compensatory strategies when making decisions on their behalf.

Another cause of experts' normally inferior performance is that some types of decisions are inherently difficult for human beings to make. As indicated in Table 1.3 (Shanteau 1992), expert audiences perform relatively well in domains that involve decisions about objects or things. These domains have a high degree of predictability and provide feedback readily. Expert audiences perform less well in domains that involve decisions about human behavior which is highly unpredictable and for which feedback is less readily available (see Bolger & Wright 1992 and Smith & Kida 1991 for reviews).

The Causes of Groups of Experts' Normally Inferior Performance

One might expect groups of experts to outperform individual experts and to match the performance of linear models. But groups tend to make decisions that are inferior

Table 1.3 The Decision Performance of Experts Depends on their Domain

Better performance (Domains concerning things)	Poorer performance (Domains concerning people)
Weather forecasting	Clinical psychology
Astronomy	Astrology
Aeronautics	Student admissions
Agriculture	Law
Chess	Behavioral research
Physics	Counseling
Mathematics	Human resources
Accounting	Parole granting
Actuarial statistics	Stock market investing

Source: Adapted from Shanteau 1992.

to those made by their most expert members and may perform considerably worse than even their average members on some tasks (Tindale 1993). Why? Because majorities/pluralities, not the most knowledgeable members, "win" most of the time. Majority/plurality rule has been observed in a variety of group-level audience decisions, including decisions made by mock juries (Kameda & Sugimori 1995; MacCoun & Kerr 1988; Tindale & Davis 1983), groups of investors (Kameda & Davis 1990), groups of voters (Stasser & Titus 1985), budgetary committees (Tindale & Davis 1985), and teams of recruiters (Kameda & Sugimori 1993).

Majority/plurality rule is particularly prevalent when the group does not share a schema for solving the problem or making the decision (Laughlin & Ellis 1986; Tindale et al. 1996). Thus, it may not enhance group performance if a minority of group members perform at a high level since group performance typically depends on the level at which the majority/plurality performs.

The Importance of Expert Audiences Despite their Limitations

While acknowledging the limitations of experts to weight decision criteria appropriately and their deviations from normative decision-making processes, professionals must still understand experts and be able to convince them. Expert audiences have the final say in most decisions and are not likely be replaced altogether by linear models any time soon. The judgments of expert audiences are perceived as fairer than the judgments of linear models (Dawes 1971). Expert audiences are still indispensable for selecting, weighting, and measuring the criteria that go into linear models (Camerer 1981; Sawyer 1966) and for discovering new decision criteria (Johnson 1988a). In addition, expert audiences have the ability to recognize rare but highly diagnostic cues that may not be accounted for in linear models (Meehl 1954). Most importantly, expert audiences are less likely than linear models to make large mistakes (Shanteau 1988).

Audience Decision-Making Expertise: Implications for Communicators

✧ The main takeaway for communicators in Chapter 1 is that expert audiences already know what information they want from professionals—the information that will fill their decision schemata. Audiences are not empty cups waiting to be filled with whatever information professionals want to give them.

✧ Use the information presented in the chapter to guide the selection of content for your documents, presentations, meetings, and interviews. The alternative is to select content based on subjective opinion or convention.

✧ Why use the information? To make your communications more persuasive, especially with expert audiences. To enable all types of audiences—experts, novices, groups, and individuals—to make more informed decisions.

✧ See Chapter 2 for techniques that make it easier to anticipate the audience's information requirements for any specific decision.

Types of Audience Decisions

It didn't help that the executive sent to deliver the decision [to lay off] the assembled staff started off with a glowing account of how well rival operations were doing, and that he had just returned from a wonderful trip to Cannes. The news itself was bad enough, but the brusque, even contentious manner of the executive incited something beyond the expected frustration. People became enraged—not just at the management decision, but also at the bearer of the news himself. The atmosphere became so threatening, in fact, that it looked as though the executive might have to call security to usher him safely from the room.

The next day, another executive visited the same staff. He took a very different approach. He spoke from his heart about the crucial importance of journalism to the vibrancy of a society, and of the calling that had drawn them all to the field in the first place. He reminded them that no one goes into journalism to get rich—as a profession its finances have always been marginal, with job security ebbing and flowing with larger economic tides. And he invoked the passion, even the dedication, the journalists had for the service they offered. Finally, he wished them all well in getting on with their careers. When this leader finished speaking, the staff cheered.

The excerpt above from *Primal Leadership* by Goleman, Boyatzis, and McKee (2002, p. 4) illustrates the importance of understanding your audience and the type of decision you want them to make. The excerpt contrasts the way two executives from the British Broadcasting Corporation (BBC) informed their audience of about 200 journalists and editors of upper management's plan to shut down their news reporting division. Notice how unsympathetic and immature the first executive appears to be as he reports on the success of the other divisions at the BBC and then adds that the apparently unprofitable news reporting division is to be shut down. Giving such a report to a different audience, say the firm's board of directors with oversight responsibility for upper management's plans, might have been totally appropriate. In order to make an informed oversight decision, most boards would appreciate the comparative information the first executive shared as well as his apparent concern for profitability. But for this audience of soon-to-be unemployed journalists, the first executive appears to have no clue to whom he is speaking or the type of decision he wants them to make—Does he want the journalists to decide to go along with upper management's plan or to fight it? No doubt this executive was surprised by the journalists' angry response to his speech; it seems likely his speaking experience was limited to delivering similar factual reports.

Notice, on the other hand, how empathetic and leader-like the second executive appears to be. The second executive addresses the group's values, their sacrifices, and the difficulties they will face. He knows his job is not simply to report the facts but to inspire and rally the journalists' flagging spirits. To inspire the group, the second executive elicits what this text terms a rallying decision from the journalists. Chapter 2 will show us how we can be more like the second executive. We too can know what to say and when to say it, even when circumstances are most trying and difficult.

As we saw in Chapter 1, to be effective communicators, professionals must first be aware of their audiences' decision schemata. But how can professionals ever prepare for such a task when the number of individual decisions their audiences make is seemingly infinite? Busy professionals do not have time to conduct a Multi-Attribute Utility Analysis, build a linear model, or engage in think-aloud research in order to discover the decision schemata of their audiences. Instead, professionals need a classification scheme that makes sense of the bewildering array of audience decisions and helps them produce the numerous documents and presentations, and orchestrate the many interactions, required to elicit those decisions.

Chapter 2 proposes a scheme that classifies a large number of audience decisions, as well as the documents, presentations, and interactions designed to elicit them, into 13 major types: *oversight, compliance, staffing, employment, exonerative, rallying, investment, lending, usage, sourcing, budgetary, borrowing*, and *policy* decisions. For example, a student's decision to apply the teacher's lesson to a situation at work, a patient's decision to follow the doctor's orders when she gets home, and a customer's decision to try a free sample based on the salesperson's product pitch can all be classified as usage decisions—decisions to use or try out certain products, services, or information. And all usage decisions require communicators to address similar decision criteria and thus to deliver similar types of information. Moreover, the teacher's lesson, the doctor's orders, and the salesperson's product pitch can all be classified as documents, presentations, or interactions whose communicative purpose is to elicit a usage decision. Interestingly, a growing number of scholars agree that the most productive way to classify any form of communication is according to its communicative purpose (cf., Askehave & Swales 2001; Bhatia 1997; Johns 1997; Nickerson 1999; Swales 1990).

The major benefit of such a classification scheme is that it can help professionals predict the information or content their audiences expect them to provide in a document, presentation, or an interaction. In contrast, knowing the format of a document, presentation, or an interaction—such as a memo, an impromptu presentation, or a team meeting—says little about the content audiences expect. Martin (1985), for example, points out that letters to the editor are usually exhortations advising needed change formatted as letters. The contents of letters to the editor are more similar to the contents of political speeches than to the contents of many other types of letters.

Likewise, knowing the source of a message says little about the content audiences require. For instance, knowing that an attorney generated a particular document says little about an audience's content expectations given the many different types of documents attorneys generate. In the same way, simply identifying the audience to whom a message is directed tells practically nothing about the content required in it. For example, consumers, one of salespeople's primary audiences, are asked to make compliance, investment, usage, sourcing, staffing, exonerative, borrowing, and rallying decisions. And again, each decision type requires professionals to provide quite different types of information to their audiences.

Such a scheme can also be used to classify *genres*, or types of discourse to which various documents, presentations, and interactions belong. For example, business genres include business plans, quarterly reports, directives, and standard operating procedures, as well as hundreds of other types of management documents and presentations. The classification scheme can deepen what Berkenkotter and Huckin (1995) call *genre knowledge* which "embraces both form and content, including a sense of what content is appropriate to a particular purpose in a particular situation at a particular point in time" (p. 13).

Classifying genres by the type of decision they are meant to elicit also reveals underlying similarities among nominally different genres. Although one might reasonably assume that all documents labeled *plans* differ from all documents labeled *reports*, an understanding of decision types reveals that strategic plans and annual reports are both designed to elicit an oversight decision, and thus both require similar information. An understanding of decision types also reveals profound differences among documents and presentations that seemingly belong to the same genre. For example, not all documents or presentations called *plans* are meant to elicit an oversight decision. Some plans are meant to elicit an investment decision (e.g., many business plans), some a lending decision (e.g., some acquisition plans), some a usage decision (e.g., most medical treatment plans), and so on.

The 13 decision types this chapter describes cover a wide range of rhetorical situations professionals face. They can be used to meaningfully group scores of genres, to address scores of different audiences, and to accomplish many different communication goals. However, some types of decisions are not included among the 13 in this classification scheme. For instance, this classification scheme does not include decisions professionals are more likely to make themselves, as opposed to ask an audience to make, such as judicial, marketing, regulatory, financing, and technical decisions. Table 2.1 illustrates a few of the many audience decisions and the documents, presentations, or interactions designed to elicit them that are readily classified as belonging to one of the 13 major decision types described in this chapter.

One of the best-known types of decisions—policy decisions—will be discussed last in this chapter. This category includes many of the decisions that world leaders, legislators, and CEOs make every day. Policy decisions are non-routine decisions to which little routine decision-making expertise can be applied. In addition, many policy decisions are quite controversial and generate much debate. Unlike routine decisions, policy decisions sometimes require professionals to generate decision criteria and to convince their audiences to accept those criteria (Beasley 1998).

The remaining twelve types of audience decisions this chapter includes can be divided into two groups of six. The first group helps audiences manage their professional

Table 2.1 Many Audience Decisions can be Classified as One of Thirteen Types

Professional	Audience	Document, presentation, or interaction	Audience decision	Decision type
Politician	Voters	Campaign speech	Vote for candidate or not	Rallying
Job applicant	Recruiters	Job interview responses	Hire applicant or not	Staffing
Attorney	Jurors	Defense arguments	Acquit defendant or not	Exonerative
Consultant	Clients	Project proposal	Hire consultants or not	Staffing
Executive	Directors	Strategic plan	Approve strategy or not	Oversight
Teacher	Students	Lesson	Apply instructions or not	Usage
Army officer	Subordinates	Intent statement	Follow orders or not	Compliance
Salesperson	Customers	Sales pitch	Buy product or not	Usage

relationships both within an organizational hierarchy and outside it. The second group helps them manage their own or their organization's financial resources. In order to understand the first group of six decision types, one must first understand the differences between principals and their agents.

Principals are the people to whom agents must answer. Principals of managers, for example, include their firm's shareholders, board members, and upper management. More broadly speaking, principals of managers can also be said to include their clients, customers, and creditors, or else anyone to whom they are contractually obligated. Managers themselves function as principals to their subordinates, suppliers, and borrowers. Principals set the terms and conditions of any principal/agent relationship. They write the employee contracts, draw up the requests for proposals, and stipulate the covenants for a loan.

Agents, on the other hand, are the people who are obligated to act on behalf of principals. Agents who are unhappy with the principal/agent relationships they have entered into may decide to leave them once they have met their obligations to the principals. Employees may resign and leave an employer; credit-card holders may transfer their balances to another bank; suppliers may refuse shipment to untrustworthy customers. Table 2.2 lists common principal/agent pairs as this text more broadly defines the terms.

Table 2.2 Examples of Principal/Agent Pairs

Principals	Agents
1. Stockholders	Board members
2. Employers	Employees
3. Supervisors	Subordinates
4. Clients	Attorneys
5. Legislators	Bureaucrats
6. Investors	Fund managers
7. Creditors	Borrowers
8. Customers	Suppliers

The six decision types concerned with the management of principal/agent relationships are oversight, compliance, staffing, employment, exonerative, and rallying decisions. These six types can be further divided into three complementary pairs, as Figure 2.1 illustrates. The first pair, oversight and compliance decisions, execute principal/agent relationships that have already been established. For example, board members make oversight decisions when they approve or reject executives' plans and when they approve or disapprove of executives' performance. And executives make compliance decisions when they decide whether to comply with directives from their board.

The second pair, staffing and employment decisions, establish principal/agent relationships within an organization. For example, employers make staffing decisions when they hire, fire, promote, or demote employees. And job applicants make employment decisions when they accept or reject a job offer.

The third pair, exonerative and rallying decisions, help maintain good principal/agent relationships. For example, customers make exonerative decisions when they decide whether to exonerate from blame a supplier who failed to meet a delivery deadline. And suppliers make rallying decisions when they decide whether to make an extra effort to provide high-quality service to their customers. In each of these three complementary pairs of decision types, one type is typically made by the principal in the principal/agent pair and the other type by the agent. The principal typically makes staffing, oversight, and exonerative decisions. The agent typically makes employment, compliance, and rallying decisions.

The six decision types concerned with the management of financial resources are investment, lending, usage, sourcing, budgetary, and borrowing decisions. These six types can be further divided into three complementary pairs as Figure 2.2 shows. The first pair, investment and lending decisions, are made in an effort to use money to make money. Investment decisions are made when people decide whether to buy equity. Lending decisions are made when people decide whether to buy debt.

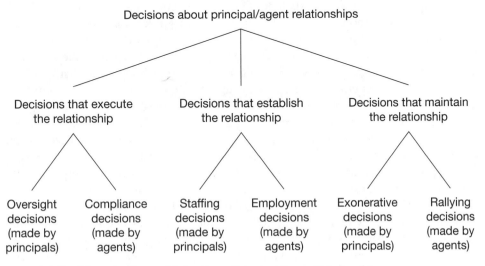

Figure 2.1 Decisions Audiences Make About Principal/Agent Relationships

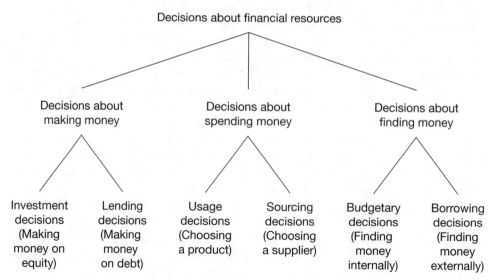

Figure 2.2 Decisions Audiences Make About Financial Resources

The second pair, usage and sourcing decisions, are made in an effort to spend money wisely. Usage decisions are made when people decide whether they can use a particular product, service, or piece of information. Sourcing decisions are made when people decide who should supply them with the product, service, or information they desire.

The third pair, budgetary and borrowing decisions, are made in order to find money from either internal or external sources to pay for the desired product, service, or information. Budgetary decisions are made when people look for money generated internally to fund what they desire. Borrowing decisions are made when people decide whether to accept others' offers to lend them money. The principal in a principal/agent relationship generally makes all six types of decisions about financial resources.

Before we go into more detail about each of the 13 major decision types the audiences of professionals make, we should be aware of several important caveats regarding decision types and the extent to which they can help professionals predict the audience's information needs. First, even when two genres are meant to elicit the same type of decision, the decision criteria audiences use to evaluate the content in one genre will vary slightly from the decision criteria they use to evaluate the content in the other genre. For instance, strategic plans and marketing plans are both meant to elicit oversight decisions. But where board members expect strategic plans to address the corporate objective, the corporate strategy, the corporate-wide action plan, and so on, top management expects marketing plans to address the marketing department's objective, the marketing department's strategy, and the marketing department's action plan. Similarly, Campbell (1981, 1984) finds that commercial bank loan officers use somewhat different financial information when making lending decisions about extending credit to small privately held companies as opposed to extending credit to large publicly held companies.

Second, audiences are free to make any type of decision they wish, no matter what type of decision a professional intends to elicit from them. For example, a supervisor might imagine her request for a productivity increase from her staff would elicit a straightforward compliance decision from them. But while considering her request, some staff members may make employment decisions instead and decide to look elsewhere for a less demanding job. Similarly, an employee might imagine his request for a salary increase would evoke a straightforward budgetary decision from his boss. But while considering the employee's request, the boss may make an oversight decision and decide to eliminate the employee's position altogether. In general, any unilateral request for change can trigger an unintended decision type.

Third, some genres, such as annual reports, are routinely used by different audiences to make different types of decisions. For example, board members and shareholders may use annual reports to make oversight decisions when casting their votes on management's recommendations. Potential investors and analysts may use them to make investment decisions when buying shares or recommending the purchase of shares of a company's stock. Job applicants may use them to make employment decisions when applying for a new position. Customers may use them to make usage decisions when educating themselves about a company's new product line. Lenders may use them to make lending decisions when considering a company's creditworthiness. Some firms try to address the information needs of their annual reports' different audiences in different sections of their annual reports. Some firms only address the needs of the primary audience—their shareholders.

Finally, a few situations exist in which a professional may not care what type of decision the audience makes or even if it makes any decision at all. Some communications may be purely perfunctory. Others may be routine exchanges of information. In these cases a professional may not need to consider the type of decision the audience will make. The following sections describe the types of audience decisions that professionals do need to attend to seriously.

AUDIENCE DECISIONS ABOUT PRINCIPAL/AGENT RELATIONSHIPS

Oversight Decisions: Responses to Requests for Permission

Audiences who are the superiors of others within an organization or to whom others are contractually obligated, in other words principals, make oversight decisions in response to their agents' requests and proposals. For example, boards of directors make oversight decisions when they decide whether to allow top management to implement a risky new strategy, clients make oversight decisions when they decide whether to allow consultants to continue with a project that is behind schedule, employers make oversight decisions when they decide whether to allow an employee to implement a creative new proposal.

Principals make oversight decisions in order to protect the interests of the organizations or the projects for which they are responsible. The oversight decisions they make either grant or deny the professionals who are their agents the authority to take the actions they request. Oversight decisions may also reward or punish agents for their performance or lack of it. For example, a board of directors reviewing a firm's performance may replace the CEO if the firm does not meet the board's performance criteria (Puffer & Weintrop 1991).

Documents and presentations agents produce in order to elicit oversight decisions from principals include *strategic plans*, *annual reports*, *marketing plans*, *progress reports*, and *operating reviews*. Documents and presentations principals produce in an attempt to communicate their decision criteria for oversight decisions to their agents include the terms and conditions of compensation packages that boards draft for top management. They also include the vision statements, goals, objectives, and corporate policies top management set and communicate to lower management.

The list of questions below provides a starting point for predicting principals' decision criteria for any particular oversight decision.

- What is the firm's or project's past financial performance?
- What are the reasons for that performance?
- What are the financial objectives for the future?
- What is the strategy for meeting those objectives?
- What is the action plan for implementing the strategy?
- What are the contingency plans for mitigating risks?

Principals' schemata for oversight decisions may also require benchmark information about a firm's or project's historical performance, the average performance in the industry, alternative strategies and plans, as well as competing firms' and projects' financial results, strategies, and plans. Agents typically show some, but not complete, awareness of principals' decision criteria and benchmarks for oversight decisions. For example, executives responsible for producing their organization's annual report usually communicate their objectives for their firm's future performance, descriptions of their firm's past performance, and the reasons for their firm's past performance, but they rarely benchmark their plans and performance against those of their competitors (Chandler 1988).

Table 2.3 displays some of the comments two experienced audience members (a Ph.D. in finance and a Ph.D. in business policy, both with high-level corporate experience) made as they read two documents produced by top management teams: a strategic plan from General Motors and the *Management's Discussion and Analysis* section of Control Data Corporation's annual report. Each expert was asked to put himself into the role of a board member of those firms and to make a decision based on the information the plan or report provided. The comments reflect the decision criteria for making oversight decisions and illustrate how important it is that they be addressed fully. All of the comments each expert made are numbered in the order they were made. Comments that did not directly reflect the experts' decision criteria, such as comprehension-related comments and complaints about superfluous information, are not included here.

Both expert audience members found the information they required about each organization's past financial performance, but both noted that the reasons for that performance were lacking. The expert reading the strategic plan was glad to see an action plan was included, but complained that the strategy for positioning the firm *vis-à-vis* its

Table 2.3 Experts' Comments that Reveal their Decision Criteria for Making Oversight Decisions

	Expert comments on a strategic plan from General Motors	Expert comments on an annual report from Control Data
Past financial performance	They've listed their own and the three major competitors' vehicle sales growth, three-year average, the three-year profitability, and market share. Again it's just a listing of data with no insights. My sense of a good strategic plan is that what one begins with is this data.[10]	They say they had a loss across the board. These are good years. These are very good years for the country. Control Data, I would think, would share in that.[5]
Reasons for performance	[This expert noted in the second sentence above that the plan lacks reasons that explain the firm's past financial performance.]	Well, at this point I still don't know what threw their earnings off. Sometimes they make phenomenal earnings, other times they don't. And other times they have phenomenal losses. So is it just that their earnings fluctuate that much even though they make that much revenue? Or is there some sort of driver involved here that's causing this? Is it correlated with something? I still don't know that yet.[9]
Proposed financial objective	[This expert did not indicate whether he noted the plan's lack of financial objectives.]	If this were a presentation to the board of directors, I would like to see the pro forma statements, too. I'd like to see what they expect income to be over the next several years, and why they think they're going to get that. This is just been a statement of the history of the company for the last three years. Nothing with respect to the future. So again from a board member's point of view, that's lacking.[59]
Proposed strategy	I am reminded that the company said it was going to move from a low cost to a differentiated position [i.e., strategy]. And that really is the crux of the issue for the company.[26] Now I realize that what is lacking in the subsequent 10 sections is any focused discussion on precisely what moving to a differentiated position means.[27]	Their strategy is to cut costs rather than progress their technology. Nobody wants to buy last year's computer even if it is a hundred dollars cheaper.[23] It doesn't look like these people are on the right track as far as I'm concerned. Yes, I think they should be concerned about cost, everybody should be. But tell me more about technology growth. How they plan to position themselves in the future.[57]

continued . . .

Table 2.3 . . . continued

	Expert comments on a strategic plan from General Motors	Expert comments on an annual report from Control Data
Proposed action plan	I think this [chart of action plans] is useful information because it's probably the important milestones in the next three or four years within the company. It would probably be useful to support this kind of chart with a little bit more discussion, since these are the actual plans that have been chosen by management.[22]	I see nothing in here or very little about developing technology. This business is what strategists would call a fast-cycle business. New technology becomes obsolete very quickly. Cost cutting won't do much. They better have good R&D going on.[54] Maybe cut the dividends. Certainly don't pay dividends and special dividends especially. Instead, go to the commercial credit paper market or the credit market to raise more cash.[55]
Contingency plans	Based on the document itself, I would *not* feel comfortable granting authority requested.[30] The document does a poor job of focusing the reader's attention on the important issues, priorities, and the major risks involved in this strategy. And those kinds of questions would be the ones I would focus on in a discussion and presentation.[31] The ability to present information in a well-organized way, either in the written form or the verbal form, in a short amount of time, say 15 minutes (which would not be unusual at the corporate level for something like this) is sufficient to either make or break a strategic plan. I've seen it happen, and make or break the individuals involved.[32]	[This expert did not indicate whether he noted the report's lack of contingency plans.]

competitors and the risks, usually included in a contingency plan, were not clearly spelled out. The expert reading the annual report complained that financial objectives for the future were not included, that the report lacked a strategy for positioning the firm, and that the action plan was too vague. Neither of the expert audience members found that enough of his decision criteria were adequately addressed and, as a consequence, each withheld his approval.

On the following three pages are slides that a team of MBAs presented to their board of directors composed of experienced top managers. The team comprised the top management of a simulated watch manufacturing firm that was in competition with four other simulated firms run by other teams of MBA students. Notice how the team's slides address each of the decision criteria for oversight decisions and provide many benchmarks for each. Unsurprisingly, the board rated the team's presentation as well above average.

Compliance Decisions: Responses to Demands

Audiences who are subordinate and/or under an obligation to another party, in other words agents, make compliance decisions in response to principals' demands. For example, employees make compliance decisions when they decide whether to take the actions management has directed them to take, customers in arrears make compliance decisions when they decide whether to pay their bills, and suppliers make compliance decisions when they decide whether to grant a dissatisfied customer's demand for a refund.

Agents make compliance decisions in order to assess the legitimacy of the demands that are made of them as well as to assess how easy those demands are to implement. Of course, for various reasons, agents do not always comply with their principals' demands. A study of US Army officers reading their commanding officers' intent statements finds that the subordinate officers took the actions that their superior officers intended them to take only 34% of the time (Shattuck 1995).

Documents and presentations that principals produce in order to evoke compliance decisions from their agents include *directives, contracts, standard operating procedures (SOPs), invoices, policies, promissory notes, reprimands,* and *purchase orders*. Documents and presentations produced to evoke compliance decisions differ in one fundamental way from those produced to evoke the other decision types. These documents and presentations not only respond to the audience's decision criteria, they also attempt to communicate the professional's decision criteria to the audience.

The list of questions below provides a starting point for predicting agents' decision criteria for making any particular compliance decision.

- What is the purpose of the demand?
- What is the due date?
- What are the steps for completion?
- What are the evaluation criteria (i.e., the communicator's decision criteria)?
- What are unwanted outcomes and the consequences for noncompliance?
- Whom should I contact if I have problems?

An MBA Team's Strategic Plan Slides (abridged)

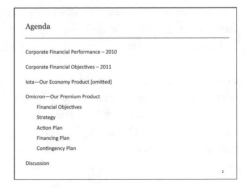

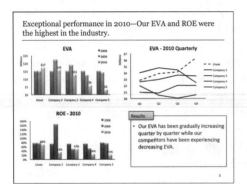

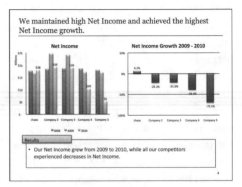

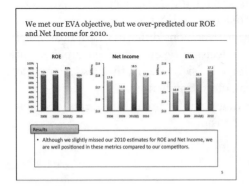

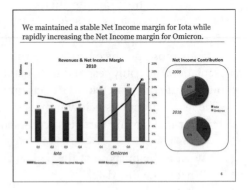

An MBA Team's Strategic Plan Slides (abridged)

Our financial objectives for next year will greatly increase shareholder value.

Next year, Lhazo will achieve the following:
- One of the top two positions for ROE
- Highest Net Income margin
- One of the top two positions for EVA

To attain these goals, we are targeting 10% increases for the subsequent year:

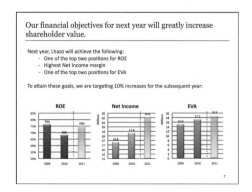

7

Our goals for Omicron in 2011 are to increase both margins and market shares in target countries.

Margin Goal:
Increase Net Income Margin for Omicron by 10 percentage points in the next year.

Market Share Goals:
Achieve 26-30% market shares in target markets.

8

Omicron's differentiation strategy worked in 2010.

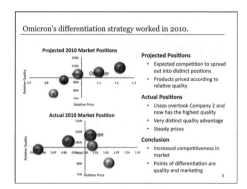

Projected Positions
- Expected competition to spread out into distinct positions
- Products priced according to relative quality

Actual Positions
- Lhazo overtook Company 2 and now has the highest quality
- Very distinct quality advantage
- Steady prices

Conclusion
- Increased competitiveness in market
- Points of differentiation are quality and marketing

9

Omicron held the second highest market share among all luxury watch brands in 2010.

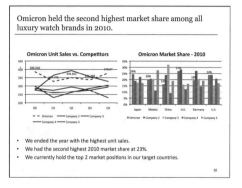

- We ended the year with the highest unit sales.
- We had the second highest 2010 market share at 23%.
- We currently hold the top 2 market positions in our target countries.

10

In 2011, we will maintain Omicron's differentiation strategy and increase prices to gain higher profitability.

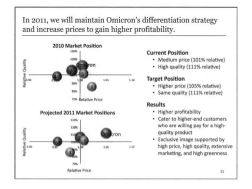

Current Position
- Medium price (101% relative)
- High quality (111% relative)

Target Position
- Higher price (105% relative)
- Same quality (111% relative)

Results
- Higher profitability
- Cater to higher-end customers who are willing pay for a high-quality product
- Exclusive image supported by high price, high quality, extensive marketing, and high greenness

11

We will accomplish our goals for Omicron through targeted marketing and price differentiation.

Target markets:
- US, UK, and Japan will continue to be Omicron's target markets
- Since high quality has been achieved, Germany is also now a target market

Marketing Changes: **Pricing Changes:**

- Continue to invest heavily in marketing in target countries
- Increase marketing in non-target countries

- Increase relative prices in the least price sensitive markets
- Decrease relative prices in price-sensitive markets

12

An MBA Team's Strategic Plan Slides (abridged)

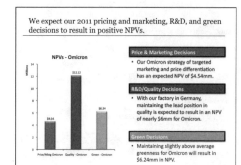

We expect our 2011 pricing and marketing, R&D, and green decisions to result in positive NPVs.

Price & Marketing Decisions
- Our Omicron strategy of targeted marketing and price differentiation has an expected NPV of $4.54mm.

R&D/Quality Decisions
- With our factory in Germany, maintaining the lead position in quality is expected to result in an NPV of nearly $6mm for Omicron.

Green Decisions
- Maintaining slightly above average greenness for Omicron will result in $6.24mm in NPV.

13

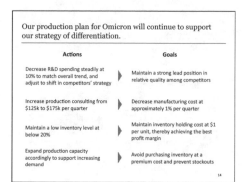

Our production plan for Omicron will continue to support our strategy of differentiation.

Actions	Goals
Decrease R&D spending steadily at 10% to match overall trend, and adjust to shift in competitors' strategy	Maintain a strong lead position in relative quality among competitors
Increase production consulting from $125k to $175k per quarter	Decrease manufacturing cost at approximately 1% per quarter
Maintain a low inventory level at below 20%	Maintain inventory holding cost at $1 per unit, thereby achieving the best profit margin
Expand production capacity accordingly to support increasing demand	Avoid purchasing inventory at a premium cost and prevent stockouts

14

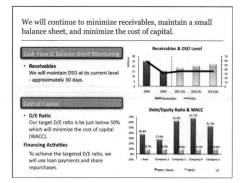

We will continue to minimize receivables, maintain a small balance sheet, and minimize the cost of capital.

Cash Flow & Balance Sheet Monitoring
- **Receivables**
  We will maintain DSO at its current level - approximately 30 days.

Cost of Capital
- **D/E Ratio**
  Our target D/E ratio is be just below 50% which will minimize the cost of capital (WACC).
- **Financing Activities**
  To achieve the targeted D/E ratio, we will use loan payments and share repurchases.

15

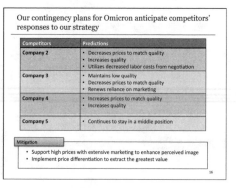

Our contingency plans for Omicron anticipate competitors' responses to our strategy

Competitors	Predictions
Company 2	• Decreases prices to match quality • Increases quality • Utilizes decreased labor costs from negotiation
Company 3	• Maintains low quality • Decreases prices to match quality • Renews reliance on marketing
Company 4	• Increases prices to match quality • Increases quality
Company 5	• Continues to stay in a middle position

Mitigation
- Support high prices with extensive marketing to enhance perceived image
- Implement price differentiation to extract the greatest value

16

In summary, we are well positioned to sustain profitability and outpace the competition.

2010 Accomplishments
- Highest ROE
- Highest increase in net income
- Premium market quality leader through strategic R&D investment

2011 Outlook
- As economic conditions improve, we are well-positioned to achieve higher levels of profitability and deliver the greatest amount of shareholder value
- Having developed a greater understanding of our competitive landscape, we are well-equipped to respond to market changes

17

Even experienced professionals may neglect to address their agents' criteria for compliance decisions. Although a content analysis of 35 intent statements by US Army commanders found that the purpose was stated in 42% of them and the steps for completion in 92%, unwanted outcomes were mentioned in just 14%, and plans for handling problems that may arise in only 37% (Klein 1994). Benchmarks that agents use to make compliance decisions include prior demands made on them by the same principal, other current demands, the terms and conditions of any relevant contracts, industry norms, or corporate policies, as well as applicable state laws and federal regulations.

Below are two versions of the same directive from a quality manager in a large engineering firm to supervisors and shop floor foremen (note: The names of the employees, the ISO 9001 auditor, and the firm's locations have been changed) as well as comments made by one of the firm's supervisors who actually received the directive. The supervisor's comments are numbered and inserted into each version in bold and brackets. The comments illustrate how important it is for principals to address each of their agents' criteria for making a compliance decision. The comments about the original version are quite negative. Much of the information included is irrelevant to the supervisor. What are missing from the original directive are clear-cut answers to the supervisor's decision criteria. Without those answers—such as a due date, specific requirements, and a procedure for implementing those requirements—the supervisor decided to disregard the directive. When the supervisor read the revised version about a week later, he came away ready to comply. Notice that the writer of the revision explicitly addresses each of the decision criteria that are typically relevant for compliance decisions. Notice also that the writer of the revised directive replaces the vague requirements of the original with a more specific, actionable, and testable requirement— a mock quality audit to be conducted by supervisors prior to the official audit.

Original Directive with a Supervisor's Comments

From: Quality Systems
Sent: Wednesday, September 09, 2009 1:15PM
To: 'ALL CALIFORNIA EMPLOYEES'
Subject: GENERAL NOTICE—QUALITY SYSTEM ASSESSMENTS **[OK, another general notice. What's this one about?[1]]**

Totalt Kvalitet Tjanster **[What the heck is that?[2]]** (TKT), OUR ISO 9001 REGISTRAR, IS SCHEDULED TO PERFORM TWO ASSESSMENTS OF OUR QUALITY SYSTEM IN 2010. **[It must be a company that will audit us. Never heard of them.[3]]** TKT will be here at our California facilities in November to continue the periodic assessments that have already been performed at our Nevada facilities over the past two years. In January, TKT will be conducting a "re-certification" assessment across the firm including our San Jose facility. The Quality Systems group of Total Quality Operations **[This must be a subgroup. They don't really need to distinguish because most people don't know who's in one group or the other. They don't explain why we should care.[4]]** will coordinate the assessments. To ensure we are ready, the following activities are planned:

— Briefings to Senior Management **[Not me.[5]]**
— Making Training and Awareness Material Available Online **[I think it is already.[6]]**
— Forming and training a team of experts from various departments to guide/escort TKT Auditors. **[This won't affect me.[7]]**

In the mean time, management and supervision should ensure:

— Procedures and work instructions are current and available and employees know how to access them. **[Supervision does not have time to update work instruction manuals. We have too many fires to put out. This is not a fire.[8]]**
— Employees know and understand our Quality Policy. **[Do they want us to quiz all of our employees?[9]]**
— Corrective actions are timely and effective. **[Corrective actions for what? I assume they want us to discipline employees who aren't up to snuff on the Quality Policy.[10]]**
— Records are properly **[Define properly.[11]]** stored, are current, and accurately reflect required data. **[This says "ensure records accurately reflect required data"—how general is that? Quality records? Job records? I don't know what they mean, and therefore, I don't know what required data they're talking about.[12]]**
— General compliance to any of our Quality System Elements that apply to your functional area.

Quality Systems will continue to communicate with managers and supervisors to provide up-to-date information on the progress of the assessments.

Rob Morton, Manager
Quality Systems

[The quality policy is frankly a bunch of lofty statements like "We are dedicated to providing the highest quality, lowest cost, most dependable products available which exceed all of our customers' expectations." In real day-to-day operations, it is pretty meaningless. We all do our jobs to the best of our abilities. The only thing of real value is the standard work procedures, but that is not kept current so even its value is limited.[13]

I won't take any action on this notice. I'll wait until I hear some requirements.[14]]

Revised Directive with a Supervisor's Comments

To: All California engineering supervisors and shop floor foremen
From: Rob Morton, Manager, Quality Systems
Date: September 9, 2009
Subject: Preparing your employees for the upcoming ISO 9001 quality audit

The purpose of preparing for the quality audit

We are being audited for conformance with ISO 9001 quality standards, and all employees must be able to pass it. In order to prepare, engineering supervisors and shop floor foremen will be responsible for conducting a mock quality audit with each employee who reports to them. **[OK, this affects me.[1]]** If we do not pass this audit, we will lose either a significant portion or all of our current government contracts. This will result in a company-wide loss of jobs. **[I guess it is worth the time to make sure we pass.[2]]**

The deadlines that you must meet

Each group's mock audit will occur October 22 through 24. The first actual quality audit will occur during the first and third weeks of November. In January, a re-certification assessment will be conducted. **[OK, we have the time to prepare.[3]]**

What you must do

Supervisors and foremen will receive a packet of instructions on how to conduct the mock audit within the next ten days. The packet will include a list of typical questions that auditors may ask. **[Good.[4]]** The answers to the auditor's questions should be contained in your group's standard work procedures. **[My work manual isn't up to date. I'll have to file the revisions.[5]]** You should identify all employees who are unable to give good answers and ensure that they receive corrective training. **[This will take some time. I hope it's really that important.[6]]**

The criteria for passing the mock audit

You must find a 95% compliance rate with ISO 9001 regulations. **[So we don't have to be perfect. That helps.[7]]**

What happens if your employees are not prepared

You must send employees who fail the mock audit to quality policy training prior to November 1. Employees who fail an actual audit will be subject to disciplinary action which may include termination of employment. **[Not a note on their permanent record![8]]**

What to do if you have questions

If you have any questions concerning the upcoming audits, please contact me directly at the Quality Systems Department at 333–2769. **[This is an excellent memo! It answers all of my questions. I think I can get the employees to prepare properly for the audit.[9]]**

Staffing Decisions: Responses to Applications

Audiences who are in the position to employ others, that is to say principals, make staffing decisions in response to applications and proposals from their agents or potential agents. For example, employers make staffing decisions when they decide whether to interview an applicant for a newly opened position, clients make staffing decisions when they decide whether to accept a consultant's proposal, and supervisors make staffing decisions when they decide whether to promote a star employee. Principals make staffing decisions in order to meet the staffing or personnel requirements of their organizations.

Documents and presentations agents or potential agents produce in order to elicit staffing decisions from principals include *résumés, cover letters for résumés, project proposals, letters of engagement, responses to RFPs,* and *letters of recommendation.* Professionals seeking employment also meet with recruiters in job interviews in order to elicit staffing decisions. Unfortunately, many types of communications intended to elicit staffing decisions fail to achieve their intended effect. A study of employers using letters of recommendation to evaluate job applicants finds a large gap between recommenders' intentions and the effects their letters have on the employers' perceptions (Doyle 1990). Documents and presentations that principals deliver to their agents or potential agents in an attempt to communicate their decision criteria for staffing decisions include job descriptions, job application forms, requests for proposals, and performance appraisals. Recruiters may also communicate their decision criteria during job interviews.

The list of questions below provides a starting point for predicting principals' decision criteria for any particular staffing decision.

- What is the applicant's or consultant's knowledge of the firm's objectives?
- What is their knowledge of the firm's requirements for the position or project?
- What is their action plan for meeting the firm's requirements?
- How do they fit with the firm's culture?
- What are their qualifications for the job?
- What steps for engagement do they propose?

When recruiters make staffing decisions, they are especially concerned about applicants having the right qualifications for the job. Corporate recruiters and line managers both rate an applicant's résumé more highly the more it reflects the abilities the specific job requires (Brown & Campion 1994). Two of the most important qualifications for college-educated applicants are their work experience and college record—together these two qualifications account for 75% of the variance in résumé ratings (Ruck 1980). Other characteristics that indicate a qualified candidate and that are positively related to the probability of being hired include having prior experience in a similar job, especially if the experience was in a prestigious company, having majored in the relevant area, and having graduated from a high-status university.

The more recruiters know about the job to be filled, the more agreement there is among recruiters' staffing decisions (Langdale & Weitz 1973) and the fewer irrelevant candidate attributes influence those decisions (Wiener & Schneiderman 1974). In addition, good staffing decisions require recruiters to have or seek benchmark information about other employees (Martin 1987), the ideal applicant (Webster 1964), and other current applicants (Highhouse & Gallo 1997).

Table 2.4 displays some of the comments of two real-world audience members as they made staffing decisions. The comments in the first column were made by the director of a firm's human resources department as she read the cover letter for an MBA's résumé. The comments in the second column were made by the director of another firm's management information systems (MIS) department as he read an 18-page project proposal sent to Pacific Bell from a consulting firm. Each expert was asked to play herself or himself and to make a decision based on the information provided. The comments displayed reflect the decision criteria for making staffing decisions and illustrate how important it is that professionals address them fully. All of the comments are numbered in the order they were made. Repetitive comments or those that did not directly reflect the experts' decision criteria, such as comprehension-related comments, are not included here.

Notice that both expert audience members complained that the potential hires lacked knowledge of their firms and their firms' requirements. Both experts questioned the qualifications of the potential hires as well as their fit with the firm's culture. In addition, the MIS director complained about the lack of specificity in the action plan of the consulting firm's proposal. And the HR director suggested that the MBA was wrong to expect the employer to suggest steps for engagement. Because so few criteria for staffing decisions were addressed, the first expert decided against interviewing the job applicant and the second was not interested in retaining the consulting firm.

On the pages that follow are résumé cover letters two MBA students produced as well as two versions of a third MBA student's résumé (note: The names and addresses of the students, the firms for which they worked, the schools they attended, and the recipients of the letters have been changed). The first cover letter requests an interview for a summer internship. It not only resulted in rejection but also provoked an angry reaction from the potential employer. Notice that it appears to be a form letter. Although the writer claims to have knowledge of the firm's objectives and requirements, he obviously does not.

The second cover letter is a request for an interview for a full-time position written by a different MBA student. It was one of several applications that student made that ultimately resulted in a job offer. Notice that the writer of the second cover letter shows real knowledge of the firm's objectives and makes the case that she can satisfy the firm's requirements. The writer also quantifies the results she has obtained for her current employer, suggesting she has an action plan ready to implement. In addition, the writer provides benchmark information about the firm that retains her and the schools she has attended.

The third MBA student's résumé is shown as originally composed and after it was revised. The original version of the student's résumé also includes comments made by a recruiter that are numbered and inserted into it in bold and brackets. The student was hoping to land a summer internship in marketing in the high-tech industry that would allow her to travel internationally. Notice that the recruiter's comments about the student's original résumé are generally quite negative. The recruiter is not convinced that she has the education, experience, and ability to deliver the results that the recruiter's high-tech marketing internship requires. In addition the small font makes the original version difficult for the recruiter to read.

The revised résumé is much easier to read and highlights the student's interest in marketing, high-tech, and international travel. It also puts greater focus on the results she achieved in prior positions. The revised résumé made a more positive impression on recruiters and ultimately helped the student land a marketing internship in high tech and to travel abroad.

Table 2.4 Experts' Comments that Reveal their Decision Criteria for Making Staffing Decisions

	Comments on an MBA's cover letter by an HR director	Comments on a consulting firm's project proposal by an MIS director
Knowledge of firm's objectives	This letter appears to be a form letter. No indication is given that research was done on our firm. The person does not appear to be very knowledgeable.[6]	There's nothing specific to what they are working off of or how much they know about Bell.[10] I feel that they had no idea about Bell in the slightest before they wrote this thing. That's deadly. They are not interested at all.[26]
Knowledge of firm's requirements	What specific job are they applying for? As the HR director at my firm, I need to be able to determine if openings are available for that position.[2]	They haven't given me a clue to that they know what's going on and that they are responding to what I specifically want and what we're all about.[11] I want to see them telling me "Yes, we know you have this request for proposal. We know generally what you are trying to do." I want to see their approach build off of this base.[24]
Proposed action plan	[Note: Entry-level managers are not ordinarily expected to provide a plan of action in their cover letters.]	They've been talking in general terms of what they're going to do and what we are going to get out of this. The essence of this is how are they going to do it? How long? What type of staffing? What's it going to cost? What is the involvement of Bell's general management and the other functional areas? How are the heads of marketing, finance etc. going to be involved in this and what type of effort do they have to give? Where's the structural approach in how they're going to conduct this study and what the impact is going to be in these functional areas? What is MIS's involvement? Role? Looks like MIS is on the sideline. Again no specifics.[17]

Fit with firm's culture	I don't get any sense of the person, their skills, experiences, interests, etc.[3]	I want to know: What are they doing in these phases? How they are going to do it? How is their staff going to be doing this? How are they going to be interfacing with MIS and user communities?[28]
		They're setting a tone that's so bad that it will screw up the morale of the entire MIS department. They're not working *with* me. They're just going to come in and rip the guts out of my company because they know better. They're going to run this and then hand it over and say "Now you can run this thing."[31]
Qualifications	Where are all their relevant experiences, qualifications, and achievements?[24]	I want to see a profile on the [consulting] company, sales, the types of things they have done, their types of clients, etc. They are not specific to what Bell is wanting. I want to know background but this section has nothing to do with the proposal.[3]
	Some experiences have been listed, manufacturing, marketing, consulting, etc. But this is too broad, no focus.[5]	I want to know who they are putting in charge of this project. What kind of structure they're going to have in your organization? Analysts? Principals? What level? Don't just throw me a wrath of résumés [*sic*].[39]
Steps for engagement	When do they plan to contact us? I hope they're not counting on us to contact them.[8]	I come away with *no* confidence that this company knows what they are doing, or how to organize it, or how to organize the attack.[36]
	Overall, this cover letter needs a lot of work to be effective in securing an interview.[9]	

Unsuccessful Cover Letter for a Résumé

2843 Congress Ave., Apt. B
Austin, TX 78704

November 20, 1998

Mr. John R. Abrams,
Chairman and CEO,
ENERglobal Corporation,
444 Fayette St.,
Houston, TX 77002

Dear Mr. Abrams:

I have become interested in your company through articles and advertisements which have appeared in several magazines. Your organization appears to be growing in a direction which parallels my interests and career goals. Through my conversations with the staff at the University Career Center and with other professionals, I have heard that your company is a dynamic and innovative one which also has a strong culture. These compliments have confirmed my initial positive impressions of your company, and I want to express my strong interest in working as a summer intern for you.

For the past academic year, I have attended our University's distinguished School of Business and expect to receive an MBA degree in May 2000.

During my first year at the Business School, I have gained an intensive education in basic managerial and quantitative skills. I am confident that these invaluable skills, in combination with my computer skills, would be beneficial to you in your assignments or projects. My interests and work at the Business School are in Finance and Information Systems. I look forward to discussing with you possible careers in your company.

I am sure that the intern you are looking for is as important to you as your firm is to me. Not only am I aware of your present needs and confident that I can fulfill them, but even more important, believe that I can be an asset for your future needs as well. I wish that you will give me an opportunity to prove my claim.

Thank you for your kind consideration of my request. If you need any additional information, please feel free to call me at (512) 521–2705. I look forward to hearing from you in the very near future.

Sincerely,

Evan Robbins

Successful Cover Letter for a Résumé

1914 Riverside Dr., Apt. #37
Paterson, NJ 07505
Phone: (973) 321–4757

October 16, 2006

Sarah Wymard
NRG Inc.
1200 Market Street
Fairfax, VA 22031

Dear Ms. Wymard:

My abilities fit the needs of NRG's energy practice. I presently provide consulting services to Edison Light's Treasury Group. My work there focuses on projects requiring expertise in both power plant engineering and corporate finance. I have four years electrical utility experience at both power plants and corporate headquarters. Three of these years were spent as an engineer working for one of the best and most innovative utilities in the U.S. at one of the most highly rated nuclear power stations in the world. My engineering and management educations are from premier schools in their fields. Finally, I greatly desire to continue a career related to electric utilities and energy generation. I sincerely believe that, when combined, these factors make me an outstanding candidate for employment at NRG.

My work with Edison Light's nuclear fuel financing is an excellent example of my unique abilities. While undertaking a review of Edison's nuclear fuel financing I found that they were not taking full advantage of the current New Jersey regulations for the recovery of nuclear fuel financing interest expense. I developed and coordinated the adoption of an accounting method which increased the recovery rate to the maximum allowed under the NJUC regulations. The changes made will reduce Edison's nuclear fuel financing costs by at least $300,000 per year. To date the present value of this and other work I have performed at Edison Light has been in excess of $2,500,000. I can safely say that my work has also saved their ratepayers approximately $8,000,000.

My desire to work with energy-related matters and my expertise in the area of electric utilities will make me a very effective NRG consultant. NRG's focus on energy consulting will in turn provide me with projects which match my interests. Therefore, I would very much appreciate the chance to interview for a position at NRG when you come to our university.

Sincerely Yours,

Davida Wilkinson

Original Résumé with a Recruiter's Comments

PATTY R. SPEAKMAN

3905 Market Street   215–687–2043
Philadelphia, PA 19104   E-Mail: pspeakman@wharton.upenn.edu
[This is killing my eyes! Nine point font is too small![1]]

EDUCATION

May 2006 UNIVERSITY OF PENNSYLVANIA   **Philadelphia, PA**

Master of Business Administration (MBA) **[So she's getting an MBA.[2]]**

Concentrations in Marketing, Information Technology and Strategy **[This résumé does not exude strategy. I want more about technology and marketing here, too.[3]]**

May 2000 CORNELL UNIVERSITY   **Ithaca, NY**

Bachelor of Science in Industrial and Labor Relations

GPA: 3.4/4.0 **[I don't care.[4]]**

Dean's List for Academic Achievement

Fall Semester at University of Brussels, International Business Program, 1999 **[Does she have any other international elements?[5]]**

EXPERIENCE

INGERSOLL-RAND COMPANY

Worldwide manufacturer of industrial equipment and machinery with sales of 12.3 billion

2002 to 2005 Project Leader

Promoted to position in Human Resources leading teams up to 10 people to restructure processes.

Developed local information system using Microsoft Access and corporate payroll software. **[Okay, so you can use Access. Why should I care?[6]]** Resulted in 100% increase in reporting and administrative productivity. **[This I care about.[7]]**

Restructured processes and teams resulting in 20% reduction of salaried employee headcount.

Developed outplacement services that enabled employees to terminate with dignity and minimized legal risks. **[I don't care.[8]]**

Led team of marketing managers to redesign departmental structure. Increased customer focus through addition of product training and market analysis of functions.

Implemented process enhancements for in-house suppliers' order entry function resulting in a 30% increase in deliver reliability and 40% decrease in backorders. **[Tell me results first. Then fill in the details.[9]]**

2002 Reengineering Team Member [I have an aversion to titles like this.[10]]

Part of cross-functional team focusing on supply chain improvements.

Achieved 60% decrease in purchase order processing time through EDI technology.

Initiated new procurement and manufacturing planning processes which resulted in a 20% increase in ability to reliably meet weekly production schedules and a 90% reduction in order fulfillment cycle time. **[Again, tell me the results first.[11]]**

2000 to 2002 Management Development Program Member

Selected from 100 candidates for program of project experience and management skills development.

Evaluated off the shelf product supporting information technology strategy for human resource management functions.

Guided general manager succession planning process approved by company Chairman.

Created orientation process which increased new employee productivity and effectiveness. **[So?[12]]**

ADDITIONAL INFORMATION

Marketing Club: Developed Marketing Club Web Page to stimulate interest in university's marketing resources. **[Result?[13]]**

Management of Technology Club: Organized plant tour and benchmarking. **[What benchmarking? For what goal?[14]]**

Graduate Women Business Network: Planned networking conference as First Year Representative on Steering Committee.

Enjoy skiing and international budget travel.

[My initial impressions: 1. East Coast. 2. Big company. 3. HR or Manufacturing.[15] We're a high tech firm planning to go international. We're looking for a marketing person. Someone familiar with intellectual property issues and the application of technology, (i.e., payroll, etc.), who has process and project management experience.[16]]

Please now turn the page for the revised résumé.

Revised Résumé

Patty R. Speakman

3905 Market Street
Philadelphia, PA 19104

215–687–2043
E-Mail: pspeakman@wharton.upenn.edu

===

Objective Marketing internship in the high technology industry.

Education

May 2006, University of Pennsylvania, Philadelphia, PA
Master of Business Administration (MBA)
- Concentrations in Marketing, Information Technology and Strategy
- Independent market research project for Nexus Corporation to develop strategy for voice command software application.
- Co-Chair of Graduate Women in Business Network. Planned first annual networking conference.
- Marketing Club webpage development team.

May 2000, Cornell University, Ithaca, NY
Bachelor of Science in Industrial and Labor Relations
- GPA: 3.4/4.0, Dean's List
- Fall Semester at University of Copenhagen, International Business Program, 1999. Studied privatization strategies of Polish and East German organizations.

Experience

Ingersoll-Rand Company, Davidson, NC
Global manufacturer of industrial equipment and machinery with sales over 12 billion

2002 to 2005 Project Leader
Promoted to position in Human Resources leading teams up to 10 people to restructure processes.
- Achieved 100% increase in reporting and administrative productivity by developing local information system using database and corporate payroll software.
- Generated 30% increase in delivery reliability and 40% decrease in backorders from in-house supplier by implementing order entry process enhancements.
- Led team of marketing managers to redesign departmental structure. Increased customer focus through addition of product training and market analysis functions.

2002 Order Fulfillment Team Member
Cross-functional team member tasked to generate supply chain improvements.
- Achieved 60% decrease in purchase order processing time through EDI implementation.

- Reduced order fulfillment cycle time by 90% and improved ability to reliably meet weekly production schedules by 20% through implementation of new procurement and manufacturing planning processes.

2000 to 2002 Management Development Program Member
One of three selected from 100 candidates for program of project experience and management skills development.
- Evaluated off the shelf product supporting information technology strategy for human resource management functions.

Interests Travel throughout Europe and Southeast Asia, skiing, soccer, and golf.

Employment Decisions: Responses to Recruiting Efforts

Employment decisions are complementary to staffing decisions and are made by agents or those who wish to become agents. Examples of employment decisions include a job-seeker's decision whether to make an application, an applicant's decision whether to accept a job offer, and a current employee's decision whether to stay with her firm.

Principals seek employment decisions from their agents or potential agents when they recruit and interview candidates for open positions and when they make counter offers to their own employees who are recruited by competing firms. Documents and presentations principals produce in order to evoke employment decisions include *recruiting literature, recruiting presentations, job descriptions, job advertisements*, and *contracts of employment*.

Job applicants appreciate job advertisements and other forms of recruiting literature that address their criteria for employment decisions. A study of nursing students evaluating job advertisements finds that the students prefer the "standard" or traditional job ad over testimonial job ads or minimal ads that contain only the job title and the employer's internet address (van Rooy, Hendriks, van Meurs, & Korzilius 2006). Standard job ads, on the other hand, include company information, a job description, job requirements, application procedure, salary, and conditions of employment. Although job applicants give most attention to location and compensation (Barber & Roehling 1993), they rate job advertisements as more effective when they also include the size of the organization (Barber & Roehling 1993), the job's attributes (Winter 1996; Yuce & Highhouse 1998), as well as the organization's staffing policy (Highhouse, Stierwalt, Bachchiochi, Elder, & Fisher 1999).

The list of questions below includes most of the criteria identified by the studies cited above and provides a starting point for predicting agents' decision criteria for any particular employment decision.

- How does the job fit with my education, experience, and career goals?
- What are the job's responsibilities and status?
- What are the job's working conditions and the firm's culture?
- What is the job location's cost of living and quality of life?

- What is the size and reputation of the employer?
- What is the job's compensation and benefits package?

Agents' schemata for employment decisions may also require benchmark information about salaries, benefits, and working conditions at competing firms and at firms in the same geographical locale. In addition, agents may also seek comparative ratings of regional educational and cultural resources as well as comparative information on job scarcity in different locales (Highhouse, Beadle, Gallo, & Miller 1998).

Exonerative Decisions: Responses to Requests for Pardon

Audiences, usually acting as principals, make exonerative decisions when they decide whether to exonerate an agent from blame. Customers make exonerative decisions when deciding whether to continue to patronize a business that has provided poor service, jurors make exonerative decisions when deciding whether to convict a business executive accused of fraud, supervisors make exonerative decisions when deciding whether to allow a routinely late employee to keep her job. Principals make exonerative decisions in order to ensure just and fair outcomes for all concerned.

Agents seek exonerative decisions from principals when they want to be, or when they want others to be, exonerated from blame. Documents and presentations agents produce in order to evoke exonerative decisions include *crisis press releases*, *media interviews*, *responses to customer complaints*, *rate hike notices*, and *defense arguments*.

Principals are more likely to assign blame when they can identify a particular person as being responsible for an event, when they believe the person should have foreseen and prevented the event, when they believe the person's actions were not justified by the situation, and when they believe the person was free to choose another course of action (Shaver 1975, 1985; Shaver & Drown 1986). The following questions expand on this list of decision criteria for exonerative decisions by adding questions related to the victims and their future:

- Who is responsible for the incident?
- What is the reason for the incident?
- Could it have been prevented?
- What has been done to relieve the victims?
- How much compensation is the responsible party prepared to offer?
- What guarantee is there that the incident will not be repeated?

Principals' schemata for exonerative decisions may also require benchmark information about the individual's or the organization's prior responses to similar situations, others' responses, possible alternative responses, as well as industry best practices in similar situations.

Sometimes principals seek, or should seek, what amounts to an exonerative decision from their agents. On the following page is a notice of organizational downsizing from a manager in a healthcare network as well as comments made by one of the employees, or agents, who actually received the notice (note: The names of the firms and employees have been changed). The employee's comments are numbered and inserted into the notice in bold and brackets. The comments about the notice are quite negative, even hostile. What are missing from the notice are clear-cut answers to the employee's decision criteria. The employee needed answers to questions such as "Who is responsible for the decision to downsize?" (see comment 5), "What was the reason?" (see comments 5 and 7), "Could the downsizing have been prevented?" (see comment 7) "How will the affected staff be assisted?" (see comment 12) and "What guarantee is there that more staff will not be affected or even laid off?" (see comment 13). Because the notice does not address those questions, the employee is left demoralized and resentful of those responsible.

Downsizing Notice with an Employee's Comments

Memo [(Shouting) If I don't know anything else I know this is a memo.[1]]

To: Alliance Health Plus Staff
RE Staff **[Is it safe to assume all us "staff" know who we are? Do the secretaries belong to the "staff"?[2]]**
From: Bob Ruston **[He should initial or sign a memo of this type.[3]]**
Date: 11/02/08
Re: Organization Changes

The purpose of this memo is to announce an organization change. **[Redundant . . . I already know this.[4]]** A decision has been made **[Who made it? Why? What was the impetus? Conversely, as a recipient who has/had no input, do I care?[5]]** to consolidate the medical management activities provided by Reliance Enterprises with the medical management provided by Medi-Serve. Both groups have been working with physicians in our networks to improve clinical performance and the outcomes for our members. **[The truth is, these groups don't really know what the other does.[6]]** By consolidating the expertise and resources of two teams, we believe that we can serve our providers more effectively. **[What was ineffective? Redundant service? Overlapping duties? Internal lost productions again? Why are we doing this?[7]]**

The combined unit will be under the leadership of Joyce O'Brien, Director of Medi-Serve. **[Why Joyce? Will this new team therefore be part of M-S?[8]]** The new team will be in place by December 1st with most transition activities complete by the end of the year. The team will include staff **[If you mention staff along with activities in paragraph one you don't need this sentence.[9]]** from both RE and M-S and provide medical management services to the entire network. Once the team is in place, a communication **[This is a very formal and stilted way of saying this. "Memo" would have sufficed. What will this communication tell us? Once the team is in place it's a little late to tell people that they are on the team. A meeting to explain new duties would be more appropriate than a memo. The only useful purpose this could be is a general informational announcement to the rest of Alliance and to outside providers to inform them of a procedure change.[10]]** will be issued. If you have any questions, please call Joyce at 699–3769.

The consolidation will result in the displacement **[Ah, now the real reason for the whole memo: job elimination. Displacement and elimination mean two different things. When will these people find out who they are, in the aforementioned "communication"?[11]]** of several staff from RE and M-S. ALLIANCE HEALTH PLUS's practice is to work with displaced staff to try to locate other comparable positions within the company. Every effort will be made to assist those individuals who have been impacted by this decision. **[Who will "assist" these people?[12]]**

[So, effective 12/1/08 the medical management activities and staff of RE and M-S will be combined and some of us may be looking for another job.[13]]

Rallying Decisions: Responses to Attempts to Inspire and Lead

Audience members, acting as agents or followers and often as a group, make rallying decisions when others try to inspire or lead them. Examples of rallying decisions include the decision of exhausted employees to work harder, the decision of a losing team to go out and "win just one for the Gipper," and the decision of a disenchanted voting block to throw its weight behind a political candidate.

Principals, acting as leaders, seek rallying decisions from followers when they attempt to boost morale or garner support for themselves, another, a project, or a mission. The show of support may take many forms—a donation (cf., Schkade & Payne 1994), an extra effort, or a vote of confidence. Documents and presentations leaders produce in order to evoke rallying decisions include introductions of new employees, participants, and speakers. They also include *pep talks, commencement speeches, elegies, farewells, campaign speeches, motivational speeches, mission statements,* and *vision statements.*

Followers' schemata for one type of rallying decision—the decision that groups make when choosing and evaluating their leaders—have been well researched. Hogg and colleagues (e.g., Hogg 2001; Hogg & Hardie 1991; Hogg & Terry 2000) investigated the schemata, or in Hogg's terms the *prototypes,* different groups use to decide which of their members should lead them (see Fiske & Taylor 1991, p. 117 and Hogg 1992, p. 115 for discussions of the terminology). A group will often choose as its leader the member who best fits the schema of the group, in other words the member who is most representative of it (Fielding & Hogg 1997). A group will also tend to rate that member as more likeable, influential, and charismatic than other group members (Hogg & Hains 1998; Platow, van Knippenberg, Haslam, van Knippenberg, & Spears 2001; van Knippenberg, Lossie, & Wilke 1994). The decision criteria groups use to choose leaders from among their members include the member's endorsement of the group's norms, goals, and aspirations as well as the member's preferential treatment of other group members.

The schemata employees and political party members use to evaluate their leaders' charisma have also been investigated (Conger & Kanungo 1988, 1998; Conger, Kanungo, Menon, & Mathur 1997). Charisma is an important attribute for leaders to possess since followers rate the performance of charismatic leaders more highly than the performance of others holding leadership positions (Shamir, House, & Arthur 1993). Followers are also more motivated by charismatic leaders, perform better for them, and are more satisfied working for them (Agle & Sonnenfeld 1994; Yammarino & Bass 1990; Zaccaro 2001). The four decision criteria followers use most often to evaluate a leader's charisma include the leader's sensitivity to the followers' needs, the leader's sensitivity to environmental constraints on the followers, the personal risk the leader takes on the followers' behalf, and the leader's vision, a vision which must embody the followers' ideals and aspirations.

The list of questions below expands on the criteria identified in the studies and provides a starting point for predicting followers' decision criteria for any particular rallying decision.

- Does the communicator endorse the values our group holds dear?
- Does the communicator understand the significance of the occasion to our group?
- Does the communicator appreciate the sacrifices our group has already made?
- Is the communicator ready to do his or her part?
- Does the communicator acknowledge the difficulty of the task that lies ahead of us?
- What is the communicator's vision for our future?

Followers' schemata for rallying decisions may also require benchmark information such as organizational or historical stories of others turning failure into success or responding to comparable challenges as well as competing visions for their future.

Getting followers to make a favorable rallying decision requires more than rational arguments, doing so requires artistry, emotion, conviction, and a sense of history. A leader's spoken delivery of her vision can have as great an impact as the content of her vision on how effective her followers perceive her to be (Awamleh & Gardner 1999). Not surprisingly, speeches that elicit rallying decisions—Abraham Lincoln's Gettysburg Address, Dr. Martin Luther King's "I have a dream" speech, John F. Kennedy's inaugural address, George Washington's farewell to the troops—are among the most memorable speeches ever made. Notice how Lincoln's speech below evokes deep emotion as it addresses each of the six key criteria listed above for rallying decisions. As we will see in Chapter 7, audiences tend to become emotionally involved in decision making any time a leader implicates the values they hold dear.

Lincoln's Gettysburg Address

With the six criteria for rallying decisions Lincoln addressed in brackets

Fourscore and seven years ago our fathers brought forth on this continent a new nation, conceived in liberty, and dedicated to the proposition that all men are created equal. **[Criterion 1. Our values: Liberty and equality.]**

Now we are engaged in a great civil war, testing whether that nation, or any nation, so conceived and so dedicated, can long endure. We are met on a great battle-field of that war. We have come to dedicate a portion of that field, as a final resting place for those who here gave their lives that that nation might live. It is altogether fitting and proper that we should do this. **[Criterion 2. The significance of the occasion: To commemorate our brave soldiers.]**

But, in a larger sense, we cannot dedicate, we cannot consecrate, we cannot hallow this ground. The brave men, living and dead, who struggled here, have consecrated it, far above our poor power to add or detract. The world will little note, nor long remember what we say here, but it can never forget what they did here. **[Criterion 3. The sacrifices already made: Our soldiers paid the ultimate price.]** It is for us the living, rather, to be dedicated here to the unfinished work which they who fought here have thus far so nobly advanced. **[Criterion 4. The president is ready to do his part to win the war.]** It is rather for us to be here dedicated to the great task remaining before us–that from these honored dead we take increased devotion to that cause for which they gave the last full measure of devotion—**[Criterion 5. The task ahead will not be easy.]** that we here highly resolve that these dead shall not have died in vain—that this nation, under God, shall have a new birth freedom—and that government of the people, by the people, for the people, shall not perish from the earth. **[Criterion 6. Lincoln's vision for the future: A nation of free people.]**

Quick Reference Guide to Decision Types

	Oversight decisions	*Compliance decisions*	*Staffing decisions*
Audience	Principals: Employers; Superiors; Clients	Agents: Employees; Customers in arrears; Suppliers	Principals: Employers; Superiors; Clients
Desired decision	Grant authority requested	Comply with legitimate demand	Hire individual or firm
Audience's task	Assess risk-adjusted return on proposed projects	Assess cost/benefit and doability	Assess fit with job description and culture
Audience's objective	Increase firm's value. Ensure targets met and laws upheld	Meet legitimate obligations in a convenient way	Increase productivity and revenue
Genres	Strategic plans; Marketing plans; Progress reports; Operating reviews	Directives; Order forms; SOPs; Invoices; Promissory notes	Résumés; Consulting proposals; Letters of engagement; Responses to RFPs
Criterion 1	Past financial performance	Purpose of demand	Knowledge of firm's objective
Criterion 2	Reason for performance	Due date	Knowledge of firm's requirements
Criterion 3	Proposed financial objectives	Steps for completion	Proposed action plan
Criterion 4	Proposed strategy	Evaluation criteria	Fit with firm's culture
Criterion 5	Proposed action plan	Consequences of noncompliance	Qualifications
Criterion 6	Contingency plans	Contact information	Steps for engagement

	Employment decisions	Exonerative decisions	Rallying decisions
Audience	Agents: Job applicants; Employees; Consultants	Principals: The Public; Superiors; Customers	Agents: Group members; Employees; Citizens
Desired decision	Apply for or maintain employment	Exonerate from blame	Support other group members or choose a leader
Audience's task	Assess fit with personal goals	Assess responsibility and adequacy of response	Assess risk and reward of giving support to the group
Audience's objective	Enhance standard of living and job satisfaction	Justice for victims	Rewarding relationships and experiences
Genres	Recruiting presentations; Job descriptions; Employment contracts	Crisis press releases; Complaint responses; Rate hike notices; Defense arguments	Introductions; Pep talks; Vision statements; Elegies; Campaign speeches
Criterion 1	Fit with education, experience, career goals	Responsibility for incident	Endorsement of group's values
Criterion 2	Job responsibilities and status	Reasons for incident	Understanding of occasion's significance
Criterion 3	Working conditions and culture	Preventable incident	Appreciation of sacrifices made
Criterion 4	Location's cost of living and quality of life	Relief of victims	Ready to do part Acknowledgement of difficulties ahead
Criterion 5	Size and reputation of employer	Compensation for damages	
Criterion 6	Compensation and benefits package	Guaranteed not repeatable	Vision for group's future

AUDIENCE DECISIONS ABOUT FINANCIAL RESOURCES

Investment Decisions: Responses to Offers to Invest

Audiences who want to choose the best investment opportunities available to them make investment decisions. For example, venture capitalists make investment decisions when they decide to buy equity in a new firm. Analysts make investment decisions when they decide to recommend a "buy" or a "sell." Private investors make these decisions when they decide to purchase shares in a mutual fund. CFOs make them when they decide to acquire another firm. These audiences make investment decisions in order to earn a good return for the amount of risk they take, and in the case of acquiring firms, to strategically position their firms against competing firms. Once an investment decision to buy is made, the audience becomes an owner and may be entitled to assume an oversight role in the firm's or the fund's management and operations.

Professionals seek investment decisions from audiences when they want to raise cash for their funds or businesses. Documents and presentations professionals produce in order to elicit investment decisions from potential investors include *business plans* (see the business plan executive summaries on pp. 12–16), *acquisition plans, acquisition announcements, prospectuses, tender offers, earnings reports, annual reports,* and *stock research reports.*

The decision criteria of several types of investors and analysts have been investigated thoroughly. For example, buy-side analysts' decision criteria for evaluating acquisitions have been shown to lead to questions about the price of the acquisition, the acquisition's financial impact on the acquirer, the likely synergies, the new management, the acquisition's fit with the acquiring firm's strategy, and the acquiring firm's implementation plan (Kuperman 2000). Similarly, CFOs' decision criteria for making acquisitions have been shown to include the strategic fit of the candidate with the acquirer, the competitive environment of the candidate, the management expertise of the candidate, the financial condition of the candidate and terms of the deal, the operational capabilities of the candidate, and the synergies between the candidate and the acquirer (Melone 1994).

Studies of venture capitalists screening business plans find that VCs' decision criteria for investing in new businesses include questions about the start-up's projected revenues and profits, its market, its product, its management, and the terms of the deal (cf., Bachher 1994; Hall & Hofer 1993; Pfeffer 1987). The list of questions below generalizes the investment-specific decision criteria identified in the studies cited above and provides a starting point for predicting an expert investor's decision criteria for any particular investment decision.

- What is the nature of the investment?
- What is the price and what are terms of the deal?
- What is the current and future value of the investment?
- What are the risks and liabilities associated with the investment?
- What are the qualifications of the management?
- What is the management's strategy and implementation plan?

In addition to these decision criteria, expert audiences' schemata for investment decisions may also require benchmark information about alternative investment opportunities, the investment's historical financial performance, as well as industry averages for similar investments (cf., Gunderson 1991; Clarkson 1962).

Table 2.5 displays some of the comments of two real-world audience members as they made investment decisions. The comments in the first column were made by a partner in a private equity firm as he read a plan developed by partners in another private equity firm to acquire a bankrupt textile manufacturer (note: The names of the firms and the partners have been changed). The comments in the second column were made by an experienced private investor as he read an analyst's stock research report on a recently listed chemical manufacturer, Georgia Gulf Corporation (GGLF). Each expert was asked to play himself and to make a decision based on the information provided. The comments displayed reflect the decision criteria for making investment decisions and illustrate how important it is that professionals address them fully. In addition, the comments show how important it is that professionals are mindful of the benchmarks experts use to evaluate new investment opportunities. All of the comments are numbered in the order they were made. Comments that were repetitive or did not directly reflect the experts' decision criteria, such as comprehension-related comments, are not included here.

Both expert investors found information about the nature of the investment in the documents they read. And both investors were either satisfied with, or had no questions about, the management of the firms. However, neither investor was satisfied with the terms of the deal. Neither investor was convinced by the arguments made for the values of the firms, neither was certain he had the information needed to ascertain the risks and liabilities associated with the proposed investment, and neither was convinced the firms had sustainable competitive strategies. Thus, although both investors found several of their decision criteria addressed, neither thought the recommended investments compared favorably with other investment opportunities, and, as a consequence, decided not to part with their money.

Lending Decisions: Responses to Requests for Loans

Audiences who want to choose the best lending opportunities available to them make lending decisions. Audiences from whom professionals seek lending decisions, and ultimately loans, include bankers, bondholders, and private individuals. These audiences make lending decisions in order to increase the value of their portfolios while keeping risk at an optimal level. To accomplish this, lenders must be able to assess the risk of any specific loan and its impact on the risk level of their portfolio as a whole. Examples of lending decisions include a commercial banker's decision to approve a new line of credit for a client company, a credit committee's decision to renegotiate an existing loan's terms for a client experiencing distress, and an investment banker's decision to underwrite a bond on behalf of a client company.

Borrowers seek lending decisions on behalf of their organizations when they need to raise capital or protect it but do not want to dilute the value of their shareholder's equity. Documents and presentations borrowers produce in order to elicit lending decisions include bankers' internal *loan recommendations*, consumers' *line of credit applications*, as well as some *business plans* and *acquisition plans*.

The 5Cs credit model with its five decision criteria—*character, capacity, capital, conditions,* and *collateral*—is a widely recognized framework for making lending decisions. A study of 104 lenders finds that experienced lenders use the 5Cs model but weight accounting-related criteria more heavily and character data less heavily than do lending novices (Beaulieu 1994). A study of international financial experts deciding whether to extend credit to construction project owners finds their decision criteria include the borrower's creditworthiness, the borrower's marketing and operating experience, the tightness of credit, and the risk at the construction site, as well as the political and economic stability of the project location (Al-Dughaither 1996). Hardin (1996) observed 10 experienced real-estate banking lenders making commercial lending decisions about an apartment complex project. Among the major reasons given by the nine lenders who approved the apartment project loan were borrower experience, a strong market, strong occupancy, and conservative underwriting.

The list of questions below generalizes the loan-specific decision criteria identified in the studies cited above and provides a starting point for predicting an expert lender's decision criteria for any particular lending decision.

Table 2.5 Experts' Comments that Reveal their Decision Criteria for Making Investment Decisions

	Comments on an acquisition plan by a partner in a private equity firm	Comments on an analyst's stock research report by a private investor
Nature of the investment	The company is in bankruptcy. They [the managing partners] are buying the assets from the receiver.[9] Based on this description, it sounds like a great company for a bankrupt company.[27] I'll read through all this stuff on their products and markets because it's useful to know, but most of my questions are going to have to do with the financial information.[34] Oh that's good they have new equipment. At least they won't have to put a lot of money into new machinery. I'm sort of familiar with this type of operation since we have experience in a similar industry.[36] I want them to say up front that they are buying this company out of bankruptcy.[50]	I assume the company's making some kind of chemicals.[1] I'd like to see what percent each chemical is of their product mix.[22] I assume that most of their products are similar chemical products. Only because my father was a chemical engineer do I understand the chemical process they just talked us through. If you weren't a chemical engineer you probably wouldn't be interested, from an investment point of view.[33]
Price/terms of the deal	So, so far they have set up the partnerships with equity—1.4 million, debt—7.2 million, but they still haven't told us, oh here it is, what the transaction is. Our equity contributions are $1,470,000. So the bank doesn't make anything, but they can put this loan on their books as secure now.[10] I want to see what are the sources and uses of the transaction, the $8,670,000 on the second page. Where do we fit into the total financial picture?[48]	Then they give me a bunch of data, the 52-week high and low, 20 to 50. So we're selling near high [note: The company's stock was currently trading at $48 per share]. That would make me wonder why we expect the stock that's more than double the price to triple within the next 12 months.[4]
Current and future value	What I usually like to see is a snapshot of the company, which it doesn't appear that they have. Just the company's financials, their sales, operating income at least, those two things, at least for the last three years. Depreciation and capital expenditures . . . some things to give an idea of cash flows. They make you	We're talking about $150 price value, that seems a little outrageous to me, but maybe these guys know something I don't.[5] They give current capitalization. And yet they said one of the reasons they recommended it was because that was changing. And they give you no idea how that's changing.[10]

	flip to the back to look through the numbers, which I will do now.[12]	Book value per share is only $5.60. And they're recommending $150 value for this company. I don't know about that.[12]
	I don't know why they're using a sales multiple of five times instead of an operating multiple and adjusted cash flow. They don't tell you what they're adjusting cash flow for. So based on who knows why they're getting an IRR of 38.9% (which is acceptable) but who knows what it's based on. In 1995 their margins are up to two million seven. I'm figuring you could sell it for say seven times that. That's about 17 million dollars and they're putting in seven million in debt and 1.5 in equity. So that would make a decent return, but not 38.9% that they claimed.[26]	They don't tell me why the current market only values it at seven times its earnings. Obviously some investors have different views.[26]
		Then they give me an Estimated Segment Earnings Model. If I was really knowledgeable in the industry that might interest me, but probably all I really care about is the bottom line, which is operating income, interest expense, pretax income, etc. and would probably just prefer a note that says if I want further information, contact my account representative.[27]
	They think they know what fair value the company has, and they think they're getting a very good price for it. But there is nothing in here that really tells me that. Nothing tells me the rationale for the price.[43]	Okay, a question that keeps coming back to my mind is that this is obviously a very cyclical industry. I take it that they're building their price estimates up to 21 P/E based on the fact that the industry is expanding. My question is, however, are investors going to buy that?[50]
	If this was any one of my partnerships, I'd be on the phone telling them this is a piece of trash.[45]	
Risks and liabilities	Murray and Robins are the managing partners, so they have the liability, everybody else is limited.[6]	So the firm's profitability is very sensitive to the chlorine open market price, for which I see no future estimates. If I were these guys, I'd surely want to make sure you were in bed with Georgia Pacific. But if GP goes down . . . I don't see any future analysis of GP's market, who is their big buyer.[40]
	I'm kind of wondering at this point why they don't say anything about the bankruptcy. This gives background information, which you have to read to find out where the company is coming from. But they're leaving out the most important information of all. Why did the company go down the tubes in the last three years?[30]	So 50% of this company's earnings appear to be tied to one industry, the paper industry. I'm not sure what that says about the future from what they're telling me.[41]
		One of the things they haven't talked about is liability. When you manufacture and sell chemicals, you have to consider any liabilities, environmental suits, etc. they may face.[56]

continued . . .

Table 2.5 ... continued

	Comments on an acquisition plan by a partner in a private equity firm	Comments on an analyst's stock research report by a private investor
Management qualifications	The two guys who are managing partners were with the Highland Company when the Highland Company bought it, so they're familiar with the business.[42]	[Note: No mention was made of management qualifications in the report or by the investor.]
Management strategy and action plan	I want them to tell me "We've had experience with this company in the past and there are two key things we need to do to turn this company around, and how we're going to do it." Something like, "We can cut costs by doing this, and we can increase sales by doing this."[51] If it's the competition that is the problem, then what are they going to do about it? They didn't talk about future at all.[52]	But I still don't see what these guys' big advantage is.[46] I don't see a good analysis of how these guys fit into the industry, and the industry's movements together.[51] One of the questions that kept coming back to my mind, is where is DuPont? Where are some of the other companies in this industry?[63] My gut reaction is, I don't understand why these guys are better than buying Dow Chemical or anybody else, and therefore I probably would not invest in them.[64] This report is very lengthy. I don't need to know or care how they make these chemicals. What I want to know is: "Is it profitable? Why is it profitable? What are their advantages?" If it's important to be technical because they have an advantage in a certain process, that's fine. But if they make it the same way everybody else does, I really don't care.[65]

- What is the amount and use of the loan applied for?
- What is the nature and character of the borrower?
- What is the borrower's current and future financial performance?
- What is the borrower's credit history and rating?
- What is the borrower's liquidity and collateral?
- What are the current conditions in the economy and the industry?

Benchmarks for lending decisions can include prior loans, alternative lending opportunities, and other loans in the lender's current portfolio.

Usage Decisions: Responses to Requests to Try Out

Audiences who want to choose the best product, service, or information available to them make usage decisions. Consumers make these decisions when they decide to try out a new product or when they give up their attempt to use a new product. Students make them when deciding to try out a technique their teacher recommends. Usage decisions grant or deny a trial use of the product, service, or information. A usage decision in the commercial environment is the first half of many purchasing decisions. The other half of a purchasing decision is a sourcing decision in which the audience decides which supplier offers them the best deal on the desired product, service, or information. Audiences make usage decisions for many different reasons, but usually in order to make their work more productive or their lives easier and more enjoyable.

Product manufacturers and service providers seek usage decisions when they want their clients and customers to use, and often times buy, their product, service, or information. Documents and presentations manufacturers and providers produce in order to elicit usage decisions include *product packages*, *direct mail ads*, *sales pitches*, *cut sheets*, *manufacturer's advertisements*, and *training manuals*.

The decision criteria of several types of users and customers have been investigated thoroughly. For example, Weitz (1978) identifies seven decision criteria purchasing agents use when asked to procure a new product: product reliability, price, after-sales support, product quality, ease of use, compatibility with existing equipment or practices, and salesperson responsiveness to questions or problems. A study of consumers choosing exercise equipment finds that consumers use higher order, abstract decision criteria similar to those listed above to make decisions about brands in different product categories (Graonic 1995). Surprisingly, consumers use similar higher-order constructs as decision criteria more often than they use product attributes even when choosing among comparable products (Walker et al. 1986). Investors who subscribe to analysts' reports tend to prefer to use the services of analysts who have higher historical accuracy, work for large brokerage firms, forecast more frequently, and have greater experience (Brown 2001; Clement & Tse 2003; Jacob, Lys, & Neale 1999).

The list of questions below generalizes the usage-specific decision criteria identified in the studies cited above and provides a starting point for predicting an expert user's decision criteria for any particular usage decision.

- What are the benefits of the product, service, or information?
- How much does it cost in terms of time and money?

- How reliable is it?
- What is the reputation of its manufacturer or provider?
- How compatible is it with prior purchases or information?
- How easy is it to use or implement?

In addition to these decision criteria, expert audiences' schemata for usage decisions also require benchmark information about competing products, services, or information, third-party ratings of the product, as well as the product, service, or information that the user has already adopted (cf., Jung 1996; Lee 1989a; Rothman et al. 2001).

On the following two pages are two versions of a direct mail letter (note: The firm's service and its benefits, the names and address of the firm and its owners, and the names of the universities have been changed) inviting potential clients to a financial planning seminar. Both versions include a description of the service provider, some of the benefits of the service, and a response form with dates and locations of the seminars. Although the original version was successful in attracting people to the seminar, the revised version more than doubled the response rate of the original. Notice how the second version addresses several of the audience's criteria for usage decisions that were not addressed in the original including the seminar's length and the ease of using the information provided. Notice also how the revised version highlights what was likely the audience's most important decision criterion—the cost of the seminar.

Sourcing decisions: Responses to Offers from Vendors

Audiences who want to choose the best supplier or vendor of a product or service make sourcing decisions. For example, purchasing agents make sourcing decisions when they choose among competing vendors or designate a preferred supplier. Consumers make them when they decide among competing fast food restaurants. Students make them when they choose among competing MBA programs.

Suppliers seek sourcing decisions when they want their clients and customers to use their firm, school, website, or store as a source of goods or services. Documents and presentations suppliers produce in order to elicit sourcing decisions include *e-commerce websites, retail advertisements, product catalogues*, and *sales presentations*.

The decision criteria for sourcing decisions of several types of consumers and buyers have been investigated thoroughly. For example, when women choose a department store at which to shop, the five criteria most important to them are ease of locating merchandise, return policy, knowledgeable salespeople, quality of fitting rooms, and store location (Williams 1990). For many customers, the two most important criteria are the store's past availability of products and its convenience (Mader 1988).

A study of purchasing agents selecting suppliers for long-term contracts finds they first eliminate vendors who have a poor record of quality, delivery, service, or a consistently higher price (Vyas 1981). After receiving quotes from the remaining vendors, the purchasing agents' decision criteria include the vendor's shipping costs, payment terms, and warranties. Only after the agents identify the vendors who meet these criteria does price become an important factor. New suppliers need to quote a price between 5% and 8% lower than existing suppliers to get a piece of the company's business.

Original Direct Mail Letter

PFA Price
Financial Associates

One Franklin Center, P.O. Box 711, Las Vegas, NV 89120   1-800-323-0410 FAX 215-323-0410
Bob Dawson • Frank Kirby • Robert Davidson • John Ableson, CLU, ChFC

Dear Mr. Jamison,

You are cordially invited to attend a financial planning seminar sponsored by our company in conjunction with Pauline Roberts, Esq., of the law firm of Roberts & Shaw. This is not a sales seminar, but rather is designed to educate you in available financial planning options. We, in conjunction with Roberts & Shaw, have been providing financial planning seminars over the last two years in Nevada with a favorable response.

Ms. Roberts, a graduate of the University of Hawaii Law School, who holds an LL.M. (masters degree in taxation) from San Francisco State University, and who practices exclusively in the area of financial planning, will discuss the following:

• The utilization of a Financial Plan to get out of debt, save money automatically, and retain control of your credit rating.

• How to prepare for the coming Social Security Crisis.

• How to discover the best credit cards, online savings accounts, and cd rates.

We have over fifty years of experience, in providing financial planning services to over 6,000 satisfied clients, and we are committed to help families utilize the financial planning tools available to minimize taxes, maximize income and get control over their finances.

Very Truly Yours,

John Abelson, CLU, ChFc

Please tear off here and return

PLEASE CHECK WHICH FUTURE SEMINAR YOU WILL ATTEND
DOWNTOWN HILTON

Tuesday,	November 10, 2009	1:00 p.m._____
Tuesday,	November 10, 2009	7:00 p.m._____

There is no charge for the Seminar and your registered guests are welcome.

(Please remember to mark your calendar with the seminar date and time you have selected)

"Serving the Tri-state area"

Revised Direct Mail Letter

Learn how your family can benefit from a Financial Plan

Attend a free Financial Planning Seminar

What you'll get from this seminar
- Learn how to protect your family from the upcoming Social Security Crisis.
- Find out the differences between systematic risk and specific risk.
- Have your individual questions answered by a financial planning attorney.
- Discover how to get the best credit cards, online accounts, and cd rates.
- See the in-depth 60-minute, full-color slide presentation.
- Hear how other high-income families have maintained dividend income even during the economic downturn.
- Take home a complete, free packet of financial planning information.

Who should attend:
1. Married couples who want to save for their child's education.
2. Working people who want to protect their hard-earned assets.
3. Family members who help their elderly parents with financial planning.

The 60-minute slide presentation: Informative and Entertaining
Sit back and be enlightened and entertained by the full-color Financial Planning slide presentation. You'll learn more about your financial planning options during this presentation than you would reading a 500 page book.

Your speaker: Acclaimed author on the benefits of Financial Plans
Your speaker for this seminar is attorney Pauline Roberts. A dynamic and highly respected financial planner, Pauline is also the author of numerous articles on the benefits of Financial Plans. She holds an advanced degree in tax law and dedicates her practice to providing Financial Plans to the people of Nevada.

The sponsors: Two trusted legal and financial firms
The sponsors of the Financial Planning seminar are two of Southern Nevada's most respected legal and financial firms: The law firm of Roberts & Shaw and Price Financial Associates. They have helped more than 6000 families build their savings and take control of their finances.

What people are saying about Pauline Robert's Seminar
"Pauline's seminar saved my family and me over $200,000!"
                    B.J., Las Vegas

"This seminar is probably the most profitable hour you'll ever spend."
                    C.P., Searchlight

- -

To reserve your seats, please return this form in the enclosed envelope to:

Price Financial Associates, One Franklin Center, Las Vegas, NV 89120

Please check the free seminar you will attend.   Your guests are also welcome.

Tuesday, December 10, 2009 at the Downtown Hilton	☐ 1:00 p.m.	Home Phone:_____
Tuesday, December 10, 2009 at the Downtown Hilton	☐ 7:00 p.m.	Work Phone:_____

Unable to attend at the times listed? Call 1-800-323-8410 for the dates of the next free seminar.

Some of the most frequently used decision criteria among professional retail buyers are the vendor's reputation, the anticipated margin, the reliability and speed of delivery, the product's reputation, and the estimated consumer demand for the product (Hirschman & Mazursky 1982). Surprisingly, buyers weight the vendor's production facilities and the gross margins on the vendor's merchandise more heavily than they do customer demand for the products (Hirschman 1981).

The list of questions below generalizes the source-specific decision criteria identified in the studies cited above and provides a starting point for predicting an expert audience's decision criteria for any particular sourcing decision.

- What are the supplier's prices?
- How available and extensive is their selection?
- How convenient is their location?
- What customer service and ambiance do they provide?
- What payment terms and delivery options do they offer?
- What return policy and after-sales service do they offer?

Benchmarks for sourcing decisions can include the supplier's historical price levels and performance, as well as competing vendors' prices, quality, and service levels.

Budgetary Decisions: Responses to Requests for Resources

Audiences who have power over other parties within an organization and who are charged with allocating the organization's resources make budgetary decisions. Such decisions grant professionals the right to spend the firm's money on projects, equipment, new personnel, and so on. Examples of budgetary decisions by upper management include decisions to allow middle managers to upgrade the firm's computer system, to add a requested line item to next year's budget, and to reject an employee's request for a raise. Budgetary decisions differ from oversight decisions. Whereas oversight decisions focus on financial objectives and the strategies necessary to achieve them, budgetary decisions focus on allocating resources appropriately and keeping costs under control.

Professionals seek budgetary decisions when they want funding from sources within their organization. Documents and presentations professionals produce in order to elicit budgetary decisions from those in charge of the purse strings include *purchase proposals*, *capital projects proposals*, *staffing proposals*, and *departmental budget proposals*.

Budgetary decisions are often political. A study of university CFOs' budget decision criteria finds that both internal and external politics play a big role in budgetary decisions, especially in the budgetary decisions of younger CFOs and CFOs with less seniority (Taggart 1993). To a large extent, top managers are able to control the outcome of budgetary decisions by selecting the people who are included in the decision-making process (Markus 1983).

Expert audiences' schemata for budgetary decisions appear to include, but are not limited to, decision criteria that lead expert audiences to ask the following questions (cf., Smotas 1996):

- What is the nature and cost of the expenditure?
- What are its impacts on the firm's strategy and operations?
- What are its financial benefits?
- What are the risks involved with its implementation?
- How urgent is the request?
- What are the qualifications of the requester?

Good budgetary decisions require audiences to have access to benchmarks such as past expenses, other divisions' expenses, and competitors' expenses.

Table 2.6 displays some of the comments of two real-world audience members as they made budgetary decisions. The comments in the first column were made by the CEO of a medium-size e-commerce firm as he read a manager's 17-page proposal to acquire a $392,515 application server. The comments in the second column were made by a manager in a large credit corporation as he read a four-page proposal one of his subordinates wrote requesting $6,240 for the purchase of an automated envelope stuffer. Each expert was asked to play himself and to make a decision based on the information provided. The comments displayed reflect the decision criteria for making budgetary decisions and illustrate how important it is that professionals address them fully. All of the comments are numbered in the order they were made. Comments the CEO made that were repetitive or did not directly reflect his decision criteria, such as format-related comments, are not included here. All of the comments the manager from the credit corporation made are included.

Notice that the CEO voices several major complaints about the proposal to purchase a new server, all of which are related to criteria for making budgetary decisions:

1) there is no evidence that the purchase will have a positive impact on the strategy and operations of his organization;
2) there are unexamined risks associated with its implementation;
3) there is no indication that the purchase is urgent or necessary; and
4) the requester has not gotten others within the organization on board with the idea.

Notice that the manager from the credit corporation has even more basic problems with the proposal to purchase an envelope stuffer:

1) the manager could not figure out what was being proposed or how much it would cost;
2) he did not understand the reason for the purchase; and
3) he was not told what the financial benefits would be.

On the pages that follow is a salary request (note: The position and its attributes, the names of the firm's employees, and the locations of the teams have been changed) from a manager in an engineering firm to his upper management. The comments are those of an experienced business manager who was asked to put himself into the role of upper management and to make a decision based on the information provided. The expert manager's comments are numbered and inserted into the salary request memo in bold and brackets.

Notice that the expert's comments about the request are quite skeptical. What is missing from the salary request is information that addresses upper management's decision criteria about the cost of the salary increase, the manager's impact on the operation of the firm, the financial benefit the manager provides to the firm, and information that shows the manager is uniquely qualified to hold his position. In addition, critical benchmark information is missing, such as the amount of the manager's current salary, the amount of competitive salaries, and the amount of work performed this year compared to the amount performed in the previous year.

Even more interesting is the way the expert shifts from thinking about the manager's request as requiring a budgetary decision (is the request justified?) to thinking about it:

1) as requiring a staffing decision (perhaps more managers are needed, or maybe the manager really just wants a promotion);
2) as requiring an oversight decision (perhaps the division is inefficiently run), and finally;
3) as requiring a policy decision (perhaps the organization needs a formal process for promotions and salary increases).

The expert's comments highlight the fact that audiences are free to make any type of decision they wish no matter what type of decision a professional intends to elicit from them and that a unilateral request for change can trigger a type of decision that the professional did not intend. The expert's comments also provide an excellent example of the critical thinking skills that top managers are able to bring to bear on business issues.

Salary Request with a High-Level Manager's Comments

```
TO:     Jennifer Junejo
FROM:   Aaron Schwark
RE:     Global Product Division
DATE:   September 14, 2009
```

Having completed two years as manager of the global product division, I would like to discuss how the responsibilities of the division have grown during that time. The product line that I manage is highly interrelated with other products at our firm. As such, I often have to be involved in cross-functional meetings or other projects that involve individuals from several departments or teams. I have had to learn—very quickly—how to manage and work with different teams of engineers, salespeople, and marketing employees from around the world.

There are now three "teams" that I must manage or interface with every day; the first is a team of development engineers located in Kyoto, Japan, the second is a worldwide sales force, and the third is a team of production technicians located in San Diego, CA. In regards to my dealings with the software development team in Japan, although this

Table 2.6 Experts' Comments that Reveal their Decision Criteria for Making Budgetary Decisions

	Comments on a purchase proposal by an e-business CEO	Comments on a purchase proposal by a manager in a credit company
Nature and cost of the expenditure	Do we have to spend that much [$392,515] *up front?* Why can't we phase this in?[1]	What exactly is it that you're proposing?[1]
	Why are you pushing JAVA? Give me some industry or company perspective on your premise.[6]	Are you also proposing changes to how the mail is processed? I can't tell from the information you provide just what you're getting at.[2]
	This techie stuff could be rolled up into concepts that map to a business goal.[7]	You indicate that there is an additional expense in re-ordering envelopes for the mail stuffer. Is this a big cost? I would have to know this in order to make a decision.[5]
Impact on strategy and operations	I would have expected business goals or something to start with. This section on background information is not the best lead material.[5]	You've provided lots of facts and figures about costs and options, but why? What problem are you trying to resolve? Your proposal just presents a lot of information, but never explains why you're providing it.[3]
	What are the factors that were used to evaluate our options? This should be shown up-front. For example, "Here are the key challenges for us. Here are the factors we used. Here's where the industry is going. Here's how we can get there."[9]	
	You get into factors like scalability and reliability but they are buried.[11]	

Financial benefits	Cost savings are *always* hard to even estimate. I would not lead with something like this.[2]	By reducing the manpower required to stuff envelopes, doesn't that save money as well? How much?[4]
Risks involved with implementation	How about the cultural fit and ability for our e-company to support this? How about vendor stability, market momentum?[12] Did anyone tire-kick this stuff by laying hands on it?[23]	[Perhaps because of the small up-front cost—$6,240, this expert did not indicate whether or not he noted the proposal's lack of a risk assessment.]
Urgency of request	Even if it is stated that we need this *now*, how do you draw this conclusion? In other words, traffic, load, etc. Do you reference our current platforms?[18]	[This expert did not indicate whether or not he noted the proposal's lack of urgency.]
Qualifications of requester	I'm not sure on the bias of the writer of this proposal. Were business unit folks consulted? At a minimum, marketing folks?[22]	[This expert knew the requester well and did not indicate a need for further information about him.]

team of engineers does not directly report to me, I have a certain level of responsibility in providing guidance so that they are using their time to work on the highest priority software issues and development requests. More and more they turn to me for advice on how to interpret given requirements, or whether or not to proceed on certain projects.

One of the more unofficial teams that I now "lead" **[I don't quite understand that[1]]** is our worldwide sales force. Even though none of these people report to me directly, I am now indirectly responsible for helping to increase their sales of my particular product. Of course, this is of mutual benefit, since the salespeople receive additional compensation and the increase in total product sales is one of the performance metrics by which I am evaluated. However in the past year, I have had to conduct many sales teleconferences with groups of salespeople from different geographical areas. These training sessions are generally requested by the regions, and not my idea. In an effort to more effectively inspire and lead these sales teams, I have begun setting up monthly or bi-monthly sales training sessions with each of the different regions.

I recently instituted monthly meetings with the development engineers, product segment manager, and representatives from marketing to discuss, prioritize and assign target development dates to new marketing or customer requirements. During this meeting, it is my responsibility—as chair of the board—to keep the meeting moving forward and keep the team focused. In addition, I am increasingly involved in conference calls between sales account managers and consultants, to help provide assistance while the two parties work through the terms of a major contract.

I would like to request a salary adjustment which would reflect the extra responsibility of these kinds of activities. I think a salary of $85,000 per year would fairly reflect the work and responsibility carried by my position.

[I would look into it, but based on this document I would not grant the request. There's not enough evidence.[2]

This does show that we have a manager that is unhappy in the position. He believes that he has taken on more responsibility, and therefore should get paid more. That may be true, if he's contributing more to the bottom line.[3]

What's wrong with this is he doesn't make a strong case. I would like to see how his responsibilities have increased, what exactly he is doing, how the sales volume's increased.[4]

Quite possibly we may just need to hire additional management for the division. Or maybe this individual would not be happy working in the product division over the next year or two and is looking for more opportunity. But you can only elicit that from a face-to-face meeting.[5]

There may be some inefficiency going on that I'd want to discuss.[6] The only thing this document would do would get me to talk to this person. But otherwise, the memo does not document enough what the contributions to the bottom line are, or how much more time is spent, how only he with his experience can do these kinds of jobs, etc.[7]

Perhaps our company needs a more formal process for promotion and salary increase. Usually what you would have would be a set of objectives that would be agreed upon at the first of the year. So that at the end of the year, I could look at your objectives and agree that you had met them.[8]]

Borrowing Decisions: Responses to Offers of Loans

Audiences, such as consumers and CFOs who are open to borrowing money in order to pay for their expenditures, make borrowing decisions. Bankers seek borrowing decisions from CFOs or consumers when they pitch a loan or a line of credit to them. Lower-level managers seek them when they ask upper management for permission to borrow funds for a costly new project. The audience's objective in borrowing may be to increase the value of the firm, to reestablish liquidity, to defer payment, or to manage its debt load.

Bankers and lending agencies seek borrowing decisions when they want to supply loans to borrowers in order to earn interest from them. Documents and presentations lenders produce in order to elicit borrowing decisions include *credit card offers, bond issuance proposals, line of credit proposals,* as well as *assessments of optimal capital structure and cost of capital.*

CFOs' decision criteria for borrowing decisions have been investigated thoroughly. When CFOs decide to take on debt, they are most concerned about maintaining the firm's financial flexibility and good credit rating (Graham & Harvey 2001). CFOs are somewhat less concerned about transactions costs, free cash flows, tax advantages, or the perceptions of customers and suppliers.

The list of questions below generalizes the borrower-specific decision criteria identified in the study cited above and provides a starting point for predicting an expert audience's decision criteria for any particular borrowing decision.

- What are the loan's or line of credit's interest rates and terms of repayment?
- What are its fees and transaction costs?
- What method of computing interest does it use?
- What are its restrictive covenants and penalties?
- What are its tax advantages?
- What effect will it have on my credit rating?

Borrowing decisions also require audiences to be familiar with a wide range of benchmarks, especially the offers of competing banks as well as the terms and conditions of other funding sources. CFOs' benchmarks when issuing debt include the debt levels of other firms in the industry, the potential costs of bankruptcy, the relative risk of other sources of funds, and the relative cost of other sources of funds (Graham & Harvey 2001).

Below is a student's revision of a complex, multi-page introduction to a student loan application form. The original version was so full of information irrelevant to a borrower's decision criteria that even experienced financial aid officers found it difficult to use. Information that addressed the borrower's decision criteria was especially hard to locate in the original version due its organization under vague headings such as "General Information." The revised version, on the other hand, directly addresses several of the student borrower's important decision criteria, omits background information irrelevant to a borrowing decision, and uses descriptive headings that speed information search.

Revised First Page of a Loan Application Form

DO YOU NEED HELP PAYING FOR COLLEGE?

If you are a student looking for financial assistance for college,
you may be interested in our Supplemental Student Loan.

Who Is Eligible?

To be eligible, you must be a U.S. Citizen or a permanent resident of the United States. You also must be enrolling or currently enrolled either full-time or part-time (at least 20 hours per week) at a college or university in our state. You must not be in default on any prior student loans.

What Schools Are Eligible?

You can obtain a loan from us to meet the costs of education at practically any accredited two or four-year college, university, graduate or professional school located in our state. You can call us at 1–800-GET-LOAN if you need to inquire about the eligibility of the school you wish to attend.

Is the Supplemental Loan Right for Me?

There are several different loan programs available to college students. You should first consider both the Guaranteed Student Loan (or GSL) and a PLUS Loan before applying for our Supplemental Loan. Both the GSL and PLUS are less expensive loans than our Supplemental Loan. You can get information about GSL and PLUS loans from any bank in your community.

What Is the Repayment Schedule?

You have ten years over which to pay back your loan. We will begin to charge you interest on the loan as soon as you receive your loan check. You are required to make monthly payments of both interest and principal.

How Much Will My Payments Be?

Since you repay your loan over ten years, your monthly payments should not be a financial burden. If you borrowed $10,000 your payments would be $130 per month. We require you to make payments of at least $50 per month. So if your loan was small, you may completely repay it in less than ten years.

How and When Should I Apply?

STEP 1: Fill out the attached Eligibility Application right now. It will take you only thirty minutes to fill out and will provide us with enough information to determine your eligibility. If you mail the completed application to us today, we will notify you about your approval by mail within thirty days. Just call us at 1–800-GET-LOAN if you have any questions about the Eligibility Application.

How Much Can I Borrow?

You can borrow a maximum of $10,000 for a single academic year. If you are borrowing a GSL or PLUS loan then these loans will be counted against the $10,000. For example, if it is your sophomore year as an undergraduate and you borrow $2,500 under GSL and $4,000 under PLUS, the maximum supplemental loan you can borrow this year is $3,500 ($10,000−$6,500). You can borrow for as many academic years as you require.

What Are the Charges and Interest Rates?

We charge a fee of 5% of your total loan. This fee will cover the costs of processing your loan. It allows us to guarantee your loan in the event you default. Your fixed interest rate will be 9.5% per year.

STEP 2: Once your eligibility has been approved, we will send you the Loan Request Form. This form asks for more detailed information about you and your credit history. This information will allow us to fully process the loan. You will need a copy of your most recent Federal Tax Return in order to fill in some sections of the Loan Request Form.

It is important to APPLY EARLY! It generally takes 30 days from the time we receive your fully completed Loan Request Form to the time you receive your loan check. By applying early you will be certain to have the money by the time classes begin.

How Do I Receive My Loan Check?

We will send your loan check directly to you. By law we cannot issue the check more than ten days before classes begin.

Quick Reference Guide to Decision Types

	Investment decisions	*Lending decisions*	*Usage decisions*
Audience	Venture capitalists; Private investors; Institutional investors	Bankers; Bond-holders; Private lenders	Users; Customers; Students
Desired decision	Invest or divest securities	Lend money	Use product, service, or information
Audience's task	Assess valuation	Assess terms and fit with portfolio's objectives	Assess cost/benefit of use
Audience's objective	Appropriate return for risk. Reasonable liquidity	Increase portfolio's value and lower its risk	Complete desired task efficiently
Genres	Acquisition plans; Business plans; Analysts' reports; Annual reports	Acquisition plans; Business plans; Credit applications; Loan recommendations	Advertisements; Product packaging; Direct mail offerings; Instructions
Criterion 1	Nature of investment	Amount and use of loan	Benefits
Criterion 2	Price and terms of deal	Borrower's character	Costs
Criterion 3	Current and future value	Borrower's current and future finances	Reliability
Criterion 4	Risks and liabilities	Borrower's credit history and rating	Reputation of manufacturer or provider
Criterion 5	Management qualifications	Borrower's liquidity and collateral	Compatibility with prior acquisitions
Criterion 6	Management strategy and action plan	Current conditions in economy and industry	Ease of use

	Sourcing decisions	Budgetary decisions	Borrowing decisions
Audience	Customers; Clients; Purchasing agents	Superiors; Committee members	CFOs; Managers; Consumers
Desired decision	Procure product or service from supplier	Supply funding requested	Request and accept financing
Audience's task	Assess cost/benefit of deal	Assess impact on budget	Assess cost/benefit of offer
Audience's objective	Get best deal on desired product or service	Control costs and manage expectations	Get necessary funding on best terms
Genres	Advertisements; E-commerce websites; Direct mailings; Catalogues; Free offers	Salary increase requests; Invitations to bid; Purchase proposals	Project financing proposals; Credit card offers; Bond issuance proposals
Criterion 1	Supplier's prices	Nature and cost of expenditure	Interest rates and terms of repayment
Criterion 2	Availability and selection	Impact on strategy and operations	Fees and transaction costs
Criterion 3	Convenience of location	Financial benefits	Method of computing interest
Criterion 4	Customer service and ambiance	Risks involved with implementation	Restrictive covenants and penalties
Criterion 5	Payment terms and delivery	Urgency of request	Tax advantages
Criterion 6	Return policy and after-sales service	Qualifications of requester	Affect on credit rating

AUDIENCE DECISIONS ABOUT ORGANIZATIONAL POLICIES

Audiences who decide whether or not to make a change that affects a group or an organization as a whole make policy decisions. Policy decisions involve deciding whether the group or organization should continue with the status quo (i.e., do nothing) or institute a new policy or pursue a new course of action. The need for a policy decision can arise any time a group or organization experiences a conflict or controversy about what to do. When making policy decisions, audiences benchmark proposed policies against each other, prior policies, competitors' policies, as well as against the current policy.

In order to elicit policy decisions from their audiences, professionals make policy arguments to them. Professionals regularly make policy arguments to their colleagues during group and committee meetings. Professionals may also make policy arguments to their clients when presenting policy recommendations to them, to their superiors when offering their advice, and most prominently to the public when engaging with opponents in political debates. For an example of policy arguments made by two MBA teams debating a business policy, see pp. 48–50.

Unlike decisions about financial resources, policy decisions can be made about any issue of importance to an organization. For example, government officials make policy decisions about a wide range of issues, including issues pertaining to international relations, public health, trade, immigration, and agriculture. Policy decisions may also need to be made about financial resources if a controversy about those resources exists within the organization.

Unlike decisions about principal/agent relationships, policy decisions are often made by groups of colleagues or by a leader who has asked for advice from subordinates or consultants (Hill 1984; Sniezek & Buckley 1995). When policy decisions are made by groups or committees, the group members act both as communicators and as the audience. As communicators, group members make policy arguments for or against alternative courses of action in order to garner support for the proposal they prefer. As the audience, group members help decide which of the proposals made to the group is best.

The Influence of Group Affiliations on Policy Decisions

Unlike most other types of decisions, the departmental affiliations and special interests of audience members will likely have a significant impact on the decision criteria audiences use to make policy decisions (Bonham, Shapiro, & Heradstveit 1988; Gallhofer & Saris 1996). The membership of a policy-making group often mirrors the structure of the organization to which the group belongs, with each member arguing for the decision criteria and proposals that promote the interests of his or her own department (Downs 1994; Drezner 2000; Hermann, Geva, & Bragg 2001). If a department or other stakeholder in the decision has no representative in the group, the policy alternative they would have recommended and the decision criteria they would have used to evaluate alternative proposals will likely be overlooked (cf., Brown 1988). Thus, organization leaders are able to exert a great deal of influence over policy decisions simply by deciding which departments should or should not be represented at a particular policy meeting (cf., Markus 1983).

Table 2.7 categorizes the statements made by Dutch cabinet members as they met to decide on the best response to Indonesia's bid for independence in 1948 (Gallhofer & Saris 1996). The numbers indicate the percentage of statements made by each Dutch minister that related to one of the six types of decision criteria discussed. The table illustrates that the types of decision criteria the group used to make its decision reflected the departmental affiliations of the ministers present. The percentages in bold show that each departmental minister's focus was on the decision criteria most relevant to his own department. Had the Minister of Justice been included in the meeting, we would expect to see more discussion of law-related decision criteria. The table also shows that the prime minister, whose power depended on domestic politics, was the group member most focused on domestic politics-related decision criteria.

The Influence of External Groups on Policy Decisions

Sometimes it is important for a group or an organization to take into account the decision criteria of external groups who have a stake in the group's policy decision. Table 2.8

lists decision criteria that the Federal Bureau of Reclamation found to be most important to the community interest groups who had a stake in the Bureau's proposed Orme Dam which was to be located near Phoenix, Arizona (Brown 1988). Interest groups included residents and business people from the area who were concerned about flooding and the resulting property damage; the League of Women Voters who wanted to provide recreational opportunities; water developers who wanted an abundant source of clean

Table 2.7 The Departmental Affiliation of Group Members Often Determines which Decision Criteria will be Used to Make a Policy Decision

Department of minister	Types of decision criteria used (Numbers indicate percent of statements made by each minister about each type of decision criterion)					
	Foreign affairs-related criteria	Defense-related criteria	Finance-related criteria	Overseas territories-related criteria	Law-related criteria	Domestic politics-related criteria
Foreign affairs	**39**	15	12	28	0	6
Defense	10	**57**	8	24	0	1
Finance	18	13	**54**	2	0	13
Overseas territories	32	6	3	**48**	1	10
Prime Minister	34	6	4	40	0	16

Source: Adapted from Gallhofer & Saris 1996, p. 211.

Table 2.8 Allowing Stakeholders to Determine Decision Criteria and to Rate Alternatives on the Basis of them Can Resolve Conflicts

Community's decision criteria	Build no dam	Build Orme Dam	Build Cliff Dam	Build Waddell Dam
Control flooding in valley	57	33	68	71
Control flooding in city	52	39	72	75
Promote recreation	62	26	68	72
Increase water supply	58	34	70	72
Protect environment	75	17	70	72
Respect Tribal property	80	16	70	74
Overall approval rating	64	28	70	73

Note: Numbers indicate average approval rating on a 100-point scale.
Source: Adapted from Brown 1988, p. 335.

water; environmental groups who wanted to protect wetlands and wildlife; and tribal representatives who wanted tribe members to be allowed to remain in their homes.

Initially, the Bureau neglected to solicit either the decision criteria of the interest groups or their ratings of alternative proposals and the status quo. It did so only after being forced to delay construction of the Orme Dam for more than 10 years due to protests from local citizens. The numbers in the table indicate the average approval rating on a scale of 1 to 100 that the groups as a whole gave each alternative for each decision criterion. Although all three alternative dams listed below met the two decision criteria of the Bureau—flood control and water storage—the community's ratings show that it much preferred the Waddell Dam to the Orme Dam. After the community ratings were published, even those public interest groups and politicians who had originally supported the Orme Dam chose to support construction of the Waddell Dam instead.

Organization-Based Decision Criteria for Policy Decisions

The list of questions below provides a starting point for predicting the decision criteria for policy decisions made by audiences in many for-profit and non-profit organizations. Each question tests the proposed new policy against the organization's established goals. The first question tests the policy against the mission and values, or high-level goals, of the organization as a whole. The remaining questions test the policy against the goals of the departments that make up many for-profit and non-profit organizations—i.e., the finance department, the strategy and marketing departments, various departments that deal with operations, the legal department, and the public relations department. For a new policy to meet the goals of the PR department, it may have to meet the goals of external stakeholders in the policy decision as well.

- Is the policy consistent with the organization's mission and values?
- Is the policy consistent with the organization's financial objectives?
- Is the policy consistent with the organization's strategy?
- Is the policy consistent with the organization's operational capabilities?
- Is the policy consistent with the organization's legal and ethical obligations?
- Will the policy generate positive PR for the organization?

The set of questions above is unlike those for other types of decisions. Professionals may need to develop different sets of questions to address the decision criteria of different types of groups and organizations. For example, decision criteria for US foreign policy decisions typically include criteria related to the policy's diplomatic, military, political, and economic implications for the country (Mintz, Geva, Redd, & Carnes 1997). As we have seen, the decision criteria used by the Dutch ministers differ from those used by the community groups with an interest in the Orme Dam, and the decision criteria of both groups differ from those used by businesses. Moreover, as we saw in the Dutch case, different department heads within the same organization focus on different decision criteria while evaluating the same set of policy options. And as we saw in the Orme Dam case, allowing external stakeholders to have a say in an organization's policy decision can dramatically affect the decision criteria and the choice of the best alternative.

Types of Audience Decisions: Implications for Communicators

✧ The main takeaway for communicators in Chapter 2 is that audiences use variations on a small number of decision schemata to make most of the decisions that professionals want them to make. Thus, the audience's information requirements are often predictable.

✧ Use the information presented in the chapter to more quickly ascertain the content that is appropriate for your communications. The alternative is to start from scratch when planning the content of your documents, presentations, meetings, or interviews.

✧ Why use the information? To save yourself time. To improve your accuracy in predicting the information your audience requires. To persuade your audience.

✧ To apply the information presented in the chapter: (1) Determine the type of decision you want your audience to make; (2) Address the decision criteria and provide the benchmarks for that type of decision; (3) Add or subtract decision criteria and other information depending on the needs and preferences of your specific audience.

CHAPTER 3

Cognitive Processes in Audience Decision Making

VP of R&D starting his presentation to his firm's board of directors: Okay. In as far as our middle sudser market goes, there is really not a better product that we can copy in our nation. We're looking around to see around the world to see if there isn't one we can copy that, come in and it has great productivity or whatever then we can use that [*sic*]. Otherwise, we have to either improve on one of the product characteristics, meaning washing power and gentleness, or else try and bring the cost down and compete on that basis. The retail high sudsers, again the competitors meaning Team 2 and Team 3, both have very good products. Our improvement research has brought our 7.5 product in washing power from a 1.5 to a 4.5 as indicated here [in the slide presentation].

Chairman of the Board: Would we be fair in assuming that what you're telling us is that we can spend our research bucks to get an expected result.

VP of R&D: In using which kind of research?

Chairman of the Board: I don't care. I mean do you have some recommendations and some ideas there on how you would like to spend the money to achieve some product improvement.

VP of R&D: Yes.

Chairman of the Board: Okay. Well from a policy setting point of view does the board have any more questions on that subject? Okay. Let's move on to the next subject on the list then.

(excerpt from Stratman & Young 1986)

What prompted the chairman's abrupt remarks to the VP of R&D, remarks excerpted from a board meeting of a simulated detergent manufacturing firm run by MBA students and overseen by a board of experienced business people? In essence, the VP had failed to activate the appropriate schema in the mind of the chairman. Had the VP activated the right schema before diving into product characteristics and competitor positions by first explaining what he would be recommending and why, the chairman might have been able to follow the VP's line of reasoning and to have made a decision about the VP's recommendation. Without knowing what the VP wanted him to do with the information being delivered, the chairman became more and more frustrated with every additional, and seemingly meaningless, detail.

Chapter 3 explores the thought processes, or cognitive processes, such as schema activation, that audiences must go through if they are to make informed decisions. Professionals who understand their audience's cognitive processes are in a better position to choose the best style, format, illustrations, and organization for their documents, presentations, and interactions.

Chapter 3 presents a model of audience decision making that consists of six fundamental cognitive processes. Four processes—*perception*, *attention*, *sentence-level comprehension*, and *schema activation*—have been studied in the context of a wide variety of reading and listening tasks. The other two processes—*information acquisition* and *information integration*—have been studied primarily in the context of decision making. All six processes come into play any time an audience reads a persuasive document or listens to a persuasive presentation in order to make a decision.

Figure 3.1 shows the model in the form of a flow chart. The flow chart is, of course, an oversimplification of a much more complex, recursive, and parallel process most of which takes place below the level of conscious awareness (cf., Velmans 1991). In the first step of the model, perception, the audience perceives, that is sees or hears, the information being presented. The audience gets frustrated if that information is illegible or inaudible. In the second step, attention, the audience pays attention to the information long enough to take the third step unless something more interesting grabs and keeps its attention. In the third step, sentence-level comprehension, the audience begins to comprehend the meaning of the information presented sentence by sentence. If the information is hard to comprehend, the audience may re-read it, paraphrase it, ask a question, or just give up. As soon as the audience starts to comprehend the first sentence it reads or hears, it tries to take the fourth step.

In step four of the model, schema activation, represented as gray diamonds and boxes, the audience seeks to activate the appropriate decision schema for interpreting the information it has received and for making a decision. Is someone asking the audience to approve a plan? To purchase a product? To hire a new employee? The model suggests the audience is forced to put its decision-making process on hold until it is successful at finding an answer to that question. Having to put his decision-making process on hold in this way was the source of the chairman's frustration with the VP in the episode recounted above. Once the audience understands the decision the professional wants it to make, it decides whether it is willing and able to make that decision. At that point, it activates the appropriate schema and takes the fifth step.

In the fifth step, information acquisition, the audience's activated decision schema guides its search for information relevant to making a good decision. Initially, the audience searches for the slot values of the recommendation and its benchmarks

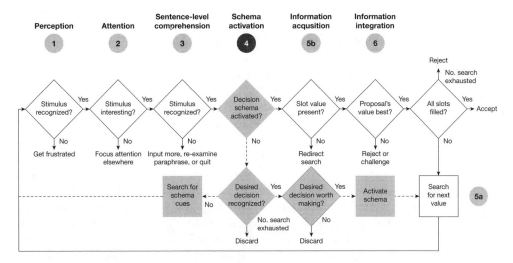

Figure 3.1 A Cognitive Process Model of Audience Decision Making

relevant to the first decision criterion in its schema. For example, if a salesperson recommends a customer buy a particular laptop, the customer's first decision criterion would likely be price. The customer would then want to know the price of the recommended laptop (say $1,999) as well as the prices of comparable laptops (which might be $2,499 and $2,599).

In step six of the model, information integration, the audience integrates the two sets of slot values by comparing the slot value of the recommendation with those of its benchmarks. If the value of the recommendation is preferable to the values of the benchmarks, for example, if the price of the recommended laptop is less than the prices of comparable laptops, then the audience will continue the decision-making process and search for the slot values relevant to the second decision criterion in its schema. However, if the slot value of the recommendation is not preferable to the values of the benchmarks, it will likely stop the decision-making process and reject the recommendation. If the audience cannot find one or more of the slot values, then it may ask the professional to provide those values or it may simply not make the decision the professional desires.

Most of the basic steps of the model have been proposed previously by other students of decision making. For example, Feltovich and colleagues (2006) propose a cognitive process model of decision making that includes four steps:

1)   the perception of data;
2)   the activation of relevant knowledge in long-term memory;
3)   the making of inferences about the data based on the activated knowledge; and
4)   a search for more data.

The four steps in their model correspond to the processes of perception, schema activation, information integration, and information acquisition in the model presented in this text.

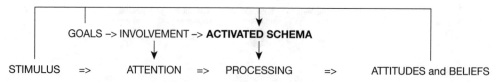

Figure 3.2 Mitchell's Cognitive Process Model of Consumers Reading Ads (source: Adapted from Mitchell 1981).

Figure 3.2 depicts a cognitive process model of audience decision making Mitchell (1981) developed to represent consumers reading advertisements. Mitchell's model highlights the role experts' schemata play in making purchasing decisions and has many similarities with the model proposed here. In Mitchell's model schema activation depends on the consumer's level of expertise and involvement. His model predicts that expert consumers who are involved in the decision-making task will activate a decision schema specific to the product category of the advertised brand and will use it to compare the values of the advertised brand against the values of other brands in the product category. He defines novice consumers as those who lack the appropriate schema and do not know which attributes (i.e., decision criteria) to use to evaluate a brand. His model predicts novice consumers will weight most heavily whatever attributes are prominent in the advertisement (cf., Wright & Rip 1980).

Like the two models of decision making just described, the model of audience decision making presented in Chapter 3, and most of the research cited in explanation of it, takes an information-processing approach to the analysis of decision making. One of the hallmarks of the information-processing approach is that it explains tasks by first breaking them into elementary cognitive processes (e.g., Busemeyer & Townsend 1993; Payne & Bettman 2004; Payne, Bettman, & Johnson 1993). The information-processing approach is most forcefully articulated by Nobel laureate Herbert Simon and his colleague Allen Newell in their seminal text, *Human Problem Solving* (1972). Despite the challenges put forward by competing theories, the information-processing approach "has become dominant in cognitive psychology" (Anderson 2004, p. 11). The information-processing approach has also become dominant in fields outside cognitive psychology that investigate the decision making of professionals. Of the research articles published in the leading accounting journals from 1995 to 2002, 87% adopted the information-processing framework (Kotchetova & Salterio 2004).

The information-processing approach is now the leading theory for explaining group as well as individual decision making. Groups can be understood as information-processing systems that encode, store, and retrieve information much like individuals (Brauner & Scholl 2000; Hinsz, Tindale, & Vollrath 1997; Larson & Christensen 1993). Hinsz and colleagues (1997) define information processing at the group level as "the degree to which information, ideas, or cognitive processes are shared or are being shared among the group members" (p. 43).

The information-processing approach is also the leading theoretical approach to the emerging field of team cognition and decision making (e.g., Albers 2002; Cooke, Salas, Kiekel, & Bell 2004; Gibson 2001). Like an individual, team members go through internalized team cognitive processes rather than automatically accepting any new information presented to them (MacMillan, Entin, & Serfaty 2004).

Figure 3.3 represents a famous early model of a simple decision-making task that inspired many researchers in human cognition to adopt the information-processing approach. In developing this model, Sternberg (1966) demonstrates that his subjects go through four elementary steps when asked to decide whether a particular one-digit number (e.g., 7) were a part of the multiple digit number (e.g., 472) that they had memorized earlier. Sternberg's model predicts his subjects would first perceive the one-digit number, then compare it to each digit in the multiple-digit number that they had memorized, make their decision, and finally generate a response. Sternberg shows that subjects took each step in the model in sequence and independently of the other steps. If Sternberg made the one-digit number blurry and hard to perceive, only the time subjects took to complete the perception step was affected. If he added a digit to the memorized multiple-digit number, subjects took an additional 38 milliseconds to complete the comparison step but took no additional time to complete the other steps. If he biased subjects to decide yes or no before they saw the one-digit number, only the time taken to complete the decision-making step was affected.

Outside the laboratory, audiences are less likely to take each subsequent step in the decision-making process than they were to take the step before it. For example, the decision to comply with warning labels and signs has been shown to be impeded because people rarely perceive the warnings in the first place (deTurck & Goldhaber 1991). Only 24% of the swimmers at a high-school pool they regularly used recalled seeing the conspicuous "NO DIVING" sign next to it. Only 20% of the students in a home economics class recalled seeing any information on an iron they regularly used for two weeks despite the fact that the iron was clearly labeled with a hazard warning (Goldhaber & deTurck 1988).

Even if audience members do perceive information, they may not attend to and comprehend it. In another study of warning labels, although 88% of the consumers in the study recalled seeing the warning on the product, only 46% read even a portion of the warning (Friedmann 1988). Moreover, only 27% made the decision to comply with the warning. Prior steps in the decision-making process can influence subsequent steps in other ways as well. For example, faster recognition of letters and words predicts better comprehension skills, whereas increases in comprehension do not predict increases in word recognition (Lesgold & Resnick 1982).

STIMULUS ⟶ PERCEPTION ⟶ COMPARISON ⟶ DECISION ⟶ RESPONSE

Example: After the subject memorized the number 472, the researcher asked, "Does the number you memorized include 7?"

7 ⟶ Perceive ⟶ 7 = 4? ⟶ 7 = 7? ⟶ 7 = 2? ⟶ Make ⟶ Generate ⟶ "Yes"
        stimulus   decision   response

Figure 3.3 Sternberg's Information-Processing Model of a Simple Decision

The information-processing approach has several other important characteristics. It focuses on the mental behaviors of individuals and views people as active, goal-oriented information processors, not as passive blank slates to be written upon. It acknowledges, for example, that audiences of presenters are far from passive even while they are sitting quietly, listening to a presentation. As audiences listen to presentations, they construct goals, evaluate information, express affective reactions, make inferences, interpret information, monitor and activate comprehension repair strategies, attend to information selectively, integrate information, and ask questions (Stein 1999). We saw the same type of active information processing during reading by the expert audiences who commented on the sample documents and presentations presented in Chapters 1 and 2.

Another important characteristic of the information-processing approach is that it is content oriented. It views content as "a substantial determinant of human behavior" (Newell & Simon 1972, p. 11). And the approach views expertise as dependent upon content-specific, schema-based, prior knowledge (cf., Anderson 2000; Feltovich et al. 2006; Glaser & Chi 1988). Thus, the information-processing approach to decision making differs from the content-free economic theories of decision making. Unlike economic theories of decision making, it does not use the concepts of probability and utility to explain decision behavior. And because it recognizes that human working memory is of limited capacity (e.g., Miller 1956), it typically characterizes decision making as an act of "satisficing" not of optimization (Simon 1955, 1956).

The sections that follow explain in detail each of the six major cognitive processes that comprise this text's model of audience decision making—perception, attention, sentence-level comprehension, schema activation, information acquisition, and information integration. The sections also compare and contrast the ways that audiences process text, speech, pictures, and graphs in each step toward their final decision.

PERCEPTION

To perceive information, audiences must be able both to register and to recognize sensory stimuli. Patients with visual agnosia are intelligent and have good eyesight but are not able to recognize the objects they see (Ratcliff & Newcombe 1982). Similarly, some patients with an injury to their left frontal lobes are intelligent and have good hearing but cannot recognize the words they hear (Goldstein 1974). Thus, neither group is able to perceive normally what their senses register. Perception in reading and listening involves both sensing and recognizing letters, phonemes, and complete words. Perception of documents and presentation slides can also involve sensing and recognizing charts, graphs, and images. An audience's perception of a document or presentation will be impaired to the extent that the words and illustrations in it are illegible, inaudible, or not recognizable to them.

Readers' Perception of Text

How do readers perceive the information professionals present to them? Research shows that readers perceive only bits and pieces of information at a time. Readers perceive text in documents and presentation slides letter by letter, word by word, line by line, left to right. The perception of written text involves two overlapping and parallel subprocesses: *word encoding* and *lexical access* (Just & Carpenter 1987). The first subprocess, word encoding, inputs the visual features of the individual letters in a word and registers their position. As readers recognize the visual features and positions of the individual letters in a word, they construct a mental representation of the visual form of the whole word and automatically map the letters onto the sounds they represent (Rayner 1998; Van Orden 1987).

The second subprocess, lexical access, inputs the encoded sound of the word, and if the word is in the reader's mental dictionary, it outputs the word's meaning (Just & Carpenter 1987). If the word's meaning is ambiguous, readers must access all its meanings before they can determine the intended meaning (Cairns & Kamerman 1975; Warren, Warren, Green, & Bresnick 1978).

Readers can recognize only those letters or words that appear in a very small area of their retinas called the *fovea*, the area in which they have maximum visual acuity. In fact, they can recognize only five to six letters on either side of the letter upon which their eyes focus or *fixate* (Pollatsek & Rayner 1990). Readers cannot recognize words on lines below the one on which they are fixating (Pollatsek, Raney, LaGasse, & Rayner 1993). Readers' ability to recognize printed letters and numbers depends on their ability to perceive each letter's or number's distinct visual features. Readers will confuse two letters only when the letters have many visual features in common, for example, *C* and *G* (Kinney, Marsetta, & Showman 1966). However, readers can recognize any letter more accurately if it is in the context of a word rather than standing alone (Nelson, Wheeler, & Engel 1970; Reicher 1969).

The amount of time readers spend fixating on any word is very brief. The average fixation time per word is about 250 milliseconds, or one-quarter of a second (Just & Carpenter 1980). Readers' fixation times on words are longer when the letters in the word are hard to perceive (Rayner, Reichle, Stroud, Williams, & Pollatsek 2006; Reingold & Rayner 2006). Readers' fixation times are also longer if the word is unfamiliar to them (Calvo & Meseguer 2002; Liversedge et al. 2004). They are longer on words that are not predictable from the preceding context (Ashby, Rayner, & Clifton 2005; Drieghe, Rayner, & Pollatsek 2005; Ehrlich & Rayner 1981). In addition, readers' fixation times are longer if the word is ambiguous or has multiple meanings (Binder 2003; Rayner & Duffy 1986; Sereno, O'Donnell, & Rayner 2006).

Readers' fixation times on pronouns are longer the farther the pronoun is from its antecedent (Garrod, Freudenthal, & Boyle 1994; O'Brien, Raney, Albrecht, & Rayner 1997). Fixation times are also longer if the antecedent violates a gender stereotype, for example a truck driver referred to as *she* (Duffy & Keir 2004; Sturt 2003; Sturt & Lombardo 2005). Readers also spend more time fixating on long words than they do on short words. In fact, the time readers spend fixating on any word increases with the number of letters in it (Just & Carpenter 1987). Readers fixate on each word an average of 30 additional milliseconds for each additional letter in the word.

Readers fixate on almost every word in a sentence (Just & Carpenter 1980). They may spend over 1,500 milliseconds on a content word that introduces the topic of a new paragraph or on a difficult or ambiguous word, but they will spend much less time on it when they encounter that same word a second time. Moreover, readers tend to fixate longer on the final word in both clauses and sentences (Rayner, Kambe, & Duffy 2000).

In a series of studies that tracked the eye movements of readers reading 15 short expository passages from *Newsweek* and *Time* magazines, Carpenter and Just (Carpenter & Just 1981, 1983; Just & Carpenter 1984) find that readers' eyes focus directly on over 80% of the content words but skip about 40% of the function words such as *the* and *a*. When the passage is difficult to comprehend, readers fixate on a larger percentage of words in the passage. But when words in the passage are highly predictable due to their context, readers are much more likely to skip over them (Gautier, O'Regan, & LaGargasson 2000; Rayner & Well 1996).

Readers' fixations account for more than 90% of the readers' total reading time. Eye movements in small jumps or *saccades* account for the other 10%. Most saccades take only about 25 to 45 milliseconds, during which time a reader's vision is blurred. When readers make regressive eye movements, or saccades to previously read words, they do not do so at random but return to the point at which they began an incorrect syntactic analysis of the sentence (Frazier & Rayner 1982; Meseguer, Carreiras, & Clifton 2002).

Figure 3.4 displays one reader's eye fixations and saccades detected by an eye-tracking device as she read an online newspaper. Notice the reader made most fixations, represented as angles in the black lines, on headlines, photographs, and the first sentences of news stories. Such a pattern is typical of audiences skilled at getting their news from either online or print newspapers.

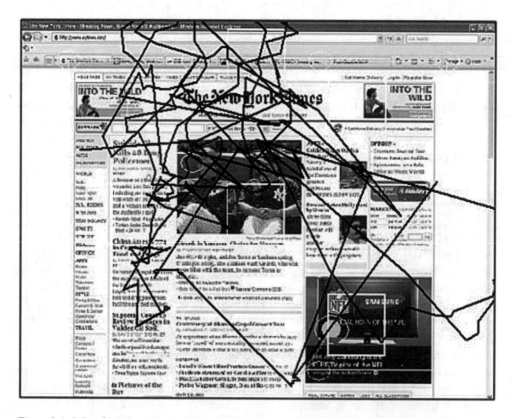

Figure 3.4 A Reader's Eye-Fixation Pattern Reading an Online Newspaper (source: Gibbs & Bernas 2009, p. 158).

Listeners' Perception of Speech

Much like the way reading audiences perceive text, listening audiences perceive speech sound by sound and word by word in the order it is spoken. But there are significant differences between speech and text that cause speech perception to be more complex than text perception. Speech is not presented as discrete units the way printed letters and words are. Instead it is presented as a continuous stream of sound. Speech sounds—the consonants and vowels that form the words of a language—overlap each other as they are spoken in a process called *coarticulation* (Liberman, Cooper, Shankweiler, & Studdert-Kennedy 1967). To make speech perception even more complex, different speakers, unlike different writers, produce the same words in different ways (Nearey 1989) and at different speaking rates (Miller 1981).

Listeners must map the acoustic signals of speech onto speech sounds or phonemes. Through a process of elimination, they are able to recognize the word being spoken even before the speaker has finished saying it (Marslen-Wilson 1987). To paraphrase Clark (in Wilson & Keil 1999, p. 688), as listeners hear each successive sound in a word, for example "elephant," they narrow down the list of possible words they might be hearing. They activate approximately 1,000 words that start with the "e" sound as soon as they perceive the "e" sound in elephant. They quickly narrow that list to about 100 words that start with "el" once they perceive the "l" sound. By the time they perceive the "f" sound, there is only one word left on their list of possible words.

Once listeners have recognized a word, for 200 to 400 milliseconds they activate all of the possible meanings of the word, even those meanings that do not fit into the context of the sentence (McQueen, Cutler, Briscoe, & Norris 1995; Swinney 1979). Although listeners typically recognize the words in clearly spoken sentences, they either fail to recognize the words in unclear speech or initially misrecognize them and then correctly recognize them as more context is provided (Bard, Shillcock, & Altmann 1988).

Viewers' Perception of Images and Graphs

Many people imagine viewers perceive pictures all at once or *holistically*. However, research shows that audiences perceive images in much the same way that they read text—by fixating on one visual feature then jumping to another part of the picture and fixating on it. Each fixation during image viewing averages about 300 milliseconds, but the duration of individual fixations can vary widely. The pattern of viewers' fixations and saccades is not random. For example, Yarbus (1967) studied the eye movements of viewers looking at images of faces. He demonstrates that viewers primarily fixate on the eyes, the mouth, and general shape of the face—the features most critical to face recognition (see Figure 3.5).

When viewers are exposed to images for longer periods, their ability to accurately recognize and recall images increases. In a study of magazine readers, Potter and Levy (1969) show that readers are able to recognize only 50% of the illustrations in a magazine when the illustrations are presented at a 500-millisecond exposure rate but that they are able to recognize 93% at a two-second exposure rate. Recognition of more complex pictures requires longer exposure rates (Fleming & Sheikhian 1972).

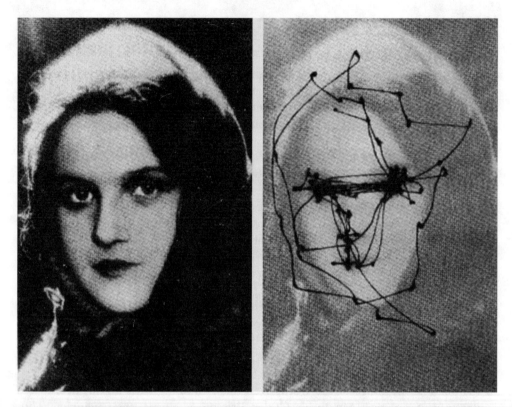

Figure 3.5 A Viewer's Eye-Fixation Pattern Looking at a Photograph (source: Yarbus 1967, p. 179).

Such longer exposure rates increase image recognition and recall independently of the viewer's opportunity to verbally label the picture (Intraub 1979). Even after a one-year delay, just two exposures enable viewers to recognize 72% of the images they view (Nickerson 1968). However, more than two exposures do not add significantly to viewers' recognition rates (Robinson 1969).

Audiences perceive charts and graphs in much the same way they perceive pictures—by fixating many times on the chart or graph's different regions and elements. In a study of viewers interpreting line graphs, viewers perceived the line graphs by making numerous fixations on different regions of the graphs (Shah 1995). In addition to fixating on the trend lines, viewers frequently fixated on the variable names, variable values, and the X and Y axes. In other words, audiences viewing a chart or graph repeatedly fixate on those elements that are most relevant to evaluating its content. Viewers spend a large portion of their viewing time fixating on the graph's captions and legends as well as on the values of the variables. In addition, viewers fixate more often when viewing complex charts and graphs as opposed to simple ones.

For a relatively simple graph, such as the line chart in Figure 3.6 below, Carpenter and Shah (1998) find that viewers average 29 fixations and spend an average of 33 seconds viewing each graph. For the more complex graphs in their study, viewers averaged 40.5 fixations and spent an average of 40.6 seconds viewing each graph.

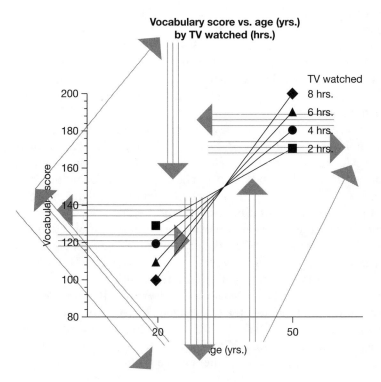

Figure 3.6 A Viewer's Eye-Fixation Pattern Interpreting a Line Chart (source: Carpenter & Shah 1998, p. 86).

ATTENTION

Audiences sense and perceive much more information peripherally than they attend to, focus on, and consciously evaluate. Their attention acts as a bottleneck that enhances the processing of the stimulus attended to and weakens the processing of all other perceived stimuli. Attention plays an important role in audience decision making. Attention during consumers' processing of advertising controls a substantial portion of the variability in their decisions (Bettman 1979). Consumers' pupil dilation, one measure of attention (cf., Beatty & Kahneman 1966; Hess & Polt 1964; Kahneman & Beatty 1966, 1967), in response to pictures of various products, is positively correlated to sales of those products, even more so than are traditional verbal measures of consumers' attitudes (Krugman 1964).

Stimulus-Driven Attention

There are two types of attention: *Task-driven* and *stimulus-driven*. An audience's attention is task-driven when the audience intentionally searches for a specific piece of information as readers do when they search a document for a particular item or as listeners do when they interrupt a speaker to ask a question. In task-driven attention, the audience's task guides and controls perception. Even the simple task of reading causes readers to shift their attention to the next word in a sentence shortly before they move their eyes to it while that word is still in a nonfoveal, or out-of-focus, region of their visual field (Hoffman & Subramaniam 1995; Kowler, Anderson, Dosher, & Blaser 1995). Task-driven attention is also called *search*. In our model, we treat search more fully in the section on the information-acquisition process.

An audience's attention is stimulus-driven when they peripherally perceive a stimulus, such as a loud noise or a flashing advertisement on a web page, and divert their attention to the stimulus. Certain types of stimuli are more attention getting than others. For example, information that has clear and direct implications for personal outcomes is more attention getting and has a greater impact on audience judgments than information that is not personally relevant (Sivacek & Crano 1982).

The audience's present intentions and goals also make certain stimuli more attention getting to them (Bruner 1957; Kahneman 1973). For example, in a study of consumers reading almost 8,000 newspaper ads, nearly twice as many prospective customers recalled seeing the target ad as did non-prospective customers, although none of the readers were intentionally searching for ads (Newspaper Advertising Bureau 1964). A later eye-tracking study shows that in 98% of the cases in which prospective customers open to a page with a target ad, they fixate on the ad at least once (Newspaper Advertising Bureau 1987). For non-prospects, the figure is 77%. Of the prospects who notice an ad, 38% read it. Only 14% of non-prospects read the ad (see Tolley & Bogart 1994). Although attention is a factor in all cognitive processes, our model depicts stimulus-driven attention occurring immediately after the audience senses and perceives stimuli.

In web-page design, stimulus-driven attention is used to support task-driven attention. Some web-page designers use eye-tracking devices to identify which parts of a web page users attend to. They then redesign web pages so that information needed to complete important tasks attracts more stimulus-driven attention. Figure 3.7 shows attention levels to different parts of the home page of the American Society of Clinical Oncology before and after its redesign. Black spots indicate a high level of attention or many eye fixations, gray spots a lesser level. Before the redesign users had difficulty finding membership information and were distracted by uninformative information on the web page. After the redesign users were quick to focus on the membership information they were searching for, indicated by the white box.

Constraints on Auditory Attention

In most cases audiences can recall very little about the stimuli they did not attend to, even when those stimuli were perfectly audible or visible (Wolford & Morrison 1980). In two seminal studies (Cherry 1953; Moray 1959), listeners were given special headphones to wear that allowed them to hear two different conversations spoken into each ear simultaneously. Listeners were then asked to selectively attend to one conversation and to tune out or not attend to the other. The only thing listeners could remember about the conversation they tuned out was whether the speakers were male or female. Listeners were not able to tell which language was spoken or to remember

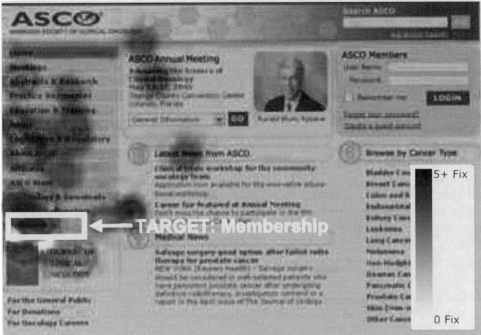

Figure 3.7 Attention to Important Information on a Home Page Increased after its Redesign (source: Bojko 2006, p. 117).

any words. In a follow-up study, listeners not only were asked to listen to two conversations simultaneously and selectively attend to one conversation but also were asked to listen for a target word in both conversations (Treisman & Geffen 1967). Although listeners recognized the target word when it was spoken in the conversation that they attended to, they did not recognize it when it was spoken in the unattended-to second conversation.

Nonetheless, listeners may perceive a fraction of the words that they do not attend to. Listeners who are asked if they recall the target words in the unattended ear immediately after each target word is spoken are able to recall the target words 25% of the time (Glucksberg & Cowen 1970). As Anderson (2000, p. 81) points out, listeners do indeed perceive two simultaneous messages simultaneously but they allocate their attention to only one message at a time. Thus, an unattended-to message delivered simultaneously can still divert a listener's attention to it, especially if it is loud, important to the listener, or relevant to the message the listener was attending to.

Constraints on Visual Attention

Viewers' visual attention works very much like listeners' auditory attention. When Rock (1977) asked viewers to attend to one set of simultaneously presented images, their processing of the other set dropped off. To conduct his experiment, Rock made a videotape showing one set of objects in silhouette moving from left to right and another set moving from right to left at the same time. The objects were large, easy to see, easy to identify, and were semitransparent so they could be seen even while they passed through each other. His results show that when viewers are asked to attend to objects moving left to right, they are able to recognize all those objects easily. The same is true for viewers asked to attend to objects moving right to left. However, in Rock's study, the first group of viewers could not remember anything about the objects that moved right to left. Neither could the second group remember anything about the objects that moved from left to right.

Readers can perceive unattended written words but do not consciously remember them. Corteen and Dunn (1974) gave mild shocks to readers as they showed them different words. The researchers then presented those same words to the readers but out of the focus of their attention. Although the readers did not attend to the words or consciously recognize them, it was clear they still perceived the words because they gave galvanic skin responses when the words were presented. In a similar way, nonfocal information in print ads can influence consumers' evaluations of brand names even when consumers do not attend to or consciously recognize that information (Janiszewski 1988, 1990).

One situation exists in which audiences can attend to two stimuli at the same time, and that is when the two stimuli are presented in different perceptual modes. Audiences who are presented with visual and auditory information in rapid succession are able to begin processing the auditory information about 60 milliseconds before they complete processing the visual information (Karlin & Kestenbaum 1968). Similarly, audiences can identify one visual and one auditory stimulus even when the two stimuli are presented simultaneously (Treisman & Davies 1973). However, as Sternberg (1999, p. 98) points out, attending to two stimuli simultaneously presented in two different modalities is difficult for anyone if both stimuli consist of verbal information. For example, for most audience members simultaneously reading a newspaper and listening to the news on TV requires extraordinary effort.

Finally, it is important to note that not all of the information an audience attends to during reading or listening comes from sensory inputs such as the written words in a professional's document or the spoken words of a presentation. An audience can also attend to information coming from non-sensory sources. For example, audiences may access information from their own long-term memories to use in decision making as when something the professional says reminds them of an important concept. Dhar and Simonson (1992) find that when consumers retrieve comparative product information from their memories, the information actually has a stronger effect on their decisions than does the comparative product information communicators provide to them. The audience may also generate information during the decision-making process, such as when they evaluate and make inferences about the information they have read or heard (see Holland, Holyoak, Nisbett, & Thagard 1986; Payne et al. 1993).

SENTENCE-LEVEL COMPREHENSION

The Sentence Comprehension Process

An audience's process for comprehending sentences involves three overlapping and parallel subprocesses: *syntactic analysis*, *semantic analysis*, and the construction of a *referential representation* or mental image of the meaning of the sentence (Just & Carpenter 1987). The first subprocess, syntactic analysis, inputs individual words from the sentence whose meanings have already been accessed during perception and outputs the grammatical role each word plays in that sentence. For instance, in the sentence "The board promoted the VP," *The board* would be recognized as a determiner and noun that constitute the subject of the verb, *promoted* would be recognized as the verb, and *the VP* recognized as a determiner and noun that constitute the object noun phrase. To demonstrate the importance of syntactic analysis to sentence comprehension, Graf and Torrey (1966) showed sentences to readers either one phrase, or syntactic unit, at a time or one randomly divided segment of a sentence at a time. Readers had better comprehension of the sentences when they read sentences one phrase at time.

The second subprocess, semantic analysis, inputs the syntax of the clause or sentence and the meaning of the verb. It outputs the conceptual relationships, or case roles, of the words and phrases in the clause or sentence (Fillmore 1968; Schank 1975). For instance, in the sentence "The board promoted the VP," *The board* would be recognized as the agent, *promoted* as the action, and *the VP* as the object of the action. In essence, semantic analysis determines who is doing what to whom. Readers may sometimes be able to bypass the syntactic analysis process if semantic cues are sufficient to provide them with the meaning of the sentence (Bever 1970).

The third subprocess, the construction of a *referential representation*, inputs the syntax and semantics of the sentence and outputs a mental image of the actual or imaginary objects and actions referred to in the sentence. The same sentence may have only one syntactic and semantic representation but may have several referential representations. For example, "He flew to Cairo," could have three different referential representations depending on how the person who is referred to flew: On a jet; in an antique biplane; or on a magic carpet (cf., Just & Carpenter 1987, p. 196). If the sentence contains a pronoun, referential processing identifies any antecedent words to which the pronoun refers as well.

Readers' Comprehension

Almost all of a reader's comprehension subprocesses concern the word they are fixating on and its relationship to the text that preceded it. For example, readers must fixate for a relatively long time on pronouns in order to assign referents to them (Carpenter & Just 1977; Ehrlich & Rayner 1983; Just & Carpenter 1987). As readers analyze each successive word in a sentence, they immediately try to integrate it with what they already know (Just & Carpenter 1987; Mason & Just 2006). Thus, readers begin to interpret a sentence even before they come to the main verb in it.

Readers pause longer at phrase and sentence boundaries because some syntactic information cannot be processed until the phrase or sentence is complete (Aaronson & Scarborough 1977). Additionally, readers have to maintain a representation of the current phrase or sentence in their memories because their interpretation of it may be wrong, and thus they may have to revise their interpretation as they read (Just & Carpenter 1987). When readers have trouble interpreting the meaning of a sentence because it is ambiguous, they must slow down and fixate on the words in it for significantly longer durations (Rayner & Frazier 1987). Just as they do for ambiguous words, readers must process all of the meanings of ambiguous sentences (Foss & Jenkins 1973; Holmes, Arwas, & Garrett 1977).

Readers can clearly remember the specific words in a sentence only while they are processing that sentence's meaning (Caplan 1972). Consequently, they often cannot recall the form or style in which a sentence was presented. Instead, they only remember the meaning of the sentence (Bransford, Barclay, & Franks 1972). For example, Anderson (1974a) asked readers to read sentences written in either the active or passive voice, to wait a few minutes, and then to decide whether a test sentence was in the same voice as a previously read sentence. None of the readers could accurately recall the voice in which the original sentence had been written.

Oftentimes when readers encounter a sentence that is difficult to comprehend, they will paraphrase it or try to put it into their own words. Sometimes readers translate individual sentences into scenarios, or story-like paraphrases (Flower, Hayes, & Swarts 1983). For example, the investor who read the executive summary of *Smartphone MBA*'s business plan in Chapter 1 translated the sentences below into a scenario in comment 3.

> Sales projections for *Smartphone MBA* estimate a subscriber base of 40,000 for the premier installment. **[What's this 40,000 for the premier installment?²]** Subscription sales are expected to quadruple to 160,000 within five years.

[They say there are two million potential subscribers out of this group, these three categories. And they have a goal of reaching an initial subscription of 40,000 and 160,000 within five years. Okay. That's understandable.³]

When the reading process is going smoothly, readers are usually unaware of it. But when something makes comprehension difficult, they often become aware of their process and may comment on it (Daneman & Carpenter 1983). For example, as the investor continued reading the executive summary of *Smartphone MBA*'s business plan, he made a comment about the difficulty of comprehending the sentence below.

> With the consent of Limited Partners holding as a group a 50% Partnership Interest in the Partnership, the General Partner may raise capital in excess of such amount by selling additional Limited Partnership Interests. **[What the heck does that mean? It says your limited partnerships start out with 15% of the partnership. This is really poorly written.¹³]**

Listeners' Comprehension

In contrast to the way readers comprehend a written sentence, listeners' comprehension of a spoken sentence depends on how the sentence is spoken, not just on its content and structure. One study of face-to-face communication concluded that only 7% of the meaning of a spoken message is communicated verbally. Because the meaning of a spoken message depends in large part on the emotion the speaker communicates, the remaining 93% of the meaning is communicated by the speaker's tone of voice and facial expression (Mehrabian & Ferris 1967). For a listener, a sarcastic versus an enthusiastic tone of voice can convey more meaning than the words in a sentence. Chapter 6 explores the process listeners go through as they infer a speaker's emotions.

Listeners base much of their syntactic analysis of spoken sentences on sentence *prosody*–the way the speaker rhythmically groups and accentuates the words in the sentences she speaks. Listeners prefer a syntactic analysis of a sentence that is consistent with the prosody over one that is not (Nespor & Vogel 1983) and base much of their semantic analysis on sentence prosody as well. They actively listen for the words speakers accentuate (Cutler 1982; Sedivy, Tanehaus, Spivey-Knowlton, Eberhard, & Carlson 1995) because they realize that accented words are cues to the meaning of the speakers' messages (Bolinger 1978; Ladd 1996).

The repeated sentence below (adapted from Knapp 1978) shows how different placements of a vocal accent can change the meaning of a sentence. The accented word in examples 1 through 5 is in bold and italicized. A final rise in intonation is added to the italicized word in example 6. One possible meaning of each of the six sentences is in parentheses.

1)   ***He's*** giving this money to Tyler. (*He* is the one giving the money; nobody else.)
2)   He's ***giving*** this money to Tyler. (He is *giving*, not lending, the money.)
3)   He's giving ***this*** money to Tyler. (The money is *this* particular money.)

4)   He's giving this *money* to Tyler. (*Cash* is being exchanged, not a check.)
5)   He's giving this money to **Tyler**. (The recipient is *Tyler*, not Evan or Ethan.)
6)   He's giving this money to **Tyler**? (Why is he giving the money to *Tyler* and not to me?)

Similar to reading audiences, listening audiences usually forget the specific words uttered in a spoken sentence almost immediately after they have heard it. Sachs (1967) asked listeners to listen to sentences and then to distinguish between the original sentence and a close paraphrase of it. Listeners' memory for the exact wording of the sentence decayed rapidly but their memory for the sentence's meaning persisted much longer. In another study of listeners' sentence comprehension, although the listeners remembered verbatim the words in the clause they were currently processing, they forgot the exact words and word order of prior clauses as soon as each sentence was spoken (Jarvella 1971).

However, listeners do tend to remember the exact wording of any message that has an emotional impact on them, as challenges or insults often do (Keenan, MacWhinney, & Mayhew 1977). The exact wording of poems, song lyrics, and important phrases are also more likely to be remembered. Wanner (1968) shows that listeners are able to remember the exact wording of a sentence but usually do not unless they are requested to do so. In his experiment, Wanner asked two groups of listeners to listen to tape-recorded instructions. The first group was told to remember the sentences in the instructions verbatim; the second group was not. Wanner then tested both groups' memory of the style and content of the instructions. The first group remembered the instructions verbatim— both style and content. The second group remembered each sentence's meaning immediately after processing it but remembered little of its exact wording.

Viewers' Comprehension

When audiences comprehend images they spontaneously assign verbal labels to them (Kunen, Green, & Waterman 1979). Older children and adults automatically assign a verbal label to all except the most complex and novel images (Pezdek & Evans 1979). Although audiences normally extract meaning from a verbal message and forget the style in which it was presented, they typically remember the exact picture they saw (Standing 1973). Asked to look at a set of 10,000 pictures, viewers were later able to identify 83% of the pictures they had seen. In a study of consumer recall of advertisements, Shepard (1967) showed consumers 600 magazine ads all containing text and pictures and found that they recognized 96.7% of the pictures immediately after viewing them, 99.7% after a two-hour delay, 92% after three days, 87% after seven days, and 57.7% after 120 days. Consumers had an 11.8% error rate in distinguishing read versus unread sentences in the ads, but only a 1.5% error rate in distinguishing viewed versus not-viewed pictures.

Before an audience can comprehend a chart or graph, they must first translate its visual features into the concepts those features represent (Kosslyn 1989). The time needed for graph comprehension is similar to that needed to read and understand a paragraph of moderate length (Shah 1995). Pinker (1990) proposes that after viewers encode the visual features in a graph, they interpret the meanings of those features as quantitative concepts. For example, viewers may recognize that a straight line in a graph represents a linear relationship. Only then do viewers identify what each feature of the graph refers to. Additional processes in Pinker's model include keeping track of multiple comparisons, performing calculations, and mentally translating from one scale to another.

In her study of viewers interpreting simple line graphs, Shah (1995) finds that the errors viewers make when interpreting line graphs primarily result from limitations in their conceptual processes rather than from inaccurate perceptual processes. All the viewers in her study accurately reproduced from memory the graphs they had seen, but many of them lacked the knowledge needed to interpret the quantitative information depicted by the graphs. One important step in interpreting the quantitative information involves relating graphic features and referents from different parts of the display to each other. For each additional proposition or fact to be comprehended, a viewer may have to re-examine different parts of the graph and re-identify the labels and values relevant to that proposition.

SCHEMA ACTIVATION

Schema Activation in Decision Making and Text-Level Comprehension

Schema activation is at the heart of information processing in general and of decision making and text-level comprehension in particular. The whole activity of "information processing may be seen as consisting of schema formation or activation, of the integration of input with these schemas, and of the updating or revision of these schemas to accommodate new input" (Markus & Zajonc 1985, p. 150). Moreover, "information processing cannot be carried out without them." Others see schema activation at the heart of the decision-making process (cf., Feltovich et al. 2006; Goldstein & Weber 1995). And after an extensive review of the research on decision making and reasoning, Anderson (2000, p. 351) confirms that both decision making and reasoning are not the application of the content-free rules of logic, syllogistic reasoning, or statistics as they are commonly thought to be, but are essentially schema-based processes.

In addition to giving audiences a framework for decision making, schemata also provide them with the interpretive framework for comprehending written discourse (Kintsch & Kintsch 1978; Rumelhart & Ortony 1976; Schank & Abelson 1977), spoken dialogue (Stokes, Kemper, & Kite 1997), and graphical displays (Randel, Pugh, & Reed 1996). "Comprehension as normally understood results in the construction of a specific instance of a schema or the accretion of schema-relevant facts. New information is *assimilated* to existing schemas" (Chi & Ohlsson 2005, p. 377).

Much of what we know about the process of schema activation comes from research on audiences reading texts in order to comprehend them. Just and Carpenter (1987) demonstrate that comprehending the meaning of texts as opposed to comprehending individual sentences depends upon schema-level processing. Their model of readers consists of processes that first activate an appropriate schema after which "the schema slots are filled in with the information from the passage" (p. 254). Other research demonstrates that schemata strongly influence not only what readers comprehend when reading a text (Spilich Vesonder, Chiesi, & Voss 1979; Sticht et al. 1986) but also what they remember from it (e.g., Bower, Black, & Turner 1979; Kintsch & Van Dijk 1978; Weldon & Malpass 1981).

Many different types of schemata are activated in the text-level comprehension process. One type of schema, often called a *script*, provides a framework for understanding events. In an effort to discover the script for dining at a restaurant, Bower and colleagues (1979) interviewed 32 people separately and asked them about the major steps involved in dining out. The restaurant script of all 32 contained the same six steps: sitting down, looking at the menu, ordering, eating, paying the bill, and leaving. Other schemata provide frameworks for understanding specific genres such as fairy tales or biographies. If expert readers are told they will read a particular genre, they will activate a schema of that genre that will guide their interpretation of the text (McDaniel & Einstein 1989; Zwaan & Brown 1996).

Other types of schemata are used to comprehend objects. Figure 3.8 is a depiction of a schema for comprehending a mechanism, such as an engine or a car's flywheel (Thibadeau, Just, & Carpenter 1982). The slots in the mechanism schema below have

Slot name	Slot value
Name	Flywheel
Goals	To store energy
Principles	Faster spinning stores up more energy
Physical properties	Made of fiberglass and rubber
Physical movements	Spinning
Made by	Humans
Used by	Humans
Exemplars	Car engine flywheels

Flywheels are one of the oldest mechanical devices known to man. Every internal-combustion engine contains a small flywheel that **converts the jerky motion** of the pistons **into the smooth flow of energy** that powers the drive shaft. The greater the mass of a flywheel and **the faster it spins, the more energy can be stored in it.** But its maximum spinning speed is limited by the strength of the material it is made from. If it spins too fast for its mass, any flywheel will fly apart. One type of flywheel **consists of** round sandwiches of **fiberglass and rubber** providing the maximum possible storage of energy when the wheel is confined in a small space **as in an automobile**. Another type, the "superflywheel," consists of a series of rimless spokes. This flywheel stores the maximum energy when space is unlimited.

Figure 3.8 A Mechanism Schema Filled in with Slot Values from the Passage Below it.

been filled in or *instantiated* with information from the expository passage below it. This schema enabled a computer model of a human reader to comprehend the expository passage and to answer questions about it.

Depending upon which schema the reader activates, the same text can be comprehended in different ways (Anderson, Reynolds, Schallert, & Goetz 1977; Spiro 1977). In a fascinating study of schema effects on readers, Anderson and Pichert (1978) asked one group of readers to assume the role of thieves and another group to assume the role of prospective homebuyers. The researchers hypothesized that the two groups would activate two different schemata. They then asked both groups to read a brief story about a very expensive house. The "thieves" recalled the valuable items described in the story that could be stolen from the house. The "home buyers," on the other hand, remembered information related to the quality of the house.

In a similar study using a videotaped conversation as the stimulus, Zadny and Gerard (1974) showed an audience a video of two men walking around in a room talking about drug use, the police, and theft. Before watching the video, audience members were primed with one of three schema-inducing ideas: two burglars; two students waiting for a friend; or two friends attempting to conceal illegal drugs. Viewers primed with the two-burglars schema recalled more theft-relevant objects and comments from the video than did those in the other two conditions. Apparently, audiences activate only one schema at a time when comprehending texts or making decisions (Malt, Ross, & Murphy 1995). For example, audiences cannot simultaneously encode information about a home from the perspective of a home-buyer and a burglar, even though both schemata are equally available to them and equally well known.

The Schema Activation Process

How do audiences activate the appropriate schemata? Readers begin reading by hypothesizing that the grammatical subject of the first or second sentence in a passage is its topic. They then activate a schema for the topic of that grammatical subject (Just & Carpenter 1987). Kieras and Bovair (1981) asked readers to think aloud and guess the theme of a short technical passage as they read it. Readers hypothesized the theme of the passage after reading the initial sentence. Readers revised their hypothesis later if subsequent sentences did not fit the theme they had hypothesized. A study of listeners listening to algebra word problems finds that early verbal cues lead listeners to activate one of several possible schemata for the word problems they hear (Hinsley et al. 1977). Half of the listeners in the study categorized problems after hearing less than one-fifth of the problem stated.

Other schemata can be internally activated by the audience's own goals for reading or listening or by schemata already activated in their minds (Markus & Zajonc 1985, p. 150). If readers believe a sentence states the main theme of a text, and is thereby capable of activating the appropriate schema, they will read it more slowly than they read other sentences (Just & Carpenter 1980). Surprisingly, readers spend more time reading sentences that introduce new topics even when paragraph boundaries are not indicated (Hyönä 1994). However, readers take just as long to read the first sentence of a text whether it is a topic sentence or, contrary to the typical reader's hypothesis, merely a supporting detail (Budd, Whitney, & Turley 1995).

Consequences of Faulty Schema Activation

If the audience is unable to activate the appropriate schema for a document or presentation, their comprehension suffers (cf., Dooling & Mullet 1973; Swaney et al. 1991). The reason a schema is not invoked may be that the audience does not possess the appropriate schema, or it may be that the wording of the text or presentation is ineffective in activating it (Anderson & Pichert 1978; Pichert & Anderson 1977; Spiro 1977). When Bransford and Johnson (1973) asked readers to read the paragraph below, they found that readers could not make sense of it as a whole although each separate sentence was easy to comprehend (p.400):

> The procedure is actually quite simple. First you arrange things into different groups. Of course, one pile may be sufficient depending on how much there is to do. If you have to go somewhere else due to a lack of facilities that is the next step, otherwise you are pretty well set. It is important not to overdo things. That is, it is better to do a few things at once than too many. In the short run this may not seem important but complications can easily arise. A mistake can be expensive as well. At first the whole procedure will seem complicated. Soon, however, it will become just another facet of life. It is difficult to foresee any end to the necessity for this task in the immediate future, but then, one never can tell. After the procedure is completed one arranges the materials into different groups again. Then they can be put into their appropriate places. Eventually, they will be used once more and the whole cycle will have to be repeated. However, that is part of life.

However, if readers were allowed to read the paragraph's title, "Washing Clothes," before they read the paragraph, then they had no difficulty understanding it. Those readers also recalled more information from the paragraph than did the readers who read the paragraph without its schema-activating title.

Although text comprehension is often understood as a left-brain activity, research in cognitive neuroscience indicates that the right hemisphere is involved in identifying the appropriate schema for making sense of a text. An fMRI study of readers reading untitled paragraphs like the one above reveals that the right hemisphere becomes more active than the left when processing untitled paragraphs, apparently indicating the attempt of the right hemisphere to activate the appropriate schema (St. George, Kutas, Martinez, & Sereno 1999). The right hemisphere also becomes more active than the left when processing schema-activating topic sentences, regardless of their location within the paragraph (Tomitch, Just, & Newman 2004).

Audiences can, of course, activate the wrong schema. The study cited earlier of listeners listening to algebra word problems and classifying them into problem types found that fully one-half of the listeners activated the wrong schema as they heard the first part of each problem (Hinsley et al. 1977). For instance, some listeners activated the schema for a triangle problem when they should have activated the schema for a distance, time, rate problem. Activating the wrong schema caused several listeners to mishear the rest of the information in the word problem as they tried to make the information they heard conform to the wrong schema or problem type.

Even activating the right schema can sometimes lead to problems. After they had identified the elements of readers' restaurant schema, Bower and coauthors (1979) asked the readers to read stories about dining in restaurants and then to recall the stories they read. Readers erroneously recalled and recognized statements that were not in the stories but that were part of their restaurant schema.

INFORMATION ACQUISITION

Information acquisition is the process by which audiences acquire information that will fill the slots of their activated schema. As Abelson and Levi (1985, p. 273) point out, there is a "tendency for schema-driven processing to be associated with search." And because search is driven by the schema that is currently activated, it is a form of task-driven, as opposed to stimulus-driven, attention. In our model information acquisition starts after schema activation. It has two steps: (1) filling in schema slots with information that has already been comprehended and identified as relevant to the schema; and (2) searching for the information that will fill the next slot in the schema.

The Process of Filling Schema Slots

The time it takes to fill a schema slot with a slot value, as opposed to search for a slot value, varies with the slot's importance. Studies of readers reading 15 expository texts showed that readers fixate longer on words that fill important schema slots than on words that fill less important schema slots (Carpenter & Just 1981; Just & Carpenter 1980; Thibadeau et al. 1982). For example, readers spent more time per word when reading about the purpose of flywheels than when reading about the physical properties of flywheels. Similarly, readers of narratives take more time to read a sentence if the information in the sentence plays a significant role in the story instead of a minor one (Cirilo & Foss 1980). Readers also remember words longer when the words fill important schema slots (Thibadeau et al. 1982).

The order in which readers search for information to fill the slots of a schema reveals each slot's relative importance to the reader's goals for a particular task. (Carpenter & Just 1981; Just & Carpenter 1980; Thibadeau et al. 1982). Readers can fill a slot quite easily if the slot value is already labeled in the text (e.g., "Exemplars include . . ."). When readers cannot locate slot values in a text, they may fill in empty schema slots with default values stored in their memories (Thibadeau et al. 1982).

Targeted versus General Search

There are two types of schema-driven search: *targeted search* and *general search*. When conducting a targeted search, the audience tries to quickly locate a particular piece of information that will fill a specific, empty schema slot. When conducting a general search, the audience reads or listens to longer passages hoping to find information that will fill several empty schema slots. An example of a targeted search is a consumer's scanning document headings, indexes, and directories for a key word such as *price* in order to fill the "price slot" in her purchasing schema. Examples of audiences conducting a general search include a trainee reading a potentially helpful chapter from a training manual line by line or a nurse listening to a drug representative's sales presentation without interrupting.

Listeners necessarily conduct general searches unless they interrupt the speaker to request specific information. Readers may conduct either type of search of the same document. In her survey of 201 instruction-manual users, Schriver (1997, p. 213), reports that only 15% of the users read the manual word for word, cover to cover. The majority conducted either general or targeted searches. Forty-six percent scanned the manuals for the major points and 35% used the manuals to find specific instructions. The remaining 4% never read them.

Viewers of images, like readers, may also conduct either type of search. Yarbus (1967) selected a painting, "An Unexpected Visitor," by the Russian artist Repin, and asked different questions of viewers while recording their eye movements and fixations. In the general search condition, viewers were allowed to view the painting as they chose. In targeted search conditions, Yarbus asked viewers about the economic status, age, activities, clothing, locations, and relationships of the people in the picture. The locus of the viewers' eye fixations varied widely according to the question he asked.

Figure 3.9 depicts some of Yarbus' results. It shows the painting and seven recordings of eye movements by the same viewer. Each recording lasted three minutes. The first recording (1) was of general search or free examination. The remaining six recordings were of targeted search. Before making each of those recordings, the author asked the viewer to perform a specific task: in the second recording (2) to estimate the economic status of the family; in (3) to give the ages of the people; in (4) to guess what the family had been doing before the "unexpected visitor" arrived; in (5) to remember the clothes the people wore; in (6) to remember the position of the people and objects in the room; and in (7) to estimate how long the "unexpected visitor" had been away (from Yarbus 1967, p. 192). As we can see, each task required the viewer to search for answers in different parts of the painting.

Targeted search of images is also associated with audience expertise. The greater the audience's expertise, the more targeted and efficient their search for information can be. For example, the pattern of eye movements expert radiologists produce as they make a diagnosis from an X-ray is far more efficient than that of novices (Nodine & Kundel 1987). Experts not only search images more efficiently than novices, they also search for different image elements. A study of the eye fixations of expert and novice art viewers finds qualitative differences in the searches experts and novices conduct as they look at paintings (Nodine, Locher, & Krupinski 1993). Viewers who are untrained in art focus their attention on elements that indicate how accurately the paintings depict "objective" reality. In contrast, art experts focus on elements that indicate the composition, balance, and symmetry of the paintings.

Viewers of charts and graphs, like readers and viewers of images, may conduct either type of search. Shah (1995) shows that graph viewers will conduct a general search if they are simply asked to describe a graph's meaning. Her viewers first read the title, inspected the graph, and then began to slowly identify the graph's variables and referents.

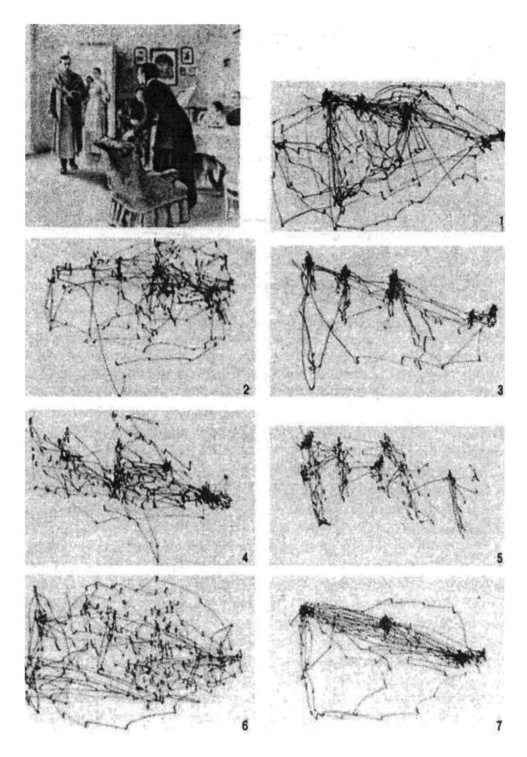

Figure 3.9 Viewers' Eye-Fixation Patterns Reveal the Information they Wish to Find
(source: Yarbus 1967, p. 174).

For example, one viewer described a line graph as follows: "This is vocabulary score vs. age by TV watched in hours. And it shows that vocabulary scores increase with age very dramatically for someone who watches a lot of TV and not so dramatically for someone who watches a little of TV" (Shah 1995, p. 61).

More often, the information an audience extracts from a graph depends on their reason for looking at the graph (Carswell & Wickens 1987). Lohse (1993) proposes a schema-driven model of graph comprehension that relies on targeted search. In the model viewers first pose a question about the variables in the graph. For example, the question, "What was average the per capita income in France in 1990?" could be answered if the graph contained three variables: *per capita income*, *France*, and *1990*. Viewers next search the graph's legend and axes for the variables in their question. In the last step viewers identify the relevant value, for example, the amount of income people in France made on average in 1990, say $26,700. In this model graph viewers do not try to comprehend everything about the graph as they would in a general search. Instead they target their search of the elements in the graph to get the answer to their particular question.

Attribute-Based versus Alternative-Based Search

When audiences conduct a targeted search within a text or table in order to make a decision, they use one of two basic search patterns. One search pattern is *attribute-based* search. Such a search pattern could also be called "criterion-based" search since attributes are one type of decision criterion. The other search pattern is *alternative-based* search (Tversky 1969). This search pattern could also be called "benchmark-based" search since alternatives are one type of benchmark.

Our model of decision making depicts attribute-based search as is illustrated in the passage below in which a renter thinks aloud as she decides which apartment to rent, A or B. Notice how she first compares both apartments with respect to the cost to rent each of them. Then she compares both apartments with respect to the noise level of each (Payne 1976, p. 378):

> OK, we have an A and a B.
> First, look at the rent for both of them.
> The rent for A is $170 and the rent for B is $140.
> $170 is a little steep, but it might have a low noise level.
> So we'll check A's noise level.
> A's noise level is low.
> We'll go to B's noise level.
> It's high.
> Gee, I can't really very well study with a lot of noise.
> So I'll ask myself the question, "Is it worth spending that extra $30 a month,
> to be able to study in my apartment?"

When conducting an attribute-based search, audience members compare the first alternative's value for the first decision criterion, in this case apartment A's cost, to the corresponding values of the other alternatives, in this case apartment B's cost, before

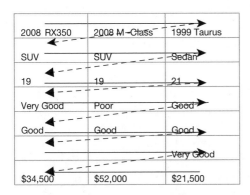

Figure 3.10 An Attribute-Based Search.

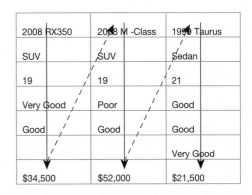

Figure 3.11 An Alternative-Based Search.

moving on to compare the first alternative's value for the second criterion, in this case apartment A's noise level, to the corresponding values of the other alternatives. Conversely, when conducting an alternative-based search, audience members input all of the attribute values of one alternative (e.g., apartment A's cost and noise level) before moving on to input all of the attribute values of the next alternative (e.g., apartment B's cost and noise level). Figures 3.10 and 3.11 illustrate the difference between the two search patterns if an audience member were to scan the cells of a decision matrix to decide among three cars.

The Audience's Preference for Attribute-Based Search

Audiences show a marked preference for making attribute-based searches. Clarkson (1962) studied an experienced trust investment officer from a large commercial bank as he chose equity stocks for a client portfolio. Before choosing to invest in a firm, the investment officer compared that firm's current value for an important attribute to the values of the other firms in the portfolio for the same attribute and then to the values of other firms in the industry as well as to mean growth rates and expected growth rates for that attribute. Then the investment officer compared that firm's current value for the next important attribute to the values of the other firms in the portfolio, and so on.

Other audiences have shown a preference for making attribute-based searches as well. In a study of auditors, Selling (1982) asked seven senior auditors to think aloud as they planned an audit of a company's internal control procedures. Selling gave the auditors the company's financial statements, company backgrounds, and flow charts of internal control procedures. Most of the auditors' time was spent making one of two types of comparisons:

1) the auditors compared two line-item amounts across years to determine if there were a significant change from one year to the next; and
2) they compared the information in the company's financial statements to their conceptions of the information a prototypical firm would disclose in its financial statements.

In the case of executive selection, high-level executives activate "their schema of what it takes to perform well in a particular position" (Sessa 2001, p. 99). They then attempt to compare each candidate to the ideal candidate using the criteria in their schema and select the candidate who best matches the ideal.

Most searches conducted by consumers as they make decisions are attribute-based. In a think-aloud protocol study of consumer decision making, Russo (1971) found that out of 80 information acquisition searches, 57 (or about 71%) were by attribute, 15 by alternative or brand, and 8 used some other search pattern. Capon and Burke (1977) also show that consumers use attribute-based search 71% of the time. A study that tracked consumers' eye movements as they decided among six used cars (alternatives) that were described in terms of three decision criteria (attributes) also finds that consumers rely most heavily on attribute-based search (Russo & Rosen 1975). Consumers' eye fixations consisted of comparing pairs of alternatives one attribute at a time. Even when consumers search by asking questions instead of reading about various products, they typically use attribute-based search, with approximately 75% of their questions being attribute-based (Ranyard & Williamson 2005).

Audiences use attribute-based search in a variety of circumstances. In field studies of consumer decision making, attribute-based search strategies are the most frequently observed (Aschenbrenner 1978; Svenson 1979). When either alternative-based or attribute-based strategies can be used, consumers overwhelmingly use attribute-based search strategies (Russo & Dosher 1983). Under time pressure, audiences' search patterns become increasingly attribute-based (Payne, Bettman, & Johnson 1988). Audiences' search patterns also become more attribute-based as the amount of information about the alternatives increases (e.g., Cook 1987; Payne 1976; Payne & Braunstein 1978).

Even when audiences initially read and search by alternative, they may have to search their notes or their memories a second time by attribute in order to make the comparisons their decision requires. In a study of new home-buyers, Svenson (1974) gave buyers written descriptions of seven houses with each house or alternative described in a separate booklet and asked them to think aloud as they read the booklets and made their decisions. In their initial reading of each booklet, buyers conducted alternative-based searches. But they conducted more attribute-based searches when looking over the booklets a second time. Russo and Dosher (1983) studied the eye movements of scholarship judges choosing among scholarship applicants who were described by three attributes. Although the judges read the information by alternative, they processed the information by attribute. Even when information was structured to bias processing by alternative, half of the judges still processed the information by attribute.

Audiences also tend to recall information that is relevant to their decisions in an attribute-based way. In a study of consumer recall, Lynch and coauthors (1988) asked consumers to read about three brands of color televisions: Sanyo, Philco, and Sharp. After a delay they asked the consumers to choose one of the brands. Consumers recalled product attributes and make attribute-based choices. Consumers did not recall their overall evaluations of the alternative brands or use them to make alternative-based choices. Thus when consumers make a decision based on memory, they conduct an attribute-based search of their memories which determines their comparison process and ultimately their choice of brands (Biehal & Chakravarti 1982, 1983).

Constraints on the Search Process

Audiences may not have time to conduct a thorough search and fill all of the slots in their activated schema. Thus, when making a decision, audiences tend to search for the values of the most important decision criteria or attributes first. Jacoby and colleagues (2002) asked consumers to choose products from three product categories: Compact disc players, clock radios, and compact refrigerators. Each product category was represented by a set of 20 attributes. The later the consumers accessed an attribute's value, the less weight they gave it when they made their decisions. When audiences face severe time pressure, they focus only on the most important attribute information (Payne et al. 1988) and rely on just a few attributes to make their choice (Wallsten 1980).

Consumers also tend to consider only a small set of alternatives when making purchasing decisions (Hauser & Wernerflt 1990; Kardes, Kalyanaram, Chandrashekaran, & Dornof 1993; Nedungadi 1990). For many product categories consumers consider between two and eight brands on average (Hauser & Wernerfelt 1990). As time pressure increases audiences may also focus on more negative information about alternatives (Payne et al. 1988; Svenson & Edland 1987; Wallsten & Barton 1982).

Even with ample time, the audience will often end the information acquisition process long before they have processed all of the information available to them due to the capacity limitations of working memory (cf., Miller 1956). For example, consumers usually process only a small proportion of the information that is relevant to deciding among products and services (Russo 1977; Russo, Staelin, Nolan, Russell, & Metcalf 1986). In addition, the goals of consumers influence the amount of attention they are willing to devote to the acquisition and interpretation of product-related information (Batra & Ray 1986; Park & Young 1986; Yalch & Elmore-Yalch 1984). As the number of attributes presented to consumers increases, the proportion of the information they search decreases (e.g., Jacoby, Speller, & Berning 1974a; Jacoby, Speller, & Kohn 1974b). Reviews of studies of consumers using information display boards (a form of decision matrix) to make decisions confirm that as the number of alternatives and attributes displayed on the boards increases, the proportion of the available information used decreases (Aschenbrenner 1978; Svenson 1979).

INFORMATION INTEGRATION

As audience members acquire the information they need to fill their schema slots, they begin to compare and integrate that information in order to arrive at a decision. The information integration process has two major stages:

1) the *valuation stage*, or the conversion of cardinal numbers into ordinal numbers or scale values; and
2) the *integration stage*, or the application of a choice rule for comparing and deciding among alternatives.

During the integration stage, audience members combine ordinal numbers or scale values using either a compensatory or non-compensatory choice rule (Anderson 1974b, 1981, 1989).

The Conversion of Cardinal Numbers into Ordinal Numbers and Scale Values

When audiences make decisions they generally do not mentally represent the values that fill the slots in their schemata as cardinal numbers (e.g., a price of $5,367,892.00) but represent them as ordinal numbers (e.g., "third highest priced") or scale values instead (Abelson & Levi 1985). In his think-aloud study of how a bank's trust officer made investment decisions for clients, Clarkson (1962) found that the trust officer tended to convert the cardinal numbers in the financial reports into scale values before comparing them. Clarkson incorporated this finding into a computer model he developed to simulate the trust officer's investment decisions by first converting numerical data for each attribute or decision criterion into a three-value scale: *Below, equal to,* or *above.*

Audiences also spontaneously transform numerical information about risk into scale values (Bottorff, Ratner, Johnson, Lovato, & Joab 1998). Consumers make similar transformations when deciding among products and assign a scale value to each attribute of the recommended product during the valuation stage of the information integration process (Anderson 1974b, 1981, 1989).

Compensatory versus Non-Compensatory Choice Rules

Many different choice rules for integrating values have been proposed (e.g., Payne et al. 1993; Tversky 1972; Wallsten 1980). The two basic rules audiences use to integrate attribute values are called *compensatory rules* and *non-compensatory rules.* When audiences use compensatory rules, they make trade offs and accept a low value on one attribute or decision criterion in order to get a high value on another attribute. For example, a car buyer may accept fewer miles per gallon in order to get an increase in safety. Such rules require the same number of attributes be examined for both alternatives. Examples of compensatory rules include the *weighted additive rule* and *the equal weight rule,* both of which rely on alternative-based search.

When audiences use the weighted additive rule, they evaluate each alternative one at a time. For each attribute or decision criterion of the alternative under consideration, they multiply the attribute's weight by the attribute's value. Next they add all of that alternative's weighted attribute values together in order to produce an overall value for that alternative. They repeat the process for each alternative. Then they compare the overall values of all the alternatives and choose the alternative with the highest overall value. Audiences go through a similar process when they use the equal weight rule. The difference is that they do not weight the relative importance of each attribute. Instead, they produce an overall value for each alternative by adding the unweighted values for each attribute of that alternative.

Unlike compensatory choice rules, non-compensatory rules do not allow trade offs among attributes. Examples of non-compensatory rules include the *elimination-by-aspects rule* and the *lexicographic rule,* two rules that rely on attribute-based search and two rules that are suggested by our model of audience decision making. When audiences use the elimination-by-aspects rule, they first rank all the attributes or decision criteria according to their importance (Tversky 1972; Tversky & Sattath 1979). Then they compare each alternative's value for the top-ranked attribute to some minimum satisfactory value and eliminate any alternative from further consideration whose value is less than the satisfactory value. For example, if safety were the most important feature to a new car buyer, then the buyer would immediately eliminate any car with a poor safety record. Next the audience eliminates alternatives that do not have satisfactory values for the second-ranked attribute. The audience continues this process of elimination until only one alternative remains.

When audiences use the lexicographic rule, they also rank each attribute or decision criterion in terms of its importance. They then compare the values of the alternatives on the highest ranked attribute and choose the alternative with the highest value on that attribute, regardless of the values the alternatives have on other attributes. If, for example, miles-per-gallon were the highest ranked attribute or decision criterion for a new car buyer and if the new Toyota Prius had the best gas mileage of all the cars under consideration, then the buyer would chose the Prius without examining other attributes. Such non-compensatory choice rules can minimize cognitive effort without severely decreasing the accuracy of the audience's decision. For example, in one experiment a simple non-compensatory rule increased the error rate from 8% to only 14% over that of the normative expected-value rule (Johnson 1979). But the time saving was dramatic. Audience members took about two minutes to apply the expected-value rule but only 15 seconds to use the non-compensatory rule.

Constraints on the Use of Compensatory Choice Rules

Can professionals predict which choice rule their audience will use? As we have seen, consumers show a strong preference to use choice rules that rely on attribute-based search and comparisons (Russo & Dosher 1980). Choice rules that rely on attribute-based search include non-compensatory rules such as the elimination-by-aspects rule and the lexicographic rule, as well as compensatory rules such as the additive-difference rule and the majority-of-confirming-dimensions rule.

When audiences choose between just two alternatives, they typically use an attribute-based compensatory choice rule (cf., Payne 1976). However, as the number of alternatives they have to consider increases, their use of compensatory choice rules decreases. For example, a study of physicians choosing among anti-infective drugs finds that physicians switch from compensatory to non-compensatory strategies as the number of alternative drugs increases from three to six (Chinburapa 1991).

When audiences have multiple alternatives to choose among, they typically use a non-compensatory choice rule such as the elimination-by-aspects rule (Johnson, Meyer, & Ghose 1989; Klayman 1985; Onken, Hastie, & Revelle 1985). Venture capitalists use the elimination-by-aspects rule to screen business plans (Pfeffer 1987). Investors use the elimination-by-aspects rule to pick stocks (Kercsmar 1985). Industrial buyers use similar non-compensatory strategies to select a supplier unless only a very few suppliers are capable of supplying the needed product and the buyer is not familiar with a viable supplier (LeBlanc 1981).

Sometimes, when faced with multiple alternatives, audience members start with a non-compensatory choice rule in order to quickly reduce the number of alternatives under consideration and then switch to a compensatory rule (Biehal & Chakravari 1986). Consumers use such a two-phase choice strategy, particularly when choosing among six or more alternative brands (Lussier & Olshavsky 1979; Svenson 1974). Consumers eliminate the unacceptable alternatives in the first phase and then compare the remaining alternatives in more detail in the second phase. For example, a study of consumers choosing among several brands of typewriters reveals that consumers first eliminate any alternative with a low value for an important criterion or attribute and then compute the total values for the remaining alternatives (Lussier & Olshavsky 1979). In a study of expert and novice consumers choosing among brands of microwave ovens, Bettman and Park (1980) find that expert consumers start with attribute-based evaluations. Then they compare alternatives to benchmark standards. Only after eliminating failing alternatives do the experts compare the remaining alternatives to each other using a compensatory strategy.

Audiences may turn to non-compensatory choice rules even when the number of alternatives stays small, especially when the decision they are making is not important to them. For example, a study of consumers choosing stores at which to shop shows that consumers use simple non-compensatory strategies to plan shopping trips for unimportant items (Peterson 1984). They only use the more complex compensatory strategies to plan shopping trips for important items.

In addition, audiences may turn to non-compensatory choice rules as the number of attributes they have to consider increases (Biggs, Bedard, Gaber, & Linsmeier 1985; Sundstrom 1987). For example, consumers tend to eliminate attributes when the initial number of attributes they are given is large (Lussier & Olshavsky 1979; van Raaij 1976). Audiences also tend to use non-compensatory choice rules when there is incomparable scaling of attribute values across alternatives (Wright 1974).

Cognitive Processes in Audience Decision Making: Implications for Communicators

✧ The main takeaway for communicators in Chapter 3 is that in order for audiences to arrive at rational decisions, they must first be able to complete a specific set of cognitive processes. The audience's decision-making process is not a black box. It is predictable and subject to many information-processing constraints.

✧ Use the information presented in the chapter to make stylistic and organizational choices that aid audience decision making, to diagnose problems with ineffective communications, and to handle communication issues with new media adaptively.

✧ Why use the information? To help your audience make decisions faster and more efficiently. To avoid making decision making difficult. To reduce the risk that your audience will discard your information because it seems unclear or disorganized to them.

✧ To apply the information presented in the chapter: (1) Identify likely problems when editing or planning communications; (2) Determine which cognitive process is affected by each problem; (3) Refer to the section of Chapter 4 dealing with proven techniques for aiding that particular process.

CHAPTER 4

Aids to Audience Decision Making

On August 5, 1977, New York State became the first state in the United States to enact a general-purpose plain English law. The impetus for the new law was a plain English loan agreement form introduced earlier that same year by Citibank (then First National City Bank). Understandably, the bank's lawyers and upper management were initially skeptical of the new form, as shown on p. 127. But when the bank finally approved it, TV and the national press saw its introduction as a major event. A bill was soon on the governor's desk requiring all consumer contracts in New York to be modeled on the new Citibank form. Within a few months, the plain English bill was signed into law.

What effect did the new loan agreement form have on the bank and its customers? Both benefited. A survey of more than 100 borrowers showed that borrowers believed the original version (Citibank 1974) contained too much information, had too much small print, was formatted in a confusing way, and was hard to read. In contrast, the borrowers said the revised form (Citibank 1977) was written in a more specific and precise style, that it gave a good breakdown of information, and that it was easy to read.

The survey also showed that the borrowers believed that banks using the two versions would be radically different. In addition, four out of five borrowers surveyed expressed positive feelings about borrowing from a bank using the new form. They also expressed interest in using the bank's other services (adapted from Felsenfeld 1991 and Felsenfeld & Siegel 1981).

Citibank's experience with the new loan agreement form illustrates just a few of the benefits to be gained when professionals are able to increase the speed and accuracy of the decisions they ask their audiences to make. To make such changes, professionals must make it easy for their audiences to complete each of the six cognitive processes required in audience decision making—perception, attention, sentence-level comprehension, schema activation, information acquisition, and information integration.

Original Citibank Loan Agreement Form

FIRST NATIONAL CITY BANK

Personal Finance Department • New York

APPLICATION	PROCEEDS TO BORROWER (1) $ _____
NUMBER	PROPERTY INS.PREMIUM (2) $ _____
ANNUAL PER-	FILING FEE (3) $ _____
CENTAGE RATE _____ %	AMOUNT FINANCED (1) ♦ (2) ♦ (3) (4) $ _____
	PREPAID FINANCE CHARGE (5) $ _____
$ _____	GROUP CREDIT LIFE INS.PREMIUM (6) $ _____
	FINANCE CHARGE (5) ♦ (6) (7) $ _____

TOTAL OF PAYMENTS (4) ♦ (7)

FOR THE VALUE RECEIVED, the undersigned (jointly and severally) hereby promises(s) to pay to FIRST NATIONAL CITY BANK (the "Bank") at it office at 399 Park Avenue, New York, New York 10022 (i) THE SUM OF

_____ ($_____) (TOTAL OF PAYMENTS) ( ) IN _____ EQUAL CONSECUTIVE MONTHLY INSTALLMENTS OF $ _____ EACH ON THE SAME DAY OF EACH MONTH, COM-MENCING _____ DAYS FROM THE DATE THE LOAN IS MADE; OR ( ) IN _____ EQUAL CONSECUTIVE WEEKLY INSTALLMENTS OF $ _____ EACH ON THE SAME DAY OF EACH WEEK, COMMENCING NOT EARLIER THAN 5 DAYS NOR LATER THAN 45 DAYS FROM THE DATE THE LOAN IS MADE; OR ( ) IN _____ EQUAL CONSECUTIVE BI-WEEKLY INSTALLMENTS OF $ _____ EACH, COM-MENCING NOT EARLIER THAN 10 DAYS NOR LATER THAN 45 DAYS FROM THE DATE THE LOAN IS MADE, AND ON THE SAME DAY OF EACH SECOND WEEK THEREAFTER; OR ( ) IN _____ EQUAL CONSECUTIVE SEMI-MONTHLY INSTALLMENTS OF $ _____ EACH, COMMENCING NOT EARLIER THAN 10 DAYS NOT LATER THAN 45 DAYS FROM THE DATE THE LOAN IS MADE, AND ON THE SAME DAY OF EACH SEMI-MONTHLY PERIOD THEREAFTER, (ii) A FINE COMPUTED AT THE RATE OF 5¢ PER $1 ON ANY INSTALMENT WHICH HAS BECOME DUE AND REMAINED UNPAID FOR A PERIOD IN EXCESS OF 10 DAYS, PROVIDED (A) IF THE PROCEEDS TO THE BORROWER ARE $10,000 OR LESS, NO SUCH FINE SHALL EXCEED $5 AND THE AGGREGATE OF ALL SUCH FINES SHALL NOT EXCEED THE LESSER OF 2% OF THE AMOUNT OF THIS NOTE OR $25, OR (B) IF THE ANNUAL PERCENTAGE RATE STATED ABOVE IS 7.50% OR LESS, THE LIMITATIONS PROVIDED IN (A) SHALL NOT APPLY AND NO SUCH FINE SHALL EXCEED $25 AND THE AGGREGATE OF ALL SUCH FINES SHALL NOT EXCEED 2% OF THE AMOUNT OF THIS NOTE, AND SUCH FINE(S) SHALL BE DEEMED LIQUIDATED DAM-AGES OCCASIONED BY THE LATE PAYMENT(S); (iii) IN THE EVENT OF THIS NOTE MATURING, SUBJECT TO AN ALLOWANCE FOR UNEARNED INTEREST ATTRIBUTABLE TO THE MATURED AMOUNTINTEREST AT A RATE EQUAL TO 1% PER MONTH AND (iv) IF THIS NOTE IS REFERRED TO AN ATTORNEY FOR COLLECTION, A SUM EQUAL TO ALL COSTS AND EXPENSES THEREOF, INCLUDING AN ATTORNEYS FEE EQUAL TO 15% OF THE AMOUNT OWNING ON THIS NOTE AT THE TIME OF SUCH REFERENCE, FOR SUCH NECESSARY COURT COSTS. THIS ACCEPTANCE BY THE BANK OF ANY PAYMENT(S) EVEN IF MARKED PAYMENT IN FULL OR SIMILAR WORDING, OR IF MADE AFTER ANY DEFAULT HEREUNDER, SHALL NOT OPERATE TO EXTEND THE TIME OF PAYMENT OF OR TO WAIVE ANY AMOUNT(S) THEN REMAINING UNPAID OR CONSTITUTE A WAIVER OF ANY RIGHTS OF THE BANK HEREUNDER.

IN THE EVENT THIS NOTE IS PREPAID IN FULL OR REFINANCED, THE BORROWER SHALL RECEIVE A REFUND OF THE UNEARNED PORTION OF THE PREPAID FINANCE CHARGE COMPUTED IN ACCORDANCE WITH THE RULE OF 78 (THE "SUM OF THE DIGITS" METHOD), PROVIDED THAT THE BANK MAY RETAIN A MINIMUM FINANCE CHARGE OF $10, WHETHER OR NOT EARNED, AND EXCEPT IN THE CASE OF A REFINANCING, NO REFUND SHALL BE MADE IF IT AMOUNTS TO LESS THAN $1. IN ADDITION, UPON ANY SUCH PREPAYMENT OR REFINANCING, THE BORROWER SHALL RECEIVE A REFUND OF THE CHARGE, IF ANY, FOR GROUP CREDIT LIFE INSURANCE INCLUDED IN THE LOAN EQUAL TO THE UNEARNED PORTION OF THE PREMIUM PAID OR PAYABLE BY THE HOLDER OF THE OBLIGATION (COMPUTED IN ACCORDANCE WITH THE RULE OF 78), PROVIDED THAT NO REFUND SHALL BE MADE OF AMOUNTS LESS THAN $1.

AS COLLATERAL SECURITY FOR THE PAYMENT OF THE INDEBTEDNESS OF THE UNDERSIGNED HEREUNDER AND ALL OTHER INDEBTEDNESS OR LIABILITIES OF THE UNDERSIGNED TO THE BANK, WHETHER JOINT, SEVERAL, ABSOLUTE, CONTINGENT, SECURED, UNSECURED, MATURED OR UNMATURED, UNDER ANY PRESENT OR FUTURE NOTE OR CONTRACT OR AGREEMENT WITH THE BANK (ALL SUCH INDEBTEDNESS AND LIABILITIES BEING HEREINAFTER COLLECTIVELY CALLED THE "OBLIGATIONS"), THE BANK SHALL HAVE, AND IS HEREBY GRANTED, A SECURITY INTEREST AND/OR RIGHT OF SET-OFF IN AND TO (a) ALL MONIES, SECURITIES AND OTHER PROPERTY OF THE UNDERSIGNED NOW OR HEREAFTER ON DEPOSIT WITH OR OTHERWISE HELD BY OR TO THE POSSESSION OR UNDER THE CONTROL OF THE BANK, WHETHER HELD FOR SAFEKEEPING, COLLECTION, TRANSMISSION OR OTHERWISE OR AS CUSTODIAN, INCLUDING THE PROCEEDS THEREOF, AND ANY AND ALL CLAIMS OF THE UNDERSIGNED AGAINST THE BANK, WHETHER NOW OR HEREAFTER EXISTING, AND (b) THE FOLLOWING DESCRIBED PERSONAL PROPERTY (ALL MONIES, SECURITIES, PROPERTY, PROCEEDS, CLAIMS AND PERSONAL PROPERTY BEING HEREINAFTER COLLECTIVELY CALLED THE "COLLATERAL"; ( ) MOTOR VEHICLE ( ) BOAT ( ) STOCKS, ( ) BONDS, ( ) SAVINGS, and/or

SEE CUSTOMER'S COPY OF SECURITY AGREEMENT(S) OR COLLATERAL RECEIPT(S) RELATIVE TO THIS LOAN FOR FULL DESCRIPTION. IF THIS NOTE IS SECURED BY A MOTOR VEHICLE, BOAT OR AIRCRAFT, PROPERTY INSURANCE ON THE COLLATERAL IS REQUIRED, AND THE BORROWER MAY OBTAIN THE SAME THROUGH A PERSON OF HIS OWN CHOICE.

IF THIS NOTE IS NOT FULLY SECURED BY THE COLLATERAL MENTIONED ABOVE, AS FURTHER SECURITY FOR THE PAYMENT OF THIS NOTE, THE BANK HAS TAKEN AN ASSIGNMENT OF 10% OF THE UNDERSIGNED BORROWER'S WAGES IN ACCORDANCE WITH THE WAGE ASSIGNMENT ATTACHED TO THIS NOTE.

In the event of default in the payment of this or any other Obligation or the performance or observance of any term or covenant contained herein or in any note or other contract or agreement evidencing or relating to any Obligation or any Collateral on the Borrower's part to be performed or observed; or the undersigned Borrower shall die; or any of the undersigned become insolvent or make an assignment for the benefit of creditors; or a petition shall be filed by or against any of the undersigned under any provision of the Bankruptcy Act; or any money, securities or property of the undersigned now or hereafter on deposit with or in the possession or under the control of the Bank shall be attached or become subject to distraint proceedings or any order or process of any court; or the Bank shall deem itself to be insecure, then and in any such event, the Bank shall have the right (at its option), without demand or notice of any kind, to declare all or any part of the Obligations to be immediately due and payable, whereupon such Obligations shall become and be immediately due and payable, and the Bank shall have the right to exercise all the rights and remedies available to a secured upon default under the Uniform Commercial Code (the "Code".) in effect in New York at the time, and such other rights and as may otherwise be provided by the law. Each of the undersigned agrees (for the purpose of the "code") that written notice of any proposed sale of, or of the Bank's election to retain, Collateral mailed to the undersigned Borrower (who is hereby appointed agent of each of the undersigned for such purpose) by first class mail, postage prepaid, at the address of the undersigned Borrower indicated below three business days prior to such sale or election shall be deemed reasonable notification thereof. The remedies of the Bank hereunder are cumulative and may be exercised concurrently or separately. If any provision of this paragraph shall conflict with any remedial provision contained in any security agreement or Collateral receipt covering any Collateral, the provision of such security agreement of Collateral, the provision of such security agreement or collateral receipt shall control.

Acceptance by the Bank of payments in shall not constitute a waiver of or otherwise affect any acceleration of payment hereunder or other right or remedy exercisable hereunder. No failure or delay on the part of the Bank in exercising, and no failure to file or otherwise perfect or enforce the Bank's security interest in or with respect to any Collateral, shall operate as a waiver of any right or remedy hereunder or release any of the undersigned, and the Obligation of the undersigned may be extended or waived by the Bank contract or other agreement evidencing or relating to any Obligation or any Collateral may be amended and any Collateral exchanged surrendered or otherwise dealt with in accordance with any agreement relative thereto, all without affecting the liability of any of the undersigned. In any litigation (whether or not arising out of or relating to any Obligation or Collateral or other matter connected herewith) in which the Bank and any of the undersigned may be adverse parties, the Bank and each such undersigned hereby waives their respective right to demand trial by jury and, additionally, each such undersigned waives his right to interpose in any such litigation any counterclaim of any nature or description which he may have against the Bank. In addition, the Bank shall not be deemed to have obtained knowledge of any fact or notice with respect to any matter relating to this note or any Collateral unless contained in a written mailed, postage prepaid, or personally delivered to the Personal Finance Department of the Bank at its address set forth above. Each of the undersigned, by his signature hereto, hereby waives presentation for payment, demand, notice of non-payment, protest and notice of protest with respect to the indebtedness evidenced by this note, and each such undersigned hereby agrees that this note shall be deemed to have been made under and shall be construed in accordance with the laws of the State of New York.

Each of the undersigned hereby authorizes the Bank to date this note as of the day the loan evidenced hereby is made to correct patent errors herein and, at its option, to cause the signatures of one or more co-makers to be added without notice of any prior obligor.

RECEIPT OF A COPY OF THIS NOTE, APPROPRIATELY FILLED IN, IS HEREBY ACKNOWLEDGED BY THE BORROWER

FULL SIGNATURE	COMPLETE ADDRESS
BORROWER _____	_____
WIFE OR HUSBAND OF BORROWER AS CO-MAKER _____	_____
CO-MAKER _____	_____
CO-MAKER _____	_____

Revised Citibank Loan Agreement Form

Consumer Loan Note   Date_____, 19____

(In this note, the words **I, me, mine** and **my** mean each and all of those who signed it. The words **you, your** and **yours** mean First National City Bank.)

Terms of Repayment
To repay my loan, I promise to pay you _____Dollars ($_____). I'll pay this sum at one of your branches in _____ uninterrupted _____ installments of $_____ each. Payments will be due _____, starting from the date the loan is made.

Here's the breakdown of my payments:

1. Amount of the Loan	$_____
2. Property Insurance Premium	$_____
3. Filing Fee for Security Interest	$_____
4. Amount Financed (1+2+3)	$_____
5. **Finance Charge**	$_____
6. Total of Payments (4+5)	$_____

Annual Percentage Rate _____%

Prepayment of Whole Note
Even though I needn't pay more that the fixed installments, I have the right to prepay the whole outstanding amount of this note at any time. If I do, or if this loan is refinanced -that is, replaced by a new note- you will refund the unearned **finance charge**, figured by the rule of 78 - a commonly used formula for figuring rebates on installment loans. However, you can change a minimum **finance charge** of $10.

Late Charge
If I fall more than 10 days behind in paying an installment, I promise to pay a late charge of 5% of the overdue installment, but no more the $5. However, the sum total of late charges on all installments can't be more than 2% of the total of payments or $25, whichever is less.

Security
To protect you if I default on this or any other debt to you, I give you what is known as a security interest in my ○ Motor Vehicle and/or_____ (see the Security Agreement I have given you for a full description of this property), ○ Stocks, ○ Bonds, ○ Savings Account (more fully described in the receipt you gave me today) **and** any account or other property of mine coming into your possession.

Insurance
I understand I must maintain property insurance on the property covered by the Security Agreement for its full insurable value, but I can buy this insurance through a person of my choosing.

Default
I'll be in default:
1. If I don't pay an installment on time; or
2. If any other creditor tries by legal process to take any money of mine in your possession.

You can then demand immediate repayment of the balance of this note, minus the part of the **finance charge** which hasn't been earned figured by the rule of 78. You will also have other legal rights, for instance, the right to repossess, sell and apply security to the payments under this note and any other debts I may then owe you.

Irregular Payments
You can accept late payments or partial payments, even though marked "payment in full", without losing any of your rights under this notice.

Delay in Enforcement
You can delay enforcing any of your rights under this note without losing them.

Collection Costs
If I'm in default under this note and you demand full payment, I agree to pay you interest on the unpaid balance at the rate of 1% per month, after an allowance for the unearned **finance charge**. If you have to sue me, I also agree to pay your attorney's fees equal to 15% of the amount due, and court costs. But if I defend and the court decides I am right, I understand that you will pay my reasonable attorney's fees and the court costs.

Comakers
If I'm signing this note as a comaker, I agree to be equally responsible with the borrower, although you may sue either of us. You don't have to notify me that this note hasn't been paid. You can change the terms of payment and release any security without notifying or releasing me from responsibility on this note.

Copy Received
The borrower acknowledges receipt of a completely filled-in copy of this note.

Signatures	Addresses
Borrower:_____	_____
Comaker: _____	_____
Comaker _____	_____
Comaker: _____	_____

Hot Line
If something should happen and you can't pay on time, please call us immediately at (212) 559-3061.

Personal Finance Department
First National City Bank

Chapter 4 describes many of the stylistic choices available to professionals and explains how each choice either helps or hinders one or more of the cognitive processes involved in audience decision making. For example, an advertiser's choice of typeface, type size, and background color can determine how easily a reading audience can perceive the words on a page. Similarly, a politician's speaking rate, volume, and prosody can determine how easily a listening audience can perceive the words being spoken.

In addition to influencing the speed and accuracy of audience decision making, stylistic choices can affect how intuitively appealing a document, presentation, or even a point made during a meeting is to an audience. The intuitive appeal of stylistic choices is the subject of Chapter 5. Other stylistic choices can affect the way the audience views the writer or speaker. Is she polite or impolite, confident or uncertain, friendly or aloof, credible or untrustworthy? Chapter 6 explores these choices.

Then there are those stylistic choices that appear to have little effect on audience decision making. For example, in a study of the responses of staff members to managers' letters that requested them to take action, Krajewski (1979) finds no correlation between the letters' organizational plans (inductive or deductive) and the likelihood that staff members would take the actions managers requested. In a study of the responses of automotive jobbers to sales letters, Wakefield (1961) finds no correlation between the letters' formats (block, marginal message, or hanging indention) or the color of the letterheads (white, pink, yellow, blue, or green) and the number of orders the jobbers placed. In a study comparing e-mailed versions of persuasive messages to printed versions, Hill and Monk (2000) find no difference in the effects of e-mail or print on the behaviors and perceptions of the message recipients.

AIDS TO PERCEPTION

Legible Characters

Readers' perception of text in a document or presentation slide depends first of all on the legibility of each letter or character of type in it. The legibility of each character of type depends on its print quality, type size, case, and typeface and its contrast with the background. Poor print quality increases the amount of time the audience needs to recognize characters and words (Becker & Killion 1977; Stanners, Jastrzembski, & Westbrook 1975). In his classic study of the decision-making process, Sternberg (1966) gave participants sets of 1 to 6 digits to memorize (e.g., 397) and then asked them to decide whether a particular digit (e.g., 1 or 9) was one of the digits they had memorized. If he made the target digit hard to perceive, only the time taken to complete the perception stage of the decision-making task was affected.

High Contrast Between Type and Background

The greatest legibility is achieved when there is maximum contrast between the type used and the background shade (Tinker 1965). Reading times are slower for color combinations with less tonal contrast between type and the background shade (e.g., black type on a dark blue background) due to the reader's need to increase eye-fixation frequency and pause duration. When the background shade is greater than 10%, readers have trouble discerning black type on it (Wheildon 1995).

Reversing the color of type (i.e., placing light type against a dark background) can affect legibility, too. When the color of the type is reversed, as it is in many slide shows, the dark background makes the type appear thinner than it actually is (Rehe 1974). If the type color is reversed over long passages, reading speed may be reduced by up to 15% (Holmes 1931; Taylor 1934).

Eleven-Point Type Size for Documents, 24 for Slides

The size of the type also affects how easily letters and words can be perceived. The most legible type size for a variety of typefaces, or fonts, in documents ranges from 9 points to 12 points (Poulton 1955). Type sizes below 6 points are hard to read (Poulton 1967). Audiences read fastest when type sizes are between 9 and 12 points and rate 11-point type as most legible (Tinker 1965). Slightly smaller type sizes may also be legible in some situations. For example, in a study of newspaper print, Davenport and Smith (1963) find little difference in legibility for type sizes between 7.5 and 9 points. Similarly, a study of instructional texts finds that type as small as 8 points is still legible for many readers (Hartley 1978). Twenty-four points is often the minimum type size recommended for slide presentations. However, type as small as 16 points may be legible to many viewers.

Lower-Case Letters

Both headings and text are less legible when typed in all upper-case letters than when typed in both upper and lower-case letters (Coles & Foster 1975; Rickards & August 1975; Tinker 1965). Because the outline of a capital letter is not as distinctive as the outline of a lower-case letter, reading speed is optimal when both upper-case and lower-case letters are used and the use of all capital letters is avoided (Just & Carpenter 1987; Rickards & August 1975; Salcedo, Reed, Evans, & Kong 1972). Words and phrases in all capital letters take about 12% longer to read (Tinker 1965). Headlines in all capital letters take between 13% and 20% longer to read (Breland & Breland 1944). See Figure 4.2 for an example of this.

Italic type can also slow readers down. When italic type is used for continuous prose, reading speed is substantially reduced (Foster & Bruce 1982). Continuous prose in italic type takes readers about 5% longer to read than continuous prose in non-italic type (Tinker 1965).

Legible Typeface

Typeface, or font, can also affect legibility. Tinker and Paterson carried out 11 studies on typography in which more than 11,000 readers took part (described in Tinker 1963, pp. 90–107). The readers preferred the most legible typefaces and their preferences for

4 point Times New Roman

5 point Times New Roman

6 point Times New Roman

7 point Times New Roman

8 point Times New Roman

9 point Times New Roman

10 point Times New Roman

11 point Times New Roman

12 point Times New Roman

14 point Times New Roman

4 point Arial

5 point Arial

6 point Arial

7 point Arial

8 point Arial

9 point Arial

10 point Arial

11 point Arial

12 point Arial

14 point Arial

4 point Courier New

5 point Courier New

6 point Courier New

7 point Courier New

8 point Courier New

9 point Courier New

10 point Courier New

11 point Courier New

12 point Courier New

14 point Courier New

Figure 4.1 Three Different Typefaces in 10 Different Sizes

BOTH HEADINGS AND TEXT ARE LESS LEGIBLE WHEN TYPED IN ALL UPPERCASE LETTERS THAN WHEN TYPED IN BOTH UPPER AND LOWERCASE LETTERS (COLES & FOSTER 1975; RICKARDS & AUGUST 1975; TINKER 1965). BECAUSE THE OUTLINE OF A CAPITAL LETTER IS NOT AS DISTINCTIVE AS THE OUTLINE OF A LOWERCASE LETTER, READING SPEED IS OPTIMAL WHEN BOTH UPPERCASE AND LOWERCASE LETTERS ARE USED AND THE USE OF ALL CAPITAL LETTERS IS AVOIDED (JUST & CARPENTER 1987; RICKARDS & AUGUST 1975; SALCEDO, REED, EVANS, & KONG 1972). WORDS AND PHRASES IN ALL CAPITAL LETTERS TAKE ABOUT 12% LONGER TO READ (TINKER 1965). HEADLINES IN ALL CAPITAL LETTERS TAKE BETWEEN 13% AND 20% LONGER TO READ (BRELAND & BRELAND 1944).

Figure 4.2 A Paragraph in All Caps.

Table 4.1 Serif versus Sans Serif Typefaces

Serif typefaces	*Sans serif typefaces*
Times New Roman	Arial
Century	Tahoma
Courier New	Helvetica
Lucida Fax	Lucida Sans
Rockwell	Microsoft Sans Serif

typefaces were highly correlated with reading speed (Tinker 1963, p. 51). Serif typefaces with their curved or straight serifs added to the ends of letters (e.g., the word "APPLE" shown here in a serif typeface) and the more block-like sans serif typefaces (e.g., the word "APPLE" shown here in a sans serif typeface) are equally preferred by readers (Hartley & Rooum 1983; Tinker 1963). Serif typefaces as illustrated in Table 4.1 may be easier to read in continuous text than sans serif typefaces (Hvistendahl & Kahl 1975; Robinson, Abbamonte, & Evans 1971; Wheildon 1995). In other reading situations serif and sans serif typefaces are likely to be read equally quickly (Gould, Alfaro, Finn, Haupt, & Minuto 1987; Hartley & Rooum 1983).

Schriver and her colleagues (as described in Schriver 1997, pp. 288–303) gave adult readers an instruction manual, tax form instructions, a business letter, and a short story all typeset both in serif and sans serif fonts. Readers had no significant overall preference for sans serif versus serif fonts. However, when readers read the long continuous prose of the short story, readers preferred serif fonts. And when readers read the highly segmented prose of the manual, they preferred sans serif fonts. Sans serif fonts are often recommended for slide presentations, perhaps because the text on slides is usually segmented into bullet points.

Ten to 12 Words per Line

The number of words per line affects the overall legibility of a page or a presentation slide. In documents, ten to 12 words per line is optimal (Tinker 1965, 1963). For most type sizes, that amounts to about 50 to 70 characters per line. A line length of 50 to 70 characters is also easiest for the eye to scan (Tinker 1965). Keeping lines to 50 to 70 characters may mean typing two or more columns to a page. When lines of type are shorter or longer than 50 to 70 characters, readers decrease their normal rate of reading (Paterson & Tinker 1942). On slides with type sizes no smaller than 24 points, bulleted lines of type will typically contain only ten words or fewer.

Some Space Between Lines

Reading audiences read faster when text has 1 to 4 points of leading, or space between the lines, than when the type is *set solid*—when no space is inserted between the lines (Becker, Heinrich, van Sichowsky, & Wendt 1970). For a 10-point type size, the space should be less than four points. Type that is set solid has a dense appearance, like the type in many credit card agreements. Readers dislike type that is set solid (Tinker 1963). At the same time, readers also dislike type with too much space between the lines. However, an added blank line between paragraphs or between bullet points on slides and a blank space between columns of type can actually increase legibility (cf., Smith & McCombs 1971).

Reading audiences read faster when text has 1 to 4 points of leading, or space between the lines, than when the type is set solid—when no space is inserted between the lines (Becker, Heinrich, van Sichowsky, & Wendt 1970). For a 10-point type size, the space should be less than four points. Type that is set solid has a dense appearance, like the type in many credit card agreements. Readers dislike type that is set solid (Tinker 1963). At the same time, readers also dislike type with too much space between the lines. However, an added blank line between paragraphs or between bullet points on slides and a blank space between columns of type can actually increase legibility (cf., Smith & McCombs 1971).

Figure 4.3 A Paragraph Set Solid.

Unjustified Right Margins

Text with unjustified right margins, or ragged edges, in documents or on presentation slides can be more legible than right-justified text that forms a straight margin down the right-hand side. Unjustified right margins can increase reading speed on-line by 10% (Trollip & Sales 1986). In a study conducted at NASA, 61% of the readers surveyed preferred unjustified right margins to justified margins when reading technical reports (Pinelli, Glassman, & Cordle 1982). However, several studies of adult readers find that justified and unjustified texts are read at similar speeds and with the same level of comprehension (Fabrizio, Kaplan, & Teal 1967; Hartley & Mills 1973; Wiggins 1967).

Short, Familiar Words

Whether spoken or written, some words are more easily perceived and recognized than others. Easily perceived and recognized words include short words, high frequency words, personal pronouns, concrete words, and words that are easy to pronounce (Cox 1978; Redish 1980; Scarborough, Gerard, & Cortese 1979). Long, difficult to understand, and less frequently used words take longer to recognize (Gibson, Bishop, Schiff, & Smith 1964; Reicher 1969; Wheeler 1970) and are harder to remember (Anderson 1974c; Jorgensen & Kintsch 1973).

Semantic variables can also influence word recognition. For example, animate nouns such as *investors* are easier to process and recall than inanimate nouns such as *investments* (Rohrman 1970). In her review of the psycholinguistic research, Holland (1981) concludes that the key to word difficulty in isolation lies not in word frequency but in the semantic variables of animateness, affirmativeness, and concreteness.

Visible Speakers

Listeners' perception of speech involves sensing and recognizing both phonemes and complete words. Speakers who allow listeners to see their faces make it easier for listeners to recognize their words, especially in a noisy room (Sumby & Pollack 1954).

Prosody, Intonation, and Articulation

Speakers who avoid speaking in a monotone also make words easier to recognize. The speaker's prosody and intonation help listeners segment the continuous stream of sounds coming from the speaker into intelligible words (Cutler & Norris 1988; Otake & Cutler 1996).

Listeners' perception of a speech will be impaired to the extent that the phonemes and words in it are inaudible, garbled, or unfamiliar. Retention of the speaker's message can be affected as well. In a test of listeners' memory for a message that contained six high-quality arguments supporting a recommended position, Eagly (1974) finds that lowering the perceptibility of the message with a poor-quality audiotape recording reliably lowers message retention.

Picture Elements in Context

Viewers' perception of images involves both sensing and recognizing visual objects and scenes and, like word perception, is highly context dependent. For example, individual facial elements, such as an eye, nose, or chin, are more difficult to recognize in isolation than when viewed in the context of a face (Palmer 1975). Biederman and coauthors (1973) show that context is also an important aid to the perception of visual scenes. The researchers presented viewers with two versions of the same street scene. The first was a normal photograph. The second was the same photograph but cut into six equal squares that were then rearranged and glued together. Viewers were much more accurate identifying the objects in the first unaltered version of the street scene.

Graphs with Easy-to-Discriminate Symbols

Viewers' perception of charts and graphs involves both sensing and recognizing graphic elements. Perceptual research indicates that small solid symbols such as triangles, squares, and circles often become difficult to perceive when clustered together in the same line graph (Chen 1982; Cleveland & McGill 1984; Kosslyn 1994). On the other hand, distinctively shaped symbols such as a solid triangle, an "x", a solid circle, and an empty square are easy to discriminate.

The use of different colors can help viewers rapidly discriminate elements of some graphs (Lewandowsky & Spence 1989). However, for people who suffer from color blindness, differences among color-coded items can be impossible to discern. Black-and-white displays with highly differentiated symbols are almost as easy for viewers with normal vision to discern as displays that use color (Schutz 1961).

AIDS TO ATTENTION

Images, Charts, and Diagrams

If documents and slide presentations are not visually appealing, audiences may decide not to attend to them (e.g., Redish 1993; Schriver, Hayes, & Steffy Cronin 1996; Wright, Creighton, & Threlfall 1982). In a study that examined the effects of adding charts and images to text, Atman and Puerzer (1995) gave readers the same text in four different formats as shown in Figure 4.4: Paragraph format, bullet point format, text block format with a flow chart, and text block format with a diagram. Although they found no significant differences in comprehension, they did find that readers overwhelmingly preferred the text block accompanied by the diagram. The researchers conclude that such a preference may encourage readers to attend to the text for longer periods of time.

Audiences tend to find photographic images in documents and slide presentations to be attention getting. Diamond (1968) studied 300 adult consumers reading magazines to determine which magazine ad formats attract the most attention. The consumers were exposed to a total of 1,070 magazine ads. Ads with more photos and fewer words attracted more attention than other ads. Moreover, ads that include images produce more definite intentions to buy the advertised product than do ads without images (Mitchell & Olson 1981; Rossiter & Percy 1978).

On the other hand, interesting but irrelevant images can degrade the decision-making process. Merely decorative images in documents or slide presentations distract readers and viewers from the content (Peeck 1987) and unlike relevant images, impair memory for the message (Levin, Anglin, & Carney 1987). Vivid images aid message recall, but only if they are congruent with the message content (Smith & Shaffer 2000). When vivid but incongruent images are added to a message, the audience's attention to the message is actually reduced.

The physical placement of charts, graphs, and images in a document or slide show also affects readers' attention. When related words and pictures are separated from each other, readers became distracted from thinking about the message and often become annoyed (Sweller, Chandler, Tierney, & Cooper 1990). Charts and graphs that are positioned at the end of a report instead of in proximity to their mention create difficulties for readers as well (Winn 1991).

White Space

Audiences find documents and slides to be more visually appealing and attention getting if they have white space. Documents with ample white space attract and hold readers' attention longer than do documents with little white space (Strong 1926). Newspaper readers rate news stories with wide margins as more appealing than the same stories with little white space, although there is no difference in the readers' understanding of the story (Smith & McCombs 1971). Similarly, teachers rate instructional materials that use white space to separate sections higher than they rate instructional materials that do not use white space (Drew, Altman, & Dykes 1971).

Prominent Size and Placement

Size and placement in a document or slide presentation can also affect audience attention. For example, magazine readers give more attention to larger magazine ads than to smaller ones (Diamond 1968). In addition, larger images increase ad recognition (Hendon 1973; Holbrook & Lehmann 1980). Magazine readers' attention also increases when the ad is placed either on a right-hand page, on the cover of the magazine, or at the beginning of the magazine.

In addition to being more attention getting, a well-designed document or slide show in terms of typography, layout, and white space aids the comprehension of poorly motivated readers (cf., McLaughlin 1966). Ultimately, layouts and formats can affect the persuasive appeal of texts. In their study of consumers reading different versions of product warning labels, Viscusi and colleagues (1986) show that different formats have varying effects on consumers' intentions to take precautions.

Titles and Section Headings

Titles and section headings can attract attention both to themselves and to the sections of text they precede. They can affect what information in a document or slide presentation is attended to and how that information gets organized in the reader's memory (cf., Kozminsky 1977). A large sample study of the effectiveness of magazine advertising inserts finds that titles and section headings are often the only verbal elements of an ad to be attended to and read. About half of the consumers who received the inserts did not read them at all. Of the 50% who read the insert, most read only the insert's headlines (Wheildon 1995).

Informative section headings increase the likelihood that readers will attend to and recall information in a document (Allen 1970; Ausubel & Fitzgerald 1961, 1962). In a test of the effects of informative section headings, Charrow and Redish (1980) gave expert consumers four warranties for new TVs written in plain English that had no

GLOBAL WARMING

What is The Greenhouse Effect?

Energy from the sun (mainly light) passes through the earth's atmosphere. Some of it is reflected back into space by clouds and light-colored parts of the earth (like snow). Most of the energy is absorbed by the atmosphere and the earth's surface. The earth and astmosphere warm up and try to radiate heat back to space.

Greenhouse gases in the atmosphere trap this energy for a time in the earth's atmosphere. Greenhouse gases include water vapor, carbon dioxide, methane, nitrous oxide and chlorofluorocarbons (CFCs). This process is called the greenhouse effect becasue the greenhouse gases trap heat in the atmosphere in the same way that glass traps heat in a greenhouse.

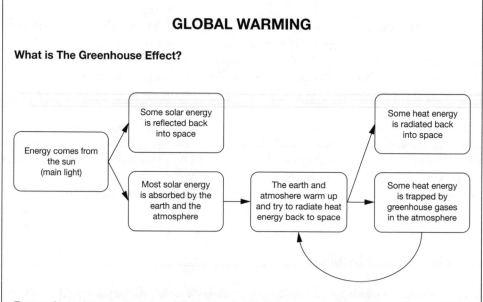

GLOBAL WARMING

What is The Greenhouse Effect?

Energy from the sun (mainly light) passes through the earth's atmosphere. Some of it is reflected back into space by clouds and light-colored parts of the earth (like snow). Most of the energy is absorbed by the atmosphere and the earth's surface. The earth and astmosphere warm up and try to radiate heat back to space. Greenhouse gases in the atmosphere trap this energy for a time in the earth's atmosphere. Greenhouse gases include water vapor, carbon dioxide, methane, nitrous oxide and chlorofluorocarbons (CFCs). This process is called the greenhouse effect becasue the greenhouse gases trap heat in the atmosphere in the same way that glass traps heat in a greenhouse.

Figure 4.4 Which Version of the Document (*above and right*) is Most Attention Getting?

GLOBAL WARMING

What is The Greenhouse Effect?

• Energy from the sun (mainly light) passes through the earth's atmosphere.

• Some of it is reflected back into space by clouds and light-colored parts of the earth (like snow). Most of the energy is absorbed by the atmosphere and the earth's surface.

• The earth and astmosphere warm up and try to radiate heat back to space.

• Greenhouse gases in the atmosphere trap this energy for a time in the earth's atmosphere. Greenhouse gases include water vapor, carbon dioxide, methane, nitrous oxide and chlorofluorocarbons (CFCs).

• This process is called the greenhouse effect becasue the greenhouse gases trap heat in the atmosphere in the same way that glass traps heat in a greenhouse.

GLOBAL WARMING

What is The Greenhouse Effect?

Energy from the sun (mainly light) passes through the earth's atmosphere. Some of it is reflected back into space by clouds and light-colored parts of the earth (like snow). Most of the energy is absorbed by the atmosphere and the earth's surface. The earth and astmosphere warm up and try to radiate heat back to space. Greenhouse gases in the atmosphere trap this energy for a time in the earth's atmosphere. Greenhouse gases include water vapor, carbon dioxide, methane, nitrous oxide and chlorofluorocarbons (CFCs). This process is called the greenhouse effect becasue the greenhouse gases trap heat in the atmosphere in the same way that glass traps heat in a greenhouse.

Figure 4.4 continued . . .

section headings and four warranties that included section headings and then tested the consumers' comprehension of the warranties. The section headings used were: "Who was covered? What was covered? What was not covered? What the manufacturer will do and for how long. What you must do. How to get warranty service." Although there was no difference in the time it took the consumers to read the warranties or in their comprehension of them, 90% of the consumers indicated that the warranties with section headings were easier to read. And 90% also indicated that the warranties with section headings motivated them to use and pay attention to the warranties.

In a study of print ads, Gardner (1981) investigated the effects of incorporating consumers' decision criteria into the headlines of print advertisements for unfamiliar brands. For example, after finding that consumers selected cooking oils partly on the basis of their scent, Gardner tested an ad headline for a fictitious brand of cooking oil that read "Pleasantly Scented Cooper's Cooking Oil." The presence of a decision criterion for the product class in an advertisement's headline facilitated recall of that criterion and inhibited recall of other decision criteria for both expert and novice consumers of cooking oils. Gardner concludes that the format, rather than the content, of an ad directs attention and determines the product attributes consumers will recall.

Color Coding and Boldface

Typographic cues can attract readers' attention as long as they are not over-used (Spyridakis 1989a, 1989b). For example, selective color coding and underlining can draw attention to important ideas (Anderson 1967; Briggs, Campeau, Gagne, & May 1966; Crouse & Idstein 1972). In most contexts, boldface attracts attention, even more so than does upper case (Coles & Foster 1975; Foster & Coles 1977). Used correctly, boldface is not only an effective attention-getting technique, it can also help readers comprehend information and follow directions more accurately (Poulton & Brown 1968; Salcedo et al. 1972). Moreover, boldface can be read as quickly as ordinary lower-case type (Tinker 1965).

As a general rule, readers pay attention to contrast among typographic elements (Spencer, Reynolds, & Coe 1974). The use of too many different highlighting techniques can be confusing and can impair readers' understanding of the text (Glynn & Di Vesta 1979; Hershberger & Terry 1965). When typographic cues are overdone, they may have the opposite effect as was intended. For example, the extensive use of italic in continuous prose may make non-italicized words more attention getting than the italicized words (Glynn, Britton, & Tillman 1985).

Personally Relevant Information

Whether in written or spoken form, some verbal content is highly attention getting. For example, personally relevant information is more attention getting and has a greater impact on the audience's judgment than information that lacks personal relevance (Sivacek & Crano 1982). Information relevant to the audience's current goals and intentions is especially attention getting (Bruner 1957; Tversky & Kahneman 1973).

For example, information about food is attention getting to audiences who are hungry, and information about entertainment is attention getting to audiences who are bored (Klinger 1975). Simply changing the pronouns in a message to enhance personal relevance (e.g., addressing the audience directly as *you* versus *one*) can increase their attention and message processing (Burnkrant & Unnava 1989).

The Verbal Style of the Powerful

The verbal style in which a message is written or spoken can influence the amount of attention that the audience will give it. Erickson and coauthors (1978) identified the verbal cues that indicate the social status and power of speakers. The "powerless" style includes frequent use of such linguistic features as intensifiers (e.g., *very, really*), hedges (e.g., *probably, I think*), hesitation forms (e.g., *uh, and uh*), and questioning intonations, whereas the "powerful" style is marked by less frequent use of these features. The researchers asked 152 undergraduates to listen to or read the testimony given by a witness who used either a powerful or a powerless style to deliver the same substantive evidence. Both the listeners and readers of the testimony given in the powerful style paid greater attention to it than did the listeners or readers of the testimony given in the powerless style.

Spoken versus Written Messages

In most cases, spoken information is more attention getting, memorable, and influential on decision making than is printed information. Grass and Wallace (1974) compared audience recall of TV commercials with specially matched print advertisements that used an image from the commercial as the pictorial component of the ad and the verbatim audio script of the commercial as the ad copy. Overall recall in the study was 81% for TV ads versus 56% for print ads. Recall of the main message point was 75% for TV ads versus 39% for print ads. The researchers hypothesize that the superior performance of TV commercials over print advertisements was due to the fact that TV commercials are more attention getting.

Even attention-getting TV commercials are susceptible to "wear out" and are likely to be ignored when they are repeated too often (e.g., Calder & Sternthal 1980; Craig, Sternthal, & Leavitt 1976). Similarly, college lectures are likely to be ignored if the students listening to them possess too much prior knowledge about the lecture's topic (Nicosia 1988).

Vocal Variety and Speed

It should come as no surprise that certain types of speech behaviors are more attention getting than others. Vocal variety—including variations in tempo, pitch, intensity, and tone quality—increases attention to speech and improves listeners' comprehension (Burgoon, Buller, & Woodall 1989).

Faster speech is more attention getting as well. In a test of listener attention, Chattopadhyay and colleagues (2003) varied three voice characteristics of broadcast ad announcers related to speech rate—syllable speed, pauses between phrases, and pitch. The increase in speech rate led listeners to attend to the ad more carefully and thereby enhanced their processing of it. Other researchers confirm that listeners pay more attention to and better comprehend messages that are delivered at rates 25% or 50% faster than the normal conversational rates (Duker 1974; LaBarbera & MacLachlan 1979). However, more complex and difficult information must be presented at a slower pace in order to avoid harming comprehension.

Expressive Nonverbal Behaviors

Expressive nonverbal behaviors can be attention getting as well. In a comparison of expressive and unexpressive nonverbal styles, Hrubes (2001) asked undergraduates to watch a video of a graduate student speaking against a ban on fraternities and sororities at a nearby college. The graduate student delivered the arguments either in an expressive nonverbal style or in an unexpressive nonverbal style. When the graduate student spoke using an expressive nonverbal style, she maintained constant eye contact with the audience, made appropriate hand and head gestures, made many facial expressions, and a varied her tone of voice. When she spoke using an unexpressive style, she made little eye contact, no hand or head gestures, few facial expressions, and spoke in a monotone voice.

Undergraduates who watched the expressive nonverbal delivery reported that they tried harder to attend to arguments than did students who watched the unexpressive delivery. In addition, the undergraduates who watched the expressive nonverbal delivery were able to discriminate strong from weak arguments better than the students who watched the unexpressive delivery.

Color Images and 3-D Effects

Although any image is likely to be attention getting, some images are more attention getting than others. For example, viewers recall more information from color than from black-and-white photographs and also rate color photographs as more attractive and attention getting (Katzman & Nyenhuis 1972). Charts and graphs that effectively use contrast and color are also more attention getting than those that do not (cf., Kosslyn 1994). Although some graphic design experts advise against it, the use of an attention-getting third dimension in charts does not necessarily reduce the viewer's accuracy or speed of making comparisons (Spence 1990). Aids to viewers' attention to other people are treated separately in Chapter 6. Emotional images that attract viewers' attention are explored in Chapter 7.

AIDS TO SENTENCE-LEVEL COMPREHENSION

Comprehension as defined in this section refers to comprehension of individual sentences and graphics as opposed to comprehension of discourse—groups of sentences in paragraphs, documents, or presentations. Discourse comprehension depends on schema activation, the topic of the next section. As Chapter 3 explains, sentence comprehension involves three major subprocesses: syntactic analysis, semantic analysis, and referential representation (Just & Carpenter 1987). Aids to each of these three subprocesses make sentence comprehension easier.

Short Words and Sentences

Aids to the first subprocess, syntactic analysis, make it easier for the audience to determine the grammatical role each word plays in a sentence. A rough measure of syntactic complexity is sentence length. For this reason, longer sentences tend to be more difficult to understand than shorter ones (see Redish 1980 for a review of the research). In addition, when the individual words that are inputs to syntactic analysis are long, complex in meaning, or infrequently used, the task of understanding a sentence becomes even more difficult (Clark 1969; Clark & Chase 1972; Just & Clark 1973). Thus, two aids to sentence comprehension would appear to be the use of short sentences and easily understood words.

Readability formulas implicitly advocate keeping words and sentences short as an aid to reading comprehension. The formulas use sentence length and measures of word difficulty to estimate the difficulty or ease of comprehending prose passages. Readability formulas are based on studies that show that vocabulary difficulty and syntactic complexity account for a large proportion of the variance in reading comprehension (Chall 1958; Klare 1963, 1984).

Three popular readability formulas are the Flesch readability formula (Flesch 1948), the FOG index readability formula (Gunning 1964), and the Dale-Chall readability formula (Dale & Chall 1948). The Flesch formula assigns passages of prose a reading ease score, 100 being the easiest and 0 being the most difficult. The FOG index and the Dale-Chall formula both assign passages a reading grade level from 1 to 12, 1 indicating that the passage could be understood by the typical first grader.

Although ideas expressed in short sentences are usually easier to understand than ideas expressed in long sentences, it is debatable whether readability formulas are useful guidelines for revising difficult-to-comprehend sentences and discourse (cf., Duffy & Kabance 1982). On the one hand, shortening long sentences has been shown to aid

Table 4.2 How Three Readability Formulas Calculate Reading Ease

The Flesch readability formula calculates reading ease as follows. Reading ease = **206.835 – 0.846 (number of syllables per 100 words) – 1.015 (average number of words per sentence)**

The FOG index is very similar: Reading grade = **0.4 (average number of words per sentence + the percent of words of more than 2 syllables)**

In the Dale-Chall formula, word familiarity replaces syllable length: Reading grade = **0.16 (percent of uncommon words) + 0.05 (average number of words per sentence)**

readers' understanding of written prose (Coleman 1962). On the other hand, a number of studies show that improving readability as measured by readability formulas does not reliably affect readers' comprehension or recall of material (Klare 1963, p. 14). Adding even more complexity is the fact that different formulas sometimes assign dramatically different reading levels to the same passage.

In a test of revised jury instructions, Charrow and Charrow (1979) show that revised instructions that simply improve readability scores result in no greater recall or ability to paraphrase than the original instructions. In a similar study, Charrow (1988) asked car owners to read three versions of an automobile recall letter. The original version of the recall letter scored "difficult" on the Flesch scale. A revision of the recall letter lowered the score to "fairly easy." Car owners who read the revised letter did not have significantly better comprehension than those who read the original version. For readability-based revisions to improve comprehension, the revisions must lower the grade level by at least 6.5 grades (Klare 1976).

Simple Sentence Structure

One reason for the seemingly contradictory findings about readability is that sentence length is only a rough measure of syntactic difficulty (Bever 1970; Fodor, Bever, & Garrett 1974). Another cause of syntactic problems is the placement of phrases and clauses within sentences. For example, sentences with subordinate clauses placed in the middle of them are more difficult to understand than are sentences with clauses placed at beginning (Clark & Clark 1968; Schwartz, Sparkman, & Deese 1970; Stolz 1967). Sentences with phrases added either to the beginning or middle are more difficult to comprehend than are sentences with phrases added to the end (Fodor et al. 1974; Hakes & Cairns 1970; Larkin & Burns 1977). And sentences with more embedded propositions take longer to read than do less syntactically complex sentences of equal length (Kintsch & Keenan 1973).

Additional reasons why readability formulas are incomplete guidelines for revision abound. Although readability formulas measure word difficulty and sentence length, they do not measure other factors that affect the audience's comprehension of a text. These factors include the text's organization and cohesiveness, the reader's prior knowledge, and how well the purpose of the text matches the purpose of the reader. In fact, readability formulas cannot distinguish a meaningful sequence of sentences from a sequence of randomly selected sentences. Even complete nonsense or scrambled sentences can score as very readable (Klare 1963, p. 162).

Parallel Sentence Structure

Another aid to syntactic analysis in particular and to comprehension in general is the use of *parallelism*, or the repetition of the syntax of a clause or sentence in the clause or sentence that immediately follows it. As illustrated in Table 4.3 below, parallelism is a technique job applicants often use when listing their accomplishments in their résumés. Notice how each bulleted sentence starts with an active verb in the past tense.

Table 4.3 Examples of Sentences Written in Parallel from an MBA's Résumé

- Achieved 100% increase in reporting and administrative productivity by developing local information system using database and corporate payroll software.

- Generated 30% increase in delivery reliability and 40% decrease in backorders from in-house supplier by implementing order entry process enhancements.

- Led team of marketing managers to redesign departmental structure. Increased customer focus through addition of product training and market analysis functions.

Sentences and clauses in parallel can be read and comprehended more quickly than those that are not. Frazier and coauthors (1984) determined how much time it took 72 undergraduates to read each sentence in a set of 60 sentences. Each sentence consisted of two clauses that either were or were not parallel. Each sentence also varied according to style (e.g., active voice versus passive voice, animate object versus inanimate object). For each style of sentence tested, the undergraduates read the second clause consistently faster when the first clause was parallel to it. A similar study of readers reading parallel clauses in compound sentences demonstrates that when syntactic structures are the same in both clauses, recall is enhanced regardless of the particular syntactic form tested (Kamil 1972).

Active Voice in Most Cases

Aids to the second subprocess in sentence comprehension, semantic analysis, make it easier for the audience to grasp the conceptual relationships, or case roles, among the words in a clause such as agent, object, instrument, or location (cf., Fillmore 1968). In other words, they make it easier to determine who did what to whom. Semantic analysis is typically easier for audiences when sentences are written in the active voice than when they are written in the passive voice (Gough 1966; Savin & Perchonock 1965; Slobin 1966).

Active voice sentence:	Our firm made a profit.
Passive voice sentence:	A profit was made by our firm.

In most cases, audiences not only find active sentences to be easier to comprehend than passive sentences, they also find them easier to recall (Clifton & Odom 1966; Kulhavy & Heinen 1977; Layton & Simpson 1975). Passive sentences are especially difficult to understand when they give sentences the wrong focus (Johnson-Laird 1968; Turner & Rommetveit 1968). For example, the passive sentence highlighted above would present even more difficulties to audiences in the context of a paragraph about "our firm" since its grammatical subject makes the focus of the sentence "a profit" as opposed to "our firm."

Sentences in which the verb expresses the action and the subject identifies the actor (as is the case for most but not all active sentences) are more concrete and easier for audiences to visualize than other types of sentences. Thus, semantic analysis goes more smoothly when the action of a sentence is expressed as an active verb rather than as a nominalized verb (Coleman 1964) or as part of a multiple-word noun string (Gleitman & Gleitman 1970).

Action as a nominalized verb:	The **expectation** was that we would get invited.
Actor as subject, action as verb:	**We expected** to get invited.
Action in a noun string:	**Event admittance tag distribution** took place yesterday.
Actor as subject, action as verb:	Yesterday, **someone distributed** tags that admit people to the event.

In a think-aloud study of readers reading hard-to-comprehend government regulations, Flower and colleagues (1983) found that readers spontaneously transformed the abstract, passive-nominal sentences in the regulations into concrete, active-verbal sentences in order to comprehend their meaning. When writers revised the sentences in the regulations by making similar transformations, readers' comprehension increased. The before and after paragraphs below from Felker and coauthors (1985, pp. 53–54) illustrate this type of revision based on semantic analysis.

Original paragraph written in an abstract, passive-nominal style

The Protocol Familiarization Period may be employed to run additional preliminary tests of the performance of the device. These tests may evaluate linearity, recovery, or any other feature not addressed in this document. The purpose of such preliminary acceptability tests should be the early discovery of any serious problems with the device. If such problems are encountered, the manufacturer should be contacted to determine the cause of error. No final judgment as to the acceptability of the device should be made from such limited tests.

Revised paragraph written in a concrete, active-verbal style

While practicing the experiment, you can also test other features of the equipment, such as linearity or recovery. Use these tests to see if there are any serious problems with the equipment. If you find any problems, contact the manufacturer to find out what is causing the problem. Don't decide if the equipment is acceptable solely on the basis of these limited, preliminary tests.

Passive Voice in Some Cases

When the object of the action is the intended focus of a sentence or paragraph, audiences find passive sentences easier to comprehend and recall than active sentences (Charrow & Charrow 1979; Hupet & Le Bouedec 1975; Johnson-Laird 1968). As illustrated in the two pairs of sentences below, passive sentences are more accurately comprehended than active sentences when the preceding sentence contains the antecedent for the subject of the passive sentence (Glucksberg, Trabasso, & Wald 1973; Olson & Filby 1972). In the first pair of sentences below, both sentences are written in the active voice. In the second pair, an active voice sentence is followed by a passive voice sentence, yet sentence pairs like this are more quickly comprehended.

> The batter hit the ball over the short stop. The left fielder caught it.
>
> The batter hit the ball over the short stop. It was caught by the left fielder.

Concrete Words

The use of concrete words aids sentence comprehension. In a study comparing concrete versus abstract language, Sadoski and coauthors (1995) asked readers to read and recall four texts that were written either in abstract or concrete language about either a familiar or an unfamiliar topic. Each of the four texts contained the same number of sentences with the same sentence lengths and scored the same when rated for cohesion and readability. Readers recalled texts about familiar topics better when they were written in concrete as opposed to abstract language. And readers recalled texts about unfamiliar topics written in concrete language just as well as they recalled texts about familiar topics written in abstract language.

Audiences more easily understand sentences rated high in imagery value than sentences rated low in imagery value (Holyoak 1974). Audiences can comprehend high-imagery sentences 30% faster on average than low-imagery sentences (Jorgensen & Kintsch 1973). High-imagery verbs can have a dramatic effect on recall. For instance, Graves and Slater (1986) asked *Time/Life* editors to revise a section of a history textbook. The *Time/Life* editors replaced less vivid verbs such as *increased* with high-imagery verbs such as *skyrocketed*. The editors also added high-imagery anecdotes and quotations from other sources. Students' recall of the textbook improved by 40%. Concrete language is more memorable because it permits pictorial as well as verbal coding by readers during the comprehension process (Sadoski & Paivio 2001).

Sentences in the Affirmative

Avoiding the use of negative words in sentences (e.g., *not, none*) simplifies semantic processing and aids sentence comprehension. The use of negative words, on the other hand, makes sentence comprehension more difficult (Jacoby, Nelson, & Hoyer 1982; Ratner & Gleason 1993; Sherman 1976). Negative words also slow down reading speed. In a study of sentences written in the negative or affirmative, Clark and Chase (1972) gave readers cards with symbols on them and asked the readers to verify true and false affirmative and negative sentences about each card. Readers took longer to verify negative sentences than they did to verify affirmative sentences and longer to identify false sentences than true sentences.

Easy-to-Identify Referents

The third subprocess in sentence comprehension is referential representation. This process identifies the references that words in a sentence make to the external world (e.g., understanding that the words *majority whip* refer to a member of Congress and not to an instrument for flogging the rest of us). The process also identifies the antecedents or referents of pronouns.

Referential representation is aided by making referents easy to identify. Readers take less time to identify the referent of a pronoun when the referent has been mentioned recently in the text than when it was mentioned earlier (Ehrlich & Rayner 1983). Each sentence that comes between a pronoun and the antecedent it refers to increases the time the audience needs to assign a referent to the pronoun (Clark & Sengul 1979). In addition, audiences make more errors in choosing the correct referent as the number of sentences between the pronoun and its antecedent increases (Daneman & Carpenter 1980).

The likelihood that the audience will choose the correct referent can be increased by the use of *the* in front of a repeated noun phrase (de Villiers 1974). It can also be increased by the use of a synonym. When a synonym is used in one sentence to refer to an object mentioned in the prior sentence (e.g., *jet* to refer to *airplane*), the time the audience needs to comprehend the sentence containing the synonym is no greater than if the same word had been used in it (Yekovich & Walker 1978). Repeating the referent instead of using a pronoun can actually slow down the comprehension process in some cases (Gordon & Chan 1995). For example, after reading the sentence "Bill bought a car," readers take longer to comprehend the sentence "Bill drove it home" than they do to comprehend the sentence "He drove it home."

Repetition of Concepts within Paragraphs

An additional aid to referential representation in particular and to comprehension in general is the repetition of concepts in the sentences within a paragraph. The number of new ideas introduced in sentences creates more comprehension problems for audiences than does the number of words in them (Kintsch & Kozminsky 1977; Kintsch & Vipond 1979). Repeated concepts in a sequence of sentences make it easier for readers to integrate their referential representations of individual sentences into a coherent whole (Just & Carpenter 1987, p. 217). Repeated references and concepts can decrease reading time and increase recall of text as an integrated unit (cf., Goetz & Armbruster 1980). Thus, readers take longer to read sentences in paragraphs that introduce many new concepts than they do to read sentences in paragraphs in which a few concepts reoccur repeatedly (Manelis & Yekovich 1976).

Reading rate and recall both increase if the number of new ideas in paragraph sentences is lowered by including examples and paraphrases in the paragraph (Wright 1968; Frase & Fisher 1976) or by restricting all the sentences in a paragraph to the amplification of just one or two main points.

Pictorial Illustrations

Pictorial illustrations can aid sentence comprehension (Glenberg & Langston 1992; Larkin & Simon 1987; Mayer & Gallini 1990). Pictorial illustrations provide visual referents to the words in sentences. Thus, words and pictures presented together can enhance recall and comprehension more than the same words and pictures presented separately (Hegarty & Just 1993; Mayer & Sims 1994).

In a review of 46 experimental studies, Levie and Lentz (1982) compared the effects of text only, of illustrations only, or of both text and illustrations on readers' comprehension. In 81% of the studies, readers' comprehension was better for text and pictures than text alone. On average, people with poor reading skills performed 44% better with text and illustrations than with text alone. More skilled readers performed 23% better. Still photographs may be just as effective in aiding sentence comprehension as video. In studies of TV news viewers, still photographs or graphics enhanced comprehension of TV news just as much as live video footage, although TV news viewers prefer as much live footage as possible (Findahl 1971; Findahl & Hoijer 1976; Gunter 1987, p. 248).

However, pictures do not always enhance sentence comprehension. In a study of instructional materials, Westendorp (1995) compared seven different picture/text combinations as consumers tried to follow a set of instructions for using a new telephone system that was loaded with features. Surprisingly, the "words only" version enabled readers to follow the instructions more quickly and accurately than the versions in which pictures accompanied text.

Illustrations will enhance comprehension only if they are of high quality and if they are relevant to the accompanying text (Duchastel 1979, 1980; Macdonald-Ross 1978). When prose and pictures intended to work together are poorly written, poorly visualized, contradictory, or not complementary, the audience's comprehension will suffer (Benson 1994; Gunter 1987; Levin et al. 1987). The audience's comprehension will also suffer if they initially focus on a sentence or headline before focusing on the picture that accompanies it, particularly if the sentence or headline is high in visual imagery (Glass, Eddy, & Schwanenflugel 1980).

Speakers' Nonverbal Behaviors

Most aids to sentence comprehension are equally helpful to both readers and listeners. Other aids are specifically helpful to listeners. For example, listeners better understand speakers' answers to their questions about the size and relative position of objects when speakers gesture while verbally describing the objects (Beattie & Shovelton 1999).

Hand gestures can play an important role in listeners' comprehension and memory especially when the speaker's message is somewhat ambiguous. Emblematic gestures, such as the OK sign and extending two fingers to signal *two,* are especially helpful in aiding memory for verbal information. In their research, Woodall and Folger (1981, 1985) find that listeners recall 34% of a message when the speaker accompanies it with emblematic gestures, 11% when the speaker accompanies it with emphasizing gestures, and only 5% when the speaker does not make any gestures.

Other nonverbal behaviors, such as nodding, eye movements, and lip and facial movements, can also improve listeners' comprehension of the speaker's message (Rogers 1978). However, some types of information may be equally well understood even when listeners cannot see the speakers' nonverbal behaviors. For example, college students who listen to audio taped lectures can comprehend just as much of the lectures as can students who view the actual lectures (Popham 1961; Menne, Klingensmith, & Nord 1969).

Labeled Plot Lines in Graphs

Placing labels next to plot lines aids graph comprehension. Audiences can comprehend graphs whose plot lines are labeled faster than they can comprehend graphs with legends (Milroy & Poulton 1978).

The Elimination of Unnecessary Graphic Elements

Avoiding the use of arbitrary symbols in graphs also aids graph comprehension (Fienberg 1979). Conversely, the use of arbitrary symbols such as stars, ships, castles, trees (Kleiner & Hartigan 1981) as well as faces (Chernoff 1973) makes graph comprehension more difficult. Audience comprehension of graphs is also easier when the quantitative relations in the graphs are plotted conventionally (Gattis & Holyoak 1996). For example, a steeper slope usually implies faster change. But if a graph is plotted unconventionally, audience members may assume a steeper slope represents a faster rate of change when it does not.

AIDS TO SCHEMA ACTIVATION

In order to comprehend and use the information in a paragraph, document, image, or presentation, the audience must first activate the appropriate schema. Audiences must activate the appropriate schema regardless of the communicator's purpose—whether it is to inform, instruct, entertain, or to persuade the audience to make a decision. Any contextual information—such as a title, section heading, or introductory paragraph— can help audiences activate the right schema. The right graph or picture can also activate the appropriate schema and portray the "big picture" at a single glance (Holliday 1975; Holliday, Brunner, & Donais 1977; Holliday & Harvey 1976).

Titles

Titles activate readers' schemata and in doing so make text easier to comprehend and recall (Bransford & Johnson 1973; von Hippel, Jonides, Hilton, & Narayan 1993). In their seminal study of titles and schema activation (described in detail on p. 114), Bransford and Johnson (1972, 1973) gave readers a paragraph that seemed nonsensical to them until they were provided with the title "Washing Clothes." The title activated the appropriate schema for interpreting the various activities involved in washing clothes that were described in the paragraph. By activating the appropriate schema, titles help readers comprehend inter-sentence coherence in paragraphs and longer passages (Anderson, Spiro, & Anderson 1978; Dansereau, Brooks, Spurlin, & Holley 1982).

In addition, titles systematically bias recall of messages in the direction of the title (Kozminsky 1977). By activating one schema as opposed to another, titles also bias comprehension. Schallert (1976) gave readers paragraphs that could be interpreted in two different ways depending on the title that introduced them. For example, the same paragraph could be interpreted as being about "the worries of a baseball team manager" or "the worries of a glassware factory manager" (Schallert 1976, p. 622). The titles determined how readers comprehended the paragraph by making one schema more accessible than another.

Section Headings

Like good titles, good section headings can aid comprehension and recall by activating the appropriate schema (Bransford & McCarrell 1972). Informative section headings aid a reader's understanding of the prose content that immediately follows (Dooling & Mullet 1973; Sjogren & Timpson 1979). In a study of the effects of section headings, Dansereau and coauthors (1982) asked students to read texts with and without embedded section headings and then tested their recall and comprehension. Students who read the texts with section headings had significantly higher scores on comprehension and recall than those who read the texts without headings.

Section headings in either statement or question form (e.g., *The Management Team Is Respected Industry Wide* versus *Who is the management team?*) can help audiences recall and retrieve information from both familiar and unfamiliar texts (Hartley & Trueman 1982). But bad section headings can mislead readers. In a study of government regulations, Swarts and coauthors (1980) discovered that the section headings of the original regulations were uninformative nouns and phrases: "Definitions," "General Policy," "Requirements," "Procedure," and "Use of Advance Payment Funds." When readers were given more informative section headings (e.g., "Setting Up the Bank Account"), they performed significantly better both in predicting what information would follow each heading and in matching headings with the appropriate text.

Topic Sentences at the Beginning of Paragraphs

Schemata can be activated by placing the topic or theme of a paragraph in the first sentence of the paragraph. The use of topic sentences improves reading speed, accuracy of recall, and the reader's ability to identify the main point of the paragraph (Kieras 1978; Kintsch 1979; Kintsch & van Dijk 1978). The systematic grouping of sentences under subordinate topics also produces better recall than random arrangements of sentences (Myers, Pezdek, & Coulson 1973; Perlmutter & Royer 1973). Hierarchically structuring major points before minor points makes prose easier to recall as well (Gardner & Schumacher 1977; Meyer & McConkie 1973).

An Introductory Decision Matrix

Novice audiences who have never made a particular type of decision before may need to see the appropriate decision schema represented as a decision matrix before they can activate it. In a think-aloud study of novice consumers reading revisions of an automobile liability insurance policy, Swaney and colleagues (1991) found that the novices had difficulty comprehending the first revision of the original policy although the writers had solved all of the lexical and structural problems in it. Novice consumers often raised the wrong questions about the revised policy. For example, they asked why the policy did not mention deductibles and their own injuries and damages. The researchers concluded that the novice consumers lacked the appropriate schema for understanding the different types of car insurance. To provide the needed schema, the researchers started the final revision with a matrix that described and contrasted different types of car insurance. Although the final revision was four times as long as the original policy, it took the novice consumers only half the time to read. In addition, the final revision had a comprehension error rate of 22% versus an error rate of 40% for the original. Moreover, the final revision evoked no complaints from the novice consumers whereas the original prompted many.

Initial Contextual Information

For titles, topic sentences, and other contextual information to have a positive effect, they must be presented first, before the rest of the message is delivered. In a test of the sequencing of contextual information, Townsend (1980) asked 48 undergraduates to listen to two ambiguous passages about familiar topics. The author gave half of the listeners the contextual information required to activate the appropriate schema either just before or just after hearing the passages. Townsend gave the other half either no contextual information or inappropriate contextual information about the passages. Listeners who were given the appropriate contextual information prior to hearing the passages had significantly higher recall of the material than did the other groups of listeners. Listeners given inappropriate contextual information recalled even less material than those given no contextual information. Readers who are given a title at the end of a message show no better recall than those who are not exposed to a title at all (Dooling & Mullet 1973).

Schemata can also be activated by starting a document or presentation with an overview of its purpose. Doing so helps the audience remember the information that follows (Hartley & Davies 1976; Luiten, Ames, & Ackerson 1980). However, introductory information may fail to increase recall if it is inconsistent with the audience's existing schemata (Morris, Stein, & Bransford 1979). In a study of patients reading health care pamphlets, Reid and colleagues (1994) found that a conflict between the pamphlets' introductory statements and the patients' existing schemata hindered the patients' comprehension of the information in the pamphlets.

Genre Labels

Audiences activate a genre schema that influences their interpretation of a text or speech when they are given a genre label such as *strategic plan*, *annual report*, or *sales pitch* (cf., McDaniel & Einstein 1989; Zwaan & Brown 1996). One study found consistent differences in an audience's interpretations of a story when they were told the story was an autobiography versus when they were told the story was fictional (Feldman & Kalmar 1996). Another found differences in an audience's interpretations of stories that were labeled either as spy stories or as travelogues (Kalmar 1996). In addition to genre labels, genre-specific textual features that are characteristic of a genre (e.g., "Once upon a time there lived . . .") may activate a genre schema.

Depending on the genre schema activated, the same sentence can serve very different functions. For example, in a descriptive message, the statement "The Bellagio hotel in Las Vegas cost $1.2 billion to build" functions to describe the amount of money it costs to build the hotel. In a persuasive message, the statement may provide a reason why the audience should decide to visit the hotel (Kricorian 2000).

The two mailings on the following two pages from a city's Chamber of Commerce (note: The names and addresses of the Chamber and Chamber member have been changed) illustrate the importance of genre labels and genre-specific textual features in eliciting the desired decision. Although both mailings had the same purpose, to collect dues from member organizations, their effectiveness varied significantly. The number of member organizations that paid their dues on time more than doubled when the revised letter was sent out in place of the original. The Chamber member's comments on the original mailing indicate he was making a budgetary decision rather than the compliance decision the Chamber wanted from him. He saw the mailing as more of a request for a donation than as a financial obligation that must be paid on time.

The revised mailing is titled with the label of the genre of the mailing—*Invoice*. In addition, the revised mailing includes textual features that are characteristic of that genre: It uses an invoice format as opposed to a letter format; it is addressed to a specific person in the accounts payable department who is responsible for paying the bills; and it demands, rather than requests, payment of the amount due.

Captions for Images

Similar to the way titles and headings aid text comprehension by activating the appropriate schema, captions can aid the activation of schemata needed for comprehending pictures and graphs. The use of captions can dramatically change how viewers interpret pictures (Bransford & Johnson 1972). Captions can also dramatically increase viewers' recall. In an innovative study of the importance of captions, Bower and coauthors (1975) asked viewers to look at two sets of line drawings of unintelligible objects called "droodles." A droodle is a hard-to-interpret drawing that has a funny meaning (see Price 1972). One set of drawings included explanatory captions for each drawing, the other set did not. Viewers recalled 70% of the captioned drawings but only 51% of the drawings without captions. The researchers conclude that a good memory for drawings and pictures depends on the audience's ability to interpret their meaning.

Would you have been able to guess what was depicted in each droodle from Bower and colleagues (1975) and reproduced in Figure 4.5 if you were not told that A is "A duck playing a trombone in a telephone booth" and that B is "An early bird who caught a very strong worm"?

Original Mailing with Comments from a Chamber Member

Titusville Chamber of Commerce

100 Main Street, Titusville, NC 27401

May 15, 2004

Nanolinc, Inc.
445 Technology Drive
Titusville, NC 27401

Dear Chamber Member, **[This letter's sent to a Chamber member. It has my address on it, but it doesn't have my name.[1]]**

Your membership in the Chamber of Commerce is set to expire at the end of this month. Please detach the lower portion of this billing and submit it with your annual dues payment of $1,250.00 to:

[It sounds like, reading this letter . . . I feel it's very . . . It's not personalized.[2]]

> Titusville Chamber of Commerce
> 100 Main Street
> Titusville, NC 27401

We appreciate your continued support. **[So I have continued to pay.[3] It doesn't create any urgency for me to pay this bill.[4] So I feel that I don't have to pay this right away. I can probably hold on to it for a little while with no repercussions and maybe pay it next quarter instead of this lump sum hitting on this quarter. So I think I'll hold on to this until, oh, until the third quarter at least. And then I'll pay my dues for the Chamber.[5]]**

Please find enclosed $1,250.00. This amount is payment in full of the dues for:

> Nanolinc, Inc.
> 445 Technology Drive
> Titusville, NC 27401

Revised Mailing

INVOICE

Invoice No: 100066
Date: May 15, 2004

From: **Titusville Chamber of Commerce**
100 Main Street
Titusville, NC 27401
Phone (336) 437–4500
Fax (336) 437–4503

To: Ms. Judy Hamric
Accounts Payable
Nanolinc, Inc.
445 Technology Drive
Titusville, NC 27401

Your Chamber membership is set to expire on June 30, 2004.

Length of membership renewal . . . . One year

TOTAL AMOUNT DUE $1,250.00

Plus additional contributions . . . . $

Amount of payment . . . . $

Please make checks payable to the Titusville Chamber of Commerce. Or try our new "Pay by Phone" service using a major credit card.

Questions about this statement? Call (336) 437–4500

Thank you for your continued support

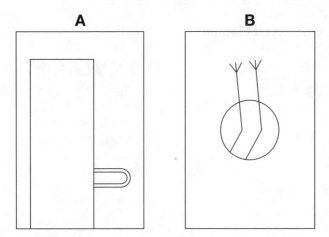

Figure 4.5 How Easy are these Drawings to Comprehend Without Captions?

AIDS TO INFORMATION ACQUISITION

After the appropriate schema for making a decision has been activated, audience members begin the information acquisition process and start to search for the information the schema requires. Section headings, global organizations, and formats that are schema based, or *task based*, can aid the audience's information-acquisition process.

Task-Based Section Headings

Task-based section headings reflect the structure and content of the audience's schema for performing a task such as operating a computer, comprehending the gist of a story, or deciding whether to buy an insurance policy. When the headings address the key questions or criteria from the audience's activated schema, they can help audiences quickly locate the information they need to complete their task (Swarts et al. 1980).

Task-Based Formats

Audiences prefer information to be expressed in the format that helps them complete their task as efficiently as possible. Consequently, audiences sometimes prefer information to be expressed in prose as opposed to chart form, as was the case for the experienced board member who commented on the strategic plan for GM in Chapter 2:

> **I'm on Section 9 looking at the McKinsey Nine Box Grid: Business Strengths, Industry Attractiveness. They indicate that they are moving**

from a low industry attractiveness today, to what they feel will be midpoint in the future with average business strengths. This kind of summary to me is not worth the paper it's written on. It could be stated in a sentence. You don't have to use a chart.[19]

At other times audiences prefer charts to prose, as was the case for the experienced investor who commented on the analyst's report on Georgia Gulf in Chapter 2:

> Salt supplied from Georgia Gulf's leased salt domes in Louisiana, is split into chlorine, caustic soda, and sodium chlorate. Annual merchant-sales capacity for these products is 118,000 tons, 501,000 tons, and 27,000 tons, respectively. **[I'd prefer that they told me what it was for each product, like 118,000 tons of chlorine, rather than otherwise.**[28]**]** The average 1987 prices of these commodities, which are collectively Inorganic Chemicals are estimated at $140 per ton, $95 per ton, and $335 per ton. **[Again, they should just chart this for me. It would be much easier to see.**[29]**]**

The best format for presenting any information—whether it be a diagram, list of bullet points, paragraph, table, or chart—varies with the purpose of the information and the task that the audience is asked to perform (Kern, Sticht, Welty, & Hauke 1977; Wright & Reid 1973). For example, graphs are a better format for helping the audience interpret trends than are tables (Wright 1977).

Task-Based Organization

Similar to task-based section headings and formats, a task-based organization of the contents of a document or presentation can help the audience locate the information it needs when it needs it. Users find training manuals easier to follow when the contents of the manuals reflect the structure of the task that they are trying to perform (Kern et al. 1977). Newspaper readers find newspaper articles easier to comprehend when their content adheres to the "newspaper schema"—headlines, leads, major events, consequences, commentaries, and evaluations (Kintsch & Yarborough 1982). In a study of story recall, Thorndyke (1977) asked one group of readers to read a story written in the conventional way and another group to read the same story with its sentences presented in a scrambled order. Readers who read the story in its original order, an order that conformed to their story schema, recalled 85% of the facts in it. Those who read the story in the scrambled order recalled only 32% of the facts in it.

Audiences make inferences about the intended reading sequence and organization of a text based on its layout on the page or presentation slide. In her study of page layouts in science textbooks, Goldsmith (1987) found that the layouts made it hard for readers to determine the order in which the information was intended to be read. Readers' actual reading order was quite different from the order the writers intended. Schriver (1997) also reports a dramatic difference between the writer's intended order and the actual order in which a two-page spread in an instruction guide was read (as described in Schriver 1997, pp. 316–320). Readers can more easily see the organization of a text when the number of different line lengths that comprise it is kept to a minimum (Bonsiepe 1968). When the layout correctly indicates the relative importance of each piece of information in it, the accuracy of readers' decisions increases (MacGregor & Slovic 1986).

The think-aloud comments in Table 4.4 below of three experts reveal the importance of task-based organization. All three experts express their frustration with the organization of the documents they are reading. Notice that the investor and the partner in the private equity firm do not wait until they run across the information they expect to be delivered, but immediately start thumbing through the long documents they have been given until they discover it.

Many documents and presentations are topic based as opposed to task based. Topic-based texts and presentations are organized around the concepts that the communicator thinks are important instead of the sequence in which the audience needs information to be presented. Topic-based texts and presentations create problems for audiences who try to use them to perform specific tasks such as make a decision or follow a set of instructions. In a study of readers' difficulties with topic-based organization, Flower and colleagues (1983) asked three experts to read and interpret a topic-based federal regulation about eligibility for Small Business Association grants and collected think-aloud comments from them. It so happened that one expert tried to use the information in the regulation to determine her own business's eligibility for a grant. During the experiment she actively searched for the information she needed. The other two experts simply followed the organization of the regulation as they read and interpreted it. The expert who actively searched for information that would help her decide if she were eligible for a grant made many more negative comments about the organization of the regulation and about the difficulty of her search process than did the other two experts. In fact, 50 of her 200 comments were complaints about the organization of the regulation.

Table 4.4 Expert Decision Makers Expect Information to be Presented in a Specific Order

---

Expert investor reading the original Smartphone MBA business plan

When I read these things I like to start off with the people involved. Is there anything in here about the background of the guy who is going to be the General Partner? [The investor then finds the General Partner's résumé in an appendix.] Oh, here he is.[12]

Partner in a private equity firm reading the acquisition plan for a textile manufacturer

What I usually like to see is a snapshot of the company, which it doesn't appear that they have. Just the company's financials, their sales, operating income at least, those two things, at least for the last three years. Depreciation and capital expenditures . . . some things to give an idea of cash flows.[11] They make you flip to the back to look through the numbers, which I will do now.[12] [The expert now turns to read Schedule A in the appendix.]

Experienced board member reading the strategic plan from General Motors

Under "Most Relevant Competitors," they've listed the three major competitor's vehicle sales growth, three-year average, the three-year profitability, and market share. Again it's just a listing of data with no insights. My sense of good strategic plan is that what one begins with is this data. One does not present data like this as a summary.[8]

The two versions of the instructions below and following illustrate the difference between topic-based and task-based organization. Both versions describe the steps soldiers must take if they are to respond quickly and effectively to chemical, biological, or radioactive attacks. However, one would expect the effectiveness of the two versions to vary considerably if soldiers were to use them in an actual attack.

We present the first version a second time in order to indicate the location in it of each step a soldier would need to take. Notice that in the original version Step 1 appears toward the end of the long paragraph and Step 5 near the beginning. Step 2 is spread throughout the paragraph. The student revision reorganizes the information in a task-based manner. It adds a section heading for each step. The revision also uses other techniques mentioned in this chapter that make it easier for readers to perceive, attend to, and comprehend the instructions.

Topic-Based Instructions

CBR: THE LOCAL ALARM
from Kern and coauthors (1977)

The local alarm (warning) is given by any person recognizing or suspecting the presence of a CBR hazard. Unit SOPs must provide for the rapid transmission of the warning to all elements of the unit and to adjacent units. Brevity codes should be used where feasible. Suspicion of the presence of a chemical hazard is reported to the unit commander for confirmation. It is important to avoid false alarms and to prevent unnecessary transmission of alarms to unaffected areas. Consistent with the mission and circumstances of the unit, the alarm will be given by use of any device that produces an audible sound that cannot be easily confused with other sounds encountered in combat. Examples of suitable devices for local alarms are empty shell cases, bells, metal triangles, vehicle horns, and iron pipes or rails. As a supplement to the audible (sound) alarms or to replace them when the tactical situation does not permit their use, certain visual signals are used to give emergency warning of a CBR hazard or attack. These visual signals consist of donning the protective mask and protective equipment, followed by an agitated action to call attention to this fact. In the event of a chemical agent attack, there is a danger of breathing in the agent if the vocal warning is given before masking. The individual suspecting or recognizing this attack will mask first and then give the alarm. The vocal alarm for chemical agent attack will be "SPRAY" for a spray attack and "GAS" for an attack delivered by other means. The vocal warning is intended for those individuals in the immediate vicinity of the person recognizing the attack. The vocal alarm does not take the place of the sound alarm or the visual signal to alert a unit of a chemical attack.

CBR: THE LOCAL ALARM
(with the location of each step indicated)

Step 2: The local alarm (warning) is given by any person recognizing or suspecting the presence of a CBR hazard. **Step 5:** Unit SOPs must provide for the rapid transmission of the warning to all elements of the unit and to adjacent units. **Step 2:** Brevity codes should be used where feasible. **Step 4:** Suspicion of the presence of a chemical hazard is reported to the unit commander for confirmation. It is important to avoid false alarms and to prevent unnecessary transmission of alarms to unaffected areas. **Step 3:** Consistent with the mission and circumstances of the unit, the alarm will be given by use of any device that produces an audible sound that cannot be easily confused with other sounds encountered in combat. Examples of suitable devices for local alarms are empty shell cases, bells, metal triangles, vehicle horns, and iron pipes or rails. **Step 2:** As a supplement to the audible (sound) alarms or to replace them when the tactical situation does not permit their use, certain visual signals are used to give emergency warning of a CBR hazard or attack. These visual signals consist of donning the protective mask and protective equipment, followed by an agitated action to call attention to this fact. **Step 1:** In the event of a chemical agent attack, there is a danger of breathing in the agent if the vocal warning is given before masking. The individual suspecting or recognizing this attack will mask first and then give the alarm. **Step 2:** The vocal alarm for chemical agent attack will be "SPRAY" for a spray attack and "GAS" for an attack delivered by other means. The vocal warning is intended for those individuals in the immediate vicinity of the person recognizing the attack. The vocal alarm does not take the place of the sound alarm or the visual signal to alert a unit of a chemical attack.

Attribute-Based Organization for Decision Making

When the audience's task is to make a decision, as opposed to follow instructions or comprehend a story, the best organization is one that promotes attribute-based processing and addresses each decision criterion in the audience's decision schema one by one (For an example, see the revised executive summary of the *Smartphone MBA* business plan on pp. 14–16).

Audiences who acquire and process information by attribute make more accurate decisions more efficiently (Payne et al. 1988). Consequently, the best decision makers are those who process by attribute, whereas the poorest decision makers are those who process by alternative (Jacoby, Kuss, Mazursky, & Troutman 1985). When audiences process by attribute, making comparisons among different alternatives is cognitively easier (Russo & Dosher 1983) and less prone to error (Jarvenpaa 1989). Interestingly, when audiences are allowed to choose an information-acquisition strategy, they tend to choose to acquire and process information by attribute (e.g., Capon & Burke 1977; Olshavsky & Acito 1980).

Although attribute-based processing affords many advantages, most audience members, especially those who are novices, generally acquire and process information in the order in which they receive it even when that order is not attribute based (Slovic 1972). Tversky (1969) suggests that if alternatives are displayed sequentially (as they are in newspaper advertisements for competing brands), processing by alternative is facilitated. If, in contrast, criteria for deciding among several alternatives are displayed simultaneously, processing by attribute is facilitated. A number of studies have verified Tversky's hypothesis. For example, a study of consumers using information displays to make decisions demonstrates that consumers tend to process information in the sequence it is displayed—either by attribute or by alternative (Jarvenpaa 1989).

Task-Based Instructions

CBR: Chemical, Biological, Radioactive

What to do in a CBR attack

"Fast action can save your life!"

Step 1: Protect yourself

Put on your gas mask. Make sure there are no gaps between your face and mask. If needed, put on other protective gear.

Step 2: Alert your neighbors

If the enemy sprays chemicals, shout "Spray!" For other attacks, shout "Gas!" Make sure the soldiers near you start to put on their masks.

If the soldiers near you don't hear you, signal to them by waving your arms and pointing to your mask. Make sure they start to put on their masks.

Step 3: Alert your entire unit

Alert the rest of your unit by banging on empty cases, ringing bells, or honking horns. Make sure all unit members start to put on their masks.

Step 4: Alert your unit commander

Run to your unit commander. Wave your arms and point to your mask. Make sure your commander sees you and nods.

Step 5: If your commander gives the "OK," alert units nearby

If your unit commander decides you are under a CBR attack, follow their instructions for alerting neighboring units.

Audiences tend to use information in the form in which it is displayed in order to reduce the cognitive effort involved in decision making (Todd & Benbasat 1991). In a study of the eye movements of consumers reading product packages, van Raaij (1976) found the package format made processing by alternative easier. In that study, fully 50% of the consumers' eye transitions were by brand (i.e., using alternative-based processing) and only 17% by attribute. Unfortunately, alternative-based organization, such as product package formats and supermarket point-of-purchase displays, hinders the ability of consumers to make product comparisons and negatively affects their ability to choose the best product (Bettman & Kakkar 1977).

One format that facilitates attribute-based processing is the matrix format. Although matrices are usually displayed as tables, both documents and presentations can reflect the matrix format and promote attribute-based processing if they address each decision criterion in the expert audience's schema one by one. All of the revised documents and effective presentation slides reproduced in this book are formatted to reflect a decision matrix in a verbal as opposed to a tabular form. The decision criteria from the audience's schema become the document's or slide presentation's outline. Keywords from the audience's decision criteria are incorporated in section headings or slide titles. Paragraphs, charts, and bullet points answer the audience's questions about each criterion and provide benchmark information for evaluating the recommended alternative.

Consumers almost always process by attribute when information about unfamiliar brands is displayed in a matrix format (Bettman & Kakkar 1977). Not only do consumers prefer the matrix format, they also make better decisions when they use it. When pricing information for competing brands is displayed in a matrix format in grocery stores, the average consumers saves about 2% more than when they view the same pricing information displayed on separate tags for each item (Russo 1977; Russo, Krieser, & Miyashita 1975).

The matrix format also outperforms other formats in terms of reducing the time audiences need to make a good decision. In a test of the matrix format, Schkade and Kleinmuntz (1994) asked 60 MBA students to choose the best loan application from sets of eight loan applications. The authors described each set of applications on four relevant attributes or criteria and presented them to the students in six different ways: Organized as a matrix or as a list, with values expressed in either verbal or numeric form, and arranged in either a sorted or random sequence. The matrix versus list organization strongly influenced the MBAs' information acquisition process and provided the largest benefit in terms of the time required to make a good decision.

Aids to Group Information Acquisition and Critical Thinking

Access to more and better information for decision making is the *raison d'être* of most groups, yet group members rarely discuss any relevant information that is not already known by the group as a whole (Gigone & Hastie 1993, 1996; Stasser & Titus 1985). Surprisingly, groups will often ignore the expertise of their most knowledgeable members (Cosier & Schwenk 1990). Thus, groups seldom realize the knowledge gains and improved decision quality that they hope for (see Mojzisch & Schulz-Hardt 2005, and Stasser & Birchmeier 2003 for reviews).

Information acquisition and decision making can be more effective when the group is small (four as opposed to eight group members) and the amount of information possessed in common by its members is minimal (Cruz, Boster, & Rodríguez 1997). If given enough time, groups overcome their tendency to discuss commonly shared information and start to discuss more information that initially is known only by single individuals within the group (Larson, Foster-Fishman, & Keys 1994). But under time pressure, groups place more emphasis on information that all members share and consequently focus on fewer alternatives (Karau & Kelly 1992; Kelly & Karau 1999).

Groups whose members propose different alternatives and have more disagreements produce better decisions than groups whose members all prefer the same alternative at the outset (Klocke 2007; Schulz-Hardt, Brodbeck, Mojzisch, Kerschreiter, & Frey 2006). In a study of groups of managers and employees, Schulz-Hardt and colleagues (2002) show that real dissent is effective in preventing a confirmatory information-acquisition bias. Simulation studies of group discussions suggest that majorities are more likely to process the information provided by dissenting minorities when the minority is able to provide more schema-relevant information than can the majority and when the minority advocates its position forcefully (Stasser & Vaughan 1996).

A number of structured group interventions have been designed to improve group information acquisition and thus enhance the quality and creativity of group decisions, but few of them have proven to be effective. Contrived dissent, encouraged by techniques such as Dialectical Inquiry and the Devil's Advocate Approach, appears to have little or no effect on decision quality or group commitment to the decision (Greitemeyer, Schulz-Hardt, Brodbeck, & Frey 2006; Robertson 2006; Schulz-Hardt et al. 2002). Brainstorming has been shown to have questionable effectiveness (Diehl & Stroebe 1987). Groups using the Stepladder Technique, a technique in which one member at a time is allowed to join the group discussion, fail to perform better than unstructured groups (Winquist & Franz 2008).

One structured technique—the multi-attribute utility decision decomposition technique—has been shown to enhance the efficient sharing of relevant information among group members and to improve decision quality (Eils & John 1980; Sainfort, Gustafson, Bosworth, & Hawkins 1990; Timmermans & Vlek 1996). This method, based on the widely used multi-attribute utility model (see Von Winterfeldt & Edwards 1986), helps group members identify and weight decision criteria, identify alternatives, assign a preference score to each alternative for each decision criteria, and determine the alternative with the highest overall score. An almost identical technique called Frame of Reference Training has also proven to be highly effective (Woehr 1994). Essentially, these techniques help group members construct a common decision matrix or shared schema and use it to determine the best alternative.

Information acquisition in groups, or the sharing of relevant unshared information during group discussions, that leads to better decisions can also be promoted by:

- Instructing the group to explicitly state its goals (Hackman 1987).
- Asking group members to keep a record of the information discussed by the group (Parks & Cowlin 1996; Sheffey, Tindale, & Scott 1989).

- Framing the group's task as a problem to be solved (Stasser & Stewart 1992). Groups given a problem/solution frame pay more attention to decision criteria that distinguish among decision alternatives than do other groups (Stewart & Stasser 1998).
- Instructing the group to think critically as opposed to asking members to reach consensus (Postmes, Spears, & Cihangir 2001).
- Making group members aware of the need to look for unshared information (Schittekatte 1996).
- Publicly designating each group member as an expert in a distinct area (Stewart & Stasser 1995).
- Asking group members to rank order decision alternatives rather than simply choose one (Hollingshead 1996).

AIDS TO INFORMATION INTEGRATION

As audience members acquire enough information to start making comparisons among alternatives, they begin to integrate that information. The information integration process is aided when documents and presentations contain only highly relevant information in limited amounts. Too much information can actually decrease the accuracy of the audience's decision. Too much information can decrease the audience's confidence in their decision as well (Heuer & Penrod 1994).

A Limited Number of Alternatives

Audiences find integrating or combining information to be easier when they are not given too many alternatives to choose among. In a study of prospective home-buyers choosing among different houses, Malhotra (1982) varied the number of alternative houses from 5 to 25. Buyers reported experiencing information overload and made significantly fewer optimal choices when the number of alternative houses reached 10. In a study that varied choice rules as well as the number of alternatives, Wright (1975) asked audiences to decide among either 2, 6, or 10 alternatives by using either the lexicographic, conjunctive, or averaging choice rule. Across all three choice rules audiences made fairly accurate decisions when deciding between 2 alternatives but they were much less accurate when deciding among 6 or 10 alternatives.

A Slightly Larger Number of Attributes

Decision quality may also decrease as the number of attributes or decision criteria increases (Keller & Staelin 1987; Sundstrom 1987). In the study described in the section above, Malhotra (1982) not only varied the number of alternative houses but also varied the number of attributes that described each house from 5 to 25. Buyers reported experiencing information overload and made significantly fewer correct choices when the number of house attributes reached 15. Malhotra concludes that when buyers face too many alternatives or attributes, they can no longer make all of the comparisons necessary to rank the alternatives.

Jacoby and colleagues (1974b) came to a somewhat different conclusion in their study of consumers choosing among various brands of laundry detergents, rice, and prepared dinners. Although they also find that consumers' accuracy decreases as the number of alternatives they consider in a product category increases, in their study consumers' accuracy increased as they considered more attributes about each alternative. How many attributes or decision criteria are too many depends in part on the amount of time the audience has available for decision making.

The Complete Set of Slot Values for Each Alternative

Audiences tend to use whatever comparative information is made available but make few additional comparisons on their own (Sheluga & Jacoby 1978). A study of consumers using information in ads to make decisions finds that 75% of the subjects who viewed comparative ads made comparisons among products whereas only 10% of those who viewed non-comparative ads did so (Walker, Swasy, & Rethans 1985). Audiences will tend to discount or ignore any comparative information they have to remember, infer, or transform (Slovic 1972). Sometimes an audience may make a decision without making the necessary comparisons because it is not aware that comparative information is missing (Fischhoff, Slovic, & Lichtenstein 1978).

Slot Values for Each Alternative in Numeric Form

Although audiences mentally convert cardinal numbers into ordinal numbers or scale values prior to making comparisons, they will integrate or combine information more accurately and efficiently when comparative information is expressed in numeric rather than verbal form (cf., Schkade & Kleinmeuntz 1994). When consumers are given numerical information, they make more attribute-based comparisons than when they are given qualitative information (Huber 1980). Conversely, when attribute values are

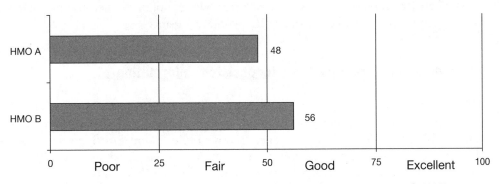

Figure 4.6 Overall Satisfaction with HMO (source: Adapted from Finucane et al. 2003).

represented as words instead of numbers, consumers make more alternative-based searches and use more non-compensatory strategies (Stone & Schkade 1991). Interestingly, audiences prefer to receive information about probabilities in numeric form but they prefer to use words (e.g., doubtful, likely) to express probabilities to others (Budescu, Weinberg, & Wallsten 1988; Erev & Cohen 1990; Wallsten 1990).

Occasionally, words or a combination of numbers and words may prove optimal. For example, consumers who were asked to choose between two health mainten-ance organizations (HMOs) on the basis of the bar chart shown in Figure 4.6 gave the numerical ratings (48% versus 56%) more weight when the qualitative verbal scale (Poor, Fair, Good, Excellent) was added to the chart (Peters, reported in Finucane, Peters, & Slovic 2003).

Comparable Slot Values

Audiences will integrate information more accurately and efficiently when comparable slot values for each alternative are expressed in comparable ways, for example when the values for several international currencies are all expressed in US dollars (Helgeson & Ursic 1993). Comparable scaling (e.g., Good, Very Good, Excellent) of slot values is another way to improve the accuracy of the audience's information integration process. Non-comparable scaling (e.g., Good, Above Average, A) across alternatives tends to decrease the audience's use of more normative compensatory strategies (Wright 1974).

The Right Graph for the Comparison

The best graph for a particular task is one that represents task information most explicitly (Carswell & Wickens 1987). In their study of graph comprehension, Simkin and Hastie (1986) show that the best graph for any particular task is also one that minimizes the number of steps needed for making the intended comparison. For example, bar charts are better than pie charts when viewers need to compare quantities because bar charts display quantities as lengths on a common scale, whereas pie charts display quantities as areas of a circle or slices and require viewers to mentally rotate the slices before making a comparison. By the same token, pie charts are better than bar charts when viewers need to make accurate part/whole judgments because pie charts give viewers a better sense of the size of the whole at a glance.

The Elimination of Irrelevant and Inconsistent Information

Irrelevant information can have an adverse or dilutive effect on the audience's information integration process and can adversely influence even experts' decisions (Gaeth & Shanteau 1984). When audiences receive irrelevant information mixed with relevant information, their predictions become more regressive and less based on the relevant information presented (Nisbett, Zukier, & Lemley 1981). Audiences also tend to decrease their use of compensatory strategies when given irrelevant data mixed with relevant data (Wright 1974). In an early information integration study, Anderson (1968) finds that mixing weak or irrelevant arguments with strong arguments lowers the overall persuasiveness of the message. And in a study of the effects of non-diagnostic, or irrelevant, information on group decision making, Young and colleagues (2001) find that non-diagnostic information produces a dilutive effect similar to its effect on individual decision making.

The think-aloud comments below, made by three experts whose comments we also saw in Chapter 2, reveal the importance of eliminating irrelevant information from business documents. All three experts express their frustration with the contents of the documents they are reading. Indeed, many think-aloud studies show that the presence of irrelevant information in business documents is pervasive and a chief complaint of the expert audiences of managers. Notice that the experienced board member dismisses as irrelevant Sections 2, 4, 5, 6, 7, 8, and 9 of the GM strategic plan, a plan that consisted of only 11 sections in total.

Inconsistent information can also have an adverse effect on the audience's information integration process. Inconsistent information takes longer to integrate because of the

Table 4.5 Expert Decision Makers are Frustrated by the Inclusion of Information Unnecessary to Their Decisions

---

Expert investor reading the original Smartphone MBA business plan

Etcetera, etcetera.[14]

Etcetera, etcetera.[16]

Blah, blah, blah.[17]

Expert investor reading the analyst's report on Georgia Gulf

Etcetera. I'm skimming it, because that's what I would have done three pages ago.[48] Talks about the different things you can do with it: put it in headliners, doors, electrical tape.[49]

This report is very lengthy. I don't need to know or care how they make these chemicals.[65]

What I want to know is: "Is it profitable?[66] Why is it profitable?[67] What are their advantages?"[68]

If it's important to be technical because they have an advantage in a certain process, that's fine. But if they make it the same way everybody else does, I really don't care.[69]

Experienced board member reading the strategic plan from General Motors

This environmental scan chart in Section 2 is something that I've not seen before. I'm looking at x's. I'm looking at the words "Market, Economics, Technical and Social." It's ranked from negative to positive on an attractiveness scale. Models like this don't impress me, because in my opinion, they are examples of a lot of information with no knowledge. I've seen all this data, now what do I do with it?[5]

The data in Sections 4 and 5 is superfluous and backup, as is the data in Section 6, and the data in Sections 7 and 8. As I said before, Section 9 is not useful to me.[28]

---

extra time the audience needs to notice and interpret the inconsistency (Greeno & Noreen 1974). Inconsistent information annoys and confuses audience members, as was the case with the experienced board member who read the strategic plan from GM:

> **They say they have a bad service record. Well, that's related to saying that they have low-quality products. But above they say their strength is high-quality products. So I'm thoroughly confused.**[15]

The two versions below of the beginning of an MBA team's strategic plan illustrate the importance of using techniques that can aid the audience's information acquisition and integration processes. The revision provides side-by-side comparisons, or benchmarks, for each quantity that it mentions. Thus, the audience can see immediately which important metrics have improved or will improve, and by how much, and will be less likely to ask for or search for that information. The revision adds a heading to the first paragraph that allows an audience who might be searching the plan for the 2009 financial results to quickly find them. Whereas the original plan expresses changes to the stock price and earnings in verbal form, the revision expresses those changes in numeric form. The vague qualitative terms used in the original—*increase significantly* and *maintaining strong earnings*—have been replaced with specific numbers. In addition, the revised version includes the comparative value for 2009's earnings per share, a slot value missing from the original.

Original first paragraphs of an MBA team's strategic plan	*Revised first paragraphs of an MBA team's strategic plan*
Coming off an outstanding year that saw our stock price *increase significantly*, Chronos Watch Company is poised to maintain earnings levels again in 2010. Chronos, the world's second largest producer of watches, posted net income of $3.0M and had an average earnings per share of $2.98, generating a net return on equity of 9%. These results handily beat our peer group average of $2.54 EPS and 9.4% ROE.	**Financial Results for 2009** 2009 was an outstanding year for Chronos Watch Company. We saw our stock price *increase more than 28%, from $83 per share to $107.* Although our average earnings per share *dropped from $3.40* to $2.98, our results handily beat our peer group average of $2.54. Today, Chronos Watch Company is the world's second largest producer of watches.
Objectives For 2010, Chronos's executive management has set certain concrete goals. In addition to *maintaining strong earnings*, Chronos expects to: • Generate a Return on Equity of 15% • Reduce Debt to Equity Ratio to from 32% to 12%	**Financial Objectives for 2010** For the year 2010, our executive management has set the following goals: • Increase Net Income from $3 M *to $3.2 M* • Increase Return on Equity from 9% to 15% • Reduce Debt to Equity from 32% to 12%

Aids to Audience Decision Making: Implications for Communicators

✧ The main takeaway for communicators in Chapter 4 is that all six of the cognitive processes audiences use to make decisions can be enhanced by a set of process-specific stylistic techniques. Thus, stylistic techniques are useful not only for enhancing audience comprehension, but also for enhancing the other major cognitive processes that make informed decision making possible.

✧ Use the information presented in the chapter to choose specific stylistic techniques that make it easy for your audience to complete each step in the decision-making process.

✧ Why use the information? To save yourself time. To improve your accuracy in predicting the techniques and organizational structures that will aid audience decision making. To combat "group think" in groups.

✧ To apply a technique presented in the chapter, simply refer to the appropriate chapter section.

PART II

Understanding Intuitive Decision Making

CHAPTER 5

Heuristics and Biases in Audience Decision Making

> In May 2000 the president and CEO of Heinz picked out his brightest young marketing executives and challenged each of them to propose a project that would significantly increase ketchup sales in the United States without spending any additional dollars. Only the best proposal would get the CEO's approval to proceed.
>
> One of the young execs chosen to propose a project to the CEO, although somewhat quiet and reserved, was a whiz at the numbers. After several months of grueling data collection and statistical analysis, the young exec made his presentation to the boss. It contained hundreds of complex charts and numbers to back up his claim that by optimizing marketing and promotion spend in each city and each grocery chain in the United States, Heinz could regain lost market share from its competitors.
>
> To the young exec's chagrin, when he concluded his presentation the CEO told him he had no idea what he was talking about but would give him a chance to try again. The CEO attended other, more engaging, presentations, but none of the proposals sold him.
>
> Soon the young exec came back to present to the CEO and other top executives in one final effort. This time, before he began, he first gave each person in the room a fleece jacket with a big red rocket logo on it. He then announced the *Red Rocket Project*—optimization of marketing spend would make Heinz ketchup sales take off!
>
> This presentation was all visual, just exciting images that illustrated the exec's key points. When he finished, the whole room was buzzing with questions, and the exec had a backup chart for each. The Red Rocket Project was a go. It soon exceeded sales expectations. Wall Street analysts loved it. And the Heinz brand was re-energized.

Why didn't the CEO approve the young executive's proposal after hearing his first presentation? Unlike his first presentation, the second was both easier for the CEO to understand and was framed by an easily visualized name—*The Red Rocket Project*, a compelling vision the CEO could get excited about.

Audiences, even expert ones like the CEO in the story above, do not always make decisions in a cold, rational, and calculating fashion, weighing each alternative's pros and cons. Instead, audiences often make decisions intuitively and revise their intuitive decisions only if they are motivated to do so. Think of the millions of consumers who have been influenced to drink Coca-Cola by slogans such as *Coke is it!* and *Live on the Coke side of life.*

When audiences make decisions primarily on the basis on their intuitions, the form or style of a message can have a greater persuasive impact on them than its content or substance. Consequently, persuasive documents and presentations must not only appeal to the audience on the rational level, they must also appeal to the audience on the intuitive level if only to ensure that competing proposals are not more persuasive for purely subjective reasons. Chapter 5 explores intuitive decision making and the techniques, such as framing, that appeal to audiences on the intuitive level.

Some of the many differences between the rational mode of decision making and the intuitive mode are highlighted in Table 5.1, adapted from a paper by Nobel laureate Daniel Kahneman and his colleague Shane Frederick (2002). Whereas rational decisions are based on objective experience and information, intuitive decisions are based on the subjective experience or the feelings of the decision maker. Unlike the rational mode, which is used consciously and only if believed to be necessary, the intuitive mode operates automatically at all times. The rational mode of decision making is a slow and deliberate process that requires effort to make the necessary comparisons, calculations, and trade offs. The intuitive mode, on the other hand, is fast and effortless, and the decisions it comes up with are not based on comparisons or calculations but on a holistic impression.

The rational mode requires abstract and quantitative information for its comparisons and calculations. It makes sense of the information it inputs using rules and deductive reasoning. The intuitive mode, in contrast, responds best to concrete and attention-getting stimuli, the photograph of a shiny red sports car, for example. It interprets the information it inputs by making associations with situations from the past that produced similar responses. In the rational mode information acquisition and integration processes are carried out in a serial sequence, one comparison at a time. In the intuitive mode audiences carry out those processes beneath conscious awareness in a parallel manner that allows them to recognize different configurations or patterns of information

Table 5.1 A Comparison of Intuitive and Rational Cognitive Processes

	Intuitive mode	*Rational mode*
Focus of awareness	Subjective experience	Objective experience
When activated	At all times	As needed
How activated	Automatically	Consciously
Speed	Rapid	Slow
Output	Holistic impression	Effortful trade offs
Stimuli	Concrete and affective	Abstract and quantitative
Comprehension	Associative, similarity-based	Deductive, rule-based
Information acquisition	Parallel	Serial
Information integration	Configural	Feature by feature

Source: Adapted from Kahneman & Frederick 2002.

immediately (e.g., Cobos, Almaraz, & Garcia-Madruga 2003; Lieberman, Gaunt, Gilbert, & Trope 2002; Whittlesea 1997).

When audiences make intuitive decisions, they are said to be using shortcuts to decision making or *heuristics*. For example, when audiences decide that a person must be a librarian because the person is dressed like a librarian, they are said to be using the *representativeness* heuristic. The person's appearance is representative or typical of a librarian's. When audiences decide that a house must be worth about $250,000 because the asking price is $250,000, they are said to be using the *anchoring* heuristic. The asking price anchors or fixes the audience's estimate of the value of the house at $250,000 simply because it is the first valuation the audience hears.

Any information may be used either heuristically or non-heuristically. Deciding someone is a librarian based on their appearance alone exemplifies using information about their appearance heuristically. Deciding someone is a librarian based on their appearance as well as all of the other relevant information available exemplifies using the same information in a non-heuristic way.

Although each individual heuristic describes a different rule by which the intuitive mode operates, all heuristics derive their persuasive power or intuitive appeal from the subjective ease of using them. Decisions based on processing information heuristically *feel* right simply because they are easy and effortless to make. When audiences use heuristics to make decisions, they give more weight to and have more confidence in information that is easy to process, even when that information is irrelevant to the decision. Audiences also tend to associate positive emotions with, and like, information that is easy to process (e.g., Garcia-Marques & Mackie 2000; Ramachandran & Hirnstein 1999; Schwarz 1990). In other words, the easier information is to process, the more it will be liked (Lee & Aaker 2004). At the same time audiences may give little or no weight to relevant information that is hard to process.

Heuristics serve the audience well in many situations and may lead them to make satisfactory decisions based on what amounts to informed guesses. In some cases, the audience's subjective feelings are the most relevant information for decision making, as is the case with judgments of liking (Schwarz & Clore 1996; Winkielman & Cacioppo 2001). More often, according to normative theory at least, the audience's subjective experiences of processing information, or feelings, should have no bearing on their decisions at all.

Heuristic use can also lead the audience to systematically distort the steps normative theory prescribes and thus result in errors and biased decisions. For example, when audiences use the representativeness heuristic to make decisions they simultaneously neglect to consider other relevant information such as base-rate information (the odds of something being true) or information about the size of the sample studied (four doctors or 4,000)—information needed to make a rational and statistically meaningful decision.

The audience's use of heuristics and their susceptibility to the resulting biases are predictable. Most audience members will use the same heuristic when processing the same information and their decisions will deviate from normative theory in the same way (Kahneman & Tversky 1982; Tversky & Kahneman 1974). For example, the moment the prices of securities reach their peak is the time most unsophisticated investors buy them. Instead of buying low and selling high, most inexperienced investors use the information about high stock prices heuristically and proceed to buy high, only to sell low when prices hit bottom.

Fortunately for the professional, the same aids to audience decision making that make it easy for the audience to process a professional's documents and presentations also bias the audience, usually in the professional's favor. When audiences use information heuristically, they choose the alternative that is presented in the style or format that:

- is easiest to perceive (e.g., Gigerenzer & Goldstein 1996; Schwarz & Vaughn 2002; Tversky & Kahneman 1973);
- is most attention getting (e.g., Kahneman & Miller 1986; Kahneman & Varey 1990);
- makes comprehension easy (e.g., Fiske, Lin, & Neuberg 1999; Kahneman & Varey 1990; Tversky & Kahneman 1983);
- makes activating a schema easy (e.g., Shah, Domke, & Wackman 2001; Simon & Hayes 1976; Tversky & Kahneman 1981, 1988);
- makes acquiring schema slot values easy (e.g., Kahneman & Tversky 1982; Tversky & Kahneman 1974);
- makes integrating schema slot values easy (e.g., Camerer & Johnson 1991; Frederick 2002).

Audiences who possess domain expertise are less likely to rely on heuristics and thus are less susceptible to bias when performing realistic tasks in their domain (e.g., Cohen 1993; Keren 1987; Shanteau 1989). For example, medical residents are less susceptible to the sunk-cost bias, less likely to "throw good money after bad," when making medical decisions than when making non-medical decisions (Bornstein, Emler, & Chapman 1999). Similarly, accountants are less susceptible to bias when making accounting than non-accounting decisions (Smith & Kida 1991). However, some experts appear to rely on heuristics routinely. For example, federal judges routinely use heuristics such as anchoring and representativeness in making their judicial decisions (Guthrie, Rachlinski, & Wistrich 2001).

Whereas expertise tends to mitigate the audience's use of heuristics and their susceptibility to bias, being part of a group often accentuates heuristic use and the audience's susceptibility to biases (cf., Castellan 1993; Kerr, MacCoun, & Kramer 1996). For example, groups tend to accentuate the bias of individual audience members to neglect base-rate information (Hinsz, Tindale, & Nagao 2008). Groups also display a more pronounced optimism bias than individual audience members do (Buehler, Messervey, & Griffin 2005). Groups are persuaded by sunk-cost arguments even when only a minority of group members mentions them as reasons for their decisions (Smith, Tindale, & Steiner 1998). Positive/negative framing effects (e.g., arguing for a medical procedure in terms of lives saved versus lives lost) at the group level tend to be stronger than those at the individual level (Paese, Bieser, & Tubbs 1993). For example, groups given the 'lives lost' version of the Asian disease problem (Tversky & Kahneman 1981) choose the riskier alternative even when a majority of the members initially favor the less risky alternative (Tindale, Sheffey, & Scott 1993).

Groups are just as susceptible as individuals to other biases. Groups are just as susceptible to the anchoring-related biases as individuals are (Whyte & Sebenius 1997).

Groups are just as susceptible to the confirmation bias as individuals are. For example, groups of managers prefer information that confirms the majority's initial decision to information that does not support it (Schulz-Hardt, Frey, Luthgens, & Moscovici 2000). Groups are equally susceptible to the conjunctive fallacy: Instead of calculating the correct response, they simply exchange information concerning their individual judgments and endorse the judgment of a single, oftentimes incorrect, group member (Tindale et al. 1998).

Some biased information processing is unique to groups. Groups may be prone to take courses of action about which all members secretly disagree (Harvey 1974). A group bias termed *pluralistic ignorance* may be caused by group members' tendency to underestimate the extent to which other group members share their concerns (Westphal & Bednar 2005). For example, outside board members are often reluctant to express their concerns about the management of under-performing firms and do not realize that other board members have similar concerns. Groups are also prone to polarize the pre-dispositions of individual members toward risk. Group polarization results in decisions that are either too risky or too conservative (see Bazerman 1994). Groups tend to produce poorly reasoned decisions when the pressure on members to conform overrides their need to produce a good decision, a group bias that Janis (1972) termed *groupthink*. More recently, groupthink has been attributed to a shared schema or a shared mental model (Fischhoff & Johnson 1997).

Note that the heuristics described in this chapter are all associated with the audience's ease of processing information, or what is called *processing fluency* (e.g., Benjamin & Bjork 1996; Johnston & Hawley 1994; Whittlesea & Williams 2001). They should not be confused with the heuristics cues identified in the dual-mode persuasion literature, cues that provide audiences with substantive information such as the communicator's level of expertise or attractiveness (see Chaiken, Liberman, & Eagly 1989; Petty & Cacioppo 1986). Dual-mode heuristic cues, as described in Chapter 6, do not make messages or arguments easier to process. Instead, they provide additional, easy-to-process information upon which an unmotivated or distracted audience may base its decisions.

Dual-mode persuasion theory predicts that even strong arguments in a message will not be persuasive unless the audience is highly motivated and attentive. More recently, researchers find that strong arguments that are easy to process will be persuasive even if the audience is not highly motivated or attentive. When the difficulty of processing arguments and dual-mode heuristic cues is controlled for, the previously found interactions with the audience's motivation and attention levels disappear (Kruglanski & Sleeth-Keppler 2007; Pierro, Mannetti, Erb, Spiegel, & Kruglanski 2005; Pierro, Mannetti, Kruglanski, & Sleeth-Keppler 2004).

PERCEPTION-RELATED HEURISTICS AND BIASES

The Perceptual Fluency Heuristic

Anything that impacts the speed and accuracy of perception and recognition can affect perceptual fluency (e.g., Jacoby, Kelley, & Dywan 1989a). For example, stimuli presented for long durations are usually easier to perceive than stimuli presented for shorter durations. Perceiving stimuli that have high clarity is easier than perceiving stimuli with low clarity. Perceiving familiar stimuli is easier than perceiving novel stimuli. Perceiving foreground stimuli or figures that contrast with their backgrounds is also easier (Winkielman, Schwarz, Reber, & Fazendeiro 2003b). In addition, certain attributes of stimuli—such as simplicity, prototypicality, symmetry, balance, as well as proportions such as the golden section—may facilitate perceptual processing and as a result give the stimuli more aesthetic appeal (e.g., Halberstadt & Rhodes 2000; Langlois & Roggman 1990; Reber, Schwarz, & Winkielman 2004).

Audiences use the perceptual fluency heuristic when their subjective experience of easily perceiving information leads them to prefer that information more, weight it more heavily, assume it is more true, or find it more persuasive than equally relevant or more relevant information that is difficult to perceive (cf., Ramachandran & Hirnstein 1999). Although anything that aids perceptual processing can lead to perceptual fluency, audiences rarely attribute the experience of perceptual fluency to its true cause. For example, audience members who have seen a particular stimulus before are likely to mistakenly believe they viewed it for a longer time period or that it possessed a higher clarity than it actually did (e.g., Whittlesea, Jacoby, & Girard 1990; Witherspoon & Allan 1985).

Figure 5.1 uses a simple flow chart to represent how the perceptual fluency heuristic can lead to perceptual biases. Irrelevant stimuli that are familiar, highly audible, highly legible, or otherwise easy to perceive lead the audience to experience positive subjective feelings about those stimuli, such as liking and certainty. The audience's positive subjective feelings, in turn, lead them to give the irrelevant stimuli undue value and weight and to place unwarranted confidence in them. On the other hand, relevant stimuli that are less familiar, less audible, less legible, or otherwise difficult to perceive lead the audience to experience negative subjective feelings about them, such as disliking and uncertainty. The audience's negative subjective feelings, in turn, lead the audience to unduly discount the relevant stimuli.

The intuitive processes, as diagrammed in Figure 5.1 and in Figures 5.2 through 5.6, are depicted as taking place every time one of the six major cognitive processes in decision making has been completed. The information on which the intuitive processes

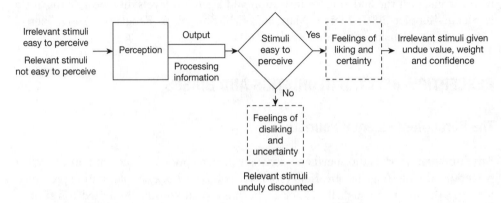

Figure 5.1 Intuitive Processes Leading to Perceptual Biases

act is not content information (i.e., what is seen, comprehended, etc.) but is processing information (i.e., the ease or difficulty with which something is seen, comprehended, and so on). Typically, the only time an audience will be consciously aware of an intuitive process is when processing becomes difficult.

Intuitive processes and the intuitive decisions that result from them are a form of metacognition (Koriat & Levy-Sadot 1999). As Petty and colleagues (2007, p. 258) observe in their review of the research on intuitive processes, "Although research has identified multiple mechanisms by which ease effects can occur, each begins with the assumption that people perceive their ease or difficulty in thinking—a metacognition. What differs in the accounts is what inferences people make based on this perceived ease." *Metacognition* is a term for the experience people have of their cognitive processes as well as for the knowledge they have about them (Flavell 1979). Although metacognition can function both to monitor and control cognition (Nelson & Narens 1990), metacognition's role as depicted here is to function solely as a monitor.

Legibility Effects: The Intuitive Appeal of Easy-to-See Messages

Audiences are more likely to be persuaded by more legible messages than less legible ones. For instance, they are more likely to judge a statement to be true when it is shown in colors that are easy to read against the background color. In a study of legibility effects, Reber and Schwarz (1999) showed statements such as "Osorno is a city in Chile" to readers and asked them to quickly decide if the statements were true. Some statements were printed in colors that were easy to read against the background color and others in colors that were hard to read. Readers were more likely to judge a statement as true when the color it was printed in made it easy to read (see also Norwick & Epley 2003; Werth & Strack 2003).

Visibility Effects: The Intuitive Appeal of Easy-to-See Images

Audiences are more persuaded by easy-to-see images than hard-to-see ones. Larger pictures of an advertised product produce stronger persuasion effects than identical but smaller pictures (Rossiter & Percy 1980). In a study of visibility effects, Pallak (1983) gave readers high-quality and low-quality arguments and high-quality and low-quality images of the source of the arguments (a color photograph versus a degraded copy of the photograph). Readers who received the sharp color photograph of the message source judged poor arguments to be as persuasive as good ones. But those who received the hard-to-see copy of the photograph judged poor arguments to be less persuasive.

Audiences are also more likely to have positive feelings about easy-to-see images. They prefer images that are prototypical, symmetrical, and simple (Cox & Cox 1988; Langlois & Roggman 1990; Martindale & Moore 1988), apparently because those image attributes increase the audience's processing fluency (Reber et al. 2004). Moreover, audiences have stronger affective responses to easy-to-process pictures than to hard to process ones (Winkielman & Cacioppo 2001). For example, audiences become more aroused by images and like them better when the images are presented on big screens than when they are presented on small screens (Detenber & Reeves 1996).

Audibility Effects: The Appeal of Easy-to-Hear Messages

Sound-related variables can influence the persuasive impact of messages as well. In a study of the persuasive effects of sound quality, Eagly (1974) asked listeners to listen to a message that contained six high-quality arguments supporting a recommended position. Lowering message perceptibility with a poor-quality audiotape recording significantly lessened the listeners' agreement with the recommended position. Conversely, enhancing the audio fidelity of a message increases both audience attention and liking (Reeves, Detenber, & Steuer 1993).

Euphonious Sound Effects: The Appeal of Melodious Messages

Words and sentences that sound good are more persuasive than those that do not sound good. For example, audiences are more likely to decide a statement is true when it is expressed in a rhyming form. Made-up sayings expressed in a rhyming form, such as "woes unite foes," are more likely to be judged as true than the same sayings expressed in a non-rhyming form, for instance "woes unite enemies" (McGlone & Tofighbakhsh 2000). Audiences are more likely to judge the rhyming statement true simply because it is easier to process (Reber et al. 2004). Political researchers find that repetition of a candidate's name is more likely to be effective when the candidate's name is euphonious, as was true in the case of a LaRouche, Illinois election in which a candidate with the name of Fairchild defeated the less euphonious sounding Sangmeister (O'Sullivan, Chen, Mohapatra, Sigelman, & Lewis 1988; Smith 1998b).

Repetition Effects: The Appeal of the Familiar

One of the best-known perceptual biases and one of the first to be identified is the mere-exposure effect (Zajonc 1968). Mere or repeated exposure to a stimulus without any reinforcement leads to easier and faster perceptual processing and a gradual increase in liking for the object or idea (Bornstein 1989; Bornstein & D'Agostino 1994; Harmon-Jones & Allen 2001).

In addition, the more often a message is repeated to an audience, the more likely that audience is to judge it as true (Bacon 1979; Hasher, Goldstein, & Toppino 1977; Schwartz 1982). A study of how rumors spread during World War II shows that the best predictor of whether an audience will believe a rumor is the number of times they have heard the rumor repeated (Allport & Lepkin 1945). Similarly, the number of times the audience is exposed to advertisements, trivia statements, or even foreign words predicts how likely they are to believe them (Brown & Nix 1996; Gilbert, Krull, & Malone 1990; Hawkins & Hoch 1992). Repeated statements are more likely to be judged true even when those statements are explicitly identified as false (Skurnik, Yoon, Park, & Schwarz 2005).

Names that the audience has been exposed to repeatedly seem more famous than names that have not been repeated (Jacoby, Woloshyn, & Kelley 1989b). Hearing the same question asked repeatedly leads audiences to increase their confidence in the answer they hear (Hastie, Landsman, & Loftus 1978). Asking an audience to repeatedly express an attitude leads them to maintain that attitude with increased certainty (Holland, Verplanken, & van Knippenberg 2003). And when the audience has already formulated a response to a piece of information, repeated exposure to it can accentuate their response (Brickman, Redfield, Harrison, & Crandall 1972). Thus, repeating information that the audience judges to be negative can make that information seem even more negative to them (Cacioppo & Petty 1989).

ATTENTION-RELATED HEURISTICS AND BIASES

The Vividness and Salience Heuristics

Audiences often neglect to use important information in decision making and instead use less important information when the less important information is presented in a more attention-getting way (MacGregor & Slovic 1986). One reason stimuli attract attention is that they are vivid. Stimuli that are vivid, such as many charts and images, are intrinsically attention getting. Thus it is not surprising that venture capitalists often cite the use of charts as an important characteristic of a good business plan (Hall & Hofer 1993).

Audiences use the vividness heuristic when their subjective experience of selectively attending to vivid information leads them to prefer it more, weight it more heavily, be more confident in it, or find it more persuasive than equally relevant or more relevant but pallid information that is not attention getting (e.g., Clark & Rutter 1985; Herr, Kardes, & Kim 1991).

Another reason stimuli attract attention is because they are salient, that is to say, because they are different from the norm (cf., McArthur & Ginsberg 1981; Nesdale & Dharmalingam 1986; Oakes & Turner 1986). Any unexpected or surprising stimulus is salient (Hastie & Kumar 1979). Audiences use the salience heuristic when their subjective experience of having their attention attracted to salient information leads them

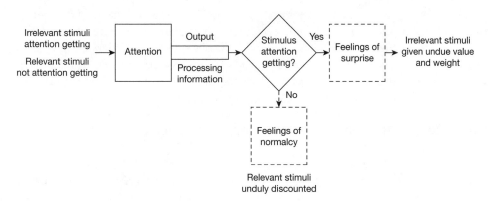

Figure 5.2 Intuitive Processes Leading to Attentional Biases

to prefer it or weight it more heavily than non-salient information. The salience heuristic is this text's term for the heuristic Kahneman and Miller (1986) dubbed the *surprise heuristic*. Kahneman and Miller (1986) explain surprise in terms of salience: The extent to which a stimulus stands out from the norm and attracts attention relative to other stimuli in its environment.

Vivid Language Effects: The Persuasive Impact of Concrete Words

Audiences are more likely to be persuaded by vivid writing and speaking styles than by pallid ones. For example, people are willing to pay more for airline travel insurance covering death from "terrorist acts" than for the more pallid but more comprehensive insurance covering death from "all possible causes" (Johnson & Tversky 1983). Vivid concrete claims in print ads produce more definite intentions to buy the advertised product than do abstract claims (Rossiter & Percy 1978). Vivid health and fear appeals are more persuasive than pallid appeals (Meyerowitz & Chaiken 1987; Robberson & Rogers 1988; Sherer & Rogers 1984).

In a study of vivid verbal claims, Rossiter and Percy (1980) find that explicit and concrete verbal claims lead the audience to have more favorable attitudes toward hypothetical brands than do implicit claims. In their study, explicit verbal claims included statements such as "Affordably priced at $1.79 per six pack" and "Winner of 5 out of 5 taste tests in the US against all major American beers and leading imports." Implicit claims included statements such as "Affordably priced" and "Great taste."

In a study of mock jurors deciding a drunk-driving case, Reyes and coauthors (1980) asked half of the jurors to read vivid (i.e., concrete and image-provoking) prosecution arguments and pallid (i.e., abstract and boring) defense arguments. Conversely, they asked the other jurors to read pallid prosecution arguments and vivid defense arguments. Initially, the decisions of the two groups of jurors were the same, but after a 48-hour delay, the jurors who read the vivid prosecution arguments judged the defendant as more likely to be guilty. On the other hand, the jurors who read the vivid defense arguments judged the defendant as more likely to be innocent.

Bell and Loftus (1988, 1989) made the language in eyewitness testimony more vivid or less vivid by varying the level of detail. When the testimony of the prosecution's eyewitness was highly detailed, mock jurors were more likely to find the defendant guilty than when the testimony contained few details. A similar study gave mock jurors testimonies that were expressed in either vivid phrases such as "a spiderweb of cracks" or pallid phrases such as "a network of cracks" (Wilson, Northcraft, & Neale 1989a). Mock jurors' verdicts and damage awards favored the side with the vivid testimonies.

Vivid Picture Effects: The Persuasive Impact of Images

Vivid pictures have a persuasive impact (Kisielius & Sternthal 1984; Smith & Shaffer 2000). Vivid pictures can also enhance the persuasive appeal of verbal information (Nisbett, Borgida, Crandall, & Reed 1982). In a study of the persuasive impact of vivid pictures, Mitchell and Olson (1981) showed consumers one version of a print ad for facial tissues that used a vivid color photograph of a fluffy kitten to communicate the attribute of softness. The other versions either stated the claim verbally or showed color photographs that were conceptually irrelevant to the product's softness. Consumers developed stronger beliefs about the softness of the brand of tissue, as well as more favorable attitudes toward the brand, when they saw the vivid color photograph of the kitten than they did when they saw the other versions of the ad.

Vivid Modality Effects: The Persuasive Impact of Speech and Video

Even more persuasive than written words or static images, are spoken words and moving images. Messages presented in the more vivid video or audiotape modality have a significantly stronger persuasive impact than do the same messages presented in the less vivid written modality (Chaiken & Eagly 1976).

The two slide presentations on the following pages illustrate the persuasive impact of information that is presented in a vivid, attention-getting style. A team of MBA students who tried to make the case that "Duke Power" should build new nuclear reactors produced the first slide presentation. A second team opposed to building new reactors developed the second slide presentation. Even without reading the text of either slide presentation, guessing which team won the debate is not difficult. Although both teams addressed the audience's decision criteria and used many facts and figures to support their claims, notice that only the second team incorporated vivid charts, graphs, and photographs. And notice that only the second team began each slide with a title that made a vivid claim.

The Negativity Bias: The Impact of Negative Information

As politicians know, negative campaign ads work. One negative fact about their opponent can outweigh 10 positive attributes. Although audiences will not judge a person's character on the basis of one socially desirable behavior, they will judge a person on the basis of one socially undesirable behavior (Reeder & Brewer 1979). One negative adjective describing a person can contribute more to an audience's overall impression of that person than many positive adjectives (Anderson 1965; Hamilton & Zanna 1972; Hodges 1974).

The reason negative information has such a powerful persuasive impact is that it is salient: Audiences pay attention to negative information because they tend to take positive information for granted (Fiske 1980). Thus, the salience of negative information leads audiences to weight it more heavily than positive information and creates a bias called the "negativity bias" (Kanouse & Hanson 1972).

Outlier Effects: The Impact of Unusual Behaviors and Events

Unusual behaviors and events are more salient and attention getting than routine ones and have a greater persuasive impact on audience decisions. Audiences remember unusual events and behaviors better than ones that are routine and thus give them more weight when predicting future events and behaviors (Pryor & Kriss 1977; Taylor & Fiske 1975). For example, if someone sees a person giving an unusually generous tip, she will

A Slide Presentation that was Rationally Appealing

Nuclear Energy:
The future of Duke Power

Agenda

- Financial Rewards
- Technology Advancements
- Environment
- Safety
- Government Incentives
- Success Story

Financial Rewards

- Nuclear Energy is Cheaper to Produce

  - Two New Reactors at Plant Vogtle
    - Construction costs expected to be $4B for two reactors (2000 MW capacity)
    - Production capacity costs $540m less than coal, $970m less than gas, by 2015
    - Rate case for $51m in nuclear studies looks positive
    - Expected NPV of approximately $2.5B using 8% IRR relative to coal

  - Government Encouraging New Nuclear
    - 1.8¢ per kWh tax credit will mean $350m per year starting in 2015
    - U.S. DOE expects 30% growth in demand in Duke's market by 2020

  - Fossil Fuel Costs are Expected to Continue Rise
    - Natural gas has seen large volatilities, making projections risky
    - Both coal and gas are subject to natural disasters, shipping, and politics
    - Uranium fuel costs declined relative to fossil fuels
    - New nuclear technology continuing to improve

Technology Advancements

- In the last two decades, technology advancements have:

  - Decreased Capital Cost
    - Advanced reactor designs have fewer valves, fewer pumps, and less pipe
    - Pebble-Bed Modular Reactor (PBMR) design, which virtually eliminates the risk of a meltdown and the need for a containment building
    - PBMR does not need safety backup and off-site emergency support

  - Decreased Recurring Cost
    - Capacity utilization of 90% vs 71% with Coal Plants
    - 30 times the energy from uranium than existing reactors
    - A Fast Reactor produces enough plutonium to make up for the uranium-235 used

  - Reduced Waste Produced
    - Fast reactor is capable of destroying the major source of long-life radiotoxicity in spent fuel

Quote

"Today, there are 103 nuclear reactors quietly delivering just 20 percent of America's electricity. Eighty percent of the people living within 10 miles of these plants approve of them (that's not including the nuclear workers). Although I don't live near a nuclear plant, I am now squarely in their camp."

- Patrick Moore, co-founder of Greenpeace, 4/16/06

Environmental Impact

- Nuclear Power creates no greenhouse gases
- Nuclear waste is controlled by plant and Department of Energy (DOE)
- Fossil fuel plants release unmanaged waste such as smoke stake waste
- A typical coal plant produces 100,000 tons of sulphur dioxide, 75,000 tons of nitrogen oxides, and 5,000 tons of fly ash
- A nuclear plant produces 0 tons of each type

A Slide Presentation that was Rationally Appealing *continued . . .*

Environmental Cost

- Nuclear waste is currently stored locally at each plant
- Nuclear waste can be stored locally for 100+ years.
- Cost of disposal is unknown as the US and other countries have not finalized disposal plans

Quote

"For the sake of economic security and national security, the United States should aggressively move forward with the construction of nuclear power plants."

-George W. Bush

Nuclear Power Safety Improvements

- Three Mile Island
  - Only Major Nuclear Plant Accident in the United States
  - No Adverse Health Effects Resultant
  - Second Generation Reactor
  - Accident Occurred Due to Instrument Failure and Poor Training
- Third Generation Plants
  - reduce possibility of core melt accidents
  - operate more easily and are less vulnerable to operational upsets due to a simpler and more rugged design
  - incorporate passive or inherent safety features
    - do rely on gravity, natural convection or resistance to high temperatures
    - do not involve electrical or mechanical operation on command

Government Incentives

- Energy Policy Act of 2005
  - Provides $13 billion in subsidies and tax incentives for nuclear industry to build new reactors
  - Provides nuclear power production tax credits of 1.8 cents per kilowatt-hour
  - Extends insurance coverage to the public in case of a reactor accident at any new plant for 20 years
  - Provides a generous production tax credit and federal loan guarantees for up to 80% of the project's cost
- Nuclear Power 2010 Initiative
  - Eases steps for issuing permits for the demonstration of two next generation nuclear reactors
  - Provides $500 million in federal matching funds
- 1992 Energy Act
  - Companies can now apply for a combined construction-and-operating license

Success Story - France

- Generated 75% of the country's electricity in 2001 from nuclear power compared to 15% in 1980
  - Energy-related carbon emissions from 1980 to 2001 decreased by 20% in France compared to a 22% increase in U.S.
  - Nuclear energy costs were comparable to fossil fuel costs (in EUR cents/kWh)
    - Nuclear costs 3.20
    - Gas costs 3.05 – 4.26
    - Coal costs 3.81 – 4.57

A Slide Presentation that was Intuitively Appealing

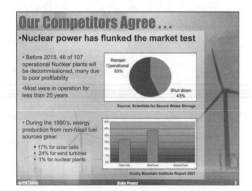

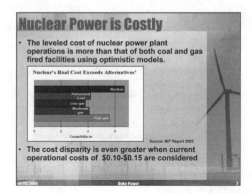

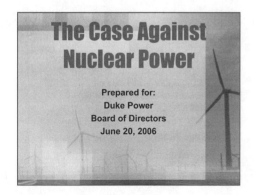

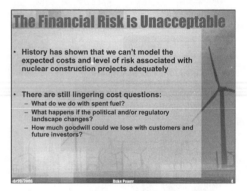

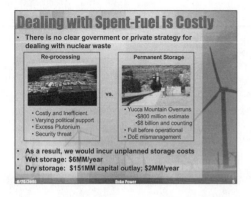

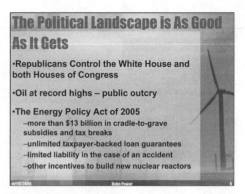

A Slide Presentation that was Intuitively Appealing *continued . . .*

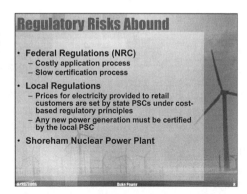

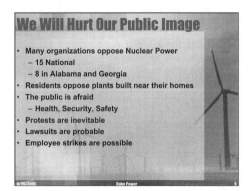

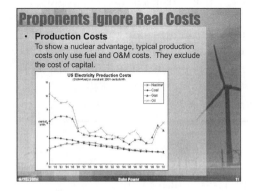

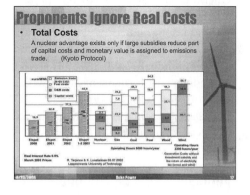

A Slide Presentation that was Intuitively Appealing *continued . . .*

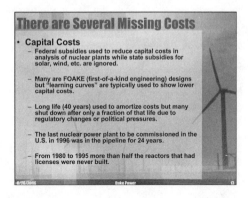

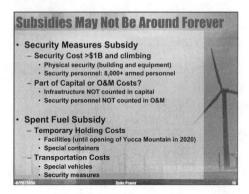

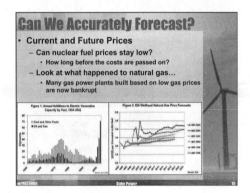

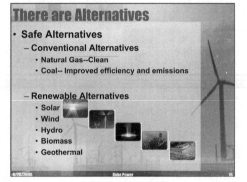

remember that event and use it to predict the size of that person's future tips (Kahneman & Tversky 1973).

In addition, audiences will be more persuaded by information related to unusual happenings than by information about happenings they consider to be normal. For example, when an audience thinks that getting a flu shot is normal, they are more persuaded by information about what happens to those who do not get vaccinated (Blanton, Stuart, & VandenEijnden 2001). When the audience views not getting a flu shot as normal, they are more persuaded by information about what happens to people who do get vaccinated.

Immediacy Effects: The Impact of Recent Trends and Events

Recent events and trends are more salient and attention getting than those that happened in the distant past or that may happen in the distant future. The salience of the present leads audiences to overreact to recent events and trends and to make predictions that are insufficiently regressive to the mean. For example, investors often assume a firm's future earnings will be directly predictable from its recent earnings. Although securities with good performance receive extremely high valuations, these valuations, on average, return to the mean (Shleifer 2000).

Even experts can make insufficiently regressive predictions and overreact to recent trends. In a study of sales forecasting, Cox and Summers (1987) asked professional retail buyers to examine one week's worth of actual sales data from two department stores for six different apparel styles and then to make sales forecasts for the following week. Although the actual sales from the first week regressed to the mean by the second week, the forecasts of the professional buyers failed to.

In a study of analysts' forecasts, De Bondt and Thaler (1990) matched analysts' earnings forecasts for one-year and two-year time horizons between 1976 and 1984 with actual stock returns and accounting numbers. In every case the analysts' forecasts failed to regress to the mean and were too extreme. The actual earnings per share (EPS) changes averaged only 65% of the forecasted one-year changes and only 46% of the forecasted two-year earnings. A strong overreaction bias in analysts' EPS forecasts has also been found between 1987 and 1995 (Amir & Ganzach 1998; Capstaff, Paudyal, & Rees 2001).

The temporal salience of the present also leads audiences to weight short-term benefits more heavily than potentially higher long-term costs. This particular bias is termed "discounting the future" (Hirshleifer 1970).

Physical Salience Effects: The Persuasive Impact of Standing Out

People and objects that stand out physically are more salient and attention getting to the audience than are people and objects that appear in the background. A person may be salient, and as a consequence more persuasive, if she is well lit and others are dimly lit, if she is moving and others are seated, if she is speaking and others are silent, if she is casually dressed and others are dressed in suits, and if she is seated in the middle of a group rather than at the extremes (cf., Fiske & Taylor 1991; McArthur & Post 1977; Raghubir & Valenzuela 2006). Leaders, in particular, have greater influence on their followers when they are physically close as opposed to distant from them (Howell & Hall-Merenda 1999).

In a study of salience created by camera effects, Lassiter (2002) finds that the camera angle used to videotape confessions and courtroom testimony can have a persuasive impact. When the camera focuses solely on the accused, mock jurors perceive the suspect to be more culpable and recommend more severe sentences than when the camera focuses equally on the prosecutor and suspect. In a similar study, Phillips and Lord (1981) varied the salience of a group's leader by changing the camera angles used in filming the group. Viewers were more likely to attribute the level of the group's performance to the leader when the camera angle made the leader stand out.

Group members who are physically salient are more likely to be chosen as group leaders. For example, group members who sit at the head of the table or who are able to have face-to-face contact with other group members are more likely to be chosen as leaders (Howells & Becker 1962; Sommer 1961). In his classic experiment, Leavitt (1951) created different types of communication networks that allowed the members of five-person groups to converse with one another. In highly centralized networks, networks in which only one group member could directly communicate with every other group member, the member in the central, and thus most salient, position was chosen to be the group leader in 100% of the groups. In the less centralized networks in which no one group member was more salient than any other, group members in every position had an equal chance to be chosen as their group's leader.

COMPREHENSION-RELATED HEURISTICS AND BIASES

The easier a message is for an audience to comprehend the more likely it is that the audience will be persuaded by it. Thus, any communication technique that makes comprehension easy will also promote heuristic processing. For example, listeners are more persuaded by spoken messages that are easy to comprehend—well organized and delivered fluently—than by either a well-organized message delivered non-fluently or by a randomly ordered message delivered fluently (McCroskey & Mehrley 1969). In a study that manipulated the comprehensibility of product information by varying information exposure time and the audience's relevant prior knowledge, Ratneshwar and Chaiken (1991) show that the same product information is more persuasive when it is easy to comprehend than when it is hard to comprehend.

The Representativeness and Causality Heuristics

Two well-studied heuristics that are related to ease of understanding and that are often contrasted with the normative rules for decision making are the representativeness heuristic and the causality heuristic.

The representativeness heuristic may be the most basic and widely used of all the heuristics (Fiske & Taylor 1991, p. 384). Audiences use the representativeness heuristic when their subjective experience of easily categorizing a stimulus described by concrete or anecdotal information leads them to give little or no weight to equally relevant or more relevant abstract, quantitative, statistical, or otherwise hard-to-comprehend information about the stimulus (Bar-Hillel & Fischhoff 1981; Kahneman & Tversky 1973; Kirsch 1985). For example, recruiters of MBAs use the representativeness heuristic any time they base their hiring decisions on the extent to which the MBAs "look like" or "act like" successful managers (cf., Griffin & Tversky 1992).

Audiences use the causality heuristic when their subjective experience of easily comprehending explanations or predictions of events presented in the form of stories leads them to give little or no weight to equally relevant or more relevant explanations or predictions presented in an abstract, quantitative, statistical, or otherwise hard-to-comprehend way (Ajzen 1977; Tversky & Kahneman 1980). Audiences automatically comprehend sequences of events in terms of stories, or causal schemata, even when they realize no causal relationship exists between the events (Michotte 1963). The ease or fluency of causal thinking makes decisions based on stories very compelling. It also

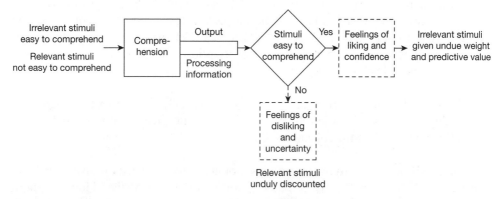

Figure 5.3 Intuitive Processes Leading to Comprehension Biases

inhibits the audience from revising its causal schemata except in rare instances (Tversky & Kahneman 1980).

Base-Rate Neglect: The Intuitive Appeal of Anecdotal Evidence

One of the most studied errors related to the representativeness heuristic is base-rate neglect. In this bias, audiences overlook relevant but difficult-to-comprehend statistical information and base their decision on easy-to-comprehend anecdotal or descriptive information instead.

In the first of a series of experiments that explored base-rate neglect, Kahneman and Tversky (1973) told one group of college students that a person had been chosen at random from a set of 100 people consisting of 70 engineers and 30 lawyers. They told a second group that the individual had been chosen from a set of 30 engineers and 70 lawyers. Both groups were able to determine the correct probability that the person chosen would be an engineer. The first group estimated a 70% probability and the second group estimated a 30% probability. Then the researchers told both groups that another person, Jack, was chosen at random from the same set of 100 people. In addition, the researchers gave both groups the following description of Jack:

> Jack is a 45-year-old man. He is married and has four children. He is generally conservative, careful, and ambitious. He shows no interest in political and social issues and spends most of his free time on his many hobbies, which include home carpentry, sailing, and mathematical puzzles.

This time, both groups estimated that there was a 90% probability that Jack was an engineer. If the second group had used the base-rate information of 30%, as Bayes Theorem demands, their probability estimate should have been much lower. Thus, the second group neglected the base-rate information and based its estimate solely on the description that seemed representative of an engineer.

In a follow-up experiment, Kahneman and Tversky (1973) told one group that there was a 70% probability that a randomly chosen person, Dick, was an engineer and told another group that there was a 30% probability that Dick was an engineer. But in this experiment they gave the two groups a description that provided no diagnostic information about Dick's profession:

> Dick is a 30-year-old man. He is married with no children. A man of high ability and high motivation, he promises to be quite successful in his field. He is well liked by his colleagues.

According to Bayes' theorem the two groups should not modify their original probability estimates of 70% and 30% since the description was not informative. However, both groups now estimated a 50% probability that Dick was an engineer. In this study both groups neglected the base-rate information and based their estimates solely on the extent to which the description seemed representative of an engineer. A number of other studies have since confirmed that audiences tend to ignore base rates when they receive less valid, but more comprehensible, anecdotal evidence (e.g., Bar-Hillel & Fischhoff 1981; Manis, Dovalina, Avis, & Cardoze 1980).

Audiences are susceptible to base-rate neglect in many different decision-making tasks (Hogarth 1980; Nisbett & Ross 1980) especially those involving person perception (Locksley, Borgida, Brekke, & Hepburn 1980; Locksley, Hepburn, & Ortiz 1982). For example, a large proportion of actual voting behavior reflects how much voters think the candidate "looks like" a competent leader (Martin 1978). Audiences making staffing decisions are also susceptible to base-rate neglect. A study of performance appraisal decisions finds that appraisers give much more weight to supervisors' subjective verbal assessments of employees than to objective statistical data about the employees' performance (Kirsch 1985). In this study, supervisors' subjective assessments accounted for 68% of the variance in the performance appraisal ratings.

Investor behavior often reflects base-rate neglect as well. For example, investors tend to predict that the future value of a company's stock will go up after they read a description of the company that "sounds good," since a good stock price will then seem to be most representative (Shefrin & Statman 1995; Solt & Statman 1989). But if they read a description that makes the company sound mediocre, a mediocre stock value will appear most representative, and investors will tend to predict that the stock price will drop. In both these cases investors are predicting the future stock values solely on the basis of company descriptions without questioning the reliability of the evidence or its statistical relevance to future profit.

Sample-Size Insensitivity: The Intuitive Appeal of Examples

A second error related to the representativeness heuristic is insensitivity to sample size. Although sample size is fundamental to statistics, Tversky and Kahneman (1974) contend that consideration of sample size is rarely a part of an audience's intuitive decision-making process. Advertisers' statements such as "Four out of five dentists surveyed recommend sugarless gum for their patients who chew gum" persuade many consumers despite the fact that the survey results are statistically meaningless without mention of the number of dentists surveyed. Even when audiences receive information about a sample's typicality, they will sometimes fail to use it (Hamill, Wilson, & Nisbett 1980).

Instead of basing their estimates and decisions on the appropriately sized sample, audiences will often over-generalize from a single, easy-to-comprehend but unrepresentative example (Nisbett & Ross 1980; Tversky & Kahneman 1974). TV viewers often base their perceptions of newsworthy events on a single example provided to them by the media (Gibson & Zillmann 1994; Zillmann, Gibson, Sundar, & Perkins 1996). The person or event featured in the news story supposedly exemplifies a whole category. Even when viewers are given contradictory survey data or base rates, frequent exposure to such exemplars may lead them to make biased decisions (Sotirovic 2001; Zillmann 2002).

A single example can have a stronger impact on decision making than statistics (cf., Feldman & March 1981; Nisbett & Ross 1980; O'Reilly 1980). For example, mock jurors in a simulated capital sentencing hearing were more persuaded by psychologists who gave their personal clinical assessment than by those who give a statistically accurate actuarial assessment (Krauss & Sales 2001). In a study that presented the same information in a statistical and non-statistical format, Koballa (1986) gave one group of high-school teachers information about a new science curriculum that was in the form of a case study written by a single teacher who had used the curriculum. The same information was given to another group but in the form of a statistical summary of the findings of 12 teachers who had used the curriculum. The high-school teachers found the case study to be much more persuasive than the statistical summary.

Audiences are especially likely to disregard sample size when they encounter extreme examples (Rothbart, Fulero, Jensen, Howard, & Birrel 1978). Audiences are also likely to disregard sample size when they encounter well-known examples. For example, audiences weight identifiable victims more heavily than statistical victims (Schelling 1984). As Loewenstein and Mather (1990) observe, when Rock Hudson and Magic Johnson were diagnosed with AIDS, the public's concern for the disease skyrocketed.

Surprisingly, experts, even expert statisticians, regularly fail to take sample size into account (Tversky & Kahneman 1971). In a study of senior auditors planning an audit of a company's internal control procedures, Selling (1982) finds that auditors do not use the optimal sample size even when given all of the necessary information. Neither do they use the sample-size selection methodology the American Institute of Certified Public Accountants (AICPA) prescribes, nor do they notice sample-size errors.

The Causality Bias: The Appeal of Narratives and Stories

Audiences give the same information more weight when it is presented to them in chronological order as an easy-to-comprehend narrative or story than when it is presented as a hard-to-comprehend random list of facts. In a study comparing two versions of a travel brochure, Adaval and Wyer (1998) asked one group of consumers to read a version of the brochure that described a vacation using a narrative form and another group to read a version that described it in a list form. Consumers evaluated the vacation more positively when it was described in a narrative form than when it was described in a list form.

Mock jurors are most likely to convict the defendant (78% chose guilty) when the prosecution presents its evidence in chronological order and the defense presents its evidence in the random order as given by the witnesses (Pennington & Hastie 1992). Mock jurors are least likely to convict when the prosecution presents evidence in random order and the defense presents it in chronological order (31% chose guilty). When attorneys on both sides of the case present evidence in chronological order or both present in random order, mock jurors choose to convict in 59% and 63% of the cases respectively.

A single story can outweigh statistics. Martin and Powers (1979, 1980) gave readers written statistical data and a verbal story and then asked them to make policy decisions. Although the statistical data influenced the readers' decisions when it was used to refute a current organizational policy, stories still tended to have a greater impact on their policy decisions. For moderately involved audiences, stories used to support arguments are at least as persuasive as statistics (Baesler 1997; Baesler & Burgoon 1994; Kazoleas 1993). In addition to activating causal schemata, narratives and stories heighten the audience's emotional reactions to claims while statistical evidence heightens the audience's rational reactions to them (Kopfman, Smith, Ah Yun, & Hodges 1998).

Syntactic and Semantic Effects: The Appeal of Simple Sentences

Audiences find information presented in easy-to-comprehend sentences to be more persuasive than the same information presented in hard-to-comprehend sentences. In a study of the effects of syntactic complexity on consumers' comprehension of advertising and on their attitudes toward the products advertised, Lowrey (1998) finds that strong arguments in advertisements are more persuasive than weak arguments only when ad sentences are syntactically simple (see also Kruglanski & Sleeth-Keppler 2007; Pierro et al. 2004, 2005). When ad sentences are syntactically complex, consumers' attitudes are not affected by the strength of the arguments in the ad. And because the semantics of active voice sentences usually makes them easier to understand, consumers perceive print ads written in the active voice to be more believable, appealing, and attractive than similar ads written in the passive voice (Motes, Hilton, & Fielden 1992).

Written Modality Effects: The Power of the Written Word

Communication modality (written, audio, or video) affects the persuasiveness of difficult-to-comprehend messages (Chaiken & Eagly 1976). Both attitude change and retention of persuasive arguments are greater when complex messages are presented in written form. The decreased persuasion observed in the audio and video modalities is due to the lesser amounts of message content that audience members are able to comprehend. The audience's comprehension of simple messages is the same regardless of the modality. However, due to the attention-getting attributes of video, attitude change for simple messages is greatest when they are presented on video and least when they are written.

SCHEMA ACTIVATION-RELATED HEURISTICS AND BIASES

The Schema Accessibility Heuristic

Before making a decision, audiences activate a schema to guide their search for information relevant to that decision. Audiences evoke what this text terms the schema accessibility heuristic when they base their search on the schema that is easiest for them to access. The schema an audience activates affects their decision-making process and its outcome. Even formally identical word problems presented in ways that activate different schemata can be vastly different in terms of the ease of solving them and the solutions arrived at (Simon & Hayes 1976).

Audiences are more likely to access a schema that is frequently and recently used than to activate other schemata (Shah et al. 2001). For expert decision makers, relevant schemata are highly accessible due to their frequent activation (cf., Fazio 1989; Higgins & King 1981; Krosnick 1988).

Both experts and novices are susceptible to activating schemata based on contextual cues or "frames" (Pan & Kosicki 2001; Tourangeau & Rasinski 1988; Tversky & Kahneman 1988). Voters may activate schemata when they hear catchphrases such as "law and order," "forced busing," and "right-wing conspiracy" that frame issues to the advantage of one politician or the other (Newman & Perloff 2004). TV news viewers may activate schemata based on the newscasters' framing of the events of the day that directly influence the decisions they make (Fredin 2001). The media can frame the news in ways that prime viewers to activate particular schemata regarding their beliefs about equality, freedom, gender, race, patriotism, international concerns, and the economy, etc. and thus lead them to attend to particular aspects of an issue and to formulate particular opinions about it (e.g., Deli Carpini 2004; Gilens 1999; Iyengar 1991).

Relying on an easily accessible schema can be appropriate in many situations (see Nisbett & Ross 1980), even when it is at the expense of statistical information. For example, in a study of medical residents at a major New York City teaching hospital, Heller and colleagues (1992) find that only first-year residents use base-rate information to make their diagnoses. Experienced residents disregard the base-rate information about the patient group and yet are more likely to make a correct diagnosis of the individual

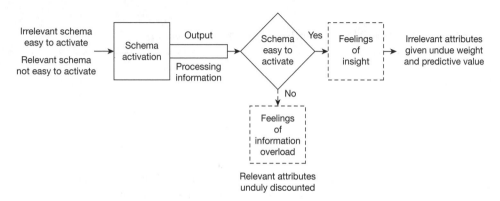

Figure 5.4 Intuitive Processes Leading to Schema Activation Biases

patient. The researchers conclude that experienced residents develop a schema that allows them to make decisions based on the symptoms as presented by the individual patient. However, relying on an easily accessible schema can also be a source of bias as the sections below indicate.

Framing Effects: The Power of Spin

Framing effects occur when two sets of information with the same meaning but different wording activate different schemata and thus lead to different decisions (Maule & Villejoubert 2007; Pan & Kosicki 2001; Simon & Hayes 1976). How many little boys would want their parents to buy them a G.I. Joe if it were called "a doll for boys" instead of "an action figure?" How many Americans would support a policy to withdraw troops from Iraq labeled "cut and run?"

There is ample empirical support for the power of framing, or "spin," to change minds. Consumers are generally more willing to pay premiums to avoid losses when the label "insurance" is used to explain those payments (Hershey & Schoemaker 1980). Consumers prefer ground beef described as 75% lean to ground beef described as 25% fat (Levin 1987). And they are more likely to make purchases when product ads are positively framed (e.g., "Save money!") versus negatively framed (e.g., "Stop wasting money!"). For example, Smith (1996) asked 390 women who either owned or were thinking about buying a video camera to read positively and negatively framed ads and to make purchase decisions. Women who read the positively framed advertising were more likely to decide to purchase the advertised camera.

Audiences other than consumers are also affected by framing. For example, voters tend to allocate more police to a community with a 3.7% crime rate as opposed to one described as 96.3% "crime free" (Quattrone & Tversky 1988). Doctors are more likely to recommend a procedure that saves 10 out of 100 lives than one that allows 90 out of 100 to die (McNeil, Pauker, Cox, & Tversky 1982). Pollsters routinely find that wording a survey question in a particular way can frame an issue and that differently worded survey questions can produce contrary results (Tumulty 1990). Changes in message frames also influence the process and outcome of a wide range of both business and political decisions (Kintsch 1988; Nelson, Oxley, & Clawson 1997; Tversky & Kahneman 1986).

Which Frame Makes the Thing Described Sound More Appealing?

"Our burgers are 25% fat"	"Our burgers are 75% lean"
Wall Street bailout	Economic rescue
Capitalism	Free enterprise
Treated wastewater	Recycled water
High-risk loans	Subprime loans
Socialized medicine	National health care

Despite the dramatic effects of frames on decision making, audiences "are normally unaware of alternative frames and of their potential effects on the relative attractiveness of options" (Tversky & Kahneman 1981, p. 457). Audiences usually fail to recognize that differently framed decision problems are similar to each other because the surface characteristics of the frames distract them (Kahneman & Tversky 1984; Tversky & Kahneman 1981). When presented with two competing frames, audiences tend to adopt the position that is consistent with their pre-existing values (Sniderman & Theriault 2004).

The influence of framing is pervasive, not only among statistical novices but also among audiences with high levels of statistical sophistication (cf., Levin, Schnittjer, & Thee 1988; Neale, Huber, & Northcraft 1987; Slovic, Fischhoff, & Lichtenstein 1982). For example, experienced physicians are as susceptible as their patients to the effects of framing alternative treatments for lung cancer described either in terms of mortality rates or survival rates (McNeil et al. 1982). Fortunately, it is sometimes possible for the audience to recognize message frames. For example, TV audiences will sometimes ignore or reject the media's frames and access frames from other sources to make sense of the news (Gamson 1992; Neuman, Just, & Crigler 1992).

Framing is most effective when the framed message recommends behaviors that are consistent with the frame. For example, in the healthcare field gain-framed messages (e.g., "Enjoy a healthy life style") that focus on the benefits of compliance are most effective when they encourage preventative behaviors such as regular physical exercise (Robberson & Rogers 1988), smoking cessation (Schneider et al. 2001b), and using sunscreen to prevent skin cancer (Detweiler, Bedell, Salovey, Pronin, & Rothman 1999). Loss-framed messages (e.g., "Stay out of the hospital") that focus on the costs of non-compliance are most effective when they encourage detection behaviors such as HIV screening (Kalichman & Coley 1995), breast self-examination (Meyerowitz & Chaiken 1987) and mammography use (Schneider et al. 2001a).

In politics, opposing sides on an issue often compete to frame the issue in the audience's mind. Framing an issue can result in a contest over the issue's scope, who is responsible for it, who is affected by it, and which values are relevant to it (Cobb & Elder 1983; Hilgartner & Bosk 1988). The success of a particular policy option often depends upon the number and influence of people who subscribe to the way it is framed (Gamson & Modigliani 1989; Snow & Benford 1988).

For politicians, framing is a strategic issue (Ryan 1991). They recognize that framing a debate takes them a long way toward winning it (Tankard 2001). In August 1990, Rep. Lee Hamilton, chairman of the House Foreign Affairs Middle East Subcommittee, spoke to Congress about the best way to frame the Persian Gulf War, saying that "The United States must not go it alone. We must frame this confrontation as a confrontation between the international community, on the one hand, and Iraq, on the other" (Keen 1990, pp. 1A, 2A). In his book *The Political Brain*, Westen (2007) makes the case that Republicans have regularly won the hearts and minds of US voters because they have been better at framing issues than Democrats:

> [Republicans] have kept government off our backs, torn down that wall, saved the flag, left no child behind, protected life, kept our marriages sacred, restored integrity to the Oval Office, spread democracy to the Middle East, and fought an unrelenting war on terror . . . I have it on good authority (i.e., off the record) that leading conservatives have chortled with joy

(usually accompanied by astonishment) as they watched their Democratic counterparts campaign by reciting their best facts and figures, as if they were trying to prevail in a high school debate tournament.

(Westen 2007, p. 36)

Films, TV news shows, newspapers, and magazines also frame issues and use specific techniques to do so (e.g., Neuman et al. 1992). Framing techniques used in the design of newspapers, such as page placement, influence the degree of concern readers express about current issues (Ghanem 1997). Framing techniques also influence the level of readership for a specific news story among the audience (McCombs & Mauro 1977). Tankard and coauthors (1991) identified 11 elements of news stories that newspapers manipulate in order to frame them:

1) headlines and kickers (small headlines over the main headlines)
2) subheads
3) photographs
4) photo captions
5) leads (the beginnings of news stories)
6) selection of sources or affiliations
7) selection of quotes
8) pull quotes (quotes that are blown up in size for emphasis)
9) logos (graphic identification of the particular series an article belongs to)
10) statistics, charts, and graphs
11) concluding statements or paragraphs of articles

Excluding information from a message frame also affects how people interpret the message (Tversky & Kahneman 1981). In a study of the effects of message framing on newspaper readers, Gitlin (1980) compared the selective publication of UPI photos of an antiwar protest by the *New York Times* with the more extensive publication of UPI photos by the *National Guardian*. The photos the *Times* editors chose to omit, or to leave outside the frame, made a significant difference in how readers interpreted the protest.

On the following pages, an experienced board member's comments about the *Chairman's Letter* from Control Data's annual report (Control Data Corporation 1986) illustrate that people are not always susceptible to framing effects. The Chairman frames the firm's problem as a lack of management focus on the firm's core businesses and promises to refocus management in the future and return the firm to profitability. Yet, the board member's final comments are quite skeptical about the firm's future. He believes that the firm's real focus is on cutting costs, and does not believe a cost-cutting strategy alone can solve the firm's problems. He thinks management should be investing heavily in R&D, and suspects the firm's creditors are the ones setting the firm's cost-cutting strategy.

The expert, whose comments on the *Management's Discussion and Analysis* from Control Data's annual report we saw in Chapter 2 (pp. 45–6) arrives at his conclusion not so much on the basis of the information the letter includes but more on the basis of what it leaves out. Although the Chairman structures the letter in a way that reflects the audience's schema for an oversight decision, he omits much information that schema requires. The letter starts by providing good information about past financial results and the reasons for them, but it commits to no specific financial goals, offers no strategy for competing, proposes no specific action plan, and fails to suggest possible contingency plans to mitigate the risk of further reductions. Certainly, there are many reasons why a chairman may decide to omit information that his audience desires, and it is rare for an annual report to provide complete coverage of all such information (cf., Chandler 1988). However, omitting critical information can create skepticism among analysts and investors about the firm's financial health and prospects (cf., Kuperman 2000).

Chairman's Letter from an Annual Report with a Board Member's Comments

Letter from the Chairman

Control Data's financial performance in 1985 was the worst in its history. Those words are difficult ones with which to begin this Annual Report. However, it is important to review for you the problems we have faced and the actions we have taken to ensure future success. With those actions and the perspectives of the past year in hand, our attention and efforts are firmly focused on 1986 and the future.

Financial Summary

Losses for the total Company amounted to $567.5 million in 1985 compared with a profit of $5.1 million for the prior year. In the computer business in 1985, the net loss totaled $562.7 million. Although operating losses of $143.3 million, together with other related charges of $65.9 million, contributed significantly to the total loss, the major component was $274.8 million resulting principally from provisions for costs and expenses associated with restructuring data storage (peripheral products) operations and the data services portion of international operations and valuation adjustments related to investments in affiliated companies. **[That was a very long sentence. It tells me, as I've seen in the financial statements, that the losses come from the peripheral devices, the data storage operations.[1]]** Operating losses of affiliates amounting to $35 million, net of minority interests, added to the loss as did a tax provision of $43.7 million related principally to the Company's international operations.

Commercial Credit, the Company's wholly-owned financial services subsidiary, also reported a net loss for 1985. Profits from continuing operations improved during the year, but the loss resulted from increased underwriting loss reserves and other charges to provide for the discontinuance of the property and casualty insurance business.

Faced with the mounting losses in 1985 and a need to conserve cash, the Company's Board of Directors decided to omit the fourth quarter dividend on common stock. **[That's a perfectly good idea.[2]]** Resumption of dividend payments on common stock will not be considered until acceptable levels of profitability have been attained and bank debt has been repaid or refinanced.

The financial reporting of Commercial Credit was deconsolidated from the parent company statements and treated on an equity basis to better present Control Data's financial condition and be more informative to shareholders and creditors. This is consistent with the current strategies the company relative to Commercial Credit and presents the computer business in a manner comparable to that of others in the industry.

Problems in Perspective

The Company's fundamental problem in 1985 was that its operations simply had become too diverse. In today's environment of intense international competition and continued rapid technological change, diversification can be highly dilutive of financial resources and, even more important, management attention. **[That can also help you in the bad times when your other investments pay off. But these people seem to have a lot of financial slack from their operations in their core business anyway. So they should be able to get rid of these businesses. Or if it were better times they could have gotten rid of these businesses, concentrated on their core, and had the financing just in case they became cash poor. Well right now I guess they can try to sell these businesses. Okay, so let's see . . .[3]]**

In key segments of the business such as the data storage products, the Company's execution of key product development had grown sluggish and inadequate to meet the changes and competitive forces in its markets. Lower demand and competitive circumstances in the market in 1985 precipitated a rapid deterioration in profits. The loss in data storage products was compounded by losses incurred in start-up service businesses in international operations and the continuing transition of the remote computing segment of U.S. data services to turnkey systems and distributed computing. **[That's a very bad sentence.[4]]** The magnitude of these losses simply overwhelmed the profits generated in other parts of the business including record performance in government systems, maintenance and other technical support services, and Arbitron Ratings. **[So they**

have rapid deterioration in their data storage business and they claim that it was competitive circumstances. It takes time for competitors to catch up in that kind of business. My guess is that new technology has come along. Competitors were already there, and they took advantage of it. Control Data was sluggish, so their data storage products are probably antiquated now. And somehow they can't create new technology in this area.[5]]

In addition, the structure of the company's assets and debt was such that liquidity became a major problem in the last half of the year. That problem had been addressed originally through the proposed divestiture of Commercial Credit in late 1984. That proposed sale, however, was withdrawn in June 1985 when it became clear that it could not be achieved on acceptable terms and conditions, in part because Commercial Credit's operations had become so diverse that no single buyer was interested in the entire company.

Following withdrawal of the sale of Commercial Credit, the Company undertook a public offering of $300 million in securities to repay existing bank debt. However, because of increasing computer business losses and a deteriorating outlook for the remainder of the year, the Company withdrew the offering in September 1985. That, in turn, resulted in the refusal of the Company's U.S. lenders to advance additional funds, forcing the Company into default on its domestic debt. **[So they're very cash poor here. That's what I get from this. And they have no access to future financing unless they give major concessions to the banks.[6]]**

Remedial Actions

Each significant problem has been addressed. The first and foremost effort was to firmly focus the organization on its core mission. All of our businesses have been and will continue to be evaluated to ensure that they have a clear and measurable potential for profitability and that they fit with the strategic thrust of the Company. Divestiture of several businesses has already been completed and some are in process.

The services businesses, both international and domestic, have also been restructured to better focus those efforts and improve profitability. **[What happened with these service businesses? Why weren't they profitable before?[7]]**

The peripherals business has been downsized, restructured and refocused toward the delivery of high-quality, cost-competitive, high-performance data storage devices, both magnetic and optical. In that regard, this segment of the Company is now named Data Storage Products rather than Peripheral Products. **[Downsizing is probably a good move. But then again, what are they going to do to make sure that this peripheral devices business can thrive in the future? Downsizing alone won't do it.[8]]**

The pain in these actions has been very great; they have resulted in pride and confidence in the future that is even greater. **[Oh really? That's interesting.[9]]**

Similarly, a program of restructuring was undertaken to reduce the scope and diversity of Commercial Credit and was essentially complete by year-end 1985. The restructuring was achieved with higher than expected value received for assets and businesses divested. It has resulted in a slimmed-down financial services company which should be more profitable. In 1986, we have undertaken further actions aimed at assuring that Commercial Credit regains its investment grade credit ratings and competitive access to capital markets.

In summary, the actions taken have meant that

- Divestitures or shut-downs of businesses representing approximately 12 percent of the 1985 revenues of the computer business and 35 percent of the revenues of Commercial Credit have been completed or are under way.

- The total work force of the Company has been reduced by approximately 10,000 through attrition, divestitures, retirements and terminations.
- Operating plant space associated primarily with peripheral equipment manufacturing was reduced by approximately 20 percent, or more than 1.2 million square feet.
- The computer business, through careful cash management and selected asset sales and asset-based financings, generated the necessary cash to sustain operations.

The Future

In February 1986, the Company reached agreement in principle with its major lenders for the restructuring of its short-term debt. However, that by no means is the total task. The highest priorities are returning to profitability and repaying domestic bank debt prior to its maturity at year-end 1986—through a major refinancing and/or additional asset sales. In addition, the Company plans to restructure its balance sheet to substantially lower the debt-to-equity ratio. Further, the major operations restructuring has been accomplished. However, the Company will continue to analyze the business segments for competitive position and potential.

The distinguishing facet of Control Data as a computer company has been its emphasis on the application of computers to solve important problems of both business and government. The common denominator is the ability to deliver value-added services which satisfy the information needs of targeted markets. Our goal for the future is to have quality and profitability join value-added as equally distinguishing characteristics. Demand will fluctuate as new technologies are absorbed and economic conditions vary, but the basic trends should assure long-term growth for the Company's products and services. **[That's the end of what they have**

for the future. So they're going to sell assets and divisions right now and lay off people to meet their pressing, short-term future debt needs. They want to return to profitability, but they don't give a clear indication as to how that's going to happen. This is a technology-driven industry. Yet I see nothing here about how they intend to come up with the next latest and greatest technology to turn things around.[10]

Board Changes

At the beginning of 1986, William C. Norris, Control Data's founder, Chairman and Chief Executive Officer for 28 years, announced his retirement from the Company. **[This is just changes in the board. They have another section here after changes in the board.[11]]** He will continue to provide his counsel to the Company as Chairman Emeritus and as a director.

Over the past year, six other directors left the board.

Marvin G. Rogers, Executive Vice President and Chief Financial Officer, and Paul G. Miller, retired Chairman of the Board of Commercial Credit Company, announced their retirements from the Board. Rogers was elected a director in 1981 and Miller in 1977.

Marilyn Carlson Nelson resigned from the Board for personal reasons in November.

Joseph W. Barr, Joseph M. Walsh and Michael W. Wright resigned from the Board because of the cancellation of the Company's directors and officers liability insurance.

The Company is grateful to each of these individuals for their dedicated service and counsel to Control Data.

In September 1985, three Company executives were appointed to the Board of Directors. They are Robert W. Duncan, Senior Vice President, Corporate Marketing and Strategic Development; Lawrence Perlman, President, Data Storage Products Group; and Henry J. White, Senior Vice President, Operation and Assistant to the President.

In January 1986, the Board elected me Chairman, Chief Executive Officer and President.

Outlook

The combined efforts and support of our many constituencies—employees, stockholders, customers, suppliers and lenders—have helped put the Company back on a track toward significant improvement. While we do not take lightly the challenges which must be successfully met in 1986 and beyond, Control Data can look forward with confidence to the coming years. **[They've given me some numbers. And they've told me that they're going to cut costs to meet the short-term needs. And they've also told me what the banks are insisting on, and that they're going to focus on their core competency. But again, these are just cost-cutting proposals. It may help them to cut off the debt but it's not going to help them become profitable in the future.[12]**

So they've said that they're back on track now and doing new things to be profitable for the future. However they haven't really stated what those things are in any specific way with respect to revenues, with respect to shoring up this sagging demand. And it's the competition that's especially killing them in the peripheral devices section.[13]

So all in all, the letter still doesn't give me confidence in the company. It seems like the creditors are starting to run the business because costs skyrocketed.[14]

The details in the annual report are the same as were summarized in the letter from the chairman: they do not address the issue of how they plan to position themselves in the future by technological change.[15]]

Robert M. Price
Chairman, President & Chief Executive Officer

March 14, 1986

Framing Effects: The Power of Analogy

Analogies can serve as powerful decision frames: They can constrain the set of alternatives the audience considers and can influence the audience's evaluations of those alternatives (Markman & Moreau 2001). Analogies have been shown to influence the decisions of many different audiences, including consumers (Gregan-Paxton & Roedder 1997), voters (Blanchette & Dunbar 2000), mock jurors (Holyoak & Simon 1999; Holyoak & Thagard 1995), and investors (Gregan-Paxton & Cote 2000).

Analogies work by activating a well-understood schema in one domain that can organize attribute information about a little-understood target in another domain (Chi & Ohlsson 2005; Gentner & Forbus 1991; Holland, Holyoak, Nisbett, & Thagard 1993). For example, what most audiences already know about the structure of the solar system—it has a number of small planets that revolve around a large central star—can be used to explain the structure of the atom—it has small electrons that revolve around a relatively large central nucleus of protons and neutrons.

Different analogies provide different frames and lead to different decisions. For example, consumers who read an ad that made an analogy between a personal digital assistant (PDA) and a librarian formed a more favorable impression of the PDA than did consumers who read an ad that made an analogy between the PDA and a secretary (Azar 1994). Similarly, consumers who read an ad that made an analogy between a digital camera and a film-based camera had a greater intention to buy the digital camera than did those who read a similar ad that made an analogy between a digital camera and a scanner (Moreau, Markman, & Lehman 2001).

Analogies can lead audiences to make biased predictions if some feature of the current situation that has no diagnostic significance has triggered the analogy. For example, Gilovich (1981) reveals that football scouts sometimes make irrelevant analogies with pro football stars when judging the talent of rookies. Football scouts tend to choose rookies who win awards named after a star football player rather than choose rookies who win equally prestigious but differently named awards.

Analogies are also useful for framing the terms of a debate in a political decision (Blanchette & Dunbar 2000, 2002) and can undermine the role of accurate information in determining causes and effects. For example, May (1973) found that US policy-makers used two analogies extensively to decide on military strategy during the pre-Vietnam era: (1) Vietnam will be another Korean War, and (2) the US experience in Vietnam will be like the French experience in Vietnam in the 1950s. Some policy-makers used the French analogy to argue against the appropriateness of the Korean analogy. They conducted this argument by comparing the two analogies to each other (Khong 1992).

Later, in the 1960s, policy-makers used the "domino theory" analogy to frame the debate about Vietnam (Glad & Taber 1990; Shimko 1994). The success of this analogy played an important role in the decision of the United States to enter into the Vietnam War (Khong 1992). Interestingly, policy-makers themselves never fully recognized the role of the analogy in framing the debate about Vietnam (Shimko 1994).

The Self-Serving Bias: The Power of Roles

When presented with identical information, different audiences activate different schemata depending on their role in the situation. The particular schema they activate tends to be the one that best promotes their perceived self-interest. For example, Democrats typically support a program if it is referred to as a Democratic program and reject the same program if it is referred to as a Republican program, and the converse is true of Republicans (Druckman 2001b). Similarly, when audience members are asked to take the role of someone personally affected by a policy they tend to make a different decision about the policy than when they are asked to take the role of the policy-maker (Wagenaar, Keren, & Lichtenstein 1988).

Psychologists call this tendency the self-serving bias (Messick & Sentis 1985). The bias is not caused by a desire to be unfair, but by a human inability to interpret information in an unbiased manner (Diekmann, Samuels, Ross, & Bazerman 1997). Furthermore, audiences tend to confuse what is beneficial to them personally with what is fair or moral. Consider the following two scenarios. Does your answer change depending on your role in it?

> **Scenario 1: An across-the-board raise to employees**
> Imagine you are an employee. Do you think a 10% raise is a good idea?
>
> Imagine you are the owner. Do you think a 10% raise is a good idea?
>
> **Scenario 2: Damages for a car accident**
> Imagine you were in a car accident. The judge determined it was *their* fault.
> Should the other driver pay for all of the damages and receive a fine?
>
> Imagine you were in a car accident. The judge determined it was *your* fault.
> Should you pay for all of the damages and receive a fine?

Even professional tax accountants, who are trained to be unbiased, tend to interpret judicial cases in a way that is consistent with their client's preferences (Cloyd & Spilker 1999). As a consequence, many recommendations made by tax accountants tend to be overly aggressive and cannot be justified when challenged by the IRS.

The self-serving bias is perhaps best known for leading people to take more responsibility for their successes than for their failures (Arkin, Appelman, & Burger 1980; Arkin, Cooper, & Kolditz 1980; Riess, Rosenfeld, Melburg, & Tedeschi 1981) and to take more credit than they deserve (Ross & Sicoly 1979). In a content analysis of one year's annual reports from Fortune 500 companies, Chandler (1988) found that CEOs whose firms had a net loss for the year took responsibility for the loss in fewer than 11% of the cases. In about 89% of these cases, the CEOs blamed external factors such as the economy, the competition, government regulations, or their employees. Conversely, CEOs whose firms had a net profit for the year took credit for their firm's profitability in fully 90% of the cases.

Priming Effects: The Power of Subtle Influences

In addition to being activated by framing techniques and the audience's role in a situation, schemata and their components can be primed—brought to mind or activated—in a number of different and sometimes subtle ways. For example, the mere presence of a television can prime a schema consistent with television content and evoke audience perceptions of violence and crime (Shrum, Wyer, & O'Guinn 1998). Music can prime consumers' schemata in subtle ways. A study of background music played in a store selling both German and French wines finds that background music from a wine's country of origin increases sales of wines from that country (North, Hargreaves, & McKendrick 1997, 1999).

Most audiences are highly susceptible to priming because they are easily influenced to interpret events with the communicator's schema (Fredin 2001). In court cases, the opening statements made by prosecution and defense attorneys prime competing schemata in the minds of the jurors (Pyszczynski & Wrightsman 1981). In this situation, the longer opening statement tends to win the competition because it primes jurors with a more complete schema for making sense of the case.

Words and captions can serve as primes for images and lead audiences to find images that are conceptually related to them to be more appealing than images that are not conceptually related (Reber, Winkielman, & Schwarz 1998; Winkielman, Schwarz, Fazendeiro, & Reber 2003a). In a study of verbal primes for images, Winkielman and Fazendeiro (2003) exposed viewers to words (e.g., "bottle") and then exposed them to pictures, some of which were associated with those words (e.g., a picture of a wineglass). Viewers preferred pictures when the pictures were shown after words that were conceptually related to them. For example, viewers rated a picture of a wineglass as more appealing when it was shown after the word "bottle" than when it was presented after an unrelated word.

Background designs and templates can serve as another subtle prime. In a study of website design, Mandel and Johnson (2002) changed the embedded designs in the background of a website to prime either product quality attributes (e.g., safety for cars, comfort for couches) or price. The prime affected the choices of both novices and experts in the product class. Note too how the background template of the intuitively appealing slide presentation shown earlier in this chapter (pp. 184–186) primes a preference for the wind-generated power alternative, whereas the background template of the more purely rational slide presentation with its symbol of the atom (pp. 182–183) may unintentionally prime fears of radioactive fallout.

Priming can determine how heavily voters will weight the criteria by which they evaluate public officials (Iyengar & Kinder 1987). For example, if last week's news stories focused on environmental issues, then voters will weight environmental criteria more heavily in their evaluation of public officials. On the other hand, if last week's news stories focused on defense issues, then voters will weight defense criteria more heavily.

Priming also makes it easier for audiences to form certain kinds of impressions of other people (Gill, Swann, & Silvera 1998). In a study of the priming effects of pre-trial publicity, Penrod and Otto (1992) asked mock jurors to render their verdicts both before and after viewing an edited videotape of an actual trial. Jurors' verdicts were significantly affected by pre-trial publicity, especially negative pre-trial publicity about the defendant's character, even when they heard the trial evidence prior to viewing the publicity. Unfortunately, a follow-up study finds that jury deliberation fails to significantly diminish the influence pre-trial publicity has on jurors' verdicts (Otto, Penrod, & Dexter 1994).

Priming can have a powerful effect on consumers' decisions. Priming the schema for a product category can change consumers' choices (Herr 1989). Priming a product feature can increase the weight consumers give to that feature (Yi 1990). Questions that prime intentions, such as "Do you intend to buy a personal computer in the next six months?" influence purchase decisions by making attitudes about products in the category more accessible (e.g., Morwitz, Johnson, & Schmittlein 1993; Morwitz & Fitzsimons 2004). The effect can last up to a year when the questions are asked as part of a consumer satisfaction survey (Dholakia & Morwitz 2002).

Primacy Effects: The Power of Being First to Frame an Issue

The schema the audience activates first will unduly influence its decision. For example, shortly before World War II began, Americans were asked if they should be allowed to join the German army. Only 23% answered "yes" when the question was presented first. However, 34% answered "yes" when the question was presented after two questions that asked if Americans should be allowed to join the French and the British armies (Rugg & Cantril 1944). Markus and Zajonc (1985) explain these results by suggesting the first presentation order activated a "loyalty and treason" schema. Americans should not help the enemy. The second presentation order, on the other hand, activated a "freedom of choice" schema. Americans should be allowed to fight in any army they choose.

INFORMATION ACQUISITION-RELATED HEURISTICS AND BIASES

The Anchoring and Availability Heuristics

Once an audience has activated a schema, it can then search for the value or information that belongs in each slot of the schema. For example, the schema home-buyers activate to decide whether to purchase a new house likely includes a slot for the monetary value of the house. When audiences allow a value that is easily acquired from an external source (e.g., a seller's asking price of $320,000) to unduly influence, or anchor, their estimate of the real slot value (e.g., the price that an appraiser might calculate after investigating the current housing market), they are said to be using the anchoring heuristic (Fischhoff & MacGregor 1980; Tversky & Kahneman 1974).

In addition to filling empty schema slots with values based on information that is easy to acquire from external sources, the audience may also fill those slots with information that is easy to imagine or to retrieve from their memories. When audiences allow a value that they can easily retrieve from their memories or imaginations (e.g., the price of the last house they purchased) to unduly influence their estimate of the actual slot value, they are said to be using the availability heuristic (Markus & Zajonc 1985; Tversky & Kahneman 1973). Information is easy for the audience to retrieve from memory if they paid close attention to it when it was presented to them, if they fully comprehended it, and if they have been exposed to it frequently (Nisbett & Ross 1980).

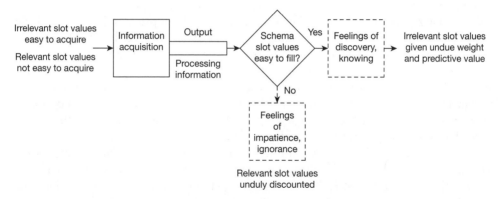

Figure 5.5 Intuitive Processes Leading to Information Acquisition Biases

Insufficient Adjustment: The Power of Easily Acquired Information

When easily acquired external information anchors an audience's estimate of a slot value, the audience rarely changes or adjusts the anchor's value sufficiently (Slovic & Lichtenstein 1971; Tversky & Kahneman 1974). For example, managers often use an employee's salary of the past year as an anchor to determine the employee's salary for the upcoming year and rarely adjust the anchor sufficiently to account for the employee's performance (Slovic & Lichtenstein 1971). Different anchors can yield different decisions about the same issue. For example, in mock negotiations between buyers and sellers, the buyer's initial offer can act as an anchor that has a dramatic effect on the final selling price (Ritov 1996).

Examples of the insufficient-adjustment bias abound. When consumers evaluate two or more items bundled together, the value of the most important item anchors their overall evaluation of the entire bundle (Yadav 1994). When mock jurors are instructed to consider the harshest verdict first, the jurors anchor on that verdict and render significantly harsher verdicts than do jurors who are told to consider lenient verdicts first (Greenberg, Williams, & O'Brien 1986). In a study of investors deciding among mutual funds, Jordan and Kaas (2002) asked 499 investors to read two versions of a print ad for a mid-cap mutual fund. Except for the names of the two funds, *Euro Star 100 Fund™* and *Euro Star 500 Fund™*, both versions of the ad were identical. Both versions presented the same product information and the same risk-return profile. Incredibly, investors anchored on the first value they read—the number in the fund's name—to determine the fund's expected return. On average, investors who read the ad for the *Euro Star 100 Fund™* said they expected a return of 11.8%. Those who read the same ad for the *Euro Star 500 Fund™* expected a 22.6% return.

Experts as well as novices make insufficient adjustment to the anchor. Northcraft and Neale (1987) find that professional real estate agents make insufficient adjustment to the anchor when they predict various values regarding houses for sale. In this study, agents were allowed to take up to 20 minutes to inspect a house before they were asked for their predictions. Agents also received one of two versions of a 10-page handout of the statistics on the house and other houses in the area. The two versions of the handout were identical except for the asking price—the first version had an asking price of $119,900; the second had an asking price of $149,900. Those agents who received the $119,900 asking price on average predicted that the appraisal value of the house would be $114,204, that the listing price would be $117,745, that the purchase price would be $111,454, and that the seller would accept an offer no lower than $111,136. On the other hand, agents who received the asking price of $149,900 on average predicted an appraisal value of $128,754, a listing price of $130,981, a purchase price of $127,318, and a lowest offer price of $123,818. Thus, the value of the asking price changed all the average predicted values by 11 to 14%.

Even financial experts are not immune to anchoring effects. Auditors from global accounting firms insufficiently adjust the anchor when asked to estimate the incidence of fraud (Joyce & Biddle 1981). Fund managers anchor on the current value of the Dow Jones Industrial Average when asked to determine what the value of the Dow would be if dividends were included in its calculation (Montier 2002). Their highest guesses only double or triple the current value even in quarters when the actual value is more than 70 times greater than the Dow's current value (Statman & Fisher 1998). When valuing firms, analysts tend to anchor on the firm's current market price and then add or subtract 5% of the price instead of calculating the firm's value using the well-accepted discounted cash flow valuation method (Montier 2002).

The most common anchor that audiences use to judge other people is themselves (Fong & Markus 1982; Markus & Smith 1981). For example, when asked questions such as, "How does your driving ability compare to that of your peers?" audiences tend to anchor on their own abilities and then adjust for the skills of their peers (Kruger 1999). Audiences also anchor on their first impressions of others. Personal traits mentioned early in impression formation tasks receive more weight than traits mentioned later. Audiences tend to rate a person described as "intelligent, slender, and suspicious" more positively than they rate a person described as "suspicious, slender, and intelligent" (Anderson 1965; Asch 1946). Invariably, when audiences try to adjust their initial impressions, they adjust too little and infer more about a person's character than is warranted (Gilbert 2002).

Anchors acquired from external sources can bias both the external search for further information and the retrieval of additional information from memory (Chapman & Johnson 1999; Jacowitz & Kahneman 1995; Mussweiler & Strack 2000). However, some easily acquired values will not serve to anchor the audience's estimates. Audiences will use a value as an anchor only when it is expressed on the same scale as the value the audience is trying to estimate. For example, an audience would not use a value expressed as a percentage as an anchor to estimate a value expressed in dollars (Kahneman & Knetsch 1993).

The Recall Bias: The Power of Easily Recalled Information

Audiences often make decisions based upon the subjective ease with which they can retrieve schema slot values from their memories. Decisions about risk (Grayson & Schwarz 1999), stereotypes (Dijksterhuis, Macrae, & Haddock 1999), and interpersonal closeness (Broemer 2001) are all influenced by ease of recall. Voters' decisions are also influenced by ease of recall. Haddock (2002) observed that voters who were asked to perform the more difficult task of retrieving eight positive attribute values regarding a politician tended to have a more negative attitude about the politician than did voters who were asked to retrieve only two positive attribute values. In addition, the easier it is for voters to retrieve arguments either for or against an issue, the more confident they are that those arguments are valid (Tormala, Petty, & Brinol 2002).

The Imagination Bias: The Power of Easily Imagined Information

Audiences may make decisions based upon the subjective ease with which they can imagine information that fills schema slots. Voters who were asked to mentally imagine a presidential election outcome later rated it more probable that the candidate they had imagined winning would actually win than did voters who had not been asked to imagine the election's outcome (Carroll 1978). Audiences who were asked to imagine experiencing a disease judged themselves as more likely to catch the disease than did others who had not been asked to imagine getting ill (Sherman, Cialdini, Schwartzman, & Reynolds 1985). Audiences asked to imagine winning a contest or being arrested for a crime decided it was more probable that those events could happen to them (Gregory, Cialdini, & Carpenter 1982). Homeowners asked to imagine watching and enjoying the benefits of a cable TV service were later more likely to subscribe to cable TV (Gregory et al. 1982). Moreover, followers find leaders who infuse their speeches with words such as *dream* and *imagine* to be more persuasive than leaders who do not (Emrich, Brower, Feldman, & Garland 2001).

Interestingly, the imagination bias also works in reverse. For example, when an event takes great effort for the audience to imagine, audience estimates of the likelihood of that event decrease rather than increase (Sherman et al. 1985).

Undue Optimism: The Power of Positive Information

Because positive information is more accessible and easier to bring to mind than negative information (Sanna & Schwarz 2004), when audiences fill schema slots with information retrieved from memory they tend to fill those slots with positive information. The audience's bias toward a positive future leads them to overestimate the likelihood that they will contribute to charity, vote in an upcoming election, and have a long-lasting romantic relationship (Epley & Dunning 2000, 2004; Sherman 1980). Similarly, college students' undue optimism leads them to over-predict their performance on examinations (Gilovich, Kerr, & Medvec 1993) and to under-predict the amount of time it will take them to complete class assignments (Newby-Clark, Ross, Buehler, Koehler, & Griffin 2000).

The Confirmation Bias: The Power of Previously Acquired Information

The confirmation bias leads audiences to frame newly acquired ambiguous or even contradictory information that fills schema slots so as to make it consistent with information they acquired earlier (e.g., Greitemeyer & Schulz-Hardt 2003; Klayman & Ha 1987; Russo, Medvec, & Meloy 1996). For example, recruiters' pre-interview impressions of job applicants significantly influence the questions they ask applicants during job interviews (Binning, Goldstein, Garcia, & Scattaregia 1988; Dougherty, Turban, & Callender 1994; Macan & Dipboye 1988). Recruiters tend to unconsciously distort the information they acquire about applicants during the interviews in order to confirm their initial expectations (Smith, Neuberg, Judice, & Biesanz 1997). In a study of pre-interview impressions, Macan and Dipboye (1994) asked 64 mock recruiters to read résumés of job applicants for a sales position and then to observe and evaluate the applicants' videotaped interviews. Mock recruiters who read more favorable résumés rated the same applicants as doing a better job in answering questions, displaying more sales-consistent traits, and making more favorable statements during the interviews.

Experts as well as novices are susceptible to the confirmation bias. Like the mock recruiters mentioned above, seasoned managers' pre-interview evaluations of job applicants influence their post-interview evaluations of applicant qualifications (Phillips & Dipboye 1989). Moreover, managers with favorable pre-interview impressions are more likely to attribute good interview performances to the applicants' qualifications for the job and to attribute poor performances to external factors.

The confirmation bias has also been found to influence juror decision making. Because jurors hear the prosecution's evidence before they hear the defendant's testimony, they are more likely to accept the prosecution's evidence, even if it is later discredited, and to become more critical of the defendant's testimony (Saunders, Vidmar, & Hewitt 1983). Defense attorneys can counteract this tendency by having their strongest witnesses testify first. Ordering witness testimony from strongest to weakest leads jurors to hand down the fewest number of guilty verdicts (Pennington 1982).

In addition to first impressions, prior decisions can also lead to the confirmation bias. For example, nine out of 10 voters who watched American presidential debates in 1960, 1976, and 1980 believed their preferred candidates won the debate (Kinder & Sears 1985). In a study of people who either supported or opposed the death penalty, Lord and coauthors (1979) asked the two groups to read two contradictory reports. The first report presented evidence that the death penalty was a deterrent to crime, whereas the second report presented evidence to the contrary. Each of the two groups claimed that the report favoring their opinion was "better conducted" and "more convincing" than the other report. Surprisingly, each group became even more convinced of the correctness of their initial opinion after reading the report that contradicted their opinion. Similarly, the more misinformed voters are about a policy, the more confident they are in their opinions about it, and the more resistant they are to changing their opinions, even when presented with factual information to the contrary (Kuklinski, Quirk, Jerit, Schwieder, & Rich 2000).

The Confirmation Bias in Groups

The confirmation bias affects the exchange of information in group discussions. Group members tend to discuss and repeat information, or schema slot values, that is consistent with their prior preferences and decisions (Dennis 1996; Schulz-Hardt et al. 2006). Group members perceive information that supports the alternative they prefer as more important than information against it (Van Swol 2007). Group members also perceive information that supports the alternative they prefer to be more credible and relevant than information that opposes it.

Even if group members are not motivated to advocate the alternative they personally prefer, they are more likely to mention information that is consistent with their preferred alternative because they regard supportive information to be of higher value (Kerschreiter, Schulz-Hardt, Faulmuller, Mojzisch, & Frey 2004). Once the group makes a decision, group members prefer information that supports the alternative favored by the majority compared to information opposing it (Schulz-Hardt et al. 2000). Groups that consistently disagree about the best alternative are less confident about the correctness of the group's decision and less committed to implementing it.

The Common Knowledge Effect in Groups

One reason people meet in groups is to allow group members to share information relevant to making a decision, in other words, to share information that fills their schema slots. Yet groups typically fail to make better decisions than individual decision makers. In a seminal study of the common knowledge effect, Gigone and Hastie (1993) asked three-person groups to use six decision criteria—aptitude test scores, high-school grade point averages, attendance, enjoyment of the course, overall workload, and self-rated anxiety—to determine the grades received by 32 students in an introductory psychology class. Each group member was exposed to all six criteria over the course of experiment's 32 decisions. For each student the group evaluated, all group members were given information about how the student performed on two of the six criteria, two of the three group members were given information about the student's performance on two other criteria, and only one group member was given information about the student's performance on the remaining two criteria.

Surprisingly, the groups consistently failed to discuss the information that was unshared or to use it to make their decisions. Even though the groups were in possession of more information than were any of the individuals, placing people in groups did not result in better judgments than would have been obtained by simply averaging together the judgments of the same individuals. Moreover, group weighting of information was a linear function of the degree of sharedness or common knowledge. The likelihood that a piece of information, or slot value, will be recalled by a group is also a function of the number of group members who share that information (Hinsz 1990; Tindale & Sheffey 2002; Vollrath, Sheppard, Hinsz, & Davis 1989).

When no single group member possesses all of the information relevant to making the decision, or the values filling all the schema slots, but the group as a whole does— a situation called the *hidden profile condition*—groups rarely discover the best alternative (e.g., Lam & Schaubroeck 2000; Schulz-Hardt et al. 2006; Van Swol, Savadori, & Sniezek 2003). Instead, groups typically choose the alternative that is supported by the information that all group members hold in common. Stasser and Titus (1985) find that only 18% of groups in a hidden profile condition choose the best alternative. In contrast, when all the relevant information is known by every group member, 83% of groups select the best alternative.

INFORMATION INTEGRATION-RELATED HEURISTICS AND BIASES

Heuristic Choice Rules

Audience members have great difficulty accurately combining or integrating the slot values they acquire for their schemata. A computer given the same information will always do as well or better than people at information integration tasks (Dawes et al. 1989). One reason for the difference between computers and people is that people attend to the values of only a few of the important attributes or decision criteria and do not combine those values with the values of other attributes (Dawes 1976, 1980).

Combining the pros and cons of many alternatives with many attributes or decision criteria can be so difficult that audience members may even make a decision opposite to the one they would have made if they could have integrated the information more easily (Hsee 1996). Because of the difficulties inherent in the information integration process, consumers are willing to pay more for products when the effort required to choose among alternatives is reduced (Garbarino & Edell 1997).

The use of heuristic choice rules enables audiences to avoid or simplify the information integration process (Payne et al. 1993; Tversky 1972). We have already examined several heuristic choice rules in Chapter 3. For example, the *elimination-by-aspects rule* and the *lexicographic rule* are heuristic choice rules because they are non-compensatory, that is to say, they do not allow trade offs (Tversky 1972).

The *equal weight rule*, although a compensatory choice rule, is a heuristic choice rule because the audience who uses it automatically assigns an equal weight to all attributes. In contrast, the *weighted additive rule* is a compensatory choice rule that is also a normative or non-heuristic rule. It demands that the audience weight every attribute or decision criteria independently and consider every value of every alternative for every attribute.

Audiences can also simplify the information integration process by quickly eliminating some alternatives from consideration on the basis of a single "if-then," or configural, heuristic choice rule. For example, a recruiter might have the rule that if a job applicant does not give her a firm handshake, then she will not hire that job applicant. Experts report that they often use such "if-then" rules to make decisions (Johnson 1988a). For example, magistrates in the UK tend to rely on "if-then" heuristic choice rules based on the prosecutor's recommendation or the age of the defendant when reaching an exonerative decision (Dhami & Ayton 2001).

Like other heuristic choice rules, "if-then" heuristic choice rules allow the audience to bypass making trade offs and avoid the difficult weighting and combination processes that are involved in normative information integration (Camerer & Johnson 1991). Although the audience's heuristic use of "if-then" choice rules can occasionally yield nearly optimal choices (Johnson & Payne 1985), their choices are usually inaccurate. When audiences formulate such rules from their experience, they tend to over-generalize from a small sample.

Audiences can avoid the difficulties of the information integration process altogether if they simply choose the same alternative they chose the last time they had to make a similar decision. Audiences rely on the habitual choice heuristic when they retrieve prior evaluations of their current options from memory and then choose the alternative they had previously evaluated most highly (Hartman, Doane, & Woo 1991).

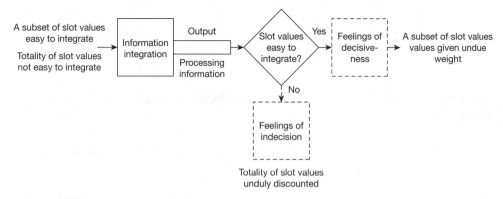

Figure 5.6 Intuitive Processes Leading to Information Integration Biases

Trade-off Avoidance: The Impact of a Dominant Attribute

In many decisions each alternative under consideration has both positive and negative slot values for different attributes or decision criteria. For example, a higher quality product usually comes with higher cost. But most people tend to avoid making trade offs (Axelrod 1976; Jervis 1976). Audiences can simplify the information integration process and avoid making trade offs by using non-compensatory choice rules.

When audiences use non-compensatory choice rules, they typically focus on one important decision criterion or attribute for which the different alternatives have different values. At the same time they avoid considering the other attributes that provide compensatory values. For many business audiences the dominant decision criterion is either a financial or legal one.

In his seminal study of trade-off avoidance, Slovic (1975) asked participants to identify pairs of alternatives that had equal value for them. For example, participants said Gift Package A below that contains $10 in cash and a book of coupons worth $32 had the same value as Gift Package B which contains twice the cash but a coupon book worth less.

	Gift Package A	*Gift Package B*
Cash	$10	$20
Coupon book worth	$32	$18

A week later, Slovic asked the participants to choose between the two alternatives. He also asked them which decision criterion—cash or coupons—they considered more important. Eighty-eight percent of the participants chose the alternative that had a higher value for the criterion the participant considered more important. Slovic (1975) obtains similar results for many different decisions, including choices among college applicants, auto tires, baseball players, and routes to work.

Slovic surmises that avoiding trade offs makes it easier for people to justify their choices to themselves and others. In a study of the written arguments of policy-makers, Gallhofer and Saris (1996) find that the policy-makers avoid arguing the pros and cons of their policy proposals. Instead they make one-sided arguments to which a simple non-compensatory choice rule can be applied.

The Mere Quantity Effect: The Impact of a Seemingly Dominant Alternative

Audiences can avoid many of the difficulties of the information integration process if they simply choose the alternative that is agreed on by the most people. In a study of the persuasiveness of multiple sources, audience members weighted trait descriptions more heavily when the descriptions were presented by multiple sources than when presented by a single source (Himmelfarb 1972). Harkins and Petty (1981) find that three speakers conveying three arguments are more persuasive than one speaker conveying the same three arguments. And audiences who lack the information or expertise to make a decision themselves are more confident in advisors' proposals when the number of advisors increases and the differences among the advisors' proposals decreases (Budescu & Rantilla 2000).

Audiences can also avoid many of the difficulties of information integration if they simply choose the alternative that is supported by the most arguments. The more arguments that are presented for a position the more likely it is that the audience will be persuaded to adopt that position (e.g., Chaiken 1980; Eagly & Warren 1976; Maddux & Rogers 1980). For example, increasing the number of arguments supporting the guilt of a defendant significantly increases mock jurors' tendency to render guilty verdicts (Calder, Insko, & Yandell 1974; Insko, Lind, & LaTour 1976). Likewise, increasing the number of not-guilty arguments increases jurors' tendency to judge the defendant innocent.

Mock jurors are also more likely to be persuaded by the number of supporting arguments made during jury deliberations than by the number of jurors who initially support a verdict (Stasser, Stella, Hanna, & Colella 1984). When audiences make no concerted effort to evaluate the quality of the arguments presented or lack the expertise to do so, they are even likely to judge a large number of irrelevant arguments to be more persuasive than a smaller number of highly relevant arguments (Petty & Cacioppo 1984; Wood, Kallgren, & Priesler 1985b).

The Common Dimension Effect: The Impact of Direct Comparisons

Audiences find comparing alternatives that have slot values for the same attributes (i.e., for the same decision criteria or dimensions) easier than comparing alternatives that have unique attributes or missing slot values. For this reason, the audience will often eliminate alternatives with unique attributes or missing slot values from consideration or else weight those attributes less heavily, a tendency called the *common dimension effect* (Hsee 1998; Markman & Moreau 2001; Tversky & Russo 1969).

When the audience is given the slot value of each attribute or decision criterion for all of the alternatives under consideration, it only needs to know the relative utility of each attribute. For example, when the audience is told that one computer has 100 GB of random access memory (RAM) and another has 200 GB of RAM, it can see the first computer has a higher value for the attribute of RAM than the second, even if it does not know the meaning of RAM. But if the audience is not given the values for some attributes or criteria, it needs to know the absolute level of utility of each attribute (Markman & Moreau 2001). For example, if the audience knows only that one computer has 100 GB of RAM, then it must know the absolute worth of that value in order to evaluate it.

Because of the difficulties involved in calculating a value's absolute worth, if the audience finds some alternatives are missing values for some attributes, they will tend to weight those attributes less heavily (Yates, Jagacinski, & Faber 1978). In a study illustrating this effect, Slovic and MacPhillamy (1974) asked judges to evaluate the grade point averages of two students, each of whom was described by two test scores. One of the test scores came from a test both students took and the other came from a test only one of the students took. Judges systematically gave more weight to the scores from the test both students took.

Audiences are susceptible to the common dimension effect even when information is presented to them in paragraph form as opposed to tabular or matrix form. Paragraph form makes finding the common attributes or decision criteria of alternatives more difficult than does a matrix format. Markman and Medin (1995) gave readers pairs of paragraph that described videogames and asked them to choose the game they thought would sell best and to justify their decision. Each pair of games had two attributes in common and two unique attributes. Readers tended to ignore the slot values of the unique attributes and to make and justify their decisions based on the different slot values each game had on the two common attributes.

In a follow-up study, Lindemann and Markman (1996) showed college students descriptions of colleges written in paragraph form. The students were asked to think aloud as they decided which college they would recommend to a younger brother or sister. They were also asked to rate the importance of all the attributes or decision criteria mentioned in the paragraphs. When making their decisions, the students discounted the slot values of the unique attributes despite claiming that they believed that information to be important.

When the format makes it difficult for audiences to compare alternatives along a common dimension or decision criterion, they may discount that dimension regardless of its importance to them. Finucane and colleagues (2003) find that an unusual display of automobile safety information in ranges, as recommended by National Academy of

Sciences in 1996, makes it hard for consumers to evaluate a car's level of safety when choosing among new vehicles. As a result, the consumers do not give safety data the weight it deserves. Instead, consumers give undue weight to less relevant but more salient slot values such as the car's color and style. Consumer decision making can be enhanced by the use of more comprehensible formats in displays of safety information that incorporate meaningful symbols such as letter grades or stars to indicate safety ratings of new cars.

Some consumers have developed strategies for avoiding the common dimension effect. Johnson (1986, 1988b) asked consumers to think aloud while making choices between comparable products (e.g., two toasters) and between non-comparable products (e.g., a toaster and a smoke detector). Consumers tended to compare slot values for concrete attributes of the comparable products, for example, the number of settings on each toaster. In contrast, consumers tended to compare slot values for abstract attributes of the non-comparable products, for example, their *need* for a toaster versus their *need* for a smoke detector. Non-comparable items have few concrete attributes in common. To choose among them, many consumers have learned to rise to a higher level of abstraction where they can identify different values on common dimensions.

The Asymmetric Dominance Effect: The Impact of a Third Option

Audiences find it easier to make trade offs between two equally desirable alternatives if given a third alternative whose slot values are clearly inferior to one alternative but not to the other. The presence of a third alternative gives audiences a compelling reason to choose one alternative over the other and is known as the *asymmetric dominance effect* (Huber, Payne, & Puto 1982; Tversky & Shafir 1992). For example, when students were given a choice between $6 and a nice pen, 64% chose the money and 36% chose the pen (Shafir et al. 1993). But when students were given a choice between $6.00, a nice pen, and a cheap pen, only 52% chose the money. Forty-six percent chose the nice pen and the remaining 2% chose the cheap pen.

The Limited Options Bias: The Appeal of Yes or No Choices

Providing audiences with too many alternatives, and thus with too many schema slot values to integrate easily, can stop them from making a decision. For example, employees' participation in 401(k) plans drops as the number of funds that their employer allows them to choose from increases (Huberman, Iyengar, & Jiang 2007). Experienced physicians are less likely to prescribe a new medication when they are asked to choose between two medications than when they are asked to decide whether or not to prescribe a single medication (Redelmeier & Shafir 1995). In a study of consumer decision making, Iyengar and Lepper (2000) set up booths in a grocery store and offered customers the opportunity to taste any of six jams at one booth, or any of 24 jams at another. At the six-jam booth, 40% of shoppers stopped to taste and 30% who tasted purchased a jam. At the 24-jam booth, 60% stopped to taste but only 3% who tasted purchased.

In a large study of the persuasive impact of single versus multiple examples on borrowers, Bertrand and colleagues (2005) examined the responses of 57,000 potential borrowers to a lender's mailing that offered them large, short-term loans. The offer letter gave either one example of a possible loan—its size, term, and monthly payments—or four examples of different loans. Borrowers were more likely to accept loans illustrated by only one example. The one-example description had the same positive effect on loan acceptance as dropping the monthly interest rate by two percentage points.

The Status Quo Bias: The Appeal of Past Decisions

The status quo bias circumvents the need to search for schema slot values and to integrate that new information. In this bias keeping things the way they are, doing things the way they have always been done, is the favorite option (Samuelson & Zeckhauser 1988). Researchers in marketing refer to this bias as *brand loyalty* (Fader & Lattin 1993). In many purchase situations, brand loyalty is the best predictor of people's future purchases (Guidagni & Little 1983).

Of course, audiences can have good reasons for maintaining the status quo. For example, untried alternatives necessarily involve more risk, the costs can be high to switch to a different alternative, and the audience may have based previous choices on good reasons they can no longer remember. Not choosing but maintaining the status quo also minimizes the negative emotions that the decision-making process sometimes creates (Luce 1998; Nowlis, Kahn, & Dhar 2002).

Heuristics and Biases in Audience Decision Making: Implications for Communicators

✧ The main takeaway for communicators in Chapter 5 is that audiences are unconsciously biased by techniques that make each of the processes in decision making easy for them to complete. Audiences do not base their decisions exclusively on facts and reason.

✧ Use the information presented in the chapter to identify techniques that make processing easy. Do not expect the facts you present to speak for themselves.

✧ Why use the information? To enhance the intuitive appeal of your communications. To compete successfully with other skilled communicators.

✧ To apply a technique that makes processing easy, refer to the section describing the appropriate process. Also, refer to the techniques described in Chapter 4 for additional ways to make the audience's decision-making process easy.

CHAPTER 6

Person Perception in Audience Decision Making

September 26, 1960, 70 million Americans saw the first televised presidential debate. The debate was between then Vice President Richard Nixon and soon-to-be President John F. Kennedy. Richard Nixon, just out of the hospital and dressed in a light-colored suit, looked pale and uncomfortable. Kennedy, fresh from a vacation and practiced in television techniques, looked tanned and relaxed.

According to the polls, radio listeners thought Nixon won the debate. But the TV audience who saw as well as heard the two candidates gave the victory to Kennedy.

Figure 6.1 Person Perception was Essential to Kennedy's TV Victory

How could such an important issue be decided by personal appearance and the color of a suit? Yet there is little doubt that person perception—the mental activity of evaluating other people—played an essential role in John F. Kennedy's victory in the televised version of the 1960 presidential debates (see Kraus 1996). Experimental studies have since verified that evaluations of political candidates by debate viewers and listeners differ significantly (McKinnon & Tedesco 1999; McKinnon, Tedesco, & Kaid 1993; Patterson, Churchill, Burger, & Powell 1992).

Skill in person perception enables audiences to recognize a professional's emotions, comprehend their character traits, and judge how well they fit a role. Person perception is typically based on direct observation of a professional's verbal behaviors (the words they write or speak), their nonverbal behaviors (their eye contact, facial expressions, tone of voice, and so on), and their appearance. Recruiters engage in this type of person perception when they interview job applicants. In fact, any number of audiences engage in this type of person perception when they listen to presentations, read reports and proposals, and talk with professionals one on one. Person perception can also be based on verbal descriptions of professionals and their behaviors. In addition, the concept of person perception can be broadened to include not only the activity of evaluating individual professionals but also the activity of evaluating groups of professionals and organizations.

Audiences incorporate their judgments of professionals into many of the types of decisions Chapter 2 reviews, including investment decisions, staffing decisions, and usage decisions. For example, most analysts would be reluctant to recommend investing in a firm whose CEO they judged to be incompetent. Most recruiters would not want to hire a job applicant they judged to be unlikable. And most consumers would be reluctant to purchase a product from a salesperson or firm they deemed unreliable.

If a professional is the source of information for an audience, the audience will also incorporate its judgment of the professional into its evaluation of the quality of information they receive. Audiences tend to discount any information they receive from sources they perceive to be biased or dishonest regardless of the type of decision they are asked to make.

THE IMPACT OF PERSON PERCEPTION ON DECISION MAKING

Person Perception and Voters' Decisions

One of the most widely known research findings from the person perception literature is that the personal characteristics of a political candidate have a greater relative impact on voters' decisions than does the candidate's stand on the issues or their party affiliation (Abelson, Kinder, Peters, & Fiske 1982; Kinder & Abelson 1981; Popkin, Gorman, Phillips, & Smith 1976). Data from the Center for Policy Studies at the University of Michigan shows that 60% of the variance in voters' preference for either Carter or Reagan in the 1980 presidential election can be accounted for by voters' perceptions of the two candidates' personal traits and emotions.

Voters' perceptions of the candidates' personalities may be based on very little information. In a study of the impact of candidates' photographs on voters, Martin

(1978) showed election photographs of 11 candidates to 33 university students and asked them to cast hypothetical votes on the basis of the photographs only. The students' voting behavior reflected their judgments of the candidates' professional competence more than judgments of the candidates' pleasantness or other traits. Interestingly, the distribution of the students' votes was significantly correlated with the distribution of votes cast in the actual election.

Person Perception and Recruiters' Decisions

The impact of person perception is especially evident in recruiters' hiring decisions, with their perceptions of applicants' nonverbal behaviors playing a significant role. In a study of how recruiters make hiring decisions, Young and Beier (1977) find that recruiters' evaluations of job applicants' nonverbal behaviors account for more than 80% of the rating variance.

Other studies confirm that recruiters weight applicants' nonverbal behaviors heavily. McGovern and Tinsley (1978) asked 52 recruiters to review one of two videotaped versions of a mock job interview. The applicant's verbal content was identical in both versions but the applicant's nonverbal behavior was systematically varied. In the first version the applicant showed minimal eye contact, low energy, lack of affect, low voice modulation, and a lack of speech fluency. In the second version the applicant engaged in the opposite behaviors. All 26 recruiters who saw the first version of the interview said they would not have invited the candidate for a second interview. Conversely, 23 of the 26 recruiters who saw the second version said they would have invited the candidate for a second interview. A follow-up study of actual job interviews found that no job candidates who had inhibited nonverbal behaviors (such as minimal eye contact, low energy, lack of affect, low voice modulation, and lack of speech fluency) during a first interview were invited back for a second interview (McGovern, Jones, & Morris 1979).

Person Perception and Job Applicants' Decisions

Just as recruiters' decisions are affected by their impressions of job applicants, job applicants' decisions to accept a job offer are significantly affected by their perceptions of recruiters. In a study of 237 college students who had been interviewed for jobs, Schmitt and Coyle (1976) asked students to describe their reactions to their recruiters and to indicate their subsequent decision. The students' perceptions of the recruiters' personalities and their manner of delivery, as well as the adequacy of information that the recruiters provided, significantly influenced the students' evaluations of the companies the recruiters represented and the likelihood that they would accept a job offer.

Person Perception and Analysts' Decisions

Analysts' investment decisions are significantly affected by their perception of the firm's management (Pincus 1986). More than 42% of the analysts surveyed responded that their personal evaluation of top management is worth 60% of their total valuation of the company's price/earnings multiple. Another 34% said that their personal appraisal of management is worth more than 33% of their total valuation.

Person Perception and the Decisions of Speakers' Audiences

Audience perceptions of the source of information can also impact their decisions. For example, consumers' perceptions of the spokespeople who advertise products influence their purchase decisions (Haley, Richardson, & Baldwin 1984). Some nonverbal behaviors of spokespeople in TV ads are even more highly correlated with an ad's persuasiveness than is the ad's verbal content (Haley 1985). The audience's initial impressions of a speaker's credibility and likeability play an especially important role in the speaker's ability to persuade them (Chaiken & Eagly 1983). And the more positive the audience's perceptions of the speaker, the more they are persuaded by the speaker's message (Carli, LaFleur, & Loeber 1995).

Sometimes the audience's perception of a speaker is the main determinant of the audience's decision, especially when their interest in the speaker's message is low (e.g., Chaiken 1980; Petty, Cacioppo, & Schumann 1983). The audience's perception of the speaker also becomes a major determinant of the audience's decision when the audience is distracted from paying attention to the message (Kiesler & Mathog 1968).

ROLE SCHEMATA OF EXPERT AUDIENCES

There has been widespread agreement among social psychologists that social knowledge and expertise are held in schemata (cf., Carlston & Smith 1996; Klimoski & Donahue 2001; Smith 1998a). At least one type of schemata—role schemata—embodies the expertise audiences use in person perception. Audiences possess role schemata for different professionals such as doctors, lawyers, and managers, as well as role schemata for leaders, job applicants, and speakers.

Role schemata play a critical role in person perception and audience decision making. Audiences depend on role schemata more than perceived personality traits to make sense of others (Andersen & Klatzky 1987). They also use role schemata more than personality traits to cue their memories of their acquaintances (Bond & Brockett 1987; Bond & Sedikides 1988). For example, it is easier for audiences to think of all the lawyers they know than to recollect all the introverts they know.

Decision Criteria in Role Schemata

Like other decision-making schemata, role schemata are organized by decision criteria. In their experiment with 104 undergraduates, McGraw and Steenbergen (1995) explored the organization of role schemata for political candidates. Students' information about political candidates appeared to be organized by attributes, or decision criteria (e.g., experience, personal characteristics, etc.), particularly among those students who were more politically expert. Political novices, lacking organized attribute information, tended to make decisions about candidates based on their more intuitive impressions of the candidates.

The decision criteria in role schemata appear to be composed of a wide range of psychological, physical, behavioral, and demographic attributes (Bond & Brockett 1987; Bond & Sedikides 1988). However, some researchers have questioned the inclusion of behaviors in role schemata. For example, Jeffrey and Mischel (1979) find that audiences organize behaviors almost completely by trait categories when asked to form an impression of a person or to make a prediction about a person's future behavior. Similarly, Markus and Zajonc (1985) conclude that when audiences are asked to form an impression of another person, they tend to organize information about the person within a schema that seldom reflects any actual behavioral details.

Benchmarks in Role Schemata

Like other decision-making schemata, role schemata include benchmarks. Audiences often judge a professional's attributes against group-specific standards and expectations (cf., Biernat, Manis, & Nelson 1991; Hogg 2001; Hogg & Terry 2000). Audiences also use themselves as a point of comparison when evaluating others (Dunning 1999). When audiences evaluate another's leadership skills and potential, they use their images of prototypical leaders as benchmarks (Lord 1985; Lord, Foti, & Phillips 1982).

Recruiters use several types of benchmarks when evaluating job applicants during employment interviews. Recruiters compare actual applicants to their image of the ideal applicant (Bolster & Springbett 1961; Hakel, Hollmann, & Dunnette 1970). Recruiters base their image of the ideal applicant on applicants from the past, on their analysis of the job, on their general impressions of good employees, and on their own image of themselves (Webster 1964). Recruiters also compare applicants to the other applicants who have recently applied for the position (Highhouse & Gallo 1997). In a study of 120 recruiters and 180 managers who were asked to watch videotaped interviews of four applicants for a management trainee position, Schuh (1978) finds that the performance of earlier applicants influences the evaluator's assessment of subsequent applicants. In a study of candidates interviewing for medical school, Kopelman (1975) finds that the performance of the two most recent candidates influences the evaluator's assessment of the current candidate.

Audiences may also use one professional in a conversation as a benchmark with which to evaluate the other professional in the conversation. In a study of viewers' perceptions of interviewees, Kepplinger and coauthors (1990) presented nine videos portraying different interviewer/interviewee nonverbal behaviors to nine groups of 25 viewers each. The viewers' perceptions of the interviewers were influenced by their perceptions of the interviewees. Aggressive interviewers caused the viewers to evaluate interviewees more positively. Obliging interviewers caused the viewers to evaluate interviewees more negatively.

When audiences receive new benchmark information during a person perception task, their judgments may exhibit the "change-of-standard effect." In the change-of-standard effect, the new benchmark information changes the audience's impressions of others as well as what the audience remembers about them (Clark, Martin, & Henry 1993; Higgins & Lurie, 1983; Higgins & Stangor 1988).

Audience Expectations about Professionals Playing their Roles

Audiences may penalize professionals whose traits do not fit their role schemata. In his study of wholesale drug salespeople and retail pharmacist buyers, Tosi (1971) shows that buyer loyalty to a given supplier is negatively related to the degree to which the salesperson's actual behavior differs from the buyer's role expectation of the salesperson. Salespeople who are uncertain about customers' expectations of them and about the best ways to fulfill their role expectations suffer from role ambiguity. The greater the salesperson's role ambiguity, the poorer their sales performance (Bagozzi 1978; Futrell, Swan, & Todd 1976; Walker, Churchill, & Ford 1975).

When audiences are asked to evaluate an individual's leadership abilities, they automatically draw on their leader schemata (Calder 1977; Eden & Leviatan 1975; Lord & Maher 1991). Audiences make leadership judgments by activating a leader schema and matching the attributes of an individual against those in their leader schema (Bartol & Butterfield 1976; Hogg 2007; Lord 1985). The better the match, the more favorable the audience's leadership perceptions (Cronshaw & Lord 1987; Fraser & Lord 1988; Lord, Foti, & de Vader 1984).

Audiences perceive leaders who behave in ways that match their leader schemata to be more effective than leaders who behave in ways that are incongruent with their leader schemata (Hains, Hogg, & Duck 1997). For example, a manager who fails to conform to her employees' schemata for business leaders will not be perceived as a leader in her organization (House & Aditya 1997). In their experiment on how leaders are rated, Maurer and Lord (1988) showed an audience videos of groups in which the target person's behavior varied on two dimensions: Prototypicality of leadership behavior and frequency of leadership behavior. Both dimensions significantly affected the audience's leadership ratings of the target person. Even more important to business professionals is the finding that managers who fail to conform to employees' leader schemata tend to be less effective than managers who do (Epitropaki & Martin 2004).

TYPES OF ROLE SCHEMATA

Occupation Schemata: How Audiences Evaluate Professionals

Audiences have role schemata for all types of professionals, for managers, teachers, engineers, politicians, as well as for those involved in other more specialized occupations (Fiske & Taylor 1991). For example, industry analysts have a clear role schema for investor-relations representatives that is very different from their role schema for high-level managers (Kuperman 2000).

As might be expected, recruiters have a highly differentiated and reliable under-standing of the personality traits specific occupations require (Jackson, Peacock, & Holden 1982). For example, recruiters expect a good applicant for an advertising position to be thrill-seeking, impulsive, changeable, attention-seeking, and fun-loving. Conversely, they expect a good applicant for an accounting position to be meek, definiteness-seeking, and orderly. And they expect applicants for supervisory and coaching positions to be dominant, ambitious, aggressive, and persistent. Interestingly, recruiters' expectations are a good match with applicants' self-reported measures of personality and vocational interests (Siess & Jackson 1970).

Leader Schemata: How Audiences Evaluate Leaders

Decision criteria in leader schemata are widely shared by people of all ages and backgrounds (Rush, Thomas, & Lord 1977; Weiss & Adler 1981). Even as early as the first grade, children can clearly differentiate leaders from non-leaders and can articulate the criteria they use to distinguish them (Matthews, Lord, & Walker 1990). Studies of group decision making also indicate that there is substantial agreement among group members about which members of the group are its leaders and which are not (see Livi, Kenny, Albright, & Pierro 2008 for a review).

Decision criteria in leader schemata are composed of the traits that audiences believe leaders should possess. A study of the leader schemata of undergraduates finds eight traits to be most important: Intelligence, sensitivity, dedication, tyranny, charisma, attractiveness, masculinity, and strength (Offermann, Kennedy, & Wirtz 1994). Another study of leader schemata identifies a somewhat different set of traits: Intelligence, understanding, friendliness, energy, honesty, and helpfulness (Winn 1984). A meta-analysis of research on leader schemata finds that three traits—intelligence, masculinity-femininity, and dominance—are significantly related to audience perceptions of leadership (Lord, de Vader, & Alliger 1986).

Audiences also have well-developed role schemata for leaders that are specific to different occupations and professions (Lord & Maher 1991; Rush & Russell 1988; Sande, Ellard, & Ross 1986). Priming different leader schemata with the appropriate labels, for instance *leader* versus *political leader*, significantly affects how the audience will perceive the target individual (Foti, Fraser, & Lord 1982). In the political world, voters possess schemata with decision criteria comprised of traits and behaviors appropriate for political leaders (Fiske & Kinder 1981). Traits in US voters' schemata for an ideal president include honesty, courage, charisma, and warmth (Kinder, Peters, Abelson, & Fiske 1980).

In the business world employees have schemata with decision criteria composed of traits and attributes appropriate for business leaders and supervisors. In their assessment of the leadership and supervisor schemata of employees, Offermann and colleagues (1994) show that the schemata employees possess for business leaders are composed of the same eight attributes as the leader schemata of the students whom they studied previously: Intelligence, sensitivity, dedication, tyranny, charisma, attractiveness, masculinity, and strength. In addition, both men and women attribute the same eight traits to leaders. Kenney and coauthors (1996) use the phrase *implicit leadership theories* (ILTs) to describe employees' schemata for business leaders. They find that employees' ILTs consist of employees' assumptions about the skills, abilities, and traits of an ideal business leader. Employees' ILTs are relatively constant across individuals and types of businesses. Stored in memory, they are activated when employees interact with business leaders.

Managers also possess schemata comprised of traits appropriate for business leaders. A cross-cultural study of 15,022 middle managers from 60 different countries asked the managers to rate the degree to which 112 leadership traits impede or facilitate effective leadership. Middle managers from all or most of the countries rated three of the traits as characteristic of outstanding leadership—charismatic, team-oriented, and participative. Middle managers from all 60 countries rated one trait, self-protective, as inhibiting leadership (Den Hartog, House, Hanges, Ruiz-Quintanilla, & Dorfman 1999).

In addition to personality traits, audiences use physical appearance as a visual cue to identify leaders and other dominant individuals. An individual's physical attractiveness is positively related to audience perceptions of dominance (Cunningham, Barbee, & Pike 1990). Furthermore, physical attractiveness actually predicts a man's leadership position in groups (Anderson, John, Keltner, & Kring 2001). Audiences also associate a mature physical appearance with leadership and dominance. Both men and women with mature facial features impress others as competent, dominant, and shrewd, whereas people with less mature features impress others as submissive, shy, and naïve (Berry 1991b). Large eyes, for example, signal low dominance (Keating & Doyle 2002).

Audiences use nonverbal behaviors as visual cues to identify leaders and other dominant individuals as well. Surprisingly, employees can accurately predict a professional's organizational status based on a few nonverbal cues depicted in photographs—downward head tilt for women, formal dress and forward lean for men (Schmid Mast & Hall 2004). The audience's perceptions of status and leadership are also linked to a closer interaction distance and more touching of others, especially to non-reciprocal touch (Henley 1995; Leary 1990). Audiences perceive those with more youthful gaits to be more powerful, regardless of their gender or age (Montepare & Zebrowitz-McArthur 1988). Audiences perceive stretching the limbs out from the body as indicating dominance typical of leaders (Argyle 1988; Eibl-Eibesfeldt 1989; Gifford 1991). In fact, audiences tend to perceive any expansive gestures, such as pointing at others or gesturing to direct others, as dominant (Andersen & Bowman 1999).

In a study of the leadership perceptions of top managers, DeGroot and Motowidlo (1999) asked 26 high-level managers to watch videotaped interviews of 22 mid-level managers from the same industry and to rate the mid-level managers' leadership potential. The high-level managers' ratings were significantly correlated with each mid-level manager's overall rating on five nonverbal visual dimensions: Physical attractiveness, amount of smiling, amount of gaze in the direction of the interviewer, amount of hand movement, and extent to which the mid-level manager leaned toward instead of away from the interviewer.

Eye contact plays an especially important role in the audience's identification of leaders. In a study that asked 120 students to watch videos in which an interviewee maintained eye contact with an interviewer for either 15, 30, or 50 seconds, Brooks and colleagues (1986) found that students perceived the interviewee to be more powerful as her eye contact increased. Another study of applicants' eye contact in job interviews finds that it is especially important for high-status applicants to maintain eye contact during their interviews (Tessler & Sushelsky 1978). It is also important for presenters to maintain good eye contact. Audience perceptions of speakers' status and power are associated with a high degree of eye contact while speaking (Dovidio & Ellyson 1982).

Audience leadership judgments rely on others' facial displays of emotions as well. Audiences infer high dominance and high likeability from happy faces, high dominance but low likeability from angry faces, and low dominance from fearful faces (Hess, Blairy, & Kleck 1997; Knutson 1996; Montepare & Dobish 2003). A leader's facial expressions of fear or evasion tend to undermine support for the leader and often disturb their followers (Chance 1976).

In addition to using nonverbal visual cues, audiences also use a number of nonverbal vocal cues to identify leaders. For example, audiences perceive people who talk more than others to be more dominant (see Schmid Mast 2002 for a review). Audiences also associate short response latencies, or pauses, as well as loudness with dominance (Burgoon 1994). Speakers with lower pitched voices are perceived to be more dominant, more competent, but less warm than those with childlike voices (Montepare & Zebrowitz-McArthur 1987). Speakers who vary the pitch of their voice also come across as more leader-like—dynamic, extroverted, benevolent, and competent—than those who speak in a monotone (Brown, Strong, & Rencher 1973; Greene & Mathieson 1989; Scherer 1979a).

In the study of nonverbal visual cues to leadership potential described above, DeGroot and Motowidlo (1999) also find that higher-level managers rate mid-level managers based on five nonverbal vocal cues: Pitch, pitch variability, speech rate, pauses, and amplitude variability. In addition, each mid-level manager's ratings based on visual cues are significantly correlated with their ratings based on vocal cues. Thus, higher-level managers perceive that mid-level managers who display leader-like visual cues in interviews also display leader-like vocal cues.

In addition to nonverbal cues, verbal cues can help audiences identify and evaluate leaders. Audiences rate both male and female speakers who use a powerful speech style higher on traits of assertiveness, politeness, and warmth than speakers who use a powerless speech style (Newcombe & Arnkoff 1979). Powerless speech styles are associated with the frequent use of verbal behaviors such as intensifiers (e.g., "really big"), hedges (e.g., "I think"), hesitation forms (e.g., "and uh"), and questioning intonations (Erickson et al. 1978). Conversely, the speech styles of powerful and high-status individuals rarely display those verbal behaviors.

A number of other verbal behaviors also lead the audience to view the speaker as dominant and leader-like. Wish and coauthors (1980) asked audience members to watch videos of sets of two people engaged in conversations and then asked them to state their impressions of each individual. The audience gave higher dominance ratings to speakers who tended to initiate new topics of conversation as opposed to react to current topics of conversation. In addition, the audience gave higher dominance ratings to speakers who made many forceful requests and lower ratings to speakers who made many weak assertions. Audience leadership judgments also rely on verbal cues to emotions. For example, the prevalence of positive emotion words is correlated with audience perceptions of leader-like dominance (Berry, Pennebaker, Mueller, & Hiller 1997).

Applicant Schemata: How Recruiters Evaluate Job Applicants

Recruiters tend to agree on the personality traits required of good job applicants (Hakel & Schuh 1971; Keenan 1976; Shaw 1972). Their evaluations of an applicant's personality traits are affected by the nonverbal visual cues that job applicants display during job interviews—cues such as physical attractiveness, eye contact, body orientation, smiling, and hand gestures (e.g., Gifford, Ng, & Wilkinson 1985; Kinicki & Lockwood 1985; Raza & Carpenter 1987). High levels of eye contact, gesturing, nodding, and smiling are all related to more favorable evaluations of applicants (e.g., Gifford et al. 1985; Imada & Hakel 1977; Parsons & Liden 1984). In fact, any time applicants exhibit highly expressive nonverbal behaviors, recruiters' ratings of them tend to increase (Rasmussen 1984).

An analysis of actual job interviews concludes that recruiters' impressions of an applicant's personality are based to a large extent on the applicant's nonverbal facial behaviors, including direct eye contact and smiling, which in turn are associated with the recruiters' hiring decisions (Anderson & Shackleton 1990). Behaviors such as avoidance glances and neutral facial expressions are typical of unsuccessful applicants (Forbes & Jackson 1980; Harris 1989).

Interestingly, the nonverbal visual cues recruiters observe in job applicants are correlated with supervisors' subsequent ratings of the applicants' performance on the job (Burnett 1993; Motowidlo & Burnett 1995). Supervisors' ratings of applicants' on-the-job performance are significantly correlated with the applicant's physical attractiveness in the interview and with the amount of time the applicant gazes at the interviewer (Burnett 1993). Moreover, interviewers' and supervisors' ratings are both significantly correlated with a composite score of the applicant's physical attractiveness, amount of gaze, amount of smiling, amount of hand movement, posture, body orientation, and dress characteristics.

In addition to visual cues, a number of vocal cues influence recruiters' perceptions of job applicants. In an analysis of the relative importance of verbal and nonverbal behaviors to hiring decisions, Hollandsworth and coauthors (1979) reveal that an applicant's speech fluency and voice level are among the top seven predictors of a job offer. In a study of the effect of accents on applicants' chances for success, Labov (1966) asked judges to rate the suitability for employment of people whose speech varied on different phonological variables such as postvocalic r. Judges rated speakers of the standard dialect as more competent and suitable for employment than speakers of nonstandard dialects.

Verbal cues are among the strongest predictors of perceived competence (Borkenau & Liebler 1992a; Feingold 1992) and of a job offer (Hollandsworth et al. 1979). Judges' perceptions of applicants' competence are inversely related to the percentage of self-referent words (e.g., I) the applicants use (Berry et al. 1997). Applicants who use a high proportion of self-referent words are generally perceived to be relatively shy and incompetent (Ickes 1982). The use of we, on the other hand, is viewed much more favorably. For example, the use of we in college applicants' essays is a strong predictor of college admissions decisions (Hatch, Hill, & Hayes 1993).

In addition to the use of self-referent words, other verbal behaviors affect the audience's perceptions of applicants' competence. In a study of audience perceptions of consulting candidates, Yates and colleagues (1996) find that audiences perceive candidates who predict extreme stock prices and earnings, either very high or very low, to be more expert than those who make less extreme predictions. Negations and negative emotion words, on the other hand, are negatively related to judges' perceptions of applicants' competence (Berry et al. 1997).

Speaker Schemata: How Audiences Evaluate Speakers

Audiences want to be informed by those who they perceive to be both competent and trustworthy, that is to say, credible. Unless the audience perceives the source of information to be credible, any attempt by the source to frame an issue will fail (Druckman 2001a). Audiences use a number of nonverbal visual cues to identify credible speakers. For example, audiences perceive speakers who smile as more credible than speakers who do not (LaFrance & Hecht 1995). Audiences view speakers who make more eye contact to be more credible as well (Argyle & Cook 1976). Audiences also view confident speakers as more credible. In a study of mock jurors evaluating the credibility of eyewitness identification of defendants, only the confidence displayed by the eyewitnesses affected juror judgments of their credibility (Cutler, Penrod, & Dexter 1990).

Studies of actual liars confirm the commonly accepted belief that people behave differently when they are lying than they do when they are telling the truth (DePaulo, Stone, & Lassiter 1985; Zuckerman, DePaulo, & Rosenthal 1981). Liars blink more, fidget more, tap more, and scratch themselves more than do people who are speaking truthfully. Liars avoid the audience's gaze unless they are being purposefully manipulative. Although liars do engage in different nonverbal behaviors, audiences still have difficulty identifying them. For example, consumers have great difficulty discriminating truthful from deceptive salespeople (DePaulo & DePaulo 1989).

Audiences also use a number of vocal cues to identify credible sources of information. For example, speech rate and fluency correlate with audience perceptions of truthfulness (Zuckerman et al. 1981). Audiences perceive fast-talking speakers as more credible than slow-talking speakers (Brown 1980; Miller, Maruyama, Beaber, & Valone 1976; Woodall & Burgoon 1983). Audiences find speakers who talk with a faster than average speech rate to be more persuasive as well (Miller et al. 1976; Smith & Shaffer 1995).

Audiences perceive speakers who frequently use hesitation forms and questioning intonations to be less credible than other speakers (Erickson et al. 1978). The more problems a speaker has speaking fluently—problems such as a repetitive use of filler words including "basically," "uh," etc., the use of long pauses and response latencies, or the unnecessary repetition of words or sounds—the lower audiences rate that speaker's competence and expertise (Burgoon, Birk, & Pfau 1990; Engstrom 1994; Scherer 1978).

Studies of actual liars confirm many of the audience's preconceptions about vocal cues to lying (DePaulo et al. 1985; Zuckerman et al. 1981). Liars typically speak less fluently, hesitate more, make more grammatical errors, and vocalize more "ums" and "ers." However, increased latency of response and slower rate of speech do not reliably discriminate between liars and speakers who tell the truth.

In addition to nonverbal cues, verbal cues can influence the audience's perceptions of a speaker's credibility. Audiences give higher credibility ratings to speakers who document their evidence (Fleshier, Ilardo, & Demoretcky 1974). Message clarity is positively related both to perceived source competence and to perceived source credibility (Hamilton & Hunter 1998). Unequivocal language can also enhance perceived source credibility, but only when the source of information uses high-quality arguments (Hamilton 1998; Hamilton & Mineo 1998). With low-quality arguments, unequivocal language decreases perceived source credibility.

Audiences perceive speakers who frequently use intensifiers and hedges to be less credible than other speakers (Erickson et al. 1978; Hosman & Siltanen 1994). Speakers who elaborate unnecessarily may also be perceived as less credible. Holtgraves and Grayer (1994) asked mock jurors to read courtroom testimony in which the defendant provided more information than the prosecutor asked for. For example, at one point when the prosecutor asked the defendant if he were an insured driver, the defendant replied, "Yes, I've never lost my insurance because of speeding tickets." The jurors judged the defendant to be guilty more often than other defendants who simply answered "Yes" or "No."

Ironically, speakers or writers who deny an assertion the audience initially believes to be false often lead the audience to conclude that the assertion must be true. Gruenfeld and Wyer (1992) asked one group of voters to read a newspaper report that denied Ronald Reagan was an alcoholic—a statement most of them believed was false. The group who read the report came to believe Reagan was an alcoholic to a greater extent than did those who did not read the report. Conversely, voters who read a newspaper report that affirmed a statement they initially believed to be true (e.g., Republican congressmen belong to elitist country clubs) came to believe the statement less than did those who did not read the report.

COGNITIVE PROCESSES IN PERSON PERCEPTION

This section presents a model of person perception that describes how audiences evaluate the professionals who communicate with them. As Blascovich and Seery (2007, p. 27) observe, social psychological processes, such as person perception, "rest on and involve more rudimentary psychological processes" such as "attention, perception, information processing, memory, etc." The model, as illustrated in Figure 6.2, consists of six basic cognitive processes—*perception, attention, comprehension, schema activation, information acquisition,* and *information integration.*

The processes described in this model of person perception are essentially the same cognitive processes as Chapter 3 describes. However, the model of person perception differs from the model of audience decision making in several ways. First the model allows for the input of professionals' nonverbal behaviors as well as the input of the verbal information they convey. Next, the model assumes audience perceptions of professionals' nonverbal behaviors are automatic and occur in parallel with their perceptions of the verbal information (cf., Langton & Bruce 2000; Langton, O'Malley, & Bruce 1996).

Finally, the model characterizes the verbal information conveyed by a professional as verbal behaviors as opposed to information about a topic. To grasp this distinction, suppose a salesman at a Toyota dealership tells a customer, "The Toyata Prius gets 60 miles per gallon in the city compared to 36 mpg for the Ford Hybrid Escape." If the customer uses the salesman's sentence to compare the two cars, the customer would be characterizing the sentence as information about the topic of the two cars' fuel efficiency. On the other hand, if the customer uses the sentence to infer the salesman's personality traits and competency as a salesperson, then the customer would be characterizing the sentence as a set of verbal behaviors (e.g., the sentence has specific quantifiable facts; it

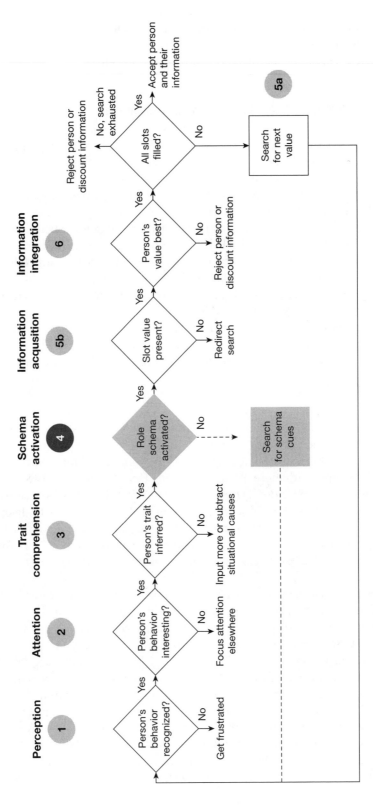

Figure 6.2 A Cognitive Process Model of Person Perception

uses correct grammar; it was spoken in an informal style, etc.). Thus, instead of thinking that the Prius is more economical than the Escape, the customer might infer that the salesman is knowledgeable, helpful, and competent at his job.

Perception of Professionals' Trait-Related Behaviors

Audiences spontaneously infer a professional's personality traits—extraversion, neuroticism, conscientiousness, agreeableness, openness, and so forth—when they perceive the professional's verbal and nonverbal behaviors (cf., Fiedler & Schenck 2001). For example, audiences infer a person is extroverted if they see that the person is dressed fashionably and has a stylish haircut (Borkenau & Liebler 1992b).

Audiences also spontaneously infer a professional's intelligence when they perceive the professional's verbal and nonverbal behaviors. For example, audiences infer a person is intelligent if they see the person is formally dressed (Behling & Williams 1991). When college students see instructors who are dressed informally they infer that the instructors are less intelligent but more friendly than their formally dressed colleagues (e.g., Davis 1992; Workman, Johnson, & Hadeler 1993).

In addition, audiences spontaneously infer the traits of others from written descriptions of their verbal and nonverbal behaviors, yet they are typically unaware that they do so (Uleman 1999; Uleman, Newman, & Moskowitz 1996; Winter & Uleman 1984).

The nonverbal cues audiences use to make trait inferences about others are most often valid (Funder & Sneed 1993). For example, the nonverbal cues audiences use to infer extraversion and aloofness accurately predict those traits (Gifford & Hine 1994). People who wear glasses do tend to be more introverted and less open to experience just as most audiences assume (Borkenau 1991). "Baby-faced" men are indeed more introverted and less assertive than those with more mature-appearing facial features (Berry & Brownlow 1989; Berry & Landry 1997; Bond, Berry, & Omar 1994). People who make less eye contact do tend to be shy and socially anxious (Asendorpf 1987; Daly 1978). People who maintain greater interpersonal distance also tend to be shy and socially anxious (Patterson & Ritts 1997; Pilkonis 1977). The ways in which people dress and move are other valid indicators of traits such as extraversion, openness, and even intelligence (Borkenau & Liebler 1995).

Like nonverbal visual cues, nonverbal vocal cues such as tone of voice are usually valid indicators of the speaker's actual traits and enable the audience to make correct trait judgments (Berry 1990, 1991a). Speakers who speak in a very loud voice do indeed tend to be extroverted (Scherer 1978). Similarly, speakers who have shorter response latencies are indeed more likely to be extroverts (Ramsey 1966). From nonverbal vocal cues alone, listeners can determine not only the speaker's personality traits (Scherer & Scherer 1981) and status in small groups (Scherer 1979b) but also their gender (Smith 1979, 1980), age (Helfrich 1979), socioeconomic background (Robinson 1979), ethnic group (Giles 1979), and place of origin (Tannen 1984).

In addition to making trait inferences on the basis of nonverbal cues, audiences also make inferences about a professional's traits based on their observation of verbal cues such as word choice (e.g., Gifford & Hine 1994; Ickes 1982; Newcombe & Arnkoff

1979). An individual's word choice plays an especially significant role in audience perceptions of their dominance, competence, trustworthiness, and cooperativeness (Berry et al. 1997; Ickes 1982; Newcombe & Arnkoff 1979).

Audiences primarily rely on verbal cues to infer an individual's intelligence, although, as we have seen, they can also use nonverbal cues to do so. Borkenau and Liebler (1993) asked audience members to view videos of speakers with and without the audio turned on and then to rate the speakers' intelligence. The audience's ratings were more influenced by the verbal content of the speech than by the speakers' nonverbal behaviors. Moreover, the audience was unable to accurately evaluate the speaker's intelligence unless the audio was turned on.

Audiences infer the traits of organizations as well as those of individuals based on verbal behaviors. The two versions of Citibank's loan agreement form (adapted from Felsenfeld & Siegel 1981) on pp. 126–7 illustrate how the audience's perceptions of the verbal behaviors of writers can affect the traits they attribute to the organizations the writers represent. The first version of the bank's loan agreement form was written by the bank's attorneys. The revision was written by a team of professionals from different areas. After the revision was completed, the bank surveyed more than 100 borrowers who had a loan other than a mortgage from a commercial bank and asked them to evaluate the two versions of the form. In addition to preferring the revised form, the borrowers inferred that the traits of banks using the two versions would be radically different. The borrowers said a bank using the old form would not be customer oriented. Conversely, they said a bank using the new form would be trustworthy, sensitive to the customer, modern, and efficient.

Audience members tend to agree with each other when they are asked to judge the personality traits of the same individuals (Borkenau & Liebler 1992a; Funder & Colvin 1991). For example, judges of college applicants' essays show substantial agreement in the personality traits they attribute to applicants based on the applicants' use of *we* vs. *I* (Hatch et al. 1993). Audience members also tend to agree even when they are asked to base their judgments on their first impressions alone (e.g., Berry & Finch Wero 1993; Kenny, Horner, Kashy, & Chu 1992; Watson 1989). Moreover, the audience's inferences about the personality traits of others are usually accurate (e.g., Albright & Forziati 1995; Borkenau & Liebler 1992b; Moskowitz 1982).

One reason that the audience's judgments about others' personality traits are usually accurate is that individuals tend to be consistent in their behavior patterns across situations. Individuals are relatively consistent in their verbal style or word choice (Pennebaker & King 1999). Individuals are also relatively consistent in their nonverbal style. Funder and Colvin (1991) asked viewers to watch videos of 164 Harvard students in three meetings with another student of the opposite sex and to rate the degree to which each student engaged in 62 different nonverbal behaviors. In the first two meetings, the students were strangers to each other and were given no prescribed topic of conversation. In the third meeting the two students from the second meeting met again and were asked to debate the issue of capital punishment. The viewers ascertained that a large number of the students' nonverbal behaviors were consistent across all three situations. The eight most consistent nonverbal behaviors are listed below in order of their degree of consistency:

1)   Speaks in a loud voice
2)   Behaves in a fearful or timid manner
3)   Expressive in face, voice, or gestures
4)   Speaks quickly
5)   Engages in constant eye contact
6)   Has high enthusiasm and energy
7)   Is reserved and unexpressive
8)   Is unconventional in appearance

Audiences' spontaneous inferences about others are not only remarkably accurate, they are also remarkably fast (Ambady, Bernieri, & Richeson 2000; Ambady & Rosenthal 1992; Gray & Ambady 2006). In one series of experiments, Ambady and Rosenthal (1993) presented college students with three 10-second video clips of unfamiliar professors and asked them to rate the professors' teaching effectiveness. Even with the sound turned off, the students had no trouble rating the professors on the basis of their nonverbal behaviors alone. Students also gave the professors similar ratings after viewing silent video clips just five-seconds and two-seconds long. Surprisingly, the students' ratings were highly correlated with ratings made by the professors' actual students after a full semester of classes.

Perception of Professionals' Emotion-Related Behaviors

For the audience to comprehend which emotions a professional is experiencing, they must first be able to see, hear, and recognize that professional's verbal and nonverbal behaviors. For example, the direction of the speaker's eye gaze is an important nonverbal visual cue to their emotions. Direct eye gaze enhances the audience's perception of anger and joy whereas averted eye gaze enhances their perception of fear and sadness (Adams & Kleck 2005). In their often cited study, Mehrabian and Ferris (1967) estimate that audience perceptions of a speaker's emotions are determined 55% by nonverbal visual cues, 38% by nonverbal vocal cues, and only 7% by the verbal content of the information they provide.

One of the most important nonverbal visual cues to others' emotions is their facial expression of emotion. There is widespread cross-cultural agreement among audiences about the emotions certain facial expressions communicate (Ekman 1973, Ekman et al. 1987). Specific emotions the audience can infer on the basis of others' facial expressions alone include happiness, anger, sadness, fear, disgust, contempt, and surprise (e.g., Fridlund, Ekman, & Oster 1987; Izard 1994). In an electromyograph (EMG) study of viewers looking at photographs of happy and sad facial expressions, Dimberg and colleagues find that audiences are able to infer emotions from facial expressions automatically (Dimberg 1997; Dimberg, Thunberg, & Elmehed 2000). Viewers smile slightly when looking at happy faces and frown slightly when looking at angry faces even when the photographs of the faces are presented to them subliminally.

Although perceiving another's emotions can be done automatically, it does take some effort. In an eye fixation study, Wong and colleagues (2005) find that viewers make significantly more fixations on faces that express emotion than on faces expressing no

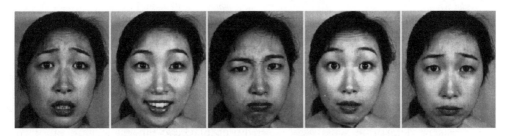

Figure 6.3 Audiences Scan Facial Expressions to Infer Emotions (source: The Japanese Female Facial Expression (JAFFE) Database. Lyons, Akamatsu, Kamachi, & Gyoba 1998).

emotion. Viewers made 11 fixations on faces that showed emotion versus 6.5 fixations on neutral faces. Moreover, the more fixations the viewers made, the more accurate was their identification of the other's emotions. When viewing a face to identify emotions, the audience must fixate on different parts of the face (Calder, Young, Keane, & Dean 2000; Ekman 1982). Anger, fear, and sadness require scanning the top half of the face. Disgust and happiness require scanning the bottom half of faces. Audiences can accurately identify surprise by scanning either the top or bottom half of the face.

Audiences are remarkably accurate at judging the emotions of other people on the basis of their facial expressions. Audiences recognize the facial expressions associated with joy and disgust with close to 100% accuracy (Ekman & Friesen 1978). Their accuracy is due to the fact that smiling for joy and nose wrinkling for disgust are highly specific expressions for those emotions. Audiences are also quite accurate in judging others' emotions even when they observe their facial expressions only briefly (Albright, Kenny, & Malloy 1988; Ambady & Rosenthal 1992; Watson 1989). However, audiences more accurately recognize the emotions expressed by others when they see videos of them making facial expressions as opposed to viewing static photographs of their faces (Wehrle, Kaiser, Schmidt, & Scherer 2000).

Audiences can also make accurate judgments of others' emotions on the basis of their nonverbal bodily postures. Coulson (2004a, 2004b) studied audiences' attributions of six emotions (anger, disgust, fear, happiness, sadness, and surprise) to static body postures. Although audiences often confuse postures that indicate happiness and surprise, they rarely confuse postures indicating the other four emotions.

In addition to using nonverbal visual clues to infer others' emotions, audiences also infer emotions on the basis of emotion-specific nonverbal vocal cues. In their analysis of listeners' evaluation of emotional speech, Banse and Scherer (1996) asked 12 professional theater actors to express 14 emotions. Listeners judged each emotion expressed by the actors, such as rage, panic, and elation, to have a distinct acoustic profile. Listeners inferred anger when speech had a high fundamental frequency, a strong fundamental frequency variation, and a significantly different energy in the lower and higher frequency bands. Listeners inferred sadness when speech had low intensity. Listeners inferred fear when speech had a fundamental frequency increase, low fundamental frequency variability, and low intensity. And listeners inferred boredom when speech had a low fundamental frequency, low intensity, and slow speech rate.

Audience recognition of vocally expressed emotion has accuracy rates of four to five times the rate expected by chance for basic emotions such as anger, fear, disgust, sadness, and happiness (Pittam & Scherer 1993). Listeners generally recognize the emotions of sadness and anger best, followed by fear (Scherer, Johnstone, & Klasmeyer 2003). Listeners can even tell whether their conversation partner on the telephone is smiling (Tartter 1980). However, the audience's recognition of vocal expressions of disgust is rarely above the level of chance.

In tests to determine which vocal attributes play the biggest role in emotion perception, Scherer (1974; Scherer & Oshinsky 1977) finds that tempo and pitch variations have the strongest influences on audience impressions of the speaker's emotions. Audiences interpret moderate pitch variations in a speaker's voice as an indication of sadness, fear, disgust, and boredom. They interpret extreme pitch variations and rising contour as indications of happiness, interest, and fear.

Members of one culture can recognize the vocal expressions of some emotions made by members of other cultures (Frick 1985; van Bezooijen, Otto, & Heenan 1983). In one cross-cultural study, people from nine countries, eight European and one Asian, listened to language-free speech samples in which vocal cues expressed emotions (Scherer, Banse, & Wallbott 2001). The listeners had an average accuracy of 66% across all emotions and countries, with the emotion of joy being recognized least accurately. In another cross-cultural study of the vocal expression of emotions, listeners associated a slow speaking rate with sadness (Breitenstein, Van Lancker, & Daum 2001). In contrast, they associated a fast speaking rate with anger, fear, or neutrality. The multi-cultural listeners in the study associated reduced pitch variation with sadness or neutrality and greater pitch variation with fear, anger, and happiness.

Apparently, speakers across the globe vocally express emotions in similar ways. In their study of the vocal expression of emotions by speakers from 27 countries on all five continents, Wallbott and Scherer (1986b) find that changes in the speakers' voices are identical for all emotions they studied.

Although audiences are able to infer emotions on the basis of the speaker's tone of voice alone, they are more accurate at inferring emotions when they can also see the speaker's facial expressions (Argyle, Alkema, & Gilmour 1971; Bugental, Kaswan, & Love 1970; DePaulo, Rosenthal, Eisenstat, Rogers, & Finkelstein 1978). In a demonstration of the greater accuracy of emotional inferences based on facial expressions, Burns and Beier (1973) asked one group of students to watch a video of speakers shown from the shoulders up who expressed anger, sadness, happiness, fear, and indifference. They asked another group to watch the same video with the audio off. They asked a third group to listen to the video's audio track without watching the visual portion. The speakers read sentences whose content was emotionally neutral, such as "Please pass the salt" and "John, there is a man at the door." Students were most accurate at identifying the speakers' emotions when they could both see and hear the speakers. Students were only slightly less accurate when they could see but not hear the speakers. When students heard the audio but could not see the speakers, their accuracy at identifying the speakers' emotions decreased significantly.

When both facial and vocal cues are available but incongruent, audiences will tend to base their evaluations of the speaker's emotions predominantly on facial cues (Graham, Ricci-Bitti, & Argyle 1975; Hess, Kappas, & Scherer 1988; Wallbott & Scherer

1986a). Even so, audiences are fastest and most accurate at identifying a speaker's emotions when the speaker speaks in a tone of voice that is emotionally congruent with the speaker's facial expression (Pell 2005; Schirmer & Kotz 2003).

In addition to nonverbal cues, audiences use verbal cues to infer speakers' emotions. One verbal cue that indicates emotional arousal is a low frequency of unique words (i.e., a smaller vocabulary). Greater numbers of unique words tend to indicate that speakers are experiencing only a low level of arousal (Sherblom & Van Rheenen 1984). Another verbal behavior that indicates the speaker is emotionally aroused is a decrease in speaking fluency. When an audience is listening to a speaker and the speaker's facial expressions are emotionally inconsistent with the verbal message, the audience will make inferences based either on the speaker's facial expressions or on the speaker's verbal message but not on both together (Shapiro 1968). In those situations facial expressions are clearly dominant over the verbal message (Leathers 1979).

Audiences also use verbal cues to infer the emotions of writers as the story of the e-mail reprimand excerpted below illustrates. Verbal behaviors indicating upset and anger in a CEO's e-mail to his managers—profanity, threats, insults, sarcasm, and ultimatums—caused a stir on Wall Street after an offended manager posted the CEO's e-mail on one of Yahoo's investor message boards. "We are getting less than 40 hours of work from a large number of our K C-based EMPLOYEES," the CEO's e-mail began. "The parking lot is sparsely used at 8 a.m.; likewise at 5 p.m. As managers—you either do not know what your EMPLOYEES are doing; or you do not CARE. You have created expectations on the work effort which allowed this to happen inside Cerner, creating a very unhealthy environment. In either case, you have a problem and you will fix it or I will replace you. NEVER in my career have I allowed a team which worked for me to think they had a 40-hour job. I have allowed YOU to create a culture which is permitting this. NO LONGER." After listing the ways employees would be punished if the company parking lot were not full between 7:30 a.m. and 6:30 p.m. and exclaiming that "what you are doing, as managers, with this company makes me SICK," the e-mail ended with "You have two weeks. Tick, tock." (adapted from Wong 2001). Almost immediately after the CEO's e-mail of March 13 was posted, the company's stock dropped 22%. The CEO apologized to his staff in a follow-up e-mail as well as in an article in the local newspaper a few days later, but his efforts were not enough. The company's stock hit bottom in early April after an article about the e-mail appeared on the front page of the business section of the *New York Times*.

Attention to Professionals and their Behaviors

Professionals can become salient for the audience and attract more attention when they are better lit than others, dressed differently than others, or walking while others are sitting (McArthur & Ginsberg 1981). A professional can also become salient if she sits down directly opposite an audience member (Taylor & Fiske 1975). In addition, unusual vocal behaviors such as an unusual pitch or a foreign accent can make a person salient. Audiences can detect less salient behaviors in other people only if they attend carefully to them (Ickes, Stinson, Bissonnette, & Garcia 1990).

When the audience is able to see a person speaking, they devote as much as 96% of their total viewing time attending to their face (Fehr & Exline 1987; Kendon 1990). The default location of audience members' eye fixations is the bridge of the speaker's nose or the eye area (Gullberg & Holmqvist 1999, 2006). Since audiences spend 96% of their viewing time on the speaker's face, they only occasionally scan the rest of the speaker's body. In fact, audiences directly fixate on only 7% of all arm and hand gestures. However, audience members' peripheral vision is sufficient to allow them to perceive the speaker's gestures and to make sense of them even while they are fixating on the speaker's face (Gullberg & Holmqvist 1999, 2006).

Audiences selectively attend to one speaker versus another depending on their current goal. For example, if two people are talking and one is a subordinate and the other a prospective client, the audience will attend to the person who is more important to them at the moment (Neuberg & Fiske 1987; Ruscher & Fiske 1990). Audiences also selectively attend to those with power over them (Erber & Fiske 1984; Ruscher & Fiske 1990), especially to leaders (Fiske & Depret 1996). They will tend to ignore those who cannot help them achieve their goals (Rodin 1987).

Unusual verbal and typographic behaviors can attract attention, too. A CEO's quarterly report to his employees (note: The firm's products, product names, and the employee's name have been changed) and one of his employee's comments about it are presented below. The CEO's use of all capital letters, block text, unusual words, extra space and punctuation, and awkward phrasing stood out to the employee. These errors and unusual practices caught the employee's attention more than the report's verbal content about the firm's progress that quarter did. Although the firm might have been on the right track financially, the CEO's verbal behaviors led the employee to infer that the management may be incompetent.

Quarterly Report from a CEO with an Employee's Comments

Sent: Monday, April 27, 2009 7:35 AM
Subject: 1st quarter results

JUST WANT TO TAKE A FEW MINUTES TO UPDATE YOU ON OUR FIRST QUARTER RESULTS. **[Why are you writing in all capital letters?[1]]** WE FINISHED THE QUARTER WITH ALL OUR WIND TURBINES ON MRP II EXCEPT x5000's WHICH WERE MISSED DUE TO LATE PARTS FROM OUR OEM. I RECENTLY VISITED OUR OEM AND HAVE BEEN ASSURED THAT THEY WILL BE BACK ON PLAN BY 5/7. TIME WILL TELL FOR THEY HAVE NOT BEEN VERY RELIABLE IN THE PAST. WE HIT OUR INVENTORY TURNS GOAL OF 16.2 WHICH WAS A GREAT ACCOMPLISHMENT. **[One single paragraph jumping from one point to the next.[2]]** WE ARE BEATING ALL OUR EH&S GOALS AND I DO NOT TAKE THIS FOR GRANTED. I KNOW IT TAKES A LOT OF WORK TO MAINTAIN A SAFE WORK ENVIRONMENT. WE HAVE HAD SOME BUMPS AND LUMPS ALONG THE WAY **["bumps and lumps" doesn't sound like the proper choice of words. Did someone actually get hurt or is he referring to negative business results?[3]]** BUT ALL OUR .NEW **[Extra space and/or punctuation.[4]]** WIND TURBINE PROGRAMS ARE IN PRETTY GOOD

SHAPE. WE WILL START ASSEMBLING THE FIRST PRODUCTION HS7000 ON MONDAY
AND I HAVE BEEN ASSURED BY ASHISH AND HIS FOLKS THAT THE TURBINE WILL
BE ASSEMBLED AND TESTED WITHIN THE NEXT DAYS. THIS HAS BEEN A SUPER
EFFORT ON BEHALF OF A LOT OF HIS FOLKS WHO HAVE PUT IN HUNDREDS OF
OVERTIME HOURS TO MAKE THIS HAPPEN. WE HAD SOME UNPLANNED COST ROLL
IN ON US THAT PUTS OUR FINANCIAL PLAN AT RISK FOR THE YEAR IF WE DO
NOT TAKE IMMEDIATE ACTION. HOWEVER, WE HAVE PUT IN PLACE A COST
ASSURANCE PLAN TO GET US BACK ON PLAN AND I WILL ENSURE THAT YOU ALL
UNDERSTAND THIS PLAN, FOR WITHOUT YOUR HELP AND COOPERATION WE WILL
FAIL. **[This sentence regarding the cost assurance plan sounds very awkward and
leaves me confused as to the CEO's intentions.[5]]**

AGAIN, WE HAVE HAD A VERY GOOD FIRST QUARTER. THANK YOU, AND I WANT
YOU TO KNOW THAT I APPRECIATE YOUR EFFORTS EVERY DAY. **[This doesn't make
me feel confident about management's ability to lead.[6]]**

Comprehension of Professionals' Traits and Emotions

Comprehension in person perception involves the audience's comprehension of
professionals' traits and emotions. How audiences infer a person's traits or comprehend
a person's character from observations of their behaviors is a central concern of the field
of person perception as well as of the field that grew out of it—social cognition (cf., Fiske
& Taylor 1991). As we have seen, audiences quickly and spontaneously encode perceived
behaviors in terms of trait categories, such as friendliness, dominance, competence,
intelligence, and so on (Gilbert 1989; Uleman et al. 1996). Audiences also quickly and
spontaneously encode perceived behaviors in terms of specific emotions, such as fear,
anger, happiness, and so forth (e.g., Albright et al. 1988; Ambady & Rosenthal 1992;
Dimberg et al. 2000).

Although spontaneous, the ability to comprehend another's traits is a learned skill
and requires more than simply perceiving their behaviors. For example, young children
do not explain others' behaviors in terms of their traits. Instead, they explain behaviors
in terms of the concrete situations that others are involved in (Kassin & Pryor 1985;
Rholes, Jones, & Wade 1988; White 1988).

Just as the ability to comprehend another person's traits is a learned skill, the ability
to comprehend another's emotions is a learned skill as well and requires more than
simply perceiving another's behaviors. Egan and coauthors (1998) asked children aged
5 to 14 years to determine whether videotaped speakers were happy, angry, sad, or
emotionally neutral. Chronological age was a significant predictor of a child's ability to
infer a speaker's emotions, with older children doing better than younger ones. Verbal
intelligence is another significant predictor of a child's ability to infer emotions.

The process of comprehending another's traits sometimes includes more than one
step. If the audience is not preoccupied with other tasks, it may use situational
information to modify or correct initial trait inferences. In their study of how audiences
comprehend speakers' traits, Gilbert and colleagues (1988) asked two groups to listen

to a speaker read either a pro-abortion or an anti-abortion speech. Both groups received the same situational information: The speaker had not written the speech but had been assigned to read a speech written by another person. One group simply listened to the speaker. The other group listened to the speaker knowing that later they would be asked to write and read aloud a speech of their own. The first group who simply listened discounted the speech's verbal content when inferring the speaker's traits. They took into account the fact that the speaker had been assigned to read a speech she had not written. In contrast, the preoccupied group inferred the speaker's traits based on the speech's verbal content and neglected to adjust their initial impressions to account for the situational information they had been given.

Just as they do in trait comprehension, audiences may also take into account situational variables when trying to comprehend another's emotions. Trope (1986) asked audience members to view ambiguous or unambiguous facial reactions of target individuals to emotional situations. When the audience tried to identify ambiguous facial expressions, the emotional situation to which the target individual was reacting had a significant influence on the audience's inferences about the target's emotions.

Activation of Role Schemata

One of the primary reasons audiences infer the traits of professionals is to determine how well they fit a particular occupational or leadership role. Does my new doctor exhibit the traits I expect in a good doctor? Does the job candidate exhibit the traits a good manager requires? To make decisions of this nature, the audience must first activate a role schema. Particular role schemata may be activated through either a bottom-up or a top-down process. Bottom-up activation may result from the perception of physical cues such as uniforms, styles of clothing, or tools (Fiske & Taylor 1991; Higgins & Bargh 1987; Lord 1985).

Top-down activation of a role schema might result from any one of several causes, including the recency of the schema's prior activation or priming (Higgins & Bargh 1987; Johnston & Dark 1986; Srull & Wyer 1979), its frequency of activation (Fiske & Taylor 1991; Wyer & Carlston 1979), or the audience's goal or purpose for observing the individual (Cohen 1981a; Ebbesen 1980).

Situational information can also activate role schemata. For example, Emrich (1999) asked two groups of mock recruiters to select job candidates to manage either in a crisis or in a tranquil situation. Both groups of recruiters received the same information about the candidates. But the recruiters who expected the candidates they interviewed to manage units in a crisis had greater false recall of leadership behaviors compared to the recruiters who expected candidates to manage units in which all was going smoothly. Emrich concluded that the crisis scenarios activated the recruiters' leadership schemata. In another study of the effects of role schema activation, Eisen and McArthur (1979) led some viewers to believe they would see a trial and other viewers to believe they would watch a social interaction. Viewers who expected to watch a trial inferred that the target individual was a defendant and decided the target was more responsible for a crime than did viewers who thought they had seen a social interaction.

Acquisition of Behavioral and Trait Information

Audiences actively search for behavioral and trait information about professionals once they have activated the appropriate role schema. The activated role schema guides the audience to attend to the behaviors and traits that are relevant to that role. In a study of how different role schemata lead viewers to observe different behaviors, Smith (1986) asked two groups of viewers to watch videos of couples interacting with each other in ways that were rated as ambiguous in terms of their degree of intimacy. One group of viewers was told they would see a couple just becoming acquainted. The other group was told they would observe a married couple. The two groups of viewers, primed with different role schemata, observed different nonverbal behaviors and made different types of inferences when making judgments about the couple.

Depending on the role schema that has been primed, viewers also infer different meaningful breaks and behaviors in the same sequence of actions or interactions. In their study of perceived breakpoints in an interaction sequence, Massad and coauthors (1979) asked two groups of viewers to watch a video of an interaction between one large and two small geometric figures that represented people of different sizes. They also asked the two groups to press a button each time they perceived a meaningful break in the action such as when the figures moved toward each other, stopped moving, or grasped each other. One group of viewers was told the large figure was a rapist (rapist role) attacking the two smaller figures (victim role). The other group was told the large figure was a "guardian of treasure" (guard role) and that the two smaller figures were burglars (thief role). The first group identified breaks in the action that were substantially different from the ones the second group identified. In his review of the breakpoint research, Ebbesen (1980) concludes that audiences are able to search for different features of others' ongoing nonverbal behaviors just as they are able to search for different verbal information in documents.

Audiences will assume that the default slot values of their activated role schema are correct unless they have access to more accurate information about the person. For example, audiences use stereotypes as an important basis for their judgment only when they have little individuating information about the target person (Baron, Albright, & Mallory 1995). In this situation the audience fills in the missing information about the particular individual with information that is true of the stereotype.

Audiences often seek less information about an individual if stereotypical information is available to them. Hattrup and Ford (1995) asked 346 undergraduates to request information describing several target individuals so that the students could form impressions of them. The targets were identified either by occupations associated with a stereotype (e.g., librarian) or by non-descriptive labels (e.g., "Person 1"). When targets were identified by occupations associated with a stereotype, students requested less information about them than when targets were identified by non-descriptive labels.

An activated role schema leads the audience to observe and remember only those behaviors and traits relevant to that role. Audience members who are told about a person's occupation before meeting them remember information about the person that is consistent with the person's occupation better than information that is inconsistent with it (Cohen 1976). In one study Cohen (1981b) asked viewers to watch a videotaped conversation between a woman and her husband. Cohen then primed two different role schemata. Half of the viewers were told the woman was a waitress; the other half were told the woman was a librarian. The videotaped woman exhibited an equal number of prototypical waitress and librarian behaviors. After watching the video viewers were able to more accurately recall behaviors consistent with the primed role schema than they were behaviors consistent with the unprimed role schema.

In another study of the effects of role schemata on information acquisition, Lingle and colleagues (1979) asked mock recruiters to read a list of traits describing a job applicant. The researchers then asked them to decide if the applicant were suitable for a particular occupation, thus activating a particular role schema. The mock recruiters later recalled applicant traits from the list that were relevant to the activated role schema better than they did irrelevant traits. Similarly, Zadny and Gerard (1974) asked students to watch another student registering for college classes. The student viewers were told that the other student was either a chemistry, music, or psychology major. Student viewers recalled significantly more facts about the other student that were consistent with the other student's supposed major than facts that were inconsistent with the other student's supposed major.

Once a role schema is activated, audiences may even confuse a person's actual behavior with the schema's default behaviors. In a test of viewers' memories of prototypical leadership behaviors, Phillips and Lord (1982) find that viewers have difficulty distinguishing between schema-consistent behaviors that were present in a target leader and those that were not. When audiences encounter behaviors that are inconsistent with the default behaviors of their activated role schema, they take longer both to encode and to acquire them (Belmore 1987; Fiske & Neuberg 1990; Jamieson & Zanna 1989).

Integration of Behavioral and Trait Information

Once the audience acquires behavioral and trait information about a professional that is relevant to their activated role schema, how does the audience combine that information to arrive at an overall impression of or attitude toward that person? In a think-aloud study of voters reading about two political candidates, Herstein (1981) found that voters rarely produced overall evaluative statements about the candidates. Instead, voters first compared the two candidates on the basis of a few traits or attributes and then chose the candidate with the highest number of favorable comparisons. Only if this comparison resulted in a tie did the voters decide on the basis of political party stereotypes. Interestingly, this model of voter decision making appears to be highly predictive of voter choice.

The choice rules that audiences most frequently use in the information integration process during person perception are the weighted additive and averaging rules (Anderson 1981). In his seminal study of information integration, Anderson (1973) asked readers to read paragraphs about several US presidents and then to rate each president's statesmanship and accomplishments on a scale that ranged from 0 to 10. For each president readers received two paragraphs that were either positive, neutral, or negative toward that president. Readers who read two positive paragraphs about a president formed a very positive impression of him. Readers who received a neutral and a positive paragraph formed a moderately positive impression. And readers who received two negative paragraphs formed an extremely negative impression. Readers who were exposed to conflicting messages formed an impression that corresponded to the average value of the unweighted messages.

Audiences use the weighted additive and averaging rules to evaluate others in a wide range of situations. In a study of personnel selection, Nagy (1981) asked personnel managers to read verbal descriptions of job applicants' personality traits. Each trait was described in terms of one of four scale values (low, below average, above average, and high). The results showed that personnel managers used a weighted averaging rule to judge the applicants. In the area of consumer decision making, Troutman and Shanteau (1976) asked parents to read verbal descriptions of pediatricians and to evaluate them. Each pediatrician was described in terms of the doctor's ability to handle children and the quality of her staff's manners. Each of these attributes varied across four scale values (low, below average, above average, and high). The parents evaluated the pediatricians by averaging the scale values of the described attributes.

Audiences use the same rules to integrate both visual and verbal information about other people. In a study of verbal/visual information integration, Nagy (1975) asked female college students to look at photographs of male college students, read descriptions of the male students' personal characteristics, and then to evaluate the male students' dating desirability. The female students used a linear averaging rule to integrate the male students' physical attractiveness with the verbal descriptions of their personal characteristics. A study of juror decision making comes to a similar conclusion: Jurors decide on the guilt or innocence of defendants by combining relevant verbal information with behavioral information using a simple linear rule (Kaplan & Kemmerick 1974).

When integrating information about other people, audiences tend to weight some types of information more heavily than other types. For example, audiences give more weight to information that is inconsistent with the other information they have about the individual (Hamilton & Zanna 1972; Hodges 1974). Audiences also weight negative information more heavily than positive information (Fiske 1980; Hodges 1974; Kanouse & Hason 1972). For example, recruiters weight negative information about job applicants more heavily than they do positive information (Hollman 1972). Recruiters appear to believe that both negative and extreme behaviors are particularly diagnostic of job applicants' personality traits (Skowronski & Carlston 1987, 1989).

BIASES IN PERSON PERCEPTION

The Attractiveness Bias: The Persuasive Appeal of Good Looks

Audiences are more likely to be biased toward and persuaded by attractive professionals than by unattractive ones (Messner, Reinhard, & Sporer 2008; Mills & Harvey 1972). For example, attractive product endorsers in advertisements are more persuasive than less attractive ones (Petty & Cacioppo 1980). Moreover, attractive professionals are equally persuasive whether or not their messages include supportive argumentation (Norman 1976).

Attractive professionals are more persuasive than less attractive ones in a variety of situations and media. In the courtroom, physically attractive surrogates who read the dispositions of expert witnesses unable to appear in court are more persuasive than less attractive surrogates (Kassin 1983). In a study of fundraisers for the American Heart Association, attractive fundraisers generated nearly twice as many donations as less attractive fundraisers (Reingen & Kernan 1993). When emotionally charged advertisements are attributed to attractive endorsers, customers tend to like the product more and express more intentions to buy (Pallak, Murroni, & Koch 1983). In a large-scale study of a lender's mailing to potential borrowers that offered them substantial, short-term loans, Bertrand and colleagues (2005) find that adding a photograph of an attractive smiling woman has the same positive effect on male borrowers' acceptance of a loan offer as dropping the monthly interest rate by 4.5%.

Audiences tend to attribute more desirable personal traits to physically attractive professionals than they do to less physically attractive ones (e.g., Cunningham 1986; Cunningham, Barbee, & Pike 1990). For example, voters attribute more desirable personal traits to physically attractive political candidates than to less attractive opposing candidates (Budesheim & DePaola 1994). Although they are unaware of the role physical appearance plays in their hiring decisions, students conducting mock job interviews are more likely to hire well-groomed but less qualified job applicants than better qualified but poorly-groomed applicants (Mack & Rainey 1990). Mock jurors are less likely to find attractive defendants guilty than unattractive defendants, unless the attractive defendants used their good looks to commit the crime (Sigall & Ostrove 1975). Indeed, courtroom evidence shows that physical attractiveness is one of the greatest advantages a defendant can have (Mazzella & Feingold 1994).

Expertise may mitigate the effects of the attractiveness bias. In contrast to the way students playing recruiters make hiring decisions, Nagy (1981) finds that experienced personnel managers make their hiring judgments exclusively on the basis of recommendations and experience. None of the personnel managers in Nagy's study showed significant effects for irrelevant attributes such as the applicants' gender, age, or physical attractiveness.

The Status Bias: The Persuasive Appeal of High Status

Audiences who believe a professional has high status are more likely to comply with the professional's requests. For example, audiences are more likely to comply with the requests of speakers who are well dressed—suits and ties for men, dress clothes for women—than they are with the requests of speakers who are poorly dressed (Bickman 1974; Kleinke 1977; Levine, Bluni, & Hochman 1998). Speakers who wear more formal and higher status clothing are especially effective at gaining compliance from lower status listeners (Segrin 1993). Movie theater audiences are more likely to comply with a request made over the public address system when the announcer uses a standard style of speaking versus a colloquial, lower-class style (Bourhis & Giles 1976). Audience attitudes toward speakers' language also play a role in medical encounters (Fielding & Evered 1978), legal settings (Seggre 1983), employment contexts (Kalin & Rayko 1980), offers of help (Gaertner & Bickman 1971), and housing discrimination hearings (Purnell, Idsardi, & Baugh 1999).

Audience evaluations of professionals are based in part on the social category their verbal behaviors activate (Pennebaker & King 1999). Sociolinguists demonstrate the existence of social class differences in several linguistic variables, including syntax (Lavandera 1978), lexical choice (Sankoff, Thibault, & Berube 1978), and intonation (Guy & Vonwiller 1984). Sociolinguists also show that audiences use linguistic cues to determine a speaker's social class (Labov 1972). When the audience attributes a higher social class to speakers based on linguistic cues, the audience is more likely to be persuaded by them. In a study of the effects of regional dialects, Giles (1973) asked 250 people from two dialect areas to listen to arguments spoken in standard dialect and regional dialects of lesser prestige. The listeners' perceptions of argument quality varied directly with prestige of the speaker's accent. Moreover, standard English speakers are evaluated more favorably than nonstandard speakers, even when information about their social class is held constant (Giles & Sassoon 1983).

Surprisingly, when listeners believe a professional to be higher in status, they perceive her speech rate to be more standard than when they believe she is lower in status (Thakerar & Giles 1981). Standard speech is not intrinsically more appealing than nonstandard speech, however. Listeners cannot discriminate among unfamiliar foreign accents on the basis of aesthetic criteria (Giles & Niedzielski 1998). Instead, listeners' evaluations of familiar accents reflect the levels of status and prestige they have learned to associate with the speakers of those accents.

The Confidence Bias: The Persuasive Appeal of Confidence

Professionals' confidence in their recommendations, regardless of their recommendations' actual validity, is one of the primary determinants of audiences' decisions (e.g., Salvadori, van Swol, & Sniezek 2001; Thomas & McFadyen 1995; van Swol & Sniezek 2002). Audiences weight the recommendations of confident speakers more heavily and are more confident when adopting them. Confident group members have more influence on group decisions than more tentative and uncertain members (Schulz-Hardt et al. 2002).

Vocal behaviors are one cue that audiences use to assess a professional's confidence. Audiences are more persuaded by speakers who express confidence by speaking in a powerful style than they are by those who speak in a style that indicates powerlessness (Burrell & Koper 1998; Erickson et al. 1978; Holtgraves & Lasky 1999). As we have seen, the frequent use of verbal behaviors such as intensifiers (e.g., "really big"), hedges (e.g., "I think"), hesitation forms (e.g., "and, uh"), and questioning intonations characterize the powerless speaking style. Conversely, the speaking styles of powerful and confident individuals rarely display those verbal behaviors. In studies of juror decision making, a confident or powerful speech style results in more favorable jury decisions than does a powerless style (Hahn & Clayton 1996). However, when audiences read written transcriptions of spoken messages delivered in a confident, powerful speech style, the persuasive effects are greatly diminished (Sparks, Areni, & Cox 1998).

Verbal behaviors are another cue that the audience uses to assess a professional's confidence. For example, clients are more persuaded by consultants who express confidence by taking an extreme position (e.g., the stock will double in value) than by those who take a more moderate position (Price & Stone 2004; Yates et al. 1996).

The Likeability Bias: The Persuasive Appeal of Friendliness

Audiences are more likely to be biased toward and persuaded by likeable professionals than by unlikeable ones (e.g., Berscheid & Reis 1998). For example, likeable job candidates tend to be rated more highly by recruiters (Keenan 1977). Likable employees tend to be rated more highly on performance appraisals by their supervisors (Cardy & Dobbins 1986). Likeable surgeons are less likely to be sued by their patients for malpractice than their equally skilled but less agreeable counterparts (Levinson, Roter, Mullooly, Dull, & Frankel 1997). Much of the reason for the difference in the patients' reactions appears to be determined by the surgeon's tone of voice (Ambady et al. 2002).

Audiences tend to like those who are expressive nonverbally more than they like those who are not expressive (Friedman, DiMatteo, & Taranta 1980b). Ratings of likeability are influenced by nonverbal cues such as smiling, expressiveness, body posture, and eye contact (Hart & Morry 1997; Hrubes 2001; Knutson 1996). In a study of the nonverbal behaviors of undergraduate business students in mock job interviews, Levine (1998) finds high likeability associated with a higher percentage of smiling.

Speaker behaviors that cue inferences of likeability and increase compliance with their requests include increased gaze, conversational proximity, touch, open body orientation, smiling, nodding, and gesturing (Baron & Bell 1976; Edinger & Patterson 1983; Kleinke 1980). Salespeople who use high levels of gaze and expressive body movements influence customers more than salespeople who are less expressive (Sommers, Greeno, & Boag 1989) as do salespeople who display happy versus negative emotions (Englis & Reid 1990). Segrin (1993) reports that gazing at listeners while making a request reliably increases the compliance rates of those listeners. However, there are some limits to the persuasive power of likeability. For example, expert audiences appear to be less biased by likeability than are novices (Wood & Kallgren 1988). And likeability makes more difference in videotaped or audio taped messages than in written messages (Andreoli & Worchel 1978; Chaiken & Eagly 1983).

The Similarity Bias: The Persuasive Appeal of Similarity

Audiences are more likely to be biased toward and persuaded by professionals they perceive to be similar to themselves than they are by those they perceive to be dissimilar. For example, consumers who perceive a salesperson as similar to themselves are more likely to make the recommended purchases (Matthews, Wilson, & Monoky 1972; Woodside & Davenport 1974). Listeners who hear a speaker's arguments spoken in their own regional dialect are more likely to be persuaded than when those same arguments are spoken in the standard dialect (Giles 1973). In a study of the effects of similar dress, Hensley (1981) finds well dressed solicitors to be more successful in gaining compliance in airports where people are typically better dressed than in bus stops where they are typically less well dressed. Conversely, casually dressed solicitors are more successful at bus stops. Audiences also tend to like others they perceive to be similar to themselves more than those they perceive to be different (e.g., Carli, Ganley, & Pierce-Otay 1991; Hill & Stull 1981).

Similarity biases a wide range of audience decisions. Mock jurors are less likely to convict when they and the defendant have similar backgrounds, ethnicity, and beliefs (Kerr, Hymes, Anderson, & Weathers 1995; Stephan & Stephan 1986). Recruiters give higher ratings to job applicants who have similar attitudes and characteristics (Graves & Powell 1988; Peters & Terborg 1975; Schmitt 1976). Similarities between a recruiter and a job applicant on demographic characteristics (Frank & Hackman 1975), attitudes (Berscheid 1985), and experience (Wade & Kinicki 1997) also affect the likelihood that the applicant will be offered a job. Studies of group decision making find that as a group becomes more tight knit, the group's evaluation of their leader's effectiveness comes to depend less on the leader's fit with a generic leader schema and more on the degree to which the leader is perceived to be prototypical of, or similar to, the specific group's membership (Hogg 2007; Hogg & van Knippenberg 2003).

Audiences also like more and are more persuaded by professionals who exhibit nonverbal behaviors similar to their own (Bailenson & Yee 2005; Bates 1975; Manusov 1993). For example, Cappella (1993) finds that people like interaction partners who mimic their smiling behaviors more than they like partners who do not. A conversational partner's similar posture can also lead to increased rapport (Scheflen 1964). Mimicking the audience's behavior without their awareness causes them to be more helpful (van Baaren, Holland, Kawakami, & van Knippenberg 2004) and in service situations, to provide bigger tips (van Baaren, Holland, Steenaert, & van Knippenberg 2003).

The Salience Bias: The Persuasive Appeal of Standing Out

Attention-getting or salient professionals are more persuasive than those who do not attract attention. Members of group discussions see attention-getting or salient group members as intrinsically persuasive. They may credit them with setting the tone of the meeting, deciding on topics to be covered, or guiding the discussion (McArthur 1981; Taylor & Fiske 1978). In addition to being more persuaded by salient individuals, participants in meetings tend to view salient individuals as representing the group to which they belong (Taylor 1981). For example, a lone marketer in a meeting of financial analysts is likely to be seen as presenting the "marketing" perspective. Audiences will also exaggerate their evaluations of salient people. When a person is salient, audiences tend to evaluate the person's positive attributes more positively and to evaluate their negative attributes more negatively than they do when the person is not salient (Taylor 1981).

Cognitive Centrality: The Power of Knowing what Others Know

Group members who possess more information other group members share (for a discussion of shared information, see Chapter 5, pp. 209–10), or who are more *cognitively central*, tend to be more persuasive in group decision making than those who possess less shared information (cf., Vaughan 1999). A study of persuasive minority members in groups finds that when the person in the minority in a three-person group possesses the most shared information, groups agree with the minority position 67% of the time (Kameda, Ohtsubo, & Takezawa 1997). When the person in the minority possesses the least amount of shared information, groups agree with the minority position only 42% of the time. On those occasions in which the minority position prevails, the person in the minority also repeats significantly more shared information than when the majority position prevails (Van Swol & Seinfeld 2006).

Group members who possess more shared information tend to participate more in group discussions, get more reactions from other group members, and agree more with the group's decision than do those who possess mostly unshared information (Sargis & Larson 2002; Schittekatte & Van Hiel 1996).

One reason that shared information enhances a group member's influence is that other group members perceive shared information to be more credible and more valuable than unshared information (Kerschreiter et al. 2004). Group members evaluate information that can be corroborated by other group members more favorably whether or not they personally can corroborate it (Mojzisch, Schulz-Hardt, Kerschreiter, Brodbeck, & Frey 2004). However, there is an important exception to the rule. Group members with more unshared information may be more influential if they possess the most complete knowledge of information relevant to the group's shared schema (cf., Larson, Sargis, Elstein, & Schwartz 2002).

Person Perception in Audience Decision Making: Implications for Communicators

✧ The main takeaway for communicators in Chapter 6 is that audience decisions are based in part on audience perceptions of how well the professionals who communicate with them play their roles. Audience decisions are also biased by additional communicator attributes. Who you are perceived to be can be as important as what you say and how you say it.

✧ Use the information presented in the chapter to adjust your behaviors and appearance to meet audience role expectations and to bias audiences in your favor. Do not expect audiences to adjust their biases to suit your personal style.

✧ Why use the information? To enhance the persuasiveness of your communications. To enhance audience perceptions of you as a leader.

✧ To become competent at the behaviors presented in the chapter, simply practice them.

PART III

Understanding Emotional Decision Making

CHAPTER 7

Emotions in Audience Decision Making

On October 3, 2000 then Vice President Al Gore and soon-to-be President George W. Bush engaged in the first of three televised debates. Minutes into the first debate, Gore and Bush exchanged views on Medicare coverage.

GORE: Under the Governor's plan, if you kept the same fee for service that you have now under Medicare, your premiums would go up by between 18% and 47%, and that is the study of the Congressional plan that he's modeled his proposal on by the Medicare actuaries. Let me give you one quick example. There is a man here tonight named George McKinney from Milwaukee. He's 70 years old, has high blood pressure, his wife has heart trouble. They have an income of $25,000 a year. They can't pay for their prescription drugs. They're some of the ones that go to Canada regularly in order to get their prescription drugs. Under my plan, half of their costs would be paid right away. Under Governor Bush's plan, they would get not one penny for four to five years and then they would be forced to go into an HMO or to an insurance company and ask them for coverage, but there would be no limit on the premiums or the deductibles or any of the terms and conditions.

BUSH: I cannot let this go by, the old-style Washington politics, if we're going to scare you in the voting booth. Under my plan the man gets immediate help with prescription drugs. It's called Immediate Helping Hand. Instead of squabbling and finger pointing, he gets immediate help. Let me say something.

MODERATOR: Your

GORE: They get $25,000 a year income; that makes them ineligible.

BUSH: Look, this is a man who has great numbers. He talks about numbers. I'm beginning to think not only did he invent the Internet, but he invented the calculator. It's fuzzy math.

(Gore & Bush 2000)

Drew Westen, in his book *The Political Brain: The Role of Emotion in Deciding the Fate of the Nation*, uses the exchange excerpted above to illustrate the difference between a highly logical and reasonable appeal to voters and an appeal based on emotions. Whereas Vice President Gore spoke in a cold and humorless manner, then Governor Bush delivered his remarks in a friendly, affable style. Whereas Gore framed his Medicare plan in the language of an economist, Bush framed his plan so as to achieve maximum emotional resonance with the voting public, calling it the "Immediate Helping Hand."

> Instead of getting voters to *feel* the difference between his concern for the welfare of seniors struggling to pay their medical bills and Bush's, Gore went to a level of numerical precision—premised on a model of expected utility, giving them every number they needed to make the appropriate calculations—that played right into Bush's strategy of portraying Gore as an emotionless policy wonk, "not a regular guy, like us."
>
> (Westen 2007, p. 33)

The ability to make an emotional connection with the audience is an essential leadership skill. Emrich and colleagues (2001) find that the use of emotion-evoking images in US presidents' speeches is directly related to the public's perception of each president's charisma and greatness. Indeed, the hallmark of truly great speeches and the leaders who deliver them is their ability to stir the audience's emotions. However, many professionals over-estimate their ability to elicit the emotions they intend. Kruger and colleagues (2005) find that audiences reading e-mails have great difficulty discerning the emotions most e-mail writers intend to convey. For example, audiences are likely to interpret e-mail messages intended to be funny as being sarcastic and insulting instead.

Obviously, emotions play an important role in audience decision making, but what are emotions anyway? Emotions are comprised of:

1) thoughts and feelings;
2) physical responses in the brain and body;
3) facial, vocal, and postural expressions; and
4) action tendencies or readiness for certain behaviors (Oatley & Jenkins 1996; Roseman 1994; Smith & Lazarus 1990).

Audience members acquire emotions early in life. By age six months children have acquired the emotions of surprise, interest, joy, anger, sadness, fear, and disgust. By age two they have acquired envy and empathy. By age three they have acquired embarrassment, pride, shame, and guilt (Lewis 1999; Mascolo & Fischer 1995; Sroufe 1995).

Psychologically, emotions alter the audience's attention, make certain behavioral responses more likely than others, and activate associative memories (Levenson 2003). Physiologically, emotions produce a bodily state in audience members that is optimal for an effective response to the perceived situation. Emotions alter the state of the audience's skeletomuscular system, their autonomic nervous system, and their endocrine system—the hormonal system that affects audience members' reflex, cardiovascular, electrodermal, gastrointestinal, and papillary activity (Cacioppo, Tassinary, & Berntson 2000). Taylor and colleagues (2005) show that threateningly worded and emotion-evoking e-mailed reprimands, like the one from the CEO quoted in Chapter 6 (p. 235), significantly increase the diastolic blood pressure of the employees reading them, compared to the diastolic blood pressure of employees reading non-threateningly worded reprimands. Emotions not only change blood pressure levels in the audience, they also change the number of immune and antibody cells in their blood (Maier & Watkins 1998).

Emotions, although similar to moods, do not last as long. Whereas audience members may experience moods for days, their emotions last only minutes or hours (Oatley & Jenkins 1996; Rosenberg 1998).

A primary function of emotions is to evaluate stimuli, to sort out which stimuli are good and which are bad, and to signal which stimuli should be approached and which should be avoided (e.g., Lang, Bradley, & Cuthbert 1990). Emotions also function to prepare audience members to respond to stimuli in particular ways researchers often refer to as "action tendencies" (Frijda 1986; Plutchik 1980; Smith & Lazarus 1990). And since emotions are usually accompanied by expressive postures, gestures, and facial and vocal expressions, emotions also serve to communicate the audience's feeling states to others (Ekman 1971; Scherer 1986). Short-circuiting the audience's rational processing of information is another primary function of emotions (Levenson 1994; Simon 1967).

In addition, emotions serve to enhance the audience's memory. Audiences are more likely to remember emotional stimuli than neutral stimuli (Brown & Kulik 1977; Buchanan & Adolphs 2002; Hamann 2001). In a study of emotional messages, Kensinger and coauthors (2005) asked adults of different ages to read sentences that were written either to stir emotions (e.g., "There was a fire in the forest") or to be emotionally neutral (e.g., "There was a road in the forest"). Both younger and older adults showed enhanced memory for emotional words (e.g., fire) compared to neutral words (e.g., road).

Audiences are also likely to remember emotional stimuli more vividly (Heuer & Reisberg 1990; Kensinger & Corkin 2003; Ochsner 2000). Many studies show enhanced "flashbulb memories" of emotionally salient public events (e.g., Cohen, Conway, & Maylor 1994; Davidson & Glisky 2002). At the same time audiences may have difficulty intentionally forgetting emotional stimuli. Although audiences can intentionally forget neutral photographs, they find it hard to forget either emotionally negative or positive photographs (Ochsner & Sanchez 2001).

THE IMPACT OF EMOTIONS ON DECISION MAKING

Emotional Decisions versus Rational Decisions

Emotions are often better predictors of audience behavior than reason (Breckler & Wiggins 1989). When emotion and reason are consistent with one another, both exert equal influence on the audience's attitudes and behaviors (Lavine, Thomsen, Zanna, & Borgida 1998). However, when emotion and reason are inconsistent with one another, emotion has a greater influence on the audience than reason.

Surprisingly, when audience decisions are based on emotions, individual audience members may agree more with other members of the audience than when their decisions are based on reason (Pham, Cohen, Pracejus, & Hughes 2001). The consensual nature of audience members' emotional responses may explain why juries often agree strongly on how they feel about legal cases yet disagree just as strongly on the amount of punitive damages to award (Kahneman, Schkade, & Sunstein 1998).

Unlike rational decisions, the emotional decisions audiences make are insensitive to quantity. For example, audiences donate less to save pandas when they are shown the number of pandas to be saved represented as dots as opposed to a photograph of a single panda (Hsee & Rottenstreich 2004). Emotional decisions are insensitive to probabilities as well (Loewenstein, Weber, Hsee, & Welch 2001). Contrary to the assumptions of economic theory, research participants are unwilling to pay more to avoid a high probability of receiving an electric shock than they are to avoid a low probability of receiving the same shock (Rottenstreich & Hsee 2001).

Up to 50% of consumer purchase decisions can be classified as emotional or impulse purchases (Bellenger, Robertson, & Hirschman 1978; Cobb & Hoyer 1986; Han, Morgan, Kotsiopulos, & Kang-Park 1991). And almost 90% of consumers make impulsive, emotion-based purchases at least occasionally (Welles 1986), and they do so across a broad range of product offerings in a variety of price ranges (Cobb & Hoyer 1986; Rook 1987; Rook & Fisher 1995).

Emotions can even determine decisions that require substantial rational thought and deliberation from the audience (Loewenstein & Lerner 2003). For example, emotions played a critical role in determining voters' decisions during the 1980 US presidential election (Abelson et al. 1982). Some theorists believe "the majority of choices people make, including economic ones, are completely or largely based on normative-affective [i.e., values and emotional] considerations" (Etzioni 1992, p. 90).

In some situations, audiences are especially likely to make emotional as opposed to rational decisions. For example, a consumer's judgments are more likely to be based on emotional considerations when the consumer is looking for a particular experience such as having fun as opposed to accomplishing a pragmatic goal such as buying groceries (Pham 1998). Consumers' decisions to buy certain types of products such as vacation packages are more likely to be based on emotions than are decisions to buy other types of products such as long-distance telephone plans (Adaval 2001). Consumers' evaluations of certain product attributes such as styling are more likely to be based on emotions than are their evaluations of other types of product attributes such as cost (Wyer, Clore, & Isbell 1999). In general, audiences rely more on emotion than reason when they have only limited motivation, ability, or opportunity to process information (e.g., Albarracín & Wyer 2001; Miniard, Bhatla, Lord, Dickson, & Unnava 1991).

An ad's ability to evoke emotions often determines the purchase intentions of its audience. In a study of ad formats, Mitchell and Olson (1981) asked consumers to read four versions of an ad for a hypothetical brand of facial tissues and to decide if they wanted to purchase the product. One version contained only a verbal claim about the product. Two versions contained the same verbal claim together with a headline and different, but emotionally positive, photographs. The fourth version contained the same verbal claim as well as a headline and an emotionally neutral photograph. The two versions containing the emotionally positive photographs elicited the most positive emotions. Moreover, the more positive a consumer's emotional reaction to a version of the ad, the greater was the consumer's intention to purchase the product. Related studies of advertising confirm that when rational responses to the product are statistically controlled for, consumers' emotional reactions to ads account for significant amounts of variance in their attitudes toward brands (Moore & Hutchinson 1983; Park & Young 1986), especially in their attitudes toward new brands (Edell & Burke 1986; Stayman & Aaker 1987).

Like consumers' decisions, jurors' verdicts are influenced by the jurors' emotional responses. In a study of the effects of pre-trial publicity, Kramer and colleagues (1990) showed mock jurors either factual news reports describing the defendant's previous convictions and the discovery of incriminating evidence or emotional pre-trial publicity that identified the defendant as a suspect in a hit-and-run killing of a child. The emotional pre-trial publicity produced a 20% higher conviction rate than did the factual pre-trial publicity, despite judicial instructions to discount the pre-trial publicity altogether.

The Positive Impact of Emotions on Decision Making

The impact of emotions on audience decision making is mostly positive. Emotions help the audience recognize the personal significance of the information they use to make judgments and decisions (Isen & Means 1983; Schwarz & Clore 1983). Emotions help the audience recognize the desirability of different alternatives (Keltner & Kring 1998; Lerner & Keltner 2000; Levenson 1994). In addition, emotions help the audience recognize the personal significance of moral and aesthetic values implicated by their decisions (Forgas 1995; Isen 1993; Lerner & Keltner 2000).

Surprisingly, audience decisions based on emotions are sometimes even more accurate than decisions based on analytic assessments. For example, the ratings of consumers who were asked how much they liked the taste of various brands of jam corresponded better with ratings of gustatory experts than did ratings of consumers who were asked to rationally justify their preferences (Wilson, Kraft, & Dunn 1989b; Wilson & Schooler 1991). In a follow-up study, consumers who were asked simply to choose the poster they liked most ended up liking the poster they chose more than did consumers who were asked to analyze each poster along several attributes or decision criteria before making their final decision (Wilson et al. 1993).

Emotions also provide the audience with the motivation necessary to implement their decisions (Frijda 1988; Frijda & Mesquita 1994; Keltner & Gross 1999). Traditional decision theory assumes that once an audience member chooses an appropriate course of action she will automatically take that course of action. But many researchers have shown that although audience members may decide to do what is best, they do not necessarily do what is best (Loewenstein 1996; Metcalfe & Mischel 1999; Mischel, Cantor, & Feldman 1996). Emotions provide the audience with the motivation to follow through.

The Negative Impact of Emotions

Emotions are well known for their negative effects on audience decision making. Emotions can cause audience members to reverse prior rational decisions, such as a decision to diet, to stop drinking, or to hold a stock that is dropping in value (Sjöberg 1980). Emotions can cause the audience to scrutinize information either too much or too little (Bless et al. 1996; Bodenhausen, Kramer, & Süsser 1994a; Bodenhausen, Sheppard, & Kramer 1994b). Emotions can cut short rational processing and cause audiences to jump to unwarranted conclusions (cf., Etzioni 1992).

Thus, emotions can potentially override rational deliberations and cause audience members to behave self-destructively (Bazerman, Tenbrunsel, & Wade-Benzoni 2005; Loewenstein 1996). Intense emotions create a sense of urgency that may lead audience members to respond only to emotion-related cues and unconscious processes (Wallace, Newman, & Bachorowski 1991) and can result in automatic, and dangerous, behaviors (Wallace & Newman 1997). In the courtroom, emotionally arousing testimony and/or evidence can inhibit rational decision making and can lead jurors to render excessively severe sentencing judgments (Myers & Greene 2004).

Emotions can distort the audience's judgment about the consequences of their decisions (Goldberg, Lerner, & Tetlock 1999; Lerner & Keltner 2001; Loewenstein et al. 2001). For example, emotions can cause investors to be excessively risk-averse and to choose safe investments such as bonds over higher-performing stocks (Loewenstein et al. 2001). Emotions can cause consumers to pay twice as much to insure a beloved antique clock as to insure a similar clock of equal value to which they have no emotional attachment, all despite the fact that the insurance pays $100 in both cases (Hsee & Kunreuther 2000). Similarly, emotions can make consumers more likely to buy a warranty on a newly purchased used car when the car is a beautiful convertible than when it is an ordinary-looking station wagon even though the expected repair expenses and the cost of the warranty are the same (Hsee & Menon 1999).

Emotions can also make audiences less sensitive to possible risks. For example, cigarette advertising designed to increase the positive emotions associated with smoking can depress the audience's perception of the risks involved with smoking (Finucane, Alhakami, Slovic, & Johnson 2000). Emotions can even hamper the audience's ability to reason logically about logic problems. In a classic study of emotion versus reason, Lefford (1946) gave participants 20 syllogisms that dealt with emotionally charged topics and 20 syllogisms that dealt with emotionally neutral topics. Participants were then asked to determine if the syllogisms were valid and to state whether they agreed with the syllogisms' conclusions. Interestingly, participants were more accurate judging the validity of the neutral syllogisms than they were judging the emotionally charged ones.

The Impact of Emotional Deficits

The audience's ability to experience emotions is essential if it is to make a rational decision. In spite of otherwise normal intellectual abilities, patients with damage to the ventromedial (VM) prefrontal cortex of their brains are unable to experience emotions and, consequently, have great difficulty making rational decisions (Bechara, Damasio, Tranel, & Anderson 1998; Damasio, Tranel, & Damasio 1990; Eslinger & Damasio 1985). These patients often make decisions against their best interests and repeat prior decisions that led to negative consequences (Bechara 2003). The decisions they make often result in financial losses, losses in social standing, and losses of family and friends.

Other symptoms of the emotional deficits caused by damage to the VM prefrontal cortex include indecisiveness, inability to prioritize, inability to plan future activity, inappropriate social manners, disregard of risks, and lack of concern for others (Bechara, Damasio, Damasio, & Anderson 1994; Bechara, Damasio, Damasio, & Lee 1999; Damasio 1994). Yet the same patients possess all of their other faculties, including normal intelligence, comprehension, memory, and attention (Anderson, Bechara, Damasio, Tranel, & Damasio 1999; Anderson, Damasio, Jones, & Tranel 1991; Bechara et al. 1998).

In his book *Descartes' Error*, Damasio describes the difficulties one VM patient had when asked to decide which of two days he would prefer to come for his next appointment with the author. "For the better part of a half-hour, the patient enumerated reasons for and against each of the two dates: previous engagements, proximity to other engagements, possible meteorological conditions . . . he was now walking us through a tiresome cost-benefit analysis, an endless outlining and fruitless comparison of options and possible consequences" (Damasio 1994, p. 193). The same patient showed no emotional reactions to grisly pictures, although he described them as "disgusting." Despite the fact the patient had an intellectual understanding of emotional states, he had no emotional experiences.

THE ANTECEDENTS OF EMOTIONAL DECISION MAKING

Audience Goals and Values

The antecedents of the audience's emotions are its goals and values (e.g., Clore & Isbell 2001; Ellsworth & Scherer 2003; Smith & Kirby 2001). Without goals or values, audiences would not experience emotions since emotions are evaluations of stimuli as they relate to audience members' goals and values (Smith & Lazarus 1990; Smith & Pope 1992). Clore and Ortony (1988) assert that emotions need not be unreasonable, but that they must by definition involve value. Similarly, Lazarus (1999) proposes that without a goal at stake, there will be no emotion.

Negative emotions result from threats to the audience's goals and values. Positive emotions result from attainment of their goals and values (e.g., Carver & Scheier 1990). The strength of an audience's emotional response to a situation is determined (1) by how relevant that situation is to their goals and values, and (2) by how invested the audience is in those goals and values (cf., Griner & Smith 2000; Ross & Conway 1986; Singer & Salovey 1996; Smith & Pope 1992). Table 7.1 indicates the values of Americans in different age groups. Although all three age groups rank freedom and self respect among their top five values, 20-year-olds tend to value freedom and happiness most highly. Older people tend to value family security and world peace most highly.

Different Goals and Values, Different Emotions

Different audience members can have different emotional reactions to the same stimulus (e.g., Shaver, Hazan, & Bradshaw 1988; Smith & Ellsworth 1987; Smith & Pope 1992).

Table 7.1 Top Five Values of Three Age Groups

Rank	20-year-olds	30-year-olds	60-year-olds
1	Freedom	Family security	World peace
2	Happiness	World peace	Family security
3	Wisdom	Freedom	Freedom
4	Self-respect	Self-respect	National security
5	Love	Wisdom	Self-respect

Source: Adapted from Rokeach 1973.

The Greek philosopher Epictetus said much the same thing more than 2,000 years ago when he observed that people are not disturbed by things but rather by their view of them. An old story illustrates this point. It describes "three persons of much the same age and temperament" traveling in the same vehicle who were told of the sudden death of another. The first person was not affected; the second started to cry; the third smiled. Why? The first person never heard of the deceased. The second person was the brother of the deceased. The third person was a long-time rival of the deceased. Thus each person had a different emotional reaction to the same event because each valued the deceased differently.

The fact that different audience members have different goals and values appears to explain many individual differences in consumer behavior and media exposure (e.g., Kahle, Beatty, & Homer 1986; Kamakura & Novak 1992; Richins 1994). For example, a cross-cultural study finds that consumers in France purchase expensive brands of wine because of their desire for social interaction, whereas consumers in the United States purchase the same brands in order to prove themselves to others (Overby, Gardial, & Woodruff 2004). Thus, an ad that motivates consumers in Los Angeles is unlikely to be effective with consumers in Paris. Likewise, because different citizens have different values that come into play when they decide whether to recycle, recycling campaigns with a single focus tend to have only limited success (Smeesters, Warlop, Vanden Abeele, & Ratneshwar 1999).

The Link Between Decision Criteria and Goals and Values

The audience's decision criteria determine which of their goals and values are implicated when they make a decision (cf., Luce 1998; Luce, Bettman, & Payne 2000). For instance, when deciding between two cars, the criterion or attribute of safety may implicate the value of personal survival, whereas the criterion of styling may implicate the value of personal expression. In addition, there is a direct connection between the goals and values that product attributes implicate and consumer purchases and preferences (e.g., Bagozzi & Dholakia 1999; Huffman, Ratneshwar, & Mick 2000; Walker & Olson 1997). Consumers are motivated to buy a product to the extent that they are able to link the product's attributes to their own goals and values (Grunert & Bech-Larsen 2005).

The values consumers link to products are often better predictors of their product preferences than are the product's attributes (Grunert & Bech-Larsen 2005; Perkins & Reynolds 1988). The values consumers link to products correlate not only with their initial purchase intentions, but also with their product and/or service evaluations and with their repeat purchases as well (Cronin, Brady, & Hult 2000; Patterson & Spreng 1997).

Much like consumers responding to products that implicate their goals and values, subordinates respond more positively to leaders who articulate the subordinates' goals and values (Conger & Kanungo 1998; Shamir et al. 1993; Sheldon & Elliot 1999). Business leaders who frame messages in terms of their subordinates' goals and values increase their employees' motivation, commitment, and satisfaction (Bono & Judge 2003).

Decision criteria or attributes with implications for the audience's more highly valued goals trigger more emotion (Luce 1998). Although economic attributes such as price may be highly important to consumers, economic attributes do not have much potential to elicit emotion, whereas other attributes such as safety features may be moderately important but easily elicit emotion (Luce et al. 2000). Decision criteria or attributes with implications for the audience's more highly valued goals are also higher in "trade-off difficulty" (Luce 1998). For instance, new parents who purchase an automobile may be very reluctant to accept losses on the attribute of safety for gains on an attribute such as greater fuel efficiency. Similarly, voters are rarely willing to trade off a positive evaluation of a candidate on an economic issue for a negative evaluation of the same candidate on a highly valued ethical issue (Shah, Domke, & Wackman 1996).

Figures 7.1 and 7.2 show a buyer's decision matrix for choosing between two cars—a Metro Car and a Cadillac SUV. In Figure 7.1 none of the decision criteria

Decision Criteria	PREFERENCES	PROPOSAL 2006 Metro Car	ALTERNATIVE 2006 Cadillac SUV	Proposal's score
Size?	> Better	¾ ton	3 ½ tons	Low
Miles per gallon?	> Better	65	16	High
Safety record?	> Better	Below average	Average	Low
Horse power?	> Better	60	345	Low
Depreciation rate?	> Better	Excellent	Poor	High
Retail price?	> Better	$20,000	$53,850	High
			Metro Car's total score	Medium
			Decision	Accept

Figure 7.1 When Decision Criteria are Not Linked to Goals and Values, Decision Making is Rational

Decision Criteria	PREFERENCES	PROPOSAL 2006 Metro Car	ALTERNATIVE 2006 Cadillac SUV	Proposal's score
Size?	> Better	¾ ton	3 ½ tons	Low
Miles per gallon?	> Better	65	16	High
Safety record?	**> Better**	**Below average**	Average	Low
Horse power?	> Better	60	345	Low
Depreciation rate?	> Better	Excellent	Poor	High
Retail price?	> Better	$20,000	$53,850	High
			Emotion generated	Fear
			Decision	Reject

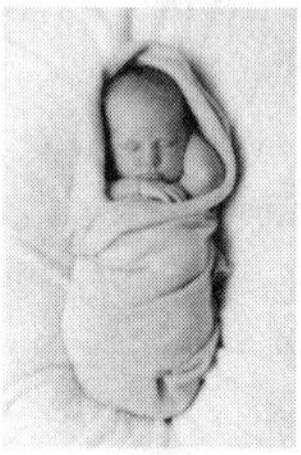

The life of my child

Figure 7.2 When Decision Criteria are Linked to Goals and Values, Decision Making is Emotional

are linked to the audience's high-level goals or values, making the Metro Car an acceptable decision from a rational point of view. But in Figure 7.2 the decision criterion of safety is linked to the car buyer's high-level value, the life of their newborn baby. From this emotional point of view, the Metro Car is not acceptable because of its below-average safety record. Consequently, the potential car buyer would make no further comparisons or trade offs before rejecting the Metro Car.

COGNITIVE AND PHYSIOLOGICAL PROCESSES IN EMOTIONAL DECISION MAKING

Unlike rational decision making, emotional decision making includes physiological as well as cognitive processes. Emotional decision making starts as soon as the audience perceives an emotionally significant stimulus or an emotionally significant attribute of a stimulus. Only those stimuli or attributes of a stimulus relevant to the audience's goals and values can be said to be emotionally significant. As we have seen, the stimulus itself does not trigger the emotion or the decisions based on it, but instead the stimulus' implications for the goals or values of the audience trigger them (Derryberry & Tucker 1992).

The model of emotional decision making proposed here and shown in Figure 7.3 builds on this understanding of emotionally significant stimuli. The model also presents an account of Simon's (1967) analysis of emotions as "interrupt mechanisms." As soon as an audience member perceives a stimulus that has emotional significance to them, the stimulus captures their attention, demands fast comprehension of its implications, and evokes an emotional response that includes a tendency to take a particular type of action such as embrace, attack, or withdraw from the stimulus. The emotional response interrupts and overrides the more deliberate and rational decision-making process of making comparisons and trade offs and leads the audience to make a decision congruent with the emotion's action tendency.

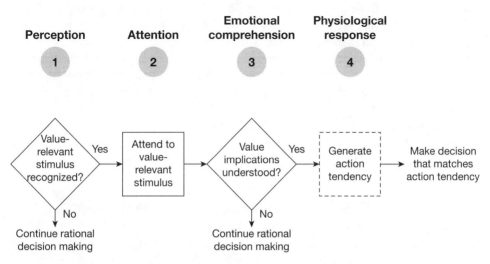

Figure 7.3 A Cognitive Process Model of Emotional Decision Making

Perception of Emotionally Significant Stimuli

Audiences perceive emotionally significant images more rapidly than emotionally neutral images (Lundqvist & Öhman 2005; Öhman, Esteves, & Soares 1995; Schupp, Junghöfer, Weike, & Hamm 2003). Although audiences need 240 milliseconds to recognize neutral pictures, they can perceive negative pictures within 105 milliseconds and positive pictures within 180 milliseconds (Carretié, Hinojosa, Martín-Loeches, Mercado, & Tapia 2004). Even abstract images are perceived more quickly if an emotion is associated with them. Batty and colleagues (2005) conditioned viewers to associate an emotionally neutral or negative valence with different abstract shapes. Viewers had faster responses to abstract stimuli that they had associated with threats.

Audiences are especially fast at perceiving emotional facial expressions, such as the facial expressions of speakers or fellow group members. Audience responses to positive versus negative facial expressions are distinguishable within just 80 to 160 milliseconds after the faces are presented (Pizzagalli, Regard, & Lehmann 1999). Even in tasks for which the emotional expression on a face is irrelevant, audience members respond to emotional faces more rapidly than neutral ones (Eger, Jedynak, Iwaki, & Skrandies 2003; Sato, Kochiyama, Yoshikawa, & Matusumura 2001). Audience responses to threatening faces are most rapid. Audiences can detect threatening faces faster and more accurately than friendly faces even when only one facial feature, such as the eyebrows, the mouth, or the eyes, conveys the threat (Lundqvist and Öhman 2005). Facial features that affect the audience's detection of most emotions in rank order are eyebrows, mouth, and eyes.

Audiences perceive emotionally significant words more quickly than emotionally neutral ones. When presented a series of words very quickly, about one every 100 milliseconds, readers are more likely to recognize emotionally significant words than neutral words (Anderson & Phelps 2001).

Some audience members can perceive and encode emotionally significant stimuli even when the stimuli are outside the focus of their attention (Compton 2003; Vuilleumier et al. 2002; White 1996). In a study of gender differences, Schirmer and colleagues (2005) asked men and women who had been induced to attend to something else to listen to syllables spoken either in an emotional or a neutral way. Although both sexes detected non-emotional acoustic changes in the speaker's voice prior to attending to those changes consciously, only women detected the changes in the emotional tone of the speaker's voice.

Neither male nor female readers perceive and recognize emotionally significant written words unless they fixate on them using their foveal vision. In an eye-tracking study of readers' eye fixations, Hyönä and Häikiö (2005) find no evidence of semantic processing of either emotional words (sex-related, threat-related, or curse words) or neutral words that are outside the reader's foveal vision but within their peripheral vision. In addition, readers' pupil size does not increase when presented with emotional words peripherally, indicating a lack of emotional response.

Attention to Emotionally Significant Stimuli

Audiences selectively attend to emotionally significant stimuli. When a neutral and an emotionally significant picture are simultaneously projected into viewers' eyes, viewers give the emotionally significant picture preferential processing (Alpers, Ruhleder, Walz, Mühlberger, & Pauli 2005). In an eye-tracking study, Calvo and Lang (2004) simultaneously presented viewers with pictures of emotionally significant scenes paired with neutral scenes. Viewers gave preferential attention at an early processing stage to the emotional scene in each pair of scenes and were more likely to fixate first and longer on either pleasant or unpleasant emotional scenes than on neutral ones.

Emotionally significant stimuli capture the audience's attention (Kensinger, Piguet, Krendl, & Corkin 2005; Mackintosh & Mathews 2003; Stormark, Nordby, & Hugdahl 1995) even when the emotional stimuli are presented simultaneously with a number of different neutral stimuli that should otherwise distract the audience's attention (Alpers et al. 2005; Calvo & Lang 2004). For example, fear-relevant stimuli (e.g., a picture of a snake or a spider) "pop out" of visual displays regardless of the number of neutral objects in the display (Hansen & Hansen 1988). An angry face among many neutral faces also yields a pop-out effect (Eastwood, Smilek, & Merikle 2001). Interestingly, the number of neutral images in a display does not influence the time the audience needs to detect a fear-relevant stimulus within that display (Öhman, Flykt, & Esteves 2001).

Emotionally significant stimuli elicit sustained attention from the audience. In a study of the eye movements and emotional responses of viewers as they examined emotionally significant and neutral pictures, Quirk and Strauss (2001) find that viewers explore emotionally significant pictures longer and more extensively than they do neutral pictures. In a study in which either an emotional or neutral word indicated the location of the next target, Stormark and coauthors (1995) find that emotionally significant words cause viewers to maintain their attention on the locations where the words are presented, leading them to have faster reactions to the targets.

Emotionally significant messages elicit increased attention and processing from the audience, as indicated by pupil dilatation (cf., Hyönä & Häikiö 2005). In a study of spoken messages, White and Maltzman (1978) asked audiences to listen to neutral, pleasant, and unpleasant verbal messages that each lasted two minutes. Changes in audience members' pupil diameter before, during, and after each passage was spoken were monitored continuously. Audience members' pupils dilated more when they listened to the pleasant and unpleasant messages than when they listened to the neutral messages.

Pupil size also increases when audiences view emotionally significant images (Hess & Polt 1960). Figure 7.4 shows the percentage of change in pupil size after viewers were given ten-second exposures to five test pictures. Male viewers showed the greatest change in pupil size in response to a picture of a nude female. Female viewers showed the greatest change in response to a picture of a mother holding a young child. In a similar study Metalis and Hess (1982) showed viewers a series of pictures related to different emotionally significant themes (e.g., disease). They found that the size of the viewers' pupils differed for each theme presented.

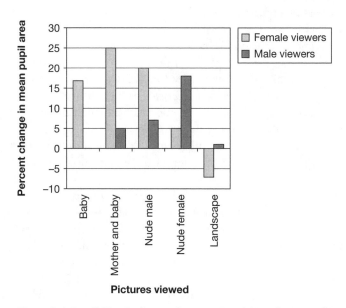

Figure 7.4 Pupil Size Indicates the Emotional Significance of Stimuli (source: Adapted from Hess & Polt 1960).

Emotionally significant stimuli evoke the orienting response in audiences (Öhman & Wiens 2003). The orienting response is associated with the emotion of surprise. When audience members are surprised, they stop whatever behavior they were engaged in and give their full attention to the stimulus (Öhman 1979). The orienting response also elicits the audience's anticipation and a readiness to respond physically (Jennings 1992; Öhman, Hamm, & Hugdahl 2000). The audience's orienting response to intensely emotional stimuli is immediate regardless of the specific emotional quality of the stimulus. When they are presented with an intensely emotional stimulus, they are compelled to divert their attention to the stimulus. However, when audience members are given a task to perform and then exposed to a mildly emotional stimulus, they can consciously avoid diverting their attention away from the task at hand (Mackintosh & Mathews 2003).

The audience's attentional biases are strongest for stimuli that are most closely related to their goals and values (e.g., MacLeod & Rutherford 1992; Mathews & Klug 1993). For example, expert bird watchers display a selective attentional bias toward bird-related words (Dalgleish 1995). In a study of smokers' reactions to smoking-related photographs, Mogg and colleagues (2003) recorded the direction and duration of the eye fixations of smokers and nonsmokers as they viewed smoking-related pictures and neutral, control pictures. Smokers, but not nonsmokers, maintained their gaze longer on smoking-related pictures than they did on pictures that were not related to smoking. The longer smokers fixated on smoking-related pictures, the more positively they rated them and the greater their urge to smoke.

In a study that compared viewers who were and who were not clinically depressed, Matthews and Antes (1992) tracked eye movements while the viewers looked at a series of pictures depicting both happy and sad events. Viewers who were not clinically depressed fixated on happy regions of the pictures significantly sooner, more often, and longer than they fixated on sad regions. Viewers who were depressed fixated more on the sad regions. Audience members in a normal mood also have a bias toward attending to positive stimuli (Gotlib, McLachlan, & Katz 1988).

The audience's attention to and memory for neutral information in scenes is substantially reduced by the presence of emotionally significant stimuli (Anderson & Phelps 2001; Kensinger et al. 2005; Libkuman, Stabler, & Otani 2004). This effect is termed the "weapon-focus" effect (Loftus 1979). When Loftus and coauthors (1987) showed audiences scenes of crimes taking place, they found that audience members spent a disproportionate amount of time looking at the weapon in the scenes (e.g., a gun). Moreover, the amount of time that audience members spent looking at the weapon was inversely related to their ability to remember peripheral information in the scene, such as the criminal.

In their review of the literature, Buchanan and Adolphs (2002) conclude that the presence of any emotionally significant element in a scene makes it less likely audiences will remember neutral elements. Instead, audience members are more likely to remember those same neutral elements if they occur in a scene without an emotional component. Emotionally significant stimuli also degrade attention to and memory for neutral stimuli that are presented immediately before the emotional stimuli (Loftus & Burns 1982; Strange, Hurleman, & Dolan 2003). For example, reading audiences are more likely to forget words that appear just before emotional stimuli than they are to forget other words in the text (Strange et al. 2003).

Comprehension or "Appraisal" of Emotionally Significant Stimuli

According to appraisal theory—the dominant psychological explanation of emotions—each distinct emotion that the audience experiences is elicited by a distinct appraisal, or understanding, of a situation (e.g., Arnold 1960; Lazarus 1991; Ortony, Clore, & Collins 1988). According to this theory, a change in an audience member's emotions, say from anger to shame after the being called on by a speaker, is caused by a change in their appraisal of the situation, in this case from blaming the speaker for calling on them to blaming themselves for being unable to answer the speaker's question (e.g., Roseman 1984; Smith & Lazarus 1990). Table 7.2 indicates the appraisals audiences are thought to make for several of the core emotions.

The appraisal process usually proceeds effortlessly, beneath the conscious awareness of audience members, and generates emotions automatically (e.g., Arnold 1960; Lazarus 1968; Scherer 1987). Surprisingly, conscious awareness is not necessary for most of the audience's cognitive processes, including perception, comprehension, learning, memory, or even the control of action (Velmans 1991).

A small number of appraisal dimensions—such as positive or negative valence and certainty or uncertainty—account for most of the different emotions that audiences experience (e.g., Izard 1977; Tomkins 1962). In their review of the appraisal literature, Smith and Kirby (2000) find substantial agreement among appraisal theorists on the appraisal dimensions that differentiate the various emotions. The five dimensions appraisal theorists have commonly proposed are unexpectedness, valence (positive or negative), certainty (certain or uncertain), agency (caused by another, oneself, or no one), and norm violation (committed by another or oneself).

Cross-cultural studies demonstrate that audiences in the United States, much of Western Europe, and parts of Africa, Asia, and South Asia use similar appraisal dimensions to evoke similar emotions (e.g., Roseman, Dhawan, Rettek, Naidu, & Thapa 1995). In one study researchers asked almost 1,000 people in the United States, Japan, and the People's Republic of China to recall emotional situations and to describe how they had appraised them (Mauro, Sato, & Tucker 1992). The researchers conclude that there are few differences from one country to another in terms of the appraisal dimensions associated with each emotion. For example, in all of the cultures studied, anger involves moderately negative valence and fairly high other-agency, whereas fear involves both negative valence and uncertainty.

Table 7.2 Each Emotion is the Result of a Distinct Appraisal

Appraisal of stimulus	*Resulting emotion*
My expectation is violated	Surprise
Something I value is available to me	Happiness
Something I value is no longer available to me	Sadness
Something I value may be taken from me	Fear
Something I value has been taken from me by someone	Anger
Something I value is available because of me	Pride
Something I value has been defiled	Disgust
Something I value has been defiled by me	Shame

The Sequence of Emotional Appraisals

Emotionally significant stimuli appear to be appraised one dimension at a time in a fixed sequence with the audience member's emotional experience changing each time a new dimension is appraised (Scherer 1984). The first appraisal audiences make is that of unexpectedness—something in their environment unexpectedly changes and attracts their attention (Ellsworth & Scherer 2003). Meyer and colleagues (1997) contend that the appraisal of unexpectedness also serves a purely rational function; it indicates to the audience that they need to update the slot values in the schema they have activated. Once the audience recognizes something unexpected has occurred, they generally display an orienting response in which they stop any ongoing activities and become ready to make additional appraisals (Ellsworth 1994; Kagan 1991). Together with the orienting response, audiences also display the emotion of surprise, with the degree of unexpectedness determining the intensity of the surprise felt (Reisenzein 2000).

The second appraisal audiences make is that of valence, positive or negative, like or dislike (Ellsworth & Scherer 2003). Liking encourages approach; disliking or aversion leads to avoidance (Schneirla 1959). Valence appraisals occur quickly, sometimes so quickly that they cannot be distinguished from the experience of attention (Ellsworth & Scherer 2003). Occasionally the same stimulus is conducive for one of the audience's goals or values and obstructive for another. When this happens the audience experiences mixed emotions and emotional conflict (Weigert 1991). For example, an employee might be both happy and somewhat sad to learn that a respected and well-liked supervisor is at last able to retire from the workforce. Although the audience can experience low levels of bad feelings with low levels of pleasant feelings at the same time, they cannot experience both strong positive and strong negative feelings simultaneously (Diener & Iran-Nejad 1986).

The third appraisal audiences make is that of certainty. Anger, disgust, and happiness are associated with the appraisal of certainty. Hope, fear, and worry are associated with the appraisal of uncertainty (Roseman 1984; Scherer 1984; Smith & Ellsworth 1985). The attribution of agency, determining who caused an event, is the fourth appraisal in the sequence. The attribution of agency is especially important in distinguishing among the negative emotions (Ellsworth & Smith 1988). Anger is evoked when the audience understands someone else to be the cause of the problem or the agent; guilt is evoked when the cause or agent is understood to be oneself, and sadness when the cause or agent is thought to be the circumstances (e.g., an avoidable accident).

The last appraisal audiences make is that of norm violation. Societies depend upon their members to abide by shared rules or norms of acceptable behaviors. Violations of norms lead audiences to experience contempt or disgust when judging the behavior of others and guilt or shame when judging themselves (Ellsworth & Scherer 2003). The emotions associated with one's own norm violations are among the last to appear developmentally (Scherer 1982). Although children experience surprise, joy, anger, sadness, and fear by the age of six months, they do not experience embarrassment, shame, or guilt until the age of three years (Lewis 1999; Mascolo & Fischer 1995; Sroufe 1995).

Figure 7.5 represents the audience's appraisal sequence as a decision tree. Each branch on the tree represents an appraisal in the appraisal sequence. An audience member either

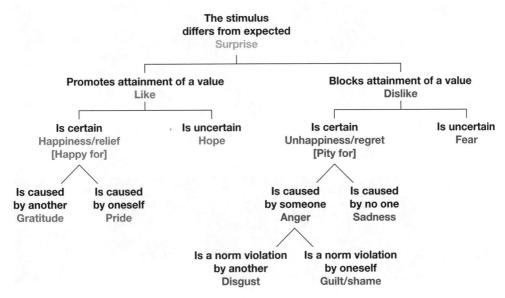

Figure 7.5 A Decision Tree Model of the Appraisal Sequence

likes or dislikes a surprising stimulus. If she likes it and it seems the stimulus is sure to happen, happiness results. If she likes it but the stimulus may not happen, hope results. Happiness may transform into gratitude if someone else is responsible for the stimulus. Happiness may transform into pride if her own efforts are responsible for the stimulus. The appraisal of a disliked stimulus is parallel to that of a liked stimulus except that a disliked stimulus may also be appraised for a norm violation.

In a study designed to elicit a wide range of emotional reactions, Kaiser and Wehrle (2001) videotaped participants as they played an interactive video game. Analysis of the game players' facial expressions supported the idea of a fixed emotional appraisal sequence. For example, whenever players encountered an event that made it difficult for them to score, they would rapidly raise their eyebrows, indicating the appraisal of unexpectedness, and then follow that behavior with an immediate frown, indicating the appraisal of negative valence.

Figure 7.6 depicts the sequence of facial reactions of three players to three videogame events. The three events elicited fear, disappointment, and anger. The first sequence shows a player's facial expressions after seeing a threatening enemy suddenly appear. The player's initial neutral expression is followed by an expression of surprise, then dislike, and finally fear. The second sequence shows a player's facial expressions after she found out the game would become much more difficult to play than she had realized. Her initial neutral expression is followed by an expression of surprise, then dislike, and finally sadness or disappointment. The third sequence shows a player's facial expressions after she was told her video assistant would no longer be there to help her. Her initial expression of surprise/dislike is followed by an expression of regret and then anger.

Response to a frightening event .

Response to a disappointing event

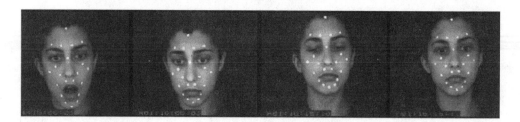

Response to an angering event

Figure 7.6 High-Speed Photography Captures the Sequence of Emotional Appraisals (source: Kaiser, Wehrle, & Schmidt 1998).

Physiological Responses to Emotional Appraisals

Emotional appraisals elicit bodily responses in audience members' autonomic nervous systems, their immune systems, their cardiovascular systems, and their digestive systems (Cacioppo et al. 2000). They elicit changes in the audience's facial expressions, somatic muscular tonus, and tone of voice. Emotional appraisals change hormone levels (Maier & Watkins 1998). The appraisal of negatively valenced pictures decelerates audience members' heart rates, whereas the appraisal of positively valenced pictures produces a large peak in heart rate acceleration (Hamm, Schupp, & Weike 2003).

Emotional appraisals elicit not only specific physiological responses but also specific action tendencies from audience members (e.g., Frijda & Mesquita 1994; Roseman 1996; Smith 1989). Plutchik (1980) proposes that the action tendency of anger is destruction;

of fear, protection; of sadness, reintegration; of joy, reproduction; and of disgust, rejection. Similarly, Lazarus (1991) proposes that the action tendency of anger is attack; of fear, escape; of sadness, withdrawal; of joy, expansiveness; of disgust, ejection; of guilt, atonement; and of shame, hiding. Table 7.3 shows the overall agreement among five prominent appraisal theorists about the action tendencies associated with eight different emotions.

Action tendencies play an influential role in audience decision making. For example, sadness amplifies the audience's tendency to hold on to their possessions, whereas disgust triggers an impulse to get rid of them (Lerner, Small, & Loewenstein 2004). Consumers who experience regret after failing to receive good service will have a different action tendency than consumers who are angry about the service. Consumers who experience regret switch to another service provider, whereas consumers who are angry actively engage in negative word-of-mouth (Zeelenberg & Pieters 1999).

The Inhibition of Information Acquisition and Integration

Because emotional appraisals automatically trigger an action tendency in response to a situation (e.g., attack, escape, dominate), they can simultaneously inhibit information acquisition or search and lead audiences to inadequately scrutinize information (Bless

Table 7.3 Researchers are in Basic Agreement about the Action Tendency Elicited by Each Emotion

Emotion	Plutchik (1980)	Frijda (1986)	Lazarus (1991)	Roseman (2001)
Surprise	Stop	Interrupt		Interrupt
Joy	Reproduce	Activate	Expand	Act
Fear	Protect	Avoid	Escape	Prevent
Anger	Destroy	Attack	Attack	Attack
Sadness	Reintegrate	Deactivate	Withdraw	Inaction
Disgust	Reject	Reject	Eject	Expel
Shame		Submit	Hide	Withdraw
Pride		Dominate	Expand	Dominate

Anger ⟶ Attack   Joy ⟶ Possess   Sadness ⟶ Withdraw   Pride ⟶ Dominate

Figure 7.7 Emotional Appraisals Trigger Action Tendencies.

et al. 1996; Nolen-Hoeksema & Morrow 1993; Nolen-Hoeksema, Morrow, & Fredrickson 1993). Research shows that emotional decisions often entail no deliberation at all—the "right" choice appears to be "self-evident" (cf., Etzioni 1992; Loewenstein & Lerner 2003; Medvec, Madey, & Gilovich 1995).

Emotional appraisals also inhibit the audience's information integration process. Whereas trade offs among decision criteria are common in rational decision making (e.g., to get better quality you may have to pay more), emotional appraisals inhibit trade offs (cf., Luce 1998; Luce, Bettman, & Payne 1997). As we have seen, product attributes with implications for highly valued goals (e.g., the attribute of automobile safety may implicate personal survival) trigger more emotion in consumers and are higher in trade-off difficulty.

Emotional appraisals inhibit trade offs in voter decision making as well. Shah and colleagues (1996) asked one group of voters to read news stories about the positions of political candidates on healthcare issues whose arguments were framed in emotional, value-laden terms. They asked another group to read similar news stories whose arguments were framed in neutral, economic terms. They then asked both groups to vote for a candidate. Voters who read the healthcare arguments framed in emotional, value-laden terms were more likely to use a non-compensatory decision strategy and thus to avoid making trade offs than were voters who read the healthcare arguments framed in neutral, economic terms.

As depicted in Figure 7.8, 41% of the voters who read the emotionally framed arguments used a non-compensatory strategy when deciding for whom to vote compared to only 16% of the voters who read the economically framed arguments.

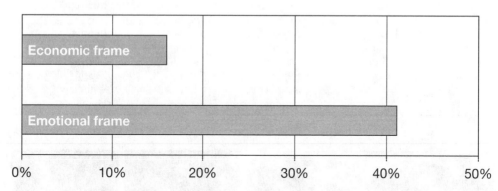

Figure 7.8 Voters Who Read Emotionally Framed Arguments were More than Twice as Likely to Avoid Making Trade offs (source: Shah, Domke, & Wackman 1996)

EMOTIONAL APPEALS AND INTENSIFIERS

Emotional Appeals

Audiences may make decisions based on emotions as opposed to reason when they are presented with emotional appeals. Emotional appeals may be presented as either words or images and consist of photographs, videos, or verbal messages (Bowers, Metts, & Duncanson 1985). Successful emotional appeals elicit real emotions from their audiences. For example, a sentence such as "Animal research causes unnecessary suffering to animals" can be used as an emotional appeal and can elicit real emotional responses in readers (Rosselli, Skelly, & Mackie 1995). Similarly, television commercials can make emotional appeals that can elicit real emotional responses in viewers (Englis 1989).

When emotional appeals are able to elicit emotions, they can have a significant impact on audience decision making. For example, fear-arousing product-warning labels have been found to significantly affect users' safety behavior (Cox, Wogalter, Stokes, & Murff 1997). Audiences with health problems who are exposed to fear-arousing appeals are more likely to try the recommended medical solutions (Das, de Wit, & Stroebe 2003; de Hoog, Stroebe, & de Wit 2005). Audiences who are exposed to inspirational appeals are more likely to give their cooperation to their colleagues and leaders (Yukl & Falbe 1990; Yukl & Tracey 1992). In a study of group decision making, members of policy-making groups rated inspirational emotional appeals as persuasive as rational appeals and more persuasive than pressure tactics, ingratiation, exchange tactics, or other types of persuasive appeals (Jensen 2007). A study of emotional appeals made during an antilittering campaign in Oklahoma City found that the campaign succeeded in large part because it was able to attach the negative emotions of shame and embarrassment to littering (Grasmick, Bursik, & Kinsey 1991).

The power of emotional appeals to affect consumer decisions is undeniable. For example, cigarette advertising designed to increase the positive emotions associated with smoking decreases consumers' perceptions of risk (Finucane et al. 2000). The joy some television commercials elicit produces a strong positive effect on consumers' intentions to purchase the products advertised (Holbrook 1986). A study of the effectiveness of TV commercials for frequently purchased products finds that emotional ads are significantly more likely to produce increases in sales than are neutral ads (MacInnis, Rao, & Weiss 2002). Furthermore, ads that produce positive emotions are more likely to produce increases in sales than are ads that produce other types of emotions. Consumers' emotional responses to commercials are also important predictors of brand and product attitudes as well as of attitude change (Holbrook & Batra 1987).

Emotional appeals can either produce the same emotional response, such as feeling anger while listening to an angry speaker, or a different but complementary emotional response, such as feeling pity when hearing an emotional plea for help (Andersen & Guerrero 1998; Miller, Stiff, & Ellis 1988; Stiff et al. 1988). In the United States, consumers commonly encounter emotional appeals designed to elicit pride, fear, joy, sadness, guilt, love, anger, and pity (Chang & Gruner 1981; Lulofs 1991; Moog 1991).

The most studied emotional appeal is the appeal to fear, although there has been some study of other emotional appeals such as appeals to pride (e.g., Aaker & Williams 1998), disgust (e.g., Nabi 1998), and guilt (e.g., Coulter & Pinto 1995). Advertisers commonly use appeals to fear to promote products such as insurance, toothpaste, deodorants, mouthwash, and detergents. Fear appeals such as these make social threats and are more effective in persuading potential consumers than fear appeals that make physical threats (Evans, Rozelle, Lasater, Dembroski, & Allen 1970). Public service announcements also use appeals to fear to discourage smoking, drinking and driving, and participation in unsafe sex. As fear appeals increase in fearfulness, they tend to become increasingly persuasive (see Boster & Mongeau 1984; Mongeau 1998; Witte & Allen 2000).

Fear appeals are more effective when the audience believes following the advice they offer helps them avoid negative consequences (Petty, DeSteno, & Rucker 2001). For example, earthquake preparedness messages are more effective when they include not only a fear appeal but also an explanation of how the recommendations will help the audience avoid an earthquake's dangers (Johnson 1994). Giving audiences information about risk as well as information on how, when, and where to take action also makes behavior change more likely (Weinstein, Lyon, Sandman, & Cuite 1998). Moreover, fear appeals immediately followed by recommendations are more effective than either recommendations followed by fear appeals or recommendations given much later (Leventhal & Singer 1966; Skilbeck, Tulips, & Ley 1977). If the audience does not believe it can cope effectively with the threat, then increasing the fear appeal of the threat tends to produce a boomerang effect (e.g., Ditto & Lopez 1992; Mulilis & Lippa 1990; Witte & Allen 1996).

Are emotional appeals always a hindrance to rational decision making? In his book *The Place of Emotion in Argument*, Walton (1992) contends that emotional appeals can play a legitimate role as persuasive arguments since emotions are indicative of one's most fundamental values. But Walton also warns of four types of emotional appeals that are often used fallaciously. The first type is *Argumentum ad baculum*, an appeal to fear. The Michelin tire slogan, "Because so much is riding on your tires," appeals to fear for one's family's safety. But it says nothing to prove that Michelin tires are any safer than other brands. The second type, *Argumentum ad misericordiam*, is an appeal to pity. Advertisements requesting donations to support medical research often include photographs of extremely ill children and their personal stories in order to elicit the reader's sympathy. However, the ads typically lack any information about the trustworthiness of the agency, the truth of their claims, or the percentage of contributions used for research.

The third type of emotional appeal often used fallaciously is *Argumentum ad populum*, an appeal to popular values or pride. Politicians appeal to popular values when they say the flag must be honored and law and order restored. However, those same politicians may neglect to prove a problem existed in the first place. The final type of emotional appeal Walton identifies as typically fallacious is *Argumentum ad hominem*, an attack against the person that is often an appeal to anger. For example, some politicians disparage their rivals as ivy-league "elitists" although they themselves are graduates of ivy-league schools.

Despite the possibility of using emotional appeals to support fallacious reasoning, many of the most memorable speeches throughout history have made strong appeals to specific emotions. We have already read the Gettysburg Address by Abraham Lincoln. Lincoln's speech is an appeal to the emotion of gratitude: Gratitude triggers the action tendency to repay the debt that is owed. Lincoln called on his audience at the memorial service in Gettysburg, Pennsylvania, to repay the debt they owed the fallen soldiers by finishing the task the soldiers had begun. Another famous speech, the "I have a dream" speech by Dr. Martin Luther King, delivered on August 28, 1963, is an appeal to the emotion of hope. Hope triggers the action tendency to prepare or to make happen (Roseman 2001). King wanted his audience to take the action necessary to turn his dream of freedom for all into a reality.

On the following pages, four other famous speeches are reproduced in part or in their entirety. The first two speeches are fictional and are excerpted from Shakespeare's *Julius Caesar*, Act III, Scene 2: The Forum. In the first speech Brutus makes a rational argument—an appeal to reason—to the crowd of onlookers. He asks them to understand that his decision to assassinate Caesar was difficult for him but was made with their best interests in mind. The crowd gives Brutus their approval. Moments later Brutus invites Antony to speak and then leaves the stage. By the time Antony finishes speaking, the same audience that had applauded Brutus for ridding Rome of a tyrant is now ready to kill him for betraying and murdering their beloved leader.

Unlike the speech Brutus gave, Antony's speech is an emotional appeal. Notice how Shakespeare, the master communicator, depicts the crowd's process of emotional decision making in sequence. Shakespeare's Antony first surprises and shocks the crowd by unexpectedly throwing off the garment that covered the dead Caesar and revealing Caesar's bloody body with its gaping knife wounds. The crowd's surprise turns to pity as they grieve for their now-beloved leader. Pity quickly turns to anger and anger to the action tendency of attack, and this is exactly what Antony wants his audience in Rome to do—to attack and kill Brutus. Audiences comprehend emotions faster and more accurately when information about others' emotional appraisals is provided to them not in random order but in sequence—unexpectedness, valence, certainty, agency, and norm violation (Scherer 1999)—just as Shakespeare does so brilliantly.

The last two speeches are the actual words of two great American leaders. The "D-day order" speech by Dwight D. Eisenhower, delivered on June 6, 1944, is an appeal to the emotion of pride. Pride triggers the action tendency to dominate (Frijda 1986; Roseman 2001), and domination of the Nazis through total victory was Eisenhower's goal. In stark contrast to Eisenhower's speech, the "Surrender" speech, by Chief Joseph of the Nez Perce, to the US Army in 1877, translated by a scout and transcribed by an artist for *Harper's Weekly* magazine and quoted in Safire (2004), is an appeal to the emotion of sadness. Sadness triggers the action tendency to withdraw (Lazarus 1991). His own robes riddled with bullet holes, his people killed or starving, Chief Joseph was convinced that further resistance was futile. It was time for him and his warriors to withdraw from the stage of history.

A Rational Argument

BRUTUS

Romans, countrymen, and lovers! hear me for my cause, and be silent, that you may hear: Believe me for mine honor, and have respect to mine honor, that you may believe: Censure me in your wisdom, and awake your senses, that you may the better judge. If there be any in this assembly, any dear friend of Caesar's, to him I say, that Brutus' love to Caesar was no less than his. If then that friend demand why Brutus rose against Caesar, this is my answer: Not that I loved Caesar less, but that I loved Rome more. Had you rather Caesar were living and die all slaves, than that Caesar were dead, to live all free men? As Caesar loved me, I weep for him; as he was fortunate, I rejoice at it; as he was valiant, I honor him: but, as he was ambitious, I slew him. There is tears for his love; joy for his fortune; honor for his valor; and death for his ambition. Who is here so base that would be a bondman? If any, speak; for him have I offended. Who is here so rude that would not be a Roman? If any, speak; for him have I offended. Who is here so vile that will not love his country? If any, speak; for him have I offended. I pause for a reply.

ALL None, Brutus, none.

BRUTUS

Then none have I offended. I have done no more to Caesar than you shall do to Brutus. The question of his death is enrolled in the Capitol; his glory not extenuated, wherein he was worthy, nor his offences enforced, for which he suffered death.

Enter ANTONY and others, with CAESAR's body

Here comes his body, mourned by Mark Antony: who, though he had no hand in his death, shall receive the benefit of his dying, a place in the commonwealth; as which of you shall not? With this I depart,–that, as I slew my best lover for the good of Rome, I have the same dagger for myself, when it shall please my country to need my death.

ALL Live, Brutus! live, live!

An Appeal to Anger

ANTONY

If you have tears, prepare to shed them now. You all do know this mantle: I remember the first time ever Caesar put it on; 'Twas on a summer's evening, in his tent, that day he overcame the Nervii: Look, in this place ran Cassius' dagger through: See what a rent the envious Casca made: Through this the well-beloved Brutus stabb'd; and as he pluck'd his cursed steel away, mark how the blood of Caesar follow'd it, as rushing out of doors, to be resolved if Brutus so unkindly knock'd, or no; for Brutus, as you know, was Caesar's angel: Judge, O you gods, how dearly Caesar lov'd him. This was the most unkindest cut of all; for when the noble Caesar saw him stab, ingratitude, more strong than traitors' arms, quite vanquish'd him: then burst his mighty heart; and, in his mantle muffling up his face, even at the base of Pompey's statue, which all the while ran blood, great Caesar fell. O, what a fall was there, my countrymen! Then I, and you, and all of us fell down, whilst bloody treason flourish'd over us. O, now you weep; and, I perceive, you feel the dint of pity: these are gracious drops. Kind souls, what, weep you when you but behold our Caesar's vesture wounded? Look you here, here is himself, marr'd, as you see, with traitors.

FIRST CITIZEN O piteous spectacle!

SECOND CITIZEN O noble Caesar!

THIRD CITIZEN O woeful day!

FOURTH CITIZEN O traitors, villains!

FIRST CITIZEN O most bloody sight!

SECOND CITIZEN We will be revenged.

ALL Revenge! About! Seek! Burn! Fire! Kill! Slay! Let not a traitor live!

An Appeal to Pride

D-Day Order Speech by Dwight D. Eisenhower

You will bring about the destruction of the German war machine, the elimination of Nazi tyranny over the oppressed peoples of Europe, and security for ourselves in a free world. Your task will not be an easy one. Your enemy is well trained, well equipped, and battle-hardened. He will fight savagely.

But this is the year 1944. Much has happened since the Nazi triumphs of 1940–41. The United Nations have inflicted upon the Germans great defeat in open battle man to man. Our air offensive has seriously reduced their strength in the air and their capacity to wage war on the ground. Our home fronts have given us an overwhelming superiority in weapons and munitions of war and placed at our disposal great reserves of trained fighting men. The tide has turned.

The free men of the world are marching together to victory. I have full confidence in your courage, devotion to duty, and skill in battle. We will accept nothing less than full victory. Good luck, and let us all beseech the blessings of Almighty God upon this great and noble undertaking.

An Appeal to Sadness

Surrender Speech by Chief Joseph of the Nez Perce

Tell General Howard I know his heart. What he told me before, I have it in my heart. I am tired of fighting. Our chiefs are killed; Looking Glass is dead, Ta-Hool-Hool-Shute is dead. The old men are all dead. It is the young men who say yes or no. He who led on the young men is dead.

It is cold, and we have no blankets; the little children are freezing to death. My people, some of them, have run away to the hills, and have no blankets, no food. No one knows where they are—perhaps freezing to death. I want to have time to look for my children, and see how many of them I can find. Maybe I shall find them among the dead.

Hear me, my chiefs! I am tired; my heart is sick and sad. From where the sun now stands I will fight no more forever.

Emotionally Significant Words and Images

Attorneys, politicians, and advertisers routinely use emotionally significant words and images to intensify the effects of their emotional appeals. An audience's emotional reaction to the emotionally charged term "child abusers" predicts how they will judge a particular child abuser better than their rational beliefs about the group of child abusers as a whole (Jussim, Nelson, Manis, & Soffin 1995). In the legal arena, emotionally charged words are highly damaging to defendants even when the words have no evidentiary value (Edwards & Bryan 1997). Unfortunately, any attempt to stifle the negative emotions jurors feel when they hear testimony using emotive language results in the jurors being even more biased by the testimony.

CEOs use emotionally significant words to appeal to the emotions of their audiences as well. When new CEOs use emotionally charged words in their initial letters to their shareholders, analysts who read the letters tend to make more favorable earnings forecasts (Fanelli, Misangyi, & Tosi 2009). The typical new CEO letter to shareholders uses negative terms to describe the past and positive words such as "faith," "challenge," and "inspiration" to describe the CEO's vision of the future and how it will be achieved. The more emotional language the new CEOs uses, the more inclined analysts are to issue favorable recommendations.

Emotionally significant images also have a significant impact on the emotions and the decisions of audiences who see them. In their study of the effects of live testimony and video recreations of the crime on mock jurors' decisions in a civil trial, Fishfader and colleagues (1996) find that jurors who either view live testimony or who view live testimony and then watch a video recreation have stronger emotional reactions to the evidence than jurors who simply read a transcript of the trial. Moreover, mock jurors who view gruesome videos have lower thresholds to convict than those who do not view the videos but who instead hear a description of the evidence (Kassin & Garfield 1991). Another study presented two groups of mock jurors with the same transcript of a murder trial but showed autopsy photographs to only one of the two groups (Douglas, Lyon, & Ogloff 1997). Although the transcript described the victim's wounds verbally, the group exposed to the autopsy photographs was twice as likely to find the defendant guilty.

In addition, the sentences mock jurors hand down are more extreme when the jurors are presented with vivid photographic evidence. Mock jurors who view highly gruesome photographic evidence are more likely to decide on the death sentence than are mock jurors who view less gruesome evidence (Nemeth 2002). Mock jurors who view photographs of a victim's injury award a greater proportion of the requested damages than do jurors who do not view the photographs (Oliver & Griffitt 1976). Moreover, when the victim's injuries are severe and the defendant is clearly to blame, mock jurors who view color photographs of the injured party give higher monetary awards than those who view either black-and-white photographs or no photographs (Whalen & Blanchard 1982).

Audiences also respond strongly to a combination of emotionally significant words and images. In their study of investor decision making, Jordan and Kaas (2002) found that emotionally significant verbal and pictorial elements in an ad for a mutual fund decreased the amount of risk that both expert and novice investors perceived. However, the emotional elements of the ad had a greater effect on novice than on expert investors.

One of the most famous examples of the use of emotionally significant words and images in a political campaign is the "Daisy" ad, created by Tony Schwartz and aired on US TV on September 7, 1964. Its purpose was to promote President Lyndon Johnson's campaign for re-election. The "Daisy" ad begins by showing a little girl slowly counting each petal she picks off a daisy. When the little girl reaches the count of "nine," a threatening male voice begins the countdown of a missile launch, at which point the little girl looks up toward the sky. As the girl looks to the sky, the camera zooms in on her eyes. Next, a nuclear bomb is shown exploding while President Johnson can be heard to say, "These are the stakes! To make a world in which all of God's children can live, or to go into the dark. We must either love each other, or we must die." Another speaker then says, "Vote for President Johnson on November 3. The stakes are too high for you to stay home." Because so many complained that President Johnson's campaign used the ad to frighten voters into believing that his opponent, Republican Barry Goldwater, would start a nuclear war, his campaign never aired the "Daisy" ad again.

Narratives and Metaphors as Emotional Intensifiers

The written word can evoke a number of different emotions in audiences (Van den Oetelaar, Tellegen, & Wober 1997), and narratives and stories are especially likely to evoke emotions in them. Readers of 4,000-word stories are aware of having about five emotions per story (Larsen & Seilman 1988). Narrative poems, such as Coleridge's "The Rime of the Ancient Mariner," can arouse readers' emotions as well (Sikora, Miall, & Kuiken 1998).

President Johnson's "Daisy" ad juxtaposed images of a little girl and a nuclear explosion

Figure 7.9 A Visual Appeal to Fear (courtesy of Democratic National Committee).

Although readers tend to respond emotionally to narrative forms of writing, they typically respond with little emotion to the style of writing newspaper reporters commonly use (Donohew 1981, 1982). Readers also respond with less emotion to logical arguments than they do to narrative persuasive messages (Kopfman, Smith, Ah Yun, & Hodges 1994). As a result, the persuasive impact of emotional appeals is stronger when they are communicated in the form of narratives and stories or when narratives and stories are included in the appeals. For example, audiences are more likely to comply with the recommendation of fear appeals that include stories as well as facts (Johnson 1994).

In addition to responding emotionally to narratives, audiences respond emotionally to metaphors as well. Metaphors can persuade audiences to change their attitudes toward various political and social topics (Bosman 1987; Read, Cesa, Jones, & Collins 1990), and the ability of metaphors to evoke particular emotions accounts for a significant part of their persuasiveness (Gibbs, Leggitt, & Turner 2002). Metaphors are particularly influential when introduced early in a persuasive communication (Sopory & Dillard 2002).

Politicians routinely use metaphors and analogies to evoke emotions and to persuade. In an analysis of the transcript of the three-day debate in the US Senate in 1991 over the Persian Gulf War, Voss and colleagues (1992) found that during the debate, both Republicans and Democrats often used metaphors to bolster their positions. For example, one Republican senator used the following metaphorical description of Saddam Hussein as a glutton to evoke the negative emotional response of disgust (Voss, Kennet, Wiley, & Schooler 1992, p. 205):

> Saddam Hussein is like a glutton—a geopolitical glutton. He is sitting down at a big banquet table, overflowing with goodies. And let me tell you—like every glutton, he is going to have them all. Kuwait is just the appetizer—He is gobbling it up—but it is not going to satisfy him. After a noisy belch or two, he is going to reach across the table for the next morsel. What is it going to be? Saudi Arabia? . . . He is going to keep grabbing and gobbling, . . . It is time to let this grisly glutton know the free lunch is over. It is time for him to pay the bill.

Believability as an Emotional Intensifier

Only when audiences believe an event is real can the event elicit their emotions (Frijda 1988). Unreal events can elicit emotions only if "the stimulating fantasy succeeds in inducing a sense of reality in the reader or viewer" (Ortony et al. 1988, p. 61). In an empirical test of this concept, Stayman and Aaker (1989) manipulated the believability of three emotional ads. The audience's emotional responses to all three ads showed significant differences due to the believability manipulation.

In another test of the effects of believability, Lazarus and Alfert (1964) asked audiences to watch a gruesome anthropological film that showed a "sub-incision" procedure adolescent boys in New Guinea must undergo. One group of viewers watched a silent film version of the excruciatingly painful procedure. A second group first received a written statement that said the procedure was actually painless before they watched the same silent version of the film. A third group watched the same film with a soundtrack added and heard a narrator claim the procedure was painless. The second and third groups responded with less emotion, as measured by changes in their electrodermal activity, than did the first group, an indication that reducing the believability of a film reduces its emotional impact.

Temporal and Physical Proximity as Emotional Intensifiers

As an emotionally significant event draws nearer in time, the emotions that the event evokes, such as fear and happiness, tend to intensify even when the audience's evaluations of the event's probability or likely outcomes stay the same (Breznitz 1983; Loewenstein 1987; Roth, Breivik, Jorgensen, & Hofmann 1996). For example, when researchers told subjects they would receive an electric shock at a specific time, they found that the subjects' levels of fear as measured by heart rates, galvanic skin conductance, and reports of anxiety all increased as the moment approached (Breznitz 1971; Monat 1976).

In a study of the effects of temporal proximity on stage fright, VanBoven and coauthors (2001) offered 49 students one dollar each to tell a joke in front of the class the next week. Only nine students accepted the offer. When the next week came all 49 students were given a chance to change their minds. Six of the nine students who had previously accepted the offer to tell a joke decided not to do so. None of the students who had initially declined the offer decided to tell a joke at the last minute.

Physical proximity can have an effect on emotions similar to the effect of temporal proximity. Physical proximity and sensory contact can lead to impulsive behavior, behavior that grocery store checkout lanes are ready to take advantage of (cf., Hoch & Loewenstein 1991).

Emotional Contagion

Professionals can elicit emotions from their audiences through their own facial expressions (e.g., Englis 1990; Friedman, DiMatteo, & Mertz 1980a), gestures, and bodily postures (e.g., Haley et al. 1984)—a phenomenon known as emotional contagion. Emotional contagion most often occurs below the level of conscious awareness and is based on automatic cognitive processes and physiological responses (e.g., Hatfield, Cacioppo, & Rapson 1994; Neumann & Strack 2000). Most displays of emotions elicit either the same or complementary emotions from others. For example, one partner's display of emotions usually elicits either the same or complementary emotions from the other partner in a relationship (Eibl-Eibesfeldt 1989).

Most facial expressions of emotions evoke complementary emotional responses in viewers (for reviews, see Dimberg & Öhman 1996; Keltner & Kring 1998). For example, photographs of angry faces tend to evoke fear, even when the viewers do not consciously perceive the faces (Esteves, Dimberg, & Öhman 1994; Öhman & Dimberg

1978). Facial expressions of distress and shame evoke compassion or sympathy (e.g., Batson and Shaw 1991; Keltner, Young, & Buswell 1997). Beginning as early as age eight months, displays of distress, including facial expressions indicating distress, evoke the child's readiness to help (Eisenberg et al. 1989; Zahn-Waxler, Radke-Yarrow, Wagner, & Chapman 1992). Facial expressions of sympathy produce increased liking and, when relevant, more forgiveness (cf., Keltner & Buswell 1997). Facial expressions of embarrassment often evoke amusement (Keltner et al. 1997).

Leaders have a special ability to elicit emotions from their audiences (cf., Cherulnik, Donley, Wiewel, & Miller 2001; Lewis 2000). Even brief, televised clips of politicians' nonverbal behaviors are capable of eliciting noticeable emotional reactions from voters (McHugo, Lanzetta, Sullivan, Masters, & Englis 1985). Voters' emotional responses to leaders' facial expressions and nonverbal behaviors can influence their attitudes toward the leader independent of the leader's verbal messages (for reviews, see Lanzetta, Sullivan, Masters, & McHugo 1985; Masters & Sullivan 1993). Moreover, the different emotions political candidates elicit have different effects on voters' attitudes toward the candidates and toward the issues on the national agenda (Englis 1994; Sullivan, Masters, Lanzetta, Englis, & McHugo 1984).

Not surprisingly, some emotional displays by leaders elicit stronger emotional responses than others. Sullivan and Masters (1988) presented voters with video recordings of national leaders who displayed either happiness and reassurance, anger and threat, or fear and evasion at different levels of consistency and intensity. Leaders who displayed emotions in a consistent and intense manner elicited much stronger emotional responses than those whose emotional displays were inconsistent or weak. Uncommitted voters were especially susceptible to influence by emotional appeals and the leaders' nonverbal displays of emotion.

Professionals can also elicit emotions in their audiences through their tone of voice. For example, Neumann and Strack (2000) asked an audience to listen to a speech that was delivered in either a slightly happy or a slightly sad voice and then to rate their own mood. Not only was the audience's mood affected by the speaker's tone of voice but when asked to repeat the message they heard, audience members spontaneously and unconsciously mimicked the speaker's tone.

Groups as well as individuals are susceptible to emotional contagion. A study of teams of nurses and accountants finds that team members' moods are shared even after controlling for shared work problems (Totterdell, Kellett, Teuchmann, & Briner 1998). A study of professional cricket teams finds similar results even after controlling for each team's status in the league (Totterdell 2000). Emotional contagion has also been found to occur in a variety of automotive, information technology, and creative advertising work groups (Bartel & Saavedra 2000).

Emotional contagion in groups can have a significant influence on group processes and outcomes (George 1989, 1990; George & Brief 1992). In a study of senior management teams, Barsade and colleagues (2000) find that a group's emotions affect both individual attitudes and team dynamics. Groups experiencing positive emotional contagion show improved cooperation, decreased conflict, and increased perceived task performance (Barsade 2002). Conversely, groups experiencing negative group emotions are less likely to cooperate and more likely to miss work (George 1990).

BIASES IN EMOTIONAL DECISION MAKING

The Effects of Moods and Emotions Triggered by Unrelated Events

Emotions triggered by related events typically have a stronger influence on audience decisions than do moods and emotions triggered by unrelated events (Raghunathan, Pham, & Corfman 2006). However, any emotion and its action tendency will linger after the triggering event has passed if the audience does not take the emotion-relieving action (Fredrickson & Levenson 1998). In such cases the action tendencies triggered by one situation may bias the audience's assessment of unrelated situations (see Keltner, Ellsworth, & Edwards 1993a; Lerner & Keltner 2000, 2001; Raghunathan & Pham 1999).

In a study of the effects of unrelieved action tendencies, Goldberg and coauthors (1999) asked one group of viewers to watch a film in which a violent criminal was punished and another group to watch a film in which the criminal evaded punishment due to a legal technicality. Both groups reported equivalent levels of anger in response to the crime. Soon afterward, the two groups were asked to read a legal case about a different crime and to recommend an appropriate punishment for the perpetrator. The residual anger of the viewers who watched the second film led them to recommend higher levels of punishment than that recommended by the viewers who watched the first film. The anger felt by the audience who watched the first film was relieved by the punishment of the criminal. But the anger felt by the audience who watched the second film went unrelieved and resulted in harsher subsequent sentences.

Other studies confirm that moods and emotions triggered by unrelated events can bias the audience's action tendencies. For example, experimentally induced anger promotes more punitive judgments of others (Lerner Goldberg, & Tetlock 1998). Readers whose anger was aroused by a story about toxic waste dumping were more likely to decide to punish the perpetrator of an unrelated incident than to help the victims of the incident (Gault & Sabini 2000, Study 4). In a study that first primed either anger or fear in two groups of participants, Nabi (2003) asked each group how they might reduce the problem of drunk driving. Sixty-five percent of the fear-primed group proposed safety or protection-oriented solutions, whereas 64% of the anger-primed group proposed punishment or blame-oriented solutions.

Moods and emotions triggered by unrelated events can also bias the cognitive processes that lead audiences to make particular decisions (e.g., Fiedler 2000; Mackie & Worth 1991; Petty, Gleicher, & Baker 1991; Schwarz & Bless 1991). They can bias perception (Niedenthal, Setterlund, & Jones 1994). They can bias the audience to selectively attend to, encode, and retrieve emotion-relevant information (Derryberry & Tucker 1994; Niedenthal & Kitayama 1994; Niedenthal & Setterlund 1994). Negative emotions triggered by unrelated events can cause audience members to narrow their focus of attention, whereas positive emotions can cause them to broaden it (Basso, Schefft, Ris, & Dember 1996; Conway & Giannopoulos 1993; Isen 1999). In addition, audiences are more likely to recall information from memory that is congruent with moods and emotions triggered by unrelated events than information that is incongruent with them (e.g. Isen 1987; Niedenthal, Halberstadt, & Innes-Ker 1999).

Moods and emotions triggered by unrelated events can bias the audience's perception of others (e.g., Forgas 1992; Hirt, Levine, McDonald, Melton, & Martin 1997; Martin, Abend, Sedikides, & Green 1997). One partner in a relationship will often interpret the other partner's emotional state to be congruent with their own. Likewise, happy people see others as happy, and sad people will often see others as sad (Metha & Clark 1994). Clark and colleagues (1984) asked one group of people to exercise immediately before viewing a person in order to put that group in a positive mood. They asked another group to view the person without exercising. The exercisers associated the person's positive verbal and nonverbal communication with more intense positive emotions than did the non-exercisers. For instance, whereas the non-exercisers saw the person expressing contentment, the exercisers saw the person expressing joy. Griffit and Veitch (1971) asked one group of people to evaluate a person while they were working in an unpleasantly hot and crowded room. They asked another group to evaluate the same person while they were working in a pleasant, uncrowded room. Interestingly, the two groups made significantly different but mood-congruent evaluations.

Moods and emotions triggered by unrelated events typically bias the decisions of novice audience members more than those of experts. In study of automotive experts and novices, Srull (1990) induced a positive, neutral, or negative mood in expert and novice groups and then asked them to read an ad for a new car. After 48 hours both groups were asked to evaluate the car. The mood the novices were in when they read the ad had a strong effect on their judgments but the mood the experts were in only had a weak effect. Surprisingly, moods and emotions triggered by unrelated events can bias experts and novices in opposing ways. Ottati and Isbell (1996) induced positive or negative moods in political experts and novices and then asked them to make political decisions. Political novices showed the typical mood congruency effects; for example, novices in positive moods made more favorable judgments of the candidates. Conversely, political experts showed a contrast effect; experts in positive moods made less favorable judgments.

The power of moods and emotions triggered by unrelated events to bias decision making can be decreased if audiences become aware that irrelevant situational factors are influencing their judgments (Keltner, Locke, & Audrain 1993b; Schwarz & Clore 1983). Keltner and coauthors (1993b) asked readers to read a sad story and then to estimate how satisfactory their lives were. Readers reduced their estimates less if they were first asked to focus on the cause of their sad feelings. Usually, people are completely unaware that a mood or an emotion triggered by one situation has influenced their judgment in another situation (Johnson & Tversky 1983; Lerner et al. 1998; Wilson & Brekke 1994).

The power of moods and emotions triggered by unrelated events to bias audience decision making also decreases when audiences are held accountable for their decisions. For example, the tendency of happy audiences to base their impressions of others on stereotypes decreases when they are held accountable for their decisions (Bodenhausen et al. 1994a, Study 4). The tendency of angry jurors to demand more severe punishment in unrelated legal cases also decreases when they are held accountable for their decisions (Lerner et al. 1998).

Being polite to the audience can reduce the biasing effects of moods and emotions triggered by unrelated events. Forgas (1998) induced a positive or negative mood in an audience and then made an unexpected request to them either in a polite or impolite manner. The audience's response to an impolite request was significantly more mood-congruent than was their response to the polite request; audience members in both moods responded positively to the polite request. Not surprisingly, audiences view senders of polite messages more positively than senders of impolite messages (Jessmer & Anderson 2001).

The Effects of Induced Happiness

Audiences put into happy moods, such as employees at an office party or viewers of a typical TV commercial, tend to overestimate the frequency of positive events and to underestimate the likelihood of negative outcomes and events (Mayer, Gaschke, Braverman, & Evans 1992; Mayer & Hanson 1995; Wright & Bower 1992). Thus, they tend to make optimistic judgments and risk-seeking decisions. For example, audiences who read happy newspaper articles subsequently are willing to take more risks than audiences who read sad articles (Johnson & Tversky 1983). However, happy audience members are actually less likely to take risks when the stakes are high and the potential for loss is genuine (Isen & Geva 1987; Isen, Nygren, & Ashby 1988; Isen & Patrick 1983).

Audiences put into happy moods tend to make more positive evaluations of other people and situations. For example, audiences put into happy moods make significantly more positive than negative evaluations of strangers, whereas those in bad moods are unlikely to allow their feelings to influence their evaluations (Forgas & Bower 1987). Consumers put into happy moods evaluate various products, brands, and ads more positively than do consumers in neutral or negative moods (Ger 1989). Interviewing a large random sample of the US population, Mayer and coauthors (1992) find that interviewees who feel good at the time of their interview are more positive in their responses than are their counterparts who are in a bad mood during their interview.

Audiences put into happy moods generally agree with persuasive messages more than audiences in other moods (McGuire 1985; Petty et al. 1991). Typically, happy people are more compliant with persuasive communications, whereas angry people are less compliant (Krugman 1983; Laird 1974; Wells & Petty 1980). The happiness an ad creates can lead consumers to adopt a positive attitude toward the advertised brand (Allen & Madden 1983; Lutz, MacKenzie, & Belch 1983; Mitchell & Olson 1981).

In most cases, audiences put into happy moods process persuasive messages without much rational thought or deliberation (Bless, Bohner, Schwarz, & Strack 1990; Bohner, Crow, Erb, & Schwarz 1992; Kuykendall & Keating 1990). Worth and Mackie (1987) asked audience members who were in a neutral mood or who were put into a positive mood to read either a strong or a weak persuasive argument. Those in a neutral mood were more persuaded by strong arguments than by the weak arguments, as they should be if their decision-making process were rational. But those put into happy moods were equally persuaded by both strong and weak arguments. Inducing happy moods can even cause audiences to perceive weak arguments to be more persuasive than strong ones. For example, the use of humor in an ad tends to produce more positive attitudes among consumers when the ad uses weak arguments, and fewer positive attitudes when the ad uses strong arguments (Cline & Kellaris 1999).

In special cases, audiences put into happy moods will process persuasive messages in a rational and deliberate way. For example, audiences put into happy moods are more influenced by strong arguments than are sad audiences when both groups believe the message causes happiness (Wegener, Petty, & Smith 1995). Compared with unhappy audience members, audiences put into happy moods show less confusion, less redundancy, and are better able to integrate task-relevant information when making decisions (Isen 2000). If happy audiences are asked to make a decision that is interesting or important, they will make the effort to process relevant information rationally and systematically (Bodenhausen et al. 1994a; Estrada, Isen, & Young 1997). And as long as the decisions to be made are interesting or important, audiences put into happy moods also make good decisions faster (Isen, Rosenzweig, & Young 1991). For example, happy consumers make the same purchasing decisions as consumers in neutral moods, but they make their decisions more quickly (Isen & Means 1983).

The Effects of Induced Sadness

Unlike happy people, audiences put into sad moods, such as the recently unemployed or viewers of distressing events shown on the evening news, tend to make pessimistic judgments and decisions (Mayer & Hanson 1995; Wright & Bower 1992). Thus, they tend to overestimate the frequency of sad events and to underestimate the likelihood of positive events (DeSteno, Petty, Wegener, & Rucker 2000; Nygren, Isen, Taylor, & Dulin 1996). Audiences who are induced to feel sad are also more likely to expect future events to result from uncontrollable situational forces (Keltner et al. 1993a). When choosing among both gambles and jobs, audiences put into sad moods prefer the high-risk/high-reward option (Raghunatham & Pham 1999).

Audiences put into sad moods generally agree with persuasive messages that emphasize saddening problems or outcomes. They have more favorable views of positions if the message argues that failing to adopt the position is likely to make bad things happen than if it argues that adopting the position will make good things happen (Wegener, Petty, & Klein 1994). In their study of the effects of induced sadness on persuasion, DeSteno and colleagues (2004) asked readers who were in a neutral mood or who were put into a sad mood to read one of two equally strong arguments for a proposed tax increase. One argument justified the proposed tax increase by claiming it would help address saddening problems (e.g., the plight of senior citizens). The other justified the increase by claiming it would address angering problems (e.g., long traffic delays). The saddening reasons, but not the angering reasons, persuaded readers in a sad mood. In addition, the sadder a reader felt, the more positively she responded to the tax proposal the saddening reasons justified. Neither type of argument persuaded people in a neutral mood.

In many cases, audiences put into sad moods will process persuasive messages in a rational and deliberate way despite their mood (cf., Bohner et al. 1992; Forgas 1998; Schwarz & Clore 1996). For example, Petty and Cacioppo (1986) asked students to read either strong or weak arguments for a proposed final examination before graduation. Students put into sad moods were persuaded only by strong arguments, whereas students put into happy moods were moderately persuaded by both strong and weak arguments.

The Effects of Induced Anger

Like happy people, audiences put into angry moods, such as listeners to politically oriented talk radio, tend to make optimistic judgments and risk-seeking decisions (Leith & Baumeister 1996). Unlike happy people, audiences put into angry moods overestimate the frequency of angering events (Lerner & Keltner 2000, 2001). Angry audiences also believe that negative events caused by human agents are more likely to occur than are sad ones (Keltner et al. 1993a). In addition, audiences put into angry moods are more likely to quickly attribute blame to others, to perceive another's ambiguous behavior as hostile, and to punish others for their mistakes (Goldberg et al. 1999; Lemerise & Dodge 1993; Quigley & Tedeschi 1996). Unlike happy people, audiences put into angry moods tend not to comply with persuasive messages (see McGuire 1985; Petty, Cacioppo, & Kasmer 1988 for reviews).

Audiences put into angry moods do tend to agree, however, with persuasive messages that emphasize angering problems. Calder and Gruder (1989) hypnotized newspaper readers to feel either anger or disgust and then asked them to read one of two reviews of a local restaurant. One review consisted of several positive comments as well as several negative comments that were associated with anger (e.g., an extremely careless waiter). The other review consisted of several positive comments as well as several negative comments that were associated with disgust (e.g., a view of the garbage). Readers put into an angry mood formed the most negative attitudes toward the restaurant after they read the comments associated with anger. In a similar study, DeSteno and colleagues (2004) put readers into an angry or a sad mood and then asked them to read arguments for a proposed tax increase. Readers in angry moods were more persuaded by arguments that described the angering consequences of inaction.

Like happy people, audiences put into angry moods tend to process persuasive messages without much rational thought or deliberation (Bodenhausen 1993; Tiedens & Linton 2001). For example, mock jurors who are put into an angry mood are more likely than sad ones to convict a defendant on the basis of an ethnic stereotype (Bodenhausen et al. 1994b). Mock jurors who are angry are also more likely to ignore opposing evidence than are jurors in neutral moods (Lerner et al. 1998).

The Effects of Induced Fear

Like people in sad moods, audiences put into fearful moods, such as employees who have received threatening reprimands, tend to make pessimistic judgments about future events. They also tend to make relatively pessimistic risk assessments and risk-averse choices (Lerner & Keltner 2000, 2001). In choices of both gambles and jobs, audiences put into fearful moods avoid taking big risks even when the reward is great (Raghunathan 2000; Raghunatham & Pham 1999). However, in special cases, audiences put into fearful moods will process persuasive messages in a rational and systematic way despite their natural inclination to make pessimistic and risk-averse decisions (cf., Nabi 2002).

Emotions in Audience Decision Making: Implications for Communicators

✧ The main takeaway for communicators in Chapter 7 is that each different emotion an audience experiences will affect its decision in an emotion-specific way.

✧ Use the information presented in the chapter to anticipate the effects of your audience's current moods and emotions on their decisions and to make appeals that affect your audience's decisions in specific ways.

✧ Why use the information? To increase the chances of the audience making the decision you desire. To enhance audience perceptions of you as a leader.

✧ If you need to improve your ability to recognize others' emotions, refer to the section on emotions in Chapter 6. You can then determine the effect of that emotion on decision making. If you need to evoke a different emotion from your audience, refer to the section on emotional appeals and intensifiers.

Conclusion

This book paints a different picture of audiences than the one many of us hold in our imaginations, and by doing so redefines our roles as communicators. In the first part of the book, we see that audiences are not empty cups waiting to be filled with whatever information we would like to pour into them but are instead highly-selective and highly-critical decision makers. Experienced audiences already know what type of information they need from us even before they sit down to read our documents or listen to our presentations. No matter how logical, reasonable, correct, and factual our communications may be, if we fail to anticipate the information needs of our audiences, we will fail to persuade them. Thus, our job in selecting persuasive content for our documents, presentations, and meetings is less subjective than we first imagined. It is tightly constrained by the audience's information requirements.

Not only is our job as communicators less subjective than we thought, it is also less formidable. A large number of our audiences' individual decisions can be viewed as instances of one of 13 major decision types. Identify the type of decision that you desire your audience to make, and you can more readily ascertain the type of information your audience will expect from you.

Perhaps the book's biggest challenge to our image of audiences is its model of the cognitive processes that underlie audience decision making. Together with Anderson (2000, p. 351), the book makes clear that real-world reasoning and decision making do not correspond to the abstract rules of logic, syllogistic reasoning, or statistics of the classroom. Nor do they correspond to preferences among formal gambles as decision researchers have often assumed. Instead, both reasoning and decision making are content-specific and schema-based processes. As Schneider and Shanteau (2003, pp. 1–2) point out, it is only within the last several years that decision researchers have come to appreciate the vital roles that context and basic psychological processes such as attention, comprehension, memory, and emotion play in determining decision strategies. And as we review communication techniques in light of our model, we soon realize that, far from being arbitrary rules or mere conventions, each communication technique directly impacts one or more of the cognitive processes involved in audience decision making.

In the second part of the book, we see that despite our audiences' insistence on being given just the right information for making rational decisions, even the most sophisticated and statistically savvy audience can be swayed as much by our style of writing or speaking as by the facts and figures we present. This section disabuses us of any notion we may have had that facts and figures speak for themselves. It also makes clear that who we are sometimes speaks louder that what we say. When we fail to play our professional roles appropriately, we risk losing out to other communicators who behave in ways that meet the audience's expectations.

In the final section of the book we come to understand that our audiences' emotions need not be viewed as antithetical to rational decision making. Instead, this section invites us to view the audience's emotions as essential to rationality and to admit that emotions quickly focus the audience's attention on the things that matter most to them. Taken together, the book's three sections present a 360° view of audience decision making, a view that offers us our best chance to be persuasive.

In addition to helping us become more persuasive, there is another equally important reason why we as professionals need to know, as precisely as possible, how our audiences make decisions—so that we can help them make good ones. Bad decisions can be very costly for those audiences who depend on our documents and presentations for critical information. Investors who make bad investment decisions can go bankrupt. Borrowers who make bad borrowing decisions can find themselves facing onerous payment schedules as well as exorbitant fees and interest rates. Medical patients who fail to make the necessary usage decisions can jeopardize their own and others' physical safety. Currently, relatively few documents and presentations are designed in such a way as to help their audiences make good decisions. Even the best documents and presentations typically contain a great deal of information that is superfluous to the audience's decision. And although they are grammatically correct and may even be easy to comprehend, most will lack much of the information that the audience needs to make a good decision. Oftentimes professionals do not realize that their audiences read documents and listen to presentations in order to make decisions. Many times professionals themselves do not know how to make a good decision of the type their audience needs to make.

Evidence suggests that the average professional may be no better at anticipating the information needs of an audience than is the average undergraduate student. For example, in what was intended to be a study of the differences between expert and novice business writers, Garay (1988) gave executives and undergraduates a business case and asked both groups to write and then revise a report to the client in the case. Contrary to the researcher's expectations, the executives made neither more nor better points in their reports than the undergraduates did. The executives' performance in Garay's study is less surprising when we consider the state of audience awareness in the field of decision support systems—a computer science field ostensibly dedicated to supporting good decisions in audiences. Incredibly, system designers "are rarely told what the key decisions are that the system must help the operator make" or how the operator will make them (Klein 1998, p. 107).

Clearly the time has come for professionals in every field to form an accurate picture of audience decision making. To do so promises high returns to any professional, organization, or student of communication who can put the lessons of this book into practice—returns in the form of greater trust, respect, and long-term success.

References

Aaker, J. L., & Williams, P. (1998). Empathy versus pride: The influence of emotional appeals across cultures. *Journal of Consumer Research, 25*(3), 241–261.

Aaronson, D., & Scarborough, H. S. (1977). Performance theories for sentence coding: Some quantitative models. *Journal of Verbal Learning & Verbal Behavior, 16*(3), 277–303.

Abelson, R. P., Kinder, D. R., Peters, M. D., & Fiske, S. T. (1982). Affective and semantic components in political person perception. *Journal of Personality and Social Psychology, 42*(4), 619–630.

Abelson, R. P., & Levi, A. (1985). Decision making and decision theory. In G. Lindzey & E. Aronson (Eds.), *The handbook of social psychology* (3rd ed., Vol. 1, pp. 231–309). New York: Knopf.

Adams, R. B., Jr., & Kleck, R. E. (2005). Effects of direct and averted gaze on the perception of facially communicated emotion. *Emotion, 5*(1), 3–11.

Adaval, R. (2001). Sometimes it just feels right: The differential weighting of affect-consistent and affect-inconsistent product information. *Journal of Consumer Research, 28*(1), 1–17.

Adaval, R., & Wyer, R. S. (1998). The role of narratives in consumer information processing. *Journal of Consumer Psychology, 7*(3), 207–245.

Agle, B. R., & Sonnenfeld, J. A. (1994). Charismatic chief executive officers: Are they more effective? An empirical test of charismatic leadership theory. *Academy of Management Best Papers Proceedings*, 2–6.

Ajzen, I. (1977). Intuitive theories of events and the effects of base-rate information on prediction. *Journal of Personality and Social Psychology, 35*(5), 303–314.

Alba, J. W., & Hutchinson, J. W. (1987). Dimensions of consumer expertise. *Journal of Consumer Research, 13*(4), 411–454.

Albarracín, D., & Wyer, R. S., Jr. (2001). Elaborative and nonelaborative processing of a behavior-related communication. *Personality and Social Psychology Bulletin, 27*(6), 691–705.

Alberdi, E., Becher, J. C., Gilhooly, K., Hunter, J., Logie, R., Lyon, A., McIntosh, N., & Reiss, J. (2001). Expertise and the interpretation of computerized physiological data: Implications for the design of computerized monitoring in neonatal intensive care. *International Journal of Human-Computer Studies, 55*, 191–216.

Albers, M. (2002). Complex problem solving and content analysis. In M. Albers & B. Mazur (Eds.), *Content and complexity: Information Design in Software Development and Documentation* (pp. 285–305). Hillsdale, NJ: Erlbaum.

Albright, L., & Forziati, C. (1995). Cross-situational consistency and perceptual accuracy in leadership. *Personality and Social Psychology Bulletin, 21*(12), 1269–1276.

Albright, L., Kenny, D. A., & Malloy, T. E. (1988). Consensus in personality judgments at zero acquaintance. *Journal of Personality and Social Psychology*, *55*(3), 387–395.

Al-Dughaither, K. A. (1996). International construction financing strategies: Influential factors and decision-making (Doctoral dissertation, Carnegie Mellon University, 1996). *Dissertation Abstracts International*, *57* (11a), 4857.

Allen, C. T., & Madden, T. J. (1983). *Examining the Link between Attitude Towards an Ad and Brand Attitude: A Classical Conditioning Approach*. Working paper.

Allen, K. (1970). Some effects of advance organizers and level of question on the learning and retention of written social studies materials. *Journal of Educational Psychology*, *61*(5), 333–339.

Allport, F. H., & Lepkin, M. (1945). Wartime rumors of waste and special privilege: Why some people believe them. *The Journal of Abnormal and Social Psychology*, *40*(1), 3–36.

Alpers, G. W., Ruhleder, M., Walz, N., Mühlberger, A., & Pauli, P. (2005). Binocular rivalry between emotional and neutral stimuli: A validation using fear conditioning and EEG. *International Journal of Psychophysiology Special Issue: Neurobiology of Fear and Disgust*, *57*(1), 25–32.

Alpert, M. I. (1971). Identification of determinant attributes: A comparison of methods. *Journal of Marketing Research*, *8*(2), 184–191.

Ambady, N., Bernieri, F. J., & Richeson, J. A. (2000). Toward a histology of social behavior: Judgmental accuracy from thin slices of the behavioral stream. In M. P. Zanna (Ed.), *Advances in experimental social psychology* (Vol. 32, pp. 201–271). San Diego, CA: Academic Press.

Ambady, N., Laplante, D., Nguyen, T., Rosenthal, R., Chaumeton, N., & Levinson, W. (2002). Surgeons' tone of voice: A clue to malpractice history. *Surgery*, *132*(1), 5–9.

Ambady, N., & Rosenthal, R. (1992). Thin slices of expressive behavior as predictors of interpersonal consequences: A meta-analysis. *Psychological Bulletin*, *111*(2), 256–274.

Ambady, N., & Rosenthal, R. (1993). Half a minute: Predicting teacher evaluations from thin slices of nonverbal behavior and physical attractiveness. *Journal of Personality and Social Psychology*, *64*(3), 431–441.

Amir, E., & Ganzach, Y. (1998). Overreaction and underreaction in analysts' forecasts. *Journal of Economic Behavior & Organization*, *37*(3), 333–347.

Andersen, P. A., & Bowman, L. L. (1999). Positions of power: Nonverbal influence in organizational communication. In L. K. Guerrero, J. A. DeVito & M. L. Hecht (Eds.), *The nonverbal communication reader: Classic and contemporary readings* (pp. 317–334). Prospect Heights, IL: Waveland.

Andersen, P. A., & Guerrero, L. K. (1998). Principles of communication and emotion in social interaction. In P. A. Andersen & L. K. Guerrero (Eds.), *Handbook of communication and emotion: Research, Theory, Applications, and Contexts* (pp. 49–96). San Diego, CA: Academic Press.

Andersen, S. M., & Klatzky, R. L. (1987). Traits and social stereotypes: Levels of categorization in person perception. *Journal of Personality and Social Psychology*, *53*(2), 235–246.

Anderson, A. K., & Phelps, E. A. (2001). Lesions of the human amygdala impair enhanced perception of emotionally salient events. *Nature*, *411*(6835), 305–309.

Anderson, C., John, O. P., Keltner, D., & Kring, A. M. (2001). Who attains social status? Effects of personality and physical attractiveness in social groups. *Journal of Personality and Social Psychology*, *81*(1), 116–132.

Anderson, J. R. (1974a). Verbatim and propositional representation of sentences in immediate and long-term memory. *Journal of Verbal Learning & Verbal Behavior*, *13*(2), 149–162.

Anderson, J. R. (2000). *Cognitive psychology and its implications* (5th ed.). New York: Worth Publishers.

Anderson, J. R. (2004). *Cognitive psychology and its implications* (6th ed.). New York: Worth Publishers.

Anderson, N. H. (1965). Averaging versus adding as a stimulus-combination rule in impression formation. *Journal of Experimental Psychology*, *70*(4), 394–400.

Anderson, N. H. (1968). A simple model of information integration. In R. B. Abelson, E. Aronson, W. J. McGuire, T. M. Newcomb, M. J. Rosenberg & P. H. Tannenbaum (Eds.), *Theories of cognitive consistency: A sourcebook* (pp. 731–743). Chicago: Rand McNally.

Anderson, N. H. (1973). Information integration theory applied to attitudes about U. S. presidents. *Journal of Educational Psychology*, *64*(1), 1–8.

Anderson, N. H. (1974b). Cognitive algebra: Integration theory applied to social attribution. In L. Berkowitz (Ed.), *Advances in experimental social psychology* (Vol. 7, pp. 1–101). New York: Academic Press.

Anderson, N. H. (1981). *Foundations of information theory.* New York: Academic Press.

Anderson, N. H. (1989). Functional memory and on-line attribution. In J. N. Bassili (Ed.), *On-line cognition in person perception* (pp. 175–220). Hillsdale, NJ: Erlbaum.

Anderson, N. H., & Shackleton, V. J. (1990). Decision making in the graduate selection interview: A field study. *Journal of Occupational Psychology, 63*(1), 63–76.

Anderson, R. C. (1967). Educational psychology. *Annual Review of Psychology, 18*, 129–164.

Anderson, R. C. (1974c). Concretization and sentence learning. *Journal of Educational Psychology, 66*(2), 179–183.

Anderson, R. C., & Pichert, J. W. (1978). Recall of previously unrecallable information following a shift in perspective. *Journal of Verbal Learning & Verbal Behavior, 17*(1), 1–12.

Anderson, R. C., Reynolds, R. E., Schallert, D. L., & Goetz, E. T. (1977). Frameworks for comprehending discourse. *American Educational Research Journal, 14*(4), 367–381.

Anderson, R. C., Spiro, R. J., & Anderson, M. C. (1978). Schemata as scaffolding for the representation of information in connected discourse. *American Educational Research Journal, 15*(3), 433–440.

Anderson, S. W., Bechara, A., Damasio, H., Tranel, D., & Damasio, A. R. (1999). Impairment of social and moral behavior related to early damage in human prefrontal cortex. *Nature Neuroscience, 2*(11), 1032–1037.

Anderson, S. W., Damasio, H., Jones, R. D., & Tranel, D. (1991). Wisconsin card sorting test performance as a measure of frontal lobe damage. *Journal of Clinical and Experimental Neuropsychology, 13*(6), 909–922.

Andreoli, V., & Worchel, S. (1978). Effects of media, communicator, and message position on attitude change. *Public Opinion Quarterly, 42*, 59–70.

Argyle, M. (1988). *Bodily communication* (2nd ed.). London: Methuen.

Argyle, M., Alkema, F., & Gilmour, R. (1971). The communication of friendly and hostile attitudes by verbal and nonverbal signals. *European Journal of Social Psychology, 1*(3), 385–402.

Argyle, M., & Cook, M. (1976). *Gaze and mutual gaze.* Oxford, UK: Cambridge University Press.

Arkin, R. M., Appelman, A. J., & Burger, J. M. (1980). Social anxiety, self-presentation, and the self-serving bias in causal attribution. *Journal of Personality and Social Psychology, 38*(1), 23–35.

Arkin, R. M., Cooper, H. M., & Kolditz, T. A. (1980). A statistical review of the literature concerning the self-serving attribution bias in interpersonal influence situations. *Journal of Personality, 48*(4), 435–448.

Arnold, M. B. (1960). *Emotion and personality.* New York: Columbia University Press.

Asch, S. E. (1946). Forming impressions of personality. *The Journal of Abnormal and Social Psychology, 41*(3), 258–290.

Aschenbrenner, K. M. (1978). Single-peaked risk preferences and their dependability on the gambles' presentation mode. *Journal of Experimental Psychology: Human Perception and Performance, 4*(3), 513–520.

Asendorpf, J. B. (1987). Videotape reconstruction of emotions and cognitions related to shyness. *Journal of Personality and Social Psychology, 53*(3), 542–549.

Ashby, J., Rayner, K., & Clifton, C. (2005). Eye movements of highly skilled and average readers: Differential effects of frequency and predictability. *Quarterly Journal of Experimental Psychology, 58A*(6), 1065–1086.

Askehave, I., & Swales, J. M. (2001). Genre identification and communicative purpose: A problem and a possible solution. *Applied Linguistics, 22*(2), 195–212.

Atman, C. J., & Puerzer, R. (1995). *Reader preference and comprehension of risk diagrams* (Tech Rep. No 95–8). Pittsburgh, PA: University of Pittsburgh, Department of Industrial Engineering.

Ausubel, D., & Fitzgerald, D. (1961). The role of discriminability in meaningful verbal learning and retention. *Journal of Educational Psychology, 52*(5), 266–274.

Ausubel, D., & Fitzgerald, D. (1962). Organizer, general background and antecedent learning variables in sequential verbal learning. *Journal of Educational Psychology, 53*(6), 243–249.

Awamleh, R., & Gardner, W. L. (1999). Perceptions of leader charisma and effectiveness: The effects of vision content, delivery, and organizational performance. *Leadership Quarterly, 10,* 345–373.

Axelrod, R. (1976). *The structure of decision.* Princeton, NJ: Princeton University Press.

Azar, P. G. (1994). Learning new-to-the-world products (cognitive processing, analogy) (Doctoral dissertation, Northwestern University, 1994). *Dissertation Abstracts International, 56* (03A), 1028.

Bachher, J. S. (1994). Decision making criteria used by Canadian equity investors to evaluate early stage technology based companies (Doctoral dissertation, University of Waterloo, 1994). *Dissertation Abstracts International, 33* (04), 1119.

Bacon, F. T. (1979). Credibility of repeated statements: Memory for trivia. *Journal of Experimental Psychology: Human Learning and Memory, 5*(3), 241–252.

Baehr, M. E., & Williams, G. B. (1968). Prediction of sales success from factorially determined dimensions of personal background data. *Journal of Applied Psychology, 52*(2), 98–103.

Baesler, E. J. (1997). Persuasive effects of story and statistical evidence. *Argumentation and Advocacy, 33,* 170–175.

Baesler, E. J., & Burgoon, J. K. (1994). The temporal effects of story and statistical evidence on belief change. *Communication Research, 21*(5), 582–602.

Bagozzi, R. P. (1978). Salesforce performance and satisfaction as a function of individual difference, interpersonal, and situational factors. *Journal of Marketing Research, 15*(4), 517–531.

Bagozzi, R. P., & Dholakia, U. (1999). Goal setting and goal striving in consumer behavior. *Journal of Marketing Special Issue: Fundamental Issues and Directions for Marketing, 63,* 19–32.

Bailenson, J. N., & Yee, N. (2005). Digital chameleons: Automatic assimilation of nonverbal gestures in immersive virtual environments. *Psychological Science, 16,* 814–819.

Banse, R., & Scherer, K. R. (1996). Acoustic profiles in vocal emotion expression. *Journal of Personality and Social Psychology, 70*(3), 614–636.

Barber, A. E., & Roehling, M. V. (1993). Job postings and the decision to interview: A verbal protocol analysis. *Journal of Applied Psychology, 78*(5), 845–856.

Bard, E. G., Shillcock, R. C., & Altmann, G. T. M. (1988). The recognition of words after their acoustic offsets in spontaneous speech: Effects of subsequent context. *Perception and Psychophysics, 44*(5), 395–408.

Bar-Hillel, M., & Fischhoff, B. (1981). When do base rates affect predictions? *Journal of Personality and Social Psychology, 41*(4), 671–680.

Baron, R. A., & Bell, P. A. (1976). Physical distance and helping: Some unexpected benefits of "crowding in" on others. *Journal of Applied Social Psychology, 6*(2), 95–104.

Baron, R. M., Albright, L., & Mallory, T. E. (1995). Effects of behavioral and social class information on social judgment. *Personality and Social Psychology Bulletin, 21*(4), 308–315.

Barsade, S. G. (2002). The ripple effects: Emotional contagion and its influence on group behavior. *Administrative Science Quarterly, 47*(4), 644–675.

Barsade, S. G., Ward, A. J., Turner, J. D. F., & Sonnenfeld, J. A. (2000). To your heart's content: A model of affective diversity in top management teams. *Administrative Science Quarterly, 45*(4), 802–836.

Bartel, C. A., & Saavedra, R. (2000). The collective construction of work group moods. *Administrative Science Quarterly, 45*(2), 197–231.

Bartol, K. M., & Butterfield, D. A. (1976). Sex effects in evaluating leaders. *Journal of Applied Psychology, 61*(4), 446–454.

Basso, M. R., Schefft, B. K., Ris, M. D., & Dember, W. N. (1996). Mood and global-local visual processing. *Journal of the International Neuropsychological Society, 2*(3), 249–255.

Bates, J. E. (1975). Effects of a child's imitation versus nonimitation on adults' verbal and nonverbal positivity. *Journal of Personality and Social Psychology, 31*(5), 840–851.

Batra, R., & Ray, M. L. (1986). Situational effects of advertising repetition: The moderating influence of motivation, ability, and opportunity to respond. *Journal of Consumer Research, 12*(4), 432–445.

Batson, C. D., & Shaw, L. L. (1991). Evidence for altruism: Toward a pluralism of prosocial motives. *Psychological Inquiry, 2*(2), 107–122.

Batty, M. J., Cave, K. R., & Pauli, P. (2005). Abstract stimuli associated with threat through conditioning cannot be detected preattentively. *Emotion, 5*(4), 418–430.

Bazerman, M. H. (1994). *Judgment in managerial decision making* (3rd ed.). New York: J. Wiley.

Bazerman, M. H., Tenbrunsel, A. E., & Wade-Benzoni, K. (2005). *Negotiating with yourself and losing: Making decisions with competing internal preferences.* Northampton, MA: Edward Elgar Publishing.

Beach, L. R., Campbell, F. L., & Townes, B. O. (1979). Subjective expected utility and the prediction of birth-planning decisions. *Organizational Behavior and Human Performance, 24*(1), 18–28.

Beasley, R. (1998). Collective interpretations: How problem representations aggregate in foreign policy groups. In D. Sylvan & J. Voss (Eds.), *Problem representation in foreign policy decision making* (pp. 80–115). New York: Cambridge University Press.

Beattie, G., & Shovelton, H. (1999). Mapping the range of information contained in the iconic hand gestures that accompany spontaneous speech. *Journal of Language and Social Psychology, 18*(4), 438–462.

Beatty, J., & Kahneman, D. (1966). Pupillary changes in two memory tasks. *Psychonomic Science, 5*(10), 371–372.

Beaulieu, P. R. (1994). Commercial lenders' use of accounting information in interaction with source credibility. *Contemporary Accounting Research, 10*(2), 557–585.

Bechara, A. (2003). Risky business: Emotion, decision-making, and addiction. *Journal of Gambling Studies, 19*(1), 23–51.

Bechara, A., Damasio, A. R., Damasio, H., & Anderson, S. W. (1994). Insensitivity to future consequences following damage to human prefrontal cortex. *Cognition, 50*(1–3), 7–15.

Bechara, A., Damasio, H., Damasio, A. R., & Lee, G. P. (1999). Different contributions of the human amygdala and ventromedial prefrontal cortex to decision-making. *Journal of Neuroscience, 19*(13), 5473–5481.

Bechara, A., Damasio, H., Tranel, D., & Anderson, S. W. (1998). Dissociation of working memory from decision making within the human prefrontal cortex. *Journal of Neuroscience, 18*(1), 428–437.

Becker, C. A., & Killion, T. H. (1977). Interaction of visual and cognitive effects in word recognition. *Journal of Experimental Psychology: Human Perception and Performance, 3*(3), 389–401.

Becker, D., Heinrich, J., van Sichowsky, R., & Wendt, D. (1970). Reader preferences for typeface and leading. *Journal of Typographic Research, 1,* 61–66.

Becker, S. A. (1998). Individual differences in juror reasoning: General intelligence, social intelligence, and the story model (Doctoral dissertation, Fairleigh Dickinson University, 1998). *Dissertation Abstracts International, 59* (08B), 4533.

Behling, D. U., & Williams, E. A. (1991). Influence of dress on perceptions of intelligence and expectations of scholastic achievement. *Clothing and Textiles Research Journal, 9*(4), 1–7.

Bell, B. E., & Loftus, E. F. (1988). Degree of detail of eyewitness testimony and mock juror judgments. *Journal of Applied Social Psychology, 18*(14), 1171–1192.

Bell, B. E., & Loftus, E. F. (1989). Trivial persuasion in the courtroom: The power of (a few) minor details. *Journal of Personality and Social Psychology, 56*(5), 669–679.

Bellenger, D. N., Robertson, D. H., & Hirschman, E. C. (1978). Impulse buying varies by product. *Journal of Advertising Research, 18,* 15–18.

Belmore, S. M. (1987). Determinants of attention during impression formation. *Journal of Experimental Psychology: Learning, Memory, and Cognition, 13*(3), 480–489.

Benjamin, A. S., & Bjork, R. A. (1996). Retrieval fluency as a metacognitive index. In L. Reder (Ed.), *Metacognition and implicit memory* (pp. 309–338). Mahwah, NJ: Erlbaum.

Benson, P. J. (1994). Problems in picturing text (Doctoral dissertation, Carnegie Mellon University, 1994). *Dissertation Abstracts International, 55* (11A), 3357.

Berkenkotter, C., & Huckin, T. N. (1995). *Genre knowledge in disciplinary communication: Cognition, culture, power.* Hillsdale, NJ: Lawrence Erlbaum Associates.

Berry, D. S. (1990). Vocal attractiveness and vocal babyishness: Effects on stranger, self, and friend impressions. *Journal of Nonverbal Behavior, 14*(3), 141–153.

Berry, D. S. (1991a). Accuracy in social perception: Contributions of facial and vocal information. *Journal of Personality and Social Psychology, 61*(2), 298–307.

Berry, D. S. (1991b). Attractive faces are not all created equal: Joint effects of facial babyishness and attractiveness on social perception. *Personality and Social Psychology Bulletin, 17*(5), 523–531.

Berry, D. S., & Brownlow, S. (1989). Were the physiognomists right? Personality correlates of facial babyishness. *Personality and Social Psychology Bulletin, 15*(2), 266–279.

Berry, D. S., & Finch Wero, J. L. (1993). Accuracy in face perception: A view from ecological psychology. *Journal of Personality Special Issue: Viewpoints on Personality: Consensus, Self-other Agreement, and Accuracy in Personality Judgment, 61*(4), 497–520.

Berry, D. S., & Landry, J. C. (1997). Facial maturity and daily social interaction. *Journal of Personality and Social Psychology, 72*(3), 570–580.

Berry, D. S., Pennebaker, J. W., Mueller, J. S., & Hiller, W. S. (1997). Linguistic bases of social perception. *Personality and Social Psychology Bulletin, 23*(5), 526–537.

Berscheid, E. (1985). Interpersonal attraction. In G. Lindzey & E. Aronson (Eds.), *Handbook of social psychology* (3rd ed., Vol. 2, pp. 413–484). New York: Random House.

Berscheid, E., & Reis, H. T. (1998). Attraction and close relationships. In D. T. Gilbert, S. T. Fiske & G. Lindzey (Eds.), *The handbook of social psychology* (4th ed., Vol. 2, pp. 193–281). New York: McGraw-Hill.

Bertrand, M., Karlan, D., Mullainathan, S., Shafir, E., & Zinman, J. (2005). *What's psychology worth?: A field experiment in the consumer credit market.* Working Paper No. 11892, National Bureau of Economic Research, Cambridge, MA.

Bettman, J. R. (1979). *An information processing theory of consumer choice.* Reading, MA: Addison Wesley.

Bettman, J. R., & Kakkar, P. (1977). Effects of information presentation format on consumer information acquisition strategies. *Journal of Consumer Research, 3*(4), 233–240.

Bettman, J. R., & Sujan, M. (1987). Effects of framing on evaluation of comparable and noncomparable alternatives by expert and novice consumers. *Journal of Consumer Research, 14*(2), 141–154.

Bettman, J. R., & Park, C. W. (1980). Effects of prior knowledge and experience and phase of the choice process on consumer decision processes: A protocol analysis. *Journal of Consumer Research, 7*(3), 234–248.

Bever, T. (1970). The cognitive basis for linguistic structures. In J. R. Hayes (Ed.), *Cognition and the development of language* (pp. 279–362). New York: Wiley.

Beveridge, M., & Parkins, E. (1987). Visual representation in analogical problem solving. *Memory & Cognition, 15*(3), 230–237.

Bhaskar, R. (1978). Problem solving in semantically rich domains (Doctoral dissertation, Carnegie Mellon University, 1978). *Dissertation Abstracts International, 41* (05B), 1826.

Bhatia, V. K. (1997). Introduction: Genre analysis and world Englishes. *World Englishes, 16*(3), 313–319.

Bickman, L. (1974). The social power of a uniform. *Journal of Applied Social Psychology, 4*(1), 47–61.

Biederman, I., Glass, A. L., & Stacy, E. W. (1973). Searching for objects in real-world scenes. *Journal of Experimental Psychology, 97*(1), 22–27.

Biehal, G., & Chakravarti, D. (1982). Information-presentation format and learning goals as determinants of consumers' memory retrieval and choice processes. *Journal of Consumer Research, 8*(4), 431–441.

Biehal, G., & Chakravarti, D. (1983). Information accessibility as a moderator of consumer choice. *Journal of Consumer Research, 10*(1), 1–14.

Biehal, G., & Chakravarti, D. (1986). Consumers' use of memory and external information in choice: Macro and micro perspectives. *Journal of Consumer Research, 12*(4), 382–405.

Biernat, M., Manis, M., & Nelson, T. F. (1991). Stereotypes and standards of judgment. *Journal of Personality and Social Psychology, 60*(4), 485–499.

Biggs, S. F. (1984). Financial analysts' information search in the assessment of corporate earning power. *Accounting, Organizations and Society, 9*(3–4), 313–323.

Biggs, S. F., Bedard, J. C., Gaber, B. G., & Linsmeier, T. J. (1985). The effects of task size and similarity on the decision behavior of bank loan officers. *Management Science, 31*(8), 970–987.

Binder, K. S. (2003). Sentential and discourse topic effects on lexical ambiguity processing: An eye-movement examination. *Memory & Cognition, 31*(5), 690–702.

Binning, J. F., Goldstein, M. A., Garcia, M. F., & Scattaregia, J. H. (1988). Effects of preinterview impressions on questioning strategies in same-and opposite-sex employment interviews. *Journal of Applied Psychology*, 73(1), 30–37.

Blanchette, I., & Dunbar, K. (2000). How analogies are generated: The roles of structural and superficial similarity. *Memory & Cognition*, 28(1), 108–124.

Blanchette, I., & Dunbar, K. (2002). Representational change and analogy: How analogical L inferences alter target representations. *Journal of Experimental Psychology: Learning, Memory, and Cognition*, 28(4), 672–685.

Blanton, H., Stuart, A. E., & VandenEijnden, R. J. (2001). An introduction to deviance-regulation theory: The effect of behavioral norms on message framing. *Personality and Social Psychology Bulletin*, 27(7), 848–858.

Blascovich, J., & Seery, M. D. (2007). Visceral and somatic indexes of social psychological constructs: History, principles, propositions, and case studies. In A. Kruglanski & E. T. Higgins (Eds.), *Social psychology: Handbook of basic principles* (2nd ed., pp. 19–38). New York: Guilford.

Bless, H., Bohner, G., Schwarz, N., & Strack, F. (1990). Mood and persuasion: A cognitive response analysis. *Personality and Social Psychology Bulletin*, 16(2), 331–345.

Bless, H., Clore, G. L., Schwarz, N., Golisano, V., Rabe, C., & Wölk, M. (1996). Mood and the use of scripts: Does a happy mood really lead to mindlessness? *Journal of Personality and Social Psychology*, 71(4), 665–679.

Bodenhausen, G. V. (1993). Emotions, arousal, and stereotypic judgments: A heuristic model of affect and stereotyping. In D. M. Mackie & D. L. Hamilton (Eds.), *Affect, cognition, and stereotyping: Interactive processes in group perception* (pp. 13–37). San Diego, CA: Academic Press.

Bodenhausen, G. V., Kramer, G. P., & Süsser, K. (1994a). Happiness and stereotypic thinking in social judgment. *Journal of Personality and Social Psychology*, 66(4), 621–632.

Bodenhausen, G. V., Sheppard, L. A., & Kramer, G. P. (1994b). Negative affect and social judgment: The differential impact of anger and sadness. *European Journal of Social Psychology Special Issue: Affect in Social Judgments and Cognition*, 24(1), 45–62.

Bohner, G., Crow, K., Erb, H. P., & Schwarz, N. (1992). Affect and persuasion: Mood effects on the processing of message content and context cues and on subsequent behaviour. *European Journal of Social Psychology Special Issue: Positiveegative Asymmetry in Affect and Evaluations: II*, 22(6), 511–530.

Bojko, A. (2006). Using eye tracking to compare web page designs: A case study. *Journal of Usability Studies*, 1(3), 112–120.

Bolger, F., & Wright, G. (1992). Reliability and validity in expert judgment. In G. Wright & F. Bolger (Eds.), *Expertise and decision support* (pp. 47–76). New York: Plenum Press.

Bolinger, D. L. (1978). Intonation across languages. In J. H. Greenberg, C. A. Ferguson, & E. A. Moravcsik (Eds.), *Universals of human language, vol. 2: Phonology* (pp. 471–524). Palo Alto, CA: Stanford University Press.

Bolster, B. I., & Springbett, B. M. (1961). The reaction of interviewers to favorable and unfavorable information. *Journal of Applied Psychology*, 45(2), 97–103.

Bond, C. F., Berry, D. S., & Omar, A. (1994). The kernel of truth in judgments of deceptiveness. *Basic and Applied Social Psychology*, 15(4), 523–534.

Bond, C. F., & Brockett, D. R. (1987). A social context-personality index theory of memory for acquaintances. *Journal of Personality and Social Psychology*, 52(6), 1110–1121.

Bond, C. F., & Sedikides, C. (1988). The recapitulation hypothesis in person retrieval. *Journal of Experimental Social Psychology*, 24(3), 195–221.

Bonham, G. M., Shapiro, M. J., & Heradstveit, D. (1988). Group cognition: Using an oil policy game to validate a computer simulation. *Simulations & Games*, 19(4), 379–407.

Bonner, S. E., Walther, B. R., & Young, S. M. (2003). Sophistication-related differences in investors' models of the relative accuracy of analysts' forecast revisions. *The Accounting Review*, 78(3), 679–706.

Bono, J. E., & Judge, T. A. (2003). Self-concordance at work: Toward understanding the motivational effects of transformational leaders. *Academy of Management Journal*, 46(5), 554–571.

Bonsiepe, G. (1968). A method of quantifying order in typographic design. *Journal of Typographic Research*, 3, 203–220.

Borcherding, K. & Rohrmann, B. (1990). An analysis of multiattribute utility models using field data. In K. Borcherding, O. I. Larichev, & D. M. Messick (Eds.), *Contemporary issues in decision making* (pp. 223–241). Amsterdam: North-Holland.

Borkenau, P. (1991). Evidence of a correlation between wearing glasses and personality. *Personality and Individual Differences, 12*(11), 1125–1128.

Borkenau, P., & Liebler, A. (1992a). The cross-modal consistency of personality: Inferring strangers' traits from visual or acoustic information. *Journal of Research in Personality, 26*(2), 183–204.

Borkenau, P., & Liebler, A. (1992b). Trait inferences: Sources of validity at zero acquaintance. *Journal of Personality and Social Psychology, 62*(4), 645–657.

Borkenau, P., & Liebler, A. (1993). Convergence of stranger ratings of personality and intelligence with self-ratings, partner ratings, and measured intelligence. *Journal of Personality and Social Psychology, 65*(3), 546–553.

Borkenau, P., & Liebler, A. (1995). Observable attributes as manifestations and cues of personality and intelligence. *Journal of Personality, 63*(1), 1–25.

Borman, W. C. (1987). Personal constructs, performance schemata, and "folk theories" of subordinate effectiveness: Explorations in an Army officer sample. *Organizational Behavior and Human Decision Processes, 40*(3), 307–322.

Bornstein, B. H., Emler, A. C., & Chapman, G. B. (1999). Rationality in medical treatment decisions: Is there a sunk-cost effect? *Social Sciences & Medicine, 49*(2), 215–222.

Bornstein, R. F. (1989). Exposure and affect: Overview and meta-analysis of research, 1968–1987. *Psychological Bulletin, 106*(2), 265–289.

Bornstein, R. F., & D'Agostino, P. R. (1994). The attribution and discounting of perceptual fluency: Preliminary tests of a perceptual fluency. *Social Cognition, 12*(2), 103–128.

Bosman, J. (1987). Persuasive effects of political metaphors. *Metaphor & Symbolic Activity, 2*(2), 97–113.

Boster, E. J., & Mongeau, P. (1984). Fear-arousing persuasive messages. In R. N. Bostrom & B. H. Westley (Eds.), *Communication yearbook, 8* (pp. 330–375). Newbury Park, CA: Sage.

Bottorff, J. L., Ratner, P. A., Johnson, J. L., Lovato, C. Y., & Joab, S. A. (1998). Communicating cancer risk information: The challenges of uncertainty. *Patient Education and Counseling, 33*(1), 67–81.

Bourhis, R. Y., & Giles, H. (1976). The language of co-operation in Wales: A field study. *Language Sciences, 42*, 13–16.

Bouwman, M. J. (1980). Application of information-processing and decision-making research, I. In G. R. Ungson & D. N. Braunstein (Eds.), *Decision making: An interdisciplinary inquiry* (pp. 129–167). Boston: Kent Publishing.

Bouwman, M. J., Frishkoff, P. A., & Frishkoff, P. (1987). How do financial analysts make decisions? A process model of the investment screening decision. *Accounting, Organizations and Society, 12*(1), 1–29.

Bower, G. H., Black, J. B., & Turner, T. J. (1979). Scripts in memory for text. *Cognitive Psychology, 11*(2), 177–220.

Bower, G. H., Karlin, M. B., & Dueck, A. (1975). Comprehension and memory for pictures. *Memory & Cognition, 3*(2), 216–220.

Bowers, J. W., Metts, S. M., & Duncanson, W. T. (1985). Emotion and interpersonal communication. In M. L. Knapp & G. R. Miller (Eds.), *Handbook of interpersonal communication* (pp. 500–550). Beverly Hills, CA: Sage.

Boyle, P. J. (1994). Expertise in a constructive product-choice process (Doctoral dissertation, Cornell University, 1994). *Dissertation Abstracts International, 55* (05a), 1323.

Bransford, J. D., Barclay, J. R., & Franks, J. J. (1972). Sentence memory: A constructive versus interpretive approach. *Cognitive Psychology, 3*(2), 193–209.

Bransford, J. D., & Johnson, M. K. (1972). Contextual prerequisites for understanding: Some investigations of comprehension and recall. *Journal of Verbal Learning & Verbal Behavior, 11*(6), 717–726.

Bransford, J. D., & Johnson, M. K. (1973). Considerations of some problems of comprehension. In W. G. Chase (Ed.), *Visual information processing* (pp. 383–438). Oxford, UK: Academic.

Bransford, J. D., & McCarrell, N. (1972, October). *A sketch of a cognitive approach to comprehension: Some thoughts about understanding what it means to comprehend.* Paper presented at the Conference on Cognition and the Symbolic Processes, Pennsylvania State University.

Brauner, E., & Scholl, W. (2000). Editorial: The information processing approach as a perspective for groups research. *Group Processes and Intergroup Relations, 3*(2), 115–122.

Breckler, S. J., & Wiggins, E. C. (1989). Affect versus evaluation in the structure of attitudes. *Journal of Experimental Social Psychology, 25*(3), 253–271.

Breitenstein, C., Van Lancker, D., & Daum, I. (2001). The contribution of speech rate and pitch variation to the perception of vocal emotions in a German and an American sample. *Cognition & Emotion, 15*(1), 57–79.

Breland, K., & Breland, M. K. (1944). Legibility of newspaper headlines printed in capitals and in lower case. *Journal of Applied Psychology, 28*(2), 117–120.

Brewer, W. F., & Nakamura, G. V. (1984). The nature and functions of schemas. In R. S. Wyer & T. K. Srull (Eds.), *Handbook of social cognition* (Vol. 1, pp. 119–160). Hillsdale, NJ: Erlbaum.

Brewer, W. F., & Tenpenny, P. L. (1996). The role of schemata in the recall and recognition of episodic information. Unpublished manuscript, University of Illinois at Urbana-Champaign.

Breznitz, S. (1971). A study of worrying. *British Journal of Social & Clinical Psychology, 10*(3), 271–279.

Breznitz, S. (Ed.). (1983). *The denial of stress.* New York: International Universities Press.

Brickman, P., Redfield, J., Harrison, A. A., & Crandall, R. (1972). Drive and predisposition as factors in the attitudinal effects of mere exposure. *Journal of Experimental Social Psychology, 8*(1), 31–44.

Briggs, L., Campeau, P., Gagne, R., & May, M. (1966) *Instructional media: A procedure for the design of multi-media instruction: A critical review of research and suggestions for future research.* Pittsburgh, PA: American Institutes for Research.

Britt, S. H., Adams, S. C., & Miller, A. S. (1972). How many advertising exposures per day. *Journal of Advertising Research, 12*(6), 3–9.

Broemer, P. (2001). Ease of recall moderates the impact of relationship-related goals on judgments of interpersonal closeness. *Journal of Experimental Social Psychology, 37*(3), 261–266.

Brooks, C. I., Church, M. A., & Fraser, L. (1986). Effects of duration of eye contact on judgments of personality characteristics. *Journal of Social Psychology, 126*(1), 71–78.

Brown, A. S., & Nix, L. A. (1996). Turning lies into truths: Referential validation of falsehoods. *Journal of Experimental Psychology: Learning, Memory, and Cognition, 22*(5), 1088–1100.

Brown, B. K., & Campion, M. A. (1994). Biodata phenomenology: Recruiters' perceptions and use of biographical information in résumé screening. *Journal of Applied Psychology, 79*(6), 897–908.

Brown B. L. (1980). Effects of speech rate on personality attributions and competency evaluations. In H. Giles, W. P. Robinson, & P. M. Smith (Eds.), *Language: Social psychological perspectives* (pp. 116–133). Oxford, UK: Pergamon Press.

Brown, B. L., Strong, W. J., & Rencher, A. C. (1973). Perceptions of personality from speech: Effects of manipulations of acoustical parameters. *Journal of the Acoustical Society of America, 54*(1), 29–35.

Brown, C. A. (1988). The central Arizona water control study: A case for multiobjective planning and public involvement. *Water Resources Bulletin, 20*(3), 331–337.

Brown, D. J., Scott, K. A., & Lewis, H. (2004). Information processing and leadership. In J. Antonakis, A. T. Cianciolo, & R. J. Sternberg (Eds.) *The nature of leadership* (pp. 125–147). Thousand Oaks, CA: Sage.

Brown, L. D. (2001). Predicting individual analyst earnings forecast accuracy. *Financial Analysts Journal, 57*(6), 44–49.

Brown, R., & Kulik, J. (1977). Flashbulb memories. *Cognition, 5*(1), 73–99.

Brucks, M. (1985). The effects of product class knowledge on information search behavior. *Journal of Consumer Research, 12*(1), 1–16.

Bruner, J. S. (1957). On perceptual readiness. *Psychological Review, 64*(2), 123–152.

Buchanan, T. W., & Adolphs, R. (2002). The role of the human amygdala in emotional modulation of long-term declarative memory. In S. C. Moore & M. Oaksford (Eds.), *Emotional cognition: From brain to behaviour* (pp. 9–34). Amsterdam, Netherlands: John Benjamins Publishing Company.

Budd, D., Whitney, P., & Turley, K. J. (1995). Individual differences in working memory strategies for reading expository text. *Memory and Cognition, 23*(6), 735–748.

Budescu, D. V., & Rantilla, A. K. (2000). Confidence in aggregation of expert opinions. *Acta Psychologica, 104*(3), 371–398.

Budescu, D. V., Weinberg, S., & Wallsten, T. S. (1988). Decisions based on numerically and verbally expressed uncertainties. *Journal of Experimental Psychology: Human Perception and Performance, 14*(2), 281–294.

Budesheim, T. L., & DePaola, S. J. (1994). Beauty or the beast? The effects of appearance, personality, and issue information on evaluations of political candidates. *Personality and Social Psychology Bulletin, 20*(4), 339–348.

Buehler, R., Messervey, D., & Griffin, D. (2005). Collaborative planning and prediction: Does group discussion affect optimistic biases in time estimation? *Organizational Behavior and Human Decision Processes, 97*(1), 47–63.

Bugental, D. E., Kaswan, J. W., & Love, L. R. (1970). Perception of contradictory meanings conveyed by verbal and nonverbal channels. *Journal of Personality and Social Psychology, 16*(4), 647–655.

Burgoon, J. K. (1994). Nonverbal signals. In M. L. Knapp & G. R. Miller (Eds.), *Handbook of interpersonal communication* (2nd ed., pp. 229–285). Thousand Oaks, CA: Sage.

Burgoon, J. K., Birk, T., & Pfau, M. (1990). Nonverbal behaviors, persuasion, and credibility. *Human Communication Research, 17*(1), 140–169.

Burgoon, J. K., Buller, D., & Woodall, G. (1989). *Nonverbal communication: The unspoken dialogue.* New York: Harper & Row.

Burgoyne, J. G. (1975). The judgment process in management students' evaluation of their learning experiences. *Human Relations, 28*(6), 543–569.

Burke, S. J. (1992). The effects of missing information and inferences on decision processing and evaluation (Doctoral dissertation, The University of Michigan, 1992). *Dissertation Abstracts International, 53* (11A), 3997.

Burnett, J. R. (1993). Utilization and validity of nonverbal cues in the structured interview (Doctoral dissertation, University of Florida, 1993). *Dissertation Abstracts International, 55* (07A), 2041.

Burnkrant, R. E., & Unnava, H. R. (1989). Self-referencing: A strategy for increasing processing of message content. *Personality and Social Psychology Bulletin, 15*(4), 628–638.

Burns, K. L., & Beier, E. G. (1973). Significance of vocal and visual channels in the decoding of emotional meaning. *Journal of Communication, 23*(1), 118–130.

Burrell, N. A., & Koper, R. J. (1998). The efficacy of powerful/powerless language on attitudes and source credibility. In M. Allen & R. W. Preiss (Eds.), *Persuasion: Advances through metaanalysis* (pp. 203–215). Cresskill, NJ: Hampton.

Busemeyer, J. R., & Townsend, J. T. (1993). Decision field theory: A dynamic-cognitive approach to decision making in an uncertain environment. *Psychological Review, 100*(3), 432–459.

Cacioppo, J. T., & Petty, R. E. (1989). Effects of message repetition on argument processing, recall, and persuasion. *Basic and Applied Social Psychology, 10*(1), 3–12.

Cacioppo, J. T., Tassinary, L. G., & Berntson, G. G. (2000). *Handbook of psychophysiology* (2nd ed.). New York: Cambridge University Press.

Cairns, H. S., & Kamerman, J. (1975). Lexical information processing during sentence comprehension. *Journal of Verbal Learning & Verbal Behavior, 14*(2), 170–179.

Calder, A. J., Young, A. W., Keane, J., & Dean, M. (2000). Configural information in facial expression perception. *Journal of Experimental Psychology: Human Perception and Performance, 26*(2), 527–551.

Calder, B. J. (1977). An attribution theory of leadership. In B. M. Staw & G. R. Salancik (Eds.), *New directions in organizational behavior* (pp. 179–204). Chicago: St. Claire Press.

Calder, B. J., & Gruder, C. L. (1989). Emotional advertising appeals. In P. Cafferata & A. Tybout (Eds.), *Cognitive and affective responses to advertising* (pp. 277–286). Lexington, MA: D.C. Heath and Company.

Calder, B. J., Insko, C. A., & Yandell, B. (1974). The relation of cognitive and memorial processes to persuasion in a simulated jury trial. *Journal of Applied Social Psychology, 4*(1), 62–93.

Calder, B. J., & Sternthal, B. (1980). Television commercial wearout: An information processing view. *Journal of Marketing Research, 17*(2), 173–186.

Calvo, M. G., & Lang, P. J. (2004). Gaze patterns when looking at emotional pictures: Motivationally biased attention. *Motivation and Emotion*, *28*(3), 221–243.

Calvo, M. G., & Meseguer, E. (2002). Eye movements and processing stages in reading: Relative contribution of visual, lexical and contextual factors. *Spanish Journal of Psychology*, *5*(1), 66–77.

Camerer, C. F. (1981). General conditions for the success of bootstrapping models. *Organizational Behavior & Human Performance*, *27*(3), 411–422.

Camerer, C. F., & Johnson, E. J. (1991). The process-performance paradox in expert judgment: How can experts know so much and predict so badly?. In K. A. Ericsson & J. Smith (Eds.), *Toward a general theory of expertise: Prospects and limits* (pp. 195–217). New York: Cambridge University Press.

Cameron, L. D., & Leventhal, H. (2003). *The self-regulation of health and illness behavior*. London: Routledge.

Campbell, J. E. (1981). An empirical investigation of the impact on the decision processes of loan officers of separate accounting standards for smaller and/or closely held companies (Doctoral dissertation, The University of Tennessee, 1981). *Dissertation Abstracts International*, *42* (09A), 4050.

Campbell, J. E. (1984). An application of protocol analysis to the "Little GAAP" controversy. *Accounting, Organizations and Society*, *9*(3, 4), 329–343.

Cannon-Bowers, J. A., & Salas, E. (2001). Reflections on shared cognition. *Journal of Organizational Behavior*, *22*(2), 195–202.

Cannon-Bowers, J. A., Salas, E., & Converse, S. (1993) Shared mental models in expert team decision making. In N. J. Castellan (Ed.), *Individual and group decision making: Current issues* (pp. 221–246). Hillsdale, NJ: Lawrence Erlbaum Associates.

Caplan, D. (1972). Clause boundaries and recognition latencies for words in sentences. *Perception & Psychophysics*, *12*(1, Pt. B), 73–76.

Capon, N., & Burke, M. (1977). Information seeking in consumer durable purchases. In B. A. Greenberg & D. N. Bellenger (Eds.), *Contemporary marketing thought, 1977 educator's proceedings* (pp. 110–115). Chicago: American Marketing Association.

Cappella, J. N. (1993). The facial feedback hypothesis in human interaction: Review and speculation. *Journal of Language and Social Psychology Special Issue: Emotional Communication, Culture, and Power*, *12*, 13–29.

Capstaff, J., Paudyal, K., & Rees, W. (2001). A comparative analysis of earnings forecasts in Europe. *Journal of Business Finance & Accounting*, *28*(5–6), 531–562.

Cardy, R. L., & Dobbins, G. H. (1986). Affect and appraisal accuracy: Liking as an integral dimension in evaluating performance. *Journal of Applied Psychology*, *71*(4), 672–678.

Carenini, G. (2001). Generating and evaluating evaluative arguments (Doctoral dissertation, University of Pittsburgh, 2001). *Dissertation Abstracts International*, *62* (05B), 2377.

Carley, K. M. (1997). Extracting team mental models through textual analysis. *Journal of Organizational Behavior*, *18*(Spec Issue), 533–558.

Carli, L. L., Ganley, R., & Pierce-Otay, A. (1991). Similarity and satisfaction in roommate relationships. *Personality and Social Psychology Bulletin*, *17*(4), 419–426.

Carli, L. L., LaFleur, S. J., & Loeber, C. C. (1995). Nonverbal behavior, gender, and influence. *Journal of Personality and Social Psychology*, *68*(6), 1030–1041.

Carlston, D. E., & Smith, E. R. (1996). Principles of mental representation. In E. T. Higgins & A. Kruglanski (Eds.), *Social psychology: Handbook of basic principles* (2nd ed., pp. 184–210). New York: Guilford Press.

Carpenter, P. A., & Just, M. A. (1977). Reading comprehension as the eyes see it. In M. A. Just & P. A. Carpenter (Eds.), *Cognitive processes in comprehension* (pp. 109–139). Hillsdale, NJ: Erlbaum.

Carpenter, P. A., & Just, M. A. (1981). Cognitive processes in reading: Models based on readers' eye fixations. In A. M. Lesgold & C. A. Perfetti (Eds.), *Interactive processes in reading* (pp. 177–213). Hillsdale, NJ: Erlbaum.

Carpenter, P. A., & Just, M. A. (1983). What your eyes do while your mind is reading. In K. Rayner (Ed.), *Eye movements in reading: Perceptual and language processes* (pp. 275–307). New York: Academic Press.

Carpenter, P. A., & Shah, P. (1998). A model of the perceptual and conceptual processes in graph comprehension. *Journal of Experimental Psychology: Applied, 4*(2), 75–100.

Carretié, L., Hinojosa, J. A., Martín-Loeches, M., Mercado, F., & Tapia, M. (2004). Automatic attention to emotional stimuli: Neural correlates. *Human Brain Mapping, 22*(4), 290–299.

Carroll, J. S. (1978). Causal attributions in expert parole decisions. *Journal of Personality and Social Psychology, 36*(12), 1501–1511.

Carroll, M. L. (1997). A comparative analysis and evaluation of knowledge structures between expert novice and struggling novice accounting students (Doctoral dissertation, Loyola University of Chicago, 1997). *Dissertation Abstracts International, 58* (03A), 0733.

Carswell, C. M., & Wickens, C. D. (1987). Information integration and the object display: An interaction of task demands and display superiority. *Ergonomics, 30*(3), 511–527.

Carter, W. B., Beach, L. R., & Inui, T. S. (1986). The flu shot study: Using multiattribute utility theory to design a vaccination intervention. *Organizational Behavior and Human Decision Processes, 38*(3), 378–391.

Carver, C. S., & Scheier, M. F. (1990). Origins and functions of positive and negative affect: A control-process view. *Psychological Review, 97*(1), 19–35.

Cassie, J. R. B., & Robinson, F. G. (1982). A decision schema approach to career decision making. *International Journal of Advances in Counseling, 5*, 165–182.

Castellan, N. J. (Ed.). (1993). *Individual and group decision making: Current issues.* Hillsdale, NJ: Lawrence Erlbaum.

Chaiken, S. (1980). Heuristic versus systematic information processing and the use of source versus message cues in persuasion. *Journal of Personality and Social Psychology, 39*(5), 752–766.

Chaiken, S., & Eagly, A. H. (1976). Communication modality as a determinant of message persuasiveness and message comprehensibility. *Journal of Personality and Social Psychology, 34*(4), 605–614.

Chaiken, S., & Eagly, A. H. (1983). Communication modality as a determinant of persuasion: The role of communicator salience. *Journal of Personality and Social Psychology, 45*(2), 241–256.

Chaiken, S., Liberman, A., & Eagly, A. H. (1989). Heuristic and systematic information processing within and beyond the persuasion context. In J. S. Uleman & J. A. Bargh (Eds.), *Unintended thought* (pp. 212–252). New York: Guilford Press.

Chall, J. S. (1958) *Readability: An appraisal of research and application.* Columbus, OH: Ohio State University. Reprinted 1974. Epping, UK: Bowker Publishing Company.

Chan, S. (1982). Expert judgments under uncertainty: Some evidence and suggestions. *Social Science Quarterly, 63*, 428–444.

Chance, M. R. A. (1976). The organization of attention in groups. In M. von Cranach (Ed.), *Methods of inference from animal to human behavior* (pp. 213–235). The Hague, Netherlands: Mouton.

Chandler, R. C. (1988). Organizational communication to corporate constituents: The role of the company annual report (Doctoral dissertation, University of Kansas, 1988). *Dissertation Abstracts International, 49* (11a), 3200.

Chang, M. J., & Gruner, C. R. (1981). Audience reaction to self-disparaging humor. *Southern Speech Communication Journal, 46*, 419–426.

Chapman, G. B., & Johnson, E. J. (1999). Anchoring, activation, and the construction of values. *Organizational Behavior and Human Decision Processes, 79*(2), 115–153.

Charrow, R., & Charrow, V. R. (1979). Making legal language understandable: Psycholinguistic study of jury instructions. *Columbia Law Review, 79*, 1306–1374.

Charrow, V. R. (1988). Readability vs. comprehensibility: A case study in improving a real document. In A. Davison & G. M. Green (Eds.), *Linguistic complexity and text comprehension: Readability issues reconsidered* (pp. 85–114). Hillsdale, NJ: Lawrence Erlbaum Associates.

Charrow, V. R., & Redish, J. (1980). *A study of standardized headings for warranties* (Document Design Project Technical Report No. 6). Washington, DC: American Institutes for Research.

Chase, W. G., & Simon, H. A. (1973). Perception in chess. *Cognitive Psychology, 4*(1), 55–81.

Chattopadhyay, A., Dahl, D. W., Ritchie, R. J. B., & Shahin, K. N. (2003). Hearing voices: The impact of announcer speech characteristics on consumer response to broadcast advertising. *Journal of Consumer Psychology, 13*(3), 198–204.

Chen, L. (1982). Topological structure in visual perception. *Science, 218*(4573), 699–700.

Chernoff, H. (1973). Using faces to represent points in k-dimensional space graphically. *Journal of the American Statistical Association, 68*, 361–368.

Cherry, E. C. (1953). Some experiments on the recognition of speech, with one and with two ears. *Journal of the Acoustical Society of America, 25*, 975–979.

Cherulnik, P. D., Donley, D. A., Wiewel, T. S. R., & Miller, S. R. (2001). Charisma is contagious: The effects of leader's charisma on observers' affect. *Journal of Applied Social Psychology, 31*, 2149–2159.

Chi, M. T. H. (2006). Two approaches to the study of expert's characteristics. In K. A. Ericsson, N. Charness, P. Feltovich, & R. Hoffman (Eds.), *The Cambridge handbook of expertise and expert performance* (pp. 21–30). Cambridge, UK: Cambridge University Press.

Chi, M. T. H., Feltovich, P. J., & Glaser, R. (1981). Categorization and representation of physics problems by experts and novices. *Cognitive Science, 5*, 121–152.

Chi, M. T. H., Glaser, R., & Rees, E. (1982). Expertise in problem solving. In R. J. Sternberg (Ed.), *Advances in the psychology of human intelligence* (Vol. 1, pp. 7–75). Hillsdale, NJ: Erlbaum.

Chi, M. T. H., & Koeske, R. D. (1983). Network representation of a child's dinosaur knowledge. *Developmental Psychology, 19*(1), 29–39.

Chi, M. T. H., & Ohlsson, S. (2005). Complex declarative learning. In K. J. Holyoak & R. G. Morrison (Eds.), *The Cambridge handbook of thinking and reasoning* (pp. 371–399). Cambridge, UK: Cambridge University Press.

Chinburapa, V. (1991). Physician prescribing decisions: The effects of situational involvement and task complexity on information acquisition and decision making (Doctoral dissertation, The University of Arizona, 1991). *Dissertation Abstracts International, 52* (04B), 1975.

Cirilo, R. K., & Foss, D. J. (1980). Text structure and reading time for sentences. *Journal of Verbal Learning and Verbal Behavior, 19*(1), 96–109.

Citibank. (1974). First National City Bank promissory note (PBR 668 REV.9–74). In C. Felsenfeld & A. Siegel, *Writing contracts in plain English* (1981 ed., p. 3). St. Paul, MN: West Publishing Co.

Citibank. (1977). Consumer Loan Note. In C. Felsenfeld & A. Siegel, *Writing contracts in plain English* (1981 ed., p. 241). St. Paul, MN: West Publishing Co.

Clark, H. H. (1969). Linguistic processes in deductive reasoning. *Psychological Review, 76*(4), 387–404.

Clark, H. H. (1999). Psycholinguistics. In R. A. Wilson & F. C. Keil (Eds.), *MIT encyclopedia of the cognitive sciences* (pp. 688–689). Cambridge, MA: MIT Press.

Clark, H. H., & Chase, W. G. (1972). On the process of comparing sentences against pictures. *Cognitive Psychology, 3*(3), 472–517.

Clark, H. H., & Clark, E. V. (1968). Semantic distinctions and memory for complex sentences. *The Quarterly Journal of Experimental Psychology, 20*(2), 129–138.

Clark, H. H., & Sengul, C. J. (1979). In search of referents for nouns and pronouns. *Memory & Cognition, 7*(1), 35–41.

Clark, L. F., Martin, L. L., & Henry, S. M. (1993). Instantiation, interference, and the change of standard effect: Context functions in reconstructive memory. *Journal of Personality and Social Psychology, 64*(3), 336–346.

Clark, M. S., Milberg, S., & Erber, R. (1984). Effects of arousal on judgments of others' emotions. *Journal of Personality and Social Psychology, 46*(3), 551–560.

Clark, N. K., & Rutter, D. R. (1985). Social categorization, visual cues, and social judgements. *European Journal of Social Psychology, 15*(1), 105–119.

Clarkson, G. P. (1962). *Portfolio selection: A simulation of trust investment*. Englewood Cliffs, NJ: Prentice Hall.

Clement, M. B., & Tse, S. Y. (2003). Do investors respond to analysts' forecast revisions as if forecast accuracy is all that matters? *The Accounting Review, 78*(1), 227–249.

Cleveland, W. S., & McGill, R. (1984). Graphical perception: Theory, experimentation, and application to the development of graphical methods. *Journal of the American Statistical Association, 77*, 541–547.

Clifton, C., Jr., & Odom, P. (1966). Similarity relations among certain English sentence constructions. *Psychological Monographs: General & Applied, 80*(5), 35.

Cline, T. W., & Kellaris, J. J. (1999). The joint impact of humor and argument strength in a print advertising context: A case for weaker arguments. *Psychology & Marketing, 16*(1), 69–86.

Clore, G. L., & Isbell, L. M. (2001). Emotion as virtue and vice. In J. H. Kuklinski (Ed.), *Citizens and politics: Perspectives from political psychology* (pp. 103–123). New York: Cambridge University Press.

Clore, G. L., & Ortony, A. (1988). The semantics of the affective lexicon. In V. Hamilton, G. H. Bower, & N. H. Frijda (Eds.), *Cognitive perspectives on emotion and motivation* (pp. 367–397). New York: Kluwer Academic/Plenum Publishers.

Cloyd, C. B., & Spilker, B. (1999). The influence of client preferences on tax professionals' search for judicial precedents, subsequent judgments, and recommendations. *The Accounting Review, 74,* 299–322.

Cobb, C. J., & Hoyer, W. D. (1986). Planned versus impulse purchase behavior. *Journal of Retailing, 62*(4), 384–409.

Cobb, R. W., & Elder, C. D. (1983). *Participation in American politics: The dynamics of agenda building.* Baltimore: Johns Hopkins University Press.

Cobos, P. L., Almaraz, J., & Garcia-Madruga, J. A. (2003). An associative framework for probability judgment: An application to biases. *Journal of Experimental Psychology: Learning, Memory, and Cognition, 29*(1), 80–96.

Cohen, C. E. (1976). Cognitive basis of stereotyping: An information processing approach to social perception (Doctoral dissertation, University of California, San Diego, 1976). *Dissertation Abstracts International, 38* (01B), 0412.

Cohen, C. E. (1981a). Goals and schemata in person perception: Making sense from the stream of behavior. In N. Cantor & J. F. Kihlstrom (Eds.), *Personality, cognition and social interaction* (pp. 45–68). Hillsdale, NJ: Lawrence Erlbaum Associates.

Cohen, C. E. (1981b). Person categories and social perception: Testing some boundaries of the processing effect of prior knowledge. *Journal of Personality and Social Psychology, 40*(3), 441–452.

Cohen, G., Conway, M. A., & Maylor, E. A. (1994). Flashbulb memories in older adults. *Psychology and Aging, 9*(3), 454–463.

Cohen, M. S. (1993). The naturalistic basis of decision biases. In G. A. Klein, J. Orasanu, R. Calderwood, & C. E. Zsambok (Eds.), *Decision making in action: Models and methods* (pp. 51–99). Norwood, NJ: Ablex.

Coleman, E. B. (1962). Improving comprehensibility by shortening sentences. *Journal of Applied Psychology, 46*(2), 131–134.

Coleman, E. B. (1964). The comprehensibility of several grammatical transformations. *Journal of Applied Psychology, 48*(3), 186–190.

Coles, P., & Foster, J. J. (1975). Typographic cuing as an aid to learning from typewritten text. *Programmed Learning and Educational Technology, 12,* 102–108.

Collins, A., Brown, J. S., & Larkin, K. M. (1980). Inference in text understanding. In R. J. Spiro, B. C. Bruce, & W. F. Brewer (Eds.), *Theoretical issues in reading comprehension* (pp. 385–407). Hillsdale, NJ: Lawrence Erlbaum Associates.

Compton, R. J. (2003). The interface between emotion and attention: A review of evidence from psychology and neuroscience. *Behavioral and Cognitive Neuroscience Reviews, 2*(2), 115–129.

Conger, J. A., & Kanungo, R. N. (1998). *Charismatic leadership in organizations.* Thousand Oaks, CA: Sage.

Conger, J. A., & Kanungo, R. N. (Eds.). (1988). *Charismatic leadership: The elusive factor in organizational effectiveness.* San Francisco: Jossey-Bass.

Conger. J. A., Kanungo. R. N., Menon. S. T., & Mathur. P. (1997). Measuring charisma: Dimensionality and validity of the Conger-Kanungo scale of charismatic leadership. *Canadian Journal of Administrative Sciences. 14*(3), 290–302.

Connelly, M. S., Gilbert, J. A., Zaccaro, S. J., Threlfall, K. V., Marks, M. A., & Mumford, M. D. (2000). Exploring the relationship of leadership skills and knowledge to leader performance. *Leadership Quarterly, 11,* 65–86.

Consumer Reports (2009). *Smart phone ratings for AT&T smart phones.* Retrieved December 16, 2009 from www.consumerreports.org/cro/electronics-computers/phones-mobile-devices/cell-phones-services/smart-phone-ratings/ratings-overview.htm.

Control Data Corporation. (1986). *Control Data (annual report).* Control Data Corporation Records, Annual and Quarterly Reports (CBI 80), Charles Babbage Institute, University of Minnesota, Minneapolis.

Conway, M., & Giannopoulos, C. (1993). Dysphoria and decision making: Limited information use for evaluations of multiattribute targets. *Journal of Personality and Social Psychology, 64*(4), 613–623.

Cook, G. J. (1987). An analysis of information search strategies for decision making (Doctoral dissertation, Arizona State University, 1987). *Dissertation Abstracts International, 48* (02A), 0430.

Cooke, N. J., Salas, E., Kiekel, P. A., & Bell, B. (2004). Advances in measuring team cognition. In E. Salas & S. M. Fiore (Eds.), *Team cognition: Understanding the factors that drive process and performance* (pp. 83–106). Washington, DC: American Psychological Association.

Corteen, R. S., & Dunn, D. (1974). Shock-associated words in a nonattended message: A test for momentary awareness. *Journal of Experimental Psychology, 102*(6), 1143–1144.

Cosier, R. A., & Schwenk, C. R. (1990). Agreement and thinking alike: Ingredients for poor decisions. *Academy of Management Executive, 4*(1), 69–74.

Coulson, M. (2004a). Attributing emotion to static body postures: Recognition accuracy, confusions, and viewpoint dependence. *Journal of Nonverbal Behavior, 28*(2), 117–139.

Coulson, M. (2004b). Erratum for attributing emotion to static body postures: Recognition accuracy, confusions, and viewpoint dependence. *Journal of Nonverbal Behavior Special Issue: Interpersonal Sensitivity, 28*(4), 297.

Coulter, R. H., & Pinto, M. B. (1995). Guilt appeals in advertising: What are their effects? *Journal of Applied Psychology, 80*(6), 697–705.

Coupey, E. (1994). Restructuring: Constructive processing of information displays in consumer choice. *Journal of Consumer Research, 21*(1), 83–99.

Cox, A. D., & Summers, J. O. (1987). Heuristics and biases in the intuitive projection of retail sales. *Journal of Marketing Research, 24*(3), 290–297.

Cox, D. S., & Cox, A. D. (1988). What does familiarity breed? Complexity as a moderator of repetition effects in advertisement evaluation. *Journal of Consumer Research, 15*(1), 111–116.

Cox, E. P., III, Wogalter, M. S., Stokes, S. L., & Murff, E. J. T. (1997). Do product warnings increase safe behavior? A meta-analysis. *Journal of Public Policy, 16*, 195–204.

Cox, W. F. (1978). Problem solving as a function of abstract or concrete words. *Contemporary Educational Psychology, 3*(1), 95–101.

Craig, C. S., Sternthal, B., & Leavitt, C. (1976). Advertising wearout: An experimental analysis. *Journal of Marketing Research, 13*(4), 365–372.

Crespin, T. R. (1997). Cognitive convergence in developing groups: The role of sociocognitive elaboration. *Dissertation Abstracts International: Section B: The Sciences and Engineering, 57*(7-B), 4758.

Cronin, J. J., Jr., Brady, M. K., & Hult, G. T. M. (2000). Assessing the effects of quality, value, and customer satisfaction on consumer behavioral intentions in service environments. *Journal of Retailing, 76*(2), 193–218.

Cronshaw, S. F., & Lord, R. G. (1987). Effects of categorization, attribution, and encoding processes on leadership perceptions. *Journal of Applied Psychology, 72*(1), 97–106.

Crouse, J., & Idstein, P. (1972). Effects of encoding cues on prose learning. *Journal of Educational Psychology, 63*(4), 309–313.

Cruz, M. G., Boster, F. J., & Rodríguez, J. I. (1997). The impact of group size and proportion of shared information on the exchange and integration of information in groups. *Communication Research, 24*(3), 291–313.

Cunningham, M. R. (1986). Measuring the physical in physical attractiveness: Quasi-experiments on the sociobiology of female facial beauty. *Journal of Personality and Social Psychology, 50*(5), 925–935.

Cunningham, M. R., Barbee, A. P., & Pike, C. L. (1990). What do women want? Facialmetric assessment of multiple motives in the perception of male facial physical attractiveness. *Journal of Personality and Social Psychology, 59*(1), 61–72.

Cutler, A. (1982). Prosody and sentence perception in English. In J. Mehler, E. C. T. Walker, & M. F. Garrett (Eds.), *Perspectives on mental representation: Experimental and theoretical studies of cognitive processes and capacities* (pp. 201–216). Hillsdale, NJ: Erlbaum.

Cutler, A., & Norris, D. (1988). The role of strong syllables in segmentation for lexical access. *Journal of Experimental Psychology: Human Perception and Performance, 14*(1), 113–121.

Cutler, B. L., Penrod, S. D., & Dexter, H. R. (1990). Juror sensitivity to eyewitness identification evidence. *Law and Human Behavior, 14*(2), 185–191.

Dale, E., & Chall, J. S. (1948). A formula for predicting readability. *Educational Research Bulletin, 27*, 11–20, 37–54.

Dalgleish, T. (1995). Performance on the emotional Stroop task in groups of anxious, expert, and control subjects: A comparison of computer and card presentation formats. *Cognition & Emotion, 9*(4), 341–362.

Daly, S. (1978). Behavioural correlates of social anxiety. *British Journal of Social & Clinical Psychology, 17*(2), 117–120.

Damasio, A. R. (1994). *Descartes' error: Emotion, reason, and the human brain.* New York: G. P. Putnam.

Damasio, A. R., Tranel, D., & Damasio, H. (1990). Individuals with sociopathic behavior caused by frontal damage fail to respond autonomically to social stimuli. *Behavioural Brain Research, 41*(2), 81–94.

Daneman, M., & Carpenter, P. A. (1980). Individual differences in working memory and reading. *Journal of Verbal Learning & Verbal Behavior, 19*(4), 450–466.

Daneman, M., & Carpenter, P. A. (1983). Individual differences in integrating information between and within sentences. *Journal of Experimental Psychology: Learning, Memory, and Cognition, 9*(4), 561–584.

Dansereau. D. F., Brooks, L. W., Spurlin, J. E., & Holley, C. D. (1982). *Headings and outlines as processing aids for scientific text* (National Institute of Education, Final Report, NIE-G-79-0157). Fort Worth, TX: Texas Christian University.

Das, E. H., de Wit, J. F., & Stroebe, W. (2003). Fear appeals motivate acceptance of action recommendations: Evidence for a positive bias in the processing of persuasive messages. *Personality and Social Psychology Bulletin, 29*(5), 650–664.

Davenport, J. S., & Smith, S. A. (1963). Effects of hyphenation, justified, and type size on readability. *Journalism Quarterly, 42*, 382–388.

Davidson, P. S. R., & Glisky, E. L. (2002). Is flashbulb memory a special instance of source memory? Evidence from older adults. *Memory, 10*(2), 99–111.

Davis, M. A. (1992). Age and dress of professors: Influence on students' first impressions of teaching effectiveness (Doctoral dissertation, Virginia Polytechnic Institute and State University, 1992). *Dissertation Abstracts International, 53* (02B), 0806.

Dawes, R. M. (1971). A case study of graduate admissions: Application of three principles of human decision making. *American Psychologist, 26*(2), 180–188.

Dawes, R. M. (1976). Shallow psychology. In J. S. Carroll & J. W. Payne (Eds.), *Cognition and social behavior* (pp. 3–12). Hillsdale, NJ: Lawrence Erlbaum Associates.

Dawes, R. M. (1980). You can't systematize human judgment: Dyslexia. In R. A. Shweder (Ed.), *New directions for methodology of social and behavioral science* (Vol. 4, pp. 67–78). San Francisco: Jossey-Bass.

Dawes, R. M., & Corrigan, B. (1974). Linear models in decision making. *Psychological Bulletin, 81*(2), 95–106.

Dawes, R. M., Faust, D., & Meehl, P. E. (1989). Clinical versus actuarial judgment. *Science, 243*(4899), 1668–1674.

Dearborn, D. C., & Simon, H. A. (1958). Selective perception: A note on the departmental identifications of executives. *Sociometry, 21*, 140–144.

De Bondt, W. F. M., & Thaler, R. H. (1990). Do security analysis overreact? *The American Economic Review, 80*(2), 52–57.

de Groot, A. D. (1965). *Thought and choice in chess.* The Hague, Netherlands: Mouton.

DeGroot, T., & Motowidlo, S. J. (1999). Why visual and vocal interview cues can affect interviewers' judgments and predict job performance. *Journal of Applied Psychology, 84*(6), 986–993.

De Hoog, N., Stroebe, W., & de Wit, J. F. (2005). The impact of fear appeals on processing and acceptance of health messages. *Personality and Social Psychology Bulletin, 31*(1), 24–33.

Deli Carpini, M. X. (2004). Mediating democratic engagement: The impact of communications on citizens' involvement in political and civil life. In L. L. Kaid (Ed.), *Handbook of political communication research* (pp. 395–434). Mahwah, NJ: Lawrence Erlbaum Associates.

Den Hartog, D. N., House, R. J., Hanges, P. J., Ruiz-Quintanilla, S. A., & Dorfman, P. W. (1999). Culture specific and cross-cultural generalizable implicit leadership theories: Are attributes of charismatic/transformational leadership universally endorsed? *Leadership Quarterly, 10,* 219–256.

Dennis, A. R. (1996). Information exchange and use in small group decision making. *Small Group Research, 27*(4), 532–550.

DePaulo, B. M., Rosenthal, R., Eisenstat, R. A., Rogers, P. L., & Finkelstein, S. (1978). Decoding discrepant nonverbal cues. *Journal of Personality and Social Psychology, 36*(3), 313–323.

DePaulo, B. M., Stone, J. I., & Lassiter, G. D. (1985). Deceiving and detecting deceit. In B. R. Schlenker (Ed.), *The self and social life* (pp. 323–370). New York: McGraw-Hill.

DePaulo, P. J., & DePaulo, B. M. (1989). Can deception by salespersons and customers be detected through nonverbal behavioral cues? *Journal of Applied Social Psychology, 19*(18, Pt. 2), 1552–1577.

Derryberry, D., & Tucker, D. M. (1992). Neural mechanisms of emotion. *Journal of Consulting and Clinical Psychology, 60*(3), 329–338.

Derryberry, D., & Tucker, D. M. (1994). Motivating the focus of attention. In P. M. Niedenthal & S. Kitayama (Eds.), *The heart's eye: Emotional influences in perception and attention* (pp. 167–196). San Diego, CA: Academic Press.

DeSteno, D., Petty, R. E., Rucker, D. D., Wegener, D. T., & Braverman, J. (2004). Discrete emotions and persuasion: The role of emotion-induced expectancies. *Journal of Personality and Social Psychology, 86*(1), 43–56.

DeSteno, D., Petty, R. E., Wegener, D. T., & Rucker, D. D. (2000). Beyond valence in the perception of likelihood: The role of emotion specificity. *Journal of Personality and Social Psychology, 78*(3), 397–416.

Detenber, B., & Reeves, B. (1996). A bio-information theory of emotion: Motion and image size effects on viewers. *Journal of Communication, 46*(3), 66–84.

deTurck, M. A., & Goldhaber, G. M. (1991). A developmental analysis of warning signs: The case of familiarity and gender. *Journal of Products Liability, 13,* 65–78.

Detweiler, J. B., Bedell, B. T., Salovey, P., Pronin, E., & Rothman, A. J. (1999). Message framing and sunscreen use: Gain-framed messages motivate beach-goers. *Health Psychology, 18*(2), 189–196.

de Villiers, P. A. (1974). Imagery and theme in recall of connected discourse. *Journal of Experimental Psychology, 103*(2), 263–268.

Dhami, M. K., & Ayton, P. (2001). Bailing and jailing the fast and frugal way. *Journal of Behavioral Decision Making, 14*(2), 141–168.

Dhar, R., & Simonson, I. (1992). The effect of the focus of comparison on consumer preferences. *Journal of Marketing Research, 29*(4), 430–440.

Dholakia, U. M., & Morwitz, V. G. (2002). The scope and persistence of mere-measurement effects: Evidence from a field study of customer satisfaction measurement. *Journal of Consumer Research, 29*(2), 159–167.

Diamond, D. S. (1968). A quantitative approach to magazine advertisement format selection. *Journal of Marketing Research, 5*(4), 376–386.

Diehl, M., & Stroebe, W. (1987). Productivity loss in brainstorming groups: Toward the solution of a riddle. *Journal of Personality and Social Psychology, 53*(3), 497–509.

Diekmann, K. A., Samuels, S. M., Ross, L., & Bazerman, M. H. (1997). Self-interest and fairness in problems of resource allocation: Allocators versus recipients. *Journal of Personality and Social Psychology, 72*(5), 1061–1074.

Diener, E., & Iran-Nejad, A. (1986). The relationship in experience between various types of affect. *Journal of Personality and Social Psychology, 50*(5), 1031–1038.

Dijksterhuis, A., Macrae, C. N., & Haddock, G. (1999). When recollective experiences matter: Subjective ease of retrieval and stereotyping. *Personality and Social Psychology Bulletin, 25*(6), 766–774.

Dimberg, U. (1997). Psychophysiological reactions to facial expressions. In U. Segerstrale & P. Molnar (Eds.), *Nonverbal communication: Where nature meets culture* (pp. 47–60). Mahwah, NJ: Lawrence Erlbaum.

Dimberg, U., & Öhman, A. (1996). Behold the wrath: Psychophysiological responses to facial stimuli. *Motivation and Emotion Special Issue: Facial Expression and Emotion–The Legacy of John T. Lanzetta, 20*(2, Pt. 1), 149–182.

Dimberg, U., Thunberg, M., & Elmehed, K. (2000). Unconscious facial reactions to emotional facial expressions. *Psychological Science, 11*(1), 86–89.

Ditto, P. H., & Lopez, D. F. (1992). Motivated skepticism: Use of differential decision criteria for preferred and nonpreferred conclusions. *Journal of Personality and Social Psychology, 63*(4), 568–584.

Donohew, L. (1981). Arousal and affective responses to writing styles. *Journal of Applied Communication Research, 9,* 109–119.

Donohew, L. (1982). Newswriting styles: What arouses the readers? *Newspaper Research Journal, 3,* 3–6.

Dooling, D. J., & Mullet, R. L. (1973). Locus of thematic effects in retention of prose. *Journal of Experimental Psychology, 97*(3), 404–406.

Dougherty, T. W., Turban, D. B., & Callender, J. C. (1994). Confirming first impressions in the employment interview: A field study of interviewer behavior. *Journal of Applied Psychology, 79*(5), 659–665.

Douglas, K. S., Lyon, D. R., & Ogloff, J. R. P. (1997). The impact of graphic photographic evidence on mock jurors' decisions in a murder trial: Probative or prejudicial? *Law and Human Behavior, 21*(5), 485–501.

Dovidio, J. F., & Ellyson, S. L. (1982). Decoding visual dominance: Attributions of power based on relative percentages of looking while speaking and looking while listening. *Social Psychology Quarterly, 45*(2), 106–113.

Downs, A. (1994). *Inside bureaucracy.* Prospect Heights, IL: Waveland.

Doyle, A. E. (1990). Readers' and writers' genre expectations in letters of recommendation: Two case studies (Doctoral dissertation, University of Illinois at Chicago, 1990). *Dissertation Abstracts International, 52* (01A), 0209.

Drew, C. J., Altman, R., & Dykes, M. K. (1971). Evaluation of instructional materials as a function of material complexity and teacher manual format (Working Paper No. 10). Unpublished manuscript, Texas University, 1971 (ERIC Document Reproduction Service No. ED 079916).

Drezner, D. W. (2000). Ideas, bureaucratic politics, and the crafting of foreign policy. *American Journal of Political Science, 44*(4), 733–749.

Drieghe, D., Rayner, K., & Pollatsek, A. (2005). Eye movements and word skipping during reading revisited. *Journal of Experimental Psychology: Human Perception and Performance, 31*(5), 954–969.

Druckman, J. N. (2001a) On the limits of framing effects: Who can frame? *Journal of Politics, 63,* 1041–1066.

Druckman, J. N. (2001b). Using credible advice to overcome framing effects. *Journal of Law, Economics, & Organization, 17,* 62–82.

Duchastel, P. C. (1979). *A functional approach to illustrations in text* (Occasional Paper 2). Bryn Mawr, PA: The American College.

Duchastel, P. C. (1980). *Research on illustrations in instructional texts* (Occasional Paper 3). Bryn Mawr, PA: The American College.

Duffy, S., & Keir, J. A. (2004). Violating stereotypes: Eye movements and comprehension processes when text conflicts with world knowledge. *Memory and Cognition, 32*(4), 551–559.

Duffy, T. M., & Kabance, P. (1982). Testing a readable writing approach to text revision. *Journal of Educational Psychology, 74*(5), 733–748.

Duker, S. (1974). *Time compressed speech: An anthology and bibliography* (Vol. 3). Metuchen, NJ: Scarecrow Press.

Dunning. D. (1999). A newer look: Motivated social cognition and the schematic representation of social concepts. *Psychological Inquiry, 10*(1), 1–11.

Eagly, A. H. (1974). Comprehensibility of persuasive arguments as a determinant of opinion change. *Journal of Personality and Social Psychology, 29*(6), 758–773.

Eagly, A. H., & Warren, R. (1976). Intelligence, comprehension, and opinion change. *Journal of Personality, 44*(2), 226–242.

Eastwood, J. D., Smilek, D., & Merikle, P. M. (2001). Differential attentional guidance by unattended faces expressing positive and negative emotion. *Perception & Psychophysics, 63*(6), 1004–1013.

Ebbesen, E. B. (1980). Cognitive processes in understanding ongoing behavior. In R. Hastie, T. M. Ostrom, C. B. Ebbesen, R. S. Wyer, D. L. Hamilton, & E. L. Carlston (Eds.), *Person memory: The cognitive basis of social perception* (pp. 179–225). Hillsdale, NJ: Lawrence Erlbaum Associates.

Eccles, D. W., & Tenenbaum, G. (2004). Why an expert team is more than a team of experts: A social-cognitive conceptualization of team coordination and communication in sport. *Journal of Sport & Exercise Psychology, 26*(4), 542–560.

Edell, J. A., & Burke, M. C. (1986). The relative impact of prior brand attitude and attitude toward the ad on brand attitude after ad exposure. In J. C. Olson & K. Sentis (Eds.), *Advertising and consumer psychology* (Vol. 3, pp. 93–107). New York: Praeger.

Eden, D., & Leviatan, U. (1975). Implicit leadership theory as a determinant of the factor structure underlying supervisory behavior scales. *Journal of Applied Psychology, 60*(6), 736–741.

Edinger, J. A., & Patterson, M. L. (1983). Nonverbal involvement and social control. *Psychological Bulletin, 93*(1), 30–56.

Edwards, K., & Bryan, T. S. (1997). Judgmental biases produced by instructions to disregard: The (paradoxical) case of emotional information. *Personality and Social Psychology Bulletin, 23*(8), 849–864.

Edwards, W., & Newman, J. R. (1986). Multiattribute evaluation. In H. R. Arkes & K. R. Hammond (Eds.), *Judgment and decision making: An interdisciplinary reader* (pp. 13–37). New York: Cambridge University Press.

Egan, G. J., Brown, R. T., Goonan, L., Goonan, B. T., & Celano, M. (1998). The development of decoding of emotions in children with externalizing behavioral disturbances and their normally developing peers. *Archives of Clinical Neuropsychology, 13*(4), 383–396.

Eger, E., Jedynak, A., Iwaki, T., & Skrandies, W. (2003). Rapid extraction of emotional expression: Evidence from evoked potential fields during brief presentation of face stimuli. *Neuropsychologia, 41*(7), 808–817.

Ehrlich, K., & Rayner, K. (1983). Pronoun assignment and semantic integration during reading: Eye movements and immediacy of processing. *Journal of Verbal Learning & Verbal Behavior, 22*(1), 75–87.

Ehrlich, S. F., & Rayner, K. (1981). Contextual effects on word perception and eye movements during reading. *Journal of Verbal Learning and Verbal Behavior, 20*(6), 641–655.

Eibl-Eibesfeldt, I. (1989). *Human ethology (foundations of human behavior).* Hawthorne, NY: Aldine de Gruyter.

Eils, L. C., & John, R. S. (1980). A criterion validation of multiattribute utility analysis and of group communication strategy. *Organizational Behavior & Human Performance, 25*(2), 268–288.

Einhorn, H. J. (1972). Expert measurement and mechanical combination. *Organizational Behavior & Human Performance, 7*(1), 86–106.

Einhorn, H. J., & Hogarth, R. M. (1981). Behavioral decision theory: Processes of judgment and choice. *Annual Review of Psychology, 32*, 53–88.

Eisen, S. V., & McArthur, L. Z. (1979). Evaluating and sentencing a defendant as a function of his salience and the perceiver's set. *Personality and Social Psychology Bulletin, 5*(1), 48–52.

Eisenberg, N., Fabes, R. A., Miller, P. A., Fultz, J., Shell, R., Mathy, R. M., & Reno, R. R. (1989). Relation of sympathy and distress to prosocial behavior: A multi-method study. *Journal of Personality and Social Psychology, 57*(1), 55–66.

Ekman, P. (1971). Universals and cultural differences in facial expressions of emotion. In J. K. Cole (Ed.), *Nebraska symposium on motivation* (pp. 207–283). Lincoln, NE: University of Nebraska Press.

Ekman, P. (1973). Cross-cultural studies of facial expression. In P. Ekman (Ed.), *Darwin and facial expression: A century of research in review* (pp. 169–222). New York: Academic Press.

Ekman, P. (1982). *Emotion in the human face* (2nd ed.). Cambridge, UK: Cambridge University Press.

Ekman, P., & Friesen, W. V. (1978). *Facial action coding system: A technique for the measurement of facial movement.* Palo Alto, CA: Consulting Psychologists Press.

Ekman, P., Friesen, W. V., O'Sullivan, M., Chan, A., Diacoyanni-Tarlatzis, I., Heider, K., Krause, R., LeCompte, W. A., Pitcairn, T., Ricci-Bitti, P. E., Scherer, K., Tomita, M., & Tzavaras, A. (1987). Universals and cultural differences in the judgments of facial expressions of emotion. *Journal of Personality and Social Psychology, 53*(4), 712–717.

Ellsworth, P. C. (1994). Levels of thought and levels of emotion. In P. Ekman & R. J. Davidson (Eds.), *The nature of emotion: Fundamental questions* (pp. 192–196). New York: Oxford University Press.

Ellsworth, P. C., & Scherer, K. R. (2003). Appraisal processes in emotion. In R. J. Davidson, K. R. Scherer, & H. H. Goldsmith (Eds.), *Handbook of affective sciences* (pp. 572–595). New York: Oxford University Press.

Ellsworth, P. C., & Smith, C. A. (1988). From appraisal to emotion: Differences among unpleasant feelings. *Motivation and Emotion, 12*(3), 271–302.

Elstein, A. S., Shulman, A. S., & Sprafka, S. A. (1978). *Medical problem solving: An analysis of clinical reasoning.* Cambridge, MA: Harvard University Press.

Emrich, C. G. (1999). Context effects in leadership perception. *Personality and Social Psychology Bulletin, 25*(8), 991–1006.

Emrich, C. G., Brower, H. H., Feldman, J. M., & Garland, H. (2001). Images in words: Presidential rhetoric, charisma, and greatness. *Administrative Science Quarterly, 46,* 527–557.

Endsley, M. R. (2006). Expertise and situation awareness. In K. A. Ericsson, N. Charness, P. Feltovich, & R. Hoffman (Eds.), *The Cambridge handbook of expertise and expert performance* (pp. 633–651). Cambridge, UK: Cambridge University Press.

Englis, B. G. (1989). The structure of self-reported emotional reactions to television advertising. Unpublished manuscript.

Englis, B. G. (1990). Consumer emotional reactions to television advertising and their effects on message recall. In S. J. Agres, J. A. Edell, & T. M. Dubitsky (Eds.), *Emotion in advertising: Theoretical and practical explorations* (pp. 231–253). New York: Quorum Books.

Englis, B. G. (1994). The role of affect in political advertising: Voter emotional responses to the nonverbal behavior of politicians. In E. M. Clark, T. C. Brock, & D. W. Stewart (Eds.), *Attention, attitude, and affect in response to advertising* (pp. 223–247). Hillsdale, NJ: Lawrence Erlbaum Associates.

Englis, B. G., & Reid, D. (1990). Salesperson expressions of emotions influence personal selling outcomes. In *Proceedings of the Society for Consumer Psychology,* 79–83.

Engstrom, E. (1994). Effects of nonfluencies on speaker's credibility in newscast settings. *Perceptual and Motor Skills, 78*(3, Pt. 1), 739–743.

Epitropaki, O., & Martin, R. (2004). Implicit leadership theories in applied settings: Factor structure, generalizability, and stability over time. *Journal of Applied Psychology, 89*(2), 293–310.

Epley, N., & Dunning, D. (2000). Feeling "holier than thou": Are self-serving assessments produced by errors in self-or social prediction? *Journal of Personality and Social Psychology, 79*(6), 861–875.

Epley, N., & Dunning, D. (2004). The mixed blessing of self-knowledge in behavioral prediction. Unpublished manuscript. Cornell University.

Erber, R., & Fiske, S. T. (1984). Outcome dependency and attention to inconsistent information. *Journal of Personality and Social Psychology, 47*(4), 709–726.

Erev, I., & Cohen, B. L. (1990). Verbal versus numerical probabilities: Efficiency, biases, and the preference paradox. *Organizational Behavior and Human Decision Processes, 45*(1), 1–18.

Erickson, B., Lind, E. A., Johnson, B. C., & O'Barr, W. M. (1978). Speech style and impression formation in a court setting: The effects of "powerful" and "powerless" speech. *Journal of Experimental Social Psychology, 14*(3), 266–279.

Ericsson, K. A. (2001). Protocol analysis in psychology. In N. Smelser & P. Baltes (Eds.), *International encyclopedia of the social and behavioral sciences* (pp. 12256–12262). Oxford, UK: Elsevier.

Ericsson, K. A. (2006). Protocol analysis and expert thought: Concurrent verbalizations of thinking during experts' performance on representative tasks. In K. A. Ericsson, N. Charness, P. Feltovich, & R. Hoffman (Eds.), *The Cambridge handbook of expertise and expert performance* (pp. 223–241). Cambridge, UK: Cambridge University Press.

Ericsson, K. A., & Lehmann, A. C. (1996). Expert and exceptional performance: Evidence on maximal adaptations on task constraints. *Annual Review of Psychology, 47,* 273–305.

Ericsson, K. A., & Simon, H. A. (1993). *Protocol analysis: Verbal reports as data* (revised edition). Cambridge, MA: Bradford Books/MIT Press.

Eslinger, P. J., & Damasio, A. R. (1985). Severe disturbance of higher cognition after bilateral frontal lobe ablation: Patient EVR. *Neurology, 35*(12), 1731–1741.

Espinosa, J. A., & Carley, K. M. (2001). *Measuring Team Mental Models.* Paper presented at the Academy of Management Conference Organizational Communication and Information Systems Division, Washington, DC.

Esteves, F., Dimberg, U., & Öhman, A. (1994). Automatically elicited fear: Conditioned skin conductance responses to masked facial expressions. *Cognition & Emotion, 8*(5), 393–413.

Estrada, C. A., Isen, A. M., & Young, M. J. (1997). Positive affect facilitates integration of information and decreases anchoring in reasoning among physicians. *Organizational Behavior and Human Decision Processes, 72*(1), 117–135.

Etzioni, A. (1992). Normative-affective factors: Toward a new decision-making model. In M. Zey (Ed.), *Decision making: Alternatives to rational choice models* (pp. 89–111). Thousand Oaks, CA: Sage.

Evans, R., Rozelle, R., Lasater, T., Dembroski, T., & Allen, B. (1970). Fear arousal, persuasion and actual vs. implied behavioral change. *Journal of Personality and Social Psychology, 16*(2), 220–227.

Fabrizio, R., Kaplan, L., & Teal, G. (1967). Readability as a function of the straightness of right-hand margins. *Journal of Typographic Research, 1*, 90–95.

Fader, P. S., & Lattin, J. M. (1993). Accounting for heterogeneity and nonstationarity in a cross-sectional model of consumer purchase behavior. *Marketing Science, 12*(3), 304–317.

Fanelli, A., Misangyi, V. F., & Tosi, H. L. (2009). In charisma we trust: The effects of CEO charismatic visions on securities analysts. *Organization Science, 20*(6), 1011–1033.

Fazio, R. H. (1989). On the power and functionality of attitudes: The role of attitude accessibility. In A. R. Pratkanis, S. J. Breckler, & A. G. Greenwald (Eds.), *Attitude structure and function* (pp. 153–179). Hillsdale, NJ: Lawrence Erlbaum Associates.

Fehr, B. J., & Exline, R. V. (1987). Social visual interaction: A conceptual and literature review. In A. W. Siegman & S. Feldstein (Eds.), *Nonverbal behavior and communication* (2nd ed., pp. 225–325). Hillsdale, NJ: Lawrence Erlbaum Associates.

Feingold, A. (1992). Good-looking people are not what we think. *Psychological Bulletin, 111*(2), 304–341.

Feldman, C., & Kalmar, D. (1996). Autobiography and fiction as modes of thought. In D. Olson & N. Torrance (Eds.), *Modes of thought: Explorations in culture and cognition* (pp. 106–122). Cambridge, UK: Cambridge University Press.

Feldman, M. S., & March, J. G. (1981). Information in organizations as signal and symbol. *Administrative Science Quarterly, 26*(2), 171–186.

Felker, D. B., Redish, J. C., & Peterson, J. (1985). Training authors of informative documents. In T. Duffy and R. Walker (Eds.), *Designing usable texts* (pp. 43–61). New York: Academic Press.

Felsenfeld, C. (1991). The plain English experience in New York. In E. R. Steinberg (Ed.), *Plain language: Principles and practice* (pp. 13–18). Detroit, MI: Wayne State University Press.

Felsenfeld, C., & Siegel, A. (1981). *Writing contracts in plain English.* St. Paul, MN: West Publishing Co.

Feltovich, P. J., Prietula, M. J., & Ericsson, K. A. (2006). Studies of expertise from psychological perspectives. In K. A. Ericsson, N. Charness, P. J. Feltovich, & R. Hoffman (Eds.), *The Cambridge handbook of expertise and expert performance* (pp. 41–67). Cambridge, UK: Cambridge University Press.

Fiedler, K. (1982). Causal schemata: Review and criticism of research on a popular construct. *Journal of Personality and Social Psychology, 42*, 1001–1013.

Fiedler, K. (2000). Toward an integrative account of affect and cognition phenomena using the BIAS computer algorithm. In J. P. Forgas (Ed.), *Feeling and thinking: The role of affect in social cognition* (pp. 223–252). New York: Cambridge University Press.

Fiedler, K., & Schenck, W. (2001). Spontaneous inferences from pictorially presented behaviors. *Personality and Social Psychological Bulletin, 27*, 1533–1546.

Fielding, G., & Evered, C. (1978). An exploratory experimental study of the influence of patients' social background upon diagnostic process and outcome. *Psychiatria Clinica, 11*(2), 61–86.

Fielding, K. S., & Hogg, M. A. (1997). Social identity, self-categorization, and leadership: A field study of small interactive groups. *Group Dynamics: Theory, Research, and Practice, 1*, 39–51.

Fienberg, S. E. (1979). Graphical methods in statistics. *The American Statistician, 33*, 165–178.

Fillmore, C. J. (1968). The case for case. In E. Bach & R. T. Harms (Eds.), *Universals of linguistic theory* (pp. 1–88). New York: Holt, Rinehart, and Winston.

Findahl, O. (1971). *The effects of visual illustrations upon perception and retention of news programmes.* Stockholm, Sweden: Swedish Broadcasting Corporation, Audience and Program Research Department.

Findahl, O., & Hoijer, B. (1976). *Fragments of reality: An experiment with news and TV visuals.* Stockholm, Sweden: Swedish Broadcasting Corporation, Audience and Program Research Department.

Finucane, M. L., Alhakami, A., Slovic, P., & Johnson, S. M. (2000). The affect heuristic in judgments of risks and benefits. *Journal of Behavioral Decision Making, 13*(1), 1–17.

Finucane, M. L., Peters, E., & Slovic, P. (2003). Judgment and decision making: The dance of affect and reason. In S. L. Schneider & J. Shanteau (Eds.), *Emerging perspectives on judgment and decision research* (pp. 327–364). New York: Cambridge University Press.

Fischhoff, B., & Johnson, S. (1997). The possibility of distributed decision making. In Z. Shapira (Ed.), *Organizational decision making* (pp. 217–237). New York: Cambridge University Press.

Fischhoff, B., & MacGregor, D. (1980). *Judged lethality.* Decision Research Report 80–4. Eugene, OR: Decision Research.

Fischhoff, B., Slovic, P., & Lichtenstein, S. (1978). Fault trees: Sensitivity of estimated failure probabilities to problem representation. *Journal of Experimental Psychology: Human Perception and Performance, 4*(2), 330–344.

Fishfader, V. L., Howells, G. N., Katz, R. C., & Teresi, P. S. (1996). Evidential and extralegal factors in juror decisions: Presentation mode, retention, and level of emotionality. *Law and Human Behavior, 20*(5), 565–572.

Fiske, S. T. (1980). Attention and weight in person perception: The impact of negative and extreme behavior. *Journal of Personality and Social Psychology, 38*(6), 889–906.

Fiske, S. T., & Depret, E. (1996). Control, interdependence and power: Understanding social cognition in its social context. In W. Stroebe & M. Hewstone (Eds.), *European Review of Social Psychology* (Vol. 7, pp. 31–61) New York: Wiley.

Fiske, S. T., & Kinder, D. R. (1981). Involvement, expertise, and schema use: Evidence from political cognition. In N. Cantor & J. Kihlstrom (Eds.), *Personality, cognition, and social interaction* (pp. 171–190). Hillsdale, NJ: Lawrence Erlbaum Associates.

Fiske, S. T., Lin, M., & Neuberg, S. L. (1999). The continuum model: Ten years later. In S. Chaiken & Y. Trope (Eds.), *Dual-process theories in social psychology* (pp. 231–254). New York: Guilford Press.

Fiske, S. T., & Neuberg, S. L. (1990). A continuum of impression formation, from category-based to individuating processes: Influences of information and motivation on attention and interpretation. In M. P. Zanna (Ed.), *Advances in experimental social psychology* (Vol. 23, pp. 1–74). New York: Academic Press.

Fiske, S. T., & Taylor, S. E. (1991). *Social cognition* (2nd ed.). New York: McGraw-Hill.

Flavell, J. H. (1979). Metacognition and cognitive monitoring: A new area of cognitive-developmental inquiry. *American Psychologist, 34*(10), 906–911.

Fleming, M. L., & Sheikhian, M. (1972). Influence of pictorial attributes on recognition memory. *AV Communication Review, 20*(4), 423–441.

Flesch, R. (1948). A new readability yardstick. *Journal of Applied Psychology, 32*(3), 221–233.

Fleshier, H., Ilardo, J., & Demoretcky, J. (1974). The influence of field dependence, speaker credibility set, and message documentation on evaluations of speaker and message credibility. *Southern Speech Communication Journal, 39*, 389–402.

Flower, L. S., & Hayes, J. R. (1978). The dynamics of composing: Making plans and juggling constraints. In L. Gregg & I. Steinberg (Eds.), *Cognitive processes in writing* (pp. 31–50). Hillsdale, NJ: Lawrence Erlbaum Associates.

Flower, L. S., Hayes, J. R., & Swarts, H. (1983). Revising functional documents: The scenario principle. In P. V. Anderson, R. J. Brockmann & C. R. Miller (Eds.), *New essays in technical and scientific communication* (pp. 41–58). New York: Baywood Press.

Fodor, J. A., Bever, T. G., & Garrett, M. F. (1974). *The psychology of language: An introduction to psycholinguistics and generative grammar.* New York: McGraw-Hill.

Fong, G. T., & Markus, H. (1982). Self-schemas and judgments about others. *Social Cognition, 1*(3), 191–204.

Forbes, R. J., & Jackson, P. R. (1980). Non-verbal behaviour and the outcome of selection interviews. *Journal of Occupational Psychology, 53*(1), 65–72.

Forgas, J. P. (1992). On mood and peculiar people: Affect and person typicality in impression formation. *Journal of Personality and Social Psychology, 62*(5), 863–875.

Forgas, J. P. (1995). Mood and judgment: The affect infusion model (AIM). *Psychological Bulletin, 117*(1), 39–66.

Forgas, J. P. (1998). Asking nicely? The effects of mood on responding to more or less polite requests. *Personality and Social Psychology Bulletin, 24*(2), 173–185.

Forgas, J. P., & Bower, G. H. (1987). Mood effects on person-perception judgments. *Journal of Personality and Social Psychology, 53*(1), 53–60.

Foss, D. J., & Jenkins, C. M. (1973). Some effects of context on the comprehension of ambiguous sentences. *Journal of Verbal Learning & Verbal Behavior, 12*(5), 577–589.

Foster, J. J., & Bruce, M. (1982). Reading upper and lower case on Viewdata. *Applied Ergonomics, 13*(2), 145–149.

Foster, J. J., & Coles, P. (1977). An experimental study of typographic cueing in printed text. *Ergonomics, 20*(1), 57–66.

Foti, R. J., Fraser, S. L., & Lord, R. G. (1982). Effects of leadership labels and prototypes on perceptions of political leaders. *Journal of Applied Psychology, 67*(3), 326–333.

Frame, C. D. (1990). Salesperson impression formation accuracy: A person-perception approach (Doctoral dissertation, Indiana University, 1990). *Dissertation Abstracts International, 51* (12A), 4199.

Frank, L. L., & Hackman, J. R. (1975). Effects of interviewer-interviewee similarity on interviewer objectivity in college admissions interviews. *Journal of Applied Psychology, 60*(3), 356–360.

Frase, L. T., & Fisher, D. (1976). *Rating technical documents,* Case 25952, Memorandum for File. Piscataway, NJ: Bell Laboratories.

Fraser, S. L., & Lord, R. G. (1988). Stimulus prototypicality and general leadership impressions: Their role in leadership and behavioral ratings. *Journal of Psychology: Interdisciplinary and Applied, 122*(3), 291–303.

Frazier, L., & Rayner, K. (1982). Making and correcting errors during sentence comprehension: Eye movements in the analysis of structurally ambiguous sentences. *Cognitive Psychology, 14*(2), 178–121.

Frazier, L., Taft, L., Roeper, T., Clifton, C., & Ehrlich, K. (1984). Parallel structure: A source of facilitation in sentence comprehension. *Memory & Cognition, 12*(5), 421–430.

Frederick, S. (2002). Automated choice heuristics. In T. Gilovich, D. Griffin, & D. Kahneman (Eds.), *Heuristics and biases: The psychology of intuitive judgment* (pp. 548–558). New York: Cambridge University Press.

Fredin, E. S. (2001). Frame breaking and creativity: A frame database for hypermedia news. In S. D. Reese, O. H. Gandy, & A. E. Grant (Eds.), *Framing public life: Perspectives on media and our understanding of the social world* (pp. 269–293). Mahwah, NJ: Lawrence Erlbaum Associates.

Fredin, E. S., Kosicki, G. M., & Becker, L. B. (1996). Cognitive strategies for media use during a presidential campaign. *Political Communication, 13,* 23–42.

Fredrickson, B. L., & Levenson, R. W. (1998). Positive emotions speed recovery from the cardiovascular sequelae of negative emotions. *Cognition & Emotion, 12*(2), 191–220.

Fredrickson, J. W. (1985). Effects of decision motive and organizational performance level on strategic decision processes. *Academy of Management Journal, 28*(4), 821–843.

Frensch, P. A., & Sternberg, R. J. (1989). Expertise and intelligent thinking: When is it worse to know better? In R. J. Sternberg (Ed.), *Advances in the psychology of human intelligence* (Vol. 5, pp. 157–188). Hillsdale, NJ: Lawrence Erlbaum Associates.

Frick, R. W. (1985). Communicating emotion: The role of prosodic features. *Psychological Bulletin, 97*(3), 412–429.

Fridlund, A. J., Ekman, P., & Oster, H. (1987). Facial expressions of emotion. In A. W. Siegman & S. Feldstein (Eds.), *Nonverbal behavior and communication* (2nd ed., pp. 143–223). Hillsdale, NJ: Lawrence Erlbaum Associates.

Friedman, H. S., DiMatteo, M. R., & Mertz, T. I. (1980a). Nonverbal communication on television news: The facial expressions of broadcasters during coverage of a presidential election campaign. *Personality and Social Psychology Bulletin, 6*(3), 427–435.

Friedman, H.S., DiMatteo, M.R., & Taranta, A. (1980b). A study of the relationship between individual differences in nonverbal expressiveness and factors of personality and social interaction. *Journal of Research in Personality, 14*, 351–364.

Friedman, K. (1988). The effect of adding symbols to written warning labels on user behavior and recall. *Human Factors, 30*, 507–515.

Frijda, N. H. (1986). *The emotions.* New York: Cambridge University Press.

Frijda, N. H. (1988). The laws of emotion. *American Psychologist, 43*(5), 349–358.

Frijda, N. H., & Mesquita, B. (1994). The social roles and functions of emotions. In S. Kitayama & H. R. Markus (Eds.), *Emotion and culture: Empirical studies of mutual influence* (pp. 51–87). Washington, DC: American Psychological Association.

Frishkoff, P., Frishkoff, P. A., & Bouwman, M. J. (1984). Use of accounting data in screening by financial analysts. *Journal of Accounting, Auditing & Finance, 8*(1), 44–54.

Funder, D. C., & Colvin, C. R. (1991). Explorations in behavioral consistency: Properties of persons, situations, and behaviors. *Journal of Personality and Social Psychology, 60*(5), 773–794.

Funder, D. C., & Sneed, C. D. (1993). Behavioral manifestations of personality: An ecological approach to judgmental accuracy. *Journal of Personality and Social Psychology, 64*(3), 479–490.

Futrell, C. M., Swan, J. S., & Todd, J. T. (1976). Job performance related to management control systems for pharmaceutical salesmen. *Journal of Marketing Research, 13*, 25–33.

Gaertner, S., & Bickman, L. (1971). Effects of race on the elicitation of helping behavior: The wrong number technique. *Journal of Personality and Social Psychology, 20*(2), 218–222.

Gaeth, G. J., & Shanteau, J. (1984). Reducing the influence of irrelevant information on experienced decision makers. *Organizational Behavior & Human Performance, 33*(2), 263–282.

Galletta, D., King, R. C., & Rateb, D. (1993). The effect of expertise on software selection. *Association for Computing Machinery, 24*(2), 7–20.

Gallhofer, I. N., & Saris, W. E. (1996). *Foreign policy decision-making: A qualitative and quantitative analysis of policy argumentation.* Westport, CT: Praeger.

Gamson, W. A. (1992). *Talking politics.* New York: Cambridge University Press.

Gamson, W. A., & Modigliani, A. (1989). Media discourse and public opinion on nuclear power: A constructionist approach. *American Journal of Sociology, 95*(1), 1–37.

Garay, M. S. (1988). Writers making points: A case study of executives and college students revising their own reports (Doctoral dissertation, Carnegie Mellon University, 1988). *Dissertation Abstracts International, 49* (12A), 3645.

Garbarino, E. C., & Edell, J. A. (1997). Cognitive effort, affect, and choice. *Journal of Consumer Research, 24*(2),147–158.

Garcia-Marques, T., & Mackie, D. M. (2000). The positive feeling of familiarity: Mood as an information processing regulation mechanism. In H. Bless & J. Forgas (Eds.), *The Message within: The role of subjective experience in social cognition and behavior* (pp. 240–261). Philadelphia: Psychology Press.

Gardner, E. T., & Schumacher, G. M. (1977). Effects of contextual organization on prose retention. *Journal of Educational Psychology, 69*(2), 146–151.

Gardner, M. P. (1981). An information processing approach to examining advertising effects (Doctoral dissertation, Carnegie Mellon University, 1981). *Dissertation Abstracts International, 43* (05A), 1662.

Gardner, M. P., Mitchell, A. A., & Russo, J. E. (1985). Low involvement strategies for processing advertisements. *Journal of Advertising, 14*(2), 4–13.

Garrod, S., Freudenthal, S., & Boyle, E. (1994). The role of different types of anaphor in the on-line resolution of sentences in a discourse. *Journal of Memory and Language, 33*(1), 39–68.

Gattis, M., & Holyoak, K. J. (1996). Mapping conceptual to spatial relations in visual reasoning. *Journal of Experimental Psychology: Learning, Memory, and Cognition, 22*(1), 231–239.

Gault, B. A., & Sabini, J. (2000). The roles of empathy, anger, and gender in predicting attitudes toward punitive, reparative, and preventative public policies. *Cognition & Emotion Special Issue: Emotion, Cognition, and Decision Making, 14*(4), 495–520.

Gautier, V., O'Regan, J. K., & LaGargasson, I. F. (2000). "The skipping" revisited in French programming saccades to skip the article "les." *Vision Research, 40*, 2517–2531.

Gentner, D., & Forbus, K. D. (1991). MAC/FAC: A model of similarity-based access and mapping. In K. J. Hammond & D. Gentner (Eds.), *Proceedings of the thirteenth annual conference of the Cognitive Science Society* (pp. 504–509). Hillsdale, NJ: Erlbaum.

George, J. M. (1989). Mood and absence. *Journal of Applied Psychology, 74*(2), 317–324.

George, J. M. (1990). Personality, affect, and behavior in groups. *Journal of Applied Psychology, 75*(2), 107–116.

George, J. M., & Brief, A. P. (1992). Feeling good-doing good: A conceptual analysis of the mood at work-organizational spontaneity relationship. *Psychological Bulletin, 112*(2), 310–329.

Ger, G. (1989). Nature of effects of affect on judgment: Theoretical and methodological issues. In P. Cafferata & A. M. Tybout (Eds.), *Cognitive and affective responses to advertising* (pp. 263–275). Lexington, MA: Lexington Books.

Ghanem, S. (1997). Filling in the tapestry: The second level of agenda setting. In M. McCombs, D. L Shaw, & D. Weaver (Eds.), *Communication and democracy* (pp. 3–15). Mahwah, NJ: Lawrence Erlbaum Associates.

Ghiselli, E. E. (1969). Prediction of success of stockbrokers. *Personnel Psychology, 22*(2), 25–130.

Ghiselli, E. E. (1973). The validity of aptitude tests in personnel selection. *Personnel Psychology, 26*(4), 461–477.

Gibbs, R. W., Jr., Leggitt, J. S., & Turner, E. A. (2002). What's special about figurative language in emotional communication?. In S. R. Fussell (Ed.), *The verbal communication of emotions: Interdisciplinary perspectives* (pp. 125–149). Mahwah, NJ: Lawrence Erlbaum Associates.

Gibbs, W. J., and Bernas, R. S. (2009) Visual attention in newspaper versus TV-oriented news websites, *Journal of Usability Studies, 4*(4), 147–165.

Gibson, C. B. (2001). From knowledge accumulation to accommodation: cycles of collective cognition in work groups. *Journal of Organizational Behavior, 22*(2), 121–134.

Gibson, E. J., Bishop, C., Schiff, W., & Smith, J. (1964). Comparison of meaningfulness and pronounceability as grouping principles in the perception and retention of verbal material. *Journal of Experimental Psychology, 67*(2), 173–182.

Gibson, R., & Zillmann, D. (1994). Exaggerated versus representative exemplification in news reports: Perception of issues and personal consequences. *Communication Research, 21*(5), 603–624.

Gick, M. L., & Holyoak, K. J. (1983). Schema induction and analogical transfer. *Cognitive Psychology, 15*(1), 1–38.

Gifford, R. (1991). Mapping non-verbal behavior on the interpersonal circle. *Journal of Personality and Social Psychology, 61*(2), 279–288.

Gifford, R., & Hine, D. W. (1994). The role of verbal behavior in the encoding and decoding of interpersonal dispositions. *Journal of Research in Personality, 28*(2), 115–132.

Gifford, R., Ng, C. F., & Wilkinson, M. (1985). Nonverbal cues in the employment interview: Links between applicant qualities and interviewer judgments. *Journal of Applied Psychology, 70*(4), 729–736.

Gigerenzer, G., & Goldstein, D. G. (1996). Reasoning the fast and frugal way: Models of bounded rationality. *Psychological Review, 103*(4), 650–669.

Gigone, D., & Hastie, R. (1993). The common knowledge effect: Information sharing and group judgment. *Journal of Personality and Social Psychology, 65*(5), 959–974.

Gigone, D., & Hastie, R. (1996). The impact of information on group judgment: A model and computer simulation. In E. H. Witte & J. H. Davis (Eds.), *Understanding group behavior, Vol. 1: Consensual action by small groups* (pp. 221–251). Hillsdale, NJ: Lawrence Erlbaum.

Gilbert, D. T. (1989). Thinking lightly about others: Automatic components of the social inference process. In J. S. Uleman & J. A. Bargh (Eds.), *Unintended thought* (pp. 189–211). New York: Guilford Press.

Gilbert, D. T. (2002). Inferential correction. In T. Gilovich, D. Griffin, & D. Kahneman (Eds.), *Heuristics and biases: The psychology of intuitive judgment* (pp. 167–184). New York: Cambridge University Press.

Gilbert, D. T., Krull, D. S., & Malone, P. S. (1990). Unbelieving the unbelievable: Some problems in the rejection of false information. *Journal of Personality and Social Psychology, 59*(4), 601–613.

Gilbert, D. T., Pelham, B. W., & Krull, D. S. (1988). On cognitive busyness: When person perceivers meet persons perceived. *Journal of Personality and Social Psychology, 54*(5), 733–740.

Gilens, M. (1999). *Why Americans hate welfare: Race, media, and the politics of antipoverty policy.* Chicago: University of Chicago Press.

Giles, H. (1973). Communicative effectiveness as a function of accented speech. *Speech Monographs, 40*(4), 330–331.

Giles, H. (1979). Ethnicity markers in speech. In K. R. Scherer & H. Giles (Eds.), *Social markers in speech* (pp. 251–289). Cambridge, UK: Cambridge University Press.

Giles, H., & Niedzielski, N. (1998) German sounds awful, but Italian is beautiful. In L. Bauer & P. Trudgill (Eds.), *Language myths* (pp. 85–93). Harmondsworth, UK: Penguin.

Giles, H., & Sassoon, C. (1983). The effect of speaker's accent, social class background and message style on British listeners' social judgements. *Language & Communication, 3*(3), 305–313.

Gill, M. J., Swann, W. B., & Silvera, D. H. (1998). On the genesis of confidence. *Journal of Personality and Social Psychology, 75*(5), 1101–1114.

Gilovich, T. (1981). Seeing the past in the present: The effect of associations to familiar events on judgments and decisions. *Journal of Personality and Social Psychology, 40*(5), 797–808.

Gilovich, T., Kerr, M., & Medvec, V. H. (1993). The effect of temporal perspective on subjective confidence. *Journal of Personality and Social Psychology, 64*, 552–560.

Gitlin, T. (1980). *The whole world is watching.* Berkeley, CA: University of California Press.

Glad, B., & Taber, C. S. (1990). Images, learning, and the decision to use force: The domino theory of the United States. In B. Glad (Ed.), *Psychological dimensions of war* (pp. 56–81). Thousand Oaks, CA: Sage.

Glaser, R., & Chi, M. T. H. (1988). Overview. In M. T. H. Chi, R. Glaser, & M. J. Farr (Eds.), *The nature of expertise* (pp. xv–xxviii). Hillsdale, NJ: Erlbaum.

Glass, A. L., Eddy, J. K., & Schwanenflugel, P. J. (1980). The verification of high and low imagery sentences. *Journal of Experimental Psychology: Human Learning and Memory, 6*(6), 692–704.

Gleitman, L. R., & Gleitman, H. (1970). *Phrase and paraphrase: Some innovative uses of language.* New York: W. W. Norton & Company.

Glenberg, A. M., & Langston, W. E. (1992). Comprehension of illustrated text: Pictures help to build mental models. *Journal of Memory and Language, 31*(2), 129–151.

Glucksberg, S., & Cowen, G. N., Jr. (1970). Memory for nonattended auditory material. *Cognitive Psychology, 1*(2), 149–156.

Glucksberg, S., Trabasso, T., & Wald, J. (1973). Linguistic structures and mental operations. *Cognitive Psychology, 5*(3), 338–370.

Glynn, S. M., Britton, B. K., & Tillman, M. H. (1985). Typographical cues in text: Management of the reader's attention. In D. H. Jonassen (Ed.), *Technology of text: Principles for structuring, designing, and displaying text* (Vol. 2, pp. 192–209). Englewood Cliffs, NJ: Educational Technology Publications.

Glynn, S. M., & Di Vesta, F. J. (1979). Control of prose processing via instructional and typographical cues. *Journal of Educational Psychology, 71*(5), 595–603.

Goetz, E. T., & Armbruster, B. B. (1980). Psychological correlates of text structure. In R. J. Spiro, B. C. Bruce & W. F. Brewer (Eds.), *Theoretical issues in reading comprehension: Perspectives from cognitive psychology, artificial intelligence, linguistics, and education* (pp. 201–220). Hillsdale, NJ: Erlbaum.

Goldberg, J. H., Lerner, J. S., & Tetlock, P. E. (1999). Rage and reason: The psychology of the intuitive prosecutor. *European Journal of Social Psychology, 29*(5–6), 781–795.

Goldberg, L. R. (1968). Simple models or simple processes? Some research on clinical judgments. *American Psychologist, 23*(7), 483–496.

Goldhaber, G. M., & deTurck, M. A. (1988). Effects of product warnings on adolescents in an education context. *Product Safety & Liability Reporter, 16*, 949–955.

Goldsmith, E. (1987). The analysis of illustration in theory and practice. In H. A. Houghton & D. M. Willows (Eds.), *The psychology of illustration: Instructional issues* (Vol. 2, pp. 53–85). New York: Springer-Verlag.

Goldstein, M. N. (1974). Auditory agnosia for speech ("pure word deafness"): A historical review with current implications. *Brain and Language, 1,* 195–204.

Goldstein, W. M., & Weber, E. U. (1995) Content and discontent: Indications and implications of domain specificity in preferential decision making. In J. Busemeyer, D. Medin, & R. Hastie (Eds.), *Decision-making from a cognitive perspective (the psychology of learning and motivation)* (Vol. 32 pp. 83–136). San Diego, CA: Academic Press.

Goleman, D., Boyatzis, R. E., & McKee, A. (2002). *Primal leadership: Learning to lead with emotional intelligence.* Cambridge, MA: Harvard Business School Press.

Gomez Borja, M. A. (2000). Effects of expertise and similarity of alternatives on consumer decision strategies and decision quality: A process tracing approach (Doctoral dissertation, Universidad de Castilla–La Mancha, 2000). *Dissertation Abstracts International, 62* (10A), 3479.

Goodman, J., Loftus, E. F., & Greene, E. (1990). Matters of money: Voir dire in civil cases. *Forensic Reports, 3,* 303–329.

Gordon, P. C., & Chan, D. (1995). Pronouns, passives, and discourse coherence. *Journal of Memory and Language, 34*(2), 216–231.

Gore, A., & Bush, G. W. (2000). *The first Gore–Bush presidential debate.* Retrieved November 9, 2009 from www.debates.org/pages/trans2000a.html.

Gotlib, I. H., McLachlan, A. L., & Katz, A. N. (1988). Biases in visual attention in depressed and nondepressed individuals. *Cognition & Emotion Special Issue: Information Processing and the Emotional Disorders, 2*(3), 185–200.

Gough, P. B. (1966). The verification of sentences: The effects of delay of evidence and sentence length. *Journal of Verbal Learning and Verbal Behavior, 5*(5), 492–496.

Gould, J. D., Alfaro, L., Finn, R., Haupt, B., & Minuto, A. (1987). Reading from CRT displays can be as fast as reading from paper. *Human Factors, 29*(5), 497–517.

Graf, R., & Torrey, J. W. (1966). Perception of phrase structure in written language. *Proceedings of the Annual Convention of the American Psychological Association,* 83–84.

Grafman, J. (1995). Similarities and distinctions among current models of prefrontal cortical functions. *Annals of the New York Academy of Sciences, 769,* 337–368.

Graham, J. A., Ricci-Bitti, P., & Argyle, M. (1975). A cross-cultural study of the communication of emotion by facial & gestural cues. *Journal of Human Movement Studies, 1*(2), 68–77.

Graham, J. R., & Harvey, C. R. (2001). The theory and practice of corporate finance: Evidence from the field. *Journal of Financial Economics, 60*(2, 3), 187–243.

Graonic, M. D. (1995). The effects of context and consumer knowledge on transferability of preferences (Doctoral dissertation, University of Minnesota, 1995). *Dissertation Abstracts International, 56* (07A), 2772.

Grasmick, H. G., Bursik, R. J., & Kinsey, K. A. (1991). Shame and embarrassment as deterrents to noncompliance with the law—The case of an antilittering campaign. *Environment and Behavior, 23,* 233–251.

Grass, R. C., & Wallace, W. H. (1974). Advertising communications: Print vs. TV. *Journal of Advertising Research, 14*(5), 19–23.

Graves, L. M., & Powell, G. N. (1988). An investigation of sex discrimination in recruiters' evaluations of actual applicants. *Journal of Applied Psychology, 73*(1), 20–29.

Graves, M. F., & Slater, W. H. (1986). Could textbooks be better written and would it make a difference? *American Educator, 10*(1), 36–42.

Gray, H. M., & Ambady, N. (2006). Methods for the study of nonverbal communication. In V. Manusov & M. L. Patterson (Eds.), *The SAGE handbook of nonverbal communication* (pp. 41–58). Thousand Oaks, CA: Sage.

Grayson, C., & Schwarz, N. (1999). Beliefs influence information processing strategies: Declarative and experiential information in risk assessment. *Social Cognition, 17*(1), 1–18.

Green, P. E., & Srinivasan, V. (1978). Conjoint analysis in consumer research: Issues and outlook. *Journal of Consumer Research, 5*(2), 103–123.

Greenberg, J., Williams, K. D., & O'Brien, M. K. (1986). Considering the harshest verdict first: Biasing effects on mock juror verdicts. *Personality and Social Psychology Bulletin, 12*(1), 41–50.

Greene M. C. L., & Mathieson L. (1989). *The voice and its disorders*. London: Whurr.

Greeno, J. G., & Noreen, D. L. (1974). Time to read semantically related sentences. *Memory & Cognition, 2*(1-A), 117–120.

Gregan-Paxton, J., & Cote, J. (2000). How do investors make predictions? Insights from analogical reasoning research. *Journal of Behavioral Decision Making, 13*(3), 307–327.

Gregan-Paxton, J., & Roedder, J. D. (1997). Consumer learning by analogy: A model of internal knowledge transfer. *Journal of Consumer Research, 24*(3), 266–284.

Gregory, W. L., Cialdini, R. B., & Carpenter, K. M. (1982). Self-relevant scenarios as mediators of likelihood estimates and compliance: Does imagining make it so? *Journal of Personality and Social Psychology, 43*(1), 89–99.

Greitemeyer, T., & Schulz-Hardt, S. (2003). Preference-consistent evaluation of information in the hidden profile paradigm: Beyond group-level explanations for the dominance of shared information in group decisions. *Journal of Personality and Social Psychology, 84*(2), 322–339.

Greitemeyer, T., Schulz-Hardt, S., Brodbeck, F. C., & Frey, D. (2006). Information sampling and group decision making: The effects of an advocacy decision procedure and task experience. *Journal of Experimental Psychology: Applied, 12*(1), 31–42.

Griffin, D., & Tversky, A. (1992). The weighing of evidence and the determinants of confidence. *Cognitive Psychology, 24*(3), 411–435.

Griffit, W., & Veitch, R. (1971). Hot and crowded: Influence of population density and temperature on interpersonal affective behavior. *Journal of Personality and Social Psychology, 17*(1), 92–98.

Griner, L. A., & Smith, C. A. (2000). Contributions of motivational orientation to appraisal and emotion. *Personality and Social Psychology Bulletin, 26*(6), 727–740.

Gruenfeld, D. H., & Wyer, R. S. (1992). Semantics and pragmatics of social influence: How affirmations and denials affect beliefs in referent propositions. *Journal of Personality and Social Psychology, 62*(1), 38–49.

Grunert, K. G., & Bech-Larsen, T. (2005). Explaining choice option attractiveness by beliefs elicited by the laddering method. *Journal of Economic Psychology, 26*(2), 223–241.

Guidagni, P. M., & Little, J. D. C. (1983). A logit model of brand choice calibrated on scanner data. *Marketing Science, 2*, 203–238.

Gullberg, M., & Holmqvist, K. (1999). Keeping an eye on gestures: Visual perception of gestures in face-to-face communication. *Pragmatics & Cognition, 7*(1), 35–63.

Gullberg, M., & Holmqvist, K. (2006). What speakers do and what addressees look at: Visual attention to gestures in human interaction live and on video. *Pragmatics & Cognition, 14*(1), 53–82.

Gunderson, E. A. W. (1991). Expertise in security valuation: Operationalizing the valuation process (Doctoral dissertation, The Union Institute, 1991). *Dissertation Abstracts International, 52* (02A), 0592.

Gunning, R. (1964). *How to take the fog out of writing*. Chicago: Dartnell.

Gunter, B. (1987). *Poor reception: Misunderstanding and forgetting broadcast news*. Hillsdale, NJ: Lawrence Erlbaum Associates.

Guthrie, C., Rachlinski, J. J., & Wistrich, A. J. (2001). Inside the judicial mind. *Cornell Law Review, 86*, 777–830.

Gutwin, C., & Greenberg, S. (2004). The importance of awareness for team cognition in distributed collaboration. In E. Salas & S. M. Fiore (Eds.), *Team cognition: Understanding the factors that drive process and performance* (pp. 177–201). Washington, DC: American Psychological Association.

Guy, G. R., & Vonwiller, J. (1984). The meaning of an intonation in Australian English. *Australian Journal of Linguistics, 4*(1), 1–17.

Hackman, J. R. (1987). The design of work teams. In J. Lorsch (Ed.), *Handbook of organizational behavior* (pp. 315–342). Englewood Cliffs, NJ: Prentice-Hall.

Haddock, G. (2002). It's easy to like or dislike Tony Blair: Accessibility experiences and the favourability of attitude judgments. *British Journal of Psychology, 93*(2), 257–267.

Hahn, R. W., & Clayton, S. D. (1996). The effects of attorney presentation style, attorney gender, and juror gender on juror decisions. *Law and Human Behavior, 20*(5), 533–554.

Haines, G. H. (1974). Process models of consumer decision making. In G. D. Hughes & M. L. Ray (Eds.), *Buyer/consumer information processing* (pp. 89–107). Chapel Hill, NC: University of North Carolina Press.

Hains, S. C., Hogg, M. A., & Duck, J. M. (1997). Self-categorization and leadership: Effects of group prototypicality and leader stereotypicality. *Personality and Social Psychology Bulletin, 23*(10), 1087–1099.

Hakel, M. D., Hollmann, T. D., & Dunnette, M. D. (1970). Accuracy of interviewers, certified public accountants, and students in identifying the interests of accountants. *Journal of Applied Psychology, 54*(2), 115–119.

Hakel, M. D., & Schuh, A. J. (1971). Job applicant attributes judged important across seven diverse occupations. *Personnel Psychology, 24*(1), 45–52.

Hakes, D. T., & Cairns, H. S. (1970). Sentence comprehension and relative pronouns. *Perception & Psychophysics, 8*(1), 5–8.

Halberstadt, J., & Rhodes, G. (2000). The attractiveness of nonface averages: Implications for an evolutionary explanation of the attractiveness of average faces. *Psychological Science, 11*(4), 285–289.

Haley, R. I. (1985). *Developing effective communication strategy: A benefit segmentation approach.* New York: Ronald Press.

Haley, R. I., Richardson, J., & Baldwin, B. M. (1984). The effects of nonverbal communications in television advertising. *Journal of Advertising Research, 24*(4), 11–18.

Hall, J., & Hofer, C. W. (1993). Venture capitalists' decision criteria in new venture evaluation. *Journal of Business Venturing, 8*(1), 25–42.

Hamann, S. (2001). Cognitive and neural mechanisms of emotional memory. *Trends in Cognitive Sciences, 5*(9), 394–400.

Hamill, R., Wilson, T. D., & Nisbett, R. E. (1980). Insensitivity to sample bias: Generalizing from atypical cases. *Journal of Personality and Social Psychology, 39*(4), 578–589.

Hamilton, D. L., & Zanna, M. P. (1972). Differential weighting of favorable and unfavorable attributes in impressions of personality. *Journal of Experimental Research in Personality, 6*(2–3), 204–212.

Hamilton, M. A. (1998). Message variables that mediate and moderate the effect of equivocal language on source credibility. *Journal of Language and Social Psychology, 17*(1), 109–143.

Hamilton, M. A., & Hunter, J. E. (1998). The effect of language intensity on receiver evaluations of message, source, and topic. In M. Allen & R. W. Preiss (Eds.), *Persuasion: Advances through meta-analysis* (pp. 99–138). Cresskill, NJ: Hampton.

Hamilton, M. A., & Mineo, P. J. (1998). A framework for understanding equivocation. *Journal of Language and Social Psychology, 17*(1), 3–35.

Hamm, A. O., Schupp, H. T., & Weike, A. I. (2003). Motivational organization of emotions: autonomic changes, cortical responses, and reflex modulation. In R. J. Davidson, K. R. Scherer, & H. H. Goldsmith (Eds.), *Handbook of affective sciences.* New York: Oxford University Press.

Han, Y. K., Morgan, G. A., Kotsiopulos, A., & Kang-Park, J. (1991). Impulse buying behavior of apparel purchasers. *Clothing and Textile Research Journal, 9*(3), 15–21.

Hansen, C. H., & Hansen, R. D. (1988). Finding the face in the crowd: An anger superiority effect. *Journal of Personality and Social Psychology, 54*(6), 917–924.

Hardin, W. G. (1996). An investigation into the information processing heuristics of private banking and real estate banking lenders in a commercial banking environment (Doctoral dissertation, Georgia State University, 1996). *Dissertation Abstracts International, 58* (11A), 4384.

Harkins, S. G., & Petty, R. E. (1981). Effects of source magnification of cognitive effort on attitudes: An information-processing view. *Journal of Personality and Social Psychology, 40*(3), 401–413.

Harmon-Jones, E., & Allen, J. J. B. (2001). The role of affect in the mere exposure effect: Evidence from psychophysiological and individual differences approaches. *Personality and Social Psychology Bulletin, 27*(7), 889–898.

Harris, M. M. (1989). Reconsidering the employment interview: A review of recent literature and suggestions for future research. *Personnel Psychology, 42*(4), 691–726.

Hart, A. J., & Morry, M. M. (1997). Trait inferences based on racial and behavioral cues. *Basic and Applied Social Psychology, 19*(1), 33–48.

Hartley, J. (1978). *Designing instructional text*. New York: Nichols Publishing Company.

Hartley, J., & Davies, I. (1976). Preinstructional strategies: The role of pretests, behavioral objectives, overviews, and advance organizers. *Review of Educational Research, 46*, 239–265.

Hartley, J., & Mills, R. (1973). Unjustified experiments in typographical research and instructional design. *British Journal of Educational Technology, 4*, 120–131.

Hartley, J., & Rooum, D. (1983). Sir Cyril Burt and typography: A re-evaluation. *British Journal of Psychology, 74*(2), 203–212.

Hartley, J., & Trueman, M. (1982, March). *Headings in text: Issues and data*. Paper presented at Annual Meeting of American Educational Research Association, New York.

Hartman, R. S., Doane, M. J., & Woo, C. K. (1991). Consumer rationality and the status quo. *The Quarterly Journal of Economics, 106*(1), 141–162.

Harvey, J. B. (1974). The Abilene Paradox and other Meditations on Management. *Organizational Dynamics, 3*(1), 63–80.

Hasher, L., Goldstein, D., & Toppino, T. (1977). Frequency and the conference of referential validity. *Journal of Verbal Learning & Verbal Behavior, 16*(1), 107–112.

Haste, H., & Torney-Purta, J. (1992). *The development of political understanding: A new perspective*. San Francisco: Jossey-Bass.

Hastie, R., & Kumar, P. A. (1979). Person memory: Personality traits as organizing principles in memory for behaviors. *Journal of Personality and Social Psychology, 37*(1), 25–38.

Hastie, R., Landsman, R., & Loftus, E. F. (1978). Eyewitness testimony: The dangers of guessing. *Jurimetrics Journal, 19*, 1–8.

Hatch, J. A., Hill, C. A., & Hayes, J. R. (1993). When the messenger is the message: Readers' impressions of writers. *Written Communication, 10*(4), 569–598.

Hatfield, E., Cacioppo, J. T., & Rapson, R. L. (1994). *Emotional contagion*. New York: Cambridge University Press.

Hattrup, K., & Ford, J. K. (1995). The roles of information characteristics and accountability in moderating stereotype-driven processes during social decision making. *Organizational Behavior and Human Decision Processes, 63*(1), 73–86.

Hauser, J. R., & Wernerfelt, B. (1990). An evaluation cost model of consideration sets. *Journal of Consumer Research, 16*, 393–408.

Hawkins, S. A., & Hoch, S. J. (1992). Low-involvement learning: Memory without evaluation. *Journal of Consumer Research, 19*(2), 212–225.

Hegarty, M., & Just, M. A. (1993). Constructing mental models of machines from text and diagrams. *Journal of Memory and Language, 32*(6), 717–742.

Helfrich, H. (1979). Age markers in speech. In K. R. Scherer & H. Giles (Eds.), *Social markers in speech* (pp. 63–107). Cambridge, UK: Cambridge University Press.

Helgeson, J. G., & Ursic, M. L. (1993). Information load, cost/benefit assessment and decision strategy variability. *Journal of the Academy of Marketing Science, 21*(1), 13–20.

Heller, R. F., Saltzstein, H. D., & Caspe, W. B. (1992). Heuristics in medical and non-medical decision-making. *The Quarterly Journal of Experimental Psychology A: Human Experimental Psychology, 44A*(2), 211–235.

HelmReich, R. L. (1997). Managing Human Error in Aviation. *Scientific American, 277*(5), 40.

Hendon, D. W. (1973). How mechanical factors affect ad perception. *Journal of Advertising Research, 13*(4), 39–46.

Henley, N. M. (1995). Body politics revisited: What do we know today? In P. J. Kalbfleisch & M. J. Cody (Eds.), *Gender, power, and communication in human relationships* (pp. 27–61). Hillsdale, NJ: Lawrence Erlbaum Associates.

Hensley, W. E. (1981). The effects of attire, location, and sex on aiding behavior: A similarity explanation. *Journal of Nonverbal Behavior, 6*, 3–11.

Hermann, C. F., Geva, N., & Bragg, B. (2001, July). *Group dynamics in conflict management strategies: An experimental analysis of the effects on foreign policy decision making*. Hong Kong: Hong Kong Convention of International Studies.

Herr, P. M. (1989). Priming price-prior knowledge and context effects. *Journal of Consumer Research*, *16*(1), 67–75.

Herr, P. M., Kardes, F. R., & Kim, J. (1991). Effects of word-of-mouth and product-attribute information on persuasion: An accessibility-diagnosticity perspective. *Journal of Consumer Research*, *17*(4), 454–462.

Hershberger, W. A., & Terry, D. F. (1965). Typographical cuing in conventional and programed texts. *Journal of Applied Psychology*, *49*(1), 55–60.

Hershey, J. C., & Schoemaker, P. J. (1980). Prospect theory's reflection hypothesis: A critical examination. *Organizational Behavior & Human Performance*, *25*(3), 395–418.

Herstein, J. A. (1981). Keeping the voter's limits in mind: A cognitive process analysis of decision making in voting. *Journal of Personality and Social Psychology*, *40*(5), 843–861.

Hess, E. H., & Polt, J. M. (1960). Pupil size as related to interest value of visual stimuli. *Science, 132*, 349–350.

Hess, E. H., & Polt, J. M. (1964). Pupil size in relation to mental activity during simple problem-solving. *Science, 143*(3611), 1190–1192.

Hess, U., Blairy, S., & Kleck, R. E. (1997). The intensity of emotional facial expressions and decoding accuracy. *Journal of Nonverbal Behavior*, *21*(4), 241–257.

Hess, U., Kappas, A., & Scherer, K. R. (1988). Multichannel communication of emotion: Synthetic signal production. In K. R. Scherer (Ed.), *Facets of emotion: Recent research* (pp. 161–182). Hillsdale, NJ: Lawrence Erlbaum Associates.

Heuer, F., & Reisberg, D. (1990). Vivid memories of emotional events: The accuracy of remembered minutiae. *Memory & Cognition*, *18*(5), 496–506.

Heuer, L., & Penrod, S. D. (1994). Trial complexity: A field investigation of its meaning and its effect. *Law and Human Behavior*, *18*(1), 29–51.

Higgins, E. T., & Bargh, J. A. (1987). Social cognition and social perception. *Annual Review of Psychology*, *38*, 369–425.

Higgins, E. T., & King, G. (1981). Accessibility of social constructs: Information-processing consequences of individual and contextual variability. In N. Cantor & J. Kihlstrom (Eds.), *Personality, cognition, and social interaction* (pp. 69–121). Hillsdale, NJ: Lawrence Erlbaum Associates.

Higgins, E. T., & Lurie, L. (1983). Context, categorization, and recall: The "change-of-standard" effect. *Cognitive Psychology*, *15*(4), 525–547.

Higgins, E. T., & Stangor, C. A. (1988). "Change-of-standard" perspective on the relations among context, judgment, and memory. *Journal of Personality and Social Psychology*, *54*(2), 181–192.

Highhouse, S., Beadle, D., Gallo, A., & Miller, L. (1998). Get' em while they last! Effects of scarcity information in job advertisements. *Journal of Applied Social Psychology*, *28*(9), 779–795.

Highhouse, S., & Gallo, A. (1997). Order effects in personnel decision making. *Human Performance*, *10*(1), 31–46.

Highhouse, S., Stierwalt, S. L., Bachchiochi, P., Elder, A. E., & Fisher, G. (1999). Effects of advertised human resource management practices on attraction of African American applicants. *Personnel Psychology*, *52*(2), 425–442.

Hilgartner. S., & Bosk, C. L. (1988). The rise and fall of social problems: A public arenas model. *American Journal of Sociology*, *94*, 53–78.

Hill, C. T., & Stull, D. E. (1981). Sex differences in effects of social and value similarity in same-sex friendship. *Journal of Personality and Social Psychology*, *41*(3), 488–502.

Hill, K., & Monk, A. F. (2000). Electronic mail versus printed text: The effects on recipients. *Interacting with Computers*, *13*(2) 253–263.

Hill, P. H. (1984). Decisions involving the corporate environment. In W. Swap (Ed.), *Group decision making*. Beverly Hills, CA: Sage.

Himmelfarb, S. (1972). Integration and attribution theories in personality impression formation. *Journal of Personality and Social Psychology*, *23*(3), 309–313.

Hinsley, D. A., Hayes, J. R., & Simon, H. A. (1977). From words to equations: Meaning and representation in algebra word problems. In M. A. Just & P. A. Carpenter (Eds.), *Cognitive processes in comprehension* (pp. 89–106). Hillsdale, NJ: Lawrence Erlbaum Associates.

Hinsz, V. B. (1990). Cognitive and consensus processes in group recognition memory performance. *Journal of Personality and Social Psychology, 59*(4), 705–718.

Hinsz, V. B., Tindale, R. S., & Nagao, D. H. (2008). Accentuation of information processes and biases in group judgments integrating base-rate and case-specific information. *Journal of Experimental Social Psychology, 44*(1), 116–126.

Hinsz, V. B., Tindale, R. S., & Vollrath, D. A. (1997). The emerging conceptualization of groups as information processes. *Psychological Bulletin, 121*(1), 43–64.

Hirschman, E. C. (1981). An exploratory comparison of decision criteria used by retailers. In W. R. Darden & R. F. Lusch (Eds.), *Proceedings of 1981 workshop in retail patronage theory* (pp. 1–5). Norman, OK: University of Oklahoma.

Hirschman, E.C., & Mazursky, D. (1982). *A trans-organizational investigation of retail buyers' criteria and information sources.* Working Paper No. 82–8. New York University Institute of Retail Management.

Hirshleifer, S. (1970). *Investment, interest and capital.* Englewood Cliffs, NJ: Prentice-Hall.

Hirt, E. R., Levine, G. M., McDonald, H. E., Melton, R. J., & Martin, L. L. (1997). The role of mood in quantitative and qualitative aspects of performance: Single or multiple mechanisms? *Journal of Experimental Social Psychology, 33*(6), 602–629.

Hitt, M. A., & Tyler, B. B. (1991). Strategic decision models: Integrating different perspectives. *Strategic Management Journal, 12*(5), 327–351.

Hoch, S. J., & Loewenstein, G. F. (1991). Time-inconsistent preferences and consumer self-control. *Journal of Consumer Research, 17*(4), 492–507.

Hodges, B. H. (1974). Effect of valence on relative weighting in impression formation. *Journal of Personality and Social Psychology, 30*(3), 378–381.

Hoffman, J. E., & Subramaniam, B. (1995). The role of visual attention in saccadic eye movements. *Perception & Psychophysics, 57*(6), 787–795.

Hogarth, R. M. (1980). *Judgment and choice.* New York: Wiley.

Hogg, M. A. (1992). *The social psychology of group cohesiveness: From attraction to social identity.* Hemel Hempstead, UK: Harvester Wheatsheaf.

Hogg, M. A. (2001). A social identity theory of leadership. *Personality and Social Psychology Review, 5,* 184–200.

Hogg, M. A. (2007). Social psychology of leadership. In A. W. Kruglanski & E. Tory Higgins (Eds.), *Social psychology: Handbook of basic principles* (2nd ed., pp. 716–733). New York: The Guilford Press.

Hogg, M. A., & Hains, S. C. (1998). Friendship and group identification: A new look at the role of cohesiveness in group think. *European Journal of Social Psychology, 28,* 323–341.

Hogg, M. A., & Hardie, E. A. (1991). Social attraction, personal attraction and self-categorization: A field study. *Personality and Social Psychology Bulletin, 17,* 175–180.

Hogg, M. A., & Terry, O. J. (2000). Social identity and self-categorization processes in organizational contexts. *Academy of Management Review, 25,* 121–140.

Hogg, M. A., & van Knippenberg, D. (2003). Social identity and leadership processes in groups. In M. P. Zanna (Ed.), *Advances in experimental social psychology* (Vol. 35, pp. 1–52). San Diego, CA: Academic Press.

Holbrook, M. B. (1986). Emotion in the consumption experience: Toward a new model of the human consumer. In R. A. Peterson, W. D. Hoyer, & W. R. Wilson (Eds.), *The role of affect in consumer behavior: Emerging theories and applications* (pp. 17–52). Lexington, MA: Lexington Books.

Holbrook, M. B., & Batra, R. (1987). Assessing the role of emotions as mediators of consumer responses to advertising. *Journal of Consumer Research, 14*(3), 404–420.

Holbrook, M. B., & Lehmann, D. R. (1980). Form versus content in predicting Starch scores. *Journal of Advertising Research, 20*(4), 53–62.

Holland, J. H., Holyoak, K., Nisbett, R. E., & Thagard, P. R. (1986). *Induction: Processes of inference, learning, and discovery.* Cambridge, MA: MIT Press.

Holland, J. H., Holyoak, K. J., Nisbett, R. E., & Thagard, P. R. (1993). Deductive reasoning. In A. I. Goldman (Ed.), *Readings in philosophy and cognitive science* (pp. 23–41). Cambridge, MA: The MIT Press.

Holland, R. W., Verplanken, B., & van Knippenberg, A. (2003). From repetition to conviction: Attitude accessibility as a determinant of attitude certainty. *Journal of Experimental Social Psychology*, *39*(6), 594–601.

Holland, V. M. (1981). *Psycholinguistic alternatives to readability formulas* (Document Design Project Tech. Rep. No. 12). Washington, DC: American Institutes for Research.

Hollandsworth, J. G., Kazelskis, R., Stevens, J., & Dressel, M. E. (1979). Relative contributions of verbal, articulative, and nonverbal communication to employment decisions in the job interview setting. *Personnel Psychology*, *32*(2), 359–367.

Holliday, W. G. (1975). The effects of verbal and adjunct pictorial-verbal information in science instruction. *Journal of Research in Science Teaching*, *12*, 77–83.

Holliday, W. G., Brunner, L. L., & Donais, E. L. (1977). Differential cognitive and affective responses for flow diagrams in science. *Journal of Research in Science Teaching*, *14*, 129–138.

Holliday, W. G., & Harvey, D. A. (1976). Adjunct labeled drawings in teaching physics to junior high school students. *Journal of Research in Science Teaching*, *13*, 37–43.

Hollingshead, A. B. (1996). The rank-order effect in group decision making. *Organizational Behavior and Human Decision Processes*, *68*(3), 181–193.

Hollman, T. D. (1972) Employment interviewers' errors in processing positive and negative information. *Journal of Applied Psychology*, *56*, 130–134.

Holmes, G. (1931). The relative legibility of black and white print. *Journal of Applied Psychology*, *15*(3), 248–251.

Holmes, V. M., Arwas, R., & Garrett, M. F. (1977). Prior context and the perception of lexically ambiguous sentences. *Memory & Cognition*, *5*(1), 103–110.

Holtgraves, T., & Grayer, A. R. (1994). I am not a crook: Effects of denials on perceptions of a defendant's guilt, personality, and motives. *Journal of Applied Social Psychology*, *24*(23), 2132–2150.

Holtgraves, T., & Lasky, B. (1999). Linguistic power and persuasion. *Journal of Language and Social Psychology*, *18*(2), 196–205.

Holyoak, K. J. (1974). The role of imagery in the evaluation of sentences: Imagery or semantic factors. *Journal of Verbal Learning & Verbal Behavior*, *13*(2), 163–166.

Holyoak, K. J. (1984). Mental models in problem solving. In J. R. Anderson & S. M. Kosslyn (Eds.), *Tutorials in learning and memory: Essays in honor of Gordon Bower* (pp. 193–218). San Francisco: Freeman.

Holyoak, K. J., & Simon, D. (1999). Bidirectional reasoning in decision making by constraint satisfaction. *Journal of Experimental Psychology: General*, *128*(1), 3–31.

Holyoak, K. J., & Thagard, P. (1995). *Mental leaps: Analogy in creative thought*. Cambridge, MA: The MIT Press.

Hooper, V. J. (1994). Multinational capital budgeting and finance decisions. In J. Pointon (Ed.), *Issues in business taxation* (pp. 211–225). Aldershot, UK: Ashgate.

Hosman, L. A., & Siltanen, S. A. (1994). The attributional and evaluative consequences of powerful and powerless speech styles: An examination of the "control over others" and "control of self" explanations. *Language & Communication*, *14*(3), 287–298.

House, R. J., & Aditya, R. M. (1997). The social scientific study of leadership: Quo vadis? *Journal of Management*, *23*, 409–473.

Howell, J. M., & Hall-Merenda, K. E. (1999). The ties that bind: The impact of leader-member exchange, transformational and transactional leadership, and distance on predicting follower performance. *Journal of Applied Psychology*, *84*, 680–694.

Howells, L. T., & Becker, S. W. (1962). Seating arrangement and leadership emergence. *Journal of Abnormal and Social Psychology*, *64*, 148–150.

Hrubes, D. A. (2001). The role of nonverbal behavior in persuasion (Doctoral dissertation, University of Massachusetts—Amherst, 2001). *Dissertation Abstracts International*, *62* (9–B), 4274.

Hsee, C. K. (1996). The evaluability hypothesis: An explanation for preference reversals between joint and separate evaluations of alternatives. *Organizational Behavior and Human Decision Processes*, *67*(3), 247–257.

Hsee, C. K. (1998). Less is better: When low-value options are valued more highly than high-value options. *Journal of Behavioral Decision Making*, *11*(2), 107–121.

Hsee, C. K., & Kunreuther, H. (2000). The affection effect in insurance decisions. *Journal of Risk and Uncertainty*, *20*, 141–159.

Hsee, C. K., Loewenstein, G. F., Blount, S., & Bazerman, M. H. (1999). Preference reversals between joint and separate evaluations of options: A review and theoretical analysis. *Psychological Bulletin*, *125*(5), 576–590.

Hsee, C. K., & Menon, S. (1999). *Affection effect in consumer choices*. Unpublished study, University of Chicago.

Hsee, C. K., & Rottenstreich, Y. (2004). Music, pandas, and muggers: On the affective psychology of value. *Journal of Experimental Psychology: General*, *133*(1), 23–30.

Huber, J., Payne, J. W., & Puto, C. (1982). Adding asymmetrically dominated alternatives: Violations of regularity and the similarity hypothesis. *Journal of Consumer Research*, *9*(1), 90–98.

Huber, O. (1980). The influence of some task variables on cognitive operations in an information-processing decision model. *Acta Psychologica*, *45*(1–3), 187–196.

Huberman, G., Iyengar, S. S., & Jiang, W. (2007). Defined contribution pension plans: Determinants of participation and contribution rates. *Journal of Financial Services Research*, *31*(1), 1–32.

Huffman, C., Ratneshwar, S., & Mick, D. G. (2000). Consumer goal structures and goal-determination processes: An integrative framework. In S. Ratneshwar, D. G. Mick, & C. Huffman (Eds.), *The why of consumption: Contemporary perspectives on consumer motives, goals, and desires* (pp. 9–35). London and New York: Routledge.

Hupet, M., & Le Bouedec, B. (1975). Definiteness and voice in the interpretation of active and passive sentences. *The Quarterly Journal of Experimental Psychology*, *27*(2), 323–330.

Hvistendahl, J. K., & Kahl, M. R. (1975). Roman v. sans serif body type: Readability and reader preference. *News Research Bulletin*, *2*, 3–11.

Hyönä, J. (1994). Processing of topic shifts by adults and children. *Reading Research Quarterly*, *29*(1), 76–90.

Hyönä, J., & Häikiö, T. (2005). Is emotional content obtained from parafoveal words during reading? An eye movement analysis. *Scandinavian Journal of Psychology*, *46*(6), 475–483.

Ickes, W. (1982). A basic paradigm for the study of personality, roles, and social behavior. In W. Ickes & E. S. Knowles (Eds.), *Personality, roles, and social behavior* (pp. 305–341). New York: Springer-Verlag.

Ickes, W., Stinson, L., Bissonnette, V., & Garcia, S. (1990). Naturalistic social cognition: Empathic accuracy in mixed-sex dyads. *Journal of Personality and Social Psychology*, *59*(4), 730–742.

Imada, A. S., & Hakel, M. D. (1977). Influence of nonverbal communication and rater proximity on impressions and decisions in simulated employment interviews. *Journal of Applied Psychology*, *62*(3), 295–300.

Insko, C. A., Lind, E. A., & LaTour, S. (1976). Persuasion, recall, and thoughts. *Representative Research in Social Psychology*, *7*(1), 66–78.

Intraub, H. (1979). The role of implicit naming in pictorial encoding. *Journal of Experimental Psychology: Human Learning and Memory*, *5*(2), 78–87.

Isen, A. M. (1987). Positive affect, cognitive processes, and social behavior. In L. Berkowitz (Ed.), *Advances in experimental social psychology* (Vol. 20, pp. 203–253). San Diego, CA: Academic Press.

Isen, A. M. (1993). Positive affect and decision making. In M. Lewis & J. M. Haviland (Eds.), *Handbook of emotions* (pp. 261–277). New York: Guilford Press.

Isen, A. M. (1999). Positive affect. In T. Dalgleish & M. J. Power (Eds.), *Handbook of cognition and emotion* (pp. 521–539). New York: John Wiley & Sons.

Isen, A. M. (2000). Some perspectives on positive affect and self-regulation. *Psychological Inquiry*, *11*(3), 184–187.

Isen, A. M., & Geva, N. (1987). The influence of positive affect on acceptable level of risk: The person with a large canoe has a large worry. *Organizational Behavior and Human Decision Processes*, *39*(2), 145–154.

Isen, A. M., & Means, B. (1983). The influence of positive affect on decision-making strategy. *Social Cognition*, *2*(1), 18–31.

Isen, A. M., Nygren, T. E., & Ashby, F. G. (1988). Influence of positive affect on the subjective utility of gains and losses: It is just not worth the risk. *Journal of Personality and Social Psychology*, *55*(5), 710–717.

Isen, A. M., & Patrick, R. (1983). The effect of positive feelings on risk taking: When the chips are down. *Organizational Behavior & Human Performance*, *31*(2), 194–202.

Isen, A. M., Rosenzweig, A. S., & Young, M. J. (1991). The influence of positive affect on clinical problem solving. *Medical Decision Making*, *11*, 221–227.

Isenberg, D. J. (1986). Thinking and managing: A verbal protocol analysis of managerial problem solving. *Academy of Management Journal*, *29*(4), 775–788.

Iyengar, S. (1991). *Is anyone responsible: How television frames political issues*. Chicago: University of Chicago Press.

Iyengar, S., & Kinder, D. R. (1987). *News that matters: Television and American opinion*. Chicago: University of Chicago Press.

Iyengar, S. S., & Lepper, M. R. (2000). When choice is demotivating: Can one desire too much of a good thing?. *Journal of Personality and Social Psychology*, *79*(6), 995–1006.

Izard, C. E. (1977). *Human emotions*. New York: Plenum Press.

Izard, C. E. (1994). Innate and universal facial expressions: Evidence from developmental and cross-cultural research. *Psychological Bulletin*, *115*(2), 288–299.

Jackson, D. N., Peacock, A. C., & Holden, R. R. (1982). Professional interviewers' trait inferential structures for diverse occupational groups. *Organizational Behavior & Human Performance*, *29*(1), 1–20.

Jacob, J., Lys, T., & Neale, M. (1999). Expertise in forecasting performance of security analysts. *Journal of Accounting and Economics*, *28*(1), 27–50.

Jacoby, J., Kuss, A., Mazursky, D., & Troutman, T. (1985). Effectiveness of security analyst information accessing strategies: A computer interactive assessment. *Computers in Human Behavior*, *1*(1), 95–113.

Jacoby, J., Morrin, M., Jaccard, J., Gurhan, Z., Kuss, A., & Maheswaran, D. (2002). Mapping attitude formation as a function of information input: Online processing models of attitude formation. *Journal of Consumer Psychology*, *12*(1), 21–34.

Jacoby, J., Nelson, M. C., & Hoyer, W. D. (1982). Corrective advertising and affirmative disclosure statements: Their potential for confusing and misleading the consumer. *Journal of Marketing*, *46*(1), 61–72.

Jacoby, J., Speller, D. E., & Berning, C. K. (1974a). Brand choice behavior as a function of information load: Replication and extension. *Journal of Consumer Research*, *1*(1), 33–42.

Jacoby, J., Speller, D. E., & Kohn, C. A. (1974b). Brand choice behavior as a function of information load. *Journal of Marketing Research*, *11*(1), 63–69.

Jacoby, L. L., Kelley, C. M., & Dywan, J. (1989a). Memory attributions. In H. L. Roediger & F. I. M. Craik (Eds.), *Varieties of memory and consciousness: Essays in honour of Endel Tulving* (pp. 391–422). Hillsdale, NJ: Lawrence Erlbaum Associates.

Jacoby, L. L., Woloshyn, V., & Kelley, C. M. (1989b). Becoming famous without being recognized: Unconscious influences of memory produced by dividing attention. *Journal of Experimental Psychology: General*, *118*(2), 115–125.

Jacowitz, K. E., & Kahneman, D. (1995). Measures of anchoring in estimation tasks. *Personality and Social Psychology Bulletin*, *21*(11), 1161–1166.

Jamieson, D. W., & Zanna, M. P. (1989). Need for structure in attitude formation and expression. In A. R. Pratkanis, S. J. Breckler, & A. G. Greenwald (Eds.), *Attitude structure and function* (pp. 383–406). Hillsdale, NJ: Lawrence Erlbaum Associates.

Janis, I. L. (1972). *Victims of groupthink: A psychological study of foreign-policy decisions and fiascoes*. Oxford, UK: Houghton Mifflin.

Janiszewski, C. (1988). Preconscious processing effects: The independence of attitude formation and conscious thought. *Journal of Consumer Research*, *15*(2), 199–209.

Janiszewski, C. (1990). The influence of nonattended material on the processing of advertising claims. *Journal of Marketing Research*, *27*(3), 263–278.

Jarvella, R. J. (1971). Syntactic processing of connected speech. *Journal of Verbal Learning & Verbal Behavior*, *10*(4), 409–416.

Jarvenpaa, S. L. (1989). The effect of task demands and graphical format on information processing strategies and decision making performance. *Management Science, 35*(3), 285–303.

Jeffrey, K. M., & Mischel, W. (1979). Effects of purpose on the organization and recall of information in person perception. *Journal of Personality, 47*, 397–419.

Jennings, J. R. (1992). Is it important that the mind is in a body? Inhibition and the heart. *Psychophysiology, 29*(4), 369–383.

Jensen, J. L. (2007). Getting one's way in policy debates: Influence tactics used in group decision-making settings. *Public Administration Review, 67*(2), 216–227.

Jervis, R. (1976). *Perception and misperception in international relations.* Princeton, NJ: Princeton University Press.

Jessmer, S., & Anderson, D. (2001). The effect of politeness and grammar on user perceptions of electronic mail. *North American Journal of Psychology, 3*(2) 331–346.

Johns, A. M. (1997). *Text, role and context: Developing academic literacies.* Cambridge, UK: Cambridge University Press.

Johnson, E. J. (1979). *Deciding how to decide: The effort of making a decision.* Unpublished manuscript, University of Chicago.

Johnson, E. J. (1981). Expertise in admissions judgment (Doctoral dissertation, Carnegie Mellon University, 1981). *Dissertation Abstracts International, 45* (06B), 1941.

Johnson, E. J. (1988a). Expertise and decision under uncertainty: Performance and process. In M. T. H. Chi, R. Glaser, & M. J. Farr (Eds.), *The nature of expertise* (pp. 209–228). Hillsdale, NJ: Lawrence Erlbaum Associates.

Johnson, E. J., Meyer, R. J., & Ghose, S. (1989). When choice models fail: Compensatory models in negatively correlated environments. *Journal of Marketing Research, 26*(3), 255–270.

Johnson, E. J., & Payne, J. W. (1985). Effort and accuracy in choice. *Management Science, 31*, 394–414.

Johnson, E. J., & Russo, J. E. (1984). Product familiarity and learning new information. *Journal of Consumer Research, 11*(1), 542–550.

Johnson, E. J., & Sathi, A. (1984). Expertise in security analysts. Working paper, Graduate School of Industrial Administration, Carnegie Mellon University, Pittsburgh, PA.

Johnson, E. J., & Tversky, A. (1983). Affect, generalization, and the perception of risk. *Journal of Personality and Social Psychology, 45*(1), 20–31.

Johnson, L. (1994). Educating about risk: Designing more effective disaster preparedness messages (earthquakes) (Doctoral dissertation, University of Washington, 1994). *Dissertation Abstracts International, 56* (04A), 1184.

Johnson, M. D. (1986). Modeling choice strategies for noncomparable alternatives. *Marketing Science, 5*(1), 37–54.

Johnson, M. D. (1988b). Comparability and hierarchical processing in multialternative choice. *Journal of Consumer Research, 15*(3), 303–314.

Johnson-Laird, P. N. (1968). The choice of the passive voice in a communicative task. *British Journal of Psychology, 59*(1), 7–15.

Johnson-Laird, P. N. (1980). Mental models in cognitive science. *Cognitive Science: A Multidisciplinary Journal, 4*(1), 71–115.

Johnston, W. A., & Dark, V. J. (1986). Selective attention. *Annual Review of Psychology, 37*, 43–75.

Johnston, W. A., & Hawley, K. J. (1994). Perceptual inhibition of expected inputs: The key that opens closed minds. *Psychonomic Bulletin and Review, 1*, 56–72.

Jordan, J., & Kaas, K. P. (2002). Advertising in the mutual fund business: The role of judgmental heuristics in private investors' evaluation of risk and return. *Journal of Financial Services Marketing, 7*(2), 129–140.

Jorgensen, C. C., & Kintsch, W. (1973). The role of imagery in the evaluation of sentences. *Cognitive Psychology, 4*(1), 110–116.

Joyce, E. J., & Biddle, G. C. (1981). Anchoring and adjustment in probabilistic inference in auditing. *Journal of Accounting Research, 19*, 120–145.

Jung, K. (1996). Line extension versus new brand name introduction: Effects of new products discrepancy and relationship to an existing brand on the information process of new product evaluation (Doctoral dissertation, University of Illinois at Urbana-Champaign, 1996). *Dissertation Abstracts International, 57* (11A), 4833.

Jussim, L., Nelson, T. E., Manis, M., & Soffin, S. (1995). Prejudice, stereotypes, and labeling effects: Sources of bias in person perception. *Journal of Personality and Social Psychology, 68*(2), 228–246.

Just, M. A., & Carpenter, P. A. (1980). A theory of reading: From eye fixations to comprehension. *Psychological Review, 87*(4), 329–354.

Just, M. A., & Carpenter, P. A. (1984). Using eye fixations to study reading comprehension. In D. E. Kieras & M. A. Just (Eds.), *New methods in reading comprehension research* (pp. 151–182). Hillsdale, NJ: Erlbaum.

Just, M. A., & Carpenter, P. A. (1987). *The psychology of reading and language comprehension.* Boston: Allyn and Bacon.

Just, M. A., & Clark, H. H. (1973). Drawing inferences from the presuppositions and implications of affirmative and negative sentences. *Journal of Verbal Learning & Verbal Behavior, 12*(1), 21–31.

Kagan, J. (1991). A conceptual analysis of the affects. *Journal of the American Psychoanalytic Association, 39*(Suppl.), 109–129.

Kahle, L. R., Beatty, S. E., & Homer, P. M. (1986). Alternative measurement approaches to consumer values: The list of values (LOV) and values and life style (VALS). *Journal of Consumer Research, 13*(3), 405–409.

Kahn, B. E., & Baron, J. (1995). An exploratory study of choice rules favored for high-stakes decisions. *Journal of Consumer Psychology, 4*(4), 305–328.

Kahneman, D. (1973). *Attention and effort.* Englewood Cliffs, NJ: Prentice Hall.

Kahneman, D., & Beatty, J. (1966). Pupil diameter and load on memory. *Science, 154*(3756), 1583–1585.

Kahneman, D., & Beatty, J. (1967). Pupillary responses in a pitch-discrimination task. *Perception & Psychophysics, 2*(3), 101–105.

Kahneman, D., & Frederick, S. (2002). Representativeness revisited: Attribute substitution in intuitive judgment. In T. Gilovich, D. Griffin, & D. Kahneman (Eds.), *Heuristics and biases: The psychology of intuitive judgment* (pp. 49–81). New York: Cambridge University Press.

Kahneman, D., & Knetsch, J. (1993). *Anchoring or shallow inferences: The effect of format.* Unpublished manuscript, University of California, Berkeley.

Kahneman, D., Knetsch, J. L., & Thaler, R. H. (1990). Experimental tests of the endowment effect and the Coase theorem. *Journal of Political Economy, 98,* 1325–1348.

Kahneman, D., & Miller, D. T. (1986). Norm theory: Comparing reality to its alternatives. *Psychological Review, 93*(2), 136–153.

Kahneman, D., Schkade, D., & Sunstein, C. R. (1998). Shared outrage and erratic awards: The psychology of punitive damages. *Journal of Risk and Uncertainty, 16*(1), 49–86.

Kahneman, D., & Tversky, A. (1973). On the psychology of prediction. *Psychological Review, 80*(4), 237–251.

Kahneman, D., & Tversky, A. (1982). On the study of statistical intuitions. *Cognition, 11*(2), 123–141.

Kahneman, D., & Tversky, A. (1984). Choices, values, and frames. *American Psychologist, 39*(4), 341–350.

Kahneman, D., & Varey, C. A. (1990). Propensities and counterfactuals: The loser that almost won. *Journal of Personality and Social Psychology, 59*(6), 1101–1110.

Kaiser, S., & Wehrle, T. (2001). Facial expressions as indicators of appraisal processes. In K. R. Scherer, A. Schorr, & T. Johnstone (Eds.), *Appraisal processes in emotion: Theory, methods, research* (pp. 285–300). New York: Oxford University Press.

Kaiser, S., Wehrle, T., & Schmidt, S. (1998) Emotional episodes, facial expressions, and reported feelings in human-computer interactions. In A. H. Fischer (Ed.), *Proceedings of the Xth Conference of the International Society for Research on Emotions* (pp. 82–86). Würzburg: ISRE Publications.

Kalichman, S. C., & Coley, B. (1995). Context framing to enhance HIV-antibody-testing messages targeted to African American women. *Health Psychology, 14*(3), 247–254.

Kalin, R., & Rayko, D. (1980). The social significance of speech in the job interview. In R. N. St. Clair & H. Giles (Eds.), *The social and psychological contexts of language* (pp. 39–50). Hillsdale, NJ: Lawrence Erlbaum Associates.

Kalmar, D. A. (1996). The effect of perspective on recall and interpretation of stories: An extension of Anderson and Pichert (Doctoral dissertation, Yale University, 1996), *Dissertation Abstracts International, 57* (06B), 4064.

Kamakura, W. A., & Novak, T. P. (1992). Value-system segmentation: Exploring the meaning of LOV. *Journal of Consumer Research, 19*(1), 119–132.

Kameda, T., & Davis, J. H. (1990). The function of the reference point in individual and group risk decision making. *Organizational Behavior and Human Decision Processes, 46*(1), 55–76.

Kameda, T., Ohtsubo, Y., & Takezawa, M. (1997). Centrality in sociocognitive networks and social influence: An illustration in a group decision-making context. *Journal of Personality and Social Psychology, 73*(2), 296–309.

Kameda, T., & Sugimori, S. (1993). Psychological entrapment in group decision making: An assigned decision rule and a groupthink phenomenon. *Journal of Personality and Social Psychology, 65*(2), 282–292.

Kameda, T., & Sugimori, S. (1995). Procedural influence in two-step group decision making: Power of local majorities in consensus formation. *Journal of Personality and Social Psychology, 69*(5), 865–876.

Kamil, M. L. (1972). Memory of repeated words and parallel structure in compound sentences. *Journal of Verbal Learning & Verbal Behavior, 11*(5), 634–643.

Kanouse, D. E., & Hanson, L. R., Jr. (1972). Negativity in evaluations. In E. E. Jones, D. E. Kanouse, H. H. Kelley, R. E. Nisbett, S. Valins, & B. Weiner (Eds.), *Attribution: Perceiving the causes of behavior* (pp. 47–62). Morristown, NJ: General Learning Press.

Kaplan, M. F., & Kemmerick, G. D. (1974). Juror judgment as information integration: Combining evidential and non-evidential information. *Journal of Personality and Social Psychology, 30*(4), 493–499.

Karau, S. J., & Kelly, J. R. (1992). The effects of time scarcity and time abundance on group performance quality and interaction process. *Journal of Experimental Social Psychology, 28*(6), 542–571.

Kardash, C. A., Royer, J. M., & Greene, B. A. (1988). Effects of schemata on both encoding and retrieval of information from prose. *Journal of Educational Psychology, 80*(3), 324–329.

Kardes, F. R., Kalyanaram, G., Chandrashekaran, M., & Dornof, R. J. (1993). Brand retrieval, consideration set composition, consumer choice, and the pioneering advantage. *Journal of Consumer Research, 20*(1), 62–75.

Kardes, F. R., & Sanbonmatsu, D. M. (1993). Direction of comparison, expected feature correlation, and the set-size effect in preference judgment. *Journal of Consumer Psychology, 2*(1), 39–54.

Karlin, L., & Kestenbaum, R. (1968). Effects of the number of alternatives on the psychological refractory period. *Quarterly Journal of Experimental Psychology, 20*, 167–178.

Karniol, R. (2003). Egocentrism versus protocentrism: The status of self in social prediction. *Psychological Review, 110*(3), 564–580.

Kassin, S. M. (1983). Deposition testimony and the surrogate witness: Evidence for a "messenger effect" in persuasion. *Personality and Social Psychology Bulletin, 9*(2), 281–288.

Kassin, S. M., & Garfield, D. A. (1991). Blood and guts: General and trial-specific effects of videotaped crime scenes on mock jurors. *Journal of Applied Social Psychology, 21*(18), 1459–1472.

Kassin, S. M., & Pryor, J. B. (1985). The development of attribution processes. In J. Pryor & J. Day (Eds.), *The development of social cognition* (pp. 3–34). New York: Springer-Verlag.

Katzman, N., & Nyenhuis, J. (1972). Color vs. black-and-white effects on learning, opinion, and attention. *AV Communication Review, 20*(1), 16–28.

Kazoleas, D. C. (1993). A comparison of the persuasive effectiveness of qualitative versus quantitative evidence: A test of explanatory hypotheses. *Communication Quarterly, 41*, 40–50.

Keating, C. F., & Doyle, J. (2002). The faces of desirable mates and dates contain mixed social status cues. *Journal of Experimental Social Psychology, 38*(4), 414–424.

Keen, J. (1990, August 21). How long will U.S. stay in the gulf? *USA Today,* pp. IA, 2A.

Keenan, A. (1976). Interviewers' evaluation of applicant characteristics: Differences between personnel and non-personnel managers. *Journal of Occupational Psychology, 49*(4), 223–30.

Keenan, A. (1977). Some relationships between interviewers' personal feelings about candidates and their general evaluation of them. *Journal of Occupational Psychology, 50*(4), 275–283.

Keenan, J. M., MacWhinney, B., & Mayhew, D. (1977). Pragmatics in memory: A study of natural conversion. *Journal of Verbal Learning & Verbal Behavior, 16*(5), 549–560.

Keeney, R. L., & Raiffa, H. (1976/1993). *Decisions with multiple objectives: Preferences and value tradeoffs.* New York: Cambridge University Press.

Keller, K. L., & Staelin, R. (1987). Effects of quality and quantity of information on decision effectiveness. *Journal of Consumer Research, 14*(2), 200–213.

Kelly, J. R., & Karau, S. J. (1999). Group decision making: The effects of initial preferences and time pressure. *Personality and Social Psychology Bulletin, 25*(11), 1342–1354.

Keltner, D., & Buswell, B. N. (1997). Embarrassment: Its distinct form and appeasement functions. *Psychological Bulletin, 122*(3), 250–270.

Keltner, D., Ellsworth, P. C., & Edwards, K. (1993a). Beyond simple pessimism: Effects of sadness and anger on social perception. *Journal of Personality and Social Psychology, 64*(5), 740–752.

Keltner, D., & Gross, J. J. (1999). Functional accounts of emotions. *Cognition & Emotion Special Issue: Functional Accounts of Emotion, 13*(5), 467–480.

Keltner, D., & Kring, A. M. (1998). Emotion, social function, and psychopathology. *Review of General Psychology Special Issue: New Directions in Research on Emotion, 2*(3), 320–342.

Keltner, D., Locke, K. D., & Audrain, P. C. (1993b). The influence of attributions on the relevance of negative feelings to personal satisfaction. *Personality and Social Psychology Bulletin, 19*(1), 21–29.

Keltner, D., Young, R. C., & Buswell, B. N. (1997). Appeasement in human emotion, social practice, and personality. *Aggressive Behavior Special Issue: Appeasement and Reconciliation, 23*(5), 359–374.

Kendon, A. (1990). *Conducting interaction: Patterns of behavior in focused encounters.* New York: Cambridge University Press.

Kenney, R. A., Schwartz-Kenney, B. M., & Blascovich, J. (1996). Implicit leadership theories: Defining leaders described as worthy of influence. *Personality and Social Psychology Bulletin, 22*(11), 1128–1143.

Kenny, D. A., Horner, C., Kashy, D. A., & Chu, L. C. (1992). Consensus at zero acquaintance: Replication, behavioral cues, and stability. *Journal of Personality and Social Psychology, 62*(1), 88–97.

Kensinger, E. A., & Corkin, S. (2003). Memory enhancement for emotional words: Are emotional words more vividly remembered than neutral words? *Memory & Cognition, 31*(8), 1169–1180.

Kensinger, E. A., Piguet, O., Krendl, A. C., & Corkin, S. (2005). Memory for contextual details: Effects of emotion and aging. *Psychology and Aging, 20*(2), 241–250.

Kepplinger, H. M., Brosius, H. B., & Heine, N. (1990). Contrast effects of nonverbal behavior in television interviews. *Communications, 15*(1–2), 121–134.

Kercsmar, J. (1985). Individual investors' information choice, information processing, and judgment behavior: a process-tracing study of the verbal protocols associated with stock selection (Doctoral dissertation, University of Houston-University Park, 1985). *Dissertation Abstracts International, 46* (09A), 2740.

Keren, G. (1987). Facing uncertainty in the game of bridge: A calibration study. *Organizational Behavior and Human Decision Processes, 39*(1), 98–114.

Kern, R. P., Sticht, T. G., Welty, D., & Hauke, R. N. (1977). *Guidebook for the development of Army training literature.* Arlington, VA: U.S. Army Research Institute for the Behavioral and Social Sciences.

Kerr, N. L., Hymes, R. W., Anderson, A. B., & Weathers, J. E. (1995). Defendant-juror similarity and mock juror judgments. *Law and Human Behavior, 19*(6), 545–567.

Kerr, N. L., MacCoun, R. J., & Kramer, G. P. (1996) "When are N heads better (or worse) than one?": Biased judgment in individuals versus groups. In E. H. Witte & J. H. Davis (Eds.), *Understanding group behavior, Vol. 1: Consensual action by small groups* (pp. 105–136). Hillsdale, NJ: Lawrence Erlbaum.

Kerschreiter, R., Schulz-Hardt, S., Faulmuller, N., Mojzisch, A., & Frey, D. (2004). *Psychological explanations for the dominance of shared and preference-consistent information in group discussions: Mutual enhancement or rational-decision making?* Working paper, Ludwig-Maximilians-University Munich.

Khong, Y. F. (1992). *Analogies at war.* Princeton, NJ: Princeton University Press.

Kier, K. L. (2000). A study of the adaptive decision making ability of pharmacists when patient counseling using a process-tracing technique (Doctoral dissertation, The Ohio State University, 2000). *Dissertation Abstracts International, 61* (02B), 807.

Kieras, D. E. (1978). Good and bad structure in simple paragraphs: Effects on apparent theme, reading time, and recall. *Journal of Verbal Learning & Verbal Behavior, 17*(1), 13–28.

Kieras, D. E., & Bovair, S. (1981, November). *Strategies for abstracting main ideas from simple technical prose.* Technical report, Arizona University of Tucson Department of Psychology. Tucson, AZ.

Kiesler, S. B., & Mathog, R. B. (1968). Distraction hypothesis in attitude change: Effects of effectiveness. *Psychological Reports, 23*(3, Pt. 2), 1123–1133.

Kinder, D. R., & Abelson, R. P. (1981, August). *Appraising presidential candidates: Personality and affect in the 1980 campaign.* Paper presented at the 1981 annual meeting of the American Political Science Association, New York.

Kinder, D. R., Peters, M. D., Abelson, R. P., & Fiske, S. T. (1980). Presidential prototypes. *Political Behavior, 2,* 315–338.

Kinder, D. R., & Sears, D. O. (1985). Public opinion and political action. In G. Lindzey & E. Aronson (Eds.), *The handbook of social psychology* (3rd ed., Vol. 2, pp. 659–743). New York: Knopf.

Kinicki, A. J., & Lockwood, C. A. (1985). The interview process: An examination of factors recruiters use in evaluating job applicants. *Journal of Vocational Behavior, 26*(2), 117–125.

Kinney, G. G., Marsetta, M., & Showman, D. J. (1966). Studies of display symbol legibility, Part XII, The legibility of alphanumeric symbols for digitalized television. ESD-TR-66–117. MTR-206. Tech Doc Rep U S Air Force Syst Command Electron Syst Div. 1–33.

Kintsch, W. (1979). On modeling comprehension. *Educational Psychologist, 14,* 3–14.

Kintsch, W. (1988). The role of knowledge in discourse comprehension: A construction-integration model. *Psychological Review, 95*(2), 163–182.

Kintsch, W., & Keenan, J. (1973). Reading rate and retention as a function of the number of propositions in the base structure of sentences. *Cognitive Psychology, 5*(3), 257–274.

Kintsch, W., & Kintsch, E. H. (1978). The role of schemata in text comprehension. *International Journal of Psycholinguistics, 5*(2), 17–29.

Kintsch, W., & Kozminsky, E. (1977). Summarizing stories after reading and listening. *Journal of Educational Psychology, 69*(5), 491–499.

Kintsch, W., & van Dijk, T. A. (1978). Toward a model of text comprehension and production. *Psychological Review, 85*(5), 363–394.

Kintsch, W., & Vipond, D. (1979). Reading comprehension and readability in education practice and psychological theory. In L. G. Nilsson (Ed.), *Perspectives on memory research: Essays in honor of Uppsala University's 500th anniversary* (pp. 329–365). Hillsdale, NJ: Erlbaum.

Kintsch, W., & Yarborough, J. (1982). The role of rhetorical structure in text comprehension. *Journal of Educational Psychology, 74*(2), 828–834.

Kirsch, M. P. (1985). The effect of information quality and type of data on information integration strategies (Master of Arts thesis, Michigan State University, 1985). *Masters Abstracts International, 24* (04), 0422.

Kisielius, J., & Sternthal, B. (1984). Detecting and explaining vividness effects in attitudinal judgments. *Journal of Marketing Research, 21*(1), 54–64.

Klare, G. M. (1963). *The measurement of readability.* Ames, IA: Iowa State University Press.

Klare, G. R. (1976). A second look at the validity of readability formulas. *Journal of Reading Behavior, 8*(2), 129–152.

Klare, G. R. (1984). Readability. In P. D. Pearson, R. Barr, M. Kamil, & P. Mosenthal (Eds.), *Handbook of reading research* (pp. 681–744). New York: Longman.

Klayman, J. (1985). Children's decision strategies and their adaptation to task characteristics. *Organizational Behavior and Human Decision Processes, 35*(2), 179–201.

Klayman, J., & Ha, Y. (1987). Confirmation, disconfirmation, and information in hypothesis testing. *Psychological Review, 94*(2), 211–228.

Klein, G. A. (1994). A script for the commander's intent statement. In A. H. Levis & I. S. Levis (Eds.), *Science of command and control: Part III: Coping with change* (pp. 75–86). Fairfax, VA: AFCEA International Press.

Klein, G. A. (1998). *Sources of power: How people make decisions.* Cambridge, MA: MIT Press.

Klein, W. M., & Weinstein, N. D. (1997). Social comparison and unrealistic optimism about personal risk. In B. P. Buunk & F. X. Gibbons (Eds.), *Health, coping; and well-being: Perspectives from social comparison theory* (pp. 25–61). Mahwah, NJ: Erlbaum.

Kleiner, B., & Hartigan, J. A. (1981). Representing points in many dimensions by trees and castles. *Journal of the American Statistical Association, 76,* 499–512.

Kleinke, C. L. (1977). Effects of dress on compliance to requests in a field setting. *Journal of Social Psychology, 101*(2), 223–224.

Kleinke, C. L. (1980). Interaction between gaze and legitimacy of request on compliance in a field setting. *Journal of Nonverbal Behavior, 5*(1), 3–12.

Klimoski, R. J., & Donahue, L. M. (2001). Person perception in organizations: An overview of the field. In M. London (Ed.), *How people evaluate others in organizations* (pp. 5–43). Mahwah, NJ: Lawrence Erlbaum Associates.

Klinger, E. (1975). Consequences of commitment to and disengagement from incentives. *Psychological Review, 82*(1), 1–25.

Klocke, U. (2007). How to improve decision making in small groups: Effects of dissent and training interventions. *Small Group Research, 38*(3), 437–468.

Knapp, M. L. (1978). *Nonverbal communication in human interaction* (2nd ed.). New York: Holt, Rinehart and Winston.

Knutson, B. (1996). Facial expressions of emotion influence interpersonal trait inferences. *Journal of Nonverbal Behavior, 20,* 165–182.

Koballa, T. R. (1986). Persuading teachers to reexamine the innovative elementary science programs of yesterday: The effect of anecdotal versus data-summary communications. *Journal of Research in Science Teaching, 23*(6), 437–449.

Kopelman, M. D. (1975). The contrast effect in the selection interview. *British Journal of Educational Psychology, 45*(3), 333–336.

Kopfman, J. E., Smith, S. W., Ah Yun, J. K., & Hodges, A. (1994, November). *Affective and cognitive reactions to narrative versus logical argument organ donation strategies.* Paper presented at the Speech Communication Association Annual Convention, New Orleans, LA.

Kopfman, J. E., Smith, S. W., Ah Yun, J. K., & Hodges, A. (1998). Affective and cognitive reactions to narrative versus statistical evidence organ donation messages. *Journal of Applied Communication Research, 26*(3), 279–300.

Koriat, A., & Levy-Sadot, R. (1999). Processes underlying metacognitive judgments: Information-based and experience-based monitoring of one's own knowledge. In S. Chaiken & Y. Trope (Eds.), *Dual-process theories in social psychology* (pp. 483–502). New York: Guilford Press.

Kosslyn, S. M. (1989). Understanding charts and graphs. *Applied Cognitive Psychology, 3*(3), 185–225.

Kosslyn, S. M. (1994). *Elements of graph design.* New York: W. H. Freeman.

Kotchetova, N., & Salterio, S. (2004). Judgment and decision-making accounting research: A quest to improve the production, certification, and use of accounting information. In D. J. Koehler & N. Harvey (Eds.), *Blackwell handbook of judgment and decision making* (pp. 547–566). Oxford, UK: Blackwell Publishing.

Kotovsky, L., & Gentner, D. (1996). Comparison and categorization in the development of relational similarity. *Child Development, 67*(6), 2797–2822.

Kowler, E., Anderson, E., Dosher, B., & Blaser, E. (1995). The role of attention in the programming of saccades. *Vision Research, 35*(13), 1897–1916.

Kozminsky, E. (1977). Altering comprehension: The effect of biasing titles on text comprehension. *Memory & Cognition, 5*(4), 482–490.

Kraiger, K., & Wenzel, L. H. (1997). Conceptual development and empirical evaluation of measures of shared mental models as indicators of team effectiveness. In M. T. Brannick, E. Salas, & C. Prince (Eds.), *Team performance assessment and measurement: Theory, methods, and applications* (pp. 63–84). Mahwah, NJ: Lawrence Erlbaum.

Krajewski, L. A. (1979). Effectiveness of the inductive and the deductive organizational plans in a special request letter (Doctoral dissertation, Arizona State University, 1979). *Dissertation Abstracts International, 40* (08A), 4368.

Lee, A. Y., & Aaker, J. L. (2004). Bringing the frame into focus: The influence of regulatory fit on processing fluency and persuasion. *Journal of Personality and Social Psychology, 86*(2), 205–218.

Lee, D. (1989a). The differential impact of comparative advertising on novice and expert consumers (Doctoral dissertation, University of Pittsburgh, 1989). *Dissertation Abstracts International, 50* (11a), 3666.

Lee, D. H. (1989b). Consumer inferencing behavior in processing product information: The roles of product class knowledge and information processing goal (Doctoral dissertation, Indiana University, 1989). *Dissertation Abstracts International, 51* (03A), 933.

Lee, D. H., & Olshavsky, R. W. (1995). Conditions and consequences of spontaneous inference generation: A concurrent protocol approach. *Organizational Behavior and Human Decision Processes, 61*(2), 177–189.

Lee, M. Y. (2008). Understanding changes in team-related and task-related mental models and their effects on team and individual performance. *Dissertation Abstracts International Section A: Humanities and Social Sciences, 69*(2-A), 491.

Lefford, A. (1946). The influence of emotional subject matter on logical reasoning. *Journal of General Psychology, 34*, 127–151.

Leith, K. P., & Baumeister, R. F. (1996). Why do bad moods increase self-defeating behavior? Emotion, risk tasking, and self-regulation. *Journal of Personality and Social Psychology, 71*(6), 1250–1267.

Lemerise, E. A., & Dodge, K. A. (1993). The development of anger and hostile interactions. In M. Lewis & J. M. Haviland (Eds.), *Handbook of emotions* (pp. 537–546). New York: Guilford Press.

Lerner, J. S., Goldberg, J. H., & Tetlock, P. E. (1998). Sober second thought: The effects of accountability, anger, and authoritarianism on attributions of responsibility. *Personality and Social Psychology Bulletin, 24*, 563–574.

Lerner, J. S., & Keltner, D. (2000). Beyond valence: Toward a model of emotion-specific influences on judgement and choice. *Cognition & Emotion Special Issue: Emotion, Cognition, and Decision Making, 14*(4), 473–493.

Lerner, J. S., & Keltner, D. (2001). Fear, anger, and risk. *Journal of Personality and Social Psychology, 81*(1), 146–159.

Lerner, J. S., Small, D. A., & Loewenstein, G. (2004). Heart strings and purse strings: Carryover effects of emotions on economic transactions. *Psychological Science, 15*(5), 337–341.

Lesgold, A. M., & Resnick, L. (1982). How reading difficulties develop: Perspectives from a longitudinal study. In J. Das, R. Mulcahey, & A. Wall (Eds.), *Theory and research in learning disabilities* (pp. 155–187). New York: Plenum Press.

Levenson, R. W. (1994). Human emotion: A functional view. In P. Ekman & R. J. Davidson (Eds.), *The nature of emotion: Fundamental questions* (pp.123–126). New York: Oxford University Press.

Levenson, R. W. (2003). Blood, sweat, and fears: The autonomic architecture of emotion. In P. Ekman, J. J. Campos, R. J. Davidson, & F. B. M. de Waal (Eds.), *Emotions inside out: 130 years after Darwin's: The expression of the emotions in man and animals* (pp. 348–366). New York: New York University Press.

Leventhal, H., & Singer, R. P. (1966). Affect arousal and positioning of recommendations in persuasive communications. *Journal of Personality and Social Psychology, 4*(2), 137–146.

Levie, W. H., & Lentz, R. (1982). Effects of text illustrations: A review of research. *Educational Communication & Technology Journal, 30*(4), 195–232.

Levin, I. P. (1987). Associative effects of information framing. *Bulletin of the Psychonomic Society, 25*(2), 85–86.

Levin, I. P., Schnittjer, S. K., & Thee, S. L. (1988). Information framing effects in social and personal decisions. *Journal of Experimental Social Psychology, 24*(6), 520–529.

Levin, J. R., Anglin, G. J., & Carney, R. N. (1987). On empirically validating functions of pictures in prose. In D. M. Willows & H. A. Houghton (Eds.), *The psychology of illustration: Basic research* (Vol. 1, pp. 51–85). New York: Springer-Verlag.

Levine, J. M., Resnick, L. B., & Higgins, E. T. (1993). Social foundations of cognition. *Annual Review of Psychology, 44*, 585–612.

Levine, L. R., Bluni, T. D., & Hochman, S. H. (1998). Attire and charitable behavior. *Psychological Reports, 83*(1), 15–18.

Levine, S. P. (1998) Implicit self-presentational goals and nonverbal behavior. *Dissertation Abstracts International: Section B: The Sciences and Engineering, 59*(10-B), 5621.

Levinson, W., Roter, D. L., Mullooly, J. P., Dull, V. T., & Frankel, R. M. (1997). Physician-patient communication: The relationship with malpractice claims among primary care physicians and surgeons. *Journal of the American Medical Association, 277*(7), 553–559.

Lewandowsky, S., & Spence, I. (1989). Discriminating strata in scatterplots. *Journal of the American Statistical Association, 84,* 682–688.

Lewis, K. M. (2000). When leaders display emotion: How followers respond to negative emotional expression of male and female leaders. *Journal of Organizational Behavior, 21,* 221–234.

Lewis, M. (1999). The role of the self in cognition and emotion. In T. Dalgleish & M. J. Power (Eds.), *Handbook of cognition and emotion* (pp. 125–142). New York: John Wiley & Sons Ltd.

Libby, R. (1976). Man versus model of man: Some conflicting evidence. *Organizational Behavior & Human Performance, 16*(1), 1–12.

Libby, R., & Frederick, D. M. (1989, February). *Expertise and the ability to explain audit findings* (University of Michigan Cognitive Science and Machine Intelligence Laboratory Technical Report No. 21).

Liberman, A. M., Cooper, F. S., Shankweiler, D. P., & Studdert-Kennedy, M. (1967). Perception of the speech code. *Psychological Review, 74*(6), 431–461.

Libkuman, T. M., Stabler, C. L., & Otani, H. (2004). Arousal, valence, and memory for detail. *Memory, 12*(2), 237–247.

Lichtenstein, S., Fischhoff, B., & Phillips, L. D. (1982). Calibration of probabilities: The state of the art to 1980. In D. Kahneman, P. Slovic, & A. Tversky (Eds.), *Judgment under uncertainty: Heuristics and biases* (pp. 306–334). New York: Cambridge University Press.

Lichtenstein, S., & Slovic, P. (1971). Reversals of preference between bids and choices in gambling decisions. *Journal of Experimental Psychology, 89*(1), 46–55.

Lieberman, M. D., Gaunt, R., Gilbert, D. T., & Trope, Y. (2002). Reflection and reflexion: A social cognitive neuroscience approach to attributional inference. In M. P. Zanna (Ed.), *Advances in experimental social psychology* (Vol. 34, pp. 199–249). San Diego, CA: Academic Press.

Lim, B. C., & Klein, K. J. (2006). Team mental models and team performance: A field study of the effects of team mental model similarity and accuracy. *Journal of Organizational Behavior, 27*(4), 403–418.

Lindemann, P. G., & Markman, A. B. (1996, July). *Alignability and attribute importance in choice.* Paper presented at the Eighteenth Annual Meeting of the Cognitive Science Society, San Diego, California.

Lingle, J. H., Geva, N., Ostrom, T. M., Leippe, M. R., & Baumgardner, M. H. (1979). Thematic effects of person judgments on impression organization. *Journal of Personality and Social Psychology, 37*(5), 674–687.

Lipp, A., Nourse, H. O., Bostrom, R. P., & Watson, H. J. (1992). The evolution of questions in successive versions of an expert system for real estate disposition. In T. W. Lauer, E. Peacock, & A. C. Graesser (Eds.), *Questions and information systems* (pp. 63–84). Hillsdale, NJ: Lawrence Erlbaum Associates.

Lipshitz, R., & Shaul, O. B. (1997). Schemata and mental models in recognition-primed decision making. In C. E. Zsambok & G. Klein (Eds.), *Naturalistic decision making* (pp. 293–303). Hillsdale, NJ: Lawrence Erlbaum Associates.

Liversedge, S. P., Rayner, K., White, S. J., Vergilino-Perez, D., Findlay, J. M., & Kentridge, R. W. (2004). Eye movements when reading disappearing text: Is there a gap effect in reading? *Vision Research, 44*(10), 1013–1024.

Livi, S., Kenny, D. A., Albright, L., & Pierro, A. (2008). A social relations analysis of leadership. *Leadership Quarterly, 19*(2), 235–248.

Locksley, A., Borgida, E., Brekke, N., & Hepburn, C. (1980). Sex stereotypes and social judgment. *Journal of Personality and Social Psychology, 39*(5), 821–831.

Locksley, A., Hepburn, C., & Ortiz, V. (1982). Social stereotypes and judgments of individuals: An instance of the base-rate fallacy. *Journal of Experimental Social Psychology, 18*(1), 23–42.

Loewenstein, G. (1987). Anticipation and the valuation of delayed consumption. *Economic Journal, 97*(387), 666–684.

Loewenstein, G. (1996). Out of control: Visceral influences on behavior. *Organizational Behavior and Human Decision Processes, 65*(3), 272–292.

Loewenstein, G., & Lerner, J. S. (2003). The role of affect in decision making. In R. J. Davidson, K. R. Scherer, & H. H. Goldsmith (Eds.), *Handbook of affective sciences* (pp. 619–642). New York: Oxford University Press.

Loewenstein, G., & Mather, J. (1990). Dynamic processes in risk perception. *Journal of Risk and Uncertainty, 3*, 155–175.

Loewenstein, G., Weber, E. U., Hsee, C. K., & Welch, E. (2001). Risk as feelings. *Psychological Bulletin, 127*(2), 267–286.

Loewenstein, J., Thompson, L., & Gentner, D. (1999). Analogical encoding facilitates knowledge transfer in negotiation. *Psychonomic Bulletin and Review, 6*(4), 586–597.

Loftus, E. F. (1979). *Eyewitness testimony*. Cambridge, MA: Harvard University Press.

Loftus, E. F., & Burns, T. E. (1982). Mental shock can produce retrograde amnesia. *Memory & Cognition, 10*(4), 318–323.

Loftus, E. F., Loftus, G. R., & Messo, J. (1987). Some facts about "weapon focus." *Law and Human Behavior, 11*(1), 55–62.

Lohse, G. L. (1993). A cognitive model for understanding graphical perception. *Human-Computer Interaction, 8*, 353–388.

London, M. (2002). *Leadership development: Paths to self-insight and professional growth*. Mahwah, NJ: Lawrence Erlbaum.

Lord, C. G., Ross, L., & Lepper, M. R. (1979). Biased assimilation and attitude polarization: The effects of prior theories on subsequently considered evidence. *Journal of Personality and Social Psychology, 37*(11), 2098–2109.

Lord, R. G. (1985). Accuracy in behavioral measurement: An alternative definition based on raters' cognitive schema and signal detection theory. *Journal of Applied Psychology, 70*(1), 66–71.

Lord, R. G., de Vader, C. L., & Alliger, G. M. (1986). A meta-analysis of the relation between personality traits and leadership perceptions: An application of validity generalization procedures. *Journal of Applied Psychology, 71*(3), 402–410.

Lord, R. G., Foti, R. J., & de Vader, C. L. (1984). A test of leadership categorization theory: Internal structure, information processing, and leadership perceptions. *Organizational Behavior & Human Performance, 34*(3), 343–378.

Lord, R. G., Foti, R. J., & Phillips, J. S. (1982). A theory of leadership categorization. In H. G. Hunt, U. Sekaran, & C. Schriescheim (Eds.), *Leadership: Beyond establishment views* (pp. 104–121). Carbondale, IL: Southern Illinois University Press.

Lord, R. G., & Maher, K. J. (1991). *Leadership and information processing: Linking perceptions and performance*. Cambridge, MA: Unwin Hyman.

Lowrey, T. M. (1998). The effects of syntactic complexity on advertising persuasiveness. *Journal of Consumer Psychology, 7*(2), 187–206.

Luce, M. F. (1998). Choosing to avoid: Coping with negatively emotion-laden consumer decisions. *Journal of Consumer Research, 24*(4), 409–433.

Luce, M. F., Bettman J. R., & Payne, J. W. (1997). Choice processing in emotionally difficult decisions. *Journal of Experimental Psychology: Learning, Memory, and Cognition, 23*(2), 384–405.

Luce, M. F., Bettman, J. R., & Payne, J. W. (2000). Minimizing negative emotion as a decision goal: Investigating emotional trade-off difficulty. In S. Ratneshwar, D. G. Mick, & C. Huffman (Eds.), *The why of consumption: Contemporary perspectives on consumer motives, goals, and desires* (pp. 59–80). London and New York: Routledge.

Luiten, J., Ames, W., & Ackerson, G. (1980). A meta-analysis of the effects of advance organizers on learning and retention. *American Educational Research Journal, 17*(2), 211–218.

Lulofs, R. S. (1991). *Persuasion: Contexts, people, and messages*. Scottsdale, AZ: Gorsuch-Scarisbrick.

Lundqvist, D., & Öhman, A. (2005). Caught by the evil eye: Nonconscious information processing, emotion, and attention to facial stimuli. In L. F. Barrett, P. M. Niedenthal, & P. Winkielman (Eds.), *Emotion and consciousness* (pp. 97–122). New York: Guilford Press.

Lussier, D. A., & Olshavsky, R. W. (1979). Task complexity and contingent processing in brand choice. *Journal of Consumer Research, 6*(2), 154–165.

Lutz, R. I., MacKenzie, S. B., & Belch, G. F. (1983). Attitude toward the ad as a mediator of advertising effectiveness: Determinants and consequences. *Advances in Consumer Research, 10*(1), 532–539.

Lynch, J. G., Marmorstein, H., & Weigold, M. F. (1988). Choices from sets including remembered brands: Use of recalled attributes and prior overall evaluations. *Journal of Consumer Research, 15*(2), 169–184.

Lyons, M. J., Akamatsu, S., Kamachi, M., & Gyoba, J. (1998). Coding facial expressions with Gabor wavelets. In *Proceedings, Third IEEE international conference on automatic face and gesture recognition* (pp. 200–205). Washington, DC: IEEE Computer Society.

Macan, T. H., & Dipboye, R. L. (1988). The effects of interviewers' initial impressions on information gathering. *Organizational Behavior and Human Decision Processes, 42*(3), 364–387.

Macan, T. H., & Dipboye, R. L. (1994). The effects of the application on processing of information from the employment interview. *Journal of Applied Social Psychology, 24*(14), 1291–1314.

MacCoun, R. J., & Kerr, N. L. (1988). Asymmetric influence in mock jury deliberation: Jurors' bias for leniency. *Journal of Personality and Social Psychology, 54*(1), 21–33.

Macdonald-Ross, M. (1978). Graphics in texts. In L. S. Shulman (Ed.), *Review of research in education* (Vol. 5, pp. 49–85). Itasca, IL: F. E. Peacock Publishers.

MacGregor, D., & Slovic, P. (1986). Graphic representation of judgmental information. *Human-Computer Interaction, 2*(3), 179–200.

MacInnis, D. J., Rao, A. G., & Weiss, A. M. (2002). Assessing when increased media weight of real-world advertisements helps sales. *Journal of Marketing Research, 39*(4), 391–407.

Mack, D., & Rainey, D. (1990). Female applicants' grooming and personnel selection. *Journal of Social Behavior and Personality, 5*(5), 399–407.

Mackie, D. M., & Worth, L. T. (1991). Feeling good, but not thinking straight: The impact of positive mood on persuasion. In J. P. Forgas (Ed.), *Emotion and social judgments* (pp. 201–219). Elmsford, NY: Pergamon Press.

Mackintosh, B., & Mathews, A. (2003). Don't look now: Attentional avoidance of emotionally valenced cues. *Cognition & Emotion, 17*(4), 623–646.

MacLeod, C., & Rutherford, E. M. (1992). Anxiety and the selective processing of emotional information: Mediating roles of awareness, trait and state variables, and personal relevance of stimulus materials. *Behaviour Research and Therapy, 30*(5), 479–491.

MacMillan, I. C., Siegal, R., & Narasimha, P. N. S. (1985). Criteria used by venture capitalists to evaluate new venture proposals. *Journal of Business Venturing, 1*(1), 119–128.

MacMillan, J., Entin, E. E., & Serfaty, D. (2004). Communication overhead: The hidden cost of team cognition. In E. Salas & S. M. Fiore (Eds.), *Team cognition: Understanding the factors that drive process and performance* (pp. 61–82) Washington, DC: American Psychological Association.

Maddux, J. E., & Rogers, R. W. (1980). Effects of source expertness, physical attractiveness, and supporting arguments on persuasion: A case of brains over beauty. *Journal of Personality and Social Psychology, 39*(2), 235–244.

Mader, F. H. (1988). The influence of multi stop decision making on store choice (Doctoral dissertation, University of Georgia, 1988). *Dissertation Abstracts International, 49* (11A), 3430.

Maheswaran, D., & Sternthal, B. (1990). The effects of knowledge, motivation, and type of message on ad processing and product judgments. *Journal of Consumer Research, 17*(1), 66–73.

Maier, S. F., & Watkins, L. R. (1998). Cytokines for psychologists: Implications of bidirectional immune-to-brain communication for understanding behavior, mood, and cognition. *Psychological Review, 105*(1), 83–107.

Maines, L. A., & McDaniel, L. S. (2000). Effects of comprehensive-income characteristics on nonprofessional investors' judgments: The role of financial-statement presentation format. *The Accounting Review, 75*(2), 79–207.

Malhotra, N. K. (1982). Information load and consumer decision making. *Journal of Consumer Research, 8*(4), 419–430.

Malt, B. C., Ross, B. H., & Murphy, G. L. (1995). Predicting features for members of natural categories when categorization is uncertain. *Journal of Experimental Psychology: Learning, Memory, and Cognition, 21,* 646–661.

Mandel, N., & Johnson, E. J. (2002). When Web pages influence choice: Effects of visual primes on experts and novices. *Journal of Consumer Research, 29*(2), 235–245.

Manelis, L., & Yekovich, F. R. (1976). Repetitions of propositional arguments in sentences. *Journal of Verbal Learning & Verbal Behavior, 15*(3), 301–312.

Manis, M., Dovalina, I., Avis, N. E., & Cardoze, S. (1980). Base rates can affect individual predictions. *Journal of Personality and Social Psychology, 38*(2), 231–248.

Manusov, V. (1993). "It depends on your perspective": Effects of stance and beliefs about intent on person perception. *Western Journal of Communication, 57*(1), 27–41.

Markman, A. B. (1999). *Knowledge representation*. Mahwah, NJ: Erlbaum.

Markman, A. B., & Medin, D. L. (1995). Similarity and alignment in choice. *Organizational Behavior and Human Decision Processes, 63*(2), 117–130.

Markman, A. B., & Moreau, C. P. (2001). Analogy and analogical comparison in choice. In D. Gentner, K. J. Holyoak, & B. N. Kokinov (Eds.), *The analogical mind: Perspectives from cognitive science* (pp. 363–399). Cambridge, MA: The MIT Press.

Marks, L. J., & Olson, J. C. (1981). Toward a cognitive structure conceptualization of product familiarity. *Advances in Consumer Research, 8*, 145–150.

Markus, D. W. (1983). The budgeting process: Decision makers' perceptions of constraints (Doctoral dissertation, Northwestern University, 1983). *Dissertation Abstracts International, 44* (09A), 2642.

Markus, H., & Smith, J. (1981). The influence of self-schemas on the perception of others. In N. Cantor & J. F. Kihlstrom (Eds.), *Personality, cognition, and social interaction* (pp. 233–262). Hillsdale, NJ: Erlbaum.

Markus, H. & Zajonc, R. B. (1985). The cognitive perspective in social psychology. In G. Lindzey & E. Aronson (Eds.), *The handbook of social psychology* (3rd ed., Vol. 1, pp. 137–230). New York: Knopf.

Marshall, S. P. (1995). *Schemas in problem solving*. Cambridge, UK: Cambridge University Press.

Marslen-Wilson, W. D. (1987). Parallel processing in spoken word recognition. *Cognition, 25*, 71–102.

Martin, D. S. (1978). Person perception and real-life electoral behaviour. *Australian Journal of Psychology, 30*(3), 255–262.

Martin, J. (1982). Stories and scripts in organizational settings. In A. M. Hastorf & A. M. Isen (Eds.), *Cognitive social psychology* (pp. 255–306). New York: Elsevier/North-Holland.

Martin, J., & Powers, M. E. (1979, September). *If case examples provide no proof, why underutilize statistical information?* Paper presented at the American Psychological Association, New York.

Martin, J., & Powers, M. E. (1980, May). *Skepticism and the true believer: The effects of case and/or baserate information on belief and commitment*. Paper presented at the Western Psychological Association meetings, Honolulu, HI.

Martin, J. R. (1985) Process and Text: Two aspects of semiosis. In J. Benson and W. Greaves (Eds.), *Systemic Perspectives on Discourse* (Vol. I: Selected Theorectical Papers from the 9th International Systemic Workshop, pp. 248–274). Norwood, NJ: Ablex.

Martin, L. L., Abend, T., Sedikides, C., & Green, J. D. (1997). How would it feel if . . .? Mood as input to a role fulfillment evaluation process. *Journal of Personality and Social Psychology, 73*(2), 242–253.

Martin, S. L. (1987). An attributional analysis of differences in rating type in a performance evaluation context: A use of verbal protocol analysis (Doctoral dissertation, The Ohio State University, 1987). *Dissertation Abstracts International, 49* (02B), 0562.

Martindale, C., & Moore, K. (1988). Priming, prototypicality, and preference. *Journal of Experimental Psychology: Human Perception and Performance, 14*(4), 661–670.

Mascolo, M. F., & Fischer, K. W. (1995). Developmental transformations in appraisals for pride, shame, and guilt. In J. P. Tangney & K. W. Fischer (Eds.), *Self-conscious emotions: The psychology of shame, guilt, embarrassment, and pride* (pp. 64–113). New York: Guilford Press.

Mason, R. A., & Just, M. A. (2006). Neuroimaging contributions to the understanding of discourse processes. In M. J. Traxler & M. A. Gernsbacher (Eds.), *Handbook of psycholinguistics* (2nd ed., pp. 765–800). London: Elsevier Inc.

Massad, C. M., Hubbard, M., & Newtson, D. (1979). Selective perception of events. *Journal of Experimental Social Psychology, 15*(6), 513–532.

Massaro, D. W., & Friedman, D. (1990). Models of integration given multiple sources of information. *Psychological Review, 97*(2), 225–252.

Masters, R. D., & Sullivan, D. G. (1993). Nonverbal behavior and leadership: Emotion and cognition in political information processing. In S. Iyengar & W. J. McGuire (Eds.), *Explorations in political psychology* (pp. 150–182). Durham, NC: Duke University Press.

Mathews, A., & Klug, F. (1993). Emotionality and interference with color-naming in anxiety. *Behaviour Research and Therapy, 31*(1), 57–62.

Mathieu, J. E., Heffner, T. S., Goodwin, G. F., Cannon-Bowers, J. A., & Salas, E. (2005). Scaling the quality of teammates' mental models: Equifinality and normative comparisons. *Journal of Organizational Behavior, 26*(1), 37–56.

Matthews, A. M., Lord, R. G., & Walker, J. B. (1990). *The development of leadership perceptions in children.* Unpublished manuscript, University of Akron.

Matthews, G. R., & Antes, J. R. (1992). Visual attention and depression: Cognitive biases in the eye fixations of the dysphoric and the non-depressed. *Cognitive Therapy and Research, 16*(3), 359–371.

Matthews, H. L., Wilson, D. T., & Monoky, J. F., Jr. (1972). Bargaining behavior in a buyer-seller dyad. *Journal of Marketing Research, 9*(1), 103–105.

Maule, J., & Villejoubert, G. (2007). What lies beneath: Reframing framing effects. *Thinking & Reasoning, 13*(1), 25–44.

Maurer, T. J., & Lord, R. G. (1988). *August IP variables in leadership perception: Is cognitive demand a moderator?* Paper presented at the annual conference of the American Psychological Association (Div. 14), Atlanta, Georgia.

Mauro, R., Sato, K., & Tucker, J. (1992). The role of appraisal in human emotions: A cross-cultural study. *Journal of Personality and Social Psychology, 62*(2), 301–317.

May, E. R. (1973). *"Lessons" of the past.* New York: Oxford University Press.

Mayer, J. D., Gaschke, Y. N., Braverman, D. L., & Evans, T. W. (1992). Mood-congruent judgment is a general effect. *Journal of Personality and Social Psychology, 63*(1), 119–132.

Mayer, J. D., & Hanson, E. (1995). Mood-congruent judgment over time. *Personality and Social Psychology Bulletin, 21*(3), 237–244.

Mayer, R. E., & Gallini, J. K. (1990). When is an illustration worth ten thousand words? *Journal of Educational Psychology, 82*(4), 715–726.

Mayer, R. E., & Sims, V. K. (1994). For whom is a picture worth a thousand words? Extensions of a dual-coding theory of multimedia learning. *Journal of Educational Psychology, 86*(3), 389–401.

Mazzella, R., & Feingold, A. (1994). The effects of physical attractiveness, race, socioeconomic status, and gender of defendants and victims on judgments of mock jurors: A meta-analysis. *Journal of Applied Social Psychology, 24*(5), 1315–1344.

McArthur, L. Z. (1981). What grabs you? The role of attention in impression formation and causal attribution. In E. T. Higgins, C. P. Herman & M. P. Zanna (Eds.), *Social cognition: The Ontario Symposium* (Vol. 1, pp. 201–246). Hillsdale, NJ: Lawrence Erlbaum Associates.

McArthur, L. Z., & Ginsberg, E. (1981). Causal attribution to salient stimuli: An investigation of visual fixation mediators. *Personality and Social Psychology Bulletin, 7*(4), 547–553.

McArthur, L. Z., & Post, D. L. (1977). Figural emphasis and person perception. *Journal of Experimental Social Psychology, 13*(6), 520–535.

McCombs, M., & Mauro, J. (1977). Predicting newspaper readership from content characteristics. *Journalism Quarterly, 54*(1), 3–49.

McCoy, M. L. (1997). Jurors' reasoning skills and verdict decisions: The effect of jury deliberations (Doctoral dissertation, University of Wyoming, 1997). *Dissertation Abstracts International, 59* (01B), 436.

McCroskey, J. C., & Mehrley, R. S. (1969). The effects of disorganization and nonfluency on attitude change and source credibility. *Speech Monographs, 36*, 13–21.

McDaniel, M. A., & Einstein, G. O. (1989). Material-appropriate processing: A contextualist approach to reading and studying strategies. *Educational Psychology Review, 1*(2), 113–145.

McGlone, M. S., & Tofighbakhsh, J. (2000). Birds of a feather flock conjointly (?): Rhyme as reason in aphorisms. *Psychological Science, 11*(5), 424–428.

McGovern, T. V., Jones, B. W., & Morris, S. E. (1979). Comparison of professional versus student ratings of job interviewee behavior. *Journal of Counseling Psychology, 26*(2), 176–179.

McGovern, T. V., & Tinsley, H. E. (1978). Interviewer evaluations of interviewee nonverbal behavior. *Journal of Vocational Behavior, 13*(2), 163–171.

McGraw, K. M., & Steenbergen, M. R. (1995). Pictures in the head: Memory representations of political candidates. In M. Lodge & K. M. McGraw (Eds.), *Political judgment: Structure and process* (pp. 15–41). Ann Arbor, MI: The University of Michigan Press.

McGuire, W. J. (1985). Attitudes and attitude change. In G. Lindsey & E. Aronson (Eds.), *Handbook of social psychology* (3rd ed., Vol. 2, pp. 233–346). New York: Random House.

McHugo, G. J., Lanzetta, J. T., Sullivan, D. G., Masters, R. D., & Englis, B. G. (1985). Emotional reactions to the expressive displays of a political leader. *Journal of Personality and Social Psychology, 49*(6), 1513–1529.

McIntyre, R. M., & Salas, E. (1995). Measuring and managing for team performance: Emerging principles from complex environments. In R. A. Guzzo & E. Salas (Eds.), *Team effectiveness and decision making in organizations* (pp. 9–45). San Francisco: Jossey-Bass.

McKeithen, K. B., Reitman, J. S., Rueter, H. H., & Hirtle, S. C. (1981). Knowledge organization and skill differences in computer programmers. *Cognitive Psychology, 13*(3), 307–325.

McKinnon, L. M., & Tedesco, J. C. (1999). The influence of medium and media commentary on presidential debate effects. In L. L. Kaid & D. G. Bystrom (Eds.), *The electronic election: Perspectives on the 1996 campaign communication* (pp. 191–206). Mahwah, NJ: Lawrence Erlbaum.

McKinnon, L. M., Tedesco, J. C., & Kaid, L. L. (1993). The third 1992 presidential debate: Channel and commentary effects. *Argumentation and Advocacy, 30*, 106–118.

McLaughlin, G. H. (1966). Comparing styles of presenting technical information. *Ergonomics, 9*(3), 257–259.

McNeil, B. J., Pauker, S. G., Cox, H. C., Jr., & Tversky, A. (1982). On the elicitation of preferences for alternative therapies. *New England Journal of Medicine, 306*, 1259–1262.

McQueen, J. M., Cutler, A., Briscoe, T., & Norris, D. (1995). Models of continuous speech recognition and the contents of the vocabulary. *Language and Cognitive Processes, 10*(3–4), 309–331.

Medvec, V. H., Madey, S. F., & Gilovich, T. (1995). When less is more: Counterfactual thinking and satisfaction among Olympic medalists. *Journal of Personality and Social Psychology, 69*(4), 603–610.

Meehl, P. E. (1954). *Clinical versus statistical prediction: A theoretical analysis and a review of the evidence.* Minneapolis, MN: University of Minnesota Press.

Mehrabian, A., & Ferris, S. R. (1967). Inference of attitudes from nonverbal communication in two channels. *Journal of Consulting Psychology, 31*(3), 248–252.

Melone, N. P. (1987). Expertise in corporate acquisitions: An investigation of the influence of specialized knowledge on strategic decision making (Doctoral dissertation, University of Minnesota, 1987). *Dissertation Abstracts International, 48* (09A), 2388.

Melone, N. P. (1994). Reasoning in the executive suite: The influence of role/experience-based expertise on decision processes of corporate executives. *Organization Science, 5*(3), 438–455.

Menne, J., Klingensmith, J., & Nord, D. (1969). Use of taped lectures to replace class attendance. *AV Communication Review, 17*, 47–51.

Meseguer, E., Carreiras, M., & Clifton, C. (2002). Overt reanalysis strategies and eye movements during the reading of mild garden path sentences. *Memory & Cognition, 30*(4), 551–561.

Messick, D. M., & Sentis, K. P. (1985). Estimating social and nonsocial utility functions from ordinal data. *European Journal of Social Psychology, 15*(4), 389–399.

Messner, M., Reinhard, M. A., & Sporer, S. L. (2008). Compliance through direct persuasive appeals: The moderating role of communicator's attractiveness in interpersonal persuasion. *Social Influence, 3*(2), 67–83.

Metalis, S. A., & Hess, E. H. (1982). Pupillary response/semantic differential scale relationships. *Journal of Research in Personality, 16*(2), 201–216.

Metcalfe, J., & Mischel, W. (1999). A hot/cool-system analysis of delay of gratification: Dynamics of willpower. *Psychological Review, 106*(1), 3–19.

Metha, P., & Clark, M. S. (1994). Toward understanding emotions in intimate relationships. In A. I. Weber & J. H. Harvey (Eds.), *Perspectives on close relationships* (pp. 88–109). Boston: Allyn & Bacon.

Meyer, B. J., & McConkie, G. W. (1973). What is recalled after hearing a passage? *Journal of Educational Psychology, 65*(1), 109–117.

Meyer, W. U., Reisenzein, R., & Schützwohl, A. (1997). Toward a process analysis of emotions: The case of surprise. *Motivation and Emotion, 21*(3), 251–274.

Meyerowitz, B., & Chaiken, S. (1987). The effect of message framing on breast self-examination attitudes, intentions, and behavior. *Journal of Personality and Social Psychology, 52*(3), 500–510.

Michotte, A. (1963). *The perception of causality.* Oxford, UK: Basic Books.

Mikulecky, L. (1981) *Job literacy: The relationship between school preparation and workplace actuality.* Bloomington, IN: Indiana University.

Miller, G. A. (1956). The magical number seven, plus or minus two: Some limits on our capacity for processing information. *Psychological Review, 63*(2), 81–97.

Miller, J. L. (1981). Effects of speaking rate on segmental distinctions. In P. D. Eimas & J. L. Miller (Eds.), *Perspectives on the study of speech* (pp. 39–74). Hillsdale, NJ: Erlbaum.

Miller, K. I., Stiff, J. B., & Ellis, B. H. (1988). Communication and empathy as precursors to burnout among human service workers. *Communication Monographs, 55*(3), 250–265.

Miller, N., Maruyama, G., Beaber, R. J., & Valone, K. (1976). Speed of speech and persuasion. *Journal of Personality and Social Psychology, 34*(4), 615–624.

Mills, J., & Harvey, J. (1972). Opinion change as a function of when information about the communicator is received and whether he is attractive or expert. *Journal of Personality and Social Psychology, 21*(1), 52–55.

Milroy, R., & Poulton, E. C. (1978). Labelling graphs for improved reading speed. *Ergonomics, 21*(1), 55–61.

Miniard, P. W., Bhatla, S., Lord, K. R., Dickson, P. R., & Unnava, H. R. (1991). Picture-based persuasion processes and the moderating role of involvement. *Journal of Consumer Research, 18*(1), 92–107.

Minionis, D. P. (1995). Enhancing team performance in adverse conditions: The role of shared team mental models and team training on an interdependent task. *Dissertation Abstracts International: Section B: The Sciences and Engineering, 56*(2-B), 1139.

Minsky, M. A. (1975). A framework for the representation of knowledge. In P. Winston (Ed.), *The psychology of computer vision* (pp. 211–277). New York: McGraw-Hill.

Mintz, A., Geva, N., Redd, S. B., & Carnes, A. (1997). The effect of dynamic and static choice sets on political decision making: An analysis of using the decision board platform. *American Political Science Review, 91*(3), 553–566.

Mischel, W., Cantor, N., & Feldman, S. (1996). Principles of self-regulation: The nature of willpower and self-control. In E. T. Higgins & A. W. Kruglanski (Eds.), *Social psychology: Handbook of basic principles* (pp. 329–360). New York: Guilford Press.

Mitchell, A. A. (1981). The dimensions of advertising involvement. *Advances in Consumer Research, 8,* 25–30.

Mitchell, A. A., & Olson, J. C. (1981). Are product attribute beliefs the only mediator of advertising effects on brand attitude? *Journal of Marketing Research, 18*(3), 318–332.

Mogg, K., Bradley, B. P., Field, M., & De Houwer, J. (2003). Eye movements to smoking-related pictures in smokers: Relationship between attentional biases and implicit and explicit measures of stimulus valence. *Addiction, 98*(6), 825–836.

Mohammed, S., & Dumville, B. C. (2001). Team mental models in a team knowledge framework: Expanding theory and measurement across disciplinary boundaries. *Journal of Organizational Behavior, 22*(2), 89–106.

Mojzisch, A., & Schulz-Hardt, S. (2005). Information sampling in group decision making: Sampling biases and their consequences. In K. Fiedler & P. Juslin (Eds.), *Information Sampling and Adaptive Cognition* (pp. 299–326). Cambridge, UK: Cambridge University Press.

Mojzisch, A., Schulz-Hardt, S., Kerschreiter, R., Brodbeck, F. C., & Frey, D. (2004). *Social validation as an explanation for the dominance of shared information in group decisions: A critical test and extension.* Working paper, Dresden University of Technology.

Monat, A. (1976). Temporal uncertainty, anticipation time, and cognitive coping under threat. *Journal of Human Stress, 2*(2), 32–43.

Mongeau, P. A. (1998). Another look at fear-arousing persuasive appeals. In M. Allen & R. W. Preiss (Eds.), *Persuasion: Advances through meta-analysis* (pp. 53–68). Cresskill, NJ: Hampton Press.

Montepare, J. M., & Dobish, H. (2003). The contribution of emotion perceptions and their overgeneralizations to trait impressions. *Journal of Nonverbal Behavior, 27*(4), 237–254.

Montepare, J. M., & Zebrowitz-McArthur, L. (1987). Perceptions of adults with childlike voices in two cultures. *Journal of Experimental Social Psychology, 23*(4), 331–349.

Montepare, J. M., & Zebrowitz-McArthur, L. (1988). Impressions of people created by age-related qualities of their gaits. *Journal of Personality and Social Psychology, 55*(4), 547–556.

Montier, J. (2002). *Behavioural finance: Insights into irrational minds and markets.* Hoboken: Wiley.

Moog, C. (1991). *Are they selling her lips? Advertising and identity.* New York: Morrow & Co.

Moore, D. L., & Hutchinson, J. W. (1983). The effects of ad affect on advertising effectiveness. *Advances in Consumer Research, 10*, 526–531.

Moray, N. (1959). Attention in dichotic listening: Affective cues and the influence of instructions. *The Quarterly Journal of Experimental Psychology, 11*, 56–60.

Moreau, C. P., Markman, A. B., & Lehmann, D. R. (2001). What is it? Categorization flexibility and consumers' responses to really new products. *Journal of Consumer Research, 27*(4), 489–498.

Morris, C. D., Stein, B. S., & Bransford, J. D. (1979). Prerequisites for the utilization of knowledge in the recall of prose passages. *Journal of Experimental Psychology: Human Learning and Memory, 5*(3), 253–261.

Morwitz, V. G., & Fitzsimons, G. J. (2004). The mere-measurement effect: Why does measuring intentions change actual behavior? *Journal of Consumer Psychology, 14*(1–2), 64–74.

Morwitz, V. G., Johnson, E., & Schmittlein, D. (1993). Does measuring intent change behavior. *Journal of Consumer Research, 20*(1), 46–61.

Moskowitz, D. S. (1982). Coherence and cross-situational generality in personality: A new analysis of old problems. *Journal of Personality and Social Psychology, 43*(4), 754–768.

Motes, W. H., Hilton, C. B., & Fielden, J. S. (1992). Language, sentence, and structural variations in print advertising. *Journal of Advertising Research, 32*, 63–77.

Motowidlo, S. J., & Burnett, J. R. (1995). Aural and visual sources of validity in structured employment interviews. *Organizational Behavior and Human Decision Processes, 61*(3), 239–249.

Mulilis, J. P., & Lippa, R. (1990). Behavioral change in earthquake preparedness due to negative threat appeals: A test of protection motivation theory. *Journal of Applied Social Psychology, 20* (8, Pt. 1), 619–638.

Mulvey, M. S., Olson, J. C., Celsi, R. L., & Walker, B. A. (1994). Exploring the relationship between means-end knowledge and involvement. *Advances in Consumer Research, 21*, 51–57.

Mumford, M. D., Marks, M. A., Connelly, M. S., Zaccaro, S. J., & Reiter-Palmon, R. (2000). Development of leadership skills: Experience and timing. *Leadership Quarterly, 11*, 87–114.

Mussweiler, T., & Strack, F. (2000). The use of category and exemplar knowledge in the solution of anchoring tasks. *Journal of Personality and Social Psychology, 78*(6), 1038–1052.

Myers, B., & Greene, E. (2004). The prejudicial nature of victim impact statements: Implications for capital sentencing policy. *Psychology, Public Policy, and Law, 10*(4), 492–515.

Myers, J. L., Pezdek, K., & Coulson, D. (1973). Effect of prose organization upon free recall. *Journal of Educational Psychology, 65*(3), 313–320.

Nabi, R. L. (1998). The effect of disgust-eliciting visuals on attitudes toward animal experimentation. *Communication Quarterly, 46*, 472–484.

Nabi, R. L. (2002). Anger, fear, uncertainty, and attitudes: A test of the cognitive-functional model. *Communication Monographs, 69*(3), 204–216.

Nabi, R. L. (2003). Exploring the framing effects of emotion: Do discrete emotions differentially influence information accessibility, information seeking, and policy preference? *Communication Research, 30*(2), 224–247.

Nagy, G. (1975). Female dating strategies as a function of physical attractiveness and other social characteristics of males. Unpublished Master's thesis, Kansas State University.

Nagy, G. (1981). How are personnel selections made? An analysis of decision strategies in a simulated personnel selection task (Doctoral dissertation, Kansas State University, 1981). *Dissertation Abstracts International, 42* (07B), 3022.

Neale, M. A., Huber, V. L., & Northcraft, G. B. (1987). The framing of negotiations: Contextual versus task frames. *Organizational Behavior and Human Decision Processes, 39*(2), 228–241.

Nearey, T. M. (1989). Static, dynamic, and relational properties in vowel perception. *Journal of the Acoustical Society of America, 85*(5), 2088–2113.

Nedungadi, P. (1990). Recall and consumer consideration sets: Influencing choice without altering brand evaluations. *Journal of Consumer Research, 17*(3), 263–276.

Neisser, U. (1976). *Cognition and reality: Principles and implications of cognitive psychology*. New York: W. H. Freeman/Times Books/Henry Holt & Co.

Nelson, D. L., Wheeler, J., & Engel, J. (1970). Stimulus meaningfulness and similarity, recall direction and rate of recall test. *Psychonomic Science, 20*(6), 346–347.

Nelson, K. (1980, September). *Characteristics of children's scripts for familiar events*. Paper presented at the meeting of the American Psychological Association, Montreal, Canada.

Nelson, T. E., Oxley, Z. M., & Clawson, R. A. (1997). Toward a psychology of framing effects. *Political Behavior, 19*(3), 221–246.

Nelson, T. O., & Narens, L. (1990). Metamemory: A theoretical framework and new findings. In G. Bower (Ed.), *The psychology of learning and motivation* (Vol. 26, pp. 125–141). New York: Academic Press.

Nemeth, R. J. (2002). The impact of gruesome evidence on mock juror decision making: The role of evidence characteristics and emotional response (Doctoral dissertation, Louisiana State University, 2002). *Dissertation Abstracts International, 63* (11B), 5546.

Nesdale, A. R., & Dharmalingam, S. (1986). Category salience, stereotyping and person memory. *Australian Journal of Psychology, 38*(2), 145–151.

Nespor, M., & Vogel, I. (1983). Prosodic structure above the word. In A. Cutler & D. R. Ladd (Eds.), *Prosody: Models and measurements* (pp. 123–140). Heidelberg: Springer.

Neuberg, S. L., & Fiske, S. T. (1987). Motivational influences on impression formation: Outcome dependency, accuracy-driven attention, and individuating processes. *Journal of Personality and Social Psychology, 53*(3), 431–444.

Neuman, R., Just, M., & Crigler, A. (1992). *Common knowledge: News and the construction of political meaning*. Chicago: University of Chicago Press.

Neumann, R., & Strack, F. (2000). "Mood contagion": The automatic transfer of mood between persons. *Journal of Personality and Social Psychology, 79*(2), 211–223.

Newby-Clark, I. R., Ross, M., Buehler, R., Koehler, D. J., & Griffin, D. (2000). People focus on optimistic and disregard pessimistic scenarios while predicting their task completion times. *Journal of Experimental Psychology: Applied, 6*(3), 171–182.

Newcombe, N., & Arnkoff, D. B. (1979). Effects of speech style and sex of speaker on person perception. *Journal of Personality and Social Psychology, 37*(8), 1293–1303.

Newell, A., & Simon, H. A. (1972). *Human problem solving*. Englewood Cliffs, NJ: Prentice-Hall.

Newman, B. I., & Perloff, R. M. (2004). Political marketing: Theory, research, applications. In L. L. Kaid (Ed.), *Handbook of political communication research* (pp. 17–43). Mahwah, NJ: Lawrence Erlbaum Associates.

Newspaper Advertising Bureau. (1964). *A study of the opportunity for exposure to national newspaper advertising*. New York: Author.

Newspaper Advertising Bureau. (1987). *An eye camera study of ads*. New York: Author.

Nicholas, S. K. (1983). A video observational study of the writing process of college students in a non-academic situation (Doctoral dissertation, Oakland University, 1983). *Dissertation Abstracts International, 44* (03A), 684.

Nickerson, C. (1999). The use of English in electronic mail in a multinational corporation. In F. Bargiela-Chiappini & C. Nickerson (Eds.), *Writing business: Genres, media and discourses* (pp. 35–56). Harlow, UK: Longman.

Nickerson, R. S. (1968). On long-term recognition memory for pictorial material. *Psychonomic Science, 11*(2), 58.

Nickles, K. R. (1995). Judgment-based and reasoning-based stopping rules in decision making under uncertainty (Doctoral dissertation, University of Minnesota, 1995). *Dissertation Abstracts International, 56* (03A), 1005.

Nicosia, G. E. (1988). College students' listening comprehension strategies in a lecture situation (Doctoral dissertation, New York University, 1988). *Dissertation Abstracts International, 49* (05A), 0998.

Niedenthal, P. M., Halberstadt, J. B., & Innes-Ker, Å. H. (1999). Emotional response categorization. *Psychological Review, 106*(2), 337–361.

Niedenthal, P. M., & Kitayama, S. (Eds.). (1994). *The heart's eye: Emotional influences in perception and attention.* San Diego, CA: Academic Press.

Niedenthal, P. M., & Setterlund, M. B. (1994). Emotion congruence in perception. *Personality and Social Psychology Bulletin, 20*(4), 401–411.

Niedenthal, P. M., Setterlund, M. B., & Jones, D. E. (1994). Emotional organization of perceptual memory. In P. M. Niedenthal & S. Kitayama (Eds.), *The heart's eye: Emotional influences in perception and attention* (pp. 87–113). San Diego, CA: Academic Press.

Nisbett, R. E., Borgida, E., Crandall, R., & Reed, H. (1982). Popular induction: Information is not necessarily informative. In D. Kahneman, P. Slovic, & A. Tversky (Eds.), *Judgments under uncertainty: Heuristics and biases* (pp. 101–116). New York: Cambridge University Press.

Nisbett, R. E., & Ross, L. (1980). *Human inference: Strategies and shortcomings of social judgment.* Englewood Cliffs, NJ: Prentice-Hall.

Nisbett, R. E., Zukier, H., & Lemley, R. E. (1981). The dilution effect: Nondiagnostic information weakens the implications of diagnostic information. *Cognitive Psychology, 13*(2), 248–277.

Nodine, C. F., & Kundel, H. L. (1987). Perception and display in diagnostic imaging. *RadioGraphs, 7,* 1241–1250.

Nodine, C. F., Locher, P. J., & Krupinski, E. A. (1993). The role of formal art training on perception and aesthetic judgment of art compositions. *Leonardo, 26,* 219–227.

Nolen-Hoeksema, S., & Morrow, J. (1993). Effects of rumination and distraction on naturally occurring depressed mood. *Cognition & Emotion, 7*(6), 561–570.

Nolen-Hoeksema, S., Morrow, J., & Fredrickson, B. L. (1993). Response styles and the duration of episodes of depressed mood. *Journal of Abnormal Psychology, 102*(1), 20–28.

Norman, R. (1976). When what is said is important: A comparison of expert and attractive sources. *Journal of Experimental Social Psychology, 12*(3), 294–300.

North, A. C., Hargreaves, D. J., & McKendrick, J. (1997). In-store music affects product choice. *Nature, 390*(6656), 132.

North, A. C., Hargreaves, D. J., & McKendrick, J. (1999). Research reports- The influence of in-store music on wine selections. *Journal of Applied Psychology, 84*(2), 271–276.

Northcraft, G. B., & Neale, M. A. (1987). Experts, amateurs, and real estate: An anchoring-and-adjustment perspective on property pricing decisions. *Organizational Behavior and Human Decision, 39*(1), 84–97.

Norwick, R., & Epley, N. (2003, February). *Experiential determinants of confidence.* Poster presented at the Society for Personality and Social Psychology, Los Angeles, California.

Novick, L. R., & Holyoak, K. J. (1991). Mathematical problem solving by analogy. *Journal of Experimental Psychology: Learning, Memory, and Cognition, 17*(3), 398–415.

Nowlis, S. M., Kahn, B. E., & Dhar, R. (2002). Coping with ambivalence: The effect of removing a neutral option on consumer attitude and preference judgments. *Journal of Consumer Research, 29*(3), 319–334.

Nygren, T. E., Isen, A. M., Taylor, P. J., & Dulin, J. (1996). The influence of positive affect on the decision rule in risk situations: Focus on outcome (and especially avoidance of loss) rather than probability. *Organizational Behavior and Human Decision Processes, 66*(1), 59–72.

Oakes, P., & Turner, J. C. (1986). Distinctiveness and the salience of social category memberships: Is there an automatic perceptual bias towards novelty? *European Journal of Social Psychology, 16*(4), 325–344.

Oatley, K., & Jenkins, J. M. (1996). *Understanding emotions.* Malden, MA: Blackwell Publishing.

O'Brien, E. J., Raney, G. E., Albrecht, J., & Rayner, K. (1997). Processes involved in the resolution of explicit anaphors. *Discourse Processes, 23,* 1–24.

Ochsner, K. N. (2000). Are affective events richly recollected or simply familiar? The experience and process of recognizing feelings past. *Journal of Experimental Psychology: General, 129*(2), 242–261.

Ochsner, K. N., & Sanchez, H. (2001). *The relation between the regulation and recollection of affective experience.* Unpublished manuscript.

Offermann, L. R., Kennedy, J. K., & Wirtz, P. W. (1994). Implicit leadership theories: Content, structure, and generalizability. *Leadership Quarterly, 5*(1), 43–58.

Ohlsson, S., & Hemmerich, J. (1999). Articulating an explanation schema: A preliminary model and supporting data. In M. Hahn & S. Stones (Eds.), *Proceedings of the Twenty First Annual Conference of the Cognitive Science Society* (pp. 490–495). Mahwah, NJ: Erlbaum.

Ohlsson, S., & Lehtinen, E. (1997). Abstraction and the acquisition of complex ideas. *International Journal of Educational Research, 27,* 37–48.

Öhman, A. (1979). The orienting response, attention, and learning: An information-processing perspective. In H. D. Kimmel, E. H. van Gist, & J. F. Orlebeke (Eds.), *The orienting reflex in humans* (pp. 443–472). Hillsdale, NJ: Lawrence Erlbaum Associates.

Öhman, A., & Dimberg, U. (1978). Facial expressions as conditioned stimuli for electrodermal responses: A case of "preparedness"? *Journal of Personality and Social Psychology, 36*(11), 1251–1258.

Öhman, A., Esteves, F., & Soares, J. J. F. (1995). Preparedness and preattentive associative learning: Electrodermal conditioning to masked stimuli. *Journal of Psychophysiology, 9*(2), 99–108.

Öhman, A., Flykt, A., & Esteves, F. (2001). Emotion drives attention: Detecting the snake in the grass. *Journal of Experimental Psychology: General, 130*(3), 466–478.

Öhman, A., Hamm, A., & Hugdahl, K. (2000). Cognition and the autonomic nervous system: Orienting, anticipation, and conditioning. In J. T. Cacioppo, L. G. Tassinary, & G. G. Berntson (Eds.), *Handbook of psychophysiology* (2nd ed., pp. 533–575). New York: Cambridge University Press.

Öhman, A., & Wiens, S. (2003). On the automaticity of autonomic responses in emotion: An evolutionary perspective. In R. J. Davidson, K. R. Scherer, & H. H. Goldsmith (Eds.), *Handbook of affective sciences* (pp. 256–275). New York: Oxford University Press.

Oliver, E., & Griffitt, W. (1976). Emotional arousal and "objective" judgment. *Bulletin of the Psychonomic Society, 8*(5), 399–400.

Olshavsky, R. W., & Acito, F. (1980). The impact of data collection procedure on choice rule. *Advances in Consumer Research, 7,* 729–732.

Olson, D. R., & Filby, N. (1972). On the comprehension of active and passive sentences. *Cognitive Psychology, 3*(3), 361–381.

Onken, J., Hastie, R., & Revelle, W. (1985). Individual differences in the use of simplification strategies in a complex decision-making task. *Journal of Experimental Psychology: Human Perception and Performance, 11*(1), 14–27.

Orasanu, J., & Salas, E. (1993) Team decision making in complex environments. In G. A. Klein, J. Orasanu, R. Calderwood, & C. E. Zsambok (Eds.), *Decision making in action: Models and methods* (pp. 327–345). Westport, CT: Ablex Publishing.

Ordonez, L. D. (1994). Expectations in consumer decision-making: A model of reference price formation (Doctoral dissertation, University of California, Berkeley, 1994). *Dissertation Abstracts International, 56* (05B), 2911.

O'Reilly, C. A. (1980). Individuals and information overload in organizations: Is more necessarily better? *Academy of Management Journal, 23*(4), 684–696.

Ortony, A., Clore, G. L., & Collins, A. (1988). *The cognitive structure of emotions.* New York: Cambridge University Press.

O'Shaughnessy, J. (1987). *Why people buy.* Oxford: Oxford University Press.

O'Sullivan, C. S., Chen, A., Mohapatra, S., Sigelman, L., & Lewis, E. (1988). Voting in ignorance: The politics of smooth-sounding names. *Journal of Applied Social Psychology, 18*(13), 1094–1106.

Otake, T., & Cutler, A. (Eds.). (1996). *Phonological structure and language processing: Cross-linguistic studies.* Berlin: Mouton.

Ottati, V. C., & Isbell, L. M. (1996). Effects on mood during exposure to target information on subsequently reported judgments: An on-line model of misattribution and correction. *Journal of Personality and Social Psychology, 71*(1), 39–53.

Otto, A. L., Penrod, S. D., & Dexter, H. R. (1994). The biasing impact of pretrial publicity on juror judgments. *Law and Human Behavior, 18*(4), 453–469.

Overby, J. W., Gardial, S. F., & Woodruff, R. B. (2004). French versus American consumers' attachment of value to a product in a common consumption context: A cross-national comparison. *Journal of the Academy of Marketing Science, 32*(4), 437–460.

Paek, S. N. (1997). A cognitive model for selecting business appraisal methods (Doctoral dissertation, University of Nebraska–Lincoln, 1997). *Dissertation Abstracts International, 58* (06A), 2283.

Paese, P. W., Bieser, M., & Tubbs, M. E. (1993). Framing effects and choice shifts in group decision making. *Organizational Behavior and Human Decision Processes, 56*(1), 149–165.

Pallak, S. R. (1983). Salience of a communicator's physical attractiveness and persuasion: A heuristic versus systematic processing interpretation. *Social Cognition, 2*(2), 158–170.

Pallak, S. R., Murroni, E., & Koch, J. (1983). Communicator attractiveness and expertise, emotional versus rational appeals, and persuasion: A heuristic versus systematic processing interpretation. *Social Cognition, 2*(2), 122–141.

Palmer, J., & Faivre, J. P. (1973). The information processing theory of consumer behavior. *European Research, 1,* 231–240.

Palmer, S. E. (1975). The effects of contextual scenes on the identification of objects. *Memory & Cognition, 3*(5), 519–526.

Pan, Z., & Kosicki, G. M. (2001). Framing as a strategic action in public deliberation. In S. D. Reese, O. H. Gandy, & A. E. Grant (Eds.), *Framing public life: Perspectives on media and our understanding of the social world* (pp. 35–65). Mahwah, NJ: Lawrence Erlbaum Associates.

Park, C. W., & Lessig, V. P. (1981). Familiarity and its impact on consumer decision biases and heuristics. *Journal of Consumer Research, 8*(2), 223–230.

Park, C. W., & Young, S. M. (1986). Consumer response to television commercials: The impact of involvement and background music on brand attitude formation. *Journal of Marketing Research, 23*(1), 11–24.

Parks, C. D., & Cowlin, R. A. (1996). Acceptance of uncommon information into group discussion when that information is or is not demonstrable. *Organizational Behavior and Human Decision Processes, 66*(3), 307–315.

Parsons, C. K., & Liden, R. C. (1984). Interviewer perceptions of applicant qualifications: A multivariate field study of demographic characteristics and nonverbal cues. *Journal of Applied Psychology, 69*(4), 557–568.

Paterson, D. G., & Tinker, M. A. (1942). Influence of line width on eye movements for six-point type. *Journal of Educational Psychology, 33*(7), 552–555.

Patterson, M. L., Churchill, M. E., Burger, G. K., & Powell, J. L. (1992). Verbal and nonverbal modality effects on impressions of political candidates: Analysis from the 1984 presidential debates. *Communication Monographs, 59*(3), 231–242.

Patterson, M. L., & Ritts, V. (1997). Social and communicative anxiety: A review and meta-analysis. In B. R. Burleson & A. W. Kunkel (Eds.), *Communication yearbook 20* (pp. 263–303). Thousand Oaks, CA: Sage.

Patterson, P. G., & Spreng, R. A. (1997). Modeling the relationship between perceived value, satisfaction and repurchase intentions in a business-to-business, services context: An empirical examination. *International Journal of Service Industry Management, 8*(5), 415–432.

Payne, J. W. (1976). Task complexity and contingent processing in decision making: An information search and protocol analysis. *Organizational Behavior & Human Performance, 16*(2), 366–387.

Payne, J. W., & Bettman, J. R. (2004). Walking with the scarecrow: The information-processing approach to decision research. In D. J. Koehler & N. Harvey (Eds.), *Blackwell handbook of judgment and decision making* (pp. 110–132). Oxford, UK: Blackwell Publishing.

Payne, J. W., Bettman, J. R., & Johnson, E. J. (1988). Adaptive strategy selection in decision making. *Journal of Experimental Psychology: Learning, Memory, and Cognition, 14*(3), 534–552.

Payne, J. W., Bettman, J. R., & Johnson, E. J. (1993). *The adaptive decision maker.* New York: Cambridge University Press.

Payne, J. W., & Braunstein, M. L. (1978). Risky choice: An examination of information acquisition behavior. *Memory & Cognition, 6*(5), 554–561.

Peeck, J. (1987). The role of illustrations in processing and remembering illustrated text. In D. M. Willows & H. A. Houghton (Eds.), *The psychology of illustration: Basic research* (Vol. 1, pp. 115–151). New York: Springer-Verlag.

Pell, M. D. (2005). Prosody-face interactions in emotional processing as revealed by the facial affect decision task. *Journal of Nonverbal Behavior, 29*(4), 193–215.

Pennebaker, J. W., & King, L. A. (1999). Linguistic styles: Language use as an individual difference. *Journal of Personality and Social Psychology, 77*(6), 1296–1312.

Pennington, D. C. (1982). Witnesses and their testimony: Effects of ordering on juror verdicts. *Journal of Applied Social Psychology, 12*(4), 318–333.

Pennington, N., & Hastie, R. (1992). Explaining the evidence: Tests of the story model for juror decision making. *Journal of Personality and Social Psychology, 62*(2), 189–206.

Penrod, S., & Otto, A. L. (1992, September). *Pretrial publicity and juror decision making: Assessing the magnitude and source of prejudicial effects.* Paper presented at the Third European Conference on Law and Psychology, Oxford, UK.

Perkins, W. S., & Reynolds, T. J. (1988). The explanatory power of values in preference judgments: Validation of the means-end perspective. *Advances in Consumer Research, 15*, 122–126).

Perlmutter, J., & Royer, J. M. (1973). Organization of prose materials: Stimulus, storage, and retrieval. *Canadian Journal of Psychology/Revue Canadienne de Psychologie, 27*(2), 200–209.

Peskin, J. (1998). Constructing meaning when reading poetry: An expert-novice study. *Cognition and Instruction, 16*(3), 235–263.

Peters, L. H., & Terborg, J. R. (1975). The effects of temporal placement of unfavorable information and of attitude similarity on personnel selection decisions. *Organizational Behavior and Human Performance, 13*(2), 279–293.

Peterson, K. (1984). An investigation of consumer patronage/shopping decision-making behavior using an information processing approach (Doctoral dissertation, The University of Wisconsin—Madison, 1984). *Dissertation Abstracts International, 45.*

Petty, R. E., Brinol, P., Tormala, A. L., & Wegener, D. (2007). The role of metacognition in social judgment. In A. W. Kruglanski & E. T. Higgins (Eds.), *Social Psychology: Handbook of basic principles* (2nd ed., pp. 254–284). New York: The Guilford Press.

Petty, R. E., & Cacioppo, J. T. (1980). Effects of issue involvement on attitudes in an advertising context. In G. Gorn & M. Goldberg (Eds.), *Proceedings of the division 23 program* (pp. 75–79). Montreal, Canada: Division 23 of the American Psychological Association (09A), 2921.

Petty, R. E., & Cacioppo, J. T. (1984). The effects of involvement on responses to argument quantity and quality: Central and peripheral routes to persuasion. *Journal of Personality and Social Psychology, 46*(1), 69–81.

Petty, R. E., & Cacioppo, J. T. (1986). *Communication and persuasion: Central and peripheral routes to attitude change.* New York: Springer-Verlag.

Petty, R. E., Cacioppo, J. T., & Kasmer, J. A. (1988). The role of affect in the elaboration likelihood model of persuasion. In L. Donohew, H. E. Sypher, & E. T. Higgins (Eds.), *Communication, social cognition, and affect* (pp. 117–146). Hillsdale, NJ: Lawrence Erlbaum Associates.

Petty, R. E., Cacioppo, J. T., & Schumann, D. (1983). Central & peripheral routes to advertising effectiveness: the moderating role of involvement. *Journal of Consumer Research, 10*(2), 135–146.

Petty, R. E., DeSteno, D., & Rucker, D. D. (2001). The role of affect in attitude change. In J. P. Forgas (Ed.), *Handbook of affect and social cognition* (pp. 212–233). Mahwah, NJ: Lawrence Erlbaum Associates.

Petty, R. E., Gleicher, F., & Baker, S. M. (1991). Multiple roles for affect in persuasion. In J. P. Forgas (Ed), *Emotion and social judgments* (pp. 181–200). Elmsford, NY: Pergamon Press.

Pezdek, K., & Evans, G. W. (1979). Visual and verbal memory for objects and their spatial locations. *Journal of Experimental Psychology: Human Learning and Memory, 5*(4), 360–373.

Pfeffer, M. G. (1987). Venture capital investment and protocol analysis (Doctoral dissertation, University of North Texas, 1987). *Dissertation Abstracts International, 49* (01A), 112.

Pham, M. T. (1998). Representativeness, relevance, and the use of feelings in decision making. *Journal of Consumer Research, 25*(2), 144–159.

Pham, M. T., Cohen, J. B., Pracejus, J. W., & Hughes, G. D. (2001). Affect monitoring and the primacy of feelings in judgment. *Journal of Consumer Research, 28*(2), 167–188.

Phillips, A. P., & Dipboye, R. L. (1989). Correlational tests of predictions from a process model of the interview. *Journal of Applied Psychology, 74*(1), 41–52.

Phillips. J. S., & Lord, R. G. (1981). Causal attributions and perceptions of leadership. *Organizational Behavior and Human Performance, 28*, 143–163.

Phillips, J. S., & Lord, R. G. (1982). Schematic information processing and perceptions of leadership in problem-solving groups. *Journal of Applied Psychology, 67*(4), 486–492.

Pichert, J. W., & Anderson, R. C. (1977). Taking different perspectives on a story. *Journal of Educational Psychology, 69*(4), 309–315.

Pierro, A., Mannetti, L., Erb, H. P., Spiegel, S., & Kruglanski, A. W. (2005). Informational length and order of presentation as determinants of persuasion. *Journal of Experimental Social Psychology, 41*(5), 458–469.

Pierro, A., Mannetti, L., Kruglanski, A. W., & Sleeth-Keppler, D. (2004). Relevance override: On the reduced impact of "cues" under high motivation conditions of persuasion studies. *Journal of Personality and Social Psychology, 86*(2), 251–264.

Pilkonis, P. A. (1977). The behavioral consequences of shyness. *Journal of Personality, 45*(4), 596–611.

Pincus, T. H. (1986). A crisis parachute: Helping stock prices have a soft landing. *The Journal of Business Strategy, 6*(4), 32–38.

Pinelli, T. E., Glassman, M., & Cordle, V. M. (1982). *Survey of reader preferences concerning the format of NASA technical reports* (NASA TM-No 84502). Washington, DC: National Aeronautics and Space Administration.

Pinker, S. (1990). A theory of graph comprehension. In R. Freedle (Ed.), *Artificial intelligence and the future of testing* (pp. 73–126). Hillsdale, NJ: Lawrence Erlbaum Associates.

Pittam, J., & Scherer, K. R. (1993). Vocal expression and communication of emotion. In M. Lewis & J. M. Haviland (Eds.), *Handbook of emotions* (pp. 185–197). New York: Guilford Press.

Pizzagalli, D., Regard, M., & Lehmann, D. (1999). Rapid emotional face processing in the human right and left brain hemispheres: An ERP study. *Neuroreport: For Rapid Communication of Neuroscience Research, 10*(13), 2691–2698.

Platow, M.J., van Knippenberg, D., Haslam, S.A., van Knippenberg, B., & Spears, R. (2001). *A special gift we bestow on you for being representative of us: Considering leader charisma from a self-categorization perspective.* Unpublished manuscript, La Trobe University.

Plutchik, R. (1980). *Emotion: A psychoevolutionary synthesis.* New York: Harper & Row.

Polansky, S. H. (1987). An information-processing analysis of the effects of product class knowledge on newspaper consumer behavior (Doctoral dissertation, The University of North Carolina at Chapel Hill, 1987). *Dissertation Abstracts International, 48* (07a), 1572.

Pollatsek, A., Raney, G. E., LaGasse, L., & Rayner, K. (1993). The use of information below fixation in reading and in visual search. *Canadian Journal of Psychology, 47*(2), 179–200.

Pollatsek, A., & Rayner, K. (1990). Eye movements and lexical access in reading. In D. A. Balota, G. B. Flores d'Arcais, & K. Rayner (Eds.), *Comprehension processes in reading* (pp. 143–163). Hillsdale, NJ: Lawrence Erlbaum Associates.

Popham, W. J. (1961). Tape recorded lectures in the college classroom. *Audiovisual Communication Review, 9*(2), 109–118.

Popkin, S., Gonnan, J. W., Phillips, C., & Smith, J. A. (1976). What have you done for me lately? Toward an investment theory of voting. *The American Political Science Review, 70*, 779–805.

Postmes, T., Spears, R., & Cihangir, S. (2001). Quality of decision making and group norms. *Journal of Personality and Social Psychology, 80*(6), 918–930.

Potter, M. C., & Levy, E. I. (1969). Recognition memory for a rapid sequence of pictures. *Journal of Experimental Psychology, 81*(1), 10–15.

Poulton, E. C. (1955). Letter differentiation and rate of comprehension of reading. *Journal of Applied Psychology, 49*, 358–362.

Poulton, E. C. (1967). Skimming (scanning) news items printed in 8-point and 9-point letters. *Ergonomics, 10*(6), 713–716.

Poulton, E. C., & Brown, C. H. (1968). Rate of comprehension of an existing teleprinter output and of possible alternatives. *Journal of Applied Psychology, 52*(1, Pt.1), 16–21.

Price, P. C., & Stone, E. R. (2004). Intuitive evaluation of likelihood judgment producers: Evidence for a confidence heuristic. *Journal of Behavioral Decision Making, 17*(1), 39–57.

Price, R. (1972). *Droodles.* Los Angeles: Price/Stern/Sloan.

Price, V., & Zaller, J. (1993). Who gets the news? Alternative measures of news reception and their implications for research. *Public Opinion Quarterly, 57*, 133–164.

Pryor, J. B., & Kriss, M. (1977). The cognitive dynamics of salience in the attribution process. *Journal of Personality and Social Psychology, 35*(1), 49–55.

Puffer, S. M., & Weintrop, J. B. (1991). Corporate performance and CEO turnover: The role of performance expectations. *Administrative Science Quarterly, 36*(1), 1–19.

Purnell, T., Idsardi, W., & Baugh, J. (1999). Perceptual and phonetic experiments on American English dialect identification. *Journal of Language and Social Psychology, 18*(1), 10–30.

Pyszczynski, T. A., & Wrightsman, L. S. (1981). The effects of opening statements on mock jurors' verdicts in a simulated criminal trial. *Journal of Applied Social Psychology, 11*(4), 301–313.

Quattrone, G. A., & Tversky, A. (1988). Contrasting rational and psychological analyses of political choice. *American Political Science Review, 82*, 719–736.

Quigley, B. M., & Tedeschi, J. T. (1996). Mediating effects of blame attributions on feelings of anger. *Personality and Social Psychology Bulletin, 22*(12), 1280–1288.

Quirk, S. W., & Strauss, M. E. (2001). Visual exploration of emotion eliciting images by patients with schizophrenia. *Journal of Nervous and Mental Disease, 189*(11), 757–765.

Raghubir, P., & Valenzuela, A. (2006). Center-of-inattention: Position biases in decision-making. *Organizational Behavior and Human Decision Processes, 99*(1), 66–80.

Raghunathan, R. (2000). What do you do when you are angry, anxious or blue? Motivational influence of negative affective states on consumer decision-making (Doctoral dissertation, New York University, 2000). *Dissertation Abstracts International, 61* (09A), 3664.

Raghunathan, R., & Pham, M. T. (1999). All negative moods are not equal: Motivational influences of anxiety and sadness on decision making. *Organizational Behavior and Human Decision Processes, 79*(1), 56–77.

Raghunathan, R., Pham, M. T., & Corfman, K. P. (2006). Informational properties of anxiety and sadness, and displaced coping. *Journal of Consumer Research, 32*(4), 596–601.

Ramachandran, V. S., & Hirstein, W. (1999). The science of art: A neurological theory of aesthetic experience. *Journal of Consciousness Studies, 6*(6–7), 15–51.

Ramsey, R. (1966). Personality and speech. *Journal of Personality and Social Psychology, 4*, 116–118.

Randel, J. M., Pugh, H. L., & Reed, S. K. (1996). Differences in expert and novice situation awareness in naturalistic decision making. *International Journal of Human-Computer Studies, 45*(5), 579–597.

Ranyard, R., & Williamson, J. (2005). Conversation-based process tracing methods for naturalistic decision making: Information search and verbal analysis. In H. Montgomery, R. Lipshitz, & B. Brehmer (Eds.), *How professionals make decisions* (pp. 305–317). Mahwah, NJ: Lawrence Erlbaum Associates.

Rasmussen, K. G. (1984). Nonverbal behavior, verbal behavior, resumé credentials, and selection interview outcomes. *Journal of Applied Psychology, 69*(4), 551–556.

Ratcliff, G., & Newcombe, F. (1982). Object recognition: Some deductions from the clinical evidence. In A. W. Ellis (Ed.), *Normality and pathology in cognitive functions* (pp. 147–171). London: Academic Press.

Ratner, N. B., & Gleason, J. B. (1993). An introduction to psycholinguistics: What do language users know? In J. B. Gleason & N. B. Ratner (Eds.), *Psycholingulstics* (pp. 1–40). Fort Worth, TX: Harcourt Brace.

Ratneshwar, S., & Chaiken, S. (1991). Comprehension's role in persuasion: The case of its moderating effect on the persuasive impact of source cues. *Journal of Consumer Research, 18*(1), 52–62.

Rayner, K. (1998). Eye movements in reading and information processing: 20 years of research. *Psychological Bulletin, 124*(3), 372–422.

Rayner, K., & Duffy, S. A. (1986). Lexical complexity and fixation times in reading: Effects of word frequency, verb complexity, and lexical ambiguity. *Memory and Cognition, 14*(3), 191–201.

Rayner, K., & Frazier, L. (1987). Parsing temporarily ambiguous complements. *The Quarterly Journal of Experimental Psychology A: Human Experimental Psychology, 39*(4, Pt. A), 657–673.

Rayner, K., Kambe, G., & Duffy, S. A. (2000). Clause wrap-up effects on eye movements during reading. *Quarterly Journal of Experimental Psychology, 53A*(4), 1061–1080.

Rayner, K., Reichle, E. D., Stroud, M. J., Williams, C. C., & Pollatsek, A. (2006). The effect of word frequency, word predictability, and font difficulty on the eye movements of young and elderly readers. *Psychology and Aging, 21*(3), 448–465.

Rayner, K., & Well, A. D. (1996). Effects of contextual constraint on eye movements in reading: A further examination. *Psychonomic Bulletin & Review, 3*(4), 504–509.

Raza, S. M., & Carpenter, B. N. (1987). A model of hiring decisions in real employment interviews. *Journal of Applied Psychology, 72*(4), 596–603.

Read, S. J., Cesa, I. L., Jones, D. K., & Collins, N. L. (1990). When is the federal budget like a baby? Metaphor in political rhetoric. *Metaphor & Symbolic Activity, 5*(3), 125–149.

Reber, R., & Schwarz, N. (1999). Effects of perceptual fluency on judgments of truth. *Consciousness and Cognition: An International Journal, 8*(3), 338–342.

Reber, R., Schwarz, N., & Winkielman, P. (2004). Processing fluency and aesthetic pleasure: Is beauty in the perceiver's processing experience? *Personality and Social Psychology Review, 8*(4), 364–382.

Reber, R., Winkielman, P., & Schwarz, N. (1998). Effects of perceptual fluency on affective judgments. *Psychological Science, 9*(1), 45–48.

Redelmeier, D. A., & Shafir, E. (1995). Medical decision making in situations that offer multiple alternatives. *Journal of the American Medical Association, 273*, 302–305.

Redish, J. C. (1980). Readability. In D. Felker (Ed.), *Document design: A review of the relevant research* (pp. 69–93). Washington, DC: American Institutes for Research.

Redish, J. C. (1993). Understanding readers. In C. M. Barnum & S. Carliner (Eds.), *Techniques for technical communicators* (pp. 14–41). New York: Macmillan.

Reeder, G. D., & Brewer, M. B. (1979). A schematic model of dispositional attribution in interpersonal perception. *Psychological Review, 86*(1), 61–79.

Reeves, B., Detenber, B., & Steuer, J. (1993, May). *New televisions: The effects of big pictures and big sound on viewer responses to the screen.* Paper presented to the Information Systems Division of the International Communication Association, Chicago.

Rehe, R. F. (1974). *Typography: How to make it legible.* Carmel, IN: Design Research International.

Reicher, G. M. (1969). Perceptual recognition as a function of meaningfulness of stimulus material. *Journal of Experimental Psychology, 81*(2), 275–280.

Reid, J. C., Kardash, C. M., Robinson, R. D., & Scholes, R. (1994). Comprehension in patient literature: The importance of text and reader characteristics. *Health Communication Special Issue: Communicating With Patients About Their Medications, 6*(4), 327–335.

Reingen, P. H., & Kernan, J. B. (1993). Social perception and interpersonal influence: Some consequences of the physical attractiveness stereotype in a personal selling setting. *Journal of Consumer Psychology, 2*(1), 25–38.

Reingold, E., & Rayner, K. (2006). Examining the word identification stages identified by the E-Z reader model. *Psychological Science, 17*(9), 742–746.

Reisenzein, R. (2000). The subjective experience of surprise. In H. Bless & J. P. Forgas (Eds.), *The message within: The role of subjective experience in social cognition and behavior* (pp. 262–282). Philadelphia: Psychology Press.

Rentsch, J. R., & Hall, R. J. (1994) Members of great teams think alike: A model of team effectiveness and schema similarity among team members. In M. M. Beyerlein & D. A. Johnson (Eds.) *Advances in interdisciplinary studies of work teams: Theories of self-managing work teams* (Vol. 1, pp. 223–261). Greenwich, CT: Elsevier Science/JAI Press.

Reyes, R. M., Thompson, W. C., & Bower, G. H. (1980). Judgmental biases resulting from differing availabilities of arguments. *Journal of Personality and Social Psychology, 39*(1), 2–12.

Rhee, J. W., & Cappella, J. N. (1997). The role of political sophistication in learning from news: Measuring schema development. *Communication Research, 24,* 197–233.

Rholes, W. S., Jones, M., & Wade, C. (1988). Children's understanding of personal dispositions and its relationship to behavior. *Journal of Experimental Child Psychology, 45*(1), 1–17.

Richins, M. L. (1994). Special possessions and the expression of material values. *Journal of Consumer Research, 21*(3), 522–533.

Rickards, E. C., & August, G. J. (1975). Generative underlining strategies in prose recall. *Journal of Educational Psychology, 67*(6), 860–865.

Riess, M., Rosenfeld, P., Melburg, V., & Tedeschi, J. T. (1981). Self-serving attributions: Biased private perceptions and distorted public descriptions. *Journal of Personality and Social Psychology, 41*(2), 224–231.

Ritchhart, R., & Perkins, D. N. (2005). Learning to think: The challenges of teaching thinking. In K. J. Holyoak & R. G. Morrison (Eds.), *The Cambridge handbook of thinking and reasoning* (pp. 775–802). Cambridge, UK: Cambridge University Press.

Ritov, I. (1996). Anchoring in simulated competitive market negotiation. *Organizational Behavior and Human Decision Processes, 67*(1), 16–25.

Robberson, M. R., & Rogers, R. W. (1988). Beyond fear appeals: Negative and positive persuasive appeals to health and self-esteem. *Journal of Applied Social Psychology, 18*(3, Pt. 1), 277–287.

Robertson, D. W. (2006). A comparison of three group decision-making strategies and their effects on the group decision-making process. *Dissertation Abstracts International Section A: Humanities and Social Sciences, 66*(10-A), 3722.

Robinson, D. O., Abbamonte, M., & Evans, S. H. (1971). Why serifs are important: The perception of small print. *Visible Language, 4,* 353–359.

Robinson, J. S. (1969). Familiar patterns are no easier to see than novel ones. *American Journal of Psychology, 82*(4), 513–522.

Robinson, R. B., Jr. (1985). Emerging strategies in the venture capital industry. *Journal of Business Venturing, 2*(1), 53–77.

Robinson, W. P. (1979). Speech markers and social class. In K. R. Scherer & H. Giles (Eds.), *Social markers in speech* (pp. 211–249). Cambridge, UK: Cambridge University Press.

Rock, I. (1977, June). *Form perception as process of description.* Presented at the 10th Symposium of the Center for Visual Science, Rochester, NY.

Rodin, M. J. (1987). Who is memorable to whom: A study of cognitive disregard. *Social Cognition, 5*(2), 144–165.

Roese, N. J., & Sherman, J. W. (2007). Expectancy. In A. W. Kruglanski & E. T. Higgins (Eds.), *Social psychology: Handbook of basic principles* (2nd ed., pp. 91–115). New York: The Guilford Press.

Rogers, W. T. (1978). The contribution of kinesic illustrators toward the comprehension of verbal behavior within utterances. *Human Communication Research, 5*(1), 54–62.

Rohrman, N. L. (1970). More on the recall of nominalizations. *Journal of Verbal Learning & Verbal Behavior, 9*(5), 534–536.

Rokeach, M. (1973). *The nature of human values.* New York: Free Press.

Rook, D. W. (1987). The buying impulse. *Journal of Consumer Research, 14*(2), 189–199.

Rook, D. W., & Fisher, R. J. (1995). Trait and normative aspects of impulsive buying behavior. *Journal of Consumer Research, 22*(3), 305–13.

Roseman, I. J. (1984). Cognitive determinants of emotion: A structural theory. *Review of Personality & Social Psychology, 5,* 11–36.

Roseman, I. J. (1994, July). *The discrete emotions form a coherent set: A theory of emotional responses.* Paper presented at the Sixth Annual Convention of the American Psychological Society, Washington, DC.

Roseman, I. J. (1996). Why these appraisals? Anchoring appraisal models to research on emotional behavior and related response systems. In N. H. Frijda (Ed.), *Proceedings of the ninth international conference of the international society for research on emotions* (pp. 106–110). Toronto, Canada: International Society for Research on Emotions.

Roseman, I. J. (2001). A model of appraisal in emotion system: Integrating theory, research, and applications. In K. R. Scherer, A. Schorr & T. Johnstone (Eds.), *Appraisal processes in emotion: Theory, methods, research* (pp. 68–91). New York: Oxford University Press.

Roseman, I. J., Dhawan, N., Rettek, S. I., Naidu, R. K., & Thapa, K. (1995). Cultural differences and cross-cultural similarities in appraisals and emotional responses. *Journal of Cross-Cultural Psychology*, *26*(1), 23–48.

Rosen, D. L., & Olshavsky, R. W. (1987). A protocol analysis of brand choice strategies involving recommendations. *Journal of Consumer Research*, *14*(3), 440–444.

Rosenberg, E. L. (1998). Levels of analysis and the organization of affect. *Review of General Psychology Special Issue: New Directions in Research in Emotion*, *2*(3), 247–270.

Ross, B. H., & Kennedy, P. T. (1990). Generalizing from the use of earlier examples in problem solving. *Journal of Experimental Psychology: Learning, Memory, and Cognition*, *16*(1), 42–55.

Ross, M., & Conway, M. (1986). Remembering one's own past: The construction of personal histories. In R. M. Sorrentino & E. T. Higgins (Eds.), *Handbook of motivation and cognition: Foundations of social behavior* (pp. 122–144). New York: Guilford Press.

Ross, M., & Sicoly, F. (1979). Egocentric biases in availability and attribution. *Journal of Personality and Social Psychology*, *37*(3), 322–336.

Rosselli, F., Skelly, J. J., & Mackie, D. M. (1995). Processing rational and emotional messages: The cognitive and affective mediation of persuasion. *Journal of Experimental Social Psychology*, *31*(2), 163–190.

Rossiter, J. R., & Percy, L. (1978). Visual imaging ability as a mediator of advertising response. *Advances in Consumer Research*, *5*(1), 621–629.

Rossiter, J. R., & Percy, L. (1980). Attitude change through visual imagery in advertising. *Journal of Advertising*, *9*(2), 10–17.

Roth, W. T., Breivik, G., Jorgensen, P. E., & Hofmann, S. (1996). Activation in novice and expert parachutists while jumping. *Psychophysiology*, *33*(1), 63–72.

Rothbart, M., Fulero, S., Jensen, C., Howard, J., & Birrel, B. (1978). From individual to group impressions: Availability heuristics in stereotype formation. *Journal of Experimental Social Psychology*, *14*(3), 237–255.

Rothman, A. J., Haddock, G., & Schwarz, N. (2001). How many partners is too many? Shaping perceptions of vulnerability. *Journal of Applied Social Psychology*, *31*(10), 2195–2214.

Rottenstreich, Y., & Hsee, C. K. (2001). Money, kisses, and electric shocks: On the affective psychology of risk. *Psychological Science*, *12*(3), 185–190.

Rouet, J. F., Favart, M., Britt, M. A., & Perfetti, C. A. (1997). Studying and using multiple documents in history: Effects of discipline expertise. *Cognition and Instruction*, *15*(1), 85–106.

Rouse, W. B., Cannon-Bowers, J. A., & Salas, E. (1992). The role of mental models in team performance in complex systems. *IEEE Transactions on Systems, Man, & Cybernetics*, *22*(6), 1296–1308.

Rouse, W. B., & Morris, N. M. (1986). On looking into the black box: Prospects and limits in the search for mental models. *Psychological Bulletin*, *100*(3), 349–363.

Ruck, H. W. (1980). A cross-company study of decision policies of manager resume evaluations (Doctoral dissertation, Stevens Institute of Technology, 1980). *Dissertation Abstracts International*, *41* (08B), 3222.

Rugg, D., & Cantril, H. (1944). The wording of questions. In H. Cantril (Ed.), *Gauging public opinion* (pp. 23–50). Princeton, NJ: Princeton University Press.

Rumelhart, D. E., & Ortony, A. (1976). The representation of knowledge in memory. In R. C. Anderson, R. J. Spiro, & W. E. Montague (Eds.), *Semantic factors in cognition* (pp. 99–136). Hillsdale, NJ: Erlbaum.

Ruscher, J. B., & Fiske, S. T. (1990). Interpersonal competition can cause individuating processes. *Journal of Personality and Social Psychology*, *58*(5), 832–843.

Rush, M. C., & Russell, J. E. (1988). Leader prototypes and prototype-contingent consensus in leader behavior descriptions. *Journal of Experimental Social Psychology*, *24*(1), 88–104.

Rush, M. C., Thomas, J. C., & Lord, R. G. (1977). Implicit leadership theory: A potential threat to the internal validity of leader behavior questionnaires. *Organizational Behavior & Human Performance*, *20*(1), 93–110.

Russo, J. E. (1971). The multi-alternative choice process as tracked by recording eye fixations (Doctoral dissertation, University of Michigan, 1971). *Dissertation Abstracts International*, *32* (03B), 1882.

Russo, J. E. (1977). The value of unit price information. *Journal of Marketing Research*, *14*(2), 193–201.

Russo, J. E., & Dosher, B. A. (1980). *Cognitive effort and strategy selection in binary choice.* Technical Report, Center for Decision Research, Graduate School of Business, University of Chicago.

Russo, J. E., & Dosher, B. A. (1983). Strategies for multiattribute binary choice. *Journal of Experimental Psychology: Learning, Memory, and Cognition, 9*(4), 676–696.

Russo, J. E., Krieser, G., & Miyashita, S. (1975). An effective display of unit price information. *Journal of Marketing, 39,* 11–19.

Russo, J. E., Medvec, V. H., & Meloy, M. G. (1996). The distortion of information during decisions. *Organizational Behavior and Human Decision Processes, 66*(1), 102–110.

Russo, J. E., & Rosen, L. D. (1975). An eye fixation analysis of multialternative choice. *Memory & Cognition, 3*(3), 267–276.

Russo, J. E., Staelin, R., Nolan, C. A., Russell, G. J., & Metcalf, B. L. (1986). Nutrition information in the supermarket. *Journal of Consumer Research, 13*(1), 48–70.

Ryan, C. (1991). *Prime time activism: Media strategies for grass roots organizing.* Boston: South End Press.

Saad, G., & Russo, J. E. (1996). Stopping criteria in sequential choice. *Organizational Behavior and Human Decision Processes, 67*(3), 258–270.

Saaty, T. L. (1980). *The analytic hierarchy process.* New York: McGraw-Hill.

Sachs, J. S. (1967). Recognition of semantic, syntactic and lexical changes in sentences. *Psychonomic Bulletin, 1*(2), 17–18.

Sadoski, M., Goetz, E. T., & Avila, E. (1995). Concreteness effects in text recall: Dual coding or context availability? *Reading Research Quarterly, 30*(2), 278–288.

Sadoski, M., & Paivio, A. (2001). *Imagery and text: A dual coding theory of reading and writing.* Mahwah, NJ: Erlbaum.

Safire, W. (2004). *Lend me your ears: Great speeches in history.* New York: Norton.

Sainfort, F. C., Gustafson, D. H., Bosworth, K., & Hawkins, R. P. (1990). Decision support systems effectiveness: Conceptual framework and empirical evaluation. *Organizational Behavior and Human Decision Processes, 45*(2), 232–252.

Salcedo, R. N., Reed, H., Evans, J. F., & Kong, A. C. (1972). A broader look at legibility. *Journalism Quarterly, 49,* 285–289.

Salvadori, L., van Swol, L. M., & Sniezek, J. A. (2001). Information sampling and confidence within groups and judge advisor systems. *Communication Research, 28*(6), 737–771.

Samuelson, W., & Zeckhauser, R. (1988). Status quo bias in decision making. *Journal of Risk and Uncertainty, 1,* 7–59.

Sanbonmatsu, D. M., Kardes, F. R., & Herr, P. M. (1992). The role of prior knowledge and missing information in multiattribute evaluation. *Organizational Behavior and Human Decision Processes, 51*(1), 76–91.

Sanbonmatsu, D. M., Kardes, F. R., Houghton, D. C., Ho, E. A., & Posavac, S. S. (2003). Overestimating the importance of the given information in multiattribute consumer judgment. *Journal of Consumer Psychology, 13*(3), 289–300.

Sandberg, W. R., Schweiger, D. M., & Hofer, C. W. (1988). The use of verbal protocols in determining venture capitalists' decision processes. *Entrepreneurship Theory and Practice, 13*(2), 8–20.

Sande, G. N., Ellard, J. H., & Ross, M. (1986). Effect of arbitrarily assigned status labels on self-perceptions and social perceptions: The mere position effect. *Journal of Personality and Social Psychology, 50*(4), 684–689.

Sankoff, D., Thibault, P., & Berube, H. (1978). Semantic field variability. In D. Sankoff (Ed.), *Linguistic variation: Models and methods* (pp. 23–44). New York: Academic Press.

Sanna, L. J., & Schwarz, N. (2004). Integrating temporal biases: The interplay of focal thoughts and accessibility experiences. *Psychological Science, 15*(7), 474–481.

Sargis, E. G., & Larson, J. R., Jr. (2002). Informational centrality and member participation during group decision making. *Group Processes & Intergroup Relations, 5*(4), 333–347.

Sato, W., Kochiyama, T., Yoshikawa, S., & Matsumura, M. (2001). Emotional processing boosts early visual processing of the face: ERP recording and its decomposition by independent component analysis. *NeuroReport, 12*(4), 709–714.

Saunders, D. M., Vidmar, N., & Hewitt, E. C. (1983). Eyewitness testimony and the discrediting effect. In S. M. A. Lloyd-Bostock & B. R. Clifford (Eds.), *Evaluating witness evidence* (pp. 57–78). New York: Wiley.

Savin, H. B., & Perchonock, E. (1965). Grammatical structure and the immediate recall of English sentences. *Journal of Verbal Learning and Verbal Behavior, 4*(5), 348–353.

Sawyer, J. (1966). Measurement and prediction, clinical and statistical. *Psychological Bulletin, 66*(3), 178–200.

Scarborough, D. L., Gerard, L., & Cortese, C. (1979). Accessing lexical memory: The transfer of word repetition effects across task and modality. *Memory & Cognition, 7*(1), 3–12.

Schallert, D. L. (1976). Improving memory for prose: The relationship between depth of processing and context. *Journal of Verbal Learning & Verbal Behavior, 15*(6), 621–632.

Schank, R. C. (1975). *Conceptual information processing.* Amsterdam: North-Holland.

Schank, R. C., & Abelson, R. P. (1977). *Scripts, plans, goals and understanding: An inquiry into human knowledge structures.* Oxford, UK: Lawrence Erlbaum.

Scheflen, A. (1964). The significance of posture in communication systems. *Psychiatry, 27,* 316–331.

Schelling, T. C. (1984). *Choice and consequence.* Cambridge, MA: Harvard University Press.

Scherer, K. R. (1974). Acoustic concomitants of emotional dimensions: Judging affects from synthesized tone sequences. In S. Weitz (Ed.), *Nonverbal communication* (pp. 105–111). New York: Oxford University Press.

Scherer, K. R. (1978). Personality inference from voice quality: The loud voice of extroversion. *European Journal of Social Psychology, 8*(4), 467–487.

Scherer K. R. (1979a). Personality markers in speech. In K. R. Scherer & H. Giles (Eds.), *Social markers in speech* (pp. 58–79). Cambridge, MA: Cambridge University Press.

Scherer, K. R. (1979b). Voice and speech correlates of perceived social influence. In H. Giles & R. St. Clair (Eds.), *The social psychology of language* (pp. 88–120). London: Blackwell.

Scherer, K. R. (1982). Emotion as a process: Function, origin and regulation. *Social Science Information, 21*(4–5), 555–570.

Scherer, K. R. (1984). Emotion as a multicomponent process: A model and some cross-cultural data. *Review of Personality & Social Psychology, 5,* 37–63.

Scherer, K. R. (1986). Vocal affect expression: A review and a model for future research. *Psychological Bulletin, 99*(2), 143–165.

Scherer, K. R. (1987). Toward a dynamic theory of emotion: The component process model of affective states. *Geneva Studies in Emotion and Communication, 1*(1), 1–98.

Scherer, K. R. (1999). On the sequential nature of appraisal processes: Indirect evidence from a recognition task. *Cognition and Emotion, 13*(6), 763–793.

Scherer, K. R., Banse, R., & Wallbott, H. G. (2001). Emotion inferences from vocal expression correlate across languages and cultures. *Journal of Cross-Cultural Psychology, 32*(1), 76–92.

Scherer, K. R., Johnstone, T., & Klasmeyer, G. (2003). Vocal expression of emotion. In R. J. Davidson, K. R. Scherer, & H. H. Goldsmith (Eds.), *Handbook of affective sciences* (pp. 433–456). New York: Oxford University Press.

Scherer, K. R., & Oshinsky, J. (1977). Cue utilization in emotion attribution from auditory stimuli. *Motivation and Emotion, 1*(4), 331–346.

Scherer, K. R., & Scherer, U. (1981). Speech behavior and personality. In J. Darby (Ed.), *Speech evaluation in psychiatry* (pp. 115–135). New York: Grune & Stratton.

Schirmer, A., & Kotz, S. A. (2003). ERP evidence for a sex-specific Stroop effect in emotional speech. *Journal of Cognitive Neuroscience, 15*(8), 1135–1148.

Schirmer, A., Striano, T., & Friederici, A. D. (2005). Sex differences in the preattentive processing of vocal emotional expressions. *Neuroreport: For Rapid Communication of Neuroscience Research, 16*(6), 635–639.

Schittekatte, M. (1996). Facilitating information exchange in small decision-making groups. *European Journal of Social Psychology, 26*(4), 537–556.

Schittekatte, M., & Van Hiel, A. (1996). Effects of partially shared information and awareness of unshared information on information sampling. *Small Group Research, 27*(3), 431–449.

Schkade, D. A., & Kleinmuntz, D. N. (1994). Information displays and choice processes: Differential effects of organization, form, and sequence. *Organizational Behavior and Human Decision Processes*, *57*(3), 319–337.

Schkade, D. A., & Payne, J. W. (1994). How people respond to contingent valuation questions: A verbal protocol analysis of willingness to pay for an environmental regulation. *Journal of Environmental Economics and Management*, *26*(1), 88–109.

Schmid Mast, M. (2002). Dominance as expressed and inferred through speaking time: A meta-analysis. *Human Communication Research*, *28*(3), 420–450.

Schmid Mast, M., & Hall, J. A. (2004). Who is the boss and who is not? Accuracy of judging status. *Journal of Nonverbal Behavior*, *28*(3), 145–165.

Schmitt, N. (1976). Social and situational determinants of interview decisions: Implications for the employment interview. *Personnel Psychology*, *29*(1), 79–101.

Schmitt, N., & Coyle, B. W. (1976). Applicant decisions in the employment interview. *Journal of Applied Psychology*, *61*(2), 184–192.

Schneider, S. L., & Shanteau, J. (2003). Introduction: Where to decision making? In S. Schneider & J. Shanteau (Eds.), *Emerging perspectives on judgment and decision research* (pp. 1–10). Cambridge, UK: Cambridge University Press.

Schneider, T. R., Salovey, P., Apanovirch, A. M., Pizarro, J., McCarthy, D., Zullo, J., & Rothman, A. J. (2001a). The effects of message framing and ethnic targeting on mammography use among low-income women. *Health Psychology*, *20*(4), 256–266.

Schneider, T. R., Salovey, P., Pallonen, U., Mundorf, N., Smith, N. F., & Steward, W. (2001b). Visual and auditory message framing effects on tobacco smoking. *Journal of Applied Social Psychology*, *31*(4), 667–682.

Schneirla, T. C. (1959). An evolutionary and developmental theory of biphasic processes underlying approach and withdrawal. In M. R. Jones (Ed.), *Nebraska symposium on motivation* (pp. 1–42). Lincoln, NE: University of Nebraska Press.

Schriver, K. A. (1992). Teaching writers to anticipate readers' needs: A classroom-evaluated pedagogy. *Written Communication*, *9*(2), 179–208.

Schriver, K. A. (1997). *Dynamics in document design: Creating text for readers*. New York: Wiley.

Schriver, K. A., Hayes, J. R., & Steffy Cronin, A. (1996). *"Just say no to drugs" and other unwelcome advice: Exploring creation and interpretation of drug education literature* (Final Rep.). Berkeley, CA, and Pittsburgh, PA: University of Califorina at Berkeley and Carnegie Mellon University, National Center for the Study of Writing and Literacy.

Schuh, A. J. (1978). Contrast effect in the interview. *Bulletin of the Psychonomic Society*, *11*(3), 195–196.

Schulz-Hardt, S., Brodbeck, F. C., Mojzisch, A., Kerschreiter, R., & Frey, D. (2006). Group decision making in hidden profile situations: Dissent as a facilitator for decision quality. *Journal of Personality and Social Psychology*, *91*(6), 1080–1093.

Schulz-Hardt, S., Frey, D., Luthgens, C., & Moscovici, S. (2000). Biased information search in group decision making. *Journal of Personality and Social Psychology*, *78*(4), 655–669.

Schulz-Hardt, S., Jochims, M., & Frey, D. (2002). Productive conflict in group decision making: Genuine and contrived dissent as strategies to counteract biased information seeking. *Organizational Behavior and Human Decision Processes*, *88*(2), 563–586.

Schupp, H. T., Junghöfer, M., Weike, A. I., & Hamm, A. O. (2003). Emotional facilitation of sensory processing in the visual cortex. *Psychological Science*, *14*(1), 7–13.

Schutz, H. G. (1961). An evaluation of methods for presentation of graphic multiple trends: Experiment III. *Human Factors*, *3*(2), 108–119.

Schwartz, D., Sparkman, J. P., & Deese, J. (1970). The process of understanding and judgments of comprehensibility. *Journal of Verbal Learning & Verbal Behavior*, *9*(1), 87–93.

Schwartz, M. (1982). Repetition and rated truth value of statements. *American Journal of Psychology*, *95*(3), 393–407.

Schwarz, N. (1990). Feelings as information: Informational and motivational functions of affective states. In E. T. Higgins & R. M. Sorrentino (Eds.), *Handbook of motivation and cognition: Foundations of social behavior* (Vol. 2, pp. 527–561). New York: Guilford Press.

Schwarz, N., & Bless, H. (1991). Happy and mindless, but sad and smart? The impact of affective states on analytic reasoning. In J. P. Forgas (Ed.), *Emotion and social judgments* (pp. 55–71). Elmsford, NY: Pergamon Press.

Schwarz, N., & Clore, G. L. (1983). Mood, misattribution, and judgments of well-being: Informative and directive functions of affective states. *Journal of Personality and Social Psychology*, 45(3), 513–523.

Schwarz, N., & Clore, G. L. (1996). Feelings and phenomenal experiences. In E. T. Higgins & A. W. Kruglanski (Eds.), *Social psychology: Handbook of basic principles* (pp. 433–465). New York: Guilford Press.

Schwarz, N., & Vaughn, L. A. (2002). The availability heuristic revisited: Ease of recall and content of recall as distinct sources of information. In T. Gilovich, D. Griffin, & D. Kahneman (Eds.), *Heuristics and biases: The psychology of intuitive judgment* (pp. 103–119). New York: Cambridge University Press.

Schweitzer, M. (1994). Disentangling status quo and omission effects: An experimental analysis. *Organizational Behavior and Human Decision Processes*, 58(3), 457–476.

Schwenk, C. R. (1984). Cognitive simplification process in strategic decision making. *Strategic Management Journal*, 5(2), 111–128.

Sedivy, J., Tanehaus, M., Spivey-Knowlton, M., Eberhard, K., & Carlson, G. (1995). Using intonationally marked presuppositional information in on-line language processing: Evidence from eye movements to a visual model. In *Proceedings of the Seventeenth Annual Conference of the Cognitive Science Society* (pp. 375–380). Hillsdale, NJ: Erlbaum.

Seggre, I. (1983). Attribution of guilt as a function of ethnic accent and type of crime. *Journal of Multilingual and Multicultural Development*, 4, 197–206.

Segrin, C. (1993). The effects of nonverbal behavior on outcomes of compliance gaining attempts. *Communication Studies*, 44, 169–187.

Selling, T. I. (1982). Cognitive processes in information system choice (Doctoral dissertation, The Ohio State University, 1982). *Dissertation Abstracts International*, 43 (08A), 2713.

Sentis, K., & Markus, H. (1986). Brand personality and self. In J. C. Olson & K. Sentis (Eds.), *Advertising and consumer psychology* (Vol. 3, pp. 132–148). New York: Praeger.

Sereno, S. C., O'Donnell, P., & Rayner, K. (2006). Eye movements and lexical ambiguity resolution: Investigating the subordinate bias effect. *Journal of Experimental Psychology: Human Perception and Performance*, 32(2), 335–350.

Serfaty, D., MacMillan, J., Entin, E. E., & Entin, E. B. (1997). The decision making expertise of battle commanders. In C. E. Zsambok & G. Klein (Eds.), *Naturalistic decision making* (pp. 233–246). Mahwah, NJ: Lawrence Erlbaum Associates.

Sessa, V. I. (2001). Executive promotion and selection. In M. London (Ed.), *How people evaluate others in organizations* (pp. 91–110). Hillsdale, NJ: Lawrence Erlbaum Associates.

Sessa, V. I., Kaiser, R., Taylor, J. K., & Campbell, R. J. (1998). Executive selection: A research report on what works and what doesn't (Rep. No. 179). Greensboro, NC: Center for Creative Leadership.

Shafir, E. (1993). Choosing versus rejecting: Why some options are both better and worse than others. *Memory & Cognition*, 21(4), 546–556.

Shafir, E., Simonson, I., & Tversky, A. (1993). Reason-based choice. *Cognition Special Issue: Reasoning and Decision Making*, 49(1–2), 11–36.

Shah, D. V., Domke, D., & Wackman, D. B. (1996). "To thine own self be true": Values, framing, and voter decision-making strategies. *Communication Research*, 23(5), 509–560.

Shah, D. V., Domke, D., & Wackman, D. B. (2001). The effects of value-framing on political judgment and reasoning. In S. D. Reese, O. H. Gandy, & A. E. Grant (Eds.), *Framing public life: Perspectives on media and our understanding of the social world* (pp. 227–243). Mahwah, NJ: Lawrence Erlbaum Associates.

Shah, P. (1995). Cognitive processes in graph comprehension (Doctoral dissertation, Carnegie Mellon University, 1995). *Dissertation Abstracts International*, 57 (03B), 2191.

Shamir, B., House, R., & Arthur, M. B. (1993). The motivational effects of charismatic leadership: A self-concept based theory. *Organization Science*, 4(4), 577–594.

Shanteau, J. (1988). Psychological characteristics and strategies of expert decision makers. *Acta Psychologica, 68*(1–3), 203–215.

Shanteau, J. (1989). Cognitive heuristics and biases in behavioral auditing: Review, comments, and observations. *Accounting Organizations and Society, 14*(1–2), 165–177.

Shanteau, J. (1992). Competence in experts: The role of task characteristics. *Organizational Behavior and Human Decision Processes Special Issue: Experts and Expert Systems, 53*(2), 252–266.

Shapiro, J. G. (1968). Variability in the communication of affect. *Journal of Social Psychology, 76*(2), 181–188.

Shattuck, L. G. (1995). Communication of intent in distributed supervisory control systems (Doctoral dissertation. The Ohio State University, 1995). *Dissertation Abstracts International, 56* (09B), 5209.

Shaver, K. G. (1975). *An introduction to attribution processes.* Cambridge, MA: Winthrop Publishing.

Shaver, K. G. (1985). *The attribution of blame: Causality, responsibility, and blame-worthiness.* New York: Springer-Verlag.

Shaver, K. G., & Drown, D. (1986). On causality, responsibility, and self-blame: A theoretical note. *Journal of Personality and Social Psychology, 50*(4), 697–702.

Shaver, P., Hazan, C., & Bradshaw, D. (1988). Love as attachment. In R. J. Sternberg & M. L. Barnes (Eds.), *The psychology of love* (pp. 68–99). New Haven, CT: Yale University Press.

Shaw, E. A. (1972). Commonality of applicant stereotypes among recruiters. *Personnel Psychology, 25*(3), 421–432.

Sheffey, S., Tindale, R. S., & Scott, L. A. (1989). Information sharing and group decision making. Paper presented at the Midwestern Psychological Association Annual Convention, Chicago.

Shefrin, H., & Statman, M. (1995). Making sense of beta, size, and book-to-market. *Journal of Portfolio Management, 21*(2), 26–34.

Sheldon, K. M., & Elliot, A. J. (1999). Goal striving, need satisfaction, and longitudinal well-being: The self-concordance model. *Journal of Personality and Social Psychology, 76*(3), 482–497.

Sheluga, D. A., & Jacoby, J. (1978). Do comparative claims encourage comparison shopping?. In J. Leigh & C. R. Martin (Eds.), *Current issues and research in advertising* (pp. 23–37). Ann Arbor, MI: University of Michigan Press.

Shepard, R. N. (1967). Recognition memory for words, sentences, and pictures. *Journal of Verbal Learning & Verbal Behavior, 6*(1), 156–163.

Sherblom, J., & Van Rheenen, D. D. (1984). Spoken language indices of uncertainty. *Human Communication Research, 11*(2), 221–230.

Sherer, M., & Rogers, R. W. (1984). The role of vivid information in fear appeals and attitude change. *Journal of Research in Personality, 18*(3), 321–334.

Sherman, M. A. (1976). Adjectival negation and the comprehension of multiply negated sentences. *Journal of Verbal Learning & Verbal Behavior, 15*(2), 143–157.

Sherman, S. J. (1980). On the self-erasing nature of errors of prediction. *Journal of Personality and Social Psychology, 39*(2), 211–221.

Sherman, S. J., Cialdini, R. B., Schwartzman, D. F., & Reynolds, K. D. (1985). Imagining can heighten or lower the perceived likelihood of contracting a disease: The mediating effect of ease of imagery. *Personality and Social Psychology Bulletin, 11*(1), 118–127.

Shimko, K. L. (1994). Metaphors and foreign policy decision making. *Political Psychology, 15*(4), 655–671.

Shleifer, A. (2000). *Inefficient markets: An introduction to behavioral finance.* New York: Oxford University Press.

Shrum, L. J., Wyer, R. S., Jr., & O'Guinn, T. C. (1998). The effects of television consumption on social perceptions: The use of priming procedures to investigate psychological processes. *Journal of Consumer Research, 24*(4), 447–458.

Siess, T. F., & Jackson, D. N. (1970). Vocational interests and personality: An empirical integration. *Journal of Counseling Psychology, 17*(1), 27–35.

Sigall, H., & Ostrove, N. (1975). Beautiful but dangerous: Effects of offender attractiveness and nature of the crime on juridic judgment. *Journal of Personality and Social Psychology, 31*(3), 410–414.

Sikora, S., Miall, D. S., & Kuiken, D. (1998). Enactment versus interpretation: A phenomenological study of readers' responses to Coleridge's "The rime of the ancient mariner." Paper presented at the Sixth Biennial Conference of the International Society for the Empirical Study of Literature. Utrecht, The Netherlands.

Simkin, D. K., & Hastie, R. (1986). An information processing analysis of graph perception. *Journal of the American Statistical Association*, *82*, 454–465.

Simon, H. A. (1955). A behavioral model of rational choice. *Quarterly Journal of Economics*, *69*, 99–118.

Simon, H. A. (1956). Rational choice and the structure of the environment. *Psychological Review*, *63*(2), 129–138.

Simon, H. A. (1967). Motivational and emotional controls of cognition. *Psychological Review*, *74*(1), 29–39.

Simon, H. A., & Hayes, J. R. (1976). The understanding process: Problem isomorphs. *Cognitive Psychology*, *8*(2), 165–190.

Simonson, I., Huber, J., & Payne, J. (1988). The relationship between prior brand knowledge and information acquisition order. *Journal of Consumer Research*, *14*(4), 566–578.

Singer, J. A., & Salovey, P. (1996). Motivated memory: Self-defining memories, goals, and affect regulation. In L. L. Martin & A. Tesser (Eds.), *Striving and feeling: Interactions among goals, affect, and self-regulation* (pp. 229–250). Hillsdale, NJ: Lawrence Erlbaum Associates.

Sivacek, J., & Crano, W. D. (1982). Vested interest as a moderator of attitude-behavior consistency. *Journal of Personality and Social Psychology*, *43*(2), 210–221.

Sjöberg, L. (1980). Volitional problems in carrying through a difficult decision. *Acta Psychologica*, *45*(1–3), 123–132.

Sjogren, D., & Timpson, W. (1979). Frameworks for comprehending discourse: A replication study. *American Educational Research Journal*, *16*(4), 341–346.

Skilbeck, C., Tulips, J., & Ley, P. (1977). The effects of fear arousal, fear position, fear exposure, and sidedness on compliance with dietary instructions. *European Journal of Social Psychology*, *7*(2), 221–239.

Skowronski, J. J., & Carlston, D. E. (1987). Social judgment and social memory: The role of cue diagnosticity in negativity, positivity, and extremity biases. *Journal of Personality and Social Psychology*, *52*(4), 689–699.

Skowronski, J. J., & Carlston, D. E. (1989). Negativity and extremity biases in impression formation: A review of explanations. *Psychological Bulletin*, *105*(1), 131–142.

Skurnik, I., Yoon, C., Park, D. C., & Schwarz, N. (2005). How warnings about false claims become recommendations. *Journal of Consumer Research*, *31*(4), 713–724.

Slobin, D. I. (1966). Grammatical transformations and sentence comprehension in childhood and adulthood. *Journal of Verbal Learning and Verbal Behavior*, *5*(3), 219–277.

Slovic, P. (1972). *From Shakespeare to Simon: Speculations–and some evidence–about man's ability to process information*. ORI research monograph, 12. Eugene, OR: Oregon Research Institute.

Slovic, P. (1975). Choice between equally valued alternatives. *Journal of Experimental Psychology: Human Perception and Performance*, *1*(3), 280–287.

Slovic, P., Fischhoff, B., & Lichtenstein, S. (1982). Facts versus fears: Understanding perceived risk. In D. Kahneman, P. Slovic, & A. Tversky (Eds.), *Judgment under uncertainty: Heuristics and biases* (pp. 463–489). New York: Cambridge University Press.

Slovic, P., & Lichtenstein, S. (1971). Comparison of Bayesian and regression approaches to the study of information processing in judgment. *Organizational Behavior & Human Performance*, *6*(6), 649–744.

Slovic, P., & MacPhillamy, D. (1974). Dimensional commensurability and cue utilization in comparative judgment. *Organizational Behavior & Human Performance*, *11*(2), 172–194.

Smeesters, D., Warlop, L., Vanden Abeele, P., & Ratneshwar, S. (1999). *Exploring the recycling dilemma: consumer motivation and experiences in mandatory garbage recycling programs*. Research report no. 9924, Department of Applied Economics, Catholic University of Leuven, Belgium.

Smith, C. A. (1989). Dimensions of appraisal and physiological response in emotion. *Journal of Personality and Social Psychology*, *56*(3), 339–353.

Smith, C. A., & Ellsworth, P. C. (1985). Patterns of cognitive appraisal in emotion. *Journal of Personality and Social Psychology, 48*(4), 813–838.

Smith, C. A., & Ellsworth, P. C. (1987). Patterns of appraisal and emotion related to taking an exam. *Journal of Personality and Social Psychology, 52*(3), 475–488.

Smith, C. A., & Kirby, L. D. (2000). Consequences require antecedents: Toward a process model of emotion elicitation. In J. P. Forgas (Ed.), *Feeling and thinking: The role of affect in social cognition* (pp. 83–106). New York: Cambridge University Press.

Smith, C. A., & Kirby, L. D. (2001). Toward delivering on the promise of appraisal theory. In K. R. Scherer, A. Schorr, & T. Johnstone (Eds.), *Appraisal processes in emotion: Theory, methods, research* (pp. 121–138). New York: Oxford University Press.

Smith, C. A., & Lazarus, R. S. (1990). Emotion and adaptation. In L. A. Pervin (Ed.), *Handbook of personality: Theory and research* (pp. 609–637). New York: Guilford Press.

Smith, C. A., & Pope, L. K. (1992). Appraisal and emotion: The interactional contributions of dispositional and situational factors. In M. S. Clark (Ed.), *Emotion and social behavior* (pp. 32–62). Thousand Oaks, CA: Sage Publications.

Smith, C. M., Tindale, R. S., & Steiner, L. (1998). Investment decisions by individuals and groups in "sunk cost" situations: The potential impact of shared representations. *Group Processes & Intergroup Relations, 1*(2), 175–189.

Smith, D. M., Neuberg, S. L., Judice, T. N., & Biesanz, J. C. (1997). Target complicity in the confirmation and disconfirmation of erroneous perceiver expectations: Immediate and longer term implications. *Journal of Personality and Social Psychology, 73*(5), 974–991.

Smith, E. (1998a). Mental representations and memory. In D. Gilbert, S. Fiske, & G. Lindzey (Eds.), *The handbook of social psychology* (4th ed., pp. 391–445). New York: McGraw-Hill.

Smith, G. E. (1996). Framing in advertising and the moderating impact of consumer education. *Journal of Advertising Research, 36*(5), 49–64.

Smith, G. W. (1998b). The political impact of name sounds. *Communication Monographs, 65*(2), 154–172.

Smith, J. F., & Kida, T. (1991). Heuristics and biases: Expertise and task realism in auditing. *Psychological Bulletin, 109*(3), 472–489.

Smith, J. M., & McCombs. E. (1971). The graphics of prose. *Visible Language, 4*(Autumn), 365–369.

Smith, P. M. (1979). Sex markers in speech. In K. R. Scherer & H. Giles (Eds.), *Social markers in speech* (pp. 109–146). Cambridge, UK: Cambridge University Press.

Smith, P. M. (1980). Judging masculine and feminine social identities from content-controlled speech. In H. Giles, W. P. Robinson, & P. M. Smith (Eds.), *Language: Social psychological perspectives* (pp. 121–126). Oxford, UK: Pergamon.

Smith, S. M., & Shaffer, D. R. (2000). Vividness can undermine or enhance message processing: The moderating role of vividness congruency. *Personality and Social Psychology Bulletin, 26*(7), 769–779.

Smith, S. M., & Shaffer, D. R. (1995). Speed of speech and persuasion: Evidence for multiple effects. *Personality and Social Psychology Bulletin, 21*(10), 1051–1060.

Smith, S. W. (1986). A social-cognitive approach to the nature of input processes in reception of nonverbal messages (Doctoral dissertation, University of Southern California, 1986). *Dissertation Abstracts International, 47* (07A), 2372.

Smith-Jentsch, K. A., Campbell, G. E., Milanovich, D. M., & Reynolds, A. M. (2001). Measuring teamwork mental models to support training needs assessment, development, and evaluation: Two empirical studies. *Journal of Organizational Behavior, 22*(2), 179–194.

Smither, J. W., & Reilly, S. P. (2001). Coaching in organizations. In M. London (Ed.), *How people evaluate others in organizations* (pp. 221–252). Mahwah, NJ: Lawrence Erlbaum.

Smotas, P. E. (1996). An analysis of budget decision criteria and selected demographic factors of school business officials of Connecticut school districts (Doctoral dissertation, The University of Connecticut, 1996). *Dissertation Abstracts International, 58* (02A), 388.

Sniderman, P. M., Brody, R. A., & Tetlock, P. E. (1991). *Reasoning and choice: Explorations in political psychology*. New York: Cambridge University Press.

Sniderman, P. M., & Theriault, S. M. (2004). The structure of political argument and the logic of issue framing. In W. E. Saris & P. M. Sniderman (Eds.), *Studies in public opinion: Attitudes, nonattitudes, measurement error and change*. Princeton, NJ: Princeton University Press.

Sniezek, J. A., & Buckley, T. (1995). Cueing and cognitive conflict in Judge-Advisor decision making. *Organizational Behavior and Human Decision Processes, 62*(2), 159–174.

Snow, D. A., & Benford, R. D. (1988). Ideology, frame resonance, and participant mobilization. In B. Klandermans, H. Kriesi, & S. Tarrow (Eds.), *From structure to action: Comparing social movement research across countries* (pp. 197–217). Greenwich, CT: JAI Press.

Soelberg, P. O. (1967). Unprogrammed decision making. *Industrial Management Review, 8*(2), 19–29.

Solt, M., & Statman, M. (1989). Good companies, bad stocks. *Journal of Portfolio Management, 15*(4), 39–44.

Sommer, R. (1961). Leadership and group geography. *Sociometry, 24*, 99–110.

Sommers, M. S., Greeno, D. W., & Boag, D. (1989). The role of nonverbal communication in service provision and representation. *Service Industries Journal, 9*(4), 162–173.

Sopory, P., & Dillard, J. P. (2002). The persuasive effects of metaphor: A meta-analysis. *Human Communication Research, 28*(3), 382–419.

Sotirovic, M. (2001). Media use and perceptions of welfare. *Journal of Communication, 51*(4), 750–774.

Sparks, J. R., Areni, C. S., & Cox, K. C. (1998). An investigation of the effects of language style and communication modality on persuasion. *Communication Monographs, 65*(2), 108–125.

Spence, I. (1990). Visual psychophysics of simple graphical elements. *Journal of Experimental Psychology: Human Perception and Performance, 16*(4), 683–692.

Spencer, H., Reynolds, L., & Coe, B. (1974). Typographic coding in lists and bibliographies. *Applied Ergonomics, 5*(3), 136–141.

Spilich, G. J., Vesonder, G. T., Chiesi, H. L., & Voss, J. F. (1979). Text processing of domain-related information for individuals with high and low domain knowledge. *Journal of Verbal Learning & Verbal Behavior, 18*(3), 275–290.

Spiro, R. J. (1977). Remembering information from text: The "state of schema" approach. In R. C. Anderson, R. J. Spiro, & W. E. Montague (Eds.), *Schooling and the acquisition of knowledge* (pp. 137–165). Hillsdale, NJ: Erlbaum.

Spyridakis, J. H. (1989a). Signaling effects: Part I. *Journal of Technical Writing and Communication, 19*(1), 227–239.

Spyridakis, J. H. (1989b). Signaling effects: Part II. *Journal of Technical Writing and Communication, 19*(4), 395–415.

Sroufe, L. A. (1995). *Emotional development: The organization of emotional life in the early years*. Cambridge, UK: Cambridge University Press.

Srull, T. K. (1983). Organizational and retrieval processes in person memory: An examination of processing objectives, presentation format, and the possible role of self-generated retrieval cues. *Journal of Personality and Social Psychology, 44*(6), 1157–1170.

Srull, T. K. (1990). Individual responses to advertising: Mood and its effects from an information processing perspective. In S. J. Agres, J. A. Edell, & T. M. Dubitsky (Eds.), *Emotion in advertising: Theoretical and practical explorations* (pp. 35–51). New York: Quorum Books.

Srull, T. K., & Wyer, R. S. (1979). The role of category accessibility in the interpretation of information about persons: Some determinants and implications. *Journal of Personality and Social Psychology, 37*(10), 1660–1672.

Standing, L. (1973). Learning 10,000 pictures. *The Quarterly Journal of Experimental Psychology, 25*(2), 207–222.

Stanners, R. F., Jastrzembski, J. E., & Westbrook, A. (1975). Frequency and visual quality in a word-nonword classification task. *Journal of Verbal Learning & Verbal Behavior, 14*(3), 259–264.

Stasser, G., & Birchmeier, Z. (2003) Group creativity and collective choice. In P. B. Paulus & B. A. Nijstad (Eds.), *Group creativity: Innovation through collaboration* (pp. 85–109). New York: Oxford University Press.

Stasser, G., Stella, N., Hanna, C., & Colella, A. (1984). The majority effect in jury deliberations: Number of supporters versus number of supporting arguments. *Law & Psychology Review, 8*, 115–127.

Stasser, G., & Stewart, D. (1992). Discovery of hidden profiles by decision-making groups: Solving a problem versus making a judgment. *Journal of Personality and Social Psychology, 63*(3), 426–434.

Stasser, G., & Titus, W. (1985). Pooling of unshared information in group decision making: Biased information sampling during discussion. *Journal of Personality and Social Psychology, 48*(6), 1467–1478.

Stasser, G., & Vaughan, S. I. (1996). Models of participation during face-to-face unstructured discussion. In E. H. Witte & J. H. Davis (Eds.), *Understanding group behavior, Vol. 1: Consensual action by small groups* (pp. 165–192) Hillsdale, NJ: Lawrence Erlbaum.

Statman, M., & Fisher, K. (1998). The DJIA crossed 652,230 (in 1998). Working paper, Santa Clara University.

Staw, B. (1981). The escalation of commitment to a course of action. *Academy of Management Review, 6*(4), 577–587.

Stayman, D. M., & Aaker, D. A. (1987). *Repetition and affective response: Differences in specific feeling responses and the mediating role of attitude toward the ad.* Working paper, University of Texas at Austin.

Stayman, D. M., & Aaker, D. A. (1989). *The role of believability in the elicitation and effect of feeling responses to advertising.* Working paper, University of Texas at Austin.

Stein, S. K. (1999). Uncovering listening strategies: Protocol analysis as a means to investigate student listening in the basic communication course (Doctoral dissertation, University of Maryland at College Park, 1999). *Dissertation Abstracts International, 61* (01A), 28.

Stephan, C. W., & Stephan, W. G. (1986). Habla Ingles? The effects of language translation on simulated juror decisions. *Journal of Applied Social Psychology, 16*(7), 577–589.

Sternberg, R. J. (1999). *Cognitive Psychology* (2nd ed.). New York: Harcourt Brace College Publishers.

Sternberg, S. (1966). High-speed scanning in human memory. *Science, 153*(3736), 652–654.

Stewart, D. D., & Stasser, G. (1995). Expert role assignment and information sampling during collective recall and decision making. *Journal of Personality and Social Psychology, 69*(4), 619–628.

Stewart, D. D., & Stasser, G. (1998). The sampling of critical, unshared information in decision-making groups: The role of an informed minority. *European Journal of Social Psychology, 28*(1), 95–113.

St. George, M., Kutas, M., Martinez, A., & Sereno, M. I. (1999). Semantic integration in reading: Engagement of the right hemisphere during discourse processing. *Brain, 122*(7), 1317–1325.

Sticht, T. G. (1977). Comprehending reading at work. In M. A. Just & P. A. Carpenter (Eds.), *Cognitive processes in comprehension* (pp. 221–246). Hillsdale, NJ: Lawrence Erlbaum.

Sticht, T. G., Armijo, L., Weitzman, R., Koffman, N., Roberson, K., Chang, F., & Moracco, J. (1986). *Progress report.* Monterey, CA: U.S. Naval Postgraduate School.

Stiff, J. B., Dillard, J. P., Somera, L., Kim, H., & Sleight, C. (1988). Empathy, communication, and prosocial behavior. *Communication Monographs, 55*(2), 198–213.

Stillwell, W. G., Barron, F. H., & Edwards, W. (1983). Evaluating credit applications: A validation of multiattribute utility weight elicitation techniques. *Organizational Behavior & Human Performance, 32*(1), 87–108.

Stokes, A. F., Kemper, K., & Kite, K. (1997). Aeronautical decision making, cue recognition, and expertise under time pressure. In C. E. Zsambok & G. Klein (Eds.), *Naturalistic decision making* (pp. 183–196). Mahwah, NJ: Erlbaum.

Stolz, W. S. (1967). A study of the ability to decode grammatically novel sentences. *Journal of Verbal Learning & Verbal Behavior, 6*(6), 867–873.

Stone, D. N., & Schkade, D. A. (1991). Numeric and linguistic information representation in multiattribute choice. *Organizational Behavior and Human Decision Processes, 49*(1), 42–59.

Stormark, K. M., Nordby, H., & Hugdahl, K. (1995). Attentional shifts to emotionally charged cues: Behavioural and ERP data. *Cognition & Emotion, 9*(5), 507–523.

Strange, B. A., Hurleman, R., & Dolan, R. J. (2003). An emotion-induced retrograde amnesia in humans is amygdala- and beta-adrenergic-dependent. *Proceedings of the National Academy of Sciences, USA, 13626–13631.*

Strater, L. D., Jones, D. G., & Endsley, M. R. (2001). Analysis of infantry situation awareness training requirements. (No. SATech 01–15). Marietta, GA: SA Technologies.

Stratman, J., & Young, R. O. (1986, April). *An Analysis of Novice Managers' Performances in Board Meetings.* Annual Conference of the Management Communication Association, Durham, NC.

Strong, E. K., Jr. (1926). Value of white space in advertising. *Journal of Applied Psychology*, *10*(1), 107–116.

Sturt, P. (2003). The time course of the application of binding constraints in reference resolution. *Journal of Memory and Language*, *48*(3), 542–562.

Sturt, P., & Lombardo, V. (2005). Processing coordinated structures: Incrementality and connectedness. *Cognitive Science*, *29*(2), 291–305.

Sullivan, D. G., & Masters, R. D. (1988). Happy warriors': Leaders' facial displays, viewers' emotions, and political support. *American Journal of Political Science*, *32*, 345–368.

Sullivan, D. G., Masters, R. D., Lanzetta, J. T., Englis, B. G., & McHugo, G. J. (1984). *The effect of President Reagan's facial displays on observers' attitudes, impressions, and feelings about him.* Paper presented at the 1984 Annual Meeting of the American Political Science Association, Washington, DC.

Sumby, W. H., & Pollack, I. (1954). Visual contribution to speech intelligibility in noise. *Journal of the Acoustical Society of America*, *26*, 212–215.

Sundstrom, G. A. (1987). Information search and decision making: The effects of information displays. *Acta Psychologica*, *65*(2), 165–179.

Svenson, O. (1974). *A note on think aloud protocols obtained during the choice of a home* (Report No. 421). Stockholm: Psychology Lab, University of Stockholm.

Svenson, O. (1979). Process descriptions of decision making. *Organizational Behavior and Human Performance*, *23*(1), 86–112.

Svenson, O. (2003). Values, affect, and processes in human decision making: A differentiation and consolidation perspective. In S. L. Schneider & J. Shanteau (Eds.), *In emerging perspectives on judgment and decision research* (pp. 287–326). Cambridge, UK: Cambridge University Press.

Svenson, O., & Edland, A. (1987). Change of preferences under time pressure: Choices and judgements. *Scandinavian Journal of Psychology*, *28*(4), 322–330.

Swales, J. (1990). *Genre analysis: English in academic and research settings*. New York: Cambridge University Press.

Swaney, J. H., Janik, C. J., Bond, S. J., & Hayes, J. R. (1991). Editing for comprehension: Improving the process through reading protocols. In E. R. Steinberg (Ed.), *Plain language: Principles and practice* (pp. 173–203). Detroit, MI: Wayne State University Press. (Original article published in 1981 as Document Design Project Tech. Rep. No. 14, Pittsburgh, PA: Carnegie Mellon University).

Swarts, H., Flower, L., & Hayes, J. R. (1980). *How headings in documents can mislead readers* (Document Design Project Tech. Rep. No. 9), Pittsburgh, PA: Carnegie Mellon University, Communications Design Center.

Sweller, J., Chandler, P., Tierney, P., & Cooper, M. (1990). Cognitive load as a factor in the structuring of technical material. *Journal of Experimental Psychology: General*, *119*(2), 176–192.

Swinney, D. A. (1979). Lexical access during sentence comprehension: (Re)consideration of context effects. *Journal of Verbal Learning & Verbal Behavior*, *18*(6), 645–659.

Taggart, B. M. (1993). An analysis of budget decision criteria and selected demographic factors of chief fiscal officers in higher education (Doctoral dissertation, The University of Connecticut, 1993). *Dissertation Abstracts International*, *54* (10A), 3674.

Tankard, J. W. (2001). The empirical approach to the study of media framing. In S. D. Reese, O. H. Gandy, & A. E. Grant (Eds.), *Framing public life: Perspectives on media and our understanding of the social world* (pp. 95–106). Mahwah, NJ: Lawrence Erlbaum Associates.

Tankard, J. W., Hendrickson, L., Silberman, J., Bliss, K., & Ghanem, S. (1991, August). *Media frames: Approaches to conceptualization and measurement*. Paper presented to the Association for Education in Journalism and Mass Communication, Boston.

Tannen, D. (1984). *Conversational style: Analyzing talk among friends*. Norwood, NJ: Ablex.

Tanofsky, R., Shepps, R. R., & O'Neill, P. J. (1969). Pattern analysis of biographical predictors of success as an insurance salesman. *Journal of Applied Psychology*, *53*(2, Pt. 1), 136–139.

Tartter, V. C. (1980). Happy talk: Perceptual and acoustic effects of smiling on speech. *Perception and Psychophysics*, *27*, 24–27.

Taylor, C. D. (1934). The relative legibility of black and white print. *Journal of Educational Psychology*, *25*(8), 561–578.

Taylor, H., Fieldman, G., & Lahlou, S. (2005). The impact of a threatening e-mail reprimand on the recipient's blood pressure. *Journal of Managerial Psychology, 20*(1) 43–50.

Taylor, S. E. (1981). A categorization approach to stereotyping. In D. L. Hamilton (Ed.), *Cognitive processes in stereotyping and intergroup behavior* (pp. 88–114). Hillsdale: Lawrence Erlbaum Associates.

Taylor, S. E., & Fiske, S. T. (1975). Point of view and perceptions of causality. *Journal of Personality and Social Psychology, 32*(3), 439–445.

Taylor, S. E., & Fiske, S. T. (1978). Salience, attention, and attribution: Top of the head phenomena. In L. Berkowitz (Ed.), *Advances in experimental social psychology* (Vol. 11, pp. 249–288). New York: Academic Press.

Tessler, R., & Sushelsky, L. (1978). Effects of eye contact and social status on the perception of a job applicant in an employment interviewing situation. *Journal of Vocational Behavior, 13*(3), 338–347.

Thakerar, J. N., & Giles, H. (1981). They are—so they spoke: Noncontent speech stereotypes. *Language & Communication, 1*(2–3), 255–261.

Thibadeau, R., Just, M. A., & Carpenter, P. A. (1982). A model of the time course and content of reading. *Cognitive Science, 6*, 157–203.

Thomas, J. P., & McFadyen, R. G. (1995). The confidence heuristic: A game-theoretic analysis. *Journal of Economic Psychology, 16*(1), 97–113.

Thorndyke, P. W. (1977). Cognitive structures in comprehension and memory of narrative discourse. *Cognitive Psychology, 9*(1), 77–110.

Tiedens, L. Z., & Linton, S. (2001). Judgment under emotional certainty and uncertainty: The effects of specific emotions on information processing. *Journal of Personality and Social Psychology, 81*(6), 973–988.

Timmermans, D., & Vlek, C. (1996). Effects on decision quality of supporting multi-attribute evaluation in groups. *Organizational Behavior and Human Decision Processes, 68*(2), 158–170.

Tindale, R. S. (1993) Decision errors made by individuals and groups. In N. J. Castellan (Ed.) *Individual and group decision making: Current issues* (pp. 109–124). Hillsdale, NJ: Lawrence Erlbaum Associates.

Tindale, R. S., & Davis, J. H. (1983). Group decision making and jury verdicts. In H. H. Blumberg, A. P. Hare, V. Kent, & M. F. Davis (Eds.) *Small Groups and Social Interaction* (Vol. 2, pp. 9–38). Chichester, UK: Wiley.

Tindale, R. S., & Davis, J. H. (1985). Individual and group reward allocation decisions in two situational contexts: Effects of relative need and performance. *Journal of Personality and Social Psychology, 48*(5), 1148–1161.

Tindale, R. S., Heath, L., Edwards, J., Posavac, E. J., Bryant, F. B., Suarez-Balcazar, Y., Henderson-King, E., & Myers, J. (1998). *Theory and research on small groups.* New York: Plenum Press.

Tindale, R. S., Kameda, T., & Hinsz, V. (2003). Group decision making: Review and integration. In M. A. Hogg & J. Cooper (Eds.), *Sage handbook of social psychology* (pp. 381–403). London: Sage.

Tindale, R. S., & Sheffey, S. (2002). Shared information, cognitive load, and group memory. *Group Processes & Intergroup Relations, 5*(1), 5–18.

Tindale, R. S., Sheffey, S., & Scott, L. A. (1993). Framing and group decision-making: Do cognitive changes parallel preference changes? *Organizational Behavior and Human Decision Processes, 55*(3), 470–485.

Tindale, R. S., Smith, C. M., Thomas, L. S., Filkins, J., & Sheffey, S. (1996) Shared representations and asymmetric social influence processes in small groups. In E. H. Witte & J. H. Davis (Eds.) *Understanding group behavior* (Vol. 1: *Consensual action by small groups*, pp. 81–103). Hillsdale, NJ: Lawrence Erlbaum Associates.

Tinker, M. A. (1963). *Legibility of print.* Ames, IA: Iowa State University Press.

Tinker, M. A. (1965). *Bases for effective reading.* Minneapolis, MN: University of Minnesota Press.

Todd, P., & Benbasat, I. (1991). An experimental investigation of the impact of computer based decision aids on decision making strategies. *Information Systems Research, 2*(2), 87–115.

Tolcott, M. A., Marvin, F. F., & Lehner, P. E. (1989). Expert decision making in evolving situations. *IEEE Transactions on Systems, Man, & Cybernetics Special Issue: Perspectives in Knowledge Engineering, 19*(3), 606–615.

Tolley, B. S., & Bogart, L. (1994). How readers process newspaper advertising. In E. M. Clark, T. C. Brock, & D. W. Stewart (Eds.), *Attention, attitude, and affect in response to advertising* (pp. 69–77). Hillsdale, NJ: Lawrence Erlbaum Associates.

Tomitch, L. M. B., Just, M. A., & Newman, S. D. (2004). Main idea identification: A functional imaging study of a complex language comprehension process. In L. M. B. Tomitch & C. Rodrigues (Eds.), *Ensaios sobre a linguagem e o cerebro humano: Contribuicoes multidisciplinares* (pp. 167–175). Porto Algre, Brazil: Artmed.

Tomkins, S. S. (1962). *Affect, imagery, consciousness: Vol. I. The positive affects.* New York: Springer Publishing.

Tormala, Z. L., Petty, R. E., & Brinol, P. (2002). Ease of retrieval effects in persuasion: The roles of elaboration and thought-confidence. *Personality and Social Psychology Bulletin, 28*(12), 1700–1712.

Tosi, H. (1971). Organizaton stress as a moderator of the relationship between influence and role response. *Academy of Management Journal, 14*, 7–20.

Totterdell, P. (2000). Catching moods and hitting runs: Mood linkage and subjective performance in professional sport teams. *Journal of Applied Psychology, 85*(6), 848–859.

Totterdell, P., Kellett, S., Teuchmann, K., & Briner, R. B. (1998). Evidence of mood linkage in work groups. *Journal of Personality and Social Psychology, 74*(6), 1504–1515.

Tourangeau, R., & Rasinski, K. A. (1988). Cognitive processes underlying context effects in attitude measurement. *Psychological Bulletin, 103*(3), 299–314.

Townsend, M. A. (1980). Schema activation in memory for prose. *Journal of Reading Behavior, 12*(1), 49–53.

Treisman, A. M., & Davies, A. (1973). Divided attention to ear and eye. In S. Kornblum (Ed.), *Attention and performance IV* (pp. 101–117). London: Academic Press.

Treisman, A. M., & Geffen, G. (1967). Selective attention: Perception or response?. *The Quarterly Journal of Experimental Psychology, 19*(1), 1–17.

Trollip, S. R., & Sales, G. (1986). Readability of computer-generated fill-justified text. *Human Factors, 28*(2), 159–163.

Trope, Y. (1986). Identification and inferential processes in dispositional attribution. *Psychological Review, 93*(3), 239–257.

Troutman, C. M., & Shanteau, J. (1976). Do consumers evaluate products by adding or averaging attribute information? *Journal of Consumer Research, 3*(2), 101–106.

Tumulty, K. (1990, September 3). Abortion polls yield contradictory results. *Austin American Statesman*, p. A29.

Turner, E. A., & Rommetveit, R. (1968). Focus of attention in recall of active and passive sentences. *Journal of Verbal Learning & Verbal Behavior, 7*(2), 543–548.

Tversky, A. (1969). Intransitivity of preferences. *Psychological Review, 76*(1), 31–48.

Tversky, A. (1972). Elimination by aspects: A theory of choice. *Psychological Review, 79*(4), 281–299.

Tversky, A., & Kahneman, D. (1971). Belief in the law of small numbers. *Psychological Bulletin, 76*(2), 105–110.

Tversky, A., & Kahneman, D. (1973). Availability: A heuristic for judging frequency and probability. *Cognitive Psychology, 5*(2), 207–232.

Tversky, A., & Kahneman, D. (1974). Judgment under uncertainty: Heuristics and biases. *Science, 185*(4157), 1124–1131.

Tversky, A., & Kahneman, D. (1980). Causal schemata in judgments under uncertainty. In M. Fishbein (Ed.), *Progress in social psychology* (pp. 49–72). Hillsdale, NJ: Erlbaum.

Tversky, A. & Kahneman, D. (1981). The framing of decisions and the psychology of choice. *Science, 211*(4481), 453–458.

Tversky, A., & Kahneman, D. (1983). Extensional versus intuitive reasoning: The conjunction fallacy in probability judgment. *Psychological Review, 90*(4), 293–315.

Tversky, A., & Kahneman, D. (1986). Judgment under uncertainty: Heuristics and biases. In H. R. Arkes & K. R. Hammond (Eds.), *Judgment and decision making: An interdisciplinary reader* (pp. 38–55). New York: Cambridge University Press.

Tversky, A., & Kahneman, D. (1988). Rational choice and the framing of decisions. In D. E. Bell, H. Raiffa, & A. Tversky (Eds.), *Decision making: Descriptive, normative, and prescriptive interactions* (pp. 167–192). New York: Cambridge University Press.

Tversky, A., & Russo, J. E. (1969). Substitutability and similarity in binary choices. *Journal of Mathematical Psychology, 6*(1), 1–12.

Tversky, A., & Sattath, S. (1979). Preference trees. *Psychological Review, 86*(6), 542–573.

Tversky, A., & Shafir, E. (1992). Choice under conflict: The dynamics of deferred decision. *Psychological Science, 3*(6), 358–361.

Tyebjee, T. T., & Bruno, A. V. (1984). A model of venture capitalist investment activity. *Management Science, 30*(9), 1051–1066.

Uleman, J. S. (1999). Spontaneous versus intentional inferences in impression formation. In S. Chaiken & Y. Trope (Eds.), *Dual-process theories in social psychology* (pp. 141–160). New York: Guilford Press.

Uleman, J. S., Newman, L. S., & Moskowitz, G. B. (1996). People as flexible interpreters: Evidence and issues from spontaneous trait inference. In M. P. Zanna (Ed.), *Advances in experimental social psychology* (Vol. 28, pp. 179–211). San Diego, CA: Academic Press.

van Baaren, R. B., Holland, R. W., Kawakami, K., & van Knippenberg, A. (2004). Mimicry and prosocial behavior. *Psychological Science, 15*, 71–74.

van Baaren, R. B., Holland, R. W., Steenaert, B., & van Knippenberg, A. (2003). Mimicry for money: Behavioral consequences of imitation. *Journal of Experimental Social Psychology, 39*, 393–398.

van Bezooijen, R., Otto, S. A., & Heenan, T. A. (1983). Recognition of vocal expressions of emotion: A three-nation study to identify universal characteristics. *Journal of Cross-Cultural Psychology, 14*(4), 387–406.

VanBoven, L., Loewenstein, G., Welch, E., & Dunning, D. (2001). *The illusion of courage: Underestimating social risk aversion in self and others.* Working paper, Carnegie Mellon University, Department of Social and Decision Sciences.

Van den Oetelaar, S., Tellegen, S., & Wober, M. (1997). Affective response to reading: A comparison of reading in the United Kingdom and the Netherlands. In S. Totosy de Zepetnek & I. Sywenky (Eds.), *The systemic and empirical approach to literature and culture as theory and application* (pp. 505–513). Siegen: LUMIS.

van Knippenberg, D., Lossie, N., & Wilke, H. (1994). In-group prototypicality and persuasion: Determinants of heuristic and systematic message processing. *British Journal of Social Psychology, 33*, 289–300.

Van Orden, G. C. (1987). A rows is a rose: Spelling, sound, and reading. *Memory & Cognition, 15*(3), 181–198.

van Raaij, W. F. (1976). *Direct monitoring of consumer information processing by eye movement recorder.* Unpublished paper, Tilburg University.

Van Rooy, L., Hendriks, B., Van Meurs, F., & Korzilius, H. (2006). Job advertisements in the Dutch mental health care sector: Preferences of potential applicants. In S. Carliner, J. P. Verckens, & C. De Waile (Eds.), *Information and document design: Varieties on recent research* (pp. 61–84). The Netherlands: John Benjamins.

Van Swol, L. M. (2007). Perceived importance of information: The effects of mentioning information, shared information bias, ownership bias, reiteration, and confirmation bias. *Group Processes & Intergroup Relations, 10*(2), 239–256.

Van Swol, L. M., Savadori, L., & Sniezek, J. A. (2003). Factors that may affect the difficulty of uncovering hidden profiles. *Group Processes & Intergroup Relations, 6*(3), 285–304.

Van Swol, L. M., & Seinfeld, E. (2006). Differences between minority, majority, and unanimous group members in the communication of information. *Human Communication Research, 32*(2), 178–197.

Van Swol, L. M., & Sniezek, J. A. (2002). *Trust me, I'm and expert: Trust and confidence and acceptance of expert advice.* Paper presented at the 8th Conference on Behavioral Decision Research in Management (BDRM), Chicago.

Vaughan, S. I. (1999). Information sharing and cognitive centrality: Patterns in small decision-making groups of executives. *Dissertation Abstracts International: Section B: The Sciences and Engineering, 60*(4-B), 1919.

Velmans, M. (1991). Is human information processing conscious? *Behavioral and Brain Sciences*, *14*(4), 651–726.

Verplanken, B. W., & Weenig, M. W. H. (1993). Graphical energy labels and consumers' decisions about home appliances: A process tracing approach. *Journal of Economic Psychology*, *14*(4), 739–752.

Viscusi, W. K., Magat, W. A., & Huber, J. (1986). Informational regulation of consumer health risks: An empirical evaluation of hazard warnings. *The RAND Journal of Economics*, *17*(3), 351–365.

Vollrath, D. A., Sheppard, B. H., Hinsz, V. B., & Davis, J. H. (1989). Memory performance by decision-making groups and individuals. *Organizational Behavior and Human Decision Processes*, *43*(3), 289–300.

von Hippel, W., Jonides, I., Hilton, J. L., & Narayan, S. (1993). Inhibitory effect of schematic processing on perceptual encoding. *Journal of Personality and Social Psychology*, *64*(6), 921–935.

Von Winterfeldt, D., & Edwards, W. (1973) *Evaluation of complex stimuli using multi-attribute utility procedures*. Ann Arbor, MI: Technical Report, Engineering Psychology Laboratory, University of Michigan.

Von Winterfeldt, D., & Edwards, W. (1986). *Decision analysis and behavioral research*. Cambridge, UK: Cambridge University Press.

Voss, J. F., Greene, T. R., Post, T. A., & Penner, B. C. (1983). Problem solving skill in the social sciences. In G. H. Bower (Ed.), *The Psychology of Learning and Motivation: Advances in Research Theory* (Vol. 17, pp. 165–213). New York: Academic Press.

Voss, J. F., Kennet, J., Wiley, J., & Schooler, T. Y. (1992). Experts at debate: The use of metaphor in the U. S. Senate debate on the Gulf Crisis. *Metaphor & Symbolic Activity Special Issue: Expertise and Metaphor*, *7*(3–4), 197–214.

Vuilleumier, P., Armony, J. L., Clarke, K., Husain, M., Driver, J., & Dolan, R. J. (2002). Neural response to emotional faces with and without awareness: Event-related fMRI in a parietal patient with visual extinction and spatial neglect. *Neuropsychologia*, *40*(12), 2156–2166.

Vyas, N. M. (1981). Observation of industrial purchasing decisions on supplier choices for long-term contracts in naturalistic settings (Doctoral dissertation, University of South Carolina, 1981). *Dissertation Abstracts International*, *42* (05A), 2275.

Wade, K. J., & Kinicki, A. J. (1997). Subjective applicant qualifications and interpersonal attraction as mediators within a process model of interview selection decisions. *Journal of Vocational Behavior*, *50*(1), 23–40.

Wagenaar, W. A., Keren, G., & Lichtenstein, S. (1988). Islanders and hostages: Deep and surface structures of decision problems. *Acta Psychologica*, *67*, 175–189.

Wakefield, D. S. (1961). A test to determine the relative effectiveness of different styles, colors, and return order solicitation methods in sales letters (Doctoral dissertation, The University of Tennessee, 1961). *Dissertation Abstracts International*, *22* (10), 3453.

Walker, B. A., Celsi, R. L., & Olson, J. C. (1986). Exploring the structural characteristics of consumers' knowledge. *Advances in Consumer Research*, *14*(1), 17–21.

Walker, B. A., & Olson, J. C. (1997). The activated self in consumer behavior: A cognitive structure perspective. In R. W. Belk (Ed.), *Research in consumer behavior* (pp. 135–171). Greenwich, CT: JAI Press.

Walker. B. A., Swasy, J. L., & Rethans, A. J. (1985). The impact of comparative advertising research. *Advances in Consumer Research*, *13*, 121–125.

Walker, O. C., Churchill, G. A., & Ford, N. M. (1975). Organizational determinants of the industrial salesman's role conflict and ambiguity. *Journal of Marketing*, *39*(1), 32–39.

Wallace, J. F., & Newman, J. P. (1997). Neuroticism and the attentional mediation of dysregulatory psychopathology. *Cognitive Therapy and Research*, *21*(2), 135–156.

Wallace, J. F., Newman, J. P., & Bachorowski, J. A. (1991). Failures of response modulation: Impulsive behavior in anxious and impulsive individuals. *Journal of Research in Personality*, *25*(1), 23–44.

Wallbott, H. G., & Scherer, K. R. (1986a). Cues and channels in emotion recognition. *Journal of Personality and Social Psychology*, *51*(4), 690–699.

Wallbott, H. G., & Scherer, K. R. (1986b). How universal and specific is emotional experience? Evidence from 27 countries on five continents. *Social Science Information*, *25*(4), 763–795.

Wallsten, T. S. (1980). Processes and models to describe choice and inference. In T. S. Wallsten (Ed.), *Cognitive processes in choice and decision behavior* (pp. 215–237). Hillsdale, NJ: Erlbaum.

Wallsten, T. S. (1990). The costs and benefits of vague information. In R. Hogarth (Ed.), *Insights in decision making: A tribute to Hillel J. Einhorn* (pp. 28–43). Chicago: University of Chicago Press.

Wallsten, T. S., & Barton, C. (1982). Processing probabilistic multidimensional information for decisions. *Journal of Experimental Psychology: Learning, Memory, and Cognition, 8*(5), 361–384.

Walsh, J. P. (1995). Managerial and organizational cognition: Notes from a trip down memory lane. *Organization Science, 6*(3), 280–321.

Walsh, J. P., Henderson, C. M., & Deighton, J. (1988). Negotiated belief structures and decision performance: An empirical investigation. *Organizational Behavior and Human Decision Processes, 42*(2), 194–216.

Walton, D. N. (1992). *The place of emotion in argument.* University Park, PA: Pennsylvania State University Press.

Wanner, H. E. (1968). On remembering, forgetting, and understanding sentences. A study of the deep structure hypothesis (Doctoral dissertation, Harvard University, 1968). *American Doctoral Dissertations,* X1968, 0158.

Warren, R. E., Warren, N. T., Green, J. P., & Bresnick, J. H. (1978). Multiple semantic encoding of homophones and homographs in contexts biasing dominant or subordinate meanings. *Memory & Cognition, 6*(4), 364–371.

Watson, D. (1989). Strangers' ratings of the five robust personality factors: Evidence of a surprising convergence with self-report. *Journal of Personality and Social Psychology, 57*(1), 120–128.

Webster, E. C. (Ed.). (1964). *Decision-making in the employment interview.* Montreal, Canada: McGill University.

Wegener, D. T., Petty, R. E., & Klein, D. J. (1994). Effects of mood on high elaboration attitude change: The mediating role of likelihood judgments. *European Journal of Social Psychology Special Issue: Affect in Social Judgments and Cognition, 24*(1), 25–43.

Wegener, D. T., Petty, R. E., & Smith, S. M. (1995). Positive mood can increase or decrease message scrutiny: The hedonic contingency view of mood and message processing. *Journal of Personality and Social Psychology, 69*(1), 5–15.

Wehrle, T., Kaiser, S., Schmidt, S., & Scherer, K. R. (2000). Studying the dynamics of emotional expression using synthesized facial muscle movements. *Journal of Personality and Social Psychology, 78*(1), 105–119.

Weigert, A. J. (1991). *Mixed emotions: Certain steps toward understanding ambivalence.* New York: State University of New York Press.

Weinstein, N. D., Lyon, J. E., Sandman, P. M., & Cuite, C. L. (1998). Experimental evidence for stages of health behavior change: The precaution adoption process model applied to home radon testing. *Health Psychology, 17*(5), 445–453.

Weiss, H. M., & Adler, S. (1981). Cognitive complexity and the structure of implicit leadership theories. *Journal of Applied Psychology, 66*(1), 69–78.

Weitz, B. A. (1978). Relationship between salesperson performance and understanding of customer decision making. *Journal of Marketing Research, 15*(4), 501–516.

Weldon, D. E., & Malpass, R. S. (1981). Effects of attitudinal, cognitive, and situational variables on recall of biased communications. *Journal of Personality and Social Psychology, 40*(1), 39–52.

Welles, G. (1986), We're in the habit of impulsive buying. *USA Today,* May 21, p. 1.

Wells, G. L., & Petty, R. E. (1980). The effects of overt head movements on persuasion: Compatibility and incompatibility of responses. *Basic and Applied Social Psychology, 1*(3), 219–230.

Wells, W. A. (1974). Venture capital decision-making (Doctoral dissertation, Carnegie Mellon University, 1974). *Dissertation Abstracts International, 35* (12A), 7475.

Werth, L., & Strack, F. (2003). An inferential approach to the knew-it-all-along effect. *Memory, 11*(4–5), 411–419.

Westen, D. (2007). *The political brain: The role of emotion in deciding the fate of the nation.* New York: Public Affairs.

Westendorp, P. (1995, June). *Testing pictures, texts, and animations for procedural instructions.* Paper presented at the Conference on Verbal Communications in Professional Settings, Utrecht, Netherlands.

Westphal, J. D., & Bednar, M. K. (2005). Pluralistic ignorance in corporate boards and firms' strategic persistence in response to low firm performance. *Administrative Science Quarterly, 50*(2), 262–298.

Whalen, D. H., & Blanchard, F. A. (1982). Effects of photographic evidence on mock juror judgement. *Journal of Applied Social Psychology, 12*(1), 30–41.

Wheeler, D. D. (1970). Processes in word recognition. *Cognitive Psychology, 1*, 59–85.

Wheildon, C. (1995). *Type and layout.* Berkeley, CA: Strathmoor Press.

White, G. L., & Maltzman, I. (1978). Pupillary activity while listening to verbal passages. *Journal of Research in Personality, 12*(3), 361–369.

White, M. (1996). Anger recognition is independent of spatial attention. *New Zealand Journal of Psychology, 25*(1), 30–35.

White, P. A. (1988). Causal processing: Origins and development. *Psychological Bulletin, 104*(1), 36–52.

Whittler, T. E. (1994). Eliciting consumer choice heuristics: Sales representatives' persuasion strategies. *Journal of Personal Selling & Sales Management, 14*(4), 41–53.

Whittlesea, B. W. (1997). Production, evaluation, and preservation of experiences: Constructive processing in remembering and performance tasks. In D. L. Medin (Ed.), *The psychology of learning and motivation: Advances in research and theory* (Vol. 37, pp. 211–264). San Diego, CA: Academic Press.

Whittlesea, B. W., Jacoby, L. L., & Girard, K. (1990). Illusions of immediate memory: Evidence of an attributional basis for feelings of familiarity and perceptual quality. *Journal of Memory and Language, 29*(6), 716–732.

Whittlesea, B. W., & Williams, L. D. (2001). The discrepancy-attribution hypothesis: II. Expectation, uncertainty, surprise and feelings of familiarity. *Journal of Experimental Psychology: Learning, Memory and Cognition, 27*(1), 14–33.

Whyte, G., & Sebenius, J. K. (1997). The effect of multiple anchors on anchoring in individual and group judgment. *Organizational Behavior and Human Decision Processes, 69*(1), 75–85.

Wiener, Y., & Schneiderman, M. L. (1974). Use of job information as a criterion in employment decisions of interviewers. *Journal of Applied Psychology, 59*(6), 699–704.

Wiggins, A. H. (1967). Effects of three typographical variables on speed of reading. *Journal of Typographic Research, 1*, 5–18.

Williams, J. M. (1990). Women's preferences for and satisfaction with the convenience services offered by a department store (Doctoral dissertation, Texas Woman's University, 1990). *Dissertation Abstracts International, 51* (06B), 2848.

Wilson, M. G., Northcraft, G. B., & Neale, M. A. (1989a). Information competition and vividness effects in on-line judgments. *Organizational Behavior and Human Decision Processes, 44*(1), 132–139.

Wilson, R. A., & Keil, F. C. (Eds.). (1999). *The MIT encyclopedia of the cognitive sciences.* Cambridge, MA: The MIT Press.

Wilson, T. D., & Brekke, N. (1994). Mental contamination and mental correction: Unwanted influences on judgments and evaluations. *Psychological Bulletin, 116*(1), 117–142.

Wilson, T. D., Kraft, D., & Dunn, D. S. (1989b). The disruptive effects of explaining attitudes: The moderating effect of knowledge about the attitude object. *Journal of Experimental Social Psychology, 25*(5), 379–400.

Wilson, T. D., Lisle, D. J., Schooler, J. W., Hodges, S. D., Klaaren, K. J., & LaFleur, S. J. (1993). Introspecting about reasons can reduce post-choice satisfaction. *Personality and Social Psychology Bulletin, 19*(3), 331–339.

Wilson, T. D., & Schooler, J. W. (1991). Thinking too much: Introspection can reduce the quality of preferences and decisions. *Journal of Personality and Social Psychology, 60*(2), 181–192.

Windschitl, P. D., & Weber, E. U. (1999). The interpretation of "likely" depends on the context, but "70%" is 70%—right?: The influence of associative processes on perceived certainty. *Journal of Experimental Psychology: Learning, Memory, and Cognition, 25*(6), 1514–1533.

Winkielman, P., & Cacioppo, J. T. (2001). Mind at ease puts a smile on the face: Psychophysiological evidence that processing facilitation elicits positive affect. *Journal of Personality and Social Psychology, 81*(6), 989–1000.

Winkielman, P., & Fazendeiro, T. A. (2003). *The role of conceptual fluency in preference and memory.* Unpublished manuscript.

Winkielman, P., Schwarz, N., Fazendeiro, T., & Reber, R. (2003a). The hedonic marking of processing fluency: Implications for evaluative judgment. In J. Musch & K. C. Klauer (Eds.), *The psychology of evaluation: Affective processes in cognition and emotion* (pp. 189–217). Mahwah, NJ: Erlbaum.

Winkielman, P., Schwarz, N., Reber, R., & Fazendeiro, T. A. (2003b). Cognitive and affective consequences of visual fluency: When seeing is easy on the mind. In L. M. Scott & R. Batra (Eds.), *Persuasive imagery: A consumer response perspective* (pp. 75–89). Mahwah, NJ: Lawrence Erlbaum Associates.

Winn, A. R. (1984). A cognitive social information processing approach to leadership perceptions (Doctoral dissertation, University of South Carolina, 1984). *Dissertation Abstracts International, 46* (02A), 0464.

Winn, W. (1991). Learning from maps and diagrams. *Educational Psychology Review, 3*(3), 211–247.

Winquist, J. R., & Franz, T. M. (2008). Does the Stepladder Technique improve group decision making? A series of failed replications. *Group Dynamics: Theory, Research, and Practice, 12*(4), 255–267.

Winter, L., & Uleman, J. S. (1984). When are social judgments made? Evidence for the spontaneousness of trait inferences. *Journal of Personality and Social Psychology, 47*(2), 237–252.

Winter, P. A. (1996). Applicant evaluations of formal position advertisements: The influence of sex, job message content, and information order. *Journal of Personnel Evaluation in Education, 10*, 105–116.

Wish, M., D'Andrade, R. G., & Goodnow, J. E. (1980). Dimensions of interpersonal communication: Correspondences between structures for speech acts and bipolar scales. *Journal of Personality and Social Psychology, 39*(5), 848–860.

Witherspoon, D., & Allan, L. G. (1985). The effect of a prior presentation on temporal judgments in a perceptual identification task. *Memory & Cognition, 13*(2), 101–111.

Witte, K., & Allen, M. (1996, November). *When do scare tactics work? A meta-analysis of fear appeals.* Paper presented at the Annual Meeting of the Speech Communication Association, San Diego, California.

Witte, K., & Allen, M. (2000). A meta-analysis of fear appeals: Implications for effective public health campaigns. *Health Education and Behavior, 27*(5), 591–615.

Woehr, D. J. (1994). Understanding frame-of-reference training: The impact of training on the recall of performance information. *Journal of Applied Psychology, 79*(4), 525–534.

Wofford, J. C., Goodwin, V. L., & Whittington, J. L. (1998). A field study of a cognitive approach to understanding transformational and transactional leadership. *Leadership Quarterly, 9*, 55–84.

Wolford, G., & Morrison, F. (1980). Processing of unattended visual information. *Memory & Cognition, 8*(6), 521–527.

Wong, B., Cronin-Golomb, A., & Neargarder, S. (2005). Patterns of visual scanning as predictors of emotion identification in normal aging. *Neuropsychology, 19*(6), 739–749.

Wong, E. (2001, April 5), A stinging office memo boomerangs; Chief executive is criticized after upbraiding workers by e-mail. *New York Times,* p. C1.

Wood, J. V., Taylor, S. E., & Lichtman, R. R. (1985a). Social comparison in adjustment to breast cancer. *Journal of Personality and Social Psychology, 49*(5), 1169–1183.

Wood, W., & Kallgren, C. A. (1988). Communicator attributes and persuasion: Recipients' access to attitude-relevant information in memory. *Personality and Social Psychology Bulletin, 14*(1), 172–182.

Wood, W., Kallgren, C. A., & Preisler, R. M. (1985b). Access to attitude-relevant information in memory as a determinant of persuasion: The role of message attributes. *Journal of Experimental Social Psychology, 21*(1), 73–85.

Woodall, W. G., & Burgoon, J. K. (1983). Talking fast and changing attitudes: A critique and clarification. *Journal of Nonverbal Behavior, 8*(2), 126–142.

Woodall, W. G., & Folger, J. P. (1981). Encoding specificity and nonverbal cue context: An expansion of episodic memory research. *Communication Monographs, 48*(1), 39–53.

Woodall, W. G., & Folger, J. P. (1985). Nonverbal cue context and episodic memory: On the availability and endurance of nonverbal behaviors as retrieval cues. *Communication Monographs, 52*(4), 319–333.

Woodside, A. G., & Davenport, W. J. (1974). The effect of salesmen similarity and expertise on consumer purchasing behavior. *Journal of Marketing Research, 11*(2), 198–202.

Workman, J. E., Johnson, K. K., & Hadeler, B. (1993). The influence of clothing on students' interpretative and extended inferences about a teaching assistant. *College Student Journal, 27*(1), 119–128.

Worth, L. T., & Mackie, D. M. (1987). Cognitive mediation of positive affect in persuasion. *Social Cognition, 5*(1), 76–94.

Wright, D. B., & Hall, M. (2007). How a "reasonable doubt" instruction affects decisions of guilt. *Basic and Applied Social Psychology*, *29*(1), 91–98.

Wright, P. (1968). Reading to learn. *Chemistry in Britain*, *4*, 445–450.

Wright, P. (1974). *The use of phased, noncompensatory strategies in decisions between multi-attribute products*. Research Paper 223. Graduate School of Business, Stanford University.

Wright, P. (1975). Consumer choice strategies: Simplifying vs. optimizing. *Journal of Marketing Research*, *12*(1), 60–67.

Wright, P. (1977). Decision making as a factor in the ease of using numerical tables. *Ergonomics*, *20*(1), 91–96.

Wright, P., Creighton, P., & Threlfall, S. M. (1982). Some factors determining when instructions will be read. *Ergonomics*, *25*(3), 225–237.

Wright, P., & Reid, F. (1973). Written information: Some alternatives to prose for expressing the outcomes of complex contingencies. *Journal of Applied Psychology*, *57*(2), 160–166.

Wright, P., & Rip, P. D. (1980). Product class advertising effects on first-time buyers' decision strategies. *Journal of Consumer Research*, *7*(2), 176–188.

Wright, W. F. (1979). Properties of judgment models in a financial setting. *Organizational Behavior & Human Performance*, *23*(1), 73–85.

Wright, W. F., & Bower, G. H. (1992). Mood effects on subjective probability assessment. *Organizational Behavior and Human Decision Processes*, *52*(2), 276–291.

Wyer, R. S., & Carlston, D. E. (1979). *Social cognition, inference, and attribution*. Hillsdale, NJ: Lawrence Erlbaum Associates.

Wyer, R. S., Clore, G. L., & Isbell, L. M. (1999). Affect and information processing. In M. P. Zanna (Ed.), *Advances in experimental social psychology* (Vol. 31, pp. 1–77). San Diego, CA: Academic Press.

Yadav, M. S. (1994). How buyers evaluate product bundles: A model of anchoring and adjustment. *Journal of Consumer Research*, *21*(2), 342–353.

Yalch, R. F., & Elmore-Yalch, R. (1984). The effect of numbers on the route to persuasion. *Journal of Consumer Research*, *11*(1), 522–527.

Yammarino, F. J., & Bass, B. M. (1990). Long-term forecasting of transformational leadership and its effects among naval officers. In K. E. Clark & M. B. Clark (Eds.), *Measures of leadership* (pp. 151–170). West Orange, NJ: Leadership Library of America.

Yarbus, A. L. (1967). *Eye movements and vision*. Translated from Russian by Basil Haigh. New York: Plenum Press.

Yates, J. F., Jagacinski, C. M., & Faber, M. D. (1978). Evaluation of partially described multiattribute options. *Organizational Behavior & Human Performance*, *21*(2), 240–251.

Yates, J. F., Price, P. C., Lee, J. W., & Ramirez, J. (1996). Good probabilistic forecasters: The "consumer's" perspective. *International Journal of Forecasting*, *12*, 41–56.

Yates, J. F., Veinott, E. S., & Patalano, A. L. (2003). Hard decisions, bad decisions: On decision quality and decision aiding. In S. L. Schneider & J. Shanteau (Eds.), *Emerging perspectives on judgment and decision research* (pp. 13–63). Cambridge, UK: Cambridge University Press.

Yekovich, F. R., & Walker, C. H. (1978). Identifying and using referents in sentence comprehension. *Journal of Verbal Learning & Verbal Behavior*, *17*(3), 265–277.

Yi, Y. J. (1990). The effects of contextual priming in print advertisements. *Journal of Consumer Research*, *17*(2), 215–222.

Young, D. M., & Beier, E. G. (1977). The role of applicant nonverbal communication in the employment interview. *Journal of Employment Counseling*, *14*(4), 154–165.

Young, G. R., II, Price, K. H., & Claybrook, C. (2001). Small group predictions on an uncertain outcome: The effect of nondiagnostic information. *Theory and Decision*, *50*(2), 149–167.

Young, R. O. (1989). Cognitive processes in argumentation: An exploratory study of management consulting expertise (Doctoral dissertation, Carnegie Mellon University, 1989). *Dissertation Abstracts International*, *50* (08B), 3764.

Yuce, P., & Highhouse, S. (1998). Effects of attribute set size and pay ambiguity on reactions to "help wanted" advertisements. *Journal of Organizational Behavior*, *19*(4), 337–352.

Yukl, G. A., & Falbe, C. M. (1990). Influence tactics and objectives in upward, downward, and lateral influence attempts. *Journal of Applied Psychology*, *75*(2), 132–140.

Yukl, G. A., & Tracey, J. B. (1992). Consequences of influence tactics used with subordinates, peers, and the boss. *Journal of Applied Psychology, 77,* 525–535.

Zaccaro, S. J. (2001). *The nature of executive leadership: A conceptual and empirical analysis of success.* Washington, DC: American Psychological Association.

Zadny, J., & Gerard, H. B. (1974). Attributed intentions and informational selectivity. *Journal of Experimental Social Psychology, 10*(1), 34–52.

Zahn-Waxler, C., Radke-Yarrow, M., Wagner, E., & Chapman, M. (1992). Development of concern for others. *Developmental Psychology, 28*(1), 126–136.

Zajonc, R. B. (1968). Attitudinal effects of mere exposure. *Journal of Personality and Social Psychology, 9*(2, Pt.2), 1–27.

Zeelenberg, M., & Pieters, R. (1999). Comparing service delivery to what might have been: Behavioral responses to regret and disappointment. *Journal of Service Research, 2,* 86–97.

Zillmann, D. (2002). Exemplification theory of media influence. In J. Bryant & D. Zillmann (Eds.), *Media effects: Advances in theory and research* (pp. 19–42). Mahwah, NJ: Lawrence Erlbaum.

Zillmann, D., Gibson, R., Sundar, S. S., & Perkins, J. W. (1996). Effects of exemplification in news reports on the perception of social issues. *Journalism & Mass Communication Quarterly, 73,* 427–444.

Zuckerman, M., DePaulo, B. M., & Rosenthal, R. (1981). Verbal and nonverbal communication of deception. In L. Berkowitz (Ed.), *Advances in experimental social psychology* (Vol. 14, pp. 1–59). New York: Academic Press.

Zwaan, R. A., & Brown, C. M. (1996). The influence of language proficiency and comprehension skill on situation-model construction. *Discourse Processes, 21*(3), 289–327.

Figure Credits

Figure 1.2, "Decision makers spontaneously create decision matrices," © The University of Chicago Press. Journal of Consumer Research, 21(1), 83-99; Coupey, E. (1994). Restructuring: Constructive processing of information displays in consumer choice.

Figure 1.5, "Decision matrices from *Consumer Reports* can provide instant expertise," copyright 2009 by Consumers Union of U.S., Inc. Yonkers, NY 10703-1057, a non-profit organization. Reprinted with permission from ConsumerReports.org® for educational purposes only. No commercial use or reproduction permitted. www.ConsumerReports.org.

Figure 3.4, "A reader's eye-fixation pattern reading an online newspaper," © UPA, Journal of Usability Studies, 4(4), 147-165; Gibbs, W. J, and Bernas, R. S. (2009). Visual Attention in Newspaper versus TV-Oriented News Websites; Figure 5. Eye path trace of most central fixation sequence for NYT, page 158.

Figure 3.7, "Attention to important information on a home page increased after its redesign," © UPA, Journal of Usability Studies, 1(3), 112-120; Bojko, A. (2006). Using Eye Tracking to Compare Web Page Designs: A Case Study, page 117.

"Chairman's Letter from an Annual Report with Comments by an Experienced Board Member." The Chairman's Letter from the 1985 Annual Report of Control Data Corporation, provided courtesy of Charles Babbage Institute, University of Minnesota, Minneapolis.

There are instances where we have been unable to trace or contact the copyright holder. If notified the publisher will be pleased to rectify any errors or omissions at the earliest opportunity.

Author Index

Subject Index

Page numbers in *italics* denotes an illustration/table.